But Not Philosophy

BY GEORGE ANASTAPLO

The Constitutionalist: Notes on the First Amendment (1971)
Human Being and Citizen: Essays on Virtue, Freedom, and the Common Good (1975)
The Artist as Thinker: From Shakespeare to Joyce (1983)
The Constitution of 1787: A Commentary (1989)
The American Moralist: On Law, Ethics, and Government (1992)
The Amendments to the Constitution: A Commentary (1995)
The Thinker as Artist: From Homer to Plato & Aristotle (1997)
Campus Hate-Speech Codes, Natural Right, and Twentieth Century Atrocities (1997, 1999)
Liberty, Equality, & Modern Constitutionalism: A Source Book (1999)
Abraham Lincoln: A Constitutional Biography (1999)
But Not Philosophy: Seven Introductions to Non-Western Thought (2002)
On Trial: From Adam & Eve to O.J. Simpson (forthcoming)
On Plato's "Meno" (with Laurence Berns) (forthcoming)
The Bible: Respectful Readings (forthcoming)

But Not Philosophy

Seven Introductions
to Non-Western Thought

George Anastaplo

LEXINGTON BOOKS
Lanham • Boulder • New York • Oxford

LEXINGTON BOOKS

Published in the United States of America
by Rowman & Littlefield Publishers, Inc.
4720 Boston Way, Lanham, Maryland 20706
www.rowmanlittlefield.com

12 Hid's Copse Road
Cumnor Hill, Oxford OX2 9JJ, England

British Library Cataloguing-in-Publication Information Available

Library of Congress Cataloging-in-Publication Data

Anastaplo, George, 1925-
    But not philosophy : seven introductions to non-Western thought / George Anastaplo.
      p. cm.
    Includes bibliographical references and index.
    ISBN 0-7391-0289-3 (alk. paper) — ISBN 0-7391-0290-7 (pbk.: alk. paper)
     1. Religions. 2. Asia—Religion. 3. Africa—Religion. I. Title.

BL80.2 .A52 2002
291–dc21

                                      2001034431

Printed in the United States of America

♾™ The paper used in this publication meets the minimum requirements of American
National Standard for Information Sciences—Permanence of Paper for Printed Library
Materials, ANSI/NISO Z.39.48-1992.

To the Memory of
L.S.
and
M.J.A.,
"the Founder[s] of the Feast!"

Contents

Foreword, by John Van Doren   ix

Preface   xv

1   Mesopotamian Thought: The *Gilgamesh* Epic   1

2   "Ancient" African (Including Egyptian) Thought   31

3   Hindu Thought: The *Bhagavad Gītā*   67

4   Confucian Thought: The *Analects*   99

5   Buddhist Thought   147

6   Islamic Thought: The Koran   175

7   North American Indian Thought   225

Appendices

     A   On Beginnings   261

     B   On the Human Soul, Nature, and the Moral Virtues   303

     C   On the Use, Neglect, and Abuse of Veils:
         The Parliaments of the World's Religions   345

Index   375

About The Author   397

Foreword

It is difficult these days for anybody to write critically—which is to say, with judgment—about the cultural achievements or characteristics of non-Western peoples as compared with our own, not to speak of the differences they can be said to have among themselves. For one thing, such has been the traffic and the spread of information among tribes and nations in our time that these differences can no longer be found anywhere with certainty in their pure form. In the remote mountain villages of Tibet they listen on their crystal radios, or did, to Michael Jackson. But even where some estimate can be arrived at in such matters, there are academic and social conventions against asserting it. The social sciences have taught us that all cultures are equal and that intellectual and moral differences are to be regarded impartially as expressions of the human spirit, wherever and however they occur. Nothing can be questioned, lest we seem culture bound. One is reminded of what John Stuart Mill observed about religious toleration, which was that, whereas it was supposed to allow everyone to speak freely about religion, in practice it has meant that nobody is allowed to bring up the subject.

Of course it would be without interest, would indeed be offensive, if someone sought to speak to us of cultural distinctions with an unexamined sense of superiority—that is, with prejudice. That was a bad habit of Westerners in the past, among them Rudyard Kipling, who has been neglected because it is supposed that he was capable of nothing else, and in whom the defect was a far more complex state of mind than appears in certain of his poems—or so Ved Mehta has recently argued, whose people suffered it. Nor does it follow that judgment, when it is offered, must be without sympathy or respect for what it presumes to doubt. If we are to take the criticism seriously, it must be the product of an effort to see why others think as they do.

George Anastaplo, the author of the essays collected here on the thought, mostly ancient, of non-Western peoples, has observed these rules, and others besides of an appropriate kind, in going about his task. I say *his* task, for it was one he set himself, though the essays themselves appeared originally, at different times, in *The Great Ideas Today*, a volume once published annually by Encyclopaedia Britannica, Inc., and that book otherwise accepted articles only by invitation; I know because I was on its editorial staff, where I agreed to what became a series on Mr. Anastaplo's initiative. The essays were his idea and his formulation, since the series was deliberately conceived as the work of a student of Western thought and culture confronting what was unfamiliar to him, but not in the least pretending that he was other than what he was, a man who had written—has written—extensively on the works of the Western mind (if we can speak of such a thing in the singular), and who had decided to see what he could make of what lies outside its limits.

I emphasize the word "thought" because Mr. Anastaplo does. It is thought, not culture or custom or belief, which interests him. The underlying assumption is that ancient peoples and their descendants did think, and do—were and are possessed of minds which can be asked to give accounts of themselves that another mind can make sense of, or, if it cannot, will feel justified in saying so, and saying why. Such an assumption is to have been expected in most cases, but even where it was not—where the people under review are usually discussed in terms of their beliefs or behavior rather than their intellectual development, of which we may lack formal expression (as in the case of the North American Indian, not "Western" culturally, or the peoples of sub-Saharan Africa), it has been consistently made. Mr. Anastaplo does not merely talk *about* the peoples he discusses, but so far as possible *to* them, or to the writings which have emanated from them, and takes it for granted that they are talking back, or at least are capable of doing so—that they have, or at least did have, their own sense of what they were about, which we must discover if we can.

Perhaps we cannot. The meeting of minds between Mr. Anastaplo and those whose thinking he undertakes to examine in these essays is in no case complete, is always imperfect. Were it otherwise there would have been no reason for the exercise, which was to see what could be made of thought which is not our thought and which we cannot expect to understand wholly; if we could, such thought would be part of Western thought, and already familiar to us. It is not familiar here; there is something strange about it, if not many things, the strangeness lying in the fact that it is inconsistent with our own thought, with which we have to reconcile it so far as possible, even if what we arrive at is an understanding of its difference. This may well involve the realization that we have something to learn about ourselves, as Mr. Anastaplo says more than once.

Which raises the question why we should not go instead to the scholars, the experts, who already "know" the thinking of these people as Mr. Anastaplo does not (he does not even know their languages), and who can give us a scholarly understanding of what that thinking is, or was. Not that Mr. Anastaplo despises scholarship—far from it, as his extensive notes testify. But the answer to this question is that experts tend to disappear into their subjects, with which they try to become one (a teacher of French aims to speak without an accent), whereas it is Mr. Anastaplo's object to remain visible, to be an outsider, retaining his own Western sense of things even as he reaches beyond it. That is the position most of the rest of us are in also, and it is likely to be instructive as expert knowledge is not. We learn better, Socrates maintains, from one who himself is learning than from one who already knows, or thinks he does.

In four cases—half the principal essays in the volume—the thought to be discussed is embodied in a single book, which becomes the object of Mr. Anastaplo's interest as an expression of the people with which it is identified. Much more can be said about such people in every case, but in the *Analects* of Confucius, the *Bhagavad Gītā* of the Hindus, the *Gilgamesh* Epic of Mesopotamia, and the Koran of Islam, the book is the locus of the thought we associate with them. The book is therefore what Mr. Anastaplo examines, making such inferences from it to the people from whom it came as seem reasonable, but deriving his understanding of them from it, rather than the other way around. He does not care if the book is old, providing it is still read. His approach is that of the student of a text, not of a time.

The other peoples whose thought he examines are not represented by a book to the same degree, or at all. In the case of the Ancient Egyptians we have in writing nothing comparable to the immense tombs they built, which say something about them, certainly, and which we can "read" in various ways—in which inscriptions are to be found (along with other writings) indicative of the thinking, at least as to the subject of death, of those who built them—but which remain enigmatic in other respects. As for the North American Indians, or whatever we choose to call them, so much of whose culture we obliterated, and the Africans of the region south of the Sahara, so many of whose people we enslaved, what is to be found—what remains—are stories and folk tales that seem to go back a long way, though they continue to be told. These are what Mr. Anastaplo has had to settle for in considering the thought of such peoples, guessing with the aid of scholarship as to what they mean. They are poems of a sort which do not tell us directly about the view of the world their creators had, but imply it. We assume we know something about those who repeated the stories simply because they did so. They may not have been able, ever, to do much more.

As to what the thought of such people—those with a book and those without one—really is, or was, it would be superfluous to restate what Mr. Anastaplo is at pains to set forth, so far as he can, in the essays themselves, which deserve a chance to make their own case. But it may be fairly noted that he is himself a philosopher by training and inclination who has read widely in, and written much about, the classic works in that field, mostly those having to do with ethics and politics. He has read with equal interest in literature, ancient and modern, as further published writings by him attest. These credits will assure the reader of this collection that its author, while confessedly not an expert on the thought of the peoples here examined, has reflected much on what constitutes the human, and has spent his life with good books. He is also widely travelled. Of course those who know him will not need any reminder of such things.

Nor do I have to defend his judgments—he does that himself—with respect to the material he investigates here, beyond saying that they are driven by a conviction that the best thought never knowingly falsifies the world for the sake of religion or poetry, nor does it allow that any subjection of human kind can be really good for it. This insistence upon inherent truth and the freedom to pursue it as the constituents of thought at its best may seem a very Western one. Mr. Anastaplo says as much. Yet he perceives and, to a point, admires the different claims of non-Western religion and poetry upon our minds, as he does non-Western strictures upon human behavior. The point is what has to be decided, and if it often strikes him as beyond where Western thought can go, implying something dubious or unsustainable, he says so with diffidence, with even admiration for the religious and poetic visions of non-Western thought and—somewhat less approvingly—its moral stance. Or its many stances, for "non-Western thought" is many things, and judgments of it must be various.

We are not obliged to agree with all the positions Mr. Anastaplo takes in such matters, to the extent that he does take them. Or to put it politely, we may reasonably wish to work our own way through some of them and see if they can survive, as mostly I think they do survive, such challenges as we can think to make. This is so even with respect to his fundamental contention that "thought" in the most serious sense of the term, which in his view is philosophic thought, requires the existence of something to be thought about, and not just anything but what Mr. Anastaplo thinks of as the whole of things, or what he calls nature. What he calls nature may be a peculiarly Western conception—he thinks it is—though by now it has spread over the entire world on the wings of science, and what is peculiar about it, as compared with what is to be found in the thought of other peoples, is that for those who have it, the world is not inscrutable but is considered to be a knowable thing—which is very far from saying that it can ever be wholly known. So conceived, it is held to have had no beginning and to be the subject of no Will in the sense of a Creator, whose work must be unfathomable because *he* is, if he exists. Or, if a Creator is acknowledged, as another part of the Western tradition holds, he tends to be thought of as having let his Creation be, or be itself, once it *was* made.

This is very different from what is found in the thought of most (it would be risky to say all) non-Western peoples, for whom the world, or the natural order, including the human, is the work of a still-active Deity whose constant intervention is required to keep it from collapsing into Chaos. So in some cases, at any rate. In others, the conviction is that the nature of things is quite fixed—too much so for Western acceptance—as in the Koran. There, what is called Creation is, as Mr. Anastaplo observes, in every detail "the manifestation of God's power and presence." Before it, as before God himself, the only proper attitude is one of prostration, with no thought of discovery. We already know, through what has been revealed to us, all that we ever can.

The difference is between a conception of things which calls on us to reason about them and one which demands merely our obedience, with moral and political implications on either side, not to speak of intellectual ones. A choice between these two views of our condition must be made. For better or worse, we in the West are reasoners who think the world can make sense, and who study it so that it should—who are indignant when we are told that it need not, as Job was, contending with his comforters. This may be a foolish conceit on our part—the Hindus for one evidently believe so—but it has *been* our conceit since the Greeks, who gave it to us (possibly from Pandora's box), and we do not see how thought—or science, as we now prefer to say—can go on without it. If we did not have it, and live by it, we should think ourselves powerless before the great process of Life as are Buddhists, or slaves as the Muslims are before Allah (but not before anybody else), for all that there is a strain in our own religious tradition which leads us to say, "Thy Will be done."

But we do not want to contend—I do not think Mr. Anastaplo would contend—that the world is not in a significant sense subject to *our* will as human beings and cannot be changed for the better or, at our peril, for the worse—altered even in its physical constituents. With knowledge comes power. We hear nowadays that bacteria defy heredity, being subject to penetration by organisms which change their make-up; if so, the fixity of evolution is not so great as we imagined, and endless possibilities present themselves. Certainly most of us believe that the conditions of existence can be better than they are for a great portion of the human world, and should be. We are not fatalists.

Still, our belief in betterment, far from denying Mr. Anastaplo's argument to the effect that the West's superiority, if it has one, is rational, that it is best for human beings to follow a rational course might be said to be the proof of it, at least as far as it implies a responsibility for things. Such is not found, or not so readily found, in non-Western peoples. It is true, we frequently fail to discharge that responsibility and are destructive of physical nature as compared, say, with the American Indians or the Arabs, who have more respect for it. This implies that they have a better sense of the matter than we do. But there remains a difference between reason, which can destroy, and custom or spiritual affinity, which can fail to save. The Indians and the Arabs have been unable to sustain the natural order when it does change with the proliferation of human kind and its consequences, and when what might be called a creative imagination, combined with knowledge, is called upon to preserve it. Is such a combination purely Western? Perhaps it is not, or not entirely. We may require a mixture of Western and other forms of thought if the natural order is to survive. Given the movement of our time among peoples, perhaps this is already beginning to function.

I need not go on. It is a pleasure to have had the chance to say something about these essays, and to have been able to publish them where they first appeared, in *The Great Ideas Today*, which ceased publication in 1998. There, for nearly forty years, thoughtful scholars and writers had room to write at length about serious issues and important ideas. It is good to remember how profitable my association was in that connection with George Anastaplo, who holds always to a high standard of both purpose and performance in everything he says and writes, and from whom I have learned much about many things.

JOHN VAN DOREN

Preface

We would have great difficulty in doing justice to [the] remote or dark side of the [ancient] city but for the work of men like Fustel de Coulanges above all others who have made us see the city as it primarily understood itself as distinguished from the manner in which it was exhibited by classical political philosophy: the holy city in contradistinction to the natural city. Our gratitude is hardly diminished by the fact that Fustel de Coulanges, his illustrious predecessor, Hegel above all, and his numerous successors have failed to pay proper attention to the philosophic concept of the city as the city is exhibited by classical political philosophy. For what is "first for us" is not the philosophic understanding of the city but that understanding which is inherent in the city as such, in the pre-philosophic city, according to which the city sees itself as subject and subservient to the divine in the ordinary understanding of the divine or looks up to it. Only by beginning at this point will we be open to the full impact of the all-important question which is coeval with philosophy, although the philosophers do not frequently pronounce it–the question *quid sit deus*.

—Leo Strauss[1]

This collection of exercises in disciplined reading offers guidance for outsiders to a half dozen "schools" of non-Western thought, with each examined for its distinctive doctrines and practices. Some of these "schools" have adherents who have reason to believe that their ways of living and of knowing are sounder, if not also far more splendid and otherwise richer, than the ways generally available in the more pedestrian, if not also the more materialistic, West.[2] The guidance offered in this collection is of the kind that I myself would have found useful, both for the materials reviewed and for the interpretations ventured, when I have conducted what are now called "multicultural" courses.[3] Each of these essays was preceded by a three-hour weekly seminar (ranging across one to three academic terms) in the Basic Program of Liberal Education for Adults at the University of

Chicago. Each seminar, beginning in the 1970s, would culminate in a public lecture by me at the University of Chicago.[4] That lecture would provide the basis in turn of my more extended, and considerably documented, presentation of its subject in *The Great Ideas Today*.[5]

My first inquiry in this generation-long series was directed to Confucian thought, which appears from the outside to be the closest of all the non-Western "schools" surveyed by me to the modes of thought that many in the West are accustomed to.[6] Mortimer J. Adler, upon reading that account almost a decade after it was first distributed, recommended it to John Van Doren, the executive editor of *The Great Ideas Today*, who supervised its publication in his 1984 volume.[7] The remainder of my series was developed once I was assured that a competent publisher was available.[8]

The first introduction to this collection has been provided by Mr. Van Doren in the foreword to this volume. That foreword reflects the intelligence, the range of informed interests, and the sensitivity to language which contributed mightily to the editorial judgment which made *The Great Ideas Today* the best annual volume of essays produced in the United States during the second half of the twentieth century.[9]

Another introduction to this collection of essays is provided by a political scientist who has done substantial work both in classical studies and in political anthropology.[10] He observes at the outset of his review of my work: "Although George Anastaplo tries to understand each non-European tradition of thought in its own terms, his assessments manifest seven themes that run throughout all his writings."[11] The first three of these themes, with an emphasis upon the discovery of *nature*, are the following:

> 1. The European tradition that began in ancient Greece is superior to other traditions of thought, Anastaplo believes, because in ancient Greece (particularly among the Socratic philosophers) one finds the first full expression of nature, natural right, philosophy, prudence, science, and natural religion.
>
> 2. The idea of nature was discovered by the Greeks when they recognized that there was a rational order in the universe and in human life as part of the universe, a rational order that is universal and unchanging and therefore distinguishable from the conventional or customary order of particular human groups. Prior to the discovery of nature, human beings looked to the ancestral customs of their society as the authoritative and even divine guides to life. The politics, art, science, and religion of the Western world all show the influence of the Greek discovery of nature. Since nature is universal, *there are intimations of nature in every tradition of human thought*, but only those traditions influenced by Greece show a fully explicit, self-conscious awareness of nature as distinguished from custom or convention.
>
> 3. From the idea of nature, the Greeks derived the idea of natural right, because in human nature they discerned natural desires and capacities that set norms of good and bad, just and unjust. Natural right or justice is that which conforms to human na-

ture and is therefore universal, whereas conventional right or justice is that which has been established by human contrivance in particular societies.[12]

At this point *philosophy* comes to view, as may be seen in the next three themes that are posited by my reviewer:

4. The discovery of nature presupposes philosophy or science as a life devoted to inquiry for its own sake in which ancestral beliefs and customs are not authoritative. Distinguishing between opinion and truth, the philosopher refuses to accept common opinions that have not been rationally demonstrated. For the philosopher or scientist, reason is superior to the ancestral.

5. With the philosophic awareness of how the universal and unchangeable order of nature differs from the particular and changeable order of custom, there also arose (particularly in Aristotle's writings) an awareness of the need for prudence or practical wisdom in judging the variable circumstances of action in the light of an invariable nature. What is naturally best for any particular society will vary according to the character of that society, so that a prudent man must judge what is practicable and what is not for the people of his society. The prudent man judges how best to approximate the dictates of nature within the historical conditions in which he finds himself.

6. Modern natural science is unique to Western thought because it is rooted ultimately in the Greek discovery of nature and of philosophy as the study of nature. Insofar as people in non-Western cultures recognize the accomplishments of modern science in comprehending and controlling nature through human reason, they concede the superiority of Greek thought.[13]

The final theme posited by this quite helpful reviewer looks to the place of theology in our understanding of things:

7. Ancestral customs were traditionally regarded as divinely sanctioned, so that religious beliefs confirmed the unquestionable authority of the ancestral. Consequently, the philosophic or scientific appeal to nature as a rational order comprehensible to human reason challenged the authority of religious belief. There seemed to be an irreconcilable conflict between reason and revelation. Under the influence of Greek philosophy, however, the theology of the Biblical religions–Judaism, Christianity, and Islam–can be interpreted as supporting a natural religion in which the dictates of God reflect the dictates of nature. The natural philosopher inquires into the causal order of the whole. The natural theologian inquires into the First Cause.[14]

However I might want to qualify this account, I am encouraged by its distillation of themes, suggesting as it does the challenges posed to those of us who look beyond the traditions and the texts familiar to the West. (Much of the looking in this collection is with a view to illuminating what *philosophy* is and is not.) I am also encouraged by the endorsements I have received from recognized authorities in various of the fields that I have presumed to write about here.[15]

Still another introduction to this collection is provided in effect by each of the seven chapters that follow. Since each essay was originally designed to stand alone in *The Great Ideas Today*, my general approach and presuppositions had to be indicated on each occasion of publication over two decades.[16] The first of the published essays, on Confucian thought, can serve (for others as it did for me) as a particularly useful entry into my series. (Much the same can be said of the second of the published essays, on Hindu thought.) The last essay published, on African thought, notices what I had come to learn about dealing with radically unfamiliar materials.[17] The "schools" studied in this collection are arranged more or less in the order in which they matured over millennia, not in the order that they may have begun nor in the order that my essays were prepared. Western thought is much in evidence throughout.

Among the things I have learned from this odyssey[18] is that it proved *for me* much more productive to approach each of these "traditions" in the manner described, that is, by first examining it in university seminars for months at a time, followed by a public lecture. One comes, thereby, to "live" with a system of thought, investigating its nooks and crannies as one spells out implications and tests conjectures in the light of the experiences, presuppositions, and speculations of one's students and hence of one's time. When I have tried to approach such matters completely on my own (that is, without extended conversations with fellow readers), that has usually proved far less productive and far less persuasive.[19] The "rhetorical" aspects of such investigations, as well as of the "schools" themselves, should not be underestimated.[20]

Experts could no doubt provide the reader better informed and more thoroughly researched introductions to each of the "schools" surveyed in this collection. But the typical student is not apt to have ready access to such experts. Nor is the typical student apt to be able to choose usefully among the many experts who do happen to be available, let alone rise to the level at which experts routinely work.[21] My essays, the explorations of a determined amateur with some practice in reading,[22] do provide preliminary screenings for other amateurs, with suggestions made about questions and issues prompted by both the education and the circumstances of the contemporary Westerner. The cross-references tying the chapters together are supplemented by the record of key notions (such as *divine*, *nature*, and *philosophy*) in the index for this collection.

Introductions to this collection of essays are also supplied by the three appendices in this volume. The multifaceted Western approach to the matters touched upon in my essays, an approach long grounded among us both in revelation and in science, is recalled in my appendices.[23] The appendices conclude with an account of the Parliament of the World's Religions convened in Chicago in 1993, a lively convention where a variety of non-Western scholars and practitioners were very much in evidence.[24]

This collection is offered, then, as a set of useful introductions to long-established and otherwise impressive traditions around the world. Even more important, perhaps, are the reminders available here of that which Westerners can learn from non-Westerners about what the West itself is like, particularly with respect to its grasp of and reliance upon the divine, its reliance upon nature and causality, and its reliance upon philosophy. It usually contributes to one's self-knowledge to secure a reliable sense of what one is *not*.[25]

Critical to all of this exercise, as well as to much else which I have studied, is an emphasis upon the vital importance of *truly reading* those texts which do permit, require, and reward careful study.[25]

Notes

1. Leo Strauss, *The City and Man* (Chicago: Rand McNally & Company, 1964), pp. 240–41. See George Anastaplo, "Leo Strauss at the University of Chicago," in Kenneth L. Deutsch and John A. Murley, eds., *Leo Strauss, the Straussians, and the American Regime* (Lanham, Md.: Rowman & Littlefield, 1999), p. 3. See also John A. Murley, "*In re* George Anastaplo," in Duetsch and Murley, *Leo Strauss*, p. 159; George Anastaplo, *The Artist as Thinker: From Shakespeare to Joyce* (Athens, Ohio: Ohio University Press, 1983), p. 249; note 14 of this preface. See as well note 15 of chapter 6 of this collection.

Introductions by me to various facets of *Western* thought, ancient and modern, are provided throughout this collection by means of citations to my publications. See note 11 of this preface.

2. Seven introductions are provided with one of them (in chapter 2) encompassing two "schools," the Egyptian and the sub-Saharan African. A study of all of these "schools" should suggest to us the limits of technology and globalization. Non-Western peoples remind us of the human aspirations and yearnings, or various facets of human nature, that we in the West sometimes lose sight of. See, e.g., note 89 of chapter 2 of this collection.

The "more pedestrian" tendencies of the West are anticipated in the "demythologizing" that Socrates is reported to have resisted on one occasion (Plato, *Phaedrus* 229B-230A):

Phaedrus: Tell me, Socrates, isn't it somewhere about here that they say Boreas seized Orithyia from the river?

Socrates: Yes, that is the story.

Phaedrus: Was this the actual spot? Certainly the water looks charmingly pure and clear; it's just the place for girls to be playing beside the stream.

Socrates: No, it was about a quarter of a mile lower down, where you cross to the sanctuary of Agra, there is, I believe, an altar dedicated to Boreas close by.

Phaedrus: I have never really noticed it, but pray tell me, Socrates, do you believe that story to be true?

Socrates: I should be quite in the fashion if I disbelieved it as the men of science do. I might proceed to give a scientific account of how the maiden, while at play with Pharmacia, was blown by a gust of Boreas down from the rocks hard by, and having thus met her death was said to have been seized by Boreas, though it may have happened on the Areopagus, according to another version of the occurrence. For my part, Phaedrus, I regard such theories as no doubt attractive, but as the invention of clever, industrious people who are not exactly to be envied, for the simple reason that they must then go on and tell us the real truth about the appearance of centaurs and the Chimera, not to mention a whole host of such creatures, Gorgons and Pegasuses and countless other remarkable monsters of legend flocking in on them. If our skeptic, with his somewhat crude science, means to reduce every one of them to the standard of probability, he'll need a deal of time for it. I myself have certainly no time for the business, and I'll tell you why, my friend. I can't as yet "know myself," as the inscription at Delphi enjoins, and so long as that ignorance remains it seems to me ridiculous to inquire into extraneous matters.

3. Such courses can include survey courses in anthropology, in comparative literature, and in world religions. Each of the "schools" of thought introduced in this collection is likely either to be grounded in or to generate a system of laws, making the materials in this collection also useful for courses in jurisprudence and in political science. See, on the current sensitivity of some of the materials one is apt to encounter in such courses, George Anastaplo, "'Racism,' Political Correctness, and Constitutional Law: A Law School Case Study," 42 *South Dakota Law Review* 108 (1997); note 47 of chapter 2 of this collection. See also George Anastaplo, *Campus Hate-Speech Codes, Natural Right, and Twentieth Century Atrocities* (Lewistown, N.Y.: Edwin Mellen Press, 1999), p. 1.

4. Some of these University of Chicago seminars were supplemented by my jurisprudence courses at Loyola University of Chicago School of Law. See, on the Basic Program of Liberal Education for Adults, Anastaplo, *The Artist as Thinker*, pp. 299–300. See also George Anastaplo, "'McCarthyism,' the Cold War, and Their Aftermath," 43 *South Dakota Law Review* 103, 163, 169 (1998). See as well note 46 of chapter 2 of this collection.

The University of Chicago lectures upon which the seven introductions in this collection are based were delivered in this order: chapter 1: September 6, 1985; chapter 2: April 17, 1994; chapter 3: April 12, 1981; chapter 4: January 18, 1974; chapter 5: September 4, 1987; chapter 6: November 6, 1977; chapter 7: April 22, 1990. See, for the dates of the original publication for these lectures, note 8 of this preface.

5. *The Great Ideas Today* was a volume issued annually by the *Encyclopaedia Britanica* between 1961 and 1998. See, for my tribute to its editors, George Anastaplo, "Law & Literature and the Bible: Explorations," 23 *Oklahoma City University Law Review* 515, 865–66 (1998). See, for John Van Doren's comments on this remarkable annual publication, the foreword to this collection. See also note 9 of this preface.

6. An abridged version of this lecture on Confucian thought was published in the summer 1974 issue of the *University of Chicago Magazine* (pp. 21–28).

7. See George Anastaplo, "An Introduction to Confucian Thought," *The Great Ideas Today*, p. 124 (1984). The instructive illustrations accompanying that article, as was the case also for all subsequent articles published by me in *The Great Ideas Today* series, were selected by the art director. The James Legge translation of the *Analects* of Confucius was included in the 1984 volume of *The Great Ideas Today*.

8. The seven introductions in this collection were published in these years in *The Great Ideas Today*: chapter 1: 1986; chapter 2: 1995; chapter 3: 1985; chapter 4: 1984; chapter 5: 1992; chapter 6: 1989; chapter 7: 1993. Sometimes my manuscript, especially its notes, was abridged for publication. See, on the illustrations for these articles, note 7 of this preface. Related materials were included in the following volumes of *The Great Ideas Today*: 1984: the *Analects* of Confucius; 1985: the *Bhagavad Gita*; 1986: the Epic of *Gilgamesh*.

9. An index for the entire series (1961-1998) may be found in the final volume of *The Great Ideas Today*. Mr. Adler was the editor and Mr. Van Doren was the executive editor during the period (1984–1995) when my seven introductions were published. Cynthia L.

Rutz, Rachel N. Ankeny, and Amanda E. Fuller (all St. John's College graduates) were editorial assistants during this period.

See, on Mortimer J. Adler, George Anastaplo, "Democracy and Philosophy: On Yves R. Simon and Mortimer J. Adler," in Michael D. Torre, ed., *Freedom in the Modern World* (American Maritain Association, 1989), p. 79. See also note 14 of this preface. See, on John Van Doren, George Anastaplo, "Lawyers, First Principles, and Contemporary Challenges: Explorations," 19 *Northern Illinois University Law Review* 353, 396 (1999); the text at note 38 of appendix B of this collection.

10. See Larry Arnhart, *Aristotle on Political Reasoning: A Commentary on the "Rhetoric"* (DeKalb, Ill.: Northern Illinois University Press, 1981); Larry Arnhart, *Darwinian Natural Right: The Biological Ethics of Human Nature* (Albany, N. Y.: State University of New York, 1998).

11. Larry Arnhart, "George Anastaplo on Non-Western Thought," 26 *Political Science Review* 214–15 (1997). This is one of seven articles contributed to the symposium, "The Scholarship of George Anastaplo," which was published in the 1997 issue of the Review. My immediate response was also published in that issue; my more extended response was published in the 1998 volume of the *Review.* See also note 14 of this preface.

See, for the scholarship discussed, "George Anastaplo: Tables of Contents for His Books and Published Collections (1950–2001)," 39 *Brandeis Law Journal* 219–87 (2000–2001); "George Anastaplo: An Autobiographical Bibliography (1947–2001)," 20 *Northern Illinois University Law Review* 579–708 (2000).

12. Arnhart, "George Anastaplo on Non-Western Thought," p. 215 (emphasis added). Much of what I have done in these introductions is a study of piety—and of how the wise can properly use piety (something which, I suspect, women are more sensitive to these days than are men). Among the topics which I consider are death, happiness, and the political order. I am concerned, in large part, with how the natural awareness of human mortality is conjured with, around the world and across millennia.

13. Arnhart, "George Anastaplo on Non-Western Thought," pp. 215–16. Some argue, of course, that philosophy has also *developed* elsewhere, independently of that Western tradition which began perhaps in sixth-century Italy, a most remarkable (if not even miraculous) beginning in that part of the Greek world. I have, in various of my introductions in this collection, questioned this proposition, along with the willingness of translators into English of ancient non-Western texts to use the term *nature.* See also appendix B of this collection. Indeed, this entire collection can be understood as an attempt to pose and to refine, if not also to answer, the question, "What is Philosophy?"

Nature is not simply that which we often mean when we refer to material properties, climate, mortality, passions, mental capacities, and the like. It includes, as particularly significant, that principle of constancy and change in things, a principle of order that is independent of a superintending Intelligence. See, on *beginnings*, note 23 of this preface; appendix A of this collection. See, on *nature* as commonly spoken of, note 42 of chapter 1 of this collection; notes 78 and 80 of chapter 3 of this collection.

14. Arnhart, "George Anastaplo on Non-Western Thought," p. 216. I observed, in my immediate response to Mr. Arnhart and his colleagues, "One of the essayists makes me more sympathetic to Muhammad than I am, while two of them make me less sympathetic to Joan of Arc than I believe myself to be." Anastaplo, "First Impressions," 26 *Political Science Review* 248, 249 (1997).

One obviously learned commentator upon this collection, after observing that my "analysis is based on a notion of 'natural right' which is similar to 'natural law' and 'natural theology,'" then added, "I thought that these notions were dead or at least disreputable in the post-modern world. At any rate it does seem to end up in 'natural religion' which had its heyday in the Eighteenth Century." Another, theology-minded, commentator on this collection has observed, "[Y]ou give a 'Straussian' reading, or at least take a 'Straussian' approach to these religions, but from a uniquely Anastaploian perspective. This means that (unlike some of our brethren, but like our teacher [Leo Strauss]), you pay utmost attention to what may be learned from religions in terms of wisdom, the love of wisdom, and the life led in search of wisdom. You do so especially as such issues are tacitly or openly confronted by the most serious religions." It *is* instructive to see intelligence and reasoning (including political prudence) at work in these ancient texts—and to see how nature somehow asserts herself even when not explicitly noticed and studied.

It should be recorded as a tribute to Mortimer J. Adler (see note 9 of this preface), that although he was vigorously opposed to Leo Strauss's mode of reading philosophical texts, he never indicated in any way that I should not try to adapt that mode to the reading of non-Western texts, which I did for the dozen or so articles I prepared for the publications he supervised. See note 1 of this preface. See also the dedication for this collection.

The concluding paragraph of another preface of mine addresses those who dismiss various old-fashioned notions as "dead or at least disreputable in the post-modern world":

A reviewer of *The Artist as Thinker* reports, "Anastaplo writes for an audience that believes there 'are moral and political standards rooted in nature and discernible by reason.' His audience died on July 14, 1789." (23 *Victorian Poetry* 290 [1985]) This [*Artist as Thinker*] book is still another contribution to the attempt to resurrect among us the vital teaching that there are indeed moral and political standards rooted in nature and discernible by reason. Is there not, in the respect still accorded generally in the modern world to common sense, a reflection of the hold upon human beings of the sound practical judgment traditionally associated with natural law or, perhaps better still, with natural right?

George Anastaplo, *The American Moralist: On Law, Ethics, and Government* (Athens, Ohio: Ohio University Press, 1992), p. xxiii.

15. Those endorsements, often qualified, have been most helpful. I have been able to refer to some of them in the notes for the seven introductions. (My most vigorous critics have been the physicists and astrophysicists who were kind enough to read the Stephen Hawking part of appendix A of this collection). Various competent experts have saved me from obvious errors throughout this collection—but they have no doubt left some for others to find.

16. See, for the dates of publications, notes 6, 7, and 8 of this preface. I was surprised to learn, upon putting this collection together, how little overlapping there had been during the decade of publication in *The Great Ideas Today* (which had been anticipated, a decade earlier, by publication of one introduction in the *University of Chicago Magazine*).

17. Oral sources had to be relied upon in studying both sub-Saharan African thought and North American Indian thought. There are special problems here because these materials had been reduced to writing by Westerners, for the most part. The Egyptian materials also depend upon "non-scriptural" materials which have been largely reconstituted by ancient historians or by modern scholars.

Chapter 1 of this collection introduces questions of *eros* and mortality, both of which are important for philosophical inquiry. Chapter 2 exhibits how "obsessed" (and yet cheerful) the ancient Egyptians became with the problem of mortality, anticipating in critical respects some movements in the United States today.

18. I, like, Odysseus, have seen (in this collection) many strange peoples and ways, but always (like him also) with a view to returning home. I attempt, in my odyssey, to remain mindful of the courses charted heretofore by Homer, Herodotus, Montesquieu, Rousseau, and Hegel.

19. Kenneth Hart Green, of the Department for the Study of Religion at the University of Toronto, has observed (in his thoughtful comments to me on these materials) that the only "major" tradition I have left out in this collection is Taoism, which is based on the Tao Te Ching of Lao Tzu. There has been in Taoism, I gather thus far, a curious movement over millennia from the more philosophical to the more mystical. This seems to be the reverse of the movement Westerners have seen in "mainstream" Christianity, and in "mainstream" Judaism, and perhaps in "mainstream" Islam. See notes 40 and 90 of chapter 4 of this collection, note 38 of chapter 5 of this collection.

20. The "rhetorical" is critical to how these traditions can be explained and understood by outsiders. It is critical also to the workings of prophecy. See, on prophecy, note 38 of chapter 4 of this collection. Relevant here are reflections on the nature of *nature* and on *beginnings*. See, e.g., notes 13 and 23 of this preface.

21. Various experts, to whom we are indebted for many of the texts we have in usable forms, are cited in each chapter of this collection. Some readers may even find my notes more useful than the discussion in my text. The experts, of course, are highly likely to know the languages of the materials with which they work. They are likely to know as well both historical antecedents and contemporary developments in "their" parts of the world. In addition, different selections of texts might have been relied upon by them.

22. My attempts at careful reading have included commentaries, elsewhere, on Plato's *Apology of Socrates* and on Shakespeare's plays. See, e.g., George Anastaplo, *Human Being and Citizen: Essays on Virtue, Freedom, and the Common Good* (Chicago: Swallow Press, 1975), p. 8; George Anastaplo, "Law & Literature and Shakespeare: Explorations," 26 *Oklahoma City University Law Review* (forthcoming). My most intensive reading thus far has been the devotion of some six hundred pages to the study of one sentence in the Constitution of the United States. See George Anastaplo, *The Constitutionalist: Notes on the First Amendment* (Dallas: Southern Methodist University Press, 1971). See also Anastaplo, *The Constitution of 1787: A Commentary* (Baltimore: Johns Hopkins University Press, 1989); Anastaplo, *The Amendments to the Constitution: A Commentary* (Baltimore: Johns Hopkins University Press, 1995).

23. Appendix A ("On Beginnings") was first published, in an abridged form, in the 1998 volume of *The Great Ideas Today*.

In order to talk sensibly about beginnings, one has to know something about the things which begin as well as about the things (if any) which are always. In addition, not only does one have to consider what it means to begin, but one has to be at least aware of the end (or the likely termination) of that which has begun. Is there also implicit in this inquiry a sense of what Nothingness (or non-being) is? Can one talk meaningfully about beginnings if one does not somehow draw upon that out of which something begins which had not been "there" before? Or must there be something which orders or requires the beginning, something other than the materials shaped or reshaped for *this* beginning. Once we are aware of all that there is, do we sense that the whole must always have existed? And yet do we not also sense that all this is highly questionable, or deficient, if we are not somehow forever part of the whole? See, on the significance of the Doctrine of the Ideas, George Anastaplo, *The Thinker as Artist: From Homer to Plato and Aristotle* (Athens, Ohio: Ohio University Press, 1997), p. 303. See, on *nature*, note 13 of this preface; appendix B of this collection. See also sections XIV and XV of chapter 3 of this collection.

24. See appendix C of this collection, on the 1993 Parliament of the World's Religions, which was preceded by the 1893 Parliament. It has now become of immediate practical importance in this country to learn something of what other "schools" of thought are like, partly because of what is happening to ethnicity here (with a higher proportion of the population being of non-European descent anticipated than ever before). Many of these people will have, after a generation or two here, only mangled memories of their heritages, with far less exposure to the relevant materials than that which I provide in this collection.

Distinctive to the West pehaps may be the longstanding tension between Revelation and Reason. Perhaps this helps us to study and to grasp radically different ways of life, ways which are apt to be revelation-based. See chapter 3 of this collection, notes 7 and 79; see chapter 4 of this collection, notes 14 and 109.

25. Socrates suggests to Chaerephon that the key question to put to Gorgias, who invites all questions, is to ask him "who he is." See Plato, *Gorgias* 447A. This kind of inquiry proceeds, in part, by eliminating what one is not. See, on nature and the human soul, appendix B of this collection. See also note 13 of this preface. See, on the nature of philosophy, section II of chapter 4 of this collection; sections XI, XII, and XIII of chapter 4 of this collection. See, for the religious foundations of the West, Anastaplo, "Law and Literature and the Bible: Explorations," 23 *Oklahoma City University Law Review* 515 (1998); Anastaplo, "Law and Literature and the Christian Heritage: Explorations," 40 *Brandeis Law Journal* (forthcoming).

Consider as well Leo Strauss, *The Rebirth of Classical Political Rationalism*, Thomas L. Pangle, ed. (Chicago: University of Chicago Press, 1989), pp. 43–44:

> Within the West the limitations of rationalism were always seen by the Biblical tradition. . . . Biblical thought is one form of Eastern thought. By taking the Bible as absolute, one blocks access to other forms of Eastern thought. Yet the Bible is the East within us, Western men. Not the Bible as Bible but the Bible as Eastern can help us in overcoming Greek rationalism.

26. My hope is to provide in this collection a somewhat better understanding of the major non-Western traditions, as seen in the light of philosophy, than has been available anywhere else in print for the general reader, so far as I know. I hope also that those competent to do so will provide whatever corrections I need in the course I have charted for this odyssey. See note 14 of this preface.

Chapter One

Mesopotamian Thought: The *Gilgamesh* Epic

Mother, mother, what shall we do?
  The leaves are turning brown!
Wetness shines on gray porch roofs,
  Fog hides all our town.

Daughter, daughter, calm yourself
  The whole world's death is a little thing.
Take your toys to another room;
  Play a while till spring.

—Sara Prince Anastaplo, *First Fall*[1]

I.

More than five thousand years ago the story was first told of a king, Gil-gamesh, who was in some ways bad, in other ways good.[2] The power of this story is attested to by the great expanse that it covered, both in time and in space—for it appeared in various ancient Mesopotamian countries (and in as many languages) and over more than a thousand years.[3] And yet it was a story that could be lost, perhaps in part because its central issues, or assumptions, became obsolete, at least until modern times.[4]

It is useful to provide, at the outset of this chapter, a summary of the prin-cipal story about Gilgamesh, who seems to have been a historical ruler in what we now know as the Middle East.[5] In fact, two summaries would be use-ful, if not even three, which is particularly appropriate considering how much use is made in the *Gilgamesh* epic itself of repetitions.[6]

Our first summary is taken from a guide to world literature, which reads,

Gilgamesh: a Babylonian epic poem (c. 2000 B.C.). From ancient records it is known that this poem was once more than twice as long as what has survived from

1

it. In its present form it is pieced together from nearly 30,000 tablets or fragments in three languages. The poem tells the adventures of Gilgamesh, who begins as a harsh ruler, has a terrific battle with a primitive figure [Enkidu] and then becomes his staunch friend, loses this friend, tries vainly to regain him, and finally confers with his shade in the land of the dead. The poem, like most primitive epics, is probably pieced together from a good many stories originally independent. One of the most interesting sections is the Babylonian tale of the Flood (Tablet XI), which is a remarkable parallel to the story of Noah's Flood in *Genesis*. The final section, which describes the world after death, is a literal translation from a Sumerian poem.[7]

It is in this final section (Tablet XII) that Gilgamesh confers with the shade of his dead friend, Enkidu.[8]

Our next summary adds a couple of essential points to the one we have just used. It is taken from the editorial comment introducing the epic in the E. A. Speiser translation:

> The theme of this epic is essentially a secular one. The poem deals with such earthy things as man and nature, love and adventure, friendship and combat—all masterfully blended into a background for the stark reality of death. The climactic struggle of the protagonist to change his eventual fate, by learning the secret of immortality from the hero of the Great Flood of long ago [Utnapishtim], ends in failure; but with the failure comes a sense of quiet resignation. For the first time in the history of the world a profound experience on such a heroic scale has found expression in a noble style. The scope and sweep of the epic, and its sheer poetic power, give it a timeless appeal. In antiquity, the influence of the poem spread to various tongues and cultures. Today it captivates student and poet alike.[9]

The considerable interest in this epic in modern times began with a fascination with its account of the Great Flood, something that very much caught the attention of Westerners steeped in the Bible. This happened when the *Gilgamesh* epic was rediscovered by English archaeologists at Nineveh in the second half of the nineteenth century.[10] The account of the Flood, which is particularly intriguing because of its parallels to the account in Genesis, did not originate in any of the stories about Gilgamesh.[11] But this Flood account, evidently developed elsewhere, is used by our poet to illuminate the primary concerns of the *Gilgamesh* epic, namely *eros* (that is, life and desire) and *death* (which, I will suggest, is understood to be critical to life).[12]

We turn now to our third summary, a somewhat more detailed one, which I have put together.[13] Gilgamesh, at the outset of this twelve-tablet Akkadian-language poem, is condemned by his people, especially by the nobles, as arrogant: he seems to be taking advantage of a royal sexual prerogative with the brides of the city of Uruk,[14] and he seems to be assigning wearisome tasks to the young men. Complaints against him are heard by the gods. It seems to be taken for granted by our poet and by his audience that, of course, the gods will do something about this oppressive king, who is recognized as a mighty man.[15] The response of the gods is a complicated one, beginning with the immediate creation of another powerful man, already fully grown, who looks very much like Gilgamesh.[16] This is Enkidu: he is shaggy all over his body; he is endowed with a head of hair like a woman's, he knows neither people nor land. In fact, he lives among the animals, moving about with them as they feed and drink.[17]

But whereas Gilgamesh had caused problems for his fellow men in the city, Enkidu causes problems for them in the countryside (or desert), since he is adept at filling pits and springing traps, thereby protecting from hunters the animals with which he associates. A hunter complains about this to his father, who advises him to go to King Gilgamesh for help. When the hunter does go to Uruk to complain to Gilgamesh, the king responds in the way that the hunter's father had anticipated;[18] a harlot is sent out from Uruk into the wild to display her charms to Enkidu, who responds as anticipated and is thereby tamed, so much so that his animal companions flee from him thereafter.[19]

The now civilized Enkidu, upon learning of Gilgamesh's notorious practice with the maids of Uruk, is shocked. Enkidu, aided by the harlot with whom he has been consorting, hastens to Uruk and stations himself at the building in which Gilgamesh goes to the women. Gilgamesh and Enkidu grapple ferociously outside the bridal chamber; the king prevails but, instead of killing his antagonist, he befriends him. They become inseparable companions and, so far as we know, Gilgamesh has nothing further to do with the maids of Uruk. (The harlot had anticipated what in fact happens, that Gilgamesh would have dreams which announced both his encounter and his future relations with Enkidu. Other dreams punctuate the story, anticipating again and again what is to happen.[20])

At Gilgamesh's insistence, and despite the protests of Enkidu and the concerns of the elders of Uruk, the two companions go to a distant land (to the Cedar Forest) to destroy the monstrous Humbaba.[21] Humbaba tries to surrender to them, but Enkidu insists upon his death. Earlier Enkidu had had to encourage Gilgamesh to continue the expedition, but thereafter had had to be encouraged himself by Gilgamesh.[22]

The two triumphant companions return home to great acclaim. There then follows in the center of the epic as we have it (Tablets VI and VII), the fatal encounter with Ishtar, a goddess who (to draw on Greek counterparts) seems to combine three elements: the eroticism of "glorious Aphrodite," the warlikeness of Athena, and the fertility of Ceres. Thus, the narrator tells us,

Gilgamesh washed his grimy hair, polished his weapons,
The braid of his hair he shook out against his back.
He cast off his soiled things, put on his clean ones,

Wrapped a fringed cloak about and fastened a sash.
When Gilgamesh had put on his tiara,
Glorious Ishtar raised an eye at the beauty of Gilgamesh:
"Come, Gilgamesh, be thou my lover!"[23]

The goddess then describes for him all the good things she will provide him as his wife. The king makes it clear, all too clear, that he wants nothing to do with her, dismissing her as unreliable. He recites a catalog of a half-dozen others whom she has loved, and who suffered because of her attentions.[24]

Gilgamesh's frank rebuke of Ishtar enrages her.[25] She goes to her father, Anu, who seems to be the first of the gods, demanding revenge. This leads, with precautions (lest all mankind be wiped out), to the despatch against Gilgamesh of the voracious Bull of Heaven. We are surprised to see that the two companions, Gilgamesh and Enkidu, are able to kill this divine instrument, dedicating its heart, with appropriate ceremonies, to the god Shamash (who had helped them against the Bull, as well as against Humbaba). Enkidu, however, adds insult to injury by throwing the right thigh of the Bull of Heaven at Ishtar, whom he sees hovering nearby and who is most disturbed by the turn of events.[26]

The heroic pair have gone too far. The gods confer, concluding that one of the heroes must die—and Enkidu is settled upon. He wastes away, and Gilgamesh becomes depressed by the decline and then the death of Enkidu.[27] His strong reaction to the death of his companion (someone very much like him) drives him to wander far (reverting to the primitive condition in which Enkidu had once been?). This long journey ends in a distant land where there is to be found Utnapishtim and his wife, who survived the Great Flood long before and who have never died.[28] During his journey, Gilgamesh is repeatedly told that he cannot avoid death. Utnapishtim tells him the same thing, even as he describes how he and his wife happened to survive the Great Flood and to win deathlessness. Finally, however, Utnapishtim tells Gilgamesh about a plant, which Gilgamesh then secures from the bottom of the sea, and which Utnapishtim says can be used to rejuvenate him. With this in hand, Gilgamesh starts home.[29]

On the way home, however, he is robbed of his plant by a serpent,[30] and so, bereft, he returns to Uruk with Utnapishtim's boatman.[31] By now Gilgamesh is more or less reconciled to his mortality. (He senses that he is bound to lose whatever he acquires in any future attempt to counter his mortality?) The eleventh tablet, and hence the story proper, concludes with Gilgamesh's showing the boatman the walls of Uruk and the temple of Ishtar. On this occasion he uses words that echo the opening lines of the first tablet of our epic.

The twelfth tablet tells a separate, yet related, story:[32] Gilgamesh once drops into the underworld some treasures which had been given him by Ishtar; Enkidu, who is still alive at the beginning of this tablet, volunteers to fetch them, but he does not follow the prudent instructions given him by Gilgamesh and so is permanently trapped in the underworld.[33] But Gilgamesh manages to secure thereafter an interview with the shade of Enkidu, who conveys to him what it means to be dead—the decay and the dissolution. The conclusion of the twelfth tablet is lost; but the fragments we do have indicate that Enkidu also tells Gilgamesh about the burial rites and services that should be provided the dead by survivors, as well as about the consequences of disposing of corpses without proper ceremony. Thus, it would seem, the twelfth (and final) tablet advocates a systematized response to death.[34]

This, then, is the *Gilgamesh* epic. More details will be drawn upon as I comment on various intriguing features of this six-thousand-year-old story, a story which has been called "the most significant literary creation of the whole of ancient Mesopotamia."[35]

II.

One challenging feature of this epic is the ambiguity in the character of Gilgamesh himself. He exhibits remarkable shifts between heroic strength and an all-too-human weakness (if not even sensuality and cowardice).[36]

Thus, Gilgamesh can dare much. He volunteers to challenge the terrible Humbaba, believing this to be the means for eliminating evil from the world.[37] Gilgamesh is heroic, but not philosophical; in fact, at times he can seem shallow. Even so, he is introduced as "he who saw everything to the ends of the land."[38]

Yet Gilgamesh *is* shown early as lustful, creating dissension (at least among the nobility) because of his exercise of his prerogatives with brides (and because of the attendant rigor evidently used to divert the young men of the city).[39] In a sense, that is, difficulties follow upon his being at the outset too much the disciple of Ishtar, the very goddess against whom he later rebels, with dire consequences for his companion.[40]

Thereafter Gilgamesh becomes remarkably demoralized, not only by the death of Enkidu, but even more by the prospect of his own death. He frantically strives to avoid death: those whom he encounters in his journey to secure immortality are quite struck by his shattered demeanor, especially considering his exploits and reputation.[41]

Thus Gilgamesh runs to extremes, whether in his pursuit of the erotic or in his turning away from it, whether in his contempt for death or in his abhorrence of it. Perhaps Mesopotamian life was always marked by these critical ambiguities.[42] Perhaps, also, deep ambiguity may naturally be found in any way of life which makes as much of sexuality and the female element in its *public* life as the ancient Mesopotamians evidently did.[43]

III.

We have already noticed the importance of Ishtar, the goddess who can be understood to stand for life itself. We have also noticed that Gilgamesh has a dramatic encounter with her (around which the twelve tablets turn), an encounter which proves decisive to the plot, leading to Enkidu's death and to what Gilgamesh does thereafter.[44]

This encounter obscures, however, just how much peaceful collaboration there is between Gilgamesh and Ishtar, both before and after this fateful encounter. It becomes evident, upon examination, that mankind has to rely upon Ishtar continuously. Thus, Gilgamesh learns from Utnapishtim how troubled Ishtar had been upon seeing mankind threatened by the Great Flood.[45] She had very much resented, on that occasion, the death of the creatures for whose existence she considered herself intimately responsible. At the end of the eleventh tablet we can hear Gilgamesh acknowledging the importance of the Temple of Ishtar as he shows off to a stranger the marvels of his city, Uruk.[46]

That Ishtar is somehow responsible for life itself is evident again and again. Thus, a barmaid encountered by Gilgamesh in the course of his pursuit of immortality seems to be an Ishtar figure: she counsels him to enjoy himself while he can, making much of food and drink and of association with one's spouse and children.[47] Indeed, Ishtar seems to be so much responsible for life that she can even threaten Anu on one occasion with bringing back to "life" on earth all of the dead, who would thus outnumber and overwhelm the living.[48]

There are other questionable features in Ishtar's character as well. These may be seen, for example, in the bridal rights that Gilgamesh has exercised, evidently as king. Ambiguities may also be seen in the perhaps related institution of temple-harlotry, which may have been drawn upon in civilizing Enkidu.[49] On the other hand, the catalog of grievances which Gilgamesh hurls at Ishtar, in rejecting her overtures, should be examined more carefully than the king himself seems able to do. That is, it is far from certain that the fates of the six lovers there described (Gilgamesh would have been her seventh) were as undeserved, or as much a reproach to Ishtar, as Gilgamesh seems to believe.[50] In fact, one can see running through these grievances references to developments that contributed to the furtherance of civilization, as happened also in the case of the use of the harlot with Enkidu.[51]

One must wonder, in short, whether Gilgamesh is able to face up to what Ishtar really means. Indeed, one must wonder, did Enkidu become for Gilgamesh a temporary substitute for the erotic? It is indicated, in several ways, that Enkidu is somehow female in his relation with Gilgamesh: for example, the head hair of Enkidu; the dreams of Gilgamesh, in which things are encountered that stand for Enkidu and are responded to as if female; and, of course, the intensity of the relationship between the two.[52] Certainly, the death of Enkidu provokes the quite unexpected response we have already noticed, a response which suggests that the loss of Enkidu dramatizes problems for Gilgamesh (perhaps with both death and the erotic) that he may have sensed all along.[53]

IV.

One is induced by this epic to wonder about the status of death, and hence of immortality, for the human race. We remember that Enkidu becomes, after his sexual encounter with the harlot, quite unlike the brutes he had freely associated with. Brutes, it can be said, really know nothing about the erotic, if only because the truly erotic has a rational component to it.[54] Should it not be said that brutes do not know anything about death either, if only because they do not understand the difference between life and death?[55] Thus, both eroticism and consciousness of mortality require understanding and are otherwise related as well.[56]

Gilgamesh, early in the story, is quite sensible about death. When Enkidu tries to discourage the dangerous expedition against the fierce Humbaba, Gilgamesh replies,

Who, my friend, can scale heaven?
Only the gods live forever under the sun.
As for mankind, numbered are their days;
Whatever they achieve is but the wind![57]

And he adds, "A name that endures I will make for me!"[58]

Thereafter, Gilgamesh engages in the slaughter of both Humbaba and the Bull of Heaven. The killings do not sober him; rather, he exults in these exploits. But the dying and death of Enkidu move him to despair, "moaning bitterly like a wailing woman."[59] Much has been made of Enkidu as someone who looks like Gilgamesh, who has his strength, and so forth.[60] The death of Enkidu means that, evidently for the first time, Gilgamesh has seen someone very much like himself die.[61] That this death is not in battle, or from any obvious affliction, suggests that it is due to the very nature (and hence to the inevitable limitations) of the human being. Death, or his own vulnerability, is brought close to home when Gilgamesh, after seven days and seven nights of watchful waiting and wailing over Enkidu's corpse, sees a worm come out of his nose.[62]

The despairing Gilgamesh is told several times that death cannot be avoided.[63] Perhaps most eloquent is the counsel of Utnapishtim, the immortal survivor of the Great Flood, which counsel includes these words:

Do we build a house forever?
Do we seal contracts forever?
Do brothers divide shares forever?

Does hatred persist forever in the land?
Does the river forever raise up and bring on floods?
The dragon-fly leaves its shell
That its face might but glance at the face of the sun.
Since the days of yore there has been no permanence;
The resting and the dead, how alike they are!
Do they not compose a picture of death,
The commoner and the noble,
Once they are near to their fate?[64]

Death is likened to sleep on more than one occasion in this epic.[65] The implications of this resemblance are suggested by an episode involving Gilgamesh, Utnapishtim, and Utnapishtim's wife. The weary Gilgamesh falls asleep, despite a determination not to (as a test of his eligibility for fending off death?). He sleeps for seven days but he insists, upon awakening, that he has slept only one night. He has to be disproved by the precautions Utnapishtim had taken in marking the passage of time (by the daily baking of wafers).[66] There is nothing explicitly said by the poet or grasped by Gilgamesh as to one critical lesson of this episode: if one can sleep a week without knowing it, and without "missing" it, why not years or decades also? And if so, why should death matter?[67]

We recall that the plant recommended by Utnapishtim is not something that grants perpetual deathlessness but merely rejuvenation, and even that plant is lost before Gilgamesh can get home. He does not thereupon try to go back to get more of that plant. Rather, he continues homeward, as if at last recognizing that his effort to fend off mortality had always been a hopeless venture.[68] But then, do we not know that the normal human being "accepts" death from a surprisingly early age? It takes very few observations or experiences to persuade us of the general mortality of all the living things we encounter. Do we come to sense it "in our bones"?

V.

Gilgamesh ends up being reconciled to death just as he has been reconciled to eros. In both cases, the reconciliation may reflect hopelessness, if not even desperation, thereby testifying to a limited understanding. That is, he finally accepts that which all somehow sense and adapt themselves to, some more naturally than does Gilgamesh.

The connection between death and eros is several times indicated. It may be seen most dramatically perhaps in the gods, who live primarily, if not only, through the mortals they get involved with. Consider the implications of words addressed by Gilgamesh to the deathless Utnapishtim shortly after they first meet:

As I look upon thee, Utnapishtim,
Thy features are not strange; even as I art thou.
Thou art not strange at all; even as I art thou.
My heart had regarded thee as resolved to do battle,
Yet thou liest indolent upon thy back?
Tell me, how joinedst thou the Assembly of the gods,
In thy quest for life?[69]

Utnapishtim then tells the story of the Great Flood.

The fact that the ancient Utnapishtim resembles Gilgamesh as much as he does suggests that we have here still another substitute for Gilgamesh, a parallel to his contemporary, Enkidu. Utnapishtim has transcended mortality somehow, evidently because of his great cunning.[70] But consider the price paid by Utnapishtim—a price of which Gilgamesh does not seem to appreciate the full significance when he says:

My heart had regarded thee as resolved to do battle,
Yet thou liest indolent upon thy back!

Is not Gilgamesh, even though he does not seem to recognize it, much more vital, much more alive, than the indolent Utnapishtim? We, in turn, can learn from all this something which the battle-oriented Gilgamesh may not learn as he wrestles with his condition.[71]

The erotic element is life-seeking, and life-giving; and it can be fully what it is (with its capacity to evoke the splendid) because of the possibility, nay, the inevitability, of death. The intimate relation between eros and death may be reflected in the status of the female element in this epic (and in the civilization which made this epic possible). Thus memorable females are shown to us—the harlot, the mother of Gilgamesh, "glorious Ishtar" herself, the barmaid, and Utnapishtim's wife.

The female is again and again presented in this story as the source of critical instruction and help. This may point up the importance of the erotic as life-serving. Are women particularly life-giving and hence death-averting? Does not the male element in this story tend to be identified more with death and destruction (as is the male god Enlil, who had commissioned Humbaba to guard the Cedar Forest, and who had long before visited the Flood upon mankind)?[72]

Did the civilization in which this story flourished go too far in its subservience to the female element? That may be seen, perhaps, in the institution of temple-harlots dedicated to Ishtar. One can usefully compare to this institution that of the Vestal Virgins in Rome. One is also reminded of how vigorously both the Israelite prophets and the early Christians attacked as abominations the kind of erotic worship associated with Ishtar.[73] Even so, there are some marvelous women in this story.

VI.

Perhaps it is because women are so prominent that dreams are as important here as they are. Certainly, the interpretation of dreams is evidently a special, but not the exclusive, province of women. As we have noticed, a harlot anticipates Gilgamesh's dreams about Enkidu. When the dreams do come, Gilgamesh goes to his mother for an authoritative interpretation.[74]

Dreams are tools in the service of humanity: they provide access to knowledge of what will be, perhaps (at least in part) by providing one with insights into one's own character. Evidently dreams are not understood to have been sent as messengers of the gods, strictly speaking. Utnapishtim was not "told" by any god about the Flood and about the boat he would need—all this evidently came to him in a dream (albeit at the prompting of a god). This, it seems, is not understood to be a *telling* by any god, since it is still up to the human being to figure out the meaning of what has been received. Do dreams reflect what we all somehow sense? Are they a special kind of thinking done by human beings? Does this suggest that everything is somehow interconnected?[75]

The gods rarely dream in Mesopotamian literature. Perhaps they do not have to, because most of them are not vulnerable in the way that human beings are. Perhaps, therefore, women are more prone than men to be adept with dreams because the female tends to be more vulnerable than the male.

VII.

To say that the gods are not time bound in the way that human beings are is not to say that they are omnipotent or omniscient. Consider, for example, what happens to the Bull of Heaven sent by the gods to punish Gilgamesh: it is killed by Gilgamesh and Enkidu. Or consider, much earlier, the fact that the god powerful enough to bring on the Great Flood could not destroy all of mankind as he had planned.[76]

I have suggested that the gods may live primarily, if not only, through the human beings with whom they become involved, at least in our epic. The gods are often portrayed as being very much like human beings in critical respects. They too can be intimidated by, and can cower in the face of, the storm that brings on the Flood. Later, they can respond greedily to the savor of the sacrifice offered by Utnapishtim.[77]

Perhaps it is because the gods are very much like human beings in critical respects that mortals can keep track of what the gods are doing. (Enkidu reports to Gilgamesh after their killing of the Bull of Heaven that the gods have just had a conference about them.) Certainly the human beings in the *Gil-*

gamesh epic are often very much aware of what the gods are up to, seen most dramatically perhaps in Gilgamesh's awareness of Ishtar's passion for him, which he resists so passionately.[78]

The two most dramatic gods in this story seem to be Ishtar, with her emphasis upon the erotic (or upon life), and Enlil, with his emphasis upon the destructive (or upon death). Far less dramatic, but perhaps even more impressive, may be the gods (and especially Anu?) who set into motion the action of this epic. Cannot the entire story be seen as a complicated divine response to the opening complaints about the arrogant Gilgamesh? All that happens thereafter may be seen as part of a great plan to instruct Gilgamesh, and other human beings who watch and learn, about the perils of arrogance (if not about the limitations of kingship itself).[79] This means, among other things, that Gilgamesh must be made to grasp what the erotic element, which he is so cavalierly exploiting, means; the king must be made to see how vulnerable even he is to death. Thus he must come to terms, in a complicated way, with both the erotic and the mortal (and hence with the restraints that mortality calls for).

VIII.

And so, at the end of the eleventh tablet (where the story can be said "properly" to end) Gilgamesh is shown celebrating the walls and the temple of Uruk. The king has thereby returned to his political (and priestly?) duties, having abandoned self-gratification either in the form of mere personal satisfaction (whether through sexuality or through adventures) or in the perhaps related form of a desperate quest for personal immortality on earth.

A proper (Mesopotamian?) recognition of the erotic may be seen, at the end, in Gilgamesh's deference to the Temple of Ishtar; a proper (political?) recognition of death may be seen in his admiration for the city walls. Temples and walls are monuments to life, and to the preservation of life in the face of death, including the indolence (a kind of death) which can accompany such human deathlessness as Utnapishtim displays.

It may well be that the twelfth (and final) tablet, an epilogue of sorts, may present a story that tells, in still another way, how life and death may be reconciled. Perhaps there is something fitting (if not even providential) in the mutilated condition of this particular tablet, which reminds us once again of how vulnerable human things can be. The story in the twelfth tablet does seem to indicate that one's last days are best served by the family and by the city, which make possible the proper rituals and a fitting burial upon death. Although the decay and the irrevocability of death are emphasized in

Enkidu's report from the underworld, there may also be an indication of better and worse earthly ways to respond to this inevitable fate. One depends upon one's survivors, at least for one's burial with appropriate rituals, if not also for life-sustaining memory. To speak of survivors, of proper burial, and of memory is to look to the city and to the family—and thus, in still another way, it is to depend both upon the city walls without and upon the Temple of Ishtar within.[80]

IX.

It seems that the poet responsible for this epic—for the final (and best) version of *Gilgamesh*—simply could not leave it at *eleven* tablets. Certainly, it is evident throughout the story that *twelve* is an important number for the Mesopotamians (as is *seven*). In any event, the adding of the final tablet (whether, providentially, as the twelfth or not) was deliberate: it was taken, as I have reported, from a poem which is also found standing alone in Mesopotamian literature. This addition can be understood to tell in still another way the entire story of the relations of Gilgamesh and Ishtar and of the effect upon Gilgamesh of Enkidu's death. Perhaps this is a retelling for the benefit of those who need something more, or something other, than the more complicated story told in the first eleven tablets of the epic.[81]

Perhaps, also, if we knew more about the conclusion of this twelfth tablet, we could better explain what it is doing here. This reminds us of how much has depended already for us upon the generations of dedicated and resourceful scholars who have put this epic back together again, starting with the remarkable nineteenth-century excavations at Nineveh and the meticulous assembly thereafter of thousands upon thousands of pieces. These scholars have retrieved this story from the dustbins of history. The account of their heroic efforts, and of their ingenuity, is itself engaging.[82]

Even more interesting is the question of how much the poet responsible for the final version of this epic was himself aware of with respect to the things I have noticed. There is exhibited in the epic a considerable sophistication, much of which is (I have suggested) related to the status of the female element in Mesopotamian affairs. That is to say, the opinions reflected here are anything but primitive, however colored (if not distorted) they may be by an acceptance of forms of the erotic which require further attention, especially from that perspective which looks to nature for a proper understanding of both eros and death, if not for a proper understanding of understanding itself.[83]

We have here, then, in the poet of the *Gilgamesh* epic, a mind to be reckoned with, someone who is remarkably adept in suggesting the complexities confronted by human beings in the world.[84] These enduring complexities require the most careful weighing of oppositions if we are to understand, and hence to accept, how things truly are.

Notes

1. See *Law and Philosophy: The Practice of Theory*, John A. Murley, William T. Braithwaite, and Robert L. Stone, eds. (Athens, Ohio: Ohio University Press, 1992), vol. 2, pp. 1033–45. See also George Anastaplo, *The Artist as Thinker: From Shakespeare to Joyce* (Athens, Ohio: Ohio University Press, 1983), pp. 422–24; *The Thinker as Artist: From Homer to Plato and Aristotle* (Athens, Ohio: Ohio University Press, 1999), p. v; *The Constitutionalist: Notes on the First Amendment* (Dallas: Southern Methodist University Press, 1971), p. 767 n.184 (to be republished in 2002). See, on Sara Prince Anastaplo, editorial note, *The Great Ideas Today*, p. 252 (1993). See also appendix A, note 114, of this collection.

The remarkable concern with death in our *Gilgamesh* story (see note 41 below) is reflected in John Gardner's comment on the final tablet of that story:

> The tablet is now half in ruin; much of what it says had fallen into the cracks of time. All we know for sure is that it's good to have sons, probably bad to fall from the mast of a ship into nothingness, good to die quickly and painlessly, good to die in battle, bad to die in the wilderness, unnoticed, and unspeakably bad to die unloved. Mainly what we know is that to die is a terrible thing, but to die without having truly lived—without having loved and left loved ones—is to be garbage surviving through eternity on garbage.

"Notes on Gilgamesh, Tablet XII," *MSS*, 2 (1983), pp. 159–64 (quoted in John Gardner and John Maier, *Gilgamesh* [New York: Alfred A. Knopf, 1984], pp. 256–57). See section VII of this chapter. See also note 29 below. (Unless otherwise indicated, all references to notes in any chapter in this collection are to the notes of that chapter.)

Compare the essay, "On Death: One by One, Yet All Together," in Anastaplo, *Human Being and Citizen: Essays on Virtue, Freedon, and the Common Good* (Athens, Ohio: Swallow Press/Ohio University Press, 1975), pp. 214f. See, on the equanimity promoted by being able to "step back," the text at note 100 of chapter 4 of this collection.

2. King David comes to mind, as does Achilles. See notes 16, 36, and 62, below. See, on David, Anastaplo, "Law and Literature and the Bible: Explorations," 23 *Oklahoma City University Law Review* 515, 641 (1998). See, on Gilgamesh's oppressiveness, Jeffrey H. Tigay, *The Evolution of the Gilgamesh Epic* (Philadelphia: University of Pennsylvania Press, 1982), pp. 180f. (Professor Tigay's book has been widely acclaimed, not least as a most useful distillation of what scholars have worked out over the past century about the considerably varied fragments on Gilgamesh that we now have.) "The most renowned of ancient Near Eastern heroes is Gilgamesh, who has been dubbed 'the hero par excellence of the ancient world' and 'the hero without peer of the entire ancient Near East.'" John H. Marks, *"Gilgamesh: An Afterword,"* in Herbert Mason, *Gilgamesh: A Verse Narrative* (New York: New American Library, Mentor Books, 1972), p. 117 (quoting S. N. Kramer). The name of the hero, as worked out from the cuneiform tablets, has been written various ways in modern times. See, e.g., Gardner and Maier, *Gilgamesh*, pp. 43 ("Bilgamesh"), 282–83; *The Babylonian Legends of the Creation* (London: British Museum, 1921), p. 2 ("Gizdubar" and "Gilgamesh"); R. Campbell Thompson, ed., *The Epic of Gilgamesh: Text,*

Transliteration, and Notes (Oxford: Clarendon Press, 1930), pp. 8–10. There is no generally accepted account of what the name means.

3. Professor Tigay speaks of the known written stages of the story extending "over a
period of at least 1,500 years down to the manuscripts of its final version." Tigay, *Evolution*, p. 1. "When this epic was first unearthed in the mid-nineteenth century, the tablets
discovered were from its latest and best-known version, that of the first millennium B.C.E.
. . .[It] is an epic poem covering twelve tablets in its latest version and written in Akkadian, the main Semitic language of ancient Babylonia and Assyria." Ibid., p. 3. (It is this
final version that I refer to in this chapter as "our epic." See note 13 below.)

"The earliest legends we have about Gilgamesh are found in Sumerian lays of the late
third millennium B.C. By a process of sifting out, adaptation, and radical transformation,
probably in the early second millennium B.C., these legends were reworked into a single
epic." William L. Moran, "Utnapishtim Revisited," *New York Times Book Review,*
November 11, 1984, p. 13. "During the seventh century B.C., to which the greater part of
the available tablets date back, the *Gilgamesh* Epic consisted of twelve large tablets, each
of which contained about three hundred lines, with the exception of the twelfth, which had
only about half as many lines." Alexander Heidel, *The Gilgamesh Epic and Old Testament
Parallels,* 2d ed. (Chicago: University of Chicago Press, 1949), p. 1. See, for an inventory
of the ancient texts, Tigay, *Evolution*, pp. 304–7. See, on the many peoples of Western Asia
who make use of the cuneiform ("wedge-shaped") script of the Sumerians (the Akkadians,
Assyrians, Babylonians, Hittites, Hurrians, Canaanites, and Elamites), Samuel Noah
Kramer, "Sumerian Literature, A General Survey," in G. Ernest Wright, ed., *The Bible and
the Ancient Near East* (Garden City, N.Y.: Doubleday, Anchor Books, 1965), p. 340. (It
should be noticed that I know none of the languages which the *Gilgamesh* tablets use.)

4. See note 49 below; "Mesopotamia" is usually taken to refer to that region of south-
western Asia between the Tigris and Euphrates Rivers, extending from the mountains of
Asia Minor to the Persian Gulf. It is possible that the extent of the influence of the Gilgamesh story, and the form that story took over millennia (including shifts in the rankings
of the gods), reflected political and social developments in that region. Thus the colophon
for Tablet IX of the epic identifies the tablet as having been made at the "Palace of Ashurbanipal, king of the world, king of Assyria." Heidel, *The Gilgamesh Epic*, p. 68. The Hebrew Bible has come down to us in its integrity, even though not preserved on anything so
durable as clay. It did have a people constantly using, and hence preserving, it—and this,
perhaps, because it was somehow sounder in its understanding of things? See Anastaplo,
"Law and Literature and the Bible," pp. 517, 521, 530, 758, 778; note 11 below. See also
Anastaplo, "How to Read the Constitution of the United States," 17 *Loyola University of
Chicago Law Journal* 55–64 (1985); *The Constitution of 1787: A Commentary* (Baltimore:
Johns Hopkins University Press, 1989), pp. 1f. See as well notes 11 and 57 below. What
should the preservation, or mutilation, of a text be taken to say about the role of divine
providence? Machiavelli, in his preface to the *Discourses*, says he will "write on all the
books of Titus Livy which have not been intercepted by the malignity of the times." (Leo
Paul S. de Alvarez translation.)

Perhaps contributing to the considerable interest in the *Gilgamesh* today is the height-
ened sensitivity in our time to both death and eros (as in the desperate art of Pablo Picasso
in his last years). It should be noticed that the Babylonian world, like ours, was quite sophisticated in commerce, having developed various kinds of contracts and perhaps even
insurance. "We could almost say that anything so profoundly human as the image of Gil-

gamesh was bound to reappear, yet we are still surprised to learn that one of the very old-est stories of man is so inherently contemporary." Mason, *Gilgamesh: A Verse Narrative,* p. 100. Certainly it is more "contemporary" than the Hebrew Bible or Classical Greek sto-ries, where the concern for death tends to be muted. Compare, however, Euripides, *Alces-tis.* (*GBWW*, vol. 5, pp. 237–47. The citations [provided by the *Great Ideas Today* editors of these seven introductions] to the *Great Books of the Western World [GBWW]*, are re-tained in the notes in this collection. The *Great Books of the Western World* series is pub-lished by the Encyclopaedia Britannica.) The *Great Ideas Today* editors, beginning with my "Buddhist Thought" article published in 1992, provided two sets of *GBWW* citations, designating the first edition by "I" and the second edition by "II." See note 42 below.

5. "This Sumerian king, who reigned in his city, Uruk, around 2650 B.C., achieved fame and honor unique in Mesopotamian history, and for more than 2,000 years he was cele-brated in cult and legend, only to disappear under the sands of Iraq and the ruins of Mesopotamian civilization. But then he reappeared a little more than a century ago—'Out of dark night where lay/The crowns of Nineveh,' in Yeats's phrase." Moran, "Utnapishtim Revisited," p. 13. "The Sumerian tales, the earliest known literary embodiment of Gil-gamesh's adventures, are separated from his lifetime by several centuries. According to the *Sumerian King List*, Gilgamesh was the fifth king of the first dynasty of Uruk, which his-torians place in the Second Early Dynastic Period of Sumer (ca. 2700–2500)." Tigay, *Evo-lution*, p. 13. "For the centuries between Gilgamesh's lifetime (between 2700 and 2500) and the earliest literary texts about him (2100–2000) or their forerunners, the narratives about him are generally presumed to have undergone a process of oral development and transmission." Ibid., p. 15. See also Gardner and Maier, *Gilgamesh*, p. 60.

Gilgamesh is more than once referred to in our story as two-thirds god, one-third human. His mother, Ninsun, is clearly a goddess. Lugalbanda is sometimes said to have been his fa-ther; and he is sometimes said to be a god, sometimes not. See, e.g., Heidel, *The Gilgamesh Epic*, pp. 4–5; Tigay, *Evolution*, p. 76 n. 10 and p. 185; Mason, *Gilgamesh*, p. 99. But what-ever combination of parents is posited, the puzzle remains of how the two-thirds/one-third ra-tio was developed. One of the solutions resorted to takes this form: "The problem thus raised casts doubt on the full-human paternity of his father, and therefore it is conceivable that . . . his father was a male vampire and neither fully divine nor mortal, by whatever daemono-genetic Mendelism the result may have been brought about." Thompson, *The Epic of Gil-gamesh*, p. 9. A simpler solution may be called for: We are familiar with stories about the mat-ings of gods and humans (as in the case of Achilles' parents). But we are also familiar with stories about matings in which the supposed male parent is human but in which the real male parent is divine (as in the case of Heracles' birth). In the latter sort of situation, can there not be said to be three parents involved? And if the mother is a goddess, the supposed father a hu-man, and the real father a god, then the offspring could be said to have been two-thirds divine, one-third human (especially if the supposed human father helped raise him, thereby impart-ing to him some of his mortality). (Perhaps even more intriguing is to have the supposed fa-ther be divine and the real father human, making the child clearly mortal "biologically.") The pretensions of Alexander the Great come to mind.) It is not irrelevant here that there is a tra-dition that Gilgamesh, like Heracles (whose mother and supposed father were human and whose real father was Zeus), eventually came to be regarded as a god. See Tigay, *Evolution*, p. 13. See also note 51 below. See as well note 34 of chapter 3 of this collection.

6. See Tigay, *Evolution*, pp. 101–3, 234, "Is *Gilgamesh* a great epic poem, even in its frag-mentary state (for several portions are still missing)? I believe that it is. Is it comparable to

Homer's *Iliad* and *Odyssey* or Virgil's *Aeneid*? No. Looked at from a purely literary stand-point, it falls short of Homer on several counts. First there is the irritating habit of Sumerian poets of repeating themselves. . . . [Still,] *Gilgamesh* is a poem of truly epic sweep and power. Its main theme is eternal: Man in his youth, prideful and adventurous, enjoying his brief period of self-fulfillment, even glory, followed by the tragedy of sickness, old age, and death." Leonard Cottrell, introduction, in William Ellery Leonard, trans., *Gilgamesh* (Lunenburg, Vt.: Made for the members of the Limited Editions Club, Avon, Conn., at the Stinchour Press, 1974), pp. vii–viii. "If not pushed too far, 'epic' is useful, but it does not translate a Sumerian or Akkadian term." Gardner and Maier, *Gilgamesh*, p. 37.

One advantage of Mesopotamian repetitiveness is that one can get a fairly reliable sense of the plot of a story, even when the text is badly mutilated. Thus, all but one of the principal adventures recapitulated by Gilgamesh toward the end of the story are by then familiar to us. (The one exception is the lion-hunting expedition to which he refers.) I do not directly concern myself with any of the Gilgamesh stories not included in our twelve-tablet "epic." See note 13 below.

7. Calvin S. Brown, ed., *The Reader's Companion to World Literature* (New York: New American Library, Mentor Book, 1956), p. 186. The first summary ever of the story is found in the opening lines of the first tablet of the epic. See, on Noah, Anastaplo, "Lessons for the Student of Law: The Oklahoma Lectures," 20 *Oklahoma City University Law Review* 19, 97 (1995). I have heard that Sumerian literature became part of the ancient, or "classical," education of the Babylonians when they became dominant in that part of the world. See note 64 below.

8. The twelfth tablet is discussed in section VII of this chapter.

9. It is the F. A. Speiser translation which is drawn upon both for the version that appears in volume 1986 of *The Great Ideas Today* and for my own quotations and discussion. (Texts in several languages, and from different times, are used in the Speiser array.) My citations are to the translation as found in James B. Pritchard, ed., *Ancient Near Eastern Texts Relating to the Old Testament*, 3d ed. (Princeton, N.J.: Princeton University Press, 1969), p. 721 (which is supplemented there by the S. N. Kramer translation of the Sumerian texts). (Hereafter, this volume will be cited as *A.N.E.T.*)

I have also found useful the Heidel translation (note 3 above), the Leonard translation (note 6 above), the Mason translation (note 2 above), and the Gardner-Maier translation (note 2 above, which includes a detailed summary of each of the six columns on each of the twelve tablets). Generations of scholars have found useful Thompson, ed., *The Epic of Gilgamesh: Text, Transliteration, and Notes* (note 2 above).

The condition of the text of the *Gilgamesh* is still so incomplete, however, that it is not yet possible to subject it to the kind of detailed analysis which I am able to attempt with the *Bhagavad Gītā* and the Confucian *Analects*. (See chapters 3 and 4 of this collection.) Some commentators would bracket many more words in the translations than I do.

We see in the quotation in the text the use of the term *nature*. There will be noticed throughout this collection many uses by translators and editors of *nature*, a term which should be questioned when attributed to non-Western thinkers in antiquity. See note 62, below. See also the preface to this collection.

10. Most of the manuscripts of the late version were discovered in the remains of Ashurbanipal's library (destroyed in 612 [B.C.E.] at Nineveh in northeastern Mesopotamia) Tigay, *Evolution*, p. 130. See note 4 above. See also the text at note 82 of this chapter.

11. There are devoted to the Flood, indirectly if not directly, two of the twelve tablets on which the *Gilgamesh* epic is inscribed. The modern reader can even find "the terrifying description of the Flood [to be] more powerful and evocative than that of the Bible." Cottrell, introduction, p. xi. It is reported that "the Flood was accepted in Assyria as a definite event." Thompson, *The Epic of Gilgamesh*, p. 71 n. 6. See, on the Flood, Heidel, *The Gilgamesh Epic*, pp. 224f.; Tigay, *Evolution*, pp. 214f.

I cannot attempt to deal here with the significance of the fact that various biblical stories are generally considered by scholars to have been written long after their counterparts in Mesopotamian literature were written. (I do not know what the accepted scholarly opinion is today as to which tradition was the earlier in *oral* form.) A proper discussion of these matters presupposes an understanding of the Bible in its integrity. Only then can one begin to understand divergences in the Bible from other traditional accounts of similar episodes. See Leo Strauss, "On the Interpretation of *Genesis*," in Kenneth Hart Green, ed., *Jewish Philosophy and the Crisis of Modernity* (Albany, N.Y.: State University of New York, 1997), pp. 359, 476; the text at note 1 of chapter 6 of this collection; Robert Sacks, "The Lion and the Ass: A Commentary on the *Book of Genesis*," *Interpretation*, vol. 8/2, 3 (May 1980), pp. 29f (the uses made of *Gilgamesh* at pp. 75 and 96 may be in need of correction). See also notes 2 and 4 above; notes 42, 57, and 70 below.

12. The story of the Great Flood in our *Gilgamesh* epic was evidently taken from other accounts now available (in parts) to us. The same is true of various other stories in the epic (such as that in Tablet XI). See section VII of this chapter.

13. I work here, as throughout this chapter, primarily from the final version of the epic. Earlier versions are drawn upon wherever the final version is too fragmented, so long as the earlier versions are not contradicted by the final version. See Tigay, *Evolution,* pp. 3f., 241f. Any summary is likely to reflect considerable commentary, if only in the determination of what is noticed.

14. Uruk (the Biblical Erech; the modern Warka) was a city-state in what is now southern Iraq. It was on the Euphrates River, just a few miles north of what we know as the Persian Gulf. (The Gulf went considerably further north at that time than it does now, since it has been filled in by deposits from the Euphrates.) Uruk, which is also referred to as Uruk-land and as Uruk-Eanna (reflecting its Temple of Anu and Ishtar), is at almost the same latitude as Jerusalem.

See, on Gilgamesh and the *jus primae noctis*, Tigay, *Evolution*, pp. 182–84. See also notes 20 and 39 below.

15. "The pattern of oppression, outcry, divine response was a known pattern in accounts of the gods' sending or creating a new character." Ibid., p. 191. "This is a stock pattern, known in several variations in cuneiform literature, in both mythological and historiographic texts." Ibid., p. 180. Does this pattern tend to ignore the place of nature (and hence of chance?) in human affairs? See note 77 below.

16. Consider the use by Zeus of Hector and the Trojans in response to Achilles' grievance against Agamemnon in the *Iliad*. Hector, when he puts on Achilles' armor, stripped from the body of Patroclus, looks very much like Achilles. See note 40 below. See also Anastaplo, *The Thinker as Artist*, p. 13. Agamemnon can be seen as somewhat in the Gilgamesh pattern, exhibiting in book 1 of the *Iliad* an eros-related oppressiveness.

17. One can be reminded of Rousseau's *Discourse upon the Origin and Foundation of the Inequality Among Mankind* (available in excellent English editions prepared by Roger

D. and Judith R. Masters for St. Martin's Press, and thereafter by Victor Gourevitch for Harper & Row). [See *GBWW*, vol. 38.) See notes 64 and 83 below.

18. On other occasions, such prescience is described as the result of interpreting a dream. See, on dreams, the text at note 20 of this chapter as well as notes 28 and 70 below.

19. One can be reminded of Delilah, a Philistine woman, who was loved by Samson and who betrayed him to the Philistines. See *Judges* 16:4f. (She is evidently distinguished from the harlot he earlier consorted with, which consorting had *not* affected his strength. See *Judges* 16:1–3. Perhaps, however, such appetites made the Delilah episode possible.) See also note 73 below.

The harlot with whom Enkidu consorts seems respectable enough, as well as good-natured and intelligent. Translators usually identify her as a temple-harlot. See, e.g., Leonard, *Gilgamesh*, p. 6 n. 1: "One of the sacred prostitutes at the temple of Ishtar (Astarte)" (after having referred to her in the text as "a priestess"). (Translators do not seem to agree as to whether this harlot is ever named in the epic. Would not lack of a name suggest that any of the temple-harlots could have done what this one did?) See, on institutional harlots, *Harper's Bible Dictionary*, M. S. Miller and J. L. Miller, eds. (New York: Harper & Brothers, 1959), p. 246:

> Wisdom writers knew and denounced their traits (*Prov.* 7:5ff., 29:3). Major prophets likened the apostasies of Israel and Judah to the harlotries of whores who frequented green trees and cultic mountain centers (*Jer.* 3:6, 8; *Ezek.* 16:15, 17, 20, 22, 30–52; *Hos.* 4:15). The Canaanite temples and Syrian shrines that Israel knew were often brothels where priests, priestesses, and cultists engaged in impure rites glorifying reproductive processes. The early Christian Church soon made a pronouncement against harlotry (*Acts* 15:20, 29), and combated it in cosmopolitan centers by teaching that the body is the temple of the Holy Spirit (*1 Cor.* 12–20).

See also the text at note 73 of this chapter and note 49 below. See, on Ishtar, the text at note 23 of this chapter. See also *Deut.* 23:18; *Judges* 2:13, 10:6; *I Kings* 11:5; *II Kings* 23:13; *Jer.* 44:17f. See as well note 13 of appendix C of this collection (for an engaging photograph of a dancing woman); note 73 below.

The response of the animals to the post-harlot Enkidu (*Gilgamesh*, I, iv, 22–29), for "he now had wisdom, broader understanding," is followed by this note in the Speiser translation: "The general parallel to *Gen.* 3:7 is highly suggestive." (*A.N.E.T.*, p. 75 n. 28.) That biblical verse reads, "And the eyes of them both were opened, and they knew that they were naked; and they sewed fig leaves together, and made themselves aprons." See the text at note 54 of this chapter. The harlot tells Enkidu, after their week-long encounter, that he was now wise, having "become like a god." *Gilgamesh*, I, iv, 33 (*A.N.E.T.*, p. 75). See *Genesis* 3:5: "you shall be as gods, knowing good and evil."

It is traditional to regard love as a civilizing force, as may even be seen in the transformation of such refined characters as both Elizabeth and Darcy in Jane Austen's *Pride and Prejudice*. See Anastaplo, *The Artist as Thinker*; p. 86; Anastaplo, "Law & Literature and the Moderns: Explorations," 20 *Northern Illinois University Law Review*, 350 (2000).

20. Nothing seems to be said about what the source is of the many dreams reported and interpreted in our epic, except perhaps in the case of the warning about the Flood which comes to Utnapishtim. See note 70 below. Was there, among the ancient Mesopotamians, an opinion about dream sources, etc., which was too obvious to state? To what extent are we to consider Gilgamesh as having been instructed by his dreams about how he should deal with Enkidu when he overcomes him? Thus, such dreams could be as much guidance

as prediction. In any event, Gilgamesh's struggle with Enkidu may have told him something about himself. Later on, Eukidu's various pieces of advice to Gilgamesh (whether or not derived from dreams) may have reflected aspects of Gilgamesh himself. See note 74 below.

Enkidu's dismay upon learning of Gilgamesh's practice with the maids of Uruk suggests that the practice was grounded in a resented local custom, not in nature. But may not such a custom have dynastic, if not eugenic, uses, since it makes it likely (if the ruler is as remarkable as Gilgamesh) that the oldest child (the heir of the family?) will be significantly stronger than his siblings as well as on good terms with the royal family?

21. It used to be said that the expedition against Humbaba (Huwawa in the Hittite language, Hubaba in the Assyrian language) was to "the cedar forests in the Lebanon region." See, e.g., Abraham Malamat, "Campaigns to the Mediterranean by Iabdunlim and Other Mesopotamian Rulers," *Assyriological Studies* (Studies in Honor of Benno Landsberger on His Seventy-Fifth Birthday), no. 16, p. 373. (I happened, while a student at the University of Chicago, to see Professor Landsberger in action: particularly engaging was the way he used to order the oddest assortment of things by telephone from Marshall Field's— and get them! This was a personal touch perhaps worthy of ancient Mesopotamian relations between gods and men.)

A shift in scholarly opinion about the location of the Cedar Forest is recorded in Gardner and Maier, *Gilgamesh*, p. 106:

> The cedar forest to which the two men will travel is to be located in what is now Syria, probably the Anti-Lebanon range of mountains. This is the beginning of the adventure that is known also from the Sumerian poem, "Gilgamesh and the Land of the Living," from the Old Babylonian *The Epic of Gilgamesh*, and from a Hittite version of the story. The cedar forest was probably in the east, in what is now Iran, and may represent a precious commodity for the relatively treeless southern Mesopotamia. The story of Gilgamesh's heroism may well have had political, economic, and historical motives behind it. The Akkadian versions have shifted the action to the west.

Gilgamesh's apprehensive mother, in praying to the sun god Shamash for her son as he embarks upon the expedition against Humbaba, asks Shamash, "Why, having given me Gilgamesh for a son, didst thou endow him with a restless heart?" See *Gilgamesh*, III, ii, 10–11 (*A.N.E.T.*, p. 81, Assyrian version).

22. This was after Enkidu's arm had been temporarily paralyzed upon opening the gate of the forest. See *Gilgamesh*, IV, vi, 23f (*A.N.E.T.*, p. 82).

One can be reminded, by Enkidu's urging the perhaps hesitant Gilgamesh to kill Humbaba, of Pylades' urging Orestes to kill Clytemnestra (in Aeschylus's *The Libation Bearers*. [*GBWW*, vol. 5, titled *Choephoroe*]).

23. *Gilgamesh*, VI, 1f. (*A.N.E.T.*, p. 83).

24. *Gilgamesh*, VI, 24f. (*A.N.E.T.*, p. 84). One can be reminded here of Euripides' *Hippolytus*. See notes 25, 26, and 76 below.

25. *Gilgamesh*, VI, 79f. (*A.N.E.T.*, p. 84). And here one can be reminded of the spurned Aphrodite in Euripides' *Hippolytus* [*GBWW*, vol. 5].

26. *Gilgamesh*, VI, 157f. (*A.N.E.T.*, p. 85). Does Enkidu regard Ishtar as his rival for Gilgamesh's favor? See note 40 below.

Some suggest that Enkidu throws the Bull's phallus at Ishtar. See, e.g., Leonard, *Gilgamesh*, p. 42 n. 2; Thompson, *The Epic of Gilgamesh*, p. 81 n. 161.

The Bull of Heaven has been identified with famine. See, e.g., ibid., p. 82 1. 23; *Gilgamesh*, VI, 101f. (*A.N.E.T.*, pp. 84–85). The Bull does kill three hundred men before being killed by Gilgamesh and Enkidu. One is reminded here, but only up to a point, of the bull sent against Hippolytus in Euripides' play. See note 76 below.

27. Is Gilgamesh particularly moved by Enkidu's death because he recognizes that it is Gilgamesh's debt that Enkidu is paying?

28. Utnapishtim is generally understood to mean "he found life." An older name for this man is Atrahasis, which means "exceedingly wise." See Tigay, *Evolution*, p. 229; *A.N.E.T.*, p. 90 n. 164; Gardner and Maier, *Gilgamesh*, p. 65. Atrahasis is used only once in our epic, at XI, 187 (*A.N.E.T.*, p. 95), when the god Ea explains how Utnapishtim had escaped drowning in the Flood. See note 70 below. See, on the Sumerian stories about the relations of Ea and Atrahasis, S. N. Kramer, *Mythologies of the Ancient World* (New York: Doubleday, Anchor Books, 1961), pp. 126–27.

Noah, we should remember, did not escape death altogether. See the text at note 70 of this chapter.

29. It was because Utnapishtim's wife urged that something be done for Gilgamesh that he was told about the plant. Gilgamesh always did depend much upon women. (The plant is prickly, which suggests that a price must be paid for whatever it offers.)

Opinions differ as to why Gilgamesh did not eat the plant immediately. "The purpose of this plant was to grant rejuvenated life; and it was to be eaten after a person had reached old age. For this reason Gilgamesh does not eat the plant at once but decides to wait until after his return to Uruk, until he has become an 'old man.'" Heidel, *The Gilgamesh Epic*, p. 92 n. 211. Compare Gardner and Maier, *Gilgamesh*, pp. 31–32:

> There is, of course, no possibility of avoiding death in *Gilgamesh*. The agonizing journey does not give Gilgamesh hope of personal immortality; nor does it bring Enkidu back to life. Yet, Gilgamesh is cleansed. He puts on the great garment after he casts away the filthy skins he had been wearing. He does return to Uruk, to his kingship, and to Ishtar. (It is important to notice that the magical plant, "The-Old-Man-Will-Be-Made-Young," given him by Utnapishtim, is not devoured by Gilgamesh. He intends to offer it, rather like the eucharist, to the citizens of Uruk. We take this as a symbol of the full renewal of Gilgamesh's public, i.e., priestly and kingly, role; and the altruism marks the transcendence of mere egoistic values.)

See also ibid., p. 251. There may be something sentimental about this interpretation and about the interpretation quoted in note 1 above.

One can be reminded by this "magical plant" of another such plant, that made available to Odysseus (another traveler quite dependent upon women) in order to be able to withstand the deadly power of Circe. It is in that context alone (and only once) that "nature" is used by Homer, evidently the earliest recorded usage of "nature" in the Greek literature that we happen to have. See *Odyssey* X, 277 et seq. See also Anastaplo, *The Thinker as Artist*, p. 27.

Utnapishtim and his wife, it seems, have a deathlessness which does *not* depend on this plant. See the text at note 70 of this chapter.

30. The plant that brings back youth is not allowed much time in the story. Is not that often the way with rejuvenating things; they are likely to be temporary in their unnatural effects? See note 35 below.

The motive and timing of the serpent here are quite different from those of the serpent in *Genesis*: there, the serpent acts to deprive man of what he already has; here, the serpent acts to acquire for itself something that man wants for himself (there is nothing "personal" in what the serpent does here, in that the primary end is not to hurt man but to help the serpent?). Does Gilgamesh ever see the serpent? Did Adam? See Anastaplo, "On Trial: Explorations," 22 *Loyola University of Chicago Law Journal* 763, 767 (1991) (to be published in book form by Rowman & Littlefield).

31. "In the loss of the plant Gilgamesh sees a sign that he should leave the ship behind and proceed by land. The boatman goes along, for, according to [XI, 235], he apparently has been banished [by Utnapishtim] from the shores of the blessed for bringing Gilgamesh there." Heidel, *The Gilgamesh Epic*, p. 92 n. 215. In any event, Gilgamesh does return home with something of Utnapishtim's.

32. It translates a much older Sumerian story. See note 81 below.

33. That is, Enkidu dies. The Leonard translation avoids the obvious problem which is posed by having Enkidu alive at the beginning of the twelfth tablet. It makes the opening conversation between Gilgamesh and Enkidu a conversation between Ninsun (Gilgamesh's mother) and Gilgamesh, with Gilgamesh preparing to commune with the already dead Enkidu. Leonard, *Gilgamesh*, pp. 101f. This is hardly instructive, except as a reminder that what the poet does here truly bears thinking about. See note 81 below.

34. One can be reminded of Antigone's concerns. See Anastaplo, "On Trial," p. 846. Gilgamesh had done well by Enkidu at his death, providing him both elaborate burial rituals and a statue. One can also be reminded of Odysseus's conversations with both Elpenor and Achilles in Hades. Consider, on the other hand, Socrates' expressed lack of concern, in the *Phaedo* [*GBWW*, vol. 7], as to what is to be done with his lifeless body. Compare the dread exhibited in like circumstances by Cyrus in Xenophon's *Cyropaedia* (the very Cyrus who had once gloated over corpses on the battlefield). See Xenophon, *Cyropaedia*, I, iv, 24; VIII, vii, 25. See also section III of chapter 2 of this collection. See as well section IX of chapter 3 of this collection.

35. Tigay, *Evolution*, p. 10 (quoting S. N. Kramer). "The Gilgamesh epic is a powerful tale in almost any telling. Rilke once called it the greatest thing one could experience, and many consider it the supreme literary achievement of the ancient world before Homer. It has something of the qualities Henry Moore once said he admired in Mesopotamian art—bigness and simplicity without decorative trimming." Moran, "Utnapishtim Revisited," p. 13.

A classical scholar has provided this useful interpretive summary of the Gilgamesh epic:

That myth exemplifies, through a legendary figure, the various attitudes to death that humans tend to adopt: theoretical acceptance, utterly destroyed by one's first close acquaintance with it in someone loved; revulsion from the obscenity of physical corruption; the desire to surmount death in one's own private case, either by means of a lasting reputation or by the desperate fantasy that oneself could be immortal. Finally, a kind of resignation—but before that, perhaps, an attempt to delay death by emulating youth.

G. S. Kirk, *Myth: Its Meaning and Functions in Ancient and Other Cultures* (Cambridge: Cambridge University Press, 1970), pp. 144–45. See note 30 above.

36. One can be reminded of this kind of shift when one compares the Achilles found first in the *Iliad* and then in the Hades scene in the *Odyssey* [*GBWW*, vol. 4]. See Kirk, *Myth*, pp. 108, 223.

37. How he got this notion (which is not borne out by the killing of Humbaba) is not clear.

38. This identification of him may also be seen in colophons. And yet are we not meant by the poet to see, and to understand, things that Gilgamesh does not? See note 81 below.

39. It should be noticed that Gilgamesh was looked to as a savior by the hunter and his family at the very time that he was considered oppressive within Uruk. One could attempt to distinguish city tastes from country tastes, but there is also the fact that Enkidu (or is he no longer really a country man?) is shocked when he learns of Gilgamesh's sexual conduct in Uruk. See the text at note 20 of this chapter. Even so, is there not something properly royal in Gilgamesh's refusal to surrender himself completely to Ishtar? See notes 50 and 51 below.

40. Thus, the gods destroy the same Enkidu that they had fashioned to use in order to control Gilgamesh. See note 16 above. Does Gilgamesh ever learn the origins (or purpose) of Enkidu? Of course, the death of Enkidu may itself be part of the divine plan to curb Gilgamesh. See the text at notes 16 and 79 of this chapter.

Does Ishtar strike at Enkidu because she sees him as a substitute for herself with Gilgamesh? See note 26 above. Is her proposal to Gilgamesh, in effect, an invitation to him to return to his old practices with the maids of Uruk? See notes 51 and 78 below. Were those practices (a kind of Sacred Marriage between Goddess and King?) related to fertility rites? But see note 49 below.

41. See *Gilgamesh*, X, i, 34f.; iii, 1f. (*A.N.E.T.*, pp. 90–91, Assyrian version). It seems to have been "the most persistent tradition" in the stories about Gilgamesh that he "was beset by a fear of death." See Paul Garelli, ed., *Gilgameš et sa légende* (Paris: Librairie C. Klincksieck, 1960), p. 51 (by W. G. Lambert). See also note 33 of chapter 2 of this collection.

42. That there is something about the Mesopotamian region itself which helps account for how things have always been done (and thought?) there is suggested by the presence there today of practices which scholars look to in order to explain obscure passages in the *Gilgamesh*. Consider the following sampling: "the usual method of sitting in the East when there is no stool" (Thompson, *The Epic of Gilgamesh*, p. 79); "the boat must be a light skiff or *bellam,* such as the Arabs of the southern marshes use to this day, either poled or paddled" (ibid., p. 85); "The punting-pole of the Mesopotamian skiff today has a knob of bitumen at the upper end and a metal socket or ferule at the lower end" (ibid., p. 85); "There are several methods in vogue in the Near East of making bread; the commonest shape is that of the flat disk of thin bread varying in size, but usually about a foot in diameter. This is probably one of the earliest forms of bread, and it is shown on the Hittite Sculptures" (ibid., p. 87); "Gilgamesh follows the custom of the pearl-divers of Bahrain, long celebrated for its pearl-fisheries [in using large stones to accelerate his descent]" (ibid., p. 88); "Some good photographs of reed houses [such as Utnapishtim's] have recently been published [in the *National Geographic Magazine,* 82 (1942), 410–11]" (Heidel, *The Gilgamesh Epic*, p. 80 n. 166); "To press the carrying strap against [the forehead]; for this method [of lifting and carrying], which is witnessed on the Ur Standard and is still practiced in modern Iraq" (*A.N.E.T.*, p. 76 n. 40). See also Gardner and Maier, *Gilgamesh*, pp. 229–30, 233 (on a large Sumerian boat made of reed-bundles built by Thor Heyerdahl). See as well note 52 below. Do we not see in these examples indications of how poetry depends upon an imitation of nature? Another facet of the poetic imitation of nature may be seen in the samples collected in note 84 below. See also note 83 below.

Thus, various remarkable continuities testify to the extent to which climate and resources (and, indeed, nature) may shape manners and customs over millennia. Consider, for example, what Machiavelli made of such factors:

> In our time, the examples of these two different kinds of government are those of the Turk and of the King of France. . . .Whoever considers, then, the one and the other of these states, will

find that it is difficult to acquire the state of the Turk, but [once] conquered, it is easy to hold. And you will find, on the contrary, that it is in some respects easier to take the state of France, but that it is more difficult to hold on to it. . . .

Now, if you will consider the nature of Darius' government, you will find it similar to the kingdom of the Turk. Therefore it was necessary for Alexander first to smash it all and seize the field; after which victory, with Darius dead, the state was left secure for Alexander. . . . But it is impossible to possess states ordered like that of France with such quiet. From whence arose each of the many rebellions of Spain, of France, and of Greece against the Romans, because of the many principates which existed in those states.

The Prince (Leo Paul S. de Alvarez translation; Irving, Tex.: University of Dallas Press, 1984), chap. 4. [See *GBWW*, vol. 23, p. 7.]

Consider also how Mesopotamia can be distinguished from ancient Egypt by Thorkild Jacobsen:

> How the Egyptian and the Mesopotamian civilizations came to acquire these very different moods—one trusting, the other distrusting, man's power and ultimate significance—is not an easy question. The "mood" of a civilization is the outcome of processes so intricate and so complex as to defy precise analysis. We shall therefore merely point to a single factor which would seem to have played a considerable role—the factor of environment. . . .
>
> Mesopotamian civilization grew up in an environment which was signally different [from Egyptian civilization]. We find there, of course, the same great cosmic rhythms—the change of the seasons, the unwavering sweep of sun, moon, and stars—but we also find an element of force and violence which was lacking in Egypt. The Tigris and Euphrates are not like the Nile; they may rise unpredictably and fitfully, breaking man's dykes and submerging his crops. There are scorching winds which smother man in dust, threaten to suffocate him; there are torrential rains which turn all firm ground into a sea of mud and rob man of his freedom of movement; all travel bogs down. Here, in Mesopotamia, Nature stays not her hand; in her full might she cuts across and overrides man's will, makes him feel to the full how slightly he matters.
>
> The mood of Mesopotamian civilization reflects this. Man is not tempted to overrate himself when he contemplates powers in nature such as the thunderstorm and the yearly flood. Of the thunderstorm the Mesopotamian said that its "dreadful flares of light cover the land like a cloth."

H. and H. A. Frankfort, eds., *Before Philosophy: The Intellectual Adventure of Ancient Man* (London: Penguin Books, 1949), pp. 137–39. See note 57 below. See, on Egyptian civilization, chapter 2 of this collection. See, on *nature*, note 13 of the preface to this collection.

Consider as well how far the case for the importance of materialistic factors may be taken:

> I have chosen this lowly topic [of the consumption of onions in ancient Mesopotamia] as a modest expression of protest against such esoteric and, in the present state of our knowledge, seemingly fruitless pursuits as those devoted to the study of the resurrection of Tammuz and of the Sumerian beliefs in afterlife. This is not a question of the relative importance of studies devoted to grammar, lexicon, or material culture as against those dealing with theological and metaphysical matters. The question is simply that of priorities. As all man's ideas about things divine are human, it is my firm belief that we shall never know what was the nectar of the gods until we learn what was the daily bread of the people.

I. J. Gelb, "The Philadelphia Onion Archive," *Assyriological Studies,* no. 16 (1965), p. 62. Even so, one must wonder what it means to say that "all man's ideas about things divine are human." See note 11 above. And it is only prudent to keep in mind, as we consider these prosaic matters, this observation: "It is safer to try to understand the low in the light of the high than the high in the light of the low. In doing the latter one necessarily distorts the high, whereas in doing the former one does not deprive the low of the freedom to reveal itself fully as what it is." Leo Strauss, *Spinoza's Critique of Religion* (New York: Schocken Books, 1965), p. 2. Not irrelevant here, especially considering Gilgamesh's surprising response to the death of Enkidu, are Mr. Strauss's remarks upon being "struck by the awesome, unfathomable experience of death, of the death of one near and dear to us." See Anastaplo, *The Artist as Thinker*, pp. 270–71; Green, ed., *Jewish Philosophy and the Crisis of Modernity*, p. 475. Gilgamesh "was to become the archetype of royal mortality." Kirk, *Myth*, pp. 9–10. See also ibid., pp. 231–32.

43. Is not the female element naturally more intimate and hence private (as well as somewhat prosaic)? Consider, in Aeschylus's *Oresteia* [*GBWW*, vol. 5], the juxtaposition of the female Furies (who guard the home) and Apollo (who looks out for kings). (See Gardner and Maier, *Gilgamesh*, p. 49 n. 42.) Consider also the fact that Socrates does go home at the very end of Plato's *Symposium* [*GBWW*, vol. 7]. Does not a home usually depend upon the female (and the resulting family life)? (The female element, aside from Socrates' own use of Diotima in his talk in the *Symposium*, had been muted in the other speeches on love on that occasion.) Consider, as well, the recourse to a prosaic everyday life in the concluding lines of the song at the end of Shakespeare's *Love's Labour's Lost* [*GBWW*, vol. 26, p. 284d].

44. See the text at notes 23–26 of this chapter.

45. *Gilgamesh*, XI, 116–23 (*A.N.E.T.*, p. 94).

46. The stranger is Utnapishtim's boatman. See note 31 above. Collaboration between Ishtar and Gilgamesh may be seen in Tablet XII of our epic. See also S. N. Kramer, *Gilgamesh and the Huluppu-Tree* (Chicago: University of Chicago Press, 1938).

47. *Gilgamesh*, X, iii, 1f (*A.N.E.T.*, p. 90) (the Old Babylonian version is drawn upon here since the Akkadian-language version is badly mutilated in places). See note 13 above. (Most translators use "ale-wife" instead of "barmaid.")

It is sometimes said that "Gilgamesh [left no] son to [his] father." Thompson, *The Epic of Gilgamesh*, p. 72. Also sometimes said is that Gilgamesh left a son and successor. See ibid., p. 9; Tigay, *Evolution*, p. 168 n. 17. In our *Gilgamesh* there is no reference to any children of Gilgamesh. This poet may have preferred to leave that an open question.

48. *Gilgamesh*, VI, 99–100 (*A.N.E.T.*, p. 84). This is when Ishtar seeks revenge after having been spurned by Gilgamesh. See note 84 below.

49. One must wonder, however, whether the poet, or his audience, ever regarded temple-harlotry as questionable—and, if not, what does this say about his or their understanding of things? (Should not a similar question be asked about Shakespeare's treatment of Jews in *The Merchant of Venice* and the expected response of his audience? [*GBWW*, vol. 26]) See Anastaplo, "On Trial," p. 935; Anastaplo, "Law & Literature and Shakespeare," part 13.)

See, on Babylonian temple-harlotry, Herodotus, *History*, I, 99 [*GBWW*, vol. 6, p. 45a]. See also note 19 above. The response by Herodotus assures us that we are not being merely modern provincials in our own negative response to this institution. (Is the Middle Eastern institution of the harem related? There, too, sexuality seems to us to be mismanaged. See note 73 below. Compare the widespread resort of Christianity to institutional celibacy. See the Koran, Sura 57, end. See, on the Koran, chapter 6 of this collection.)

Upon confronting temple-harlotry one wonders, "What *could* they have been thinking of?" And one must also wonder whether it is possible truly to understand such people, especially when Sacred Marriage is confused with institutionalized prostitution. See note 40 above. What is for them the meaning of sexuality, of divinity, of nature? We can see in the opening chapters of Aristotle's *Politics* an account of what happens when male and female mate, how children (and the family) result, how the family can be extended, and how eventually the village and the city emerge. But should not the Aristotelian be shocked to have simple, healthy sexuality transformed into the kind of institution so much taken for granted (it seems) in ancient Mesopotamia? See the text at note 4 of this chapter. See also the text at note 73 of this chapter. See, for the Laurence Berns translation of the beginning of the *Politics*, Anastaplo, ed., *Liberty, Equality, and Modern Constitutionalism: A Source Book* (Newburyport, Mass.: Focus, 1999), vol. 1, p. 215.

50. See note 24 above. Does Gilgamesh resent being chosen, rather than choosing (as he had done, for example, with the maids of Uruk and then with Enkidu)? A transition may be seen here by some from a matriarchal to a patriarchal society. See note 39 above, note 75 below.

51. Central to this array of lovers (with Gilgamesh selected as the seventh) is a stallion: "Then a stallion thou lovedst, famed in battle; the whip, the spur, and the lash thou ordainedst for him." *Gilgamesh*, VI, 53–54 (*A.N.E.T.*, p. 84). Certainly, Ishtar is not ashamed of having tamed the stallion: she can even offer Gilgamesh chariot horses which "shall be famed for racing." *Gilgamesh*, VI, 20 *(A.N.E.T.,* p. 84). Perhaps it can be said that Gilgamesh "identifies" himself with the stallion.

I suspect the poet of our epic appreciated at least as much as we can the salutary consequences of various of the six developments that Gilgamesh regards as grievances. (Had not some of Ishtar's lovers been properly punished for misconduct or presumptuousness? See Kirk, *Myth*, p. 104.) The purposefulness of this listing *in our epic* is suggested, it seems to me, by the following report (the import of which may not have been noticed by the scholars):

> In *Gilgamesh and the Bull of Heaven*, according to Kramer, the gifts offered Gilgamesh by the goddess Inanna (the Sumerian counterpart of Ishtar) are quite different from those that Ishtar offers in [our] epic; scholars have since come to doubt that Inanna proposed to Gilgamesh at all in the Sumerian tale.

Tigay, *Evolution*, p. 24. Thus, "her spurned proposal of marriage to Gilgamesh may have been original with the Akkadian versions." Ibid., p. 70. (The first of the allegedly ill-treated lovers Gilgamesh brings up is Tammuz, "the lover of [her] youth." Would not the poet have expected his thoughtful reader to recognize the considerable regard Ishtar had had for Tammuz? See S. H., Langdon, *Tammuz and Ishtar; A Monograph upon Babylonian Religion and Theology* (Oxford: Clarendon Press, 1914). Compare Kramer, *Mythologies of the Ancient W*orld, pp. 106–15. Particularly intriguing is this observation: "The worship of this goddess from the earliest period centred at Erech, modern Warka, a city in the extreme south of Mesopotamia, on the eastern bank of the Euphrates. The epic of Gilgamish relates that this city was founded by Gilgamish, who as we have seen was a deified king and identified with Tammuz." Ibid., p. 54. See note 81 below.

Be all this as it may, cannot it be said that Ishtar proposed to Gilgamesh as perhaps Gilgamesh's goddess mother had done to Gilgamesh's human father? Does Gilgamesh's rejection of Ishtar suggest that there will not be another Gilgamesh? "For Ishtar's lovers compare Diodorus, II, 8, about Semiramis." Thompson, *The Epic of Gilgamesh*, p. 81. See note 5 above. See also note 40 above. For a modern version of this episode, see Robert Silverberg, *Gilgamesh the King* (Toronto: Bantam Books, 1985), pp. 174f., 291f.

52. See *Gilgamesh*, e.g., I, v, 25f.; V, i, 5 (*A.N.E.T.*, pp. 75–76, 82). Consider also Enkidu's distress upon hearing about Gilgamesh's Humbaba proposal, *Gilgamesh*, III, i, 13f. (*A.N.E.T.*, pp. 78–79, Old Babylonian version). See as well the text at note 59 of this chapter.

Is sexuality a substitute for the deepest friendship (possible only between males?)? "To this day, one can see young Arab men in the Near East walking with interlocked fingers without any implications of homosexuality." Tigay, *Evolution*, p. 184 n. 22. See note 42 above. Such contacts between males could also be seen in Greece up until perhaps about a generation or so ago.

53. We are not the only ones surprised by Gilgamesh's response to the death of Enkidu: those whom he encounters on his way to Utnapishtim also express surprise. See note 41 above.

54. See note 19 above and note 83 below. See also Anastaplo, *Human Being and Citizen*, p. 123 (on obscenity). The culmination of the erotic, or at least one remarkable manifestation of it, may be philosophy. See note 71 below.

55. See Edwin Muir, "The Animals"; Anastaplo, *The Artist as Thinker*, pp. 357–62. See also note 68 below. See as well "Tokens of Ourselves," *The Great Ideas Today*, pp. 383f. (1984).

56. See, e.g., *Genesis*, chapters 2 and 3.

57. *Gilgamesh*, III, iv, 5–8 (*A.N.E.T.*, p. 79, Old Bonian version). Compare this observation on the durability of the clay tablets used by the ancient Mesopotamians:

> Clay tablets can be baked as hard as brick so that they endure forever. Our paper today decomposes, and does not last a fraction of the time that the Gilgamesh tablets have already survived. Clay is also by its nature fireproof. When a library burns down today, the books perish. When the libraries of Mesopotamia burned down, the ashes of the buildings simply buried the clay tablets for future archaeologists to find. The only effect fire has on tablets is to bake them harder and preserve them better than ever.

Cyrus H. Gordon, "Origins of the Gilgamesh Epic," in Anita Feagles, *He Who Saw Everything: The Epic of Gilgamesh* (New York: Young Scott Books, 1966), pp. 57–58. It has been noticed that the Egyptians expected their greatest buildings to last "forever," while the Mesopotamians expected theirs to crumble away. See Frankfort and Frankfort, eds., *Before Philosophy*, p. 137; note 42 above. See also chapter 2 of this collection. But the Mesopotamian clay tablets seem to have outlasted Egyptian papyrus, "all other things being equal." See notes 4 and 11 above.

58. *Gilgamesh*, III, v, 7 (*A.N.E.T.*, p. 80, Old Babylonian version).

59. *Gilgamesh*, VIII, ii, 3 (*A.N.E.T.*, p. 87). Of course, neither Humbaba nor the Bull of Heaven was human. See note 26 above.

60. *Gilgamesh*, II, v, 13f. (*A.N.E.T.*, p. 78, Old Babylonian version).

61. We are not told in our epic whether Gilgamesh ever knew his father. Only in the twelfth tablet is there any serious indication of a life beyond the grave, and *that* is hardly attractive. See Heidel, *The Gilgamesh Epic*, pp. 137f. ("Death and the Afterlife").

62. See, e.g., *Gilgamesh*, X, ii, 1–9 (*A.N.E.T.*, pp. 89–90, Old Babylonian version). Compare *2 Samuel* 12:18–23. See also notes 2, 35 above. That which is essential "to the very *nature* of the human being" can be sensed among a people, even where the idea of nature had not been explicitly grasped. See note 9 above, note 78 below. See also the preface to this collection; appendix B of this collection.

63. See, e.g., *Gilgamesh*, X, i, 5f.; iii, 1f. (*A.N.E.T.*, pp. 89, 90, Old Babylonian version).

64. *Gilgamesh*, X, vi, 26–35 (*A.N.E.T.*, pp. 92–93). Have there not "always" (naturally) been for mankind "days of yore"? See, e.g., note 7 above.

65. See Tigay, *Evolution*, p. 5 n. 2; Anastaplo, *Human Being and Citizen*, p. 219. See also Hamlet's famous soliloquy.

66. See *Gilgamesh*, XI, 200f. (*A.N.E.T.,* p. 95). Utnapishtim warns his wife here about Gilgamesh, "Since to deceive is human, he will seek to deceive thee." Does not Utnapishtim "project" onto Gilgamesh his own legendary cunning? See the text at note 70 of this chapter.

67. See the concluding lines of Plato's *Apology* [*GBWW*, vol. 7, pp. 211–12]. See also Anastaplo, *Human Being and Citizen*, p. 8.

68. See *Gilgamesh*, XI, 290f. (*A.N.E.T.*, p. 96). The snake does become deathless, but it is only a snake. See Aldous Huxley, *After Many a Summer Dies the Swan* (New York: Harper, 1939), pp. 42–44, 345–46, 349–56. See also the text at note 55 of this chapter.

69. *Gilgamesh*, XI, 1–7 (*A.N.E.T.*, p. 93).

70. Utnapishtim (pursuant to instructions from the god Ea) deceives his fellow citizens as to why he is building a boat, thereby inducing others (who are no less deserving of salvation than he is?) to help him build. *Gilgamesh*, XI, 34f. (*A.N.E.T.*, p. 93). "It was his cunning, however, rather than his heroic deeds (Herakles) or his piety (Noah), that marked him as special." Gardner and Maier, *Gilgamesh*, p. 7. See note 29 above.

Is the cunning of old Ea to be contrasted to the wisdom of the god of light Shamash? See Gardner and Maier, *Gilgamesh*, pp. 291f., 299–300. "Ea's speech is about language. Only the cunning one, the poet, can lead into the archaic and lead us back to Uruk." Ibid., p. 300. What is the poet of the *Gilgamesh* suggesting about what he is doing? Our epic "has the god instruct the hero in a ruse to fool the townspeople, whereas the [older] version simply described its perpetration by the hero." Tigay, *Evolution*, p. 224. Does the poet want us to wonder whether Utnapishtim is to be believed when he says that he got all this, including instructions in deception, from Ea? See note 81 below.

In any event, is not Ea presented as deceiving the other gods (especially Enlil) as to what he did in warning Utnapishtim? "It was not I who disclosed the secret of the great gods. I let Atrahasis see a dream, and he perceived the secret of the gods." *Gilgamesh*, XI, 185–86 (*A.N.E.T.*, p. 95). Why is the old name (Atrahasis) used here for Utnapishtim? Is something "premodern" in the relations of gods and men being alluded to?

No reason is given for the Flood except the unexamined enmity of one god, who was opposed by the other gods. Enlil is angry that anyone escaped destruction, and then he oddly grants two of the survivors deathlessness. *Gilgamesh*, XI, 189f. (*A.N.E.T.*, p. 95). Do not the differences among the gods, evident again and again in the *Gilgamesh*, suggest that such gods do not really know what they are doing? See Plato, *Euthyphro* 8A, 9C-D [*GBWW*, vol. 7, pp. 194b-c, 195a-b]. Perhaps, indeed, they are not truly gods?

71. It has been suggested that the lounging Utnapishtim is really imitating "the resting figures of the gods," thus combining in him the human and the divine. See Gardner and Maier, *Gilgamesh*, p. 228. But may not this also suggest that there is something deeply questionable about the lives of the gods themselves? Is there an intimation *in Gilgamesh* which anticipates what is developed by Plato about the necessity of eros for the highest development of the life of reason (that is, of philosophy)? See notes 43 and 54 above. Life as fully life must have an erotic element—otherwise one has the indolent Mycroft Holmes instead of an energetic Sherlock Holmes? See, on Sherlock Holmes and his brother, Anastaplo, "Law & Literature and

the Moderns," p. 464. Is not Gilgamesh closer to the inspired Arjuna of the *Bhagavad Gita* (chapter 3 of this collection) than he is to Utnapishtim?

72. Of course, Ishtar had tried to destroy (the antierotic?) Gilgamesh with the Bull of Heaven—and on that occasion the male god Anu had been concerned to provide for the general protection of mankind. The male god Shamash had also been protective of Gilgamesh.

73. Do we not also see in all this some indication of the pervasive Mesopotamian attitude toward the erotic that Muhammad had to deal with (and come to terms with) when he appeared in nearby Arabia? (His way was different from both Judaism and Christianity. See note 19 above. See also chapter 6 of this collection. Muhammad condemned those who pray to "female beings." Koran, Sura 4, 1. 117. See note 50 above.) The pervasive Middle Eastern eroticism is suggested by Montesquieu's *Persian Letters*. Even Solomon, we should remember, had a harem. See, on Solomon, Anastaplo, "Law and Literature and the Bible," p. 653. See, for what *can* arouse erotic impulses, *The Great Ideas Today*, p. 42 (1994); appendix C of this collection, note 13. See also note 19 above.

The seduction of Enkidu by the harlot did not depend on language or ideas but rather on an elementary (even animalistic) appeal. The story is frank (but not as vivid as the Gardner and Maier translation?) about what was done—and perhaps it is even more significant that both the hunter's father and Gilgamesh "naturally" resorted to the use of the harlot as a remedy. This bears upon what I have suggested about a critical problem being that temple-harlotry is evidently not seen as a problem by the Mesopotamians. See note 49 above.

The harlot, in describing to Enkidu the merits of Uruk, spoke of it as a place where "each day is made a holiday." *Gilgamesh*, I, v, 8 (*A.N.E.T.*, p. 75). What does the poet suggest about the everyday life of Uruk when he can later have Utnapishtim describe the holiday spirit among his fellow citizens who are doomed for destruction? *Gilgamesh*, XI, 70f. (*A.N.E.T.*, p. 93). Is not holidaying often an effort to forget about death? On death, see Anastaplo, *Human Being and Citizen*, p. 214.

See, on the perverted place of the erotic among the pagans, and on Christianity as a cure for that, G. K. Chesterton, *St. Francis of Assisi* (New York: Doran, 1924), pp. 36f. ("Venus was nothing but venereal vice." Ibid., p. 43).

74. Later, of course, Gilgamesh and Enkidu interpret their own dreams, perhaps because they have learned something about the art from the women they have associated with. Are the dreams in our epic to be seen as *predictions* rather than as *disguises* (for one's passions, etc.)? Should we interpret these dreams as they are interpreted in the story? Or can we (should we? are we intended to? are we able to?) go beyond where the people in the story go? That is, are the dreams even more revealing than they are taken in the story to be? See, on the difficulty of subjecting ancient dream reports to psychoanalytical inquiry, A. Leo Oppenheim, *The Interpretation of Dreams in the Ancient Near East* (Philadelphia: American Philosophical Society, 1956), pp. 185, 219. See also note 20 above.

75. See, on what Ea says he did and did not do in alerting Utnapishtim about the Flood, note 70 above. See, on the interconnectedness of all things, Plato, *Meno* 81C-E [*GBWW*, vol. 7, p. 180a-b]. See, on the *Meno*, Anastaplo, *Human Being and Citizen*, p. 74. Laurence Berns and I are currently preparing a translation of Plato's *Meno* for publication by Focus Publishing having been inspired to do so by the late John Gormly.

76. Compare the overpowering bull sent by Poseidon in Euripides' *Hippolytus: that* divine agent is not going to be killed by any mortals! See note 26 above.

77. See *Gilgamesh*, XI, 112f., 159–61 (*A.N.E.T.*, pp. 94, 95). (Again and again, one must wonder how Utnapishtim is supposed to know what he does about the doings and sayings of the gods. Perhaps the gods have nothing better to do than to tell him stories?) The conduct of the gods in response to the sacrifice calls to mind Aristophanes' *Birds* [*GBWW*, vol. 5]. See Anastaplo, *The Thinker as Artist*, p. 157. One can see in Homer also how much the gods like the sacrifices offered by human beings. Compare Tigay, *Evolution*, pp. 228–29.

In any event, it seems to be assumed throughout that the gods are responsible for famines, floods, etc. Such depredations are not regarded as simply natural occurrences, it seems. See note 15 above and note 82 below. See also note 13 of the preface to this collection.

78. But then, one might have wondered, why had Gilgamesh "dolled" himself up, if not to win such esteem as Ishtar responded with? And had he done so only in order to be able to repel (somewhat perversely?) the advances by Ishtar which (naturally?) follow upon such esteem. See notes 40 and 51 above. We can see, again and again in ancient texts, that *nature* can be sensed and relied upon without its being discussed and understood. See note 62 above.

79. See the end of note 42 above. We can again be reminded of the doings of Anu, and of the Zeus of the *Iliad*. See notes 16 and 40 above. (Anu, as the first among the gods if not even the god of creation, is made much more of in other Mesopotamian stories. Enlil, it should be noticed, is *not* the god of the underworld.)

80. See, on Gilgamesh's own descendants, note 47 above. See, on the burial of Socrates, note 34 above.

What is the significance, for us, of the fact that this story was almost permanently lost? Does this not point up the problem with any attempt to guarantee one's memory in the distant future? See Percy B. Shelley, "Ozymandias." Yet we recall that Confucius could be described as the man who "knows it's no use, but keeps on doing it." See note 100 of chapter 4 of this collection. See also note 4 above.

81. Uses of both *seven* and *twelve* abound in our epic and, evidently, elsewhere in Mesopotamian literature. See, on the importance of *twelve* in ancient Mesopotamia, Eric Voegelin, *Order and History* (Baton Rouge: Louisiana State University Press, 1956), vol. 1, pp. 29–35.

Perhaps the most important fact about the twelfth tablet is something so obvious that it can easily be overlooked: the poet of our epic evidently wanted to make it apparent that he has here, as distinct from what he has done elsewhere throughout the epic, incorporated the old material he took from the tradition with very few changes. He thereby puts the perceptive reader on notice that he is perhaps providing an orthodox alternative in the twelfth tablet to the unorthodox probing of fundamental issues in his first eleven tables. See note 33 above. See, on anticipations of Tablet XII in Tablet VI, Kirk, *Myth*, p. 143 n. 11.

The poet of our epic can be understood to see things differently from his predecessors. He differs as well, it seems, from Gilgamesh himself, whose accounts of his career (as he meets strangers on his way to Utnapishtim) and whose exhibition of walls and temple back in Uruk suggest the sort of thing *he* said when he recorded "all is toil . . . on a stone stela." *Gilgamesh*, I, i, 8 (*A.N.E.T.*, p. 73). See note 51 above.

An indication of Mesopotamian opinions about the relation of body to soul may be seen in the instructions Gilgamesh gives, in the twelfth tablet, to Enkidu before his Descent. *Gilgamesh*, XII, 10f. (*A.N.E.T.*, p. 97). (Enkidu is quite rash in the twelfth tablet, just as he had been in the earlier account [with the assault on Ishtar], contributing "once again" to his premature death. He generally is even less thoughtful than Gilgamesh.)

One of the changes made by the poet upon appending to our epic (with relatively few changes) the story portion now found in the twelfth tablet, is the addition of an appeal to the moon god Sin. *Gilgamesh*, XII, 62–69 (*A.N.E.T.*, p. 98). Perhaps this is a playful allusion to the name of the poet traditionally associated with our epic, Sin Leqi-Unninni.

82. See, e.g., Thompson, *The Epic of Gilgamesh*, pp. 5–6; Heidel, *The Gilgamesh Epic*, pp. 2–3. One can see again and again (especially upon consulting Professor Tigay's detailed compilation of the work of so many of his predecessors) how much we do rely upon scrupulous, hardworking, and quite learned scholars to establish the texts we (sometimes perhaps too cavalierly) speculate about.

83. Vital to an enduring understanding of understanding itself, I argue throughout this collection, is an informed awareness of the nature of *nature*. See, e.g., sections XI, XII, and XIII, of chapter 4 of this collection. See, for my suggestions about the absence of the notion of *nature* in both the Hindu and the Confucian thought of antiquity, chapters 3 and 4 of this collection. Similar suggestions can be made about ancient Mesopotamian thought. See note 77 above. See also note 13 of the preface. Compare note 42 above. (But here, at least, the modern reader is not likely to be misled by translators improperly using *nature* upon rendering the *Gilgamesh* into English. In fact, I do not recall any instance of the use of *nature* in any of the translations I have consulted. It might be instructive to consider why translations of this epic have been more careful, if they have been, than translations of the *Analects* or of the *Bhagavad Gita* in this respect. Is it partly because the *Analects* and the *Gita are* more thoughtful, thereby inclining translators to use *nature*?) See, for challenging suggestions about "the [primarily intuitive] confrontation between nature and culture" in the *Gilgamesh* epic, Kirk, *Myth*, pp. 148, 152. See also ibid., pp. 145f., 151. See as well note 17 above. See, on nature and the human things, appendix B of this collection.

84. The quality of this poet, or at least of the tradition upon which he so aptly draws, is further suggested by this sampling of seven passages which retain their appeal even in translation: (1) an apprehensive Enkidu says to Gilgamesh, "A cry, my father, chokes my throat" (literally, "has bound my neck veins"); (2) Ishtar warns her father, Anu, "I will raise up the dead eating and alive, so that the dead shall outnumber the living!"; (3) a startled Enkidu awakens from a dream to ask, "My friend, why are the great gods in council?"; (4) a bereaved Gilgamesh asks, "When I die, shall I not be like Enkidu?"; (5) a god advises Utnapishtim before the Great Flood, "Tear down this house, build a ship! Give up possessions, seek thou life. Forswear worldly goods, and keep the soul alive!"; (6) the storm of the Flood begins, "The wide land was shattered like a pot! For one day the south-storm blew, gathering speed as it blew, submerging the mountains, overtaking the people like a battle. No one can see his fellow, nor can the people be recognized from heaven"; (7) Utnapishtim reports on what happened after the Flood subsided, "When the seventh day arrived, I sent forth and set free a dove. The dove went forth, but came back; since no resting-place for it was visible, she turned round. Then I sent forth and set free a swallow. The swallow went forth, but came back; since no resting-place for it was visible, she turned around; Then I sent forth and set free a raven. The raven went forth and, seeing that the waters had diminished, he eats, circles, caws, and turns not round. Then I let out all to the four winds and offered a sacrifice." *Gilgamesh*, III, ii, 40; VI, 99–100, VI, 194; IX, i, 3; XI, 24–26; XI, 107–112; XI, 145f. (Pritchard, ed., *Ancient Near Eastern Texts*, pp. 79, 84, 85, 88, 93, 94, 94–95). See note 42 above.

Chapter Two

"Ancient" African (Including Egyptian) Thought

There is always something new from Africa.

—Pliny the Elder[1]

I.

Two major branches of African thought have come down to us from antiquity. One stems from North Africa, principally Egypt, which had substantial contacts to the west with the Libyans, to the south with the Nubians and Ethiopians, to the east with the people of the Fertile Crescent in Asia Minor and, very late, with the Arabs, and to the north with the Greeks and the Romans. The other branch of African thought stems from sub-Saharan Africa, made up of hundreds of tribes or peoples, similar in their diversity to the ancient tribes of the Western Hemisphere.[2] But however diverse these sub-Saharan African tribes may be, they are (and are generally recognized to be) critically different from the rest of the world which they were largely cut off from for so long.[3]

In antiquity, one "half" of Africa seems to have had little awareness of the other "half." The ancient Egyptians were part of the Mediterranean world, though deeply involved in the Nilotic world as well. The sub-Saharan Africans, although largely isolated for so long from the rest of the human race, may have a more influential worldwide presence in the coming century than the *ancient* Egyptians.[4] One notices in the novels of Naguib Mahfouz how little influence ancient Egypt seems to have even in the life of Egyptians in the twentieth century.[5]

We can see on display in Africa the "oldest" and the "youngest" of the races of mankind. "Human beings are widely thought to have originated in Africa."[6] It is sometimes said that the Pygmies, who roam the forests of a

31

small part of central Africa, exhibit the earliest form of human organization.[7] In this sense the tribes of sub-Saharan Africa may show human beings in their earliest, or youngest, condition, whereas the ancient Egyptians in their later dynasties (but before the Alexandrian and Roman conquests) show what thousands of years of development, and hence aging, of a stable civil order can lead to.

My personal experiences of Africa came in the course of my service as a flying officer in the United States Army Air Corps at the end of the Second World War. Stationed at our air bases in Egypt and Saudi Arabia, I learned to enjoy both the Nile and the desert, as well as the sounds and smells of North Africa. My service in that part of the world included flights to Dakar (in Senegal) and to Liberia. My most vivid recollection of Liberia is of the occasion when I was rebuked by a fellow officer for paying a boy too much to climb up and cut me a bunch of bananas. I believe I gave him a dime instead of a nickel. I fondly recall Dakar nights without electric lights, where I could watch people enjoying themselves around unlikely campfires on street corners.[8] My exposure to sub-Saharan Africa continues, of course, in the contacts one has in the United States with people of African descent (destined, in part by racial prejudice, to remain somewhat distinctive) who have helped convey to us some of the music, folk stories, colors, and foods of Africa.

II.

A special, if not even exotic, view of the Egyptian Africa of antiquity is provided by the great museums of the world—in Chicago, New York, London, Paris, Berlin, and Rome, to say nothing of what may still be seen in Egypt to this day. Ancient Egypt, which extended over some five thousand years of recorded history,[9] is distinguished by the monumental character of its structures. These structures, which are illuminated by extensive literary remains, are on a scale unmatched in the ancient world, except perhaps for the Great Wall of China. Egyptian civilization, despite its many changes in dynasties, was remarkably stable. So remarkable was the span of time evident throughout Egyptian life that the ancient Greeks could be dismissed by the Egyptians as "children."[10] Egyptian history, since decipherment of the language with the help of the Rosetta Stone, has been largely knowable by us, the moderns.

The West has long been fascinated by Egypt—and, indeed, by all of Africa, a strange place to which Westerners seem always to respond with ambivalence. Ethiopians, who represent a mixture of Egypt (including the Palestine that Egyptians long controlled) and sub-Saharan Africa, are noticed in the Greek fables of Aesop:

> A man bought an Ethiopian, thinking that his color was the result of the neglect of his former owner. He took him home and used all kinds of soap on him and tried all kinds of baths to clean him up. He couldn't change his color, but he made him sick with all his efforts.[11]

To this story (which can serve also as an allegory of the West's treatment of Africa in recent centuries) is added the moral, "Natures remain just as they first appear."[12] That an attempt to wash away an Ethiopian's color could be used in this way in a story attributed to Aesop (who evidently lived in the sixth century B.C.) suggests that the darker Africans were not familiar to some Greeks, although the effectiveness of the story does depend upon its audience recognizing the folly of this slave owner's efforts.

The Egyptians, on the other hand, had long been known to the Greeks. It is likely that Herodotus, when he wrote about the Egyptians in the fifth century B.C., expressed an assessment of them already shared by other Greeks, that the Egyptians were the most religious of men.[13]

III.

The great monuments of ancient Egypt, which are notable not only for their size, but also for what can be called their *determination*, seem to be devoted primarily to the care of the dead. The same can be said about many, if not most, of the literary remains of ancient Egypt. So overwhelming was the challenge of death for the Egyptians that elaborate measures were taken corpse by corpse, perhaps reinforcing thereby a radical individualism. Thus, each of the great pyramids, which could easily have housed the remains of all of the pharaohs, was devoted primarily to the needs of one royal corpse alone.[14]

Was death somehow to be overcome by the kind of display of ingenuity and energy seen in ministering to the dead? A pyramid, for example, is skillfully crystallized energy on a grand scale. Is not a preoccupation with death likely to be, in effect, a desperate effort to insure the preservation of life? Much of what one sees and reads from ancient Egypt is dedicated to the proposition that life after death can and should continue much as it had during one's time on earth. The measures resorted to in order to preserve the corpses of the deceased testify to how vital an earthly existence is to human life, so much so that proper care of one when dead permits one's spirit to come and go on earth as one wishes. (Compare the Platonic, and later the Christian, insistence upon the truly human coming into its own only when one is relieved of one's bodily attributes.) Although an occasional ancient representation can suggest that the Egyptians were not without an openness to the erotic aspects of bodily activities and human relations, such eroticism seems to have been consistently subordinated to their pursuit of immortality or, rather, of deathlessness.

Parodies of the Egyptian approach to death may be seen in the attention lavished for decades on Lenin's corpse in the Soviet Union and in the expenditures (very much in the service of a quest for eternal youth) that are devoted in the United States to the cosmetic and celebratory aspects of the funeral industry.[15]

The dead of Egypt, it sometimes seems, did not have anything better to do than to revisit their earthly habitats. No fundamental distinction seems to be recognized between the future and the past. This can mean, in effect, that the present is both everything and nothing. This is an approach that is different both from the reincarnation expected among, say, the Hindus and some sub-Saharan Africans and from the desire for release from earthly limitations seen among, say, the Christians, the Muslims, and the seekers of Nirvana.[16]

What *is* the understanding of life, or of living, that is assumed by the Egyptians? To make as much as they do of continuing after death with everyday activity as it happens to be organized by us may be to subvert life as we can know it. Is tragedy, for example, somehow lost sight of and made virtually impossible because of the impermanence of death?[17]

On the other hand, there was among the ancient Egyptians considerable emphasis not only upon rituals and formulas, but also upon the moral purity of the deceased. It was in the interest of the deceased to be able to pass muster with respect to such matters as those collected in the following recapitulation of a man's career:

I have come from my town,
I have descended from my [district],
I have done justice for its lord,
I have satisfied him with what he loves.
I spoke truly, I did right,
I spoke fairly, I repeated fairly,
I seized the right moment
So as to stand well with people.
I judged between two so as to content them,
I rescued the weak from one stronger than he
As much as was in my power.
I gave bread to the hungry, clothes to the naked,
I brought the boatless to land.
I buried him who had no son,
I made a boat for him who lacked one.
I respected my father, I pleased my mother,
I raised their children.[18]

We have no problem recognizing the merits of most, if not all, of these actions.

IV.

We have noticed the recourse of the ancient Egyptians to elaborate rituals and detailed formulae, especially with a view to a proper transition of human beings to eternal life. A kind of magic seems to have been relied upon here, however reasonable and even sophisticated that people must have been with respect to such disciplines as civil engineering, mechanical and hydraulic transportation, agriculture, and masonry. Magic means, among other things, that what one knows—and hence what one says and does—can be important, even decisive, for perpetual happiness. This too reflects the role of reason in human affairs. Again and again there are prescriptions such as the following: "If this chapter be known by [the deceased] he shall come forth by day, he shall rise up to walk upon the earth among the living, and he shall never fail and come to an end, never, never, never."[19] Another one reads: "If this composition be known [by the deceased] upon earth he shall come forth by day, and he shall have the faculty of traveling about among the living, and his name shall never perish."[20] Still another one reads:

> If this chapter be known [by the deceased] upon earth, [or if it be done] in writing upon [his] coffin, he shall come forth by day in all the forms which he is pleased [to take], and he shall enter in to [his] place and shall not be driven back. And cakes, and ale, and joints of meat upon the altar of Osiris shall be given unto him; . . . and he shall do whatsoever it pleaseth him to do, even as the company of the gods which is in the underworld, continually, and regularly, for millions of times.[21]

In these and other matters, the ancient Egyptians (like the Hindus) always "thought big," contemplating a universe with millions upon millions of years already past as well as to come.[22]

The rituals and invocations that the Egyptians relied upon were in the service of the fundamentals of their religion. These basic ideas were summed up by a Western scholar at the beginning of the twentieth century under six headings:

I. Belief in the immortality of the soul and the recognition of relatives and friends after death.

II. Belief in the resurrection of a spiritual body, in which the soul lived after death.

III. Belief in the continued existence of the heart-soul, the *ka* (the double), and the shadow.

IV. Belief in the transmutation of offerings, and the efficacy of funerary sacrifices and gifts.

V. Belief in the efficacy of words of power, including names, magical and religious formulas, &c.

VI. Belief in the Judgment, the good being rewarded with everlasting life and happiness, and the wicked with annihilation.[23]

This scholar then added, "All of the above appears to be indigenous [North?] African beliefs, which existed in the Predynastic Period, and are current under various forms at the present day among most of the tribes of the Sudan who have any religious belief at all."[24]

We may well wonder what the sources were of all the information inherited and relied upon by the Egyptians, much of which had been transmitted to them for centuries if not for millennia. We may also wonder about the significance of the fact that such information was once known only to a relatively few in antiquity and that it has long since been either lost or abandoned. We wonder, in short, about the nature of revelation, its reception, and its staying power.

V.

Critical to Egyptian thought, and to its preoccupation with a proper response to (if not conquest of) death, is its understanding of the divine. A standard reference book opens its account of Egypt with these observations:

> No one who strolls through the Egyptian galleries of a museum can fail to be struck by the multitude of divinities who attract attention on all sides. Colossal statues in sandstone, granite and basalt, minute statuettes in glazed composition, bronze, even in gold, portray gods and goddesses frozen in hierarchical attitudes, seated or standing. Sometimes these male or female figures have heads with human features. More often they are surmounted by the muzzle of an animal or the beak of a bird. The same divinities, receiving adoration and offerings or performing ritual gestures for the benefit of their worshipers, can be seen again on the bas-reliefs of massive sarcophagi or sculptured on funerary stelae and stone blocks stripped from temple walls. They recur on mummy cases and in the pictures which illuminate the papyri of the *Book of the Dead*.[25]

Further on in this account a partial list is given of the animals whose heads appear on Egyptian divinities: the bull, the cat, the cow, the crocodile, the dog-faced ape, the donkey, the falcon, the frog, the hippopotamus, the ibis, the jackal, the lion, the lioness, the ram with curved horns, the ram with wavy horns, the scarab, the scorpion, the serpent, the uraeus, the vulture, and the wolf.[26]

We are told that only the myth of Osiris, who was one of the greatest gods in the Egyptian pantheon, has been transmitted in detail to us—and this, evidently, because of the writings of Plutarch. "Plutarch, though Greek and writing of times already long past, was evidently well informed."[27] The story of Osiris's dismemberment and the subsequent reassembly of his corpse by his sorrowing mother became important in Egypt to the preservation of human corpses and to an insistence upon proper burial rites.[28]

We have noticed that knowing prescribed things was believed critical for the well-being of the deceased. We have also noticed that morality, or a proper kind of conduct, was considered important in the judging of the deceased. Even so, knowing key things may not be the same as understanding them. The names of gods and of their parts and functions are emphasized, just as may be the proper names, not only the generic names, of, say, the various parts of the ship that is to carry the deceased to perpetual bliss.[29] But little is said in the materials we have about why these things are as they are, or even why they are named as they are. This deficiency is related to the question I have raised about the source and authority for all of this supposedly useful, indeed vital, information.

Is there in all this what we might call a parody of philosophy, or is it also a step toward philosophy, just as we see astrology as a parody of and yet a contribution to astronomy? In any effort to understand the vast Egyptian lore, especially about gods such as Osiris and about human death, one must have an awareness of what can and cannot be.[30] The same can be said about any effort to understand the stories we have from sub-Saharan Africa. It is helpful, in coming to terms with the Egyptian preoccupation with serving the dead, to compare the philosophical response exhibited by Socrates in Plato's dialogues, where he (unconcerned about funeral rites) accepts with apparent equanimity the prospect of total annihilation of himself at death.[31] We ourselves can notice that, so far as we know, our personal nonexistence before conception was anything but distressing.

The elaborateness of both the doctrines and the rituals of the Egyptians may have eventually been self-defeating. For one thing, it must have become harder and harder to make sense of all the lore that had been accumulated in these matters—and the conditions of the country were such that there *was* a literate class with leisure to think about things, if so minded.[32] Furthermore, the richly adorned corpses and tombs proved attractive to thieves, especially those criminals who could not see that any divine retribution followed from their larcenous incursions. But perhaps most important, the complexity, if not even what seems to us the inherent improbability, of their pantheon may eventually have made the Egyptians susceptible to the appeal of so single-minded, rigorous, and even pure message as that offered by Islam, a religion which (unlike Christianity) does not seem to depend upon any story of the death and resurrection of a divinity such as Osiris.[33]

VI.

However separated North Africa and sub-Saharan Africa were by a vast oceanlike desert, both the Nile and trans-Saharan caravans permitted some movement north and south. For example, an occasional dancing Pygmy could delight the court of a pharaoh.[34] Also, there seems always to have been some traffic in slaves and animals from south to north down the Nile. Peculiar combinations of human beings and animals could be conjured up in stories both north and south of the Sahara Desert. In Egypt, we have seen, there were tales of gods with animal parts; in sub-Saharan African tales, humans and animals could also be mixed up, even sexually, without regard to species differentiations, and much could be made of animal stories.

But the differences north and south can still be striking. There is relatively little said in the stories of the sub-Saharan Africans (whom I will now call simply Africans) about burial rites, however important the social participation in African funerals remains down to this day.[35] Also, unlike the Egyptian stories we have, the African stories are filled with resurrections of all kinds. Further distinctions from the Egyptian approach to things may be seen in the opening passage of an article, "Mythology of Black Africa":

> In Black Africa religion has nowhere reached a definitive form. Everywhere we find the worship of the forces of Nature personified—sun, moon, sky, mountains, rivers. But the undisciplined native imagination prevented the religion of Nature from expanding into poetic myths like those of India or Greece. . . .
>
> Among the Africans sorcery is very powerful. Every medical treatment has all the characteristics of exorcism, since magic remains secret while religion is open to all. Amulets and gri-gris are the usual manifestations of magic among the Africans. The object of these talismans is to protect their owner against diseases, wounds, thieves and murderers, or to increase his wealth—in brief, to procure him everything profitable.
>
> The African native thinks that the world and everything in it must be obedient to sorcerers, magicians who have the power of commanding the elements. This belief is bound up with another—the continuing existence of the soul after death. Magicians are able to call on souls to aid their powers. The souls of the dead often transmigrate into the bodies of animals, or may even be re-incarnated in plants, when the natives think themselves bound to such by a close link of kinship. Thus the Zulus refrain from killing certain species of snakes which they think are the spirits of their relatives.
>
> Africans attribute a spirit to every animate and inanimate object, and these spirits are the emanations of deities. Moreover, they are distinct from one another, for there are spirits of natural phenomena and spirits of the ancestors.[36]

The opinions, traits, and practices described here are drawn, for the most part, from the old stories that have come down to us. No doubt, most modern Africans have questioned, if not abandoned, many of the opinions of their ancestors about such things. It is not, however, the opinions of our contemporaries in sub-Saharan Africa or anywhere else with which we are now primarily concerned, just as it was not with the opinions of our contemporaries in Egypt.[37]

Much of the African past has long been a mystery not only to Europeans (among whom I here include most Americans heretofore), but also to Africans themselves. The lack of records and of much in the way of archaeological evidence makes it difficult to piece together Africa's history. Whatever great cities, art, or writing there may once have been, not many traces seem to be left with which investigators can work. In a sense, for most Africans (unlike for the Egyptians) there has been heretofore neither past nor future, but only a perpetual present.[38]

Up to the twentieth century, therefore, Africa could be regarded as the Dark Continent and as a "latecomer" upon the world's stage.[39] Its problems, particularly in the raising of sufficient food for its fast-growing population, remain chronic, contributing to devastating famines in some countries. It is not generally recognized that the amount of arable land in regions south of the Sahara is quite small (less than 10 percent). Matters are not helped by the widespread African practice of relying upon women, already burdened with child rearing and other household duties, for much of the agricultural work of the community.[40]

It is also hard to see Africa and Africans properly after centuries of slavery. Slavery, which seems to have been indigenous to Africa (as in other parts of the ancient world) well before the fierce depredations of the Arabs and the Europeans (and which may continue, in the hundreds of thousands, in parts of Africa and the Middle East today), affects how some Africans, as well as many non-Africans, regard Africans to this day. It can be hard not only to *get* past, but also to *see* past such brutal subjugation and exploitation. However destructive Africans have been in wars among themselves from time to time—and this they *have* been—it is not likely that they have ever inflicted upon themselves the spiritual as well as the material damage that non-Africans (both Islamic and Christian) did for several centuries with their slave trade.[41] Some hope for African self-fulfillment can be gleaned, however, from the history of the successful Slavs of Eastern Europe, a people whose very name reminds everyone, including them, of their centuries of enslavement. Non-African respect can follow upon noticing what it is that Africans (despite, if not partly because of, slavery) grasp which Westerners do not.

VII.

When there is no generally authoritative text available—such as the Bible, Homer's epics, the *Gilgamesh*, the Confucian *Analects*, the *Bhagavad Gita*, the Buddhist scriptures, or the Koran—it is difficult to determine where to begin in grasping the thought of an ancient people.[42] The principal access we have to ancient sub-Saharan thought is through the African folk stories, myths, and other tales that have been recorded, often by Europeans. These stories, collected by many outsiders for at least two centuries now, pose obvious problems with respect to the reliability of their transmission. We must do the best that we can, aware both of our shortcomings and of the weaknesses of those who collected these tales.[43] This is the approach we have to take also in our study of North American Indian thought.[44] I am somewhat reassured, in making the use I do of these very old stories for investigating ancient, *not* contemporary, African thought, when I notice that these stories are repeatedly drawn upon, in a casual and relaxed fashion, in the novels and other writings of contemporary Africans, such as Chinua Achebe and Wole Soyinka.[45] This is in marked contrast to a novelist such as Naguib Mahfouz, who barely mentions ancient Egypt in his marvelous novels of *The Cairo Trilogy*.

One massive fact about the old African tales should be noticed: they are not, by and large, charming or attractive stories.[46] One encounters in the African tales considerable callousness, gratuitous cruelty, casual betrayal, and other severe moral limitations. To some extent these bleak responses may be traced back to prolonged adversities, especially chronic famine conditions, in much of Africa.[47]

The Western reader can find oppressive such a story as the following, which is *not* exceptional in the African corpus: A farmer provides refuge within his body to a snake being pursued by men. When the men leave, the snake refuses to come out of the farmer's body, finding it comfortable there. "The farmer's belly was now so puffed out that you would have thought that he was a woman with child." The farmer enlists the help of a heron, who manages to pull the snake out of the farmer's body and to kill it. All this, with the snake's ingratitude leading to its destruction, is bad enough—but, unfortunately, the fate of the snake does not serve to make others act better toward their benefactors in turn:

> The farmer got up and said to the heron, "You have rid me of the snake, but now I want a potion to drink because he may have left some of his poison behind." "You must go and find six white fowls," said the heron, "and cook and eat them—that's the remedy." "Come to think of it," said the farmer, "you're a white fowl, so you'll do for a start."
>
> So saying he seized the heron, tied it up, and carried it off home. There he hung it up in his hut while he told his wife what had happened. "I'm surprised at you," said his wife. "The bird does you a kindness, rids you of the evil in your belly, saves your life, in fact, and yet you catch it and talk of killing it." With that she released the heron and it flew away.[48]

There is something noble about this woman's response, exhibiting by the way the important (and often dominant) role that women have in African stories, even in polygamous households. But, unfortunately for our sensibilities, this story does not end there but continues. "With that she released the heron and it flew away. But as it went, it gouged out one of her eyes." I recognize that there may be something so outlandish and grotesque about such a series of betrayals that an audience could find it laughable.[49] But the teaching or moral with which this story ends is one that would apply to a significant proportion of the African stories that we happen to have available: "That is all. When you see water flowing uphill, it means that someone is repaying a kindness."[50]

To draw such a moral is, of course, to repudiate selfishness and betrayal. But it is also to recognize, and one story after another bears this out, that one should not expect much gratitude in this world. Is not the teaching of that lesson likely to discourage kindness and self-sacrifice? The disbelief with which Westerners greet such stories is echoed in an account that reached us from Rwanda during the fierce 1994 massacres:

> "To be in the middle of all this, to watch them turn from the most wonderful, the most smiling, the most gentle of people, to such treacherous murderers is beyond comprehension," said Dr. Per Housmann, a dentist who runs the Adventist clinic [in Kigali, Rwanda]. "It is almost as if someone flips a switch."[51]

No doubt, explanations (grounded in a long history of abuses and grievances, some of them due to colonial mismanagement) can be developed to help account for such atrocities, just as explanations can be developed to help account for what the highly cultured Germans did to millions of their victims during the Second World War and what the Europeans and Americans did to millions of civilians in the bombing of cities during the same war.[52] But such explanations should not keep us from being appalled at what we witness— and from attempting to figure out what these aberrations suggest about the souls of a people.

Among the aberrations in the collections we have of African stories are slavery, cannibalism (with several stories even of the casual eating of mothers by their own children), and betrayals (sometimes just for the fun of it, it seems) of relatives and friends. On the other hand, an eminent Senegalese poet and statesman recorded a condemnation of white men as cannibals for what they have done to African life.[53] And Africans could describe their colonial masters as men who practiced "the art of conquering without being in the right."[54] In more ways than one, therefore, the Westerner who studies ancient African thought should be open to seeing himself better as a result of, as well as a condition for, such an inquiry.[55]

VIII.

I suspect that the moral ambiguity which we find in old African stories is intimately related to another peculiar feature of those stories: it is often difficult to figure out why things happen the way they do. "Cause and effect" relations do not seem to be regarded the way they are in the European (or, for that matter, in the Asian and many other) stories that I happen to know. Thus one can encounter in African stories the animate instruments and the repeated spontaneous resurrections to which I have referred. This is aside from the deliberate or obvious uses in sub-Saharan Africa of magic, spirit doctors, sorcerers, and the like.[56]

This makes it difficult for us to anticipate, or to remember, what happens in many African stories. All too often, they simply do not make sense to us, even though there is no indication that anything has been omitted that the audience expects. Something of this may also be seen in modern African novels, such as three by Achebe: *Things Fall Apart, The Arrow of God*, and *A Man of the People*. Here, too, it can often be said, "It is almost as if someone flips a switch"—in the sense that dramatic and largely unanticipated reversals suddenly dominate the story.[57] Things can sometimes work out well in African stories, but the European observer often does not understand why. Perhaps a benevolent but mysterious ordering of the universe is seen as occasionally at work. It may even be believed that the ultimate government of the world is well-disposed to the living things of the earth. Animism and witchcraft, for good as well as for ill, find a fertile field here.[58]

Things can be expected to work out fairly well in adverse circumstances when there are, as is sometimes assumed in African stories and is often evident in African life, family cohesiveness, respect for elders, and what we call the work ethic. It has been pointed out that Africans have a love of justice.[59] The subordination of "cause and effect" considerations in storytelling may contribute to a kind of vitality among the Africans, a vitality reflected in the music, especially that of the drum, and in the colors and sculpture that have proved so influential in twentieth-century Western art.[60]

IX.

The general order that tends to assert itself in African thought is grounded in communalism, not individualism, however self-interested the popular (somewhat Odyssean) Trickster figure may be. Such communalism can even find all forms of life to be intimately interconnected. Along with this there is in the old stories an organization of human life in fairly small communities where everyone knows everyone else who matters.[61]

One may even wonder whether the malevolent cunning and extreme self-ishness in many of the old stories were a kind of reaction to, if not "compensation" for or relief from, the pervasiveness and intensity of the constraints that everyone had to live with.[62] Perhaps that intensity contributes also to the fierceness that tribal conflicts provoke. The passions and aggressiveness that are routinely suppressed among one's kin can find "legitimate" expression either in stories about social relations or against outsiders who can come to be regarded as barely human.[63] In critical respects, tribalism is like individualism, but on a much larger scale: the personal and the intimate, rather than the political, color one's actions. It is no wonder, then, that a continent that is still very much dominated by tribalism as well as by a "worldview" strongly influenced by beliefs in spirits and witchcraft, should generally be in chaos, politically and economically speaking.[64]

Deficiencies with respect to the political, as distinguished from the tribal, may even have contributed to the centuries-long African susceptibility to slavery at the hands of ruthless exploiters both among Africans and among outsiders. But there was also a remarkable resiliency in the African character, which permitted so many Africans to submit to and to survive (if not eventually to benefit from) North American enslavement and cruelty in a way that the perhaps more spirited (and hence less resilient) North American Indians could not.[65]

Richard Weaver has suggested that the "mind of logical simplicity," such as is promoted by modern bourgeois society, is ill equipped to deal with those "regions where mystery and contingency are recognized," "a world of terrifying reality to which the tidy moralities" of contemporary Western life do not seem applicable.[66] He then adds:

> An anthropologist related to me that certain Negro tribes of West Africa have a symbol for the white man consisting of a figure seated on the deck of a steamer in a position of stiffest rigidity. The straight, uncompromising lines are the betrayal; the primitive artist has caught the white man's unnatural rigor, which contrasts, ominously for him, with the native's sinuous adaptation.[67]

X.

What is the African grasp of that which we know as *nature*? This is an underlying question in our effort to understand the ancient African stories and hence African thought. (This kind of question is addressed repeatedly in other chapters of this collection.) The Egyptians may have blurred the distinctions between the living and the dead; the Africans may have blurred the distinctions between the human and the nonhuman, as well as between the animate and the inanimate. One form that many African stories take is that of efforts to account for natural phenomena (especially what we regard as instinctive behavior by animals) as results of "historic" events, often with acts of will (sometimes by a divinity) following upon critical events, thereby permanently establishing the characteristics of a species.[68]

The distinctions blurred here may permit, if they do not contribute to, the widespread popularity in Africa of animism and witchcraft. These can take the form among Africans in the Western Hemisphere (especially when combined with Christian elements) of voodooism, the Santeria cult, and the like.[69] This is related to what I have suggested about "cause and effect"—and this, in turn, bears upon the African sense of time, which seems to be markedly different (in some ways better, in some ways worse) than that in the West. This ill equips Africans for—or, should we say, this spares them from?—thoroughgoing and hence often dehumanizing industrialization.[70]

The fact that in many old African stories things somehow fit together and work out in desirable ways that we do not expect or understand may mean that the ancient African storytellers did not have the grasp of nature that we in the West do, a grasp among us that goes back in effect to philosophical and other developments in Greece and Rome (influenced thereafter by the Bible) more than twenty-five hundred years ago. It may also mean, of course, that Africans grasp something about the very nature of things that we Westerners have never grasped or have had to give up in pursuit of the enlightenment, self-determination, and progress that we treasure.[71]

XI.

The subtlety and rationality, in the Western sense, of ancient African thought are suggested by the not infrequent recourse in African stories to well-constructed riddles of some complexity, a recourse more frequent there than in other collections of ancient stories that I have seen from other peoples.

Here is one version of the simpler riddling stories among Africans:

> An old man had three children, all boys. When they had grown up to manhood, he called them together and told them that now he was very old and no longer able to provide, even for himself. He ordered them to go out and bring him food and clothing.
>
> The three brothers set out, and after a very long while they came to a large river. As they had gone on together for such a time, they decided that once they got across they would separate. The eldest told the youngest to take the middle road, and the second to go to the right, while he himself would go to the left. Then, in a year's time, they would come back to the same spot.

So they parted, and at the end of a year, as agreed, they found their way back to the riverside. The eldest asked the youngest what he had gotten during his travels, and the boy replied: "I have nothing but a mirror, but it has wonderful power. If you look into it, you can see all over the country, no matter how far away." When asked, in turn, what he had gotten, the second brother replied: "Only a pair of sandals that are so full of power, that if one puts them on one can walk at once to any place in the country in one step." Then, the eldest himself said: "I, too, have obtained but little, a small calabash of medicine, that is all. But let us look into the mirror and see how father fares."

The youngest produced his mirror, and they all looked into it and saw that their father was already dead and that even the funeral custom was finished. Then the elder said: "Let us hasten home and see what we can do." So the second brought out his sandals, and all three placed their feet inside them and, immediately, they were borne to their father's grave. Then the eldest shook the medicine out of his bag, and poured it over the grave. At once their father arose, as if nothing had been the matter with him. Now which of these three sons has performed the best?[72]

Notice how the authority of, as well as a duty to, a father is taken for granted.[73]

The African riddling story, for which there is neither an obvious nor a "trick" solution, reflects an awareness of limitations. Considerable sophistication is exhibited.[74] What *is* obvious is that the story is so designed as to invite and permit extended discussion among listeners. Such stories, if they are to endure, cannot have been crafted without a reliable grasp of how things work, if not perhaps of what makes them work as they do.[75]

Audience participation seems to be taken for granted. Perhaps that is also true for many of the other African stories that we find puzzling or incomprehensible: the audience may have been expected to suggest explanations and to account otherwise for "cause and effect." Such audience participation, or rather social involvement, carries over in this country in the lively responses depended upon by preachers in African American church services. Common sense and the general experience of the community can be brought to bear upon what the storyteller says, thereby filling out a story in such a way as to permit the audience to consider it just as much theirs as it is the storyteller's. This can make for a richness of communal discourse that we are no longer familiar with at a time when our "entertainment" encourages us to be ever more passive. It is like the difference between playing a musical recording in one's home and gathering around a piano to sing.[76]

To whom should the prize in the story of the three sons go? To the son with the mirror, to the son with the sandals, or to the son with the medicine? The answer to this question should not depend upon whether such communication, travel, or healing are now routinely possible. That is not what the story seems to be about.[77]

XII.

The constancy of human nature (whether or not nature is explicitly recognized as such) may be seen in how stories are responded to. We can see in the African stories some that may be variations upon stories taken from the Bible.[78] Other stories are similar to, but yet sometimes quite different from, counterparts in Europe.[79]

Particularly illuminating is an African story shared with Aesop. Perhaps the two stories—one from Greece, the other from Ghana—were first put into circulation about the same time. I suspect that one of them was influenced by the other. What is more intriguing here is not which of the two might have been first, but rather what is distinctive to each version. Most intriguing of all, perhaps, is that the subtlety and humor of the episode must have appealed both to Greek and to African audiences. Here is the Greek version:

> Two friends were traveling along the same road. When a bear suddenly appeared, one of them quickly climbed a tree and hid. The other was about to be caught but fell down on the ground and played dead. When the bear put its muzzle up close and smelled all around him, he held his breath, for they say that the animal will not touch a dead body. When the bear went away, the man up in the tree asked him what the bear had said in his ear. He replied, "Not to travel in the future with friends who won't stand by you in danger."[80]

The moral associated with this Aesopian fable is, "The story shows that hardships test true friends."[81]

Now here is the African version, in which the dangerous animal is a lion:

> There were once two friends, Kwasi and Kwaku, and one day they went to the bush. They had been playing there for some time when they saw a lion coming. Straightway, Kwasi climbed the nearest tree. Kwaku tried to follow him, but he couldn't climb very well, and he had to give up. He was very frightened and called up to his friend, "Eh, Kwasi, I can't climb. What shall I do?" Kwasi said, "Ah, I don't know, you must look out for yourself."
>
> Now Kwaku had heard somewhere that a lion doesn't eat dead meat, so he lay down and feigned death. The lion came up to him and sniffed around for a while, and then went off. Kwasi came down from the tree and said to Kwaku, "Oh, Kwaku, I thought you were dead. What was the lion saying to you just now?"
>
> Kwaku told Kwasi, "Well, Kwasi, he said a lot of things to me, but the most important one was that I should choose my friends better. So when we leave here, you and I will part company for good."[82]

A few differences are worth noticing, however briefly. The African story is almost twice the length of the Greek one.[83] The personal touch is provided in the African story by naming the two friends. The African version has the desperate man ask his friend for help, only to be explicitly rebuffed. Similarly, when the survivor of the lion's attentions reports in the African version on what the lion had said, he makes explicit what he intends to do with the lion's advice.

Is explicitness, or a kind of expansiveness, more likely in African than in Greek stories? Is there in this a kind of realism, or less reliance here upon the imagination of the audience? Or does it reflect primarily the difference between an oral and a written presentation?

I suspect that Aesop's Greek audience did not believe that the bear said anything to the "corpse," but merely nosed around it—and that the speech given to the bear is entirely the man's. What, on the other hand, would an African audience have been inclined to believe—and why?[84]

The differences between these two accounts are worth exploring. Perhaps one can begin with speculations about why the Aesop story has the two men traveling together while the African story has them playing in the nearby bush.[85]

XIII.

A few more points about the stories that I have discussed can usefully be noticed before we conclude our visit to Africa. Erotic relations are far less important in these African stories than they would be in stories among us today in the West. A village mentality is evident in these stories, as may be seen as well in much of the life today in even the larger African (as also in the larger modern Greek) cities. One can easily lose sight of the "national" interest in such circumstances; it may not even be given lip service (as may be seen in Achebe's *A Man of the People*). We are surprised to learn, in Achebe's *Things Fall Apart*, that one of the great battles (if not wars) in his hero's youth had seen only a dozen men killed.[86]

Our inquiry, here as elsewhere, obliges us to wonder, What is the truly human life? What does "Africa" contribute to the "mix" that the human race, which was once divided up more distinctly than it is now, seems to be developing worldwide? In a sense, much of what distinguishes the United States from Europe can be attributed to the contributions that Africa has made to this country, far more than it seems to have made to Europe.[87] Is the special vitality and resiliency, as well as the intriguing unpredictability, of American life in part due to the African elements among us?

All this bears upon the worldwide political and social developments to be expected in the twenty-first century. A commentary both upon traditional

African thought and upon the special influence of the United States in the modern world may be found in W. E. B. Du Bois's 1897 declaration:

> We are Americans, not only by birth and by citizenship, but by our political ideals, our language, our religion. Farther than that, our Americanism does not go. At that point, we are Negroes, *members of a vast historic race that from the very dawn of creation has slept,* but half awakening in the dark forests of its African fatherland. We are the first fruits of this new nation, the harbinger of that black to-morrow which is yet destined to soften the whiteness of the Teutonic to-day. We are that people whose subtle sense of song has given America its only American music, its only American fairy tales, its only touch of pathos and humor amid its mad money-getting plutocracy. As such, it is our duty to conserve our physical powers, our intellectual endowments, our spiritual ideals; as a race we must strive by race organization, by race solidarity, by race unity in the realization of that broader humanity *which freely recognizes differences in men, but sternly deprecates inequality in their opportunities of development.*[88]

Particularly significant here, in considering how African thought is to be assessed, is Du Bois's insistence that the African American, as "the harbinger of [a] black to-morrow," was in the vanguard of the African people of the world. This suggests that the West, or at least the United States, has provided Africans something that they, insofar as they are a distinct race, must have if they are to come to terms with the modern world. In 1903 Du Bois argued, "[T]here are to-day no truer exponents of the pure human spirit of the Declaration of Independence than the American Negroes." He also said on that occasion, "[W]e black men seem the sole oasis of simple faith and reverence in a dusty desert of dollars and smartness."[89]

But one caution is in order for the Africans assessing what they might usefully, and safely, take from the West. It would be a mistake for Africans to do what all too many Americans (including, of course, African Americans) tend to do: that is, it is a mistake to make far more of *action* than of *understanding*, a tendency which does not appreciate sufficiently what the discovery of *nature* in the West suggests about the best possible life for human beings.

Even so, it is humane (as well as in our interest as a people dedicated to the pursuit of happiness)—it is humane and just to respect an anthropologist's loving description of the life of the Pygmies, perhaps the most "ancient" and hence the "youngest" of the peoples of Africa:

> The Pygmies were more than curiosities to be filmed, and their music was more than a quaint sound to be put on records. They were a people who had found in the forest something that made their life more than just worth living, something that made it, with all its hardships and problems and tragedies, a wonderful thing of joy and happiness and free of care.[90]

This is a people which can treasure that great song of praise, a song which Socrates would have found intriguing: "If Darkness *is*, Darkness is Good."[91]

Notes

1. Pliny the Elder, *Natural History*, VIII, 77 (a classical proverb). See, on race, law, and civilization, George Anastaplo, *Human Being and Citizen: Essays on Virtue, Freedom, and the Common Good* (Chicago: Swallow Press, 1975), pp. 175–99. See also note 46 below. (Unless otherwise indicated, all references to notes in any chapter of this collection are to the notes of that chapter.)

2. See, on North American Indian thought, chapter 6 of this collection. See also notes 46 and 47 below.

3. Similarly, the many Christian sects, along with the Jews, probably appeared alike in critical respects to various Asian observers upon being first exposed to the West. Similarly, also, the Unionists and Confederates who fought each other so desperately in North America between 1861 and 1865 could appear to the rest of the world as very much alike. See, for the similarities in their constitutions, with of course significant differences, Anastaplo, *Amendments to the Constitution of the United States: A Commentary* (Baltimore: Johns Hopkins University Press, 1995), pp. 125, 344. See, on Abraham Lincoln's Emancipation Proclamation, Anastaplo, *Abraham Lincoln: A Constitutional Biography* (Lanham, Md.: Rowman & Littlefield, 1999), p. 197. See also note 89 below.

4. In a sense, the sub-Saharan Africans, like the Jews and the Greeks, may have found their highest modern development in their *diaspora* rather than in their homeland.

5. See, e.g., Naguib Mahfouz, *The Cairo Trilogy* (New York: Doubleday, 1990–1992), vol. 3 (*Sugar Street*), pp. 43–44.

6. "Africa," *Encyclopaedia Britannica*, 15th ed. (1993 printing), vol. 1, p. 132.

7. See, e.g., Colin M. Turnbull, *The Forest People: A Study of the Pygmies of the Congo* (Anchor Books; Doubleday, 1962), pp. 4–6. See also note 62 below.

8. See, on my impressions of Cairo, chapter 6 of this collection, notes 90, 91, 93. (The bananas I got in Liberia, a country founded in 1822 with American support, I eventually took to someone I knew in London who had not seen bananas since the war began in 1939.) A series of productive meetings by my wife and me in the summer of 1992 with a young Senegalese selling attractive women's clothing in Roman street markets depended upon his confidence both that like-minded people will repeatedly find each other in quite different parts of a large city and that things somehow work out for the best.

9. See "Africa," *Encyclopaedia Britannica*, vol. 1, p. 132. Egypt was described, for the Islamic ruler whose forces conquered it in the late seventh century, in terms that could probably have been used many centuries earlier as well:

O commander of the faithful, Egypt is a compound of black earth and green plants, between a pulverized mountain and a red sand. The distance from Syene to the sea is a month's journey for a horseman. Along the valley descends a river, on which the blessing of the Most High reposes both in the evening and morning, and which rises and falls with the revolutions of the sun and moon. When the annual dispensation of Providence unlocks the springs and fountains that nourish the earth, the Nile rolls his swelling and sounding waters through the realm of Egypt: the fields are overspread by the salutary flood; and the villages communicate with each other by their pointed barks. The retreat of the inundation deposits a fertilizing mud for the reception of the various needs: the crowds of husbandmen who blacken the land may be compared to a swarm of industrious ants; and their native indolence in quickened by the lash of the taskmaster and the promise of the flowers and fruits of a plentiful increase. Their hope is seldom deceived; but the riches which they extract from the wheat, the barley, and the rice, the legumes, the fruit-trees, and the cattle, are unequally shared between those who labour and those who possess. According to the vicissitudes of the seasons, the face of the country is adorned with a *silver* wave, a verdent *emerald*, and the deep yellows of a *golden* harvest.

Edward Gibbon, *The Decline and Fall of the Roman Empire* (New York: Modern Library, n.d.), vol. 3, 179–80 (chap. 51). (*GBWW* [*Great Books of the Western World*], I: vol. 41, pp. 253–88; II: vol. 38, pp. 253–88).

10. See Plato, *Timaeus* 22B. (*GBWW*, I: vol. 7, p. 444; II: vol. 6, p. 444). See also the text at note 99 of chapter 4 of this collection.

11. *Aesop Without Morals*, Lloyd W. Daly, trans. (New York: Thomas Yoseloff, 1961), pp. 219–20.

12. Ibid., p. 301. This is no. 11 in the Bude edition of Aesop. It does not appear to be in the Penguin edition.

13. See *Larousse Encyclopedia of Mythology* (London: Paul Hamlyn, 1959), p. 47. Still, Plutarch suggested, "the element of health [was, among the Egyptians,] no less important than that of piety." *Isis and Osiris* 383B (in Plutarch's *Moralia*, trans. Frank Cole Babbitt [Cambridge, Mass.: Loeb Classical Library, Harvard University Press, 1936]).

14. Ancient Egypt is referred to by a Mahfouz character, upon visiting the Great Pyramids, as "a nation whose most notable manifestations are tombs and corpses." Mahfouz, *The Cairo Trilogy*, vol. 2 (*Palace of Desire*), p. 178. See also note 33 below.

15. See, on the inept efforts made to preserve in perpetuity the body of Mao Tse-tung, Zhisui Li, *The Private Life of Chairman Mao* (New York: Random House, 1994), pp. 16–25, 629–30. See also note 35, below. See, on the relation of body to soul, note 11 of chapter 3 of this collection. See, on Egyptian eroticism, Lise Manniche, *Sexual Life in Ancient Egypt* (London: KPI Ltd., 1987); *The Tale of Sinuhe* (c. 1870 B.C.).

16. See, on the Hindus, chapter 3 of this collection. See, on the Muslims, chapter 6 of this collection. See, on Nirvana, chapter 5 of this collection. See, on the African blending of the spiritual and the physical, note 42 below.

17. Christianity, for this reason, may also make tragedy highly unlikely, if not simply impossible. Whether, however, the common man was as much influenced in North Africa by the dominant ancient Egyptian priestly doctrines as he later was in Europe by the dominant Christian church doctrines is uncertain. Consider, also, this New Kingdom love poetry:

If I stare hard enough at the gate
My darling will come to me.
Eyes on the road, ears straining,
I wait for him who avoids me,
Because loving him is all I can do.
My heart won't shut up about him.
It sends me a fleet-footed messenger
That goes about everywhere, telling me:
"He deceives you," and more,
"He has found another woman

Who dazzles his eyes."
Why do you torture me with leaving?

Elizabeth J. Sherman, "Delving into the Mysteries of Woman's Lives in Old Egypt," *Washington Times*, October 10, 1993, p. B7 (citing Papyrus Harris 500). (This author, who has a doctorate in Egyptology, dismisses Martin Bernal's *Black Athena* (1987) as "bloated and garbled" and Erich von Däniken's *Chariot of the Gods?* (1970) as "laughable." Ibid. See also Jonathan Rauch, "Academic Left vs. Science," *Wall Street Journal*, April 19, 1994, p. A16. See as well note 37 below.

18. *Ancient Egyptian Literature*, Miriam Lichtheim, ed. (Berkeley: University of California Press, 1973), vol. I, p.17. See also *The Book of the Dead*, E. A. Wallis Budge, ed. (New York: Arkana [Penguin Group], 1989), pp. 26, 360f, 366f.

19. *The Book of the Dead*, p. 155. A dim reflection of Egyptian formulas and rituals may be seen in the Masonic rites drawn upon in Mozart's *The Magic Flute* (1791).

20. *The Book of the Dead*, p. 236.

21. Ibid, p. 343. See also ibid., pp. 233, 269, 273, 284, 302, 306, 417.

22. See, e.g., ibid., p. 14.

23. Ibid., p. ccxxi.

24. Ibid., p. ccxi.

25. *Larousse Encyclopedia of Mythology*, p. 9.

26. Ibid., p. 48. The uraeus was a representation of the sacred asp on the headdress of ancient Egyptian rulers. It served as a symbol of sovereignty. Consider the response to all of this by Plutarch, who was somewhat of a Platonist:

> But the great majority of the Egyptians, in doing service to the animals themselves and in treating them as gods, have not only filled their sacred offices with ridicule and derision, but this is the least of the evils connected with their silly practices.

Isis and Osiris 379E. See also note 27 below. See, on "doing service to the animals" in sub-Saharan Africa, John S. Mbiti, *African Religions and Philosophy* (Garden City, N.Y.: Anchor Books, Doubleday, 1970), p. 62f. See also note 42 below. Plutarch, in his last years, is said to have held a priesthood connected with the shrine of Apollo at Delphi.

27. *Larousse Encyclopedia of Mythology*, p. 9. See *Isis and Osiris*, in Plutarch's *Moralia*, vol. 5, pp. 1–191. The cult of Isis and Osiris is important for Masonic rituals. See note 19 above.

28. The possible influence here upon later Christian imagery is obvious. The Israelites evidently recalled many Egyptian beliefs and practices that they wanted to have nothing to do with once they were liberated. One consequence to this day seems to be the Jewish practice of immediate burial without treatment of the corpse. See note 33 below.

29. Consider also the distinctions made in Homer's *Iliad* between the names used by human beings and those used by the gods for the same persons and things. See Plato, *Cratylus*.

30. See, e.g., Hellmut Fritzsche, "Of Things That Are Not," in John A. Murley, Robert L. Stone, and William T. Braithwaite, eds., *Law and Philosophy* (Athens, Ohio: Ohio University Press, 1992), vol. 1, pp. 3–18.

31. See Plato, *Apology* 40A et seq.; (*GBWW*, I: vol. 7, p. 211; II, vol. 6, p. 211).

32. Consider, for example, Socrates' evident lack of concern about what should be done with his corpse. See Plato, *Phaedo* (*GBWW*, I: vol. 7, pp. 220–51; II: vol. 6, pp.

220–51).Compare the death-defying concern about such matters exhibited in Sophocles' *Antigone*. See, on the Socratic response to Antigone's (as well as to the Egyptian?) approach to these matters, Anastaplo, "On Trial: Explorations," 22 *Loyola University of Chicago Law Journal* 1054 n. 348 (1991). See also ibid., pp. 846–54. See as well note 26 above.

33. See notes 16 and 28 above. G. W. F. Hegel sums up in this fashion the nineteenth-century understanding of the Egyptian treatment of death (*The History of Philosophy* [New York: Dover Publications, 1956], pp. 217–18):

> After the death of an Egyptian, judgment was passed upon him. One of the principal represen-
> tations on the sarcophagi is the judicial process in the realm of the dead. Osiris–with Isis behind
> him–appears, holding a balance, while before him stands the soul of the deceased. But judgment
> was passed on the dead by the living themselves; and that not merely in the case of a private per-
> sons, but even of kings. . . .
>
> If Death thus haunted the minds of the Egyptians during life, it might be supposed that their
> disposition was melancholy. But the thought of death by no means occasioned depression. At
> banquets they had representations of the dead (as Herodotus relates), with the admonition: "Eat
> and drink—such a one wilt though become, when thou art dead." Death was thus to them rather
> a call to enjoy Life. Osiris himself dies, and goes down into the realm of death. . . . In many
> places in Egypt, the sacred grave of Osiris was exhibited. But he was also represented as presi-
> dent of the Kingdom of the Invisible Sphere, and as judge of the dead in it.

See also note 13 above, note 46 below. On Islam, see chapter 6 of this collection. Compare, for the traumatic response by Gautama to the discovery of human mortality, chapter 5 of this collection. See, for Gilgamesh's desperate response to such a discovery, chapter 1 of this collection.

34. See *Ancient Egyptian Literature*, vol. 1, pp. 26–27, 48. See also Turnbull, *The Forest People*, pp. 4–6. The story of *Homo sapiens*, we are told,

> appears to begin 1.8 million years ago, in the region of Africa south of the Sahara that is said to
> be the cradle of humanity, judging from the wealth of ancestral bones that have been found
> there. It was there that a species of early human [*Homo erectus*] lived a simple foraging exis-
> tence, although its way of life was no doubt considerably more sophisticated than that of any
> ape-like animal which had lived before.

Clive Gamble, "March of the Timewalkers," *The Independent on Sunday*, April 10, 1994, p. 66. Compare "One Giant Step for Mankind," *Time*, July 22, 2001, p. 54.

35. See, on African funerals, Mbiti, *African Religions and Philosophy*, pp. 195f. Much more effort had to be made among the Africans in their sub-Saharan climate, than among the Egyptians in their climate, to preserve things, including corpses and art. In addition, the Egyptians had much more stone to work with. Conditions in sub-Saharan Africa led to constant improvisation by the Africans, especially as both rapid decay and a steady growth of vegetation confronted them in their more fertile areas.

36. *Larousse Encyclopedia of Mythology*, p. 480. See also notes 42 and 58 below.

37. Far more is said in this chapter about sub-Saharan thought than about the much better known Egyptian thought. One opinion of a few of our contemporaries in this country is that the Egyptians are really substantially Negroid in origins. Another such opinion is that these Egyptians are primarily responsible for the flowering of Greek civilization. See, e.g., Lerone Bennett Jr., *Before the Mayflower: A History of Black America* (New York: Penguin Books, 1993), pp. 3–9. These are opinions for which there has yet to be devel-

oped sufficient evidence to persuade many scholars. See, e.g., note 17, above. More persuasive among scholars today is the argument that Joseph Conrad's influential *Heart of Darkness* is a distorted account of the life of the natives on that other great African river, the Congo. See, e.g., Chinua Achebe, *Hopes and Impediments* (New York: Anchor Books, Doubleday, 1989), pp. 1–20.

38. See, on Edwin Muir's "The Animals," Anastaplo, *The Artist as Thinker: From Shakespeare to Joyce* (Athens, Ohio: Ohio University Press, 1983), pp. 257–63. Consider, also, the discovery of the *Gilgamesh* epic which unearthed a remarkable but long forgotten way of life. See chapter 1 of this collection. Compare Robert Farris Thompson, *Flash of the Spirit: African and Afro-American Art and Philosophy* (New York: Vintage Books, 1984), pp. xiv, xv, 3, 13, 227, 298 n. 1. The accomplishments of Yoruban letters, city building, and art are summed up thus:

> Like ancient Greece, Yorubaland consisted of self-sufficient city-states characterized by artistic and poetic richness. The Yoruba themselves cherish the creators of their aesthetic world, as one of their hunters' ballads states: "not the brave alone, they also praise those who know how to shape images in wood or compose a song."

Ibid., p. 5. See also notes 50 and 91 below.

39. See, e.g., Herbert Storing, ed., *What Country Have I?*, *Political Writings of Black Americans* (New York: St. Martin's, 1970), pp. 16, 19, 23 (Augustus Washington), 32–33, 38, 39–40 (Frederick Douglass). A South Carolina medical scholar depicted the African thus in an 1824 report justifying slavery:

> History cannot designate the time when the Caucasian was a savage—Caucasian races have often been plunged by circumstances into barbarism, but never as far as we know, into savageism. Cannibalism appears to belong exclusively to the African and Oceanic Negroes—the Bushman, the Hottentots, and perhaps the Caribs; but history does not tell us when and where the Caucasian has gorged his appetite on human flesh and blood.
>
> We can carry back the history of the Negro (though imperfectly) for 4,000 years: we know that he had all the physical characteristics then which he has now, and we have good grounds for believing that he was morally and intellectually the same then as now. One generation does not take up civilization where the last left it and carry it on as does the Caucasian—there it stands immovable; they go as far as instinct extends and no farther. Where, or when I would ask, has a Negro left his impress upon the age in which he lived? Can any reasoning mind believe that the Negro and Indian have always been the victim of circumstances? No, nature has endowed them with an inferior organization, and all the powers of earth cannot elevate them above their destiny.

Josiah C. Nott, *Two Lectures on the Natural History of the Caucasian and Negro Races* (1844), in Drew Gilpin Faust, ed., *The Ideology of Slavery: Proslavery Thought in the Antebellum South, 1830–1860* (Baton Rouge: Louisiana State University Press, 1981), p. 235. See, on nature, note 71 below. See also note 1 above, notes 53, 65, and 89 below.

40. Molara Ogundipe-Leslie, a Nigerian writer, replied, upon being asked whether the African woman writer was different from her counterparts elsewhere:

> I don't know if the African woman writer is different from woman writers in other parts of the world. I can only hazard some guesses. . . . Because of the definitely patriarchal arrangements

of [African] society, publicly and privately, most women bear a double workload, if not a triple one. Hence they have even less time and leisure than their western counterparts to think or write.

Adeola James, ed., *In Their Own Voices: African Women Writers Talk* (London: James Currey, 1990), p. 67. Virginia Woolf has developed this theme in *A Room of One's Own* (1929). Compare note 61 below. See, on the Woolf theme, George Anastaplo, "Law & Literature and the Austen-Dostoyevsky Axis: Explorations," 46 *South Dakota Law Review* (forthcoming), part 3.

41. See, on how slavery can be taken for granted in African stories, Kathleen Arnott, ed., *African Myths and Legends* (Oxford: Oxford University Press, 1989), pp. 144, 179, 184. Rough estimates of the slave population in the North American colonies by 1776 suggest the scope of the slave trade in the Western Hemisphere:

> The African Negro—imported very slowly, at first, and at times received with strong misgivings even by persons that most needed his toil—was suited to the miasmic lowland plantations: being cheap and easily managed, he rendered planting on a large scale both stable and profitable. According to one author's conclusions from various authorities, there were only 300 Negroes in Virginia in 1650 and 2,000 in 1671. By 1721, they comprised one-seventh of New York's population, one-thirteenth of Pennsylvania's, nearly one-half of Maryland's, more than one-half of Virginia's, one-third of North Carolina's and four-sevenths of South Carolina's. It is supposed that in all the continental colonies there were about 75,000 slaves in 1725, a little more than 250,000 in 1750, and about 500,000 in 1776.

Frederic Bancroft, *Slave Trading in the Old South* (New York: Frederick Ungar, 1959), p. 2 (citing W. E. B. Du Bois, *Suppression of the African Slave-Trade*, 5). Allan Nevins speaks of the Bancroft book as treating "perhaps the ugliest and saddest chapter in the whole history of American life." Ibid., p. ix. See note 3 above, note 89 below. Kofi Awoonor, a Ghanian writer and former delegate to the United Nations, has said, "I believe there is a great psychic shadow over Africa, and it has to do with our guilt and denial of our [the African] role in the slave trade. We, too, were blameworthy in what was essentially one of the most heinous crimes in human history." Howard W. French, "On Slavery, Africans Say the Guilt Is Theirs, Too," *New York Times*, December 27, 1994, p. A5. European trading companies carried over 600,000 Africans into slavery from Ghana's coastline in the eighteenth century alone. See ibid., p. A5. See, also, Vincent Harding, *There Is a River: The Black Struggle for Freedom in America* (San Diego: Harcourt Brace Jovanovich, 1981), pp. 6–7:

> Of course, long before the ships of Europe arrived, there was a form of human bondage in Africa, just as there was on most of the world's continents. But there is no evidence that the kind of chattel slavery which Europe was to perfect in the New World had taken root in West Africa. The slavery in existence [in West Africa] was—as slavery goes—far more humane, since it was only for prescribed periods of time, and involved no laws aimed at dehumanization. This slavery was not established by the Africans primarily for profit; it did not impose on the victims a mark of essential, intrinsic inferiority; and it was not necessarily passed on to the children of the bondsmen. When the ships came, they brought with them the European passion for profits, the European disease of racism, and the European fondness for power of arms. When these forces encountered all the weaknesses—all the tendencies to fear, deception, and greed—that Africans share with the rest of humankind, the earlier more flexible patterns of African bondage degenerated into the African slave trade—financed, fueled, and directed by the peoples of Europe, and all too often aided and abetted by African allies.

It has been noticed, "It is a platitude to say that the Western world only grudgingly conceded the status of natural beings to Africans, especially in the slave-trade era." Fedelis U. Olafor, "Issues in African Philosophy Re-examined," *International Philosophical Journal*, vol. 23, no. 1, p. 92 (1991). See also note 71 below. Consider as well the somewhat self-imposed slavery in Africa, as elsewhere, of the ferocious AIDS epidemic. See note 64 below.

42. See, on the Bible, Anastaplo, "On Trial," pp. 821f, 854f, 882f, 900f; Anastaplo, "Law and Literature and the Bible: Explorations," 23 *Oklahoma City University Law Review* 515 (1998). See, on Homer, Anastaplo, *The Artist as Thinker*, p. 492. See, on the Confucian *Analects*, chapter 4 of this collection. See, on the *Bhagavad Gita* and on the Koran, note 8 above, and on Buddhism, note 16 above. See also note 46 below.

It is well to keep the following caution in mind:

> Traditional religions are not universal; they are tribal or national. Each religion is bound and limited to the people among whom it has evolved. One traditional religion cannot be propagated in another tribal group. This does not rule out the fact that religious ideas may spread from one people to another. But such ideas spread spontaneously, especially through migrations, intermarriage, conquest, or expert knowledge being sought by individuals of one tribal group from another. Traditional religions have no missionaries to propagate them; and one individual does not preach his religion to another. [Would it be like an individual "preaching" his language to another?]
>
> Similarly, there is no conversion from one traditional religion to another. Each society has its own religious system, and the propagation of such a complete system would involve propagating the entire life of the people concerned. Therefore a person has to be born in a particular society in order to assimilate the religious system of the society to which he belongs. An outsider cannot enter or appreciate fully the religion of another society. Those few Europeans who claim to have been "converted" to African religions—and I know some who make such fantastic claims!—do not know what they are saying. To pour out libations or observe a few rituals like Africans, does not constitute conversion to traditional religion.

Mbiti, *African Religions and Philosophy*, p. 5 (bracketed question added). It has been noticed, "Africans are notoriously religious, and each people has its own religious system with a set of beliefs and practices. . . . We speak of African traditional religions in the plural because there are about one thousand African peoples (tribes), and each has its own religious system." Ibid., p. 1. It has also been noticed (ibid., p. 38):

> African knowledge of God is expressed in proverbs, short statements, songs, prayers, names, myths, stories and religious ceremonies. All these are easy to remember and pass on to other people, since there are no sacred writings in traditional societies. One should not, therefore, expect long dissertations about God. But God is no stranger to African peoples, and in traditional life there are no atheists. This is summarized in an Ashanti proverb that "no one shows a child the Supreme Being." That means that everybody knows of God's existence almost by instinct, and even children know Him.

It has been noticed as well (ibid., p. 6):

> Belief in the continuation of life after death is found in all African societies, as far as I have been able to discover. But this belief does not constitute a hope for a future and better life. To live here and now is the most important concern of African religious activities and beliefs. There is little, if any, concern with the distinctly spiritual welfare of man apart from his physical life. No line is drawn between the spiritual and the physical. Even life in the hereafter is conceived in materialistic and physical terms. There is neither paradise to be hoped for or hell to be feared in the hereafter. The soul of man does not long for spiritual redemption, or for closer contact with God in the next world. This is an important element in traditional religions, and one which will

help us to understand the concentration of African religiosity on earthly matters, with man at the center of his religiosity.

See note 26 above, note 58 below.

43. See "Africa," *Encyclopaedia Britannica*, vol. 1, p. 133.

44. See chapter 7 of this collection.

45. "Ngugi [wa Thiong'o] has argued that a study of the Oral Tradition would be 'important' not only in rehabilitating our minds, but also in helping African writers to innovate and break away from the European mainstream.'" Steven R. Carter, "Decolonization and Detective Fiction," in Eugene Schleh, ed., *Mysteries of Africa* (Bowling Green, Ohio: Bowling Green State University Popular Press, 1991), p. 87. Ngugi has questioned whether African experience can be honestly and fully portrayed in a European language or art form. See ibid., p. 74. See, on an advocacy of *négritude* as resistance to that European assimilationism which suppresses African culture, R. N. Egidu, *Modern African Poetry and the African Predicament* (London: Macmillan, 1978), pp. 30–32.

46. See, for exceptions, some of the stories in Arnott, ed., *African Myths and Legends*, e.g., pp. 32–34, 53–55. (But, it should be noticed, the stories in the Arnott collection have been "retold" by the editor.) This is quite different from the typical Western reader's impression of, say, many of the North American Indian stories (collected, as the African stories probably have been, mainly by missionaries and anthropologists). The half-dozen introductions to non-Western "schools" of thought incorporated in this collection have drawn upon year-long University of Chicago adult education seminars I have conducted in which the relevant literature was discussed in each case (for about one hundred hours). (See the preface to this collection.) By far the most resistance I encountered was when we read several collections of sub-Saharan African stories: the students were, almost from the beginning, so depressed by the moral tone of what they were reading that their class attendance declined steadily during the year, something that never occurred before or after in my experience with this adult-education seminar. (The year before we had studied North American Indian stories; the year after we studied scientific classics beginning with Aristotle and Galileo.) See notes 47 and 49 below. See also the text at note 63 of chapter 7 of this collection. The Egyptian materials we read were far less troubling for these adult students than the morally disorienting materials from sub-Saharan Africa, even though the Egyptian materials we read were preoccupied with the prospects of and responses to death.

It is only prudent to record the following caution here:

> Preliterate societies have their own kinds of wisdom, no doubt, and primitive Papuans probably have a better grasp of their myths than most educated Americans have of their own literature. But without years of study we can't begin to understand a culture very different from our own. The fair thing, therefore, is to make allowance for what we outsiders cannot hope to fathom in another society and grant that, as members of the same species, primitive men are as mysterious or as monstrous as any other branch of humankind.

Saul Bellow, "Papuans and Zulus," *New York Times*, March 10, 1994, p. A12.

It is also prudent to notice the observations, a half century ago, by an eminent anthropologist who intended "to correct the erroneous impression, still widely current, that native African folk-literature is mainly animal tales and to bring home the fact that it is possibly the most sophisticated and realistic of all aboriginal literature." Max Radin, ed., *African Folktales* (New York: Schocken Books, 1983), p. vii. "The creators of African literature," Professor Radin argued in 1952, "can at times be as skeptical and ironical as the Greeks. It would be difficult, indeed, to find a match for irony and sophistication comparable to the traditional beginning of an Ashanti tale: 'We do not really mean, we do not really mean, that what we are going to say is true.' Or the traditional ending: 'This, my story which I have related, if it be sweet or if it be not sweet, take some elsewhere and let some come back to me.'" Ibid., p. 19. The introduction to the Radin collection of folktales includes these observations (ibid., p. 4):

> The first salient trait to be stressed is that native African folk-literature constitutes a single unit. Of no other region of comparable size in the world does this hold true. The similarities extend not merely to the types of plot-construction and to specific subject-matter, but to literary devices as well—for example, the role played by the songs in the prose text, the frequency of moralistic endings, and the marked prevalence of etiological explanations.
>
> But even more striking and more fundamental than the similarities just mentioned are the stark realism, the insistent emphasis upon man in all his moods, the emphasis upon the contemporary scene, and the high degree of sophistication pervading the whole of native African oral literature. Rarely has man been depicted as more completely and inextricably anchored in this world, more obsessively earthbound. Contrary to the belief wide-spread throughout the world, man in aboriginal Africa is never thought of as having once possessed a portion of divinity and having subsequently lost it. Even in the few myths that deal with the so-called high gods and the heavenly deities, one detects an almost obsessive egocentrism.

Professor Radin noticed the cynicism in some of the these folktales, even as he insisted that "African realism is not always nor generally accompanied by cynicism." Ibid., p. 5. "Yet, in the main," he added, "little romanticism is found in African myths and definitely no sentimentality. It is emphatically not a literature in which wish-fulfillment plays a great role, not one where one can assume that the hero will triumph at the end or that wrongs will always be righted. How are we to explain this?" Ibid., p. 5. The Radin explanation includes these observations (ibid., pp. 8–9):

> It goes without saying that the conflict and disorganization engendered in people by a forced acculturation extending over so many centuries would leave a permanent residue in their oral literature. Folktales which were predominantly wish-fulfillment fantasies . . . were pushed into the background. Human heroes with plots taken from purely human situations forged to the front. In the latter, with uncompromising realism, man was pitted against man, as is inevitably the case when individuals are living in an economically and politically disturbed and insecure world.
>
> Assuredly we have the right to infer that it is largely because these people are living in an insecure and semi-chaotic world, with its loss of values and its consequent inward demoralization, that cruelty and wanton murder loom so large in many of their tales. So it does among the Eskimo, where the environment is so persistently inimical, and so it did in the Russia of the nineteenth century.

See, on the differences as well as the similarity between "the Jewish and Negro question," Anastaplo, "On Trial," p. 1058 n. 398. See, on distinguishing the High and the Low, chapter 1 of this collection, note 47. See, on the Hobbesian man evident in "an economically and politically disturbed and insecure world," Laurence Berns, "Thomas Hobbes," in Leo Strauss and Joseph Cropsey, eds., *History of Political Philosophy* (Chicago: Rand McNally, 1963), p. 354.

47. The only things comparable in the North American Indian stories are the scalping parties that young men might go on and the fiendish delight taken in the torture of prisoners before their execution. See chapter 7 of this collection. But these atrocities do not dominate the Indian stories we happen to have, even though there is the reference in the Declaration of Independence to "the merciless Indian Savages." See note 3 of the

preface to this collection. See, on famines being regarded as routine in Africa, Arnott, ed., *African Myths and Legends*, pp. 82, 83, 108, 124. See, for the foiling of the bad, ibid., pp. 15, 24, 31, 186f. See, for gratuitous cruelty, ibid., pp. 77, 93, 104. See, for the unexplained kindness of a witch, ibid., p. 148.

48. Roger D. Abrahams, ed., *African Folktales* (New York: Pantheon Books, 1983), p. 145.

49. Penina Muhando, a Tanzanian playwright has this to say about African audiences that she has observed:

> There is definitely an African aesthetic, which has been down-played because of our colonial history. There are certain elements of the African traditional performance which can best be understood and enjoyed by an African audience. . . . There is still much more to be done with the African tradition. To give this simple example, I have noticed the way the African audience laughs, even when the play is tragic. The point is, that Africans are not callous people, it doesn't mean they enjoy seeing people murdered, *it means they have a different perception*. Maybe they are laughing at the perfection of the acting, seeing that the actor has managed to imitate the action so well. I don't know, but these are things to be researched.

James, ed., *In Their Own Voices*, p. 88 (emphasis added). (I have recently [2001] heard a Lyric Opera of Chicago production of *Tosca* commended for the villainy of its villain.) Also to be researched are both the causes and the consequences of the ever growing amount of violence to be observed (and enjoyed?) in American film and television. See, e.g., Anastaplo, "Artists Fed on 'Raw Meat'—and the Proper Support of the Arts in the United States," in Andrew Patner, ed., *Alternative Futures: Challenging Designs for Arts Philanthropy* (Washington, D.C.: Grantmakers in the Arts, 1994), pp. 72–73. See, for a proposal to abolish broadcast television in the United States, Anastaplo, *The American Moralist: On Law, Ethics, and Government* (Athens, Ohio: Ohio University Press, 1992), pp. 245–74. See also note 89 below.

50. See Abrahams, ed., *African Folktales*, p. 145. Consider the comment we sometimes hear, "No good deed goes unpunished." Compare Arnott, ed., *African Myths and Legends*, pp. 94f. But see note 46 above; ibid., pp. 29–30, 135–39, 150–52. Compare also the magnaminity exhibited by African warriors at the end of the 1963 movie *Zulu*. See "The Zulu Warrior: Then and Now," *Wall Street Journal*, May 12, 1994, p. A15. Compare, as well, Thompson, *Flash of the Spirit*, p. 13:

> Generosity, the highest form of morality in Yoruba traditional terms, is suggested yet another way by the symbolized offering of something by a person to a higher force through the act of kneeling.

See, for a more comprehensive account of Yoruban thought, ibid., pp. 5–6:

> The Yoruba religion, the worship of various spirits under God, presents a limitless horizon of vivid moral beings, generous yet intimidating. . . . The supreme diety, God Almighty, is called in Yoruba *Olorum*, master of the skies. Olorum is neither male nor female but a vital force. In other words, Olorum is the supreme quintessence of `*ashe*.
>
> When God came down to give the world `*ashe*, God appeared in the form of certain animals. `*Ashe* descended in the form of the royal python (*ere*), the gabon viper (*oka oushere*), the earthworm (*ekolo*), the white snail (*lakoshe*), and the woodpecker (*akoko*). God, within these animals, had, according to Yoruba belief, bestowed upon us the power-to-make-things-happen, morally neutral power, power to give, and to take away, to kill and to give life, according to the purpose and the nature of its bearer. The messengers of `*ashe* reflect this complex of powers. Some are

essentially dangerous, with curved venomous fangs. Others are patient and slow-moving, teaching deliberation in their careful motion. Even the earthworm has its power, "ventilating and cooling the earth without the use of teeth."

The origins both of the Yoruban people and of `ashe had been noticed earlier (ibid., p. xv):

[This book] opens with a discussion of the art and ideals of the Yoruba, black Africa's largest population, creators of one of the premier cultures of the world. The Yorubas believe themselves descended from goddesses and gods, from an ancient spiritual capital, Ile-Ile. They show their special concern for the proprieties of right living through their worship of major goddesses and gods, each essentially a unique manifestation of `ashe, the power-to-make-things-happen, a key to futurity and self-realization in Yoruba terms.

See note 38 above, notes 85 and 91 below.

51. William E. Schmidt, "Refugee Missionaries from Rwanda Speak of Their Terror, Grief, and Guilt," *New York Times*, April 12, 1994, p. A6. See the text at note 48 of chapter 5 of this collection.

52 See, on German atrocities, Anastaplo, "On Trial," pp. 977–94. See, on the bombing of cities, Anastaplo, "On Freedom Exploration," 17 *Oklahoma City University Law Review* 465, 645–66 (1992).

53. Leopold Sedar Senghor, *Prose and Poetry* (London: Oxford University Press, 1965), p. 29:

"White men are cannibals," an old sage from my own country told me a few years ago. "They have no respect for life." It is this process of devouring which they call "humanizing nature" or more exactly "domesticating nature." "But," went on the sage, who had seen and heard much and reflected deeply, "what they don't take into account, these whites, is that life cannot be domesticated, nor especially can God who is the source of all life, in whom all life shares." And finally: "It is life which makes human, not death. I am afraid it may all turn out very badly. The whites by their madness will in the end bring down trouble upon us."

See, on African eroticism, sensuality, and musical sense, ibid., pp. 30–32. "George Hardy wrote: 'The most civilized African, even in a dinner jacket, still quivers at the sound of a drum.' He was right." Ibid., p. 31. See also note 89 below. Compare note 39 above.

54. Achebe, *Hopes and Impediments*, p. 52.

55. See, on the moral conditions for a sound understanding of human conduct, Anastaplo, *The Artist as Thinker*, pp. 1–14. See, on helpfulness that does *not* depend on a sound understanding, Arnott, ed., *African Myths and Legends*, pp. 114, 121f. See, also, Senghor, *Prose and Poetry*, p. 82: "Under the forms of the Lion, the Elephant, the Hyena, the Crocodile, the Hare and the Old Women, we read plainly with our ears of our social structures and our passions, the good as well as the bad." See as well ibid., p. 85.

56. The ancient Egyptian stories now available to us do not show everyday life confronting such events, however fanciful their pantheon may be.

57. See, on art and probability, Aristotle, *Poetics*, chap. 9 (*GBWW*, I: vol. 9, p. 686; II: vol. 8, p. 686).

58. See, on animism, *Encyclopedia of Religion* (New York: Macmillan, 1987), vol. 1, p. 296; *Poems of Black Africa*, Wole Soyinka, ed. (New York: Hill and Wang, 1975), pp. 37f, 59f; Senghor, *Prose and Poetry*, pp. 29–30, 32, 34–35; Mbiti, *African Religions and Philosophy*, pp. 9–18, 97–118; note 36 above. See, on the spirit world of the ancestors in

Africa, "Interview of Thomas Adeoye Lambo," *Omni*, February 1992, p. 71. "In Africa, the gods are still alive." Ibid., p. 103. See also Achebe, *Things Fall Apart* (London: Heineman, 1958), p. 114; note 78 below. See, on the curious but not irrational mixing of modern technology and traditional beliefs about spirits, the following account from Ethiopia:

> The Emperor [Haile Selassie] had lent [Lord Mountbatten's party] his personal Cadillac and motor-cycle escort, a signal honour but somewhat inconvenient, since every road they travelled was strewn with the bodies of peasants seeking to present petitions to what they imagined must be their imperial master. "Another charming habit of Ethiopians who believe themselves to be pursued by evil spirits is to dash across the road in front of the car, timing matters in such a way that they will just not be run over, while the evil spirit is of course cut off by the car."

Philip Ziegler, *Mountbatten: The Official Biography* (London: Collins, 1985), p. 511. But putting modern technology to good use, including against evil spirits, does not mean that the principles (or the ideas about nature) implicit in the modern science upon which modern technology is based are either understood or accepted. See note 42 above. See, on European witches, note 69 below.

59. A fourteenth-century Muslim visitor to Mali reported, "The Negroes possess some admirable qualities. They are seldom unjust, and have a greater abhorrence of injustice than any other people." See Kevin Shillington, *History of Africa* (New York: St. Martin's, 1989), p. 99. See also Lloyd A. Fallers, *Law without Precedent: Legal Ideas in Action in the Courts of Colonial Busoga* (Chicago: University of Chicago Press, 1969); Mbiti, *African Religions and Philosophy*, pp. 266f.

60. See William Rubin, ed., *"Primitivism" in the Twentieth Century: Affinity of the Tribal and the Modern* (New York: Museum of Modern Art, 1984), e.g., vol. 1, pp. 125f.

61. See "Africa," *Encyclopaedia Britannica*, vol. 1, p. 133. It is, we are told, an African adage. "It takes a village to raise a child." See, e.g., Barbara Ehrenreich, "The Bright Side of Overpopulation," *Time*, September 26, 1994, p. 86. When the African community is properly constituted, we are also told, the place of woman is preeminent. See Senghor, *Prose and Poetry*, pp. 44–45:

> In Africa, woman occupies the first place: perhaps we should say, once occupied it, for Arabo-Berber and then European influence, the influence that is of nomadic civilizations, has continuously reduced her role. The agrarian character of the African world explains this role, although there is more to it than this. . . . Because she does not leave the family and is the giver of life, woman has been made the source of the life-force and guardian of the house, that is to say, the depository of the clan's past and the guarantor of its future. In the fairly recent past and in some places still today, a person belongs to the family of his mother. The family régime was a *matriarchate*. . . . Among most African people one belongs to one's mother's clan. Nobility and inheritance are transferred through the mother. . . . This explains the place occupied by the women, the mother, in the family, the importance of the role she plays, the respect with which she is surrounded, the liberty which she enjoys. Contrary to what is often thought to-day, the African woman does not need to be liberated. She has been free for many thousands of years.

Compare Mwana Kupona, who lived during the first half of the nineteenth century. She sums up her advice to her daughter on how to minister to her husband with this assurance: "Be gay with him that he be amused. Do not oppose his authority. If he brings you ill God will defend you." *Anthology of Swahili Poetry*, Ali A. Jahadhmy, ed. (London: Heinemann, 1977), p. 33. See, on nature-based standards and the practice of female circumcision (which does seem to be common in "matriarchate" Africa), Larry Arnhart, "Feminism, Primatology, and Ethical Naturalism," *Politics and the Life Sciences*, August 1992, pp. 164–66, 177–78. See also Mbiti, *African Religions and Philosophy*, pp. 165–71. See as well note 40 above, note 71 below. See on polygamy in Africa, ibid., p. 186f. Consider also ibid., p. 3: "Traditional [African] religions are not primarily for the individual, but for his community of which he is a part. . . . One of the sources of severe strain for Africans exposed to modern change is the increasing process (through education, urbanization and industrialization) by which individuals become detached from their traditional environment."

62. Those constraints are graphically described in Colin Turnbull's remarkable account of life among the Pygmies of Central Africa. See note 7 above. See also note 49 above, and the text at notes 90 and 91 of this chapter.

63. Consider how the victims of Hitler and Stalin "had" to be spoken of by their oppressors. See e.g., Anastaplo, "On Trial," p. 1089 n. 720. See also note 39 above.

64. See, on Africa today, "Darkest Africa: Bits of It Are Disintegrating into Chaos," *Economist*, February 13, 1993, p. 17; Thomas W. Hazlett, "The Forgotten Continent," *Wall Street Journal*, March 17, 1993, p. A12; Bill Keller, "Blind Eye: Africa Allows Its Tragedies to Take Their Own Course," *New York Times*, August 7, 1994, sec. 4, p. 1; William Pfaff, "The Europeans Should Go Back to Africa," *Chicago Tribune*, August 14, 1994, sec. 4, p. 3; Liz Sly, "Blind Failures: West Must Act Earlier to Forestall African Crises," *Chicago Tribune*, August 14, 1994, sec. 4, p. 1; John Darnton, "Africa's Move to Political Freedom Liberates Ethnic Hatred as Well," *International Herald Tribune*, June 22, 1994, p. 7; Susan Okie, "AIDS Overwhelms a Continent: Epidemic Is Global, but Africa Bears Most of the Burden," *Minneapolis Star Tribune*, August 20, 1994, p. 4A (also in the *Washington Post*); Wole Soyinka, "Nigeria's Long, Steep, Bloody Slide," *New York Times*, August 22, 1994, p. A11; Soyinka, "Nigeria Spits Defiance in the World's Face," *Guardian Weekly*, November 21, 1994, p. 12. "Today the total wealth of Africa, with twice the population of the United States, is little more than that of Belgium." "Africa: A Flicker of Light," *Economist*, March 5, 1994, p. 21. See note 89 below.

65. See on the Americanization of the African slave in the United States, this passage from Frederick Douglass, "The Destiny of Colored Americans" (1849):

> [I]t is clear that [the United States] must continue to be the home of the colored man so long as it remains the abode of civilization and religion. For more than two hundred years we have been identified with its soil, its products, and its institutions. . . . The persecuted red man of the forest, the original owners of the soil, has, step by step, retreated from the Atlantic lakes and rivers; escaping, as it were, before the footsteps of the white man, and gradually disappearing from the face of the country. . . . He spurns the civilization—he hates the race which has despoiled him, and unable to measure arms with his superior, he dies.
>
> Not so with the black man. More unlike the European in form, feature and color—called to endure greater hardships, injuries and insults than those to which the Indians have been subjected, he yet lives and prospers, under every disadvantage.

Storing, ed., *What Country Have I?*, p. 39. See note 46 above, note 89 below.

Consider also this provision in the 1817 petition of "free people of color" in Philadelphia with respect to the prospect of their being colonized in Africa:

> Resolved, That without arts, without science, without prior knowledge of government, to cast into the savage wilds of Africa the free people of color, seems to us the circuitous route through which they must return to perpetual bondage.

Herbert Aptheker, *A Documentary History of the Negro People in the United States* (New York: Citadel, 1951), p. 71.

Apologists for African slavery also explained in this way why the North American Indians could not be enslaved. "The Indian is by nature a savage, and a beast of the forest like the Buffalo—can exist in no other state, and is exterminated by the approach of civilization. You cannot make a slave of him like a Negro, his spirit is broken and he dies like a wild animal in a cage." Nott, *Two Lectures*, p. 235. See note 39 above. Consider, as well, Harding, *This Is a River*, p. 7:

> Attempts had already been made in various places [before large numbers of Africans were imported] to use the indigenous peoples of the Western Hemisphere, as well as poor white prisoners and indentured servants from England and the continent, as slave workers in the Americas, but none of these experiments had proven successful. In the case of the Indians, escape was too easy on their own native ground. Besides, their numbers were limited, and few had any preparation for the heavy agricultural work and metal mining which European exploitation demanded. In many cases, when they resisted European demands for such slave workers, the native peoples were simply destroyed. On the North American continent—where the need for such work was focussed—two other considerations emerged, as well. The enslaving of Indians was a direct invitation to their armed retaliation against some of the isolated frontier settlements, which the Europeans did not readily invite. In addition, one important early source of income for the Europeans in North America was the fur trade with the Indians, which enslavement of the latter would endanger. For these and other reasons, the practice never developed beyond relatively isolated instances.

66. Richard M. Weaver, *Ideas Have Consequences* (Chicago: University of Chicago Press, 1948), p. 107. See also note 42 above.

67. Ibid., pp. 107–08.

68. See, e.g., *Poems of Black Africa*, pp. 57–58 (a sequence of creations). This sort of thing may also be seen in, among other places, North American Indian stories. See chapter 7 of this collection.

69. See, on the shaping of species, Arnott, ed., *African Myths and Legends*, pp. 21, 32–34, 39, 53–55, 63, 104, 132, 134, 150f. See, on witchcraft in sub-Saharan Africa, ibid., pp. 93, 142f, 280; Mbiti, *African Religions and Philosophy*, p. 153f. See, on the terrors addressed by the European witch trials, Anastaplo, "Church and State: Explorations," 19 *Loyola University of Chicago Law Journal* 62, 65–86 (1987). Consider, on the terror of the dark among adults reported from still another part of the world, Paul Gauguin, *Noa Noa: The Tahitian Journal* (New York: Dover, 1985), pp. 33–34. See also note 78 below. Compare note 91 below.

70. See, on Adam Smith's approach to these matters, Anastaplo, *The Constitutionalist: Notes on the First Amendment* (Dallas: Southern Methodist University Press, 1971), p. 690 n. 42 (to be reprinted in 2002).

71. See, on nature as a guide to right living, appendix B of this collection. See also notes 41 and 61 above.

72. Abrahams, ed., *African Folktales*, pp. 114–15.

73. See also ibid., pp. 125, 131, 134; note 77 below. See as well ibid., the epigraph for the Abrahams volume.

74. Consider the title story in Frank R. Stockton, *The Lady, or the Tiger? and Other Stories* (New York: Charles Scribner's Sons, 1884). See also Arnott, ed., *African Myths and Legends*, pp. 40–42.

75. Consider, on the use of "second sight" in a Greek village, Anastaplo, *The American Moralist,* p. 388. See note 78 below.

76. See, on Willa Muir and the old games and songs of Scottish school children, Anastaplo, *The Constitutionalist,* p. 556 n. 136. See also chapter 7 of this collection, note 62.

77. The story, or problem, might have to be changed if the powers inherent in one or more of the sons' possession should become routine in their operations. We notice that it is taken for granted in this story that such powers are occasionally available to human beings, although nothing is said explicitly about how the powers happened to be allocated among the three sons. We should also notice that it is the eldest son who seems to direct the action throughout, once their father has spoken.

78. Or, some might say, these are stories that provide the basis for biblical stories. See, for variations on the story of Joseph and his brothers, Arnott, ed., *African Myths and Legends,* pp. 160f, 195f, 200f. See, on the influence of Christianity upon Yoruban art and vice versa, Thompson, *Flash of the Spirit,* passim. See, on Christianity and Islam in Africa, Mbiti, *African Religions and Philosophy,* pp. 299f; note 42 above. See also Larry Rohter, "In a Harsh Land, Faith at Christmas," *New York Times,* December 25, 1994, sec. 4, p. 1:

> Missionaries and clergy here [in Haiti] often say that while 80 percent of Haitians are Roman Catholics and 20 percent are Protestants, all 100 percent believe in voodoo. Because voodoo by its nature blends symbols and concepts from various sources, most followers do not even consider themselves members of a separate religion. Instead, they look upon themselves as faithful Roman Catholics who simply "serve the spirits" and are trying to live morally in circumstances that are often difficult.

This article also reports (ibid., pp. 1, 10):

> Protestants, whose numbers are growing, have a more complex relationship with voodoo. "A good number of our converts come to us not because they no longer believe in voodoo, but because they believe our magic is stronger," one American missionary who has worked in rural Haiti for nearly a decade conceded reluctantly. "Some of them are church-goers by day, but still go to the voodoo temples at night because they want the extra protection."
>
> But for the average Haitian, especially those who live in the countryside, voodoo does more than provide a spiritual foundation. In the absence of an effective and impartial government apparatus, it also provides an alternative system of justice. Without having to resort to the police or the courts, which are seen as unreliable or worse, transgressors are punished by the community, acting through the houngan, or voodoo priest. . . .
>
> In that context, legends such as that of the zombie function . . . as a valuable tool for maintaining social order. To a Haitian peasant, being transformed into a zombie is a fate worse than death because it means eternal slavery instead of returning to Guinee, the ancestral African homeland of the soul. [It is said] that zombies are not random victims of sorcery, but those who are being punished for crimes such as "any action that unjustly keeps another from working the land" or "excessive material advancement at the obvious expense of family and dependents."

See notes 58 and 69 above. See also note 75 above.

79. See, e.g., Jack Berry, ed., *West African Folktales* (Evanston, Ill.: Northwestern University Press, 1991), pp. 146–47 (on the most efficient sequence of ferrying vulnerable things across a river). See, for a happy variation of the Oedipus story, Arnott, ed., *African Myths and Legends,* pp. 167f.

80. *Aesop without Morals*, p. 120.

81. Ibid., p. 274.

82. Berry, ed. *West African Folktales*, p. 144.

83. The typical Aesop fable is far shorter than the typical African story in the collections of materials cited in this chapter. Is this partly because the Aesop fable was apt to be reduced to writing?

84. See, on a lion's leaving corpses alone, William Shakespeare, *As You Like It*, IV, iii, 115. (*GBWW*, I: vol. 26, p. 620; vol. 24, p. 620).

85. For Aesop's Greeks, it seems, such encounters with wild animals were not part of everyday life at home. Do the African names used here mean anything? It should also be observed that gratitude for favors received is not uncommon in the Aesop fables. See, e.g., *Aesop without Morals*, pp. 156, 209. Compare note 49 above.

86. See Achebe, *Things Fall Apart*, p. 141.

87. See note 65 above. One great European exception, however, is Alexander Pushkin, the national poet of Russia. The contributions of the Jews in the United States are also special, partly because of the status first recognized for them here. See, for George Washington's 1790 letter to the Hebrew Congregation in Newport, Rhode Island, Anastaplo, *The Amendments to the Constitution*, p. 407 n. 69.

88. W. E. B. Du Bois, *Writings* (New York: Library of America, 1986), p. 822 (emphasis added). See note 1 above.

89. Ibid., p. 370. See also note 61 (end), above. See, on dubious legacies from Africa (including a tradition with an occasional human sacrifice), ibid., p. 499. See also "Interview of Thomas Adeoye Lambo," *Omni*, February 1992, p. 96:

> There's no doubt human sacrifice was practiced as recently as ten years ago. Certain tribes in remote parts may still practice it. Practitioners [of human sacrifice] claim that the oracle or some other voice tells them that the blood of a human being must be sacrificed, otherwise the community will be wiped out by famine or another malevolent force. Men also kill to enhance their sense of maleness and potency.

See as well Mbiti, *African Religions and Philosophy*, p. 79. "The Africans are usually dismissed [by Western mystery writers who set their stories in colonial Africa] as inefficient, slow, superstitious, witchcraft ridden, having no sense of time, *or just having different thought processes*." Schleh, "Colonial Mysteries," *Mysteries of Africa*, p. 6 (emphasis added). See, on the African sense of time, Mbiti, *African Religions and Philosophy*, pp. 6, 19–36. The "thought processes" distinction may be at the heart of the matter, with the Africans open to a way of life which the West simply cannot appreciate. See Senghor, *Prose and Poetry*, pp. 33–34. See also note 53 above. See, as to the African American serving "in the vanguard of the African people of the world," French, "On Slavery, Africans Say the Guilt Is Theirs, Too," p. A5:

> [B]lack American [festival visitors in Ghana] were challenged to re-examine [their] relationship with the continent. They were told in animated conversations and in editorial commentary during the festival that their relationship has often not risen above sugary romantic cravings that are satisfied by donning African outfits and learning a phrase or two in the local language.
> "Miserable Africa had expected these wealthy brothers and sisters from the diaspora who claim a sentimental, historical and blood attachment to the motherland to bring home the dollar, the big dollar, as their contribution to salvaging Africa from the doldrums," a [Cape Coast,

Ghana] editorialist wrote, complaining that black Americans had never materially supported the African continent. . . . Some [also] said that visitors from the United States had not been sufficiently interested in Africa's halting moves toward democracy, and that Americans had offered little in the way of comment or even criticism to help the process.

See notes 1 and 64 above. See, on the Americanization of the African American, Anastaplo, "Neither Black nor White," in "Slavery and the Constitution," 20 *Texas Tech Law Review* 677, 766–79 (1989). See, on race relations in the Republic of South Africa, ibid., pp. 780–84. See also Bill Keller, "Apartheid's Grisly Aftermath: 'Witch Burning,'" *New York Times*, September 18, 1994, sec. Y, p. 3:

> In this season of South Africa's rebirth, the rural villages of the dry northeastern scrubland have been seized by a passion for witch burning unlike anything the area has seen before.

One can be reminded of the escalation of violence in the United States (on inner-city streets and at abortion clinics) upon the end of the Cold War. See note 49 above. See, on "the pure human spirit of the Declaration of Independence," Anastaplo, *Abraham Lincoln*, pp. 11f.

90. Turnbull, *The Forest People*, p. 17.

91. Ibid., p. 292. Consider also these lines from Alexander Pope's *Essay on Man* (I, 293):

> And spite of Pride, in the erring Reason's spite,
> One thing is clear, *Whatever is, is right.*

This sentiment was anticipated by Democritus's observation, "What is is right." Diogenes Laertius, *Democritus*, IX, 45. See, on the relation between goodness and beauty, Arnott, ed., *African Myths and Legends*, p. 92. See, on Martin Heidegger's Nazified dedication to Being, Anastaplo, *The American Moralist*, pp. 155–56; note 17 of chapter 4 of this collection. See also Laurence Berns, "Heidegger and Strauss: Temporality, Religion, and Political Philosophy," *Interpretation*, vol. 27, pp. 99, 102–3, 103 n.11 (1999–2000). See, on religion "gone mad," note 56 of chapter 3 of this collection.The best among the Egyptians, the Greeks, and the Africans would have endorsed these lines from a Yoruban poem:

> A man may be very, very handsome
> Handsome as a fish within the water
> But if he has no character
> He is no more than a wooden doll.

Thompson, *Flash of the Spirit*, p. 11. Compare note 69 above. See note 46 above.

Chapter Three

Hindu Thought: The *Bhagavad Gītā*

This is the way it is, men of Athens, in truth. Wherever someone stations him-self, holding that it is best, or wherever he is stationed by a ruler, there he must stay and run the risk, as it seems to me, and not take into account death or any-thing else compared to what is shameful.

–Socrates[1]

I.

This chapter is an introduction—an indication of the kinds of things one might consider in approaching Hindu thought or, for that matter, any appar-ent alien thought of a serious character. It is, of course, but one introduction: one, in the sense of the approach taken; one, also, in the sense of the text used to get into Hindu thought—that is, the *Bhagavad Gītā*, which has been called "the most revered and celebrated text in Hinduism."[2]

The *Bhagavad Gītā* can be usefully compared to the Confucian *Analects*.[3] The *Analects*, it can be argued, is a less philosophical work than it seems; the *Gītā*, despite its mystical elements, is a somewhat more philosophical work than it may seem. Certainly, the *Analects* can be said to be more "worldly" and to make more than the *Gītā* ultimately does of "one's own," especially of immediate family ties.[4]

The *Gītā's* mystical character is suggested by this summary:

The war between the Pandavas and the Kauravas, two great opposing parties, is about to ensue. Arjuna, one of the Pandava brothers, develops second thoughts about the purpose and justness of this war. He conveys his doubts to Krishna, his chari-oteer. Krishna answers; but he does so not merely as a fellow warrior and friend but as a spiritual preceptor instructing his pupil. Still more: Krishna is none other than

God,[5] Vishnu himself, and [in chapter XI of the *Gītā*] he reveals himself in his full divine glory to Arjuna.[6]

Before proceeding to a discussion of this work, it would be useful to notice the context in which it is found.

II.

The general context for the *Bhagavad Gītā* is the body of ancient Sanskrit texts of which it constitutes a very small part. Hindu materials—even if one limits oneself, as I propose to do here to what we would call "religious" thought—are vast. There are (among other texts) the *Vedas*, the collections of hymns which are considered fundamental to Hindu thought and which are believed to go back three to four thousand years.[7] There are the *Upanishads*, which serve, in large part, as ancient commentaries upon the *Vedas* (and which have had, in turn, considerable commentary upon themselves, down to our day). And there are such "literary" texts as the *Mahābhārata*, that mammoth epic which may have taken centuries to put together and which is much longer than the *Iliad*, the *Odyssey*, and the Bible combined.[8]

It is this epic which provides the immediate context for the *Gītā*. The gigantic *Mahābhārata* describes the complicated family and political relations between the Pāndavas and the Kauravas, the repeated efforts that the Pāndavas make to save their inheritance (the rule of much of India) from the conniving usurpations by the Kauravas; the tremendous battle (taking more than a fortnight) in which the Pāndavas virtually annihilate their cousins; the subsequent rule by the five Pāndava brothers; and then their final pilgrimage, death, and apotheosis.[9]

The *Gītā* with which we are primarily concerned here seems to have been composed about 300 B.C., drawing perhaps on much earlier materials. It is generally believed to have been developed as a separate work and inserted into the *Mahābhārata* at that point where the great battle is about to begin.[10] Arjuna, the hero upon whom the Pāndava forces most depend, chooses this moment to wonder whether he should be fighting at all. At hand to minister to Arjuna's doubts is his gifted charioteer, who, it has already been noted, turns out to be Krishna, an incarnation of the god Vishnu.[11]

One difficulty with one's reading of the *Gītā* is that it is but a part, and a quite small part, of a grand whole. What happens before and after the episode recounted in the *Gītā* may affect one's understanding of the *Gītā* itself, even though most commentators do consider the *Gītā* to be capable of standing alone. In any event, the *Gītā* shows one of the principal characters of the *Mahābhārata*, a great warrior, in need of counsel from a god as to why he should fight in the impending cataclysmic battle among relatives to which the

Mahābhārata is devoted. The god, at the conclusion of his conversation with the warrior, considers the *Gītā* episode a colloquy on duty.[12]

III.

Another difficulty, perhaps an even more critical one, awaits the reader of the *Bhagavad Gītā*. It is said by many critics to be a book without any obvious order. We are told that one should not "seek systematic consistency in the *Gītā*," that it represents no system of thought.[13]

We must wonder how we could read such a book. One recalls Edmund Burke's observation that "good order is the foundation of all good things."[14] Is it possible truly to think about anything which does not manifest, or rest upon, "good order"?

Still, it may be that the *Gītā* rests upon an order which, although perhaps not apparent, "feels right" to the reader. People may instinctively respond to this order in the work, sensing something that helps account for the remarkable durability and popularity of the poem.[15]

We have then, at the outset of our inquiry, the decisive problem of whether there is indeed an order, a problem which bears on the question of whether we ought to take this book seriously, paying close attention to what it seems to say.

I suggest here a half dozen ways in which the book does exhibit or depend upon order. These suggestions may serve not only to reassure Western readers that the *Gītā* bears thinking about, but also to introduce them to various of its features.[16]

IV.

The sequence of the conversation between the warrior and the god is itself a reflection of order. Even those who consider the *Bhagavad Gītā* to be unsystematic and illogical can speak of it in the following fashion, thereby developing some of the points I have already touched upon and to which I will add others later:

> In form, it consists mainly of a long dialog, which is almost a monolog. The principal speaker is Krishna, who in his human aspect is merely one of the secondary heroes of the *Mahābhārata*. . . . But, according to the *Gītā* itself, he is in truth a manifestation of the Supreme Deity in human form. Hence the name—the Song (*gītā*) of the Blessed One or the Lord (*Bhagavad*). (More fully and exactly, the title of the work is "the mystic doctrines [*Upanishad*] sung [or proclaimed] by the Blessed One.") The other speaker in the dialog is Arjuna, one of the five sons of Pāndu who are the principal heroes of the *Mahābhārata*. The conversation between Arjuna and Krishna is supposed to take place just before the battle which is the main theme of the great epic. Krishna is acting as Arjuna's charioteer. Arjuna sees in the ranks of the opposing army a large number of his

own kinsmen and intimate friends. He is horror-stricken at the thought of fighting against them, and forthwith lays down his weapons, saying he would rather be killed than kill them. Krishna replies, justifying the fight on various grounds, the chief of which is that man's real self or soul is immortal and independent of the body; it "neither kills nor is killed"; it has no part in either the actions or the sufferings of the body. In response to further questions by Arjuna, [Krishna] gradually develops views of life and destiny as a whole, which it is the purpose of this book to explain. In the course of the exposition he declares himself to be the Supreme Godhead, and reveals to Arjuna, as a special act of grace, a vision of his mystic supernal form. All this apparently goes on while the two armies stand drawn up in battle array, waiting to attack each other.[17]

A further indication of the sequence of developments in this colloquy between Krishna and Arjuna can be gotten by glancing at thirteen short excerpts in which the warrior's opinions are recorded. The pattern of this sequence is fairly evident without interpretation by me:[18]

1. At the outset, the warrior asks his charioteer (II, 4–6),

> How, O Madhusudana [Krishna], shall I attack, with arrows in battle, Bhīshma and Drona who are worthy of worship, O slayer of enemies?
>
> It would be better [to live] in this world by begging than to slay these noble teachers. For by slaying these teachers who desire wealth, I would enjoy only blood-smeared delights.

The reference here to arrows prompts us to observe that the narrator, in the last stanza of the *Gītā*, refers to the by then dutiful warrior (for the first time in the poem) as "Pārtha the archer" (XVIII, 78).[19]

2. The warrior is persuaded by the god to be steadfast. And so he asks (II, 54),

> What is the description of the man of steady mind who is fixed in concentration, O Keshava [Krishna]? How might the man of steady mind speak, how might he sit, how might he walk?[20]

3. The god's answer to these questions, an answer which makes much of one's state of mind, prompts the warrior to ask further (III, 1),

> If it be thought by Thee, O Janārdana [Krishna], that [the path of] knowledge is superior to [the path of] action, then why dost Thou urge me, O Keshava [Krishna], in this terrible deed?[21]

4. The answer here, put in terms of one's duty to one's clan (in this case, the warrior clan), I will discuss later. Because of the god's emphasis upon that necessity which determines all action in accordance with the divine will, the warrior goes on to ask (III, 36),

> Then by what is a man impelled to [commit] sin against his will, as if compelled by force, O Vārshneya [Krishna]?[22]

5. The force of desire is explained by the god, who counsels both renunciation of all actions and disciplined conduct (*karma yoga*). This prompts the warrior to ask (V, 1),

> Thou praiseth renunciation of actions, O Krishna, and again [*karma*] *yoga*. Tell me definitely which one of these is the better.[23]

6. He is instructed at length about what renunciation of actions means, what the discipline of meditation requires, and what knowledge of and dedication to the Brahman (or Supreme Divinity) consists of. This prompts the warrior at ask these vital questions (VIII, 1–2),

> What is that Brahman? . . . How art Thou to be known at the time of death by men of self-control?

7. The god's answers to these questions, in the center of the *Gītā*, lead to the following request by the warrior to the god (XI, 3–4):

> I desire to see Thy godly form, O Purushottama! If Thou thinkest that it can be seen by me, O Lord, then reveal Thy immortal Self to me, O Lord of Yoga![24]

8. The Vision then displayed to the warrior so fills him with amazement that his hair stands erect (XI, 14). He is moved to say to the go (XI, 31),

> Tell me who Thou art with so terrible a form! Salutation to Thee, O best of gods, be merciful! I wish to know Thee, the primal one; for I do not understand Thy ways.[25]

9. After having been overwhelmed by the divine vision and being instructed about it, the warrior can develop further an earlier inquiry about meditation (XII, 1):

> Those devotees who are always disciplined and honor Thee, and those who worship the Imperishable and the Unmanifest—which of these are more learned in yoga?[26]

10. The warrior is instructed about the three *gunas* (or strands of human existence) which are rooted in the material body and which should be transcended. He can then ask (XIV, 21),

> What are the marks of one who has transcend the three *gunas*, O Lord? What is his conduct? How does he go beyond these three *gunas*?[27]

11. The immediate response by the god, developed in the two following chapters of the *Gītā*, describes the effects of such transcendence upon the enlightened man (XIV, 26–27):

> He who serves Me with unswerving *bhakti yoga*, having transcended these *gunas*, is fit to become Brahman.
> For I am the abode of Brahman, of the immortal and imperishable, of eternal righteousness and of absolute bliss.[28]

12. All this leads to the warrior announcing, in the opening stanza of the final chapter (XVIII, 1),

> I desire to know, O mighty-armed one, the true essence of renunciation and of abandonment, O Hrishīkesha, and the distinction between them, O Keshinishudana.[29]

He is told that, according to the wise, giving up all acts of desire is called *renunciation* and that disregarding the fruits (or consequences) of all the actions one does perform is called *abandonment* (XVIII, 2).

13. The warrior (in his final speech in the *Gītā*, at the end of the colloquy with the god), can report to him (XVIII, 73):

> My delusion is destroyed and I have gained memory [understanding] through Thy grace, O Acyuta! I stand firm with my doubts dispelled; I shall act by Thy word.[30]

It should be evident, even from this sampling of disjointed quotations (some of which could easily have been replaced by others to similar effect) that a pattern, or order, to the *Gītā* can be discerned, however puzzling various of the distinctions drawn by the god may ultimately remain.

Other features of the book, to which we now turn, can also be understood to point to the overall order of a colloquy which culminates in, but does not end with, a Vision of the divine.

V.

Various numbers in the *Bhagavad Gītā* provide further assurance of a deliberate order to this sedentary, yet lively, story.

There are eighteen chapters in the *Gītā*. These chapters are to be found in the *Mahābhārata*, itself made up of eighteen books, which is devoted in its entirety to an epic battle that takes eighteen days.[31]

Fortunately, it seems that these texts, and especially the *Gītā*, have come down to us in remarkably good shape, with their divisions evidently having been made very early, if not originally, by someone who understood the entire work.[32]

Further suggestive of orderliness is the fact that there are in the *Gītā* exactly seven hundred four-line slokas (or stanzas).[33] Of these, about 10 percent are devoted to the speeches of the warrior, about 5 percent to observations by the narrator, and the rest to the speeches of the god.

It would be difficult to overestimate the significance of numbers for Hindus both past and present. One can see again and again in their ancient literature the considerable emphasis placed upon counting. Thus, for example, five and eight are particularly significant.[34]

There seem to be, in the colloquy between the god and the warrior, forty-one speeches.[35] Central to them is the twenty-first, in which a vital set of questions,which I have already indicated, is put to the god by the warrior (VIII, 1–2):

> What is that Brahman? What is the supreme Self and action, O best of beings? What is said to be the material domain and what is declared to be the domain of the divine?
>
> How and what is the domain of sacrifice here in this body, O Madhusūdana? How art Thou to be known at the time of death by men of self-control?

VI.

I have suggested that various number patterns in the *Bhagavad Gītā* testify to the ordering principle exhibited in the work. But before we do more with numbers, consider what the uses of epithets in the book also suggest about an intrinsic order. By epithets, I mean the names by which the god and the warrior address each other.

The warrior uses at least thirty-nine different epithets for the god, employing them some seventy-two times; the god uses at least twenty-two different epithets for the warrior, employing them some one hundred and sixty-two times.[36] The warrior, in his first speech to the god (who, we should remember, appears in the guise of a charioteer), addresses him only as "Acyuta" (I, 21); in his final speech (XVIII, 73), the warrior again addresses him only as "Acyuta" (having done so but one other time since the beginning).[37] Thus, all that transpires in the extended colloquy between the warrior and the god may be considered as implicit in what this mortal senses about divinity from the beginning. Does the colloquy "merely" confirm what the pious man is "always" aware of? Indeed, is this warrior able to have the experience of the divine he does because of the kind of man he is (which includes the things he is already aware of)? We return to these questions shortly.

We notice, also, that the god addresses the warrior thirty-eight times as "Pārtha" (the most used epithet by far), twenty-four times as "son of Bhārata," and twenty times as "son of Kuntī." Thus, more than half of the god's one hundred and sixty-two uses of epithets for the warrior remind him of his family status and thereby, as we shall further see, of his duty to fight and to kill in the prescribed manner. How much is made of family ties will be evident hereafter.[38]

VII.

Other indications are available as to the aptness of the epithets employed at various stages of the colloquy. Thus, the warrior, when he explains to his charioteer how the killing of relatives can lead to a lawlessness that will corrupt women and thereby family life, addresses the god as a fellow clansman, "O Vārshneya" (I, 41). The only other time he addresses the god as a kinsman is just after he has been instructed by the god in the duties of the warrior caste to which they both belong (III, 36). Thus, also, the warrior addresses the god with such epithets as "O Madhusūdana" (slayer of Madhu) when the god's insistence upon killing becomes particularly acute.[39]

Shortly after the warrior is exhorted to abstain from acquisition and possession (II, 45), he is twice addressed for the first time by the god as "Dhananjaya" (winner of wealth) (II, 48–49). In the last stanza of his final speech to the warrior, the god addresses him as "Dhananjaya," as well as "Pārtha" (XVIII, 72).[40]

Consider, also, how the warrior speaks to the god upon being shown the full divine majesty (XI, 41–42):

> For whatever I said in rashness from negligence or even from affection thinking Thou art my friend, and not knowing Thy greatness, calling Thee "O Krishna, O Yādava, O comrade."
>
> And whatever disrespect I showed Thee for the sake of jesting, whether at play, on the bed, seated or at meals, whether alone or in the company of others, Acyuta, I pray forgiveness from thee, the boundless one.

What is curious here is that, when the warrior recalls and repents his former names for the god—that is, when presumably he is most sensitive to the names he has been using—he again says "Acyuta," the epithet for the god, which he has not used since the opening speech and (as we have seen) will not use again until the very end. Does he implicitly reaffirm his original relations with the god, despite all he is saying here, thereby suggesting that even when he was perhaps unduly familiar with the god, incarnated as his charioteer, he had still been inspired to address him, on special occasions, by the "Acyuta" title which, appropriately enough, connotes changelessness? The warrior has referred to the god simply as "Krishna" seven times. After this abjuration of his earlier familiarity, he refers to him as "Krishna" only once more (XVII, 1). This is in the context of a discussion about those who neglect the law's injunction. Does the warrior thereby tacitly recognize that he, too, is capable of neglecting the law's injunction, by ignoring the restriction (or law) he has in effect laid down for himself about the use of the name, "Krishna"?[41]

On the other hand, the narrator (as distinguished from the warrior) who has used "Krishna" only once (XI, 35) before the warrior's abjuration, never uses it again after the abjuration, except when coupled with the phrase "the Lord of Yoga" (XVIII, 75, 78).

In fact, after the Vision scene the narrator never uses *any* of the names he has used for Krishna earlier. The names thereafter used by the narrator for the god are used for the first time by him only after the Vision begins.[42]

This care by the narrator with respect to the names he uses for the god should be compared with the names used by the narrator for the warrior after the Vision: no new names for the warrior are introduced (except for the attributes, "Kirītī" [or "diademed"] [XI, 35] and "archer" [XVIII, 78]). Rather, the narrator uses for the warrior, after the Vision begins, various of the names he has used before (such as "Pāndava," "Dhananjaya," "Pārtha." "Arjuna").

Thus, it can be said, the Vision changes the narrator's view of the god, not his view of the warrior. But it can also be said—and this may be less obvious—that the narrator may learn even more about the god from the Vision than does the warrior. This may be reflected in the fact that the narrator, even more than the warrior, adjusts his names for the god after the Vision.[43]

The epithets do seem to be sensitive, if not even playful at times. (If playful, an orderliness would be suggested, in that there can be playfulness only when there is an apparent overall order?) Of course, epithets cannot themselves readily establish an order, nor are they a substitute for an ordering principle. Still, they may provide grace notes, as well as clues and qualifications, for what is otherwise said in the *Gītā*.[44]

VIII.

Also sensitive, and evidently deliberate, are the first and last words in the speeches of the warrior and of the god.

The warrior's first word (in the Sanskrit original) is "armies" (I, 21). It is fitting that he should speak first of the armies all around him, for much of the *Bhagavad Gītā* consists of the warrior's coming to recognize what is called for in the military situation which he confronts. The god's first word is "behold," pointing to the armies assembled for the impending battle (I, 25).[45]

This use of "behold" by the god anticipates the principal use of this word later, when the great beholding, in the form of the Vision in chapter XI, is provided for the warrior. The uses of "behold" suggest that that which is shown in the extraordinary Vision may have been anticipated from the very beginning of the *Gītā*.[46]

Thus, the teachings of the *Gītā* follow from what the warrior and the god each stands for. The "personal" character of this colloquy, and the fact that it *is* a colloquy between this warrior and this god, may be indicated by the fact that the very last word used by each of them (in the Sanskrit original) is "your" (XVIII, 72, 73).[47]

The "personal" character of all this, and hence the importance of the circumstances, is further indicated by the fact that the very last word used by the narrator (in the Sanskrit original), and hence in the *Gītā* as a whole, is "my." And so, the narrator can conclude by saying that it is his belief that various good things can be expected when the god and the warrior collaborate. Thus, a poem full of remarkable revelations ends with a reliance on the opinion of the narrator upon whom—it should become evident on examination—all this must rest.[48]

The most remarkable revelation in the *Gītā* is, of course, the famous Vision to which I have several times referred already, and about which more may now be said.

IX.

What is said in the *Bhagavad Gītā* turns around the central six chapters, thereby reinforcing the impression of the order we have been noticing. These chapters culminate in the divine Vision (in chapter XI) that is granted to the warrior.[49]

The Vision is repeatedly characterized by the narrator as marvelous.[50] The narrator's short description of the Vision moves systematically from the god as something physical to the god as light, and then to the god as encompassing the universe (XI, 10–13).

The warrior's description of what he sees differs considerably from what the narrator describes.[51] Particularly vivid for the warrior, perhaps because he *is* a warrior, are the multitudes, especially of armed men, he sees pulverized in the many mouths of the god (XI, 26–27).[52]

How is the god's swallowing of "all the worlds" to be understood? The description does reflect a simple fact of life, which *should* be rooted somehow in divinity (if anything is): all that we do observe around us is destined for destruction. It is in this context alone that the god is referred to by the warrior as Vishnu.[53]

Although everything in the universe is marked for destruction, the same should not be said about the god himself: in one of the two central stanzas of the seven hundred stanzas in the *Gītā*, there may be found this assertion by the god to the warrior: "But the great-souled, O Pārtha, who abide in the divine nature, worship Me with undeviating mind, knowing Me as the imperishable source of all beings" (IX, 13).[54] The imperishable Brahman, we are given to understand, is at the center of things; he is the foundation of all; he accounts for everything.[55]

X.

Much is said in the *Bhagavad Gītā*, of course, about the divine character further uniting the parts of that book. Particularly striking in the Hindu account of things is the relation of the one to the many. The divine manifestations can all be reduced to one, but most Hindus do not so reduce them, nor would they want to do so. There is, in the appearances of things, an obvious variety that seems to be respected by the Hindus—as may be seen, for example, in the many epithets used for the god.[56]

Those who see the divine as multitudinous are destined for an existence commensurate with their (unpurified?) perception. It takes many births, the warrior is told by the god, before "the man of wisdom" approaches the god in his unity (VII, 19). Those of more limited understanding settle for gods, rather than for *the* god. And so it can be said by the god, "Those who worship the gods go to the gods; My devotees come to Me" (VII, 23). That each gets what is due him is elaborated further on: "The worshipers of the gods go to the gods; the worshipers of the ancestors go to the ancestors; sacrificers of the spirits go to the spirits; and those who sacrifice to Me come to Me" (IX, 25).[57] Good works, it is recognized, can lead to rewards, but not to that release from earthly travail provided by freedom from rebirth (IX, 21). Only one who knows ("comes to") this one god goes no more from life to life (that is, from death to death) (VIII, 16).

At the heart of this theology is the opinion that the god is the source of all being.[58] This is the god who can say of himself that he is the superlative form, and hence the origin, of all things. A sampling from some eighty manifestations, proclaimed by the god about himself, should suffice to indicate the god's range:

I am the Self seated in the hearts of all beings, O Gudākesha [Arjuna];
I am the beginning, the middle, and also the end of all beings. [X, 20][59]

Of cows I am Kāmadhuk [the cow of plenty]. [X, 20][60]

Of guardians I am Yama [the god of death]. [X, 29]

Of rivers I am the Ganges. [X, 31][61]

I am the gambling of the dishonest; the splendor of the splendid; . . . I am the goodness of the good. [X, 36][62]

The god can conclude this inventory, "But what is all this detailed knowledge to thee, O Arjuna? I stand supporting this entire world with only a single fraction of Myself" (X, 42). Early in his instruction of the warrior the god can say, "Of non-being there is no coming to be; of being there is no ceasing to be" (II, 16).

XI.

A sense of duty permeates this "sacred colloquy" (XVIII, 70). What one's duty is seems to be determined primarily by the circumstances into which one is born.[63] The god enumerates, in the final chapter of the *Bhagavad Gītā*, the attributes of the four classes (XVIII, 42–44):

1. Calmness, self-control, austerity, purity, patience, uprightness, wisdom, knowledge and religious belief are the actions of the Brahmin, born of his nature.

2. Heroism, majesty, firmness, skill and not fleeing in battle, generosity and lordship, are the actions of the Kshatriya [the royal warrior], born of his nature.

3. Agriculture, cattle-tending and trade are the actions of a Vaishya, born of his nature;

4. Action whose character is service is likewise that of the Shudra, born of his nature.[64]

Much is made of these distinctions and of preserving them, even though it has been said that such distinctions do not really matter to one who knows the whole (V, 18 et seq.).

But it is difficult truly to know the whole. If one could see the whole, the god says, one would be reconciled to one's duty. Instead, human beings usually see only the middle of things, not their beginning or their end (I, 28). Do not our own experiences support this teaching? Thus, apparent calamities sometimes turn out well for us, even as we come to suffer from what seemed blessings.

In any event, the warrior is given to understand that he really has no choice as to whether he will kill the enemy: he will do that, and he will be victorious. The only question is how he will regard what he is destined to do. The entire action of the book is with a view to moving the warrior to understand

and accept his fate. He is not asked to enjoy that fate: rather, he is to kill without passion (II, 48, 56, 63–65). But, he is told, one can neither slay nor be slain (II, 19).[65]

There is very little in this book about virtue, in the traditional Western sense; there is much more about subordination and piety. We should remember that Aristotle, who said little about piety, argued that, by and large, the truly virtuous man enjoys doing what he should do.[66]

But to be virtuous in the Aristotelian sense, the *Gītā* seems to say, is to rely too much on private judgment.[67] Thus, the warrior's reluctance to fight is a reflection of his own desires. He does invoke the clan's interest in preserving its purity, but he is reminded of a whole which is threatened by his personal preferences. His pacifist sentiments would tend to win favor among us today, but perhaps that is partly because we, too, do not see the whole available to be seen.[68]

The Hindu view of things is such, we are told, that mere life is not to be greatly respected.[69] Glory and dishonor matter enough to be invoked by the god in his first efforts to recall the warrior to his duty (II, 31–36). But, if they matter, it is with the reminder that gold and stones and earth are one, that the conventional distinctions here do not ultimately matter.[70]

Indeed, there is something radical and radicalizing in the *Gītā's* disparagement both of conventional distinctions and of everyday rituals and concerns. The god is said to appear directly to a warrior (not to a Brahmin, or priest, it should be noticed). Moreover, when the god thus appears, he seems to liberate his protégé from received opinions (in their multiplicity?) by explaining to him how things truly are.[71]

And yet, however freshening the spirit of the *Gītā* may be, the fact remains that the warrior is recalled to his duty: after all is said and done, a warrior who would have gone his own way, preferring rather to be killed than to kill, is moved to fight. The duty to which he is recalled, keyed as it is to family ties and class obligations, is defined by long-established law. It would seem that this law, or custom, is not to be disregarded; rather, it is to be routinely conformed to. Thus, the *Gītā*, however bold it is in its apparent departure from the established way, seems deeply rooted in the received opinions of Hindu life.[72]

XII.

The warrior, in attempting to think for himself, has to be reined in by his charioteer. He must be told, in no uncertain terms, that it is presumptuous (if not even heretical?) to strike out for oneself when one does not have an adequate sense of the whole, something which it may be impossible for earthly creatures to have.

And so he must be taught, among other things, why this god (for the moment in human form) can be before another person in time (Vivasvant, the sun god) and yet after him (IV, 4). He is further taught, "Many are My past lives and thine, O Arjuna; I know all of them but thou knowest them not, O oppressor of the foe" (IV, 5). In short, the god knows what is bound to happen.

What does happen—indeed, what *is*—depends upon the constant efforts of this god. He must continually work to prevent chaos in the universe (III, 22–24). The warrior is told that he should do his duty, just as the god does his. There is nothing in it for the god—no ordinary pleasure, certainly—and yet the world depends upon him (X, 42).

It is a dutiful god who directs the warrior to do *his* duty, instructing him that to do one's duty, even if imperfectly, is much better than to do another's duty, even if perfectly (III, 35; XVIII, 47).

XIII.

There can be something paralyzing about the god's insistence that things simply are not what they seem to be. This means that common sense, which must rely upon appearances to a considerable extent, can easily be disparaged.[73] Also subject to disparagement would be any civic-mindedness which moves the citizen to do more, and in some cases to do other, than what the law requires.

One can understand, that is, why it can be lamented today that "modern India is full of frustration and has suffered from too much quietism." Such a lament can be followed by a celebration of the *Bhagavad Gītā* as a "call to action" which makes "a special appeal."[74] No doubt the *Gītā* can inspire men to dedicate themselves to "ideals," whatever those ideals may happen to be.[75] But we must wonder whether its typical effect, in the community at large, is not simply to encourage acquiescence: after all, passivity may be displayed even in vigorously executing, without question, whatever is expected of one.

The serious limitations of the human soul, and hence of one's ability to figure things out for oneself, is suggested by the semblance of a smile with which the god receives the warrior's assertion, "I will not fight" (II, 9). Early on, the warrior is told by the god something he will be told in a variety of ways in the course of this fateful colloquy (II, 11–13):

> Thou grievest for those thou shouldst not grieve for, and yet thou speakest words that sound like wisdom. Wise men do not mourn for the dead or for the living.
>
> Never was there a time when I did not exist, nor thou, nor these rulers of men; nor will there ever be a time hereafter when we shall all cease to be.

As the soul in this body passes through childhood, youth and old age, so [after departure from this body] it passes on to another body. The sage is not bewildered by this.[76]

Thus, the god treats the questioning warrior as if he were a child in need of the most obvious instruction. His smile (restrained lest the feelings of the child be hurt?) may be particularly revealing.

XIV.

I have suggested in these remarks the order which shapes the *Bhagavad Gītā*. A few general observations upon the book and its author will bring to a close this introduction to Hindu thought.

To say that the god must keep working to prevent chaos means, in effect, that there is no *nature*.[77] True, translators from the Sanskrit freely use the word *nature*, but that, I suspect, is because they have not thought through the implications of what is being assumed and said in the text. The god's constant effort would not be needed if nature, in the Western sense of the term, governed the world.[78]

Yet, we must wonder, what is the god guided by in keeping order? Is not a sense of order looked to by the god, just as, I have suggested, it is evident overall in the *Gītā*? Indeed, is not a sense of order evident as well in the universe described in this book? And what, we must wonder, can that order be, other than nature itself?

All this points to the possibility of nature being present in things, and in everyone's understanding of things, even if only tacitly. May not nature be evident even when all things are said to be dependent on fate? But to see that nature is no more than tacitly relied upon in the *Gītā* is to recognize that it is not deliberately examined—and this suggests, among other things, that *philosophy*, in the strictest sense of the term, is not to be found in ancient Hindu thought.[79]

To say this, however, is not to deny that there is here something knowable. In fact, Hindu thought can be quite sophisticated—and, in some ways, it is on the verge of philosophy. Thus, for example, the ancient Indians insisted that opposites (including the opposites of being and nonbeing) must be brought together if the whole is to be understood. The god can say that he is both what is and what is not.

Must not one, in order to understand the whole, have an intimation of what has never been—of the alternatives which have never been realized—as well as a grasp of that which has been, is now, or will be?[80]

XV.

Nature is seen also in the fact that the *Bhagavad Gītā* is a work of considerable art. Art depends, whether consciously or not, upon nature. And art (and hence nature) may be seen in the language of the poem—not only in the effects of the sounds, meter, and the like (which effects are rarely available to us in translation), but also in images and descriptions that even we outsiders can glimpse. A sampling of images should suffice for our purposes here.

The steadfast man can be described by the god in this fashion: "When he completely withdraws his senses from the objects of sense, as a tortoise draws in his limbs, his mind is firmly established" (II, 58).[81]

Further on, the god says of the man who abandons attachment to the things of this world, "[He] is not affected by sin, just as a lotus leaf is not affected by water" (V, 10).

Our third artistic image comes from the warrior's description of the things that go to their doom into the mouths of the god, seen by Arjuna in the overwhelming Vision of Vishnu-Krishna (XI, 28–29):

As the many water currents of rivers race headlong to the ocean, so these heroes of the world of men enter into Thy flaming mouths.
    As moths swiftly enter a blazing fire and perish there, so these creatures swiftly enter Thy mouths and perish.

Such images testify not only to the art of the *Gītā*, but to an awareness (albeit an unarticulated awareness) of nature upon which that art draws. An awareness of nature may be seen as well in an observation by Samkara, one of the great commentators upon the *Gītā*, more than a thousand years ago: "If a hundred scriptures should declare that fire is cold or that it is dark, we would suppose that they intend quite a different meaning from the apparent one!"[82]

A further awareness of nature may be seen in the understanding reflected in the *Gītā* of its characters, divine as well as human. As we have already noticed, when the warrior stoutly (and childishly?) insists that he will not fight, the god, who knows all and who certainly knows what is to happen, answers him with a semblance of a smile (II,10). Is it not a tribute to the art of the *Gītā*, and its awareness of human nature, that the Indians one meets today typically exhibit a considerable fondness for Arjuna when they are asked about the poem?

But mere awareness of nature is not sufficient for philosophy, however much Indian, as well as Western, commentators may speak of Hindu thought as "philosophy." Of course, the truth seems to have been important in ancient Hindu thought, but primarily for what the truth can do for one, particularly with respect to liberation from the unwelcome cycles of rebirth. Knowledge, when approached in this fashion, tends to be regarded as having magical properties. Among the things one may be taught when nature is made an explicit concern of the reason is that the supreme use to which reason may be put is to seek and grasp the truth for its own sake.[83]

XVI.

One more topic must be touched upon before we conclude this introduction to Hindu thought. We have spoken of art and nature. We have yet to speak of the artist.

Two, perhaps three, artists are evident in the *Bhagavad Gītā*. There is the narrator, Sanjaya, who tells his blind king (Dhritarāshtra) the story of the "sacred colloquy." There is Vyāsa, who is said not only to recount the *Mahābhārata,* but also to participate (as does Sanjaya) in some of its actions.[84] The third artist may be a poet who sees and tells all—the man (a Brahmin, perhaps, who uses the warriors?)—the man (or woman) who tells the story of Sanjaya and Vyāsa telling their stories.[85]

We have already noticed Sanjaya's uses of names for Krishna and Arjuna, and how they compare, for example, with the epithets used by Krishna and Arjuna for each other. What *he* sees—for example, in the Vision of the god—seems to be less "dramatic," if perhaps more "cosmic," than what the warrior sees.

Where and how did Sanjaya, the narrator, get all that he reports to his king? It seems to be suggested that he got it from Vyāsa, who had himself gotten it from the god (XVIII, 75). That is to say, perhaps there was no warrior with this particular experience, but only the narrators Vyāsa and Sanjaya (or, behind them, the anonymous poet) and this "experience" of the god. Does the master-poet thus present, in a form accessible to different kinds of men, what was revealed to or somehow seen by him?

However this may be, it should be noticed as well that the teachings of the *Gītā* result from inquiries *initiated* by human beings, not from interventions by any god. The artists responsible for this story are themselves human beings. No muse or other divine being is invoked here in *the telling* of the story.[86]

XVII.

All this bears on a major puzzle of the *Bhagavad Gītā*. An injunction of secrecy is several times laid down by the god for the warrior with respect to what is revealed to him.[87] Has Sanjaya or Vyāsa or the anonymous poet improperly revealed the secrets entrusted to the warrior? Or is it that the warrior does retain his own secrets, whereas no poet has any restrictions placed on his sharing with others whatever *he* is inspired to see (that is, whatever he figures out)? In any event, does the poet report only the surface of the colloquy, that surface the confusion of which the critics *do* notice? Only a few are likely to figure out in turn what is truly being said in the book, including what is being indicated about such things as rituals and the status of the ancient hymns, the *Vedas*.[88] It is evident in the *Gītā* that the truly learned and responsible human being should be cautious. Consider the warning of the god about the effects in the world of what we would today call militant atheists (XVI, 8–9):

> They say that the world is without truth, without a moral basis, without a God, that it is not originated by regular causation, but that it is caused by desire.
>   Holding fast to this view, these lost souls of little intelligence and of cruel deeds come forth as enemies for the destruction of the world.[89]

The secrets made available by the god to the gifted and privileged warrior may be preserved by the poet simply because few are equipped and disciplined enough to pursue the truth systematically. The god instructs the warrior, "Among thousands of men, perchance one strives for perfection, and of those who strive and are successful, perhaps one knows Me in essence" (VII, 3).[90] We thus confirm that rare as perfection in action is, perfection in attaining to the truth is even rarer.

It should be evident as well that we would need to see what is truly being said in this and other such books—and the consequences of such opinions—in order to be able to investigate properly the organized religion and the complicated Hindu community somehow rooted in and no doubt illuminating these opinions.[91]

Epilogue

I trust I have said enough in this introduction to suggest that the *Bhagavad Gītā* is a book capable of being read as a work of the mind; to suggest how we might begin to read it and similar books from other ways of life; and finally, to suggest how we might undertake to read first-rate books, "secular" as well as "religious," of our very own.

Notes

1. Plato, *Apology of Socrates* 28D (trans. Thomas G. West and Grace Starry West).

2. Eliot Deutsch, trans., *The Bhagavad Gītā* (New York: Holt, Rinehart and Winston, 1968), p. 3. Mr. Deutsch adds, "Countless orthodox Hindus recite passages from [the *Gītā*]

daily, and on special occasions the entire work is recited by groups of devotees." See on the dating of the *Bhagavad Gītā*, chapter 5 of this collection, note 52.

Wilhelm von Humboldt has been quoted as describing the *Gītā* as "the most beautiful, perhaps the only true philosophical song, existing in any known tongue." Jawaharlal Nehru, *The Discovery of India* (Garden City, N.Y.: Anchor Books, 1960), p. 62.

A. L. Basham, perhaps the most distinguished Western Indologist today, has described the *Gītā* as "the most exalted and beautiful of India's religious poems, which teaches a fully-fledged theism and is part of the more recent Hinduism, rather than of the old Brahmanism, which slowly changed from a religion of sacrifice to one of devotion." *The Wonder That Was India* (New York: Grove Press, 1959), p. 253. "No other religious-philosophical work of a comparable size, whether from China, Japan, the West or India itself, has quite captured the attention in the 20th century that this work has." A. L. Herman, trans., *The Bhagavad Gītā* (Springfield, Ill.: Charles C. Thomas, 1973), p. 3.

Interest in Hindu thought, of which the *Gītā* is the most widely known expression, is evident in works as diverse as G. W. F. Hegel's *Philosophy of History* and T. S. Eliot's *Waste Land*. "In the traditional form the chief distinguishing features of Hinduism are the doctrine of the transmigration of souls, with its corollary that all living beings are the same in essence; a complex polytheism, subsumed in a fundamental monotheism by the doctrine that all lesser divinities are subsidiary aspects of the one God; a deep-rooted tendency to mysticism and monistic philosophy; a stratified system of social classes, generally called castes, which is given religious sanction; and a propensity to assimilate rather than to exclude. This last feature divides Hinduism sharply from the religions of the West, based on Judaism. The latter, at least in their earlier forms, generally reject as false all other religious beliefs and practices; Hinduism, on the other hand, concedes some validity to them all. The Western attitude is expressed by the words of Yahweh on Sinai, 'You shall have no other gods before me' (*Exod.* xx, 3); in the *Bhagavad Gītā*, the incarnate god Krishna says, 'Whatever god a man worships, it is I who answer the prayer.'" "Hinduism," *Encyclopaedia Britannica*, 14th ed. See *Bhagavad Gītā*, IV, 11.

All quotations from the *Bhagavad Gītā* in my text are taken from the Deutsch translation. That translation may be found in the 1985 volume of *The Great Ideas Today*. All citations in both the text of this chapter and in these notes are, unless otherwise indicated, to the *Gītā* by chapter and stanza. All citations to sections are, unless otherwise indicated, to the sections of this chapter.

I have been encouraged by the generous response to this chapter by Wendy Doniger of the University of Chicago.

3. See chapter 4 of this collection. Various things I say there about Confucian thought apply here as well, not only suggestions about how and and why one should read books from a radically different way of life, but also observations about philosophy, about nature, and about my purposes and limitations. It should be understood that just as I do not know Chinese, so I do not know Sanskrit. Compare note 37 below. (Unless otherwise indicated, all references to notes in any chapter in this collection are to the notes of that chapter.)

4. Immediate family ties *are* made much of in the Confucian *Analects*. In Hinduism, the family, vital (if not even oppressive) as it can be, is decisively guided by class (or caste) requirements. Even so, much, perhaps most, worship is based in the household.

5. Krishna, although the name of a god, is to this day a name which may be given to a son. Krishna, as Arjuna's charioteer, is his older cousin. Family and other relations get rather complicated in the ancient Hindu stories, especially when transmigration of souls

and earlier divine incarnations are taken into account. It can be said that even Krishna had to learn, in the course of his human life, of his miraculous birth and his divine status. See, e.g., *The Bhagavad Gītā*, Winthrop Sargeant, trans. (Garden City, N.Y.: Doubleday, 1979), p. 25. See also J. A. B. van Buitenen, *The Bhagavad Gītā in the Mahābhārata* (Chicago: University of Chicago Press, 1981), pp. 5, 28; note 52, below.

Even more complicated may be the relations among the gods. The following account should suffice as an introduction to the subject for the reader of this chapter: "The word *brahma* is primarily and originally neuter in gender, and remains so usually throughout the *Upanishads* and the *Bhagavad Gītā*; but occasionally it acquires a personality, as a sort of creating and ruling deity, and then it has masculine gender. It thus becomes the god Brahmā, familiar to later Hinduism as the nominal head of the Triad consisting of Brahmā the Creator, Vishnu the Preserver, and Shiva the Destroyer. This trinity appears only in comparatively late *Upanishads*, and no clear mention of it is found in the *Bhagavad Gītā*, although the *Gītā* at least once refers to the masculine and personal Brahmā, 'the Lord sitting on the lotus-seat' [XI, 15]. . . . Vishnu and Shiva, under various names and forms, are the real gods of later India. Shiva-worship, though certainly much older than the *Bhagavad Gītā*, hardly appears therein and may therefore be left out of consideration in this book. (Shiva, under various of his innumerable names, is however mentioned [e.g., X, 23].) But we must say a few words about Vishnu, since he was identified with Krishna, the *Gītā's* God, or regarded as incarnate in Him. This identification seems to me to appear clearly in the *Gītā* itself [XI, 24, 30]. The *Upanishads* add nothing to the history of Vishnu. They— that is, the older ones, those which antedate the *Gītā*—mention his name only three or four times, and quite in the style of the Middle-Vedic period. But suddenly, in the *Gītā* and other contemporary writings, we find Vishnu recognized as a supreme monotheistic deity, worshiped either under his own name, or in the form of various incarnations, the chief of which is Krishna. . . . We have, then, finally, a union of at least three strands in the monotheistic deity of the *Bhagavad Gītā*: a popular god-hero of a local tribe, an ancient Vedic deity belonging to the hieratic ritual religion, and the philosophic Absolute of the *Upanishads*." Franklin Edgerton, trans., *The Bhagavad Gītā* (Cambridge, Mass.: Harvard University Press, 1972), pp. 133–35. See Basham, *The Wonder That Was India*, p. 238.

Are we to understand that the divine is implicit in all human beings, if not even in all living things?

6. Kees W. Bolle, trans., *The Bhagavadgītā* (Berkeley: University of California Press, 1979), p. 219. "Sanjaya, the old king's personal bard, acts as his reporter on the progress of the war between the Pandavas, his nephews, and the Kauravas, his sons." J. A. B. van Buitenen, trans., *The Bhagavad Gītā in the Mahābhārata*. This king, Dhritarāshtra, is blind. See note 86 below.

In this chapter, the spelling and italicizing of names in quotations are made uniform by me.

7. The most venerable of the *Vedas* is the *Rig Veda*, of which it can be said that its sound is as important as its sense. Particularly challenging for its sense is the hymn at *Rig Veda*, X, 129, which concludes, "Whence all creation had its origin, he, whether he fashioned it or whether he did not, he who surveys it all from highest heaven, he knows—or maybe even he does not know." See Basham, *The Wonder That Was India*, pp. 247–48. *Veda*, we are told, comes from the root, *vid*, "to know." See Nehru, *The Discovery of India* pp. 42f. See also notes 71 and 90 below.

In ancient times, descriptions of the capacity of battle leaders would refer not only to their skill in war, but also to their being conversant with the *Vedas*. Religion "has always been the central and supreme activity of the Hindu Society." Arnold J. Toynbee, *A Study of History* (London: Oxford University Press, 1935), II, 75. Thus, the contemporary distinction between "secular" and "religious" is largely Western. It is a distinction with which the present Indian constitution wrestles. See, on the relation of Reason to Revelation, note 79 below; chapter 4 of this collection, notes 14 and 109. See also chapter 6 of this collection, note 101.

8. "About 112 *Upanishads* have been printed in Sanskrit, but the most important ones are about eighteen." Juan Mascaro, trans., *The Bhagavad Gītā* (Baltimore: Penguin Books, 1962), p. 13. "The term *Upanishad* means literally 'a session', sitting at the feet of a master who imparts esoteric doctrines." Basham, *The Wonder That Was India*, p. 250. Sometimes the *Bhagavad Gītā* is itself regarded as an *Upanishad*. See, e.g., the colophon for chapter 1 of the *Gītā*.

"The word *Mahābhārata*, meaning the great Bhārata, reminds us of Bhārata, . . . the founder of a dynasty of Indian kings." Mascaro, *The Bhagavad Gītā*, p. 21.

9. Useful day-by-day summaries of the *Mahābhārata* may be found in Sargeant, pp. 21f, 40f. See also Basham, *The Wonder That Was India*, p. 407f; R. K. Narayan, *The Mahabharata: A Shortened Modern Prose Version of the Indian Epic* (New York: Viking Press, 1978). Graham Greene has said of Mr. Narayan, the grand patriarch of Indo-Anglican writers, "Without him I could never have known what it is like to be Indian." S. S. Moorty, book review, *Liberal and Fine Arts*, vol. 4 (January 1984), p. 67. See, as a reminder that the often bizarre episodes in ancient Indian literature are not merely things of the past, James P. Sterba, "In a Temple in India, the Rats Don't Bite, but They Do Tickle: Today's Rodents at the Shrine of Karni Mata Might Be Tomorrow's Town Elders," *Wall Street Journal*, January 9, 1985, p. 1.

10. The *Gītā* constitutes chapters 23–40 of the sixth book of the eighteen-book *Mahābhārata*. See van Buitenen, *The Bhagavadgītā*, pp. 5–6. Suppositions about the date of its *composition* range from 500 B.C. to A.D. 200. I find rather charming the following suggestions as to when the *Mahābhārata*'s war was *fought*: "Indian scholars like C. V. Vaidya, Karandikar and others are of opinion that the war commenced in December on the 11th or on the 13th day of the white part of the month of Margasirsa, 3102 B.C., and that the *Bhagavad Gītā* was preached on the morning of that very day. Prof. V. B. Athavale of Nasika has recently fixed 3018 B.C. as the year when the Kuru war commenced." Umesha Mishra, *The Bhagavad Gītā: A Critical Study* (Allahabad, India: Tirabhukti Publications, 1967), p. 27. More sober estimates place the war itself at about 900 B.C. See, e.g., Ann Stanford, trans., *The Bhagavad Gītā* (New York: Herder and Herder, 1970), p. xvii.

11. See note 6 above. Readers of the *Iliad* and of the *Odyssey* will remember that divinities such as Athena appeared on occasion in human form. Compare Hans-Georg Gadamer, *Truth and Method* (New York: Seabury Press, 1975), pp. 378–79: "There is, however, an idea that is not Greek and that does more justice to the nature of language and prevented the forgetfulness of language in Western thought from being complete. This is the Christian idea of incarnation. Incarnation is obviously not embodiment. Neither the idea of the soul nor of God that is connected with embodiment corresponds to the Christian idea of incarnation. The relation between soul and body conceived in these theories, as, for instance, in Platonic and Pythagorean philosophy, and corresponding to the religious idea of the migration of souls, assumes the complete separateness of the soul from the body. The soul retains its own separate nature throughout all its embodiments, and the separation from the body it regards as a purification, i.e.,

as a restoration of its true and real being. Even the appearance of the divine in human form, which makes Greek religion so human, has nothing to do with incarnation. God does not become man, but shows himself to men in human form, while wholly retaining his superhuman divinity. As opposed to this, that God became man, as understood in the Christian religion, involves the sacrifice that the crucified Christ accepts as the Son of Man, namely a relationship that is strangely different and is expressed theologically in the doctrine of the Trinity." See Plato, *Timaeus* 81D-E (*GBWW* [*Great Books of the Western World*], vol. 7, pp. 471d–72a). See also Philostratus, *The Life of Apollonius* (Loeb Classical Library, 1912), I, 269f; II, 455f, 479.

12. See *B. Gītā*, XVIII, 70. See also section XI of this chapter.

13. Edgerton, *The Bhagavad Gītā*, p. 99 n. 5. See also ibid., pp. 106, 108, 193. See, as well, Bolle, p. 219. The lack of an apparent order is suggested by efforts to ascribe various parts of the *Gītā* to different authors. See, e.g., Gajanan S. Khair, *Quest for the Original Gita* (Bombay: Somaiya Publications, 1969). Professor Basham, in his 1985 American Council of Learned Societies account, reported that scholars have discerned as many as a dozen contributors to the *Gītā*. He considers the original text to end with II, 38. He himself believes there are three principal authors of the *Gītā*. This diverse authorship accounts, in his opinion, for the contradictions he sees in the *Gītā* (as, for example, between V, 23–28 and V, 29). Even so, must not *someone* have believed that these verses could be plausibly connected thus? How is *that* to be accounted for?

14. *Reflections on the Revolution in France* (Indianapolis: Bobbs Merrill, 1955), p. 287. See also Mortimer J. Adler, *Aristotle for Everybody* (New York: Macmillan, 1978), p. 77. See as well appendix B of this collection, note 39.

15. See, for similar observations about Charles Dickens's *A Christmas Carol* and Lewis Carroll's *Alice* books, Anastaplo, *The Artist as Thinker: From Shakespeare to Joyce* (Athens, Ohio: Swallow Press/Ohio University Press, 1983), pp. 123f, 166f.

16. For the most part, I limit myself on this occasion to recording intriguing, and I hope instructive, features of the *Gītā* that I have not seen noticed elsewhere in those parts of the vast literature which I have sampled. Those who know this poem, Hindu literature, and India herself far better than I ever will may find it useful to take account of, even as they correct, what I have noticed.

17. Edgerton, p. 105. See, for another summary of the *Gītā*, Narayan, *The Mahabharata*, p. 145f. See also Basham, *The Wonder That Was India*, pp. 340–42.

18. Some critics tend to neglect Arjuna's questioning, regarding the *Gītā* as virtually a monologue by Krishna. But the most instructive presentation of divine things may perhaps be found in what is said in response to human concerns, questions, and limitations.

19. "Madhusūdana" means "slayer of the demon Madhu." See the text at note 35 and at note 39 of this chapter. Evidently, there have always been in Hinduism epic struggles between gods and demons. See note 29 below. See, on the epithets, sections VI and VII of this chapter. See, on the meanings of the epithets and other names, the glossary which follows the text of the *Gītā* in the 1985 volume of *The Great Ideas Today*.

The use of "archer," in XVIII, 78, is anticipated not only in II, 4 (and elsewhere), but also by the god's calling the warrior "Savyasācin" ("ambidextrous") in XI, 33, referring to his prowess with the bow. (It had been a feat of archery which had permitted Arjuna to win Draupadī who, because of a quirk, became the joint wife of the five Pāndava brothers.) Another troubled archer who had to be brought around to what was decreed for him to do in a great enterprise was Philoctetes. He, too, was moved by a great vision (in the form of

Heracles, another slayer of demons). Thus, he also had to be induced to see and to accept what was fated. See Sophocles, *Philoctetes* (*GBWW*, vol. 5, pp. 182–95).

20. See, on the "great-souled man," Aristotle, *Nicomachean Ethics*, IV, 3 (*GBWW*, vol. 9, pp. 370b–72b). See also Philostratus, *The Life of Apollonius*, I, 183f, 249, 267f, 291f.

21. "Janārdana" means "agitator of men" (if not "savior of men" or "liberator of men").

22. See the text at note 39 of this chapter.

23. The van Buitenen translation renders this passage thus, "You praise the relinquishment of acts and at the same time the practice of them, Krishna. Now tell me decidedly which is the better of the two."

24. Compare *Exodus* 33:8–23, *Deuteronomy* 4:12, 34:10. See *Job* 41:32.

Is it not signficant that the warrior does assume, if he does not "know," that there is something special to be *seen*? See notes 51, 71, and 90 below.

25. See Sophocles, *Oedipus Tyrannus*, 938 ("What have you designed, O Zeus, to do with me?").

26. The van Buitenen translation renders this passage thus, "Who are the foremost adepts of yoga: those who attend on you with the devotion they constantly practice, or those who seek out the imperishable that is unmanifest?"

27. "As both Samkara (A.D. 700–750) and Rāmānuja (A.D. 1017–1137) point out [in their great Sanskrit commentaries], these are the essential characteristics of the three 'Strands' of nature: 'goodness, passion, and darkness' respectively." Edgerton, *The Bhagavad Gītā*, p. 100. See, on the commentators, Basham, *The Wonder That Was India*, p. 328f.

28. See, on the divine Brahman, note 6 above, and the text at note 35 of this chapter. See, on the priestly Brahman, the text at note 64 of this chapter.

29. "Keshinishūdana" means "slayer of the demon Keshin." See note 19 above. "Hrishikesha" means "bristling-haired one."

"The teaching of the *Bhagavad Gītā* is summed up in the [somewhat Kantian?] maxim, 'Your business is with the deed, and not with the result'. In an organized society each individual has his special part to play, and in every circumstance there are actions which are intrinsically right—from the point of view of the poet who wrote the *Gītā* they are those laid down by the Sacred Laws of the Aryans and the traditions of class and clan. The right course must be chosen according to the circumstances, without any considerations of personal interest or sentiment. Thus man serves God, and in so far as he lives up to this ideal he draws near to God." Basham, *The Wonder That Was India*, pp. 341–42. See the text at note 65 of this chapter. See, on Kant, George Anastaplo, *The American Moralist: On Law, Ethics, and Government* (Athens, Ohio: Ohio University Press, 1992), p.27.

30. See, on the "Acyuta" epithet, section VI of this chapter. This epithet is also used by Arjuna at I, 21, and at XI, 42 (although it is a rare translator who will use "Acyuta" at all three places in his translation). See note 37 below. See also note 36 below.

See, on the linking of understanding to memory, Plato, *Meno* (*GBWW*, vol. 7). See also *B. Gītā*, XVIII, 76–77; Anastaplo, *Human Being and Citizen* (Chicago: Swallow Press, 1975), p. 82f; note 11, above. See as well Anastaplo, "Teaching, Nature, and the Moral Virtues," *The Great Ideas Today*, p. 2 (1997).

31. It has been suggested that the *Gītā* is actually finished in the seventeenth chapter, and that the eighteenth is a kind of epilogue summing up the topics discussed before. See, e.g., A. C. Bhaktivedanta Swami Prabhupada, trans., *Bhagavad-gītā As It Is* (New York: Macmillan, 1972), p. 780.

Why eighteen? It does *not* seem otherwise to be a significant number for Hindus. Compare the text at note 34 of this chapter. (Eighteen *can* be seen to reflect a symmetry using more important numbers: five plus eight plus five.) See, for one derivation of eighteen, *The Upanishads*, F. Max Muller, ed. (New York: Dover, n.d.), I, 184 (*Aitareya-Aranyaka*, I, iii, 7). See, for other literary divisions by eighteen, "Sanskrit Literature," *Encyclopædia Britannica*, 14th ed. See, on the ordinariness of eighteen, Philostratus, I, 297.

Subrahmanyan Chandrasekhar, of the University of Chicago, has suggested to me, in conversation, that recollection of an eighteen-day battle (real or supposed) may have guided the authors of the *Mahābhārata* and of the *Gītā* in making their divisions. That is, he starts (in a scientific fashion?) from what might have actually been, if only accidentally. Even so, such authors might still have had to decide whether this number (as distinguished from others no doubt also available from "history") was particularly significant. See, on Mr. Chandrasekhar, note 85 of appendix A of this collection.

It seems that eighteen can be an important number among Jews: it is evidently the numerical equivalent of the Hebrew word for *life* (*het-yod*). See also chapter 7 of this collection, note 16.

32. See chapter 4 of this collection, notes 7, 29, and 52.

33. The typical stanza has thirty-two syllables. See Stanford, p. xxii. A few editors add a stanza, in the form of a question by Arjuna, at the beginning of chapter XIII. See Sargeant, *The Bhagavad Gītā*, p. 540; Khair, *Quest for the Original Gita*, p. 133; Prabhupada, *Bhagavad-Gītā As It Is*, p. 620. But much is to be said for, and about, seven hundred.

34. The significance of five and eight for the Hindus is comparable to that of three, seven, nine, ten, twelve, and thirteen, and perhaps seventeen and twenty-six as well, in the West. On five, see, e.g., *Gītā*, XVIII, 13 et seq.; Muller, *The Upanishads* I, 23f, 46f, 76f, 82–84, 221, 223, 232f; II, 23, 46f, 83–84, 234; Narayan, *The Mahabharata*, pp. 32, 33, 37, 38; Basham, *The Wonder That Was India*, pp. 497, 499. On eight, see, e.g., *Gītā*, VII, 4 et seq.; Muller, *The Upanishads*, I, 1–2, 16–17; II, 149; Narayan, *The Mahabharata*, p. 1; Khair, *Quest for the Original Gītā*, pp. 70–71; Basham, pp. 385, 417, 420, 504. Panini's great Sanskrit grammar (in antiquity) consisted of eight lectures. See, on the relation of eight to five and three, van Buitenen, *The Bhagavad Gītā*, p. 28. See, for samplings of correspondences between numbers and things, Muller, *The Upanishads* I, 160–61, 165, 171–73, 181–82, 186, 187f, 191, 192, 193f, 214, 220, 234, 258. See, for various suggestions about how many gods there are, Muller, *The Upanishads* II, 139f (with one curious suggestion, at p. 142, being "one and a half"). See also note 5 of chapter 1 of this collection. See, on numbering, Anastaplo, *The Artist as Thinker*, p. 397. See also note 62 below.

35. I take Arjuna's "I will not fight" in II, 9, to be part of his speech in II, 4–8. That is, this is all one response to what Krishna had said in II, 2–3. (Of course, if an extra stanza is added as some would have it at the beginning of chapter XIII of the *Gita*, there would be forty-three speeches. See note 33, above. But that would mar the discipline evidently sought in having exactly seven hundred stanzas. The Kashmir recension of the *Gītā* is said to have an additional verse after II, 11. See Herman, *The Bhagavad Gītā*, p. 113.)

An attractive feature of forty-one, at least for us, is that twenty-one (three times seven) should be its center. There are forty-one names indicated in the genealogy provided in *Exodus* 6:14–25 and in the generations provided in *Matthew* 1:1–17.

36. There *is* a problem counting epithets, especially if one has to rely on translations. There is no translator into English, of the dozen I have examined, who is completely faith-

ful to the text in this respect. (It is tempting to try to make the number of epithets "come out right" by, for example, having Arjuna use forty [five times eight] and having Krishna use twenty-four [three times eight]. But I must leave this exercise to someone who knows Sanskrit.) In any event, it should be noticed that the warrior uses many more different epithets than does the god, even though the warrior speaks much, much less.

37. The second use of "Acyuta" (XI, 42) may be found in my text at note 40 of this chapter; the third use (XVIII, 73) may be found in my text at note 30 of this chapter. "Acyuta" has been translated as "sinless one" at XI, 42 of the Deutsch translation, and as "immovable one" at I, 21 of the Deutsch translation. Others have translated it as "unshaken one" and "changeless one" (Edgerton) and as "unshakable one" and "imperishable Lord" (Bolle). It has been defined as "not fallen, unchanging, imperishable, unshaken, firm." Sargeant, *The Bhagavad Gītā*, p. 71.

The god may be recognized by the warrior as unchanging, but the warrior's perceptions of the god *do* keep changing, perhaps because the god is so complicated and because the warrior is subject to human frailties in perception and in powers of expression. This makes the steadfastness of the "Acyuta" epithet even more striking by comparison. (I did use the original text, transliterated, to develop the data I present here. Compare note 2 above.)

38. "Pārtha" and "Kuntī" refer to the warrior's mother. (Thus, the god is much steadier in the epithets he employs.) A commentator on II, 14, observes, "In the beginning of the verse, where the nature of heat and cold is declared, Arjuna is addressed as the son of his mother,—Kuntī; but when he is exhorted to abandon pleasure and pain, he is reminded of his heroic ancestor Bhārata, from whom India is called by her people 'the land of Bhārata'." M. Chatterji, *The Bhagavad Gītā* (New York: Julian Press, 1960), p. 34.

I suspect that a thorough study of the *Gītā* would bring to light the appropriateness of the use of each epithet in the circumstances in which it is used. Consider, for example, this sequence: After the warrior addresses the god for the first time as "best of beings" (or "Supreme Person" [as in the van Buitenen translation]) (VIII, 1), he is thereafter addressed for the first (and only) time as "best of embodied ones" (VIII, 4)—and this comes immediately after the warrior had asked how the god is "to be known at the time of death" (VIII, 2). (See the text at note 35 of this chapter.) Cannot dying be considered "dis-embodying"? Is it indicated that neither "dis-embodiment" nor "embodiment" (that is, neither death nor life, on earth) means much to the god? See note 11, above.

It has been suggested, of course, that epithets are often chosen because their sound is appropriate in the lines where they are found. See, e.g., Stanford, *The Bhagavad Gītā*, p. 139. Compare ibid., p. 140.

39. See, e.g., I, 35; II, 4. See also note 19 above.

40. See also note 49 below. The question remains as to what that wealth consists of which is truly worth winning. (The warrior's noble teachers had become too desirous of conventional wealth? See II, 5. See also the text at note 19 of this chapter.) The considerable significance of "Dhananjaya" as an epithet for the warrior and of "Vāsudeva" (and hence of the present incarnation of this god?) as an epithet for the god is pointed up by the god at X, 37. (This is the last of the "divine manifestations" stanzas to use proper names.) See also VII, 19. (The god's "Vāsudeva" epithet again reminds us of the importance of the maternal line, since Krishna is the son of Vāsudeva, who is related to Arjuna's mother.) The great treasure which Dhananjaya (Arjuna) wins is the teaching by Vāsudeva (Krishna) which is made available (to us?) with the help of the sage Vyāsa. See notes 59 and 84 below. Thus, X, 37, is a most remarkable stanza, bringing together (and extolling with

superlatives) three of those responsible for the *Gītā* (Krishna, Arjuna, and Vyāsa). Is San-jaya the narrator "represented" (perhaps even superseded) by the fourth name here, "the poet Ushanā"? See the text at note 85 of this chapter.

41. See, on the restrictions placed in the Hebrew Bible and elsewhere on how the divine is referred to, Anastaplo, "Censorship," *Encyclopaedia Britannica*, 15th ed.

42. Thus, the narrator uses "Hari" as the Vision begins (at XI, 9) and again at the end of the *Gītā* (at XVIII, 72). See, for other noteworthy Visions, chapter 6 of this collection, note 64.

43. After all, the warrior, as distinguished from the narrator, is someone who was from the beginning considered worthy of being personally instructed by the god. "And although one ought not to reason of Moses, he having been a mere executor of the things that were ordained by God, he ought yet to be admired, if only for the grace which made him worthy to speak with God." Niccolo Machiavelli, *The Prince*, Leo Paul S. de Alvarez, trans. (Irving, Tex.: University of Dallas Press, 1980), p. 33 (see *GBWW*, vol. 23, p. 9a).

44. Much more can be said about the epithets—about, for example, those shared by the god and the warrior. Thus, both the warrior and the god can be addressed as "*Mahabaho*" ("great-armed one"). I have noticed three places where the warrior uses this form of address for his companion (VI, 38; XI, 23; XVIII, 1), and eleven places where the god uses this form of address for his companion (II, 26, 68; III, 28, 43; V, 3, 6; VI, 35; VII, 5; X, 1; XIV, 5; XVIII, 13). Does such sharing of epithets suggest that the god and the warrior do not differ in kind, at least with respect to prowess in battle? ("Bhārata," conjuring up as it does the common ancestor, can be shared as an epithet by Dhritarāshtra and Arjuna, in the *Gītā*, and by others in the *Mahābhārata*.

See, for a pioneering study of epithets, Seth G. Benardete, "Achilles and Hector: The Homeric Hero" (University of Chicago doctoral dissertation, 1955).

45. The word for *armies* is *senayor* (I, 21) and for *behold* is *pasyaitan* (I, 25). There seem to be differences in the editions and translations as to whether the god's first word to the warrior is "Pārtha" (one of his family names) or "behold." If "Pārtha" *is* used by the god, rather than by the narrator, then the second word used by the god is "behold" (with the god pointing to the assembled army).

46. "Behold" had been used even earlier by the somewhat villainous Duryodhana (the leader of the army opposed to the Pāndavas). Indeed, it is the first word used by Duryodhana himself (I, 3): that the grasping Duryodhana should use "behold" with his teacher, as the god uses "behold" with his student (Arjuna), may suggest Duryodhana's willingness, even eagerness, to dispense with reliance upon salutary conventions. Arjuna, on the other hand, instinctively defers to his teacher and hence to the divine. Thus, we again notice the noteworthy piety of Arjuna reflected throughout (as in his well-timed uses of "Acyuta"). Thus, also, we are encouraged to notice the care with which this poem has been put together *by someone*, however many hands contributed to the fashioning of the materials that went into it. See, on comparable care used by a master poet with the materials gathered into the *Iliad*, Anastaplo, *The Constitutionalist: Notes on the First Amendment* (Dallas: Southern Methodist University Press, 1971), p. 807.

47. The last word used by the god is *te*, that used by the warrior is *teva*. This god can appear differently to, and mean quite different things for, others. To young women, for example, he can appear as a dancer, perhaps even as a lover. "When peasants or old women suffer a grievous loss, their natural exclamation is, *Krishnarpanamastus*, Surrendered to Krishna." Khair, *Quest for the Original Gītā*, p. vii.

48. The last word used by the narrator is *mama* ("my" or "I"). The last two words, *matir mama*, have been translated as "I am certain" (Bolle), "I ween" (Edgerton), "I hold" (van Buitenen), and "so I believe" (Deutsch). The first word used in the poem (after "Dhritarāshtra said") is *Dharma*. This word, which is rendered as "righteousness" in the Deutsch translation, has been defined as "established order, rule, duty, virtue, moral merit, right, justice, law (in an eternal sense)." Narayan, *The Mahabharata,* p. 181. On the *Gītā* as a reaffirmation of the established way—but a way that has been refined as much as it is advisable to do in the circumstances, see the text at note 72 of this chapter.

We are once again encouraged to notice the care lavished upon this poem, further attesting to its likely unity and overall thoughtfulness. It is evident, upon close examination, that it *has* been put together by someone who is remarkably restrained, who relies to a considerable extent on argument, and who again and again takes common sense for granted, even as he is quite willing to draw upon the general opinion among his audience with respect both to miracles and to ancient stories and characters. (Compared to the rest of the *Mahābhārata,* the *Gītā* is [especially for its time] remarkably free of the immediately miraculous—and this despite the spectacular vision seen [by one man only?] in chapter XI. See note 56 below.) In short, this poet may be much more subtle and hence sophisticated than most twentieth-century scholars. See, on the limitations of the most fashionable literary criticism today, Anastaplo, *The Artist as Thinker,* pp. 470–72.

49. See Stanford, pp. xviii–xxi. The names for the warrior used by the narrator just before and after the Vision is granted are "Pārtha" and "Dhananjaya," the names that the god finally settles upon in the last stanza of his last speech to the warrior. See XI, 9, 14; XVIII, 72. Does the poet, in thus bracketing the Vision, deliberately use something he has learned from the *Gītā*-experience as a whole? See note 40 above.

50. Our contemporaries are also impressed. Thus, the Vision can be referred to as "the marvelous transfiguration of chapter XI." Van Buitenen, *The Bhagavadgītā,* p. 12.

51. Does the narrator see everything that the warrior does? The warrior *is* given a special power, by which he can see the Vision (XI, 8). We must again wonder whether the narrator sees the Vision at all. Or does he describe what he "sees" on the basis of what he hears the warrior describing? In any event, was the Vision necessary to intensify, if not even to confirm, the god's teaching for the warrior? And if necessary, what is to be the status of such teaching for those of us who have not seen the Vision?

It does seem that we naturally regard sight as more reliable than hearing. See Muller, II, 197. But do not thoughts and ideas depend more on words (that is, heard things) than they do on seen things? Certainly, what is told to the warrior is more important than what is shown to him, especially if all this *is* ultimately for the benefit of the poet's audience. See note 85 below.

52. One can be reminded here of the three-jawed Lucifer at the very bottom of Dante's Inferno. The story is told, in the *Bhagavata Purana,* of Krishna's unsuspecting human mother's looking into her child's mouth, where she is astonished to see "the whole eternal universe." *Hindu Myths,* Wendy D. O'Flaherty, ed. (Penguin Books, 1975), p. 220. She is then made to forget what she had seen, as she continues to love Krishna as her son.

53. See XI, 24, 30. See also X, 21. See, as well, note 5 above.

54. The second half of the central pair in the 700 stanzas is IX, 14: "Always glorifying Me and striving with steadfast resolve, and honoring Me with devotion, they worship Me ever-disciplined." Thus, centrality here is seen as the 350th and 351st stanzas.

It might be instructive to consider as central in another way the final stanza of the ninth chapter and the opening stanza of the tenth chapter (that is, the places where the two central chapters meet). Akin to the first of the "central" pair quoted in the text (IX, 13) *is* the first of this other pair (IX, 34): "Fix the mind on Me, be devoted to Me, worship Me, salute Me; thus having disciplined the self and having Me as the supreme goal, thou shalt come to Me."

55. See, on "Brahman" (or "Brahmā"), note 5 above. See Philostratus, *The Life of Apollonius*, II, 315.

56. Such multiplication of divine ascriptions may be seen as well both in Christianity and in Islām. See also *Exodus* 34:6–7. See as well Moses Maimonides, *The Guide of the Perplexed*, e.g., I, 54; note 24, above.

Is not any persistent conception of the divine ultimately monotheistic? When, for example, it is determined by a people what is and what is not divine, is not a standard drawn upon which is implicitly monotheistic? And does not such a standard depend upon some awareness of *being* and of the natural? But what is meant when one observes that a religion has "gone mad"? See, e.g., John F. Muehl, *Interview with India* (New York: John Day, 1950), p. 252. See also notes 79 and 80 below. See as well note 91 of chapter 2 of this collection.

57. See the note on this passage in van Buitenen, *The Bhagavadgītā*, p. 166.

58. See IX, 5; X, 1 et seq., 28, 42; XIII, 14 et seq.

59. "Gudākesha" evidently means "thick-haired one." (Some suggest that it means "one who conquers sleep." Chatterji, *The Bhagavad Gītā*, p. 163; Prabhupada, *Bhagavad-gītā As It Is*, p. 51.) In this list of divine manifestations, the warrior himself appears (with the name, "Dhananjaya") as the peak of the Pāndavas (X, 37). In that same stanza, Vyāsa is recognized as the peak of the sages.

60. "Professor Godbole's conversations frequently culminated in a cow." E. M. Forster, *A Passage to India* (New York: Harvest Book, Harcourt, Brace & World, n.d.), p. 179. See also Basham, pp. 120, 194–95, 319. Considering what Hindus are able to perceive in a cow, it should be no wonder that Arjuna saw what he did in (or through or because of) his talented charioteer? Still, "Oh cows, cows" can be a derogatory remark. Narayan, *The Mahabharata*, p. 68. See also Anastaplo, *The Constitutionalist*, pp. 605–6.

61. "*Yama*, lord of the dead, was a sort of Adam, the first man to die, who became guardian of the World of the Fathers, where the blessed dead, those who have performed the rites of the Aryans, feast in bliss forever." Basham, *The Wonder That Was India*, p. 238. See also ibid., pp. 242, 313–14.

An English woman in *A Passage to India* says of the Ganges, "What a terrible river! what a wonderful river!" Forster, p. 32. See also ibid., pp. 7, 123; Basham, *The Wonder That Was India*, p. 320; *Chicago Tribune*, September 14, 1984, sec. 5, p. 1.

62. The troubles of the Pāndava brothers are intensified by the weakness for gambling in the oldest of them, Yudhishthira. See Deutsch, *The Bhagavad Gītā*, p. 141; Narayan, *The Mahabharata*, pp. 52, 67, 80. One of the hymns of the *Rig Veda* is the lament of a ruined gambler. See also Basham, *The Wonder That Was India*, pp. 37, 90, 207–8, 403–5; Edgerton, p. 98. Is the significance of gambling related to a fascination with numbers? See note 34 above.

63. See II, 31. See, for an indication of the origins of classes (or castes), IV, 13. See also Nehru, *The Discovery of India*, p. 76; Basham, *The Wonder That Was India*, pp. 34–35, 137f, 146f, 483, 484. See, as well, Friedrich Nietzsche, *Twilight of the Idols*, secs. 3–5; *Anti-Christ*, secs. 56–57; *Beyond Good and Evil*, sec. 61; Leonard Feinberg, *Asian Laughter* (New York: Weatherhill, 1971), pp. 438–39.

"In India, as in China, learning and erudition have always stood high in public esteem. . . . Before the learned man, the ruler and the warrior have always bowed. . . . The warrior class, though not at the top, held a high position, and was not, as in China, looked upon with contempt." Nehru, *The Discovery of India*, p. 51. See also Narayan, *The Mahabharata*, pp. 28, 31, 79.

64. See, on the Kantian approach, note 29 above. It should be noticed that there is no provision here for "untouchability." See, on the daily life of the lowest class, Mulk Raj Anand, *Untouchable* (Bombay: Jaico Publishing House, 1956; first published in 1935).

65. Compare Xenophon, *Cyropaedia*, I, iv, 24; VIII, vii, 26. See also Plato, *Republic* 439E-440E (*GBWW*, vol. 7, pp. 352d–53b). See, as well, Ralph Walso Emerson, "Brahma."

66. See, for a list of Hindu virtues, XVI, 1 et seq. See also Narayan, *The Mahabharata*, pp. 90–92. Compare Plato, *Laws* 657C, 658E (*GBWW,* vol. 7, pp. 655b, 656a); Adler, *Aristotle for Everybody,* pp. 89f, 154–55; Anastaplo, "Aristotle on Law and Morality," *Windsor Yearbook of Access to Justice*, vol. 3, 1983, p. 458.

67. See XVIII, 59. See also note 29, above.

68. Does one not need a sound appreciation of the entire *Mahābhārata*, its circumstances and its consequences, in order to make an informed judgment about all this?

See, for a somewhat sentimental effort by modern pacifism to accomodate itself to the *Gītā*, Edgerton, *The Bhagavad Gītā*, p. 140, n. 7. Compare Ved Mehta, "Personal History," *New Yorker*, February 11, 1985, p. 57: "Christians are taught love and compassion while we Hindus are taught only fate and duty." But does not the *Gītā* make it clear that Arjuna's compassion is preferable to Duryodhana's ruthlessness? Arjuna himself can run wild when the killing becomes frenzied enough in the *Mahābhārata,* more so than his brother Yudhishthira. See, for his brother's instructive respect for protocol, van Buitenen, *The Bhagavadgītā,* p. 145f.

69. See IV, 9. See also II, 11. Yet Indians can develop a remarkable, even fanatical, respect for life, as exhibited by the Jains. See, e.g., Basham, *The Wonder That Was India*, p. 287f. See also appendix C of this collection.

70. See, e.g., VI, 8–9; XIII, 12; XIV, 24. See also R. K. Narayan, *The Printer of Malgudi* (Lansing: Michigan State University Press, 1957), p. 76. What is generally said about wealth in the *Gītā* (see note 40 above) leads us to wonder whether the seeming naturalness and hence rigidity of classes make possible the extreme asceticism and the disregard for practical considerations that some Hindus seem to exhibit down to our day. Perhaps the inexorable movement of the classes, as they go about their duties, permits the community to support those who do immobilize themselves in the everyday world. One can be reminded here of the most Orthodox Jews in the modern context.

71. But then, there *are* the narrator and the poet: of what class are they? See section XVI of this chapter. Or should it be recognized that it is as true among the Hindus, as it is in the West, that one who truly understands is confined by neither class nor gender?

72. But see van Buitenen, *The Bhagavadgītā,* p. 12: "For despite his perfunctory bows to received orthodoxy, Krishna is quite aware that he has new things to say, disguised as old things, older than the oldest brahmin." Compare ibid., p. 10. See Friedrich Nietzsche, *Unpublished Letters* (London: Peter Owen, 1960), pp. 135–37; Basham, *The Wonder That Was India*, pp. 341–42. See also note 48 above.

73. See Troy Organ on polarity in Hinduism, *Philosophy East and West* (January 1976).

74. Nehru, p. 63. See also ibid., pp. 47, 56, 278. See, as well, Philostratus, *The Life of Apollonius*, II, 593f; Narayan, *The Printer of Malgudi*, pp. 11–12; Muehl, pp. 8–9, 58f, 126–27, 184f, 301.

75. These can include the nonviolence ideals of a Mohandas Gandhi. See Nehru, *The Discovery of India*, pp. 63, 277; Herman, p. 6; Calvin Kytle, *Gandhi, Soldier of Nonviolence* (Cabin John, Md.: Seven Locks Press, 1982), pp. 38, 83–84; Basham, *The Wonder That Was India*, p. 483.

76. See, on transmigration and reincarnation, *B. Gita,* V, 6, VIII, 15, IX, 22; R. K. Narayan, *The Teacher* (Chicago: University of Chicago Press, 1980), pp. 26, 94–96, 100, 106f, 117f, 163, 184 (originally published under the title *Grateful to Life and Death*); Wendy D. O'Flaherty, *Karma and Rebirth in Classical Indian Tradition* (Berkeley: University of California Press, 1980). See also note 23 of the preface to this collection. Compare Aristotle, *Nicomachean Ethics* 1166a18 et seq. (*GBWW*, vol. 9, p. 419b et seq.); Thomas Aquinas, *Summa Theologica*, I, Q. 23, A. 5 (*GBWW*, vol. 19, pp. 135d–37d) (on "a former life" and predestination); note 11, above.

77. See section XII of chapter 4 of this collection.

78. Various *Gītā* passages I have quoted in this chapter use *nature* (often for *prakriti*). It can be argued that various terms do have, in Sanskrit, the "function" of *nature*. No doubt, the same can be said of the expression translated from the Hebrew Bible as "each after its kind." But see Chatterji, *The Bhagavad Gītā*, p. 97: "In the teaching of the Blessed Lord [Krishna], the independent existence of Nature is never asserted." See also ibid., pp. 148–50. Compare van Buitenen, *The Bhagavadgītā*, pp. 22–23.

May not the status of nature among the Hindus help account for the often noticed fact that there are no tragedies in Indian literature? See, e.g., Nehru, *The Discovery of India*, p. 100; Basham, *The Wonder That Was India*, pp. 416–17. Consider, also, Nietzsche, *Beyond Good and Evil*, sec. 30: "There are heights of the soul from which even tragedy ceases to have a tragic effect." May not both classical tragedy and philosophy depend upon a mature grasp of *nature*? See, e.g., note 13 of the preface to this collection; appendix B of this collection.

79. Is all this another form of the tension, familiar to the West, between Reason and Revelation? Is not Krishna more like Moses or the God of Job than like Socrates or Plato? See the preface to this collection, note 24.

80. See IX, 19. See also XI, 37; XIII, 12. See as well V, 1; note 23 of the preface to this collection. Is not a superior *beingness* assumed in Hindu thought, something which is beyond change? Is not this intuition related to investigations by modern physicists into such things as "antimatter," as part of their efforts to understand the nature of matter itself? See appendix A of this collection. The need to combine opposites in order to grasp the whole may be reflected in the productive collaboration in the *Gītā* of Krishna and Arjuna, whose names mean "black" (or "dark") and "white" (or "silver"), respectively. See *Rig Veda*, X, 129 (note 7, above); van Buitenen, *The Bhagavadgītā*, p. 160 n. 50; Forster, *A Passage to India*, p. 177f. See also Muller, The Upanishads, I, 230–32, 312; II, 176; *B. Gītā*, VIII, 26.

See, on the status of common sense in Hindu thought, the text at note 70 of this chapter. Did not the Socratic school (including Aristotle) regard common sense, in its rough reflection of nature, as a necessary point of departure for philosophy? See Adler, *Aristotle for Everybody*, pp. xi–xiv; chapter 4 of this collection, note 9. See also note 13 of the preface to this collection.

81. See also II, 68. See as well VI, 19; X, 19 et seq. See, on the dependence of art upon nature, Aristotle, *Poetics* (*GBWW*, vol. 9); Philostratus, *The Life of Apollonius*, I, 173f; Laurence Berns, "Aristotle's *Poetics*," in Joseph Cropsey, ed., *Ancients and Moderns* (New York: Basic Books, 1964); Anastaplo, *The Artist as Thinker*, pp. 275f, 284f, 310f, 494 ("nature").

82. Mascaro, *The Bhagavad Gītā*, p. 26. See also the opening chapters of Maimonides' *The Guide of the Perplexed*. See, as well, Cropsey, *Ancients and Moderns*, p. 95; Anastaplo, *The Artist as Thinker*, p. 3f. Compare Muller, *The Upanishads*, I, 75 ("If you were to tell [a certain teaching] to a dry stick, branches would grow, and leaves spring from it." [*Khandogya-Upanishad*, V, i]); II, 266.

83. Or so the philosophers have said. See Edgerton, *The Bhagavad Gītā*, pp. 108–9, 139; Forster, p. 317 ("He knew that few Indians think education good in itself.") Compare note 20 above.

84. See, on Vyāsa, B. *Gītā*, X, 13, 37; XVIII, 75; Narayan, *The Mahabharata*, pp. vii–viii, 6–7, 28, 131; Sargeant, *The Bhagavad Gītā*, pp. 23, 435, 748; van Buitenen, *The Bhagavadgītā*, p. 161 (chap. 16, n. 2); note 40 above. "Vyāsa" is sometimes taken to mean "the arranger" or "the reviser."

85. See note 40 above. The narrator Sanjaya is like the god Krishna in our story about Arjuna, in that he too is the charioteer to his companion (in Sanjaya's case, the king Dhritarāshtra). Is Sanjaya, then, also somewhat divine, at least in being inspired? In any event, Sanjaya tells a story to his blind king—that is, to someone who is like us in not being able to see for himself what is being described. See note 51 above. A charioteer is also important, as an instructor, in chapter 5 of this collection.

86. Thus, the *Gītā*, as we have it, depends for its form on two mortals: the blind king and the compassionate warrior both ask questions of their respective charioteers. Are not both questioners somewhat defective (at least for the moment, in the case of the warrior) for their respective duties? (This king's claim to rule *is* compromised by his blindness.)

87. See, e.g., IX, 1; XV, 20; XVIII, 63–64, 67–68.

88. See, e.g., II, 46. Who does and who does not have secrecy injunctions laid upon him? The warrior himself does not report to anyone else anything said to him, it seems. Nor does he know that a poet "hears" his conversation with the god or his description of the Vision. Does the god prefer to have a poet report the entire story? Is this, in part, because of the discipline and limitations of warriors? They cannot be depended upon to use their judgment properly here? Does not all this reflect the division of labor which the elaborate Hindu caste system very much depends upon, promotes, and perhaps perverts? See note 70 above.

Be all this as it may, what *does* the poet do? Consider, e.g., Muller, *The Upanishads,* I, 227: "Poets through their understanding discovered [the god] Indra dancing an Anushtubh [a kind of meter]." How many of the things reported in sacred literature (including the *Gītā*) are really the "discoveries" of poets? What does it say about inspiration (prophetic or poetic) if one insists, as Maimonides did, that a prophet must be quite intelligent? See Anastaplo, *The Artist as Thinker*, p. 11. See also note 79 above. See as well chapter 4 of this collection, note 38.

89. One can be reminded here of Lucretius and the Epicureans. One can be reminded as well of Molly Bloom's scorn for atheists as recorded in her grand soliloquy in James Joyce's *Ulysses*. See Anastaplo, *Law & Literature and the Moderns*, p.514. See, as instructive guides to the study of divine things, Mortimer J. Adler, *How to Think about God* (New York: Macmillan, 1980); Leo Strauss, "On the Interpretation of *Genesis*," in Kenneth Hart Green, ed., *Jewish Philosophy and the Crisis of Modernity* (Albany: State University of New York Press, 1997), p. 359. See also the preface to this collection, note 14.

90. What is required for one truly to know? Is it not to proceed as we have been able to do in this chapter, as well as elsewhere in this collection, both to assume and to confirm

the sovereignty of nature and reason and hence of natural right and perhaps of philosophy? See notes 3, 56, and 79 above. See also the preface to this collection, note 13.

91. A sampling of observations by three Westerners in the twentieth century can serve to remind us of how varied foreign responses to India can be:

A British policeman, in *A Passage to India*, says to a compatriot, "Read any of the Mutiny records; which, rather than the *Bhagavad Gita*, should be your Bible in this country. Though I'm not sure that the one and the other are not closely connected." Forster, p. 169. (Is not Hegel's instructive account of Hinduism in this spirit? Compare chapter 6 of this collection, note 33.)

Winston Churchill reports that upon arriving, as a young army officer, in Bombay Harbor, he "pulled up the curtain on what might well have been a different planet." And he could add, "One voyage to India is enough; the others are merely repletion." *My Early Life: A Roving Commission* (New York: Charles Scribner's Sons, 1930), pp. 101, 122. (Compare N. G. Jog, *Churchill's Blind Spot: India* [Bombay: New Book Co., 1944], especially chap. XXII, "Churchill and Gandhi"; Nehru, p. 353f.)

And a scholar who has devoted a long career to the study of India can prophesy, "Hindu civilization will, we believe, retain its continuity. *The Bhagavad Gītā* will not cease to inspire men of action, and the *Upanishads* men of thought. The charm and graciousness of the Indian way of life will continue, however much affected it may be by the labour-saving devices of the West. People will still love the tales of the heroes of the *Mahābhārata* and the *Ramayana*. . . . The quiet and gentle happiness which has at all times pervaded Indian life where oppression, disease and poverty have not overclouded it will surely not vanish before the more hectic ways of the West." Basham, *The Wonder That Was India*, p. 484. The Gītā, I have argued, should challenge and hence inspire "men of thought" as well.

Chapter Four

Confucian Thought: The *Analects*

And whether anyone in the city is of high or low birth, or what evil has been inherited by anyone from his ancestors, male or female, are matters to which
[philosophers] pay no more attention than to the number of pints in the sea, as
the saying goes. [The philosopher] does not keep aloof from these things for the
sake of gaining reputation, but really it is only his body which has its place and
home in the city; his thought, considering all these things petty and of no account, disdains them and is borne in all directions, as Pindar says, "both below
the earth," and measuring the surface of the earth, and "above the sky," studying the stars, and investigating the universal nature of every thing that is, each
in its entirety, never lowering itself to anything close at hand.

—Socrates[1]

I.

This chapter is an introduction—an indication of the kinds of things one might
consider in approaching Confucian thought or, for that matter, any apparently
alien thought of a serious character. It is, moreover, but *one* introduction: one,
in the sense of the approach taken (which may be dependent somewhat upon
chance, some will say); one, also, in the sense of the text used to get into Confucian thought—that is, the *Analects*, that compilation of sayings which has
been called the "best single source for the ideas of Confucius."[2]

I refer to Confucian *thought*, not as some do to *philosophy*. I am aware that
philosophy and *philosopher* are terms used by Confucian translators and
scholars. But it remains to be seen (and indeed it should be one of the principal concerns of any serious study *by us* of Confucian thought, or of any corpus of non-Western thought), whether the term *philosophy* is a proper one to
be used in this connection.[3] I refer to *Confucian* thought, rather than to the

thought of Confucius. My usage here reflects serious problems with the texts from which one has to work.

Confucius himself, it is said, probably did not write anything. In this respect, it seems, he was like Socrates and Jesus—or strictly speaking, they were like him, since he lived and died before either of them was born. That is, Confucius is said to have died in 479 B.C., the year of the Battle of Plataea (toward the end of the Great War between the Greeks and the Persians), about a decade before the birth of Socrates. The name "Confucius" is a Latinized version of "K'ung Fu-tzu," which means (I am told) "Master K'ung."[4] It should go without saying, since it will soon be evident, that I know absolutely no Chinese at all. So much, then, for preliminaries.

Not only did Confucius not write anything, he may well not have said many of the things which have been attributed to him.[5] However, all the thought which is traditionally called Confucian is such in the sense that it was promulgated in various and varying editions by the Confucian school—by the men who considered themselves (and who were generally considered) Confucius' disciples and successors.[6]

The typical Western reader must sometimes wonder whether the organizing principle for collections of Confucian passages is one that has as little relation to the originally intended thought of the passages collected as a comprehensive book of quotations does among us. Furthermore, there have been textual disputes among the editors of the writings over the centuries—indeed, over the millennia—which we, of course, are not in a position to settle.[7]

But, then, we have no immediate need, for our purposes, to try to resolve such differences. What unites Chinese scholars during the five hundred or so years after Confucius's death (the period during which the authoritative texts were evidently put together in the forms we now have) is, at least in Western eyes, far greater than what divides them. That which unites them, and which they take for granted, is a pervasive sense of what Confucian thought is all about, something that we in the West find it hard to get more than a glimpse of. One must wonder whether Confucian thought *is* to be grasped, in the first instance, through a book.[8] Was it intended that writings would do no more than refine and stabilize what had already been ordained both by the community and by centuries of exposure to a way of life?[9]

Some might even suggest that what made Confucius as influential as he was—an influence for which it is difficult to imagine the books we do have to be alone responsible—was that he was able, through the force of his personality and in the kind of language he used (neither of which is likely to be accessible to us), to confirm and thereafter to build upon a deeply engrained tendency among the Chinese people. Thus understood, Confucian thought would not be the product of a single mind at work but rather the "spirit" of a people expressing itself. Such an account of Confucius would make him seem more historical and accidental and hence less philosophical (less knowing and knowable) than an influential teacher might otherwise be.[10]

But it might also be suggested—and this permits more of a philosophical approach—that there was a significant oral tradition which accompanied, explained, and made use of the compilations of Confucius's teachings which we have. Whether the original oral tradition is still available, I do not know; one who is ignorant of the Chinese language does not easily run across it. But there certainly is available a considerable body of written commentary on the surviving texts, to which I venture to contribute on this occasion.[11]

II.

One of our purposes on this occasion is to understand ourselves by stepping somewhat away from our usual way of thinking, examining indirectly thereby how we do think about the things we take for granted. We will see, by the way, that those Westerners who believe, on the basis of the smattering of information they pick up here and there, that they are following Eastern ways may be badly deceived and, to the extent that others follow them, quite deceiving. The most they may get thereby are superficial and probably harmless intimations of another way of life. Of course, they can also cut themselves loose from their moorings and set themselves adrift on a boundless sea, enjoying first the exhilaration of liberty and experiencing thereafter the despair of homelessness, if not even of purposelessness.[12]

Truly to understand others requires an effort to understand them as they understood themselves.[13] Thus, our concern is not that of the anthropologist, who tends to see the sayings and doings of other people in terms of preconceived psychic and social "forces." Or, rather, the study of a "high civilization"—and the Chinese is certainly that—may be the "anthropology" most worth taking seriously. Examination of a high civilization can truly help us look at ourselves: another way of life puts to us the challenge of considering whether it has anything decisive to offer us, anything which calls for fundamental changes in our way of life. Critical to Western life is the implicit understanding that it is open to improvement, that it is not necessarily the best way of life. There is even a sense that only a way of life which is open (as the West has long been) to philosophy can begin truly to understand both itself and other ways of life.[14]

Only a civilization which has itself been exposed to philosophy can consider seriously whether philosophy exists elsewhere. Philosophy is that organized and deliberate inquiry which strives for knowledge of the whole.

"The whole," Leo Strauss has observed, "is the totality of the parts. The whole eludes us but we know parts: we possess partial knowledge of the parts."[15] I assume that he says "partial knowledge" because it would require complete knowledge of the whole, which may be unattainable by us in our temporal circumstances, to put the (somewhat known) parts in their places and thus fully to know even them.

Political philosophy—and here we come closer to Confucius's evident concerns—is that interest in political things which is illuminated by philosophy. Political philosophy, Mr. Strauss has said, is "the attempt to understand the nature of political things."[16] And, it should be added, one may speak sensibly about political things without being a political philosopher. Thus, Mr. Strauss has also said, "A political thinker who is not a philosopher is primarily interested in, or attached to, a specific order or policy; the political philosopher is primarily interested in, or attached to, the truth."[17]

Was Confucius himself, or anyone working in the tradition he evidently established, a political philosopher? Political philosophy recognizes, among other things, that the highest human concern may be philosophy itself. One's way may *depend* upon a "theory"—on an opinion about the whole (and Confucius's way may well do *that*, just as does, say, Homer's or Pindar's). But such a way need not be concerned *with* theory. Thus the underlying theory for a way of life may be no more than a kind of "given," the unexamined foundation upon which everything else rests.

Someone might say, in defense of a nonphilosophical Confucius, that whoever takes philosophy most seriously (as the political philosopher does, or as the modern intellectual seems to do) is in a way irresponsible: he selfishly cares more for the truth than he cares for good order and the general welfare. An inquiry into Confucian thought, therefore, can oblige (and permit) us to examine and thus to know ourselves a little better than we otherwise might.

Let us turn then to the Confucian texts. How are they to be read?

III.

One should read these texts with a great deal of trepidation; that is, one must recognize from the outset how limited our access to the Confucian texts is.[18] A typical effect on the Western reader of a Confucian text is a sense of disorientation. He gets the impression that he has wandered in on the middle of conversations at a great dance, that he hears snatches of exchanges here and there as he moves around the ballroom floor.[19] He also gets the impression that those engaged in the conversations he overhears do understand the many allusions and references being exchanged. The Westerner is an outsider.

Consider, for example, chapters 18 and 19 of book XV. I will use, in this chapter on Confucian thought, primarily the old-fashioned James Legge translation, which seems to me somewhat more reliable than anything else available in English:[20]

18. The Master [Confucius] said, "The superior man is distressed by his want of ability. He is not distressed by men's not knowing him."
19. The Master said, "The superior man dislikes the thought of his name not being mentioned after his death."

Chapter 18 fits in well with what is said in book I, at the end of chapter 1, where Confucius is reported to have said, "Is he not a man of complete virtue, who feels no discomposure though men may take no note of him?" But how is chapter 18 of book XV to fit in with chapter 19 of book XV? The Arthur Waley translation has this for chapter 19: "The Master said, A gentleman has reason to be distressed if he ends his days without making a reputation for himself." And Waley adds, in a note, "[This] contradicts the saying before. As both sayings completely lack context, it would be a waste of time to try to reconcile the contradiction."[21] We notice, by the way, that Legge may have smoothed over somewhat the contradiction by the way he had translated chapter 19.[22]

Waley may be correct: the originally different contexts of the two sayings may explain the apparent discrepancy. Some scholars, by the way, would question the accuracy here of the Chinese text itself or would suggest there has been an interpolation into the compilation of one or the other saying—but that approach can explain away *all* apparent contradictions, intended ones as well as unintended ones. This could be a loss, for the probing of such a contradiction in, say, a Platonic text can guide one to subtle elements in Plato's thought.[23] But, in Plato's case, we *can* fairly safely depend on the accuracy of the available text and we are fairly sure of the contexts of the apparently contradictory remarks.

If their original contexts (that is, prior to their compilation into the *Analects*) account for each of these Confucian statements, thereby eliminating the contradiction apparent in the compilation, how can we be sure about *any* of the shorter statements? That is, we cannot know about any of them what the "whole" is of which they were originally intended to be parts; we cannot know whether the "remainder" of the statement (that is, the original context) would change the meaning, however evident that meaning may now happen to seem in the compilation in which it is found.

What did the more thoughtful Confucian students do with such passages? Did they rely upon textual emendations and upon explanations keyed to "contexts" only as a last resort? I detect, on the basis of what I have seen in and around the *Analects*, a prudent tradition in which it is insisted that one must work with the compilation as it has come down for centuries, if not even millennia, from competent, knowledgeable editors.[24] Thus, the accepted exercise might well have been (as it should be with Platonic or with Aristotelian texts) to try to fit together everything traditionally ascribed to a thinker. Is not one obliged to consider, as the relevant context, that which does appear to be provided where the passages are now to be found? Let us try with the two passages quoted from book XV.

Is one reconciled, during one's lifetime, to the lack of recognition only so long as hope remains of eventual recognition? It is not easy—is it too much to expect? is it inhuman?—that one should not care *at all* about what is *ever* thought of one. And if one's emphasis is upon practice—upon doing something in this world—then the total lack of recognition suggests a complete failure to move others. On the other hand, to be overly concerned about recognition, as one goes along, may lessen one's effectiveness and hence the prospect of an enduring recognition. One should be most concerned during one's life, therefore, with making oneself so worthy of one's duties that one is entitled to eventual recognition. But, we might ask, what good is recognition at the end of or after one's life? Perhaps the response would be—in the discussion we are positing among various students of Confucius—"Of course, one must be concerned with one's standing on earth after death. Does not this fit in with our respect for the ancestral? Does this not tie civilized generations together?"

Thus the probing would proceed, a probing which seems to be invited by Confucius's suggestive hints, a constant probing which trains and qualifies one to join the select circle of those who have learned how to think subtly and responsibly. Indeed, it sometimes seems to the Western reader that the Confucian texts must be read almost as one would read poetry, if not even the many enigmatic nursery rhymes we have inherited. Much depends upon the nuance, upon the particular circumstances, of an observation. One is encouraged to settle on particular passages for a leisurely discussion. (I have heard that one might devote a day to each Confucian chapter, even to a chapter of only a few lines.) An authoritative moral tone is assumed and reinforced thereby.[25]

Exhortation and example are exhibited in the Confucian texts as more important, or at least as more influential, than reasoning and intellectual organization. Certainly, the philosophical texts with which we in the West are familiar are much more obviously organized.[26] Systematization means more for us, as do definitions, which themselves reflect a comprehensive order and, ultimately, nature. What do these different approaches—the Confucian and the more familiar philosophical—say, or assume, about "reality"? What *is* "the world" like? The difference in approaches may reflect a difference in ultimate purposes: one can pursue either a life of action, with an emphasis upon proper everyday conduct, or a life of contemplation, for which a more or less systematic, examined, and disciplined view of the whole is needed.

We sense that we get much, if not most, of what Socrates was like through the Platonic dialogues. But we simply do not have that impression of the Confucius glimpsed through the Chinese texts. Why should this be so? Are the Chinese texts deliberately fragmentary? For Socrates, whatever the force of his remarkable "personality" might have been, the critical thing seems to have been the *thinking*, something which can be expressed in words—and this may be captured somewhat on paper. For Confucius, the critical thing seems to have been the social influence, something which is difficult to put on paper.[27]

We turn now—and here we *are* in the Confucian tradition—to exegeses of a half dozen sample passages from the *Analects*. I believe it is safe to assume, and this our inquiry should confirm, that Confucius is intelligent, thoughtful, and subtle. I cannot do more than make suggestions about texts which no doubt require much more examination than I am able to give them here.

We proceed, in a more or less straightforward fashion, with samples drawn from the *Analects* as presented in the Legge translation.[28] These examinations are necessarily tentative, permitting us to weave together what we see in the work as a whole as we enter into a way of reading and indeed into a way of life which are both unfamiliar and instructive.[29]

IV.

Book I, chapter 1 of the *Analects* reads:[30]

> 1. The Master [Confucius] said, "Is it not pleasant to learn with a constant perseverance and application?
> 2. "Is it not delightful to have friends coming from distant quarters?
> 3. "Is he not a man of complete virtue, who feels no discomposure though men may take no note of him?"

Notice what comes into view at the outset of the *Analects*: a "disquisition" on pleasure and pain—on what provides pleasure, on what should *not* be painful. First of all in the *Analects*, in fact, is an observation about the pleasure of learning. Thus, there *are* things to be learned, and the human being is capable of learning them. We recall, by comparison, the confession of ignorance in the opening words of the dialogue with which the study of Plato traditionally begins, "How you, men of Athens, have been affected by my accusers, I do not know."[31]

We recall as well the Socratic insistence upon an awareness of ignorance as being one mark of a truly wise man. The emphasis does seem different in the *Analects*: there *are* things to be learned and Confucius is in a position to teach them to men of ability who want to learn. What are the learnable things? *That* may be the key question of the *Analects*. The learnable things—the things which may be learned *and which may be worth learning*—seem to bear directly upon how one should conduct oneself. (Chapter 2 of book I proceeds immediately to the desirability of "filial piety and fraternal submission.") However that may be, it seems to be recognized from the outset of Confucian thought that there is pleasure in learning. And, *we* would add, only the truly knowable can be learned; only that can provide us genuine pleasure. Something of this may be detected in book II, chapter 17 of the *Analects*: "The Master said, 'Yu, shall I teach you what knowledge is? When you know a thing, to hold that you know it; and when you do not know a thing, to allow that you do not know it—this is knowledge.'"[32]

We also notice, upon returning to chapter 1 of book I, that the orientation at the outset of the *Analects* seems self-centered. (I have several times said "outset," even though it does appear that things are somehow "in progress": we come on in the middle of things, with no introduction of "characters," no background information. In this we are reminded of some of the Platonic dialogues.) Is it not assumed that friends are good to have, and that they can live far off? What is good about the visits of friends? Do they add to what one learns? Does this, too, indicate what there is to be learned? It does seem proper, perhaps even necessary, to travel a lot: friends (and they are called that here, despite prolonged or distant separation?) are expected to go to one another, thus to give pleasure to one another, to enjoy telling each other what has been happening. Is the coming of such friends recognition enough for the truly virtuous man?[33]

Perhaps it should be added that this opening chapter may indicate that the entire *Analects*, too, is essentially learnable. Does this also mean that the text is so organized as to make sense? It depends upon whether the truly learnable things are only those shaped by reason, in which principles control. What comes with friends from afar? Perhaps reports on experiences—that is, reports on things happening elsewhere, not demonstrations which have been worked out. If knowledge is primarily dependent upon the latter type of intellectual activity, travel may not be needed; it may even interfere with a steady investigation into the things that are.

We thus return to the question: What are the learnable things? I have called this perhaps the key question of the *Analects*. I should now qualify what I have said. This may well be the key question *for us* in our examination of the *Analects*. Or rather, the key question, at least here, may truly be whether the author of the *Analects* (the editor, say, who understood it all and put it together?) recognizes this as the key question: What are the learnable things?

So much then for our first extended exercise in exegesis.

V.

Consider now what can be said about book I, chapter 15: something which should help us recognize that Confucian thought can be most subtle.

This chapter of the *Analects* reads:[34]

> 1. Tsze-kung said, "What do you pronounce concerning the poor man who yet does not flatter, and the rich man who is not proud?" The Master replied, "They will do; but they are not equal to him who, though poor, is yet cheerful, and to him who, though rich, loves the rules of propriety."
>
> 2. Tsze-kung replied, "It is said in the Book of Poetry, 'As you cut and then file, as you carve and then polish.' The meaning is the same, I apprehend, as that which you have just expressed."
>
> 3. The Master said, "With one like Ts'ze [Tsze-kung], I can begin to talk about the odes. I told him one point, and he knew its proper sequence."

We start here with a recognition of the existence of the rich and the poor. The problems of the rich and the poor, including the problem of the relation of rich and poor to one another, are always with us, whether the decisive wealth is gold or political power or physical aptitudes. How does one deal with such problems? And how does one speak about how one deals with such problems? The Confucian answer seems to be that one should speak discreetly, so that the truly privileged class which emerges can be both dutiful and self-perpetuating. But I anticipate my analysis of this passage.

We see here the tendencies to which human beings are prone in varying circumstances.[35] It is most likely (that is, unless corrected and guarded against) that the poor *will* flatter and the rich *will* be proud (Waley: "will swagger"). It is something of an accomplishment if the poor do not flatter and if the rich do not swagger. But it would be even better (but unusual, it seems) for the poor to be cheerful, for the rich to observe rituals carefully, to respect the propriety reflected in such rituals.[36] The poor man does tend to feel vulnerable. He needs all the help he can get; he very much depends upon rituals; *he* does not need to be encouraged to observe them. (In fact, one might even suspect that ritual observance fits in with the marked tendency of the poor to flatter. Do we go too far if we suggest that Confucius hinted at this?)

The rich man, on the other hand, tends to feel invulnerable. Money, or power, shields him from many of the vicissitudes of life. He can hire grocers and doctors and guards. He does not have to be encouraged to be cheerful, to enjoy himself; nor does he ordinarily need whatever it is that many believe ritual to promise mankind.[37] It is useful, then, if the rich man should be obliged to flatter *someone*, if he should be made aware of his own limitations and vulnerability as a human being, and if he should be thereby restrained in the exercise of his power.

A query: Does Confucius himself flatter when he partakes in ritual? Or is this for him primarily a way of teaching, and thereby of restraining, others?[38] This points to a major question running through the texts of the Confucian tradition, a question which we can do no more than touch upon here: What are man's innate inclinations? Do improper desires have to be suppressed? Or does an innate goodness have to be liberated (or protected)?[39]

These Confucian observations about the rich and the poor are part of a "hard headed" approach to social relations, an approach evident throughout the *Analects*. This approach is to be contrasted to both "idealism," which can turn into sentimentality, and "cynicism," which some might call "realism" but which can also mean "nihilism." Idealism can fail to recognize how things are and are always likely to be. This can lead to resentment because of disappointed expectations, and that in turn can lead to anger and upheaval. What I have called cynicism fails to recognize the partial amelioration which is sometimes possible in human relations. Such failure can lead in turn to malaise, spiritedlessness, and disintegration, perhaps eventually to tyranny as an attempt to return to a healthier (natural) condition of life.[40]

I should add that although the rich and the poor—each group with its special failings—will always be with us, that need not mean that they cannot be improved, each group in its own way. I should also add that Confucius elsewhere counsels rulers on what they should do about the poor. He recognizes, that is, that there is a limit to exhortations to cheerfulness: impoverished people *can* become desperate.[41]

All this reminds Tsze-kung of an old poem: he sees what Confucius has just said as an application of something in that poem, a poem which they may have discussed on another occasion.[42] It is significant that there *is* recourse to an old poem. What Confucius is saying fits in with, *or can be made to fit in with*, ancient authority. This shows the attentive Chinese reader familiar with his heritage how well-established poems can be reinterpreted in the light of Confucian thought, how they can be used to advantage by a man such as Confucius. One may even suspect that Confucius deliberately made things which were somewhat new with him seem much older than they were.[43]

Consider the parallels between the old poem and the Confucian observation. These are raw materials to be worked on. Men are always in particular circumstances, sometimes in critical circumstances such as poverty or wealth. The raw materials must be cut and filed, must be carved and polished.[44] The parallel here extends to the assumption that there *are* two kinds of materials and hence two refining processes. Is not the first process (cut and file) cruder than the second (carve and polish)? The poor are mentioned first; they can be cut and filed down. The rich can be carved and polished. This suggests that a tougher piece can be made of the poor, a more exquisite piece of the rich? Such is indicated in the sequence in the poem as well: on the one hand, metal, on the other, jade.[45]

But notice: is there not evident in all this a third kind of man as well—the man who cuts and files, the man who carves and polishes? Such a man is neither rich nor poor. He is "above it all"? He knows how to handle such matters. He knows what a Confucian does about the position and duties of the third kind of man.[46] In a sense, he is rich, but only in that which is truly worth having—not gold or power or jade, but rather knowledge of what human beings are like and how they should conduct themselves. Some might be inclined to call this attitude "philosophical." Would they be rich in so doing?

The third part of this chapter confirms what we have heard, that Confucius's style can be both allusive and illusory; he often does no more than point to his opinions, and to the connections among the things which have been mentioned. All this implies that the truth is hard to come by, that one has to work for it; that great care is needed; that it may even be a disservice, both to the learner and to the community, if things are spelled out fully; that a sense of self-restraint is called for on the part of those whom we would today call intellectuals.[47]

In any event, fruitful inquiry depends, Confucius indicates, upon disciplined conduct. Stability is thereby promoted, and an atmosphere of care and of responsible special privilege is created. It is evident that much is always left concealed, that much is left unsaid. Does not this reflect an old-fashioned understanding of the relation between reason and community? If this is so, can philosophy be far behind?

VI.

Let us now lighten the atmosphere a little. Our next exercise in exegesis permits us to see, among other things, one form a poor man's flattery can take.

Book II, chapter 24 of the *Analects* reads:[48]

> 1. The Master said, "For a man to sacrifice to a spirit which does not belong to him is flattery.
> 2. "To see what is right and not to do it is want of courage."

Where is the flattery (Waley: "presumption") here? Who is flattered? The now living descendants of the spirit sacrificed to, it seems. Why is this flattery? Because one may say, by sacrificing to another's spirit, "Your ancestor was a remarkable man. I wish he were mine." Or, perhaps one says, "You are so remarkable that I adopt your ancestor." (This is to be distinguished from public sacrifices, such as those to a George Washington or an Abraham Lincoln.) Might not even we, in this more permissive age, regard such behavior as troublesome, or at least as questionable, this appropriation by one man of another's ancestor? After all, what are genealogical societies for, if not to keep such matters in order? Even so, Confucius does seem to make more than we would today of sacrifices, of mourning, and of rituals.[49] We will return to the significance of this. It suffices to say at this point that respect for the ancestral contributes to continuity from one generation to another and thus promotes stability.[50]

The two sections of this *Analects* chapter could well have been put in separate chapters. That is, adjoining chapters in the *Analects* often have as much, and as little, obvious connection with one another as do the two sections in this chapter. So, to join these two is to indicate how chapters might be connected. I have found when I have tried to connect chapters in various books of the *Analects*—to work out a sequence—that it can be done in a plausible way, that there is a sense to that part of the whole.[51] I suspect, although, as I have indicated, most scholars do not, that the same might well be done with the *Analects* as a whole *if* the text is reasonably close to the condition in which it was put by a perceptive editor in antiquity. What one has to do—and such an attempt would require much more space than is available here—is to work out what might be called the suppressed transitions.[52]

What is the connection between the two sections of chapter 24 of book II? Is not flattery a kind of cowardice, a refusal to live with or face up to the facts? Is not such flattery, such ancestor sacrifice, a taking for one's own of what belongs to another, and hence an injustice?[53] In neither case—either that of flattery or that of cowardice—does one do what is appropriate, what is expected. In neither case does one act justly.

Something more should be said about all this, but in doing so we must speak from the Socratic perspective, which may well be a higher perspective. Who would be flattered by such appropriation by another of one's ancestor? A vain man? We can imagine this in a Molière play. Try also to imagine the response of a Socratic to such an episode. That is, we must see what Confucius sees—and what he may not see. Is sacrifice for Confucius too serious a matter to provide an occasion for amusement? It seems that the social order very much depends, for him, upon such things.[54] Thus, one can imagine a Homeric character protesting as Confucius does against the misappropriation of an ancestor, but not Socrates. When one asks how Socrates would respond, one notices how sober Confucius is (despite his usual sense of humor).[55] Does he not take everyday morality more seriously than does Socrates? Does he not restrain himself, more than does Socrates, from lifting the veil and playfully exposing for inspection the things that human beings take so seriously?[56]

But *is* there not something rather amusing about the flatterer's conduct? We might even take pleasure in learning about it. Does this indicate, however, our corruption? That is, do we make too much of learning? Even so, this points to a problem, from the Socratic perspective, with the second section of this *Analects* chapter: cowardice is not distinguished from injustice. In fact, may not all misbehavior be reduced to cowardice by this Confucian approach? This would fail to distinguish among the vices as they "really" are (as, for instance, Aristotle presents them).[57] Yet it does not reduce the vices to the one cause of which Plato's Socrates so often speaks as fundamental, which is ignorance. Knowledge does not seem to be, at least in Confucius's public teaching, the critical thing for virtuous activity, but rather the will. Confucius seems to say that for most practical purposes, the good is known by all. The only question is likely to be with respect to one's willingness to do what is called for. If the will is critical, then courage—at least, moral courage–can become the most important virtue.[58]

We thus see where the fundamental difference, rooted ultimately in the status of knowledge (what it is to know and what is knowable), may lie between classical political philosophy and Confucian thought.

VII.

Chapter 25 of book XI seems to be the longest chapter in the *Analects*. I will deal with it relatively briefly. It reads:[59]

1. Tsze-lu, Tsang Hsi, Zan Yu, and Kung-hsi Hwa were sitting by the Master.

2. He said to them, "Though I am a day or so older than you, do not think of that.

3. "From day to day you are saying, 'We are not known.' If some ruler were to know you, what would you like to do?"

4. Tsze-lu hastily and lightly replied, "Suppose the case of a State of ten thousand chariots; let it be straitened between other large States; let it be suffering from invading armies; and to this let there be added a famine in [wheat] and in all vegetables—if I were entrusted with the government of it, in three years' time I could make the people to be bold, and to recognize the rules of righteous conduct." The Master smiled at him.

5. Turning to Yen Yu [Zan Yu], he said, "Ch'iu, what are your wishes?" Ch'iu replied, "Suppose a State of sixty or seventy li square, or one of fifty or sixty, and let

me have the government of it—in three years' time, I could make plenty to abound among the people. As to teaching them the rules of propriety, and music, I must wait for the rise of a superior man to do that."

6. "What are your wishes, Ch'ih," said the Master next to Kung-hsi Hwa. Ch'ih replied, "I do not say that my ability extends to these things, but I should wish to learn them. At the services of the ancestral temple, and at the audiences of the princes with the sovereign, I should like, dressed in the dark square-made robe and the black linen cap, to act as a small assistant."

7. Last of all, the Master asked Tsang Hsi, "Tien, what are your wishes?" Tien, pausing as he was playing on his lute, while it was yet twanging, laid the instrument aside, and rose. "My wishes," he said, "are different from the cherished purposes of these three gentlemen." "What harm is there in that?" said the Master; "do you also, as well as they, speak out your wishes." Tien then said, "In this, the last month of spring, with the dress of the season all complete, along with five or six young men who have assumed the cap, and six or seven boys, I would wash in the Yi, enjoy the breeze among the rain altars, and return home singing." The Master heaved a sigh and said, "I give my approval to Tien."[60]

8. The three others having gone out, Tsang Hsi remained behind, and said, "What do you think of the words of these three friends?" The Master replied, "They simply told each one his wishes."

9. Hsi pursued, "Master, why did you smile at Yu?"

10. He was answered, "The management of a State demands the rules of propriety. His words were not humble; therefore I smiled at him."

11. Hsi again said, "But was it not a State which Ch'iu proposed for himself?" The reply was, "Yes; did you ever see a territory of sixty or seventy li, or one of fifty or sixty, which was not a State?"

12. Once more, Hsi inquired, "And was it not a State which Ch'ih proposed for himself?" The Master again replied, "Yes; who but princes have to do with ancestral temples, and with audiences but the sovereign? If Ch'ih were to be a small assistant in these services, who could be a great one?"[61]

Four men speak to Confucius. I will identify them by the order in which they are first named. One commentator suggests that they are listed thus according to age, with the oldest first. It would be useful, perhaps even necessary for the full teaching of this *Analects* chapter, to *know* that. This does seem likely. Certainly, the four men are initially named, probably according to some principle, in an order different from their speaking order.

Number One presumes to speak "hastily and lightly" in response to Confucius's general invitation. It is almost as if he wants to revive the prerogatives of age which Confucius has just set aside. The others are called on by Confucius. Confucius knows what he is doing; he saves the best for the last. (But perhaps Number One's attempted "revival" of the prerogatives of age had some effect: once Number Two is skipped over, Number Three and Number Four *are* called upon in the "proper" order.) Number Two, the last in the order of speaking, evidently wanted to continue with his music and to observe the other three. The others all wanted to assert themselves, it turned out. But were they honest with themselves about what they wanted?

Is Number Two (the final speaker) the only one who wondered at Confucius's smile? Certainly, he is the only one who remained behind to learn more. The smile is a subtle way of rebuking Number One and of teaching Number Two and perhaps the others. When does Confucius smile at us also?

Number One's desires and consequent happiness depends upon his country's miseries.[62] He needs war and famine to do his best; he answers hastily; he is a vigorous fellow; he makes a good deal of physical courage which, it is evident elsewhere in the *Analects*, is far from sufficient. Thus, we see that "personality" and "opinions" go together; one's character is likely to be revealed by the desires one expresses.[63]

Number Three does not posit the miseries that Number One does—but perhaps he also needs to find his country not at its best: for then he, too, could make it prosperous. He recognizes that ritual is needed, but he cannot provide it himself. He knows that a better man is needed for that. There is no immediate response to this by Confucius. Perhaps Number Three had spotted Confucius's smile as well and thereby recognized a problem. That is, the smile triggers off a chain reaction.

Number Four (the reaction continues) disparages himself as the required better man. In fact, he so disparages himself as to ask for a "subordinate" assignment. He also acknowledges the importance of ritual, in which he will be an assistant. He does not know enough, perhaps, to do more than that. Even so, we later learn, it seems that his rank or station in life is too high for him to be a subordinate in the setting he posits for himself. That is, he is really asking for much the same as Number One and Number Three, but he seems to have learned caution from Confucius's responses to them.

Number Two, it seems, would pursue a more harmonious course. He, the final speaker, knows what is appropriate to the seasons. He limits his personal desires. Is this the proper way to get or to hold power? One shows thereby that one knows what one is doing—and how men are shaped. Would Number Two rule at all? Would he rule the young men and the boys in the ritual he describes? If not, there may be no rule at all by him. And yet, he may well be the "superior man" deferred to by Number Three, the man who can teach others the principles of propriety and music. Has Number Two astutely shown his qualifications for the recognition that Number Three is willing to concede?

But, it should be added, even Number Two is not as astute as Confucius, for Number Two did not recognize fully the royal desires of the other three. I restate what has happened: Number One was explicit in his royal ambition (he relies on arms only, and there are no practical limits for him); Number Three asked for something big enough to require a ruler (he wants to rule, but he may somewhat recognize his limits); Number Four (responding in his own way to what Number Three had said about the principles of propriety?) asked for a ritual role in such a small place as to make him in effect the chief man. (He somewhat recognizes his limitations also, even as he pretends he does not want to rule.) Did only Number Two, who provided a musical accompaniment to all this, show himself fit to rule? Does he thus sense his superiority? And, throughout all this, does not Confucius recognize his own superiority? And do not others also?[64]

For whose sake is this exhibition of gradations elicited by Confucius? For Number Two or for anyone who may hear of this conversation? Does not Confucius expect Number Two to stay behind and to talk further with him? Is Number Two being told, in effect, that he is a fit ruler? Certainly Number Two (who can distinguish himself from "these three friends") is fit to be talked to intimately.

Certainly, also, it is assumed throughout the *Analects* that one who is fit to rule should do so. The life of practice, it would seem, would be the highest. Confucius, it is indicated in various places, wanted to rule. He is not "merely" a theoretical man; he wants to shape regimes, and that is presupposed here.[65]

In any event, we see how Confucius interprets what people say, and this should alert us as to what Confucius reveals to others and to us and how that too is in need of interpretation.[66]

We may also wonder, about all this, whether there is, somehow showing through, an editor superior even to Confucius. Is that superior editor the embodiment of Reason itself—something which would be philosophical in its inclinations, whatever many have been the case of Confucius himself? Dare we suggest, that is, that Confucius himself was not a philosopher but that one of his editors might have been disposed in that direction?[67]

However that may be, we do notice that this *Analects* chapter ends on an ironic note. We see at its beginning that if one is properly respectful—that is, before one's elders—one moderates one's desires, even if only in their expression. Then, as the conversation develops, we see that Confucius implicitly moderates their desires further—but on a better basis than respect for age. We also notice that the man who seems to be oldest among the four happens to be the least restrained. That is, age does not suffice, however useful it may be to encourage, as Confucius does again and again encourage, a respect for age.

May not the same be said of the related respect, in Confucian thought, for ritual?[68] Confucius "liberates" these four men in order to "work" on them.[69] Does not his "working" of the four men suggest what moderation and self-restraint, as well as rituals and respect for the customary, serve? Whom does it show all this? Perhaps to Number Two—and certainly to those who read the *Analects* carefully.

It should be noticed that Number Two was the only one of the four who is reported to have risen when he responded to Confucius: *he* cannot forget that Confucius does remain "a day or so older" than they are. Is not Number Two a natural ruler in that he truly knows what is "altogether fitting and proper"?[70]

VIII.

Let us now turn to book XV, chapter 32:

> 1. The Master said, "When a man's knowledge is sufficient to attain, and his virtue is not sufficient to enable him to hold, whatever he may have gained, he will lose again.
> 2. "When his knowledge is sufficient to attain, and he has virtue enough to hold fast, if he cannot govern with dignity, the people will not respect him.
> 3. "When his knowledge is sufficient to attain, and he has virtue enough to hold fast; when he governs also with dignity, yet if he try to move the people contrary to the rules of propriety—full excellence is not reached."

Waley suggests that the placement here of ritual (or the rules of propriety) "on a pinnacle far above Goodness" (or virtue) is "certainly one of the later additions to the book."[71] I would agree with Waley, on the basis of what we have just seen in our discussion of book XI, chapter 25, that ritual is not for Confucius the very highest thing. But more interesting for our immediate purposes, and regardless of what might have been added long after Confucius, is the distinction made here among "knowledge," "virtue," "dignity," and "ritual." We again see that knowledge is not, according to Confucian opinion, the ultimate cause of virtue.[72]

Consider also chapter 18 of book VI, where Confucius is reported to have said, "They who know the truth are not equal to those who love it, and they who love it are not equal to those who delight in it." Waley suggests that for "truth" one should read "the Way."[73] But however this is read, it is significant for our purposes that there is a distinction made between knowing, on the one hand, and loving or delighting in the truth (or the Way), on the other. In short, knowing is not enough. Is this not substantially the popular understanding, down to our day? The will is critical.[74] But the philosopher would be inclined to ask, "How well does one 'know the truth'—truly know it—if one is not moved to delight in it, and to live in accordance with it?"[75]

IX.

Our next exercise in exegesis deals with what seems to be the second longest chapter in the *Analects*, book XVI, chapter 1. This chapter, which is made of thirteen sections in the Legge translation, reads:

1. The head of the Chi family was going to attack Chwan-yu.
2. Zan Yu and Chi-lu had an interview with Confucius, and said, "Our chief, Chi, is going to commence operations against Chwan-yu."
3. Confucius said, "Ch'iu [Zan Yu], is it not you who are at fault here?
4. "Now, in regard to Chwan-yu, long ago a former king appointed its ruler to preside over the sacrifices to the eastern Mang; moreover, it is in the midst of the territory of our State; and its ruler is a minister in direct connection with the sovereign—What has your chief to do with attacking it?"
5. Zan Yu said, "Our master wishes the thing; neither of us two ministers wishes it."
6. Confucius said, "Ch'iu, there are the words of Chau Zan, 'When he can put forth his ability, he takes his place in the ranks of office; when he finds himself unable to do so, he retires from it. How can he be used as a guide to a blind man, who does not support him when tottering, nor raise him up when fallen?'
7. "And further, you speak wrongly. When a tiger or rhinoceros escapes from his cage; when a tortoise or piece of jade is injured in its repository—whose is the fault?"
8. Zan Yu said, "But at present, Chwan-yu is strong and near to Pi; if our chief do not now take it, it will hereafter be a sorrow to his descendants."
9. Confucius said, "Ch'iu, the superior man hates that declining to say, 'I want such and such a thing,' and framing explanations for his conduct.
10. "I have heard that rulers of States and chiefs of families are not troubled lest their people should be few, but are troubled lest they should not keep their several places; that they are not troubled with fears of poverty, but are troubled with fears of a want of contented repose among the people in their several places. For when the people keep their several places, there will be no poverty; when harmony prevails, there will be no scarcity of people; and when there is such a contented repose, there will be no rebellious upsettings.
11. "So it is. Therefore, if remoter people are not submissive, all the influences of civil culture and virtue are to be cultivated to attract them to be so; and when they have been so attracted, they must be made contented and tranquil.
12. "Now, here are you, Yu [Chi-lu] and Ch'iu [Zan Yu], assisting your chief. Remoter people are not submissive, and with your help, he cannot attract them to him. In his own territory there are divisions and downfalls, leavings and separations, and, with your help, he cannot preserve it.
13. "And yet he is planning these hostile movements within the State. I am afraid that the sorrow of the Chi-sun family will not be on account of Chwan-yu, but will be found within the screen of his own court."

We make a preliminary examination of this *Analects* chapter, section by section ("the narrator" refers to the authoritative Chinese editor of this text in antiquity):

1. Why have the ministers come to Confucius? Are they uncertain? Troubled? Curious? We are told by the narrator—this is our point of departure—that there was indeed an attack imminent. The narrator wants us to know that. It should help us understand the subsequent exchanges.

2. A guarded report is made to Confucius about what is going to happen: "Our chief, Chi, is going to commence operations. "A euphemism is used: not "attack," but "commence operations." This suggests the ministers' awareness of the dubiousness of their ruler's impending action.

3. Confucius's response is not euphemistic. His way of talking here is quite different from theirs. He tacitly repudiates their approach. He speaks frankly and brutally—and he selects out one man (the elder or more active or senior minister?) as the one to be addressed, even though both had reported to him at the outset. He is precise about where the fault lies.[76]

4. Confucius then explains why what they plan to do is a crime. We notice that he uses the word *attack*, just as had the narrator at the very beginning. Confucius puts his emphasis on the ritual duties involved and on legal (historic?) obligations. In addition, "feudal" relations, of a privileged character, seem to be referred to. Thus, Confucius seems to object on the basis of the status quo. Does he suspect that there are no good reasons for what is planned, since the ministers began by disguising the impending attack as they did? Or is it that Confucius (and the ancient Chinese reader) knew the facts—the geography, history, etc.—which make it clear that the attack would be improper, especially if sacrilegious or in the nature of a civil war?

5. The minister who had been singled out concedes Confucius's criticism. He tries to shift the blame to his ruler; or, failing that, he tries to shift part of the blame to his companion minister. (He himself did not get to be a minister for nothing? Is not the ruler being criticized as well throughout, but with the appropriate outward forms of respect preserved?[77])

6. Confucius again addresses the senior minister. There is a tacit rebuke: Confucius will not permit him to shift the blame to the ruler or to the other minister, relying first on a quotation from someone else. That is, Confucius shares the task of criticism: *he* succeeds in sharing, something which the senior minister had not done. This, Confucius suggests, is how to share: attach yourself to a wise man. (Is not Confucius himself available? And he, unlike Socrates, it should again be noted, very much wanted to share in the political life of whatever community he happened to be in. Also, unlike Socrates, he evidently liked, or at least was willing, to travel.) This quotation from Chau Zan also shows that Confucius's criticism of the ministers is based on an old teaching: that is, the ministers should have known better even before this conversation with Confucius. Thus, Confucius is, in effect, citing *his* superior—a wise man. He points to the alternative of resigning when an improper course is

being pursued by one's nominal superior. It is evidently not clear in the manuscripts whether the last sentence of this section is part of the Chau Zan quotation or whether it is a homely example supplied by Confucius to bring the
ancient teaching closer to home.[78] In any event, the ministers' ruler is shown
as tottering, not strong, even though he is about to become an aggressor.

7. Confucius then makes the ruler into a wild animal, like a tiger or a rhinoceros, and then into something precious, like a tortoise or jade. Thus, however one regards the ruler, whether he is weak or fierce or precious or exalted,
there is a proper duty for the ministers. Confucius thereby forecloses various
excuses. The result is to make both ministers move closer to facing up to the
truth. (Is this intended to be the central teaching of the chapter?)

8. The senior minister now gives a justification for the aggression. National security, or at least the national interest, especially on behalf of future
generations, is invoked. A country's leaders must look ahead, just as Confucius had looked ahead and stripped the ministers of their defense. But what
they do not try to explain is why all this is a problem now. Why is a change
in policy now called for? Is the ministers' silence suspicious?

9. Confucius responds to the invocation of the national interest: You still
have not given a good reason. You should have resigned.

10. He then goes on to diagnose the trouble. There is indeed something
wrong in their country. National security is not the problem, nor is poverty, except the lack of harmony and proper sharing. (Has not Confucius already
shown them what is proper and what is improper sharing?)

11. Much more needs to be done with the long concluding speech by Confucius, which began in the ninth section of this *Analects* chapter, than I can
provide here. Has not everything which has gone before empowered Confucius to say what he does? One should consider, for instance, what authority
he relies upon here and what kind of argument. Certainly, he rules them by
directing them to look homeward—and inward—for correction. He argues
that if their country is well governed, other countries will want to join them;
there will be no need for aggression; there will then be no threat to their security. This kind of imperialism through virtue may be seen advocated again
and again in the *Analects*. To be well governed, it should be noticed, depends
not on the rule of law but on the rule by good men under law, including the
considerable customary law. It is significant for the political thought of Confucius that no limit is set on the proper size of a community. This, too, reminds us of differences from classical political philosophy.

12. Confucius now addresses both ministers directly. Is the junior minister
being urged to do more, perhaps even to supplant his colleague? (Not only is
the junior minister addressed by name for the first time, but his name is put
before that of his companion minister.) However that may be, the fundamen-

tal character of the country is not due just to what is happening at the moment. Both ministers are told either to resign or to attempt to reform the ruler of their country. (Had the junior minister, if he *is* junior, been troubled enough to induce his senior colleague to consult Confucius? Otherwise, the senior minister, if sufficiently troubled, would have come to Confucius alone? Here, as elsewhere in this chapter on Confucian thought, my own quite limited knowledge of Chinese things may manifest itself.)

13. Confucius concludes by addressing, in effect, the ruler of the country. Perhaps he is even suggesting—but in such a way that the ministers may convey, unawares, his message to the ruler[79]—that the ruler should move against his ministers rather than against the proposed enemy. The ruler is asked to face up to his true problem. It is indicated that genuine security depends upon one's own character and hence upon the effects of one's character on others. Is it not assumed, here and elsewhere in the *Analects*, that the truth about regimes is fairly evident, and people generally know whose rule is good and whose is not, and that the consequences of good and bad rule are fairly predictable? It should be noticed, by the way, that this emphasis upon the ruler's character may be one of the reasons why the size of the country should not matter. Did Confucius believe that there is no innate limit to the extension of the institutions which reflect the appropriate character?[80]

We are left to wonder what happens after this conversation.[81] If the character of a ruler is as decisive as Confucius argues, here and elsewhere, and if Confucius rules the ministers, then there should have been peace as a result of this conversation. But does not the Confucian intervention depend, for its effectiveness, upon opportunity? Confucius, after all, is not their ruler. Perhaps the most he can do is to induce these ministers to resign—and then what would happen? Perhaps we are intended to recognize that even the very best advice cannot suffice, that much also depends upon the occasion if political evil is to be prevented. But one does not need "the right occasion" in order to behave oneself personally.

More needs to be said about what the silent Chi-lu may have thought about throughout this conversation—and afterward.[82]

X.

Our final passage for exegesis is chapter 3 of book XX, the final chapter in the *Analects* (at least final in the edition that has come down to us). It reads:[83]

1. The Master said, "Without recognizing the ordinances of Heaven, it is impossible to be a superior man.

2. "Without an acquaintance with the rules of propriety, it is impossible for the character to be established.

3. "Without knowing the force of words, it is impossible to know men."

One is thus directed, in the conclusion of the *Analects*, to look at heaven, at "the rules of propriety" (or "rites," in Waley) and at the words of men. Is heaven the supposed source of rituals, which are set forth in words? And is not all this with a view to action? The *Analects* does seem to end on a more or less practical note. Once again, one is obliged to wonder: Do the rituals come from heaven? Or from men's words alone–with a useful attribution of them to heaven? Do the rituals matter? Certainly, the political philosopher does not stress as Confucius does the importance either of ritual or even of courage in the life of a community.[84]

Perhaps ritual is for many, as we have seen, an assurance, if not a source, of order in the cosmos. Adherence to long-established rites or manners by a ruler means considerable self-restraint on his part. One recalls the swaggering rich man in book I, chapter 15. Both tyranny and anarchy are made less likely if there should be scrupulous regard for *any* well-established and humane ritual. This is aside from the validity of the authority for such rituals: it may be even better if that authority is concealed or obscure and hence less vulnerable to examination. Are not rituals most useful if they are not obviously utilitarian in purpose? If a ritual makes some sense, one may more easily feel entitled to adjust it, to rationalize changes in it to suit one's passions, or otherwise to question and thus to undermine it, all in the name of serving its evident utilitarian purpose. Does Confucius in the *Analects*, therefore, speak only covertly about the authority and purpose of ritual? Certainly, he indicates that it is better not to make the purpose an issue.[85] Certainly, also, both the supernatural and the possibility of life after death are muted throughout the *Analects*.[86]

Be all this as it may, Confucius seems to say, rituals help keep things working and help keep men humane. Does his silence about the origins reflect a suspicion, to say the least, that rituals are man-made? Did he indicate that it is not useful to look into such matters because it could be subversive of public order to do so? Or because there is little to be learned about the origins anyway?

In short, Confucius seems to anticipate the position of classical political philosophy in that he endorses moderation in public discourses about these matters.[87]

XI.

If we are to practice what both Confucius and classical political philosophy preach, should not moderation be displayed here also? A series of exegeses, such as we have just been through, is, I gather, in the Confucian tradition. There is, Confucius might add, no need for generalization: general observations are not likely to be anchored sufficiently to particulars to be both instructive and safe; enough has been said to suggest both that the *Analects is* a text worth reading and how to begin to read it. But since we are not likely to be dealing here with readers able to proceed on their own in the Confucian manner, some general observations should perhaps be ventured.

What remains to be done, then, is both much and little; it is little in that it would only spell out, in general terms, various of the points which have been touched upon or implied in what has already been said here; it is much in that it would take considerable space to do "only" that. Perhaps I can proceed in a Confucian manner, compressing in a few pages what could be a quite extended discourse—and then leave it to my readers to develop these matters further than I do here.

The family unit is, in much of Confucian thought, critical to the ordering of the community. An emphasis upon the family reinforces continuity and promises stability. But every family depends upon various unexamined—and, for the health of the family, unexaminable—premises. Does Confucius recognize the constant tension and the potential conflict between the family and the city, and between both of them and any reliance on serious questioning?[88] If the family *is* the critical association, then the size of the city or country may indeed not matter. One should, Confucius indicates, respect one's own, but that "own" can be primarily the family unit, which is established and reinforced by various age-old rituals, independent of obvious political concerns.[89]

One's place in the family is critical: one's age or gender is critical. It matters whether one is a parent or a child, a father or a mother, an older or a younger brother. Parents are dominant, of course, but they, in turn, are held in check by duties to their ancestors. Philosophy, on the other hand, almost inevitably calls such things into question: public order tends to be sacrificed thereby to serious inquiry.[90]

Another way of putting all this is the following: One can ask about the Confucian doctrine, "Where are books VI-X?" That is, much of what *is* in the *Analects* may be found in the first five books of Aristotle's *Nicomachean Ethics.*[91] But where are the last five books of the *Ethics*, in which the intellectual virtues are examined and in which the superiority of the contemplative life is ratified?[92]

Socrates was very much interested in questions about the origins of things—that is, about the nature of things—while rituals usually present themselves as sufficient accounts of such matters. It is in the absence of an explicit concern about nature—the absence of an informed awareness of what "the natural" means—which may be most revealing about Confucian thought.

Without such an awareness and concern, genuine philosophy is hardly likely to emerge. Nor can there be a systematic teaching about the best possible regime or about what we know as natural right. The implied "theoria" of Confucian thought seems to rest upon a radical utilitarianism: a tradition is accepted as "the given," and that tradition, rather than nature, is then emphasized by Confucius.[93]

XII.

Nature may be the key term, the term which educated Westerners versed in the Chinese language should consider carefully for us in studying the Confucian texts.[94] Why did not Confucius address himself explicitly to the "big questions" about the nature of things?[95]

Philosophy does shake things up, so that one can get a better look at them. Confucius, on the other hand, may have been philanthropic in his cautiousness about inquiry for its own sake. He may not have thought it good for human beings to be thus diverted. We are familiar with the concern evident here.[96]

In addition, Confucius may have seen such an inquiry as ultimately fruitless and even harmful, as something which could not help but lead to error and frustration. Consider how Ezra Pound, in the introduction to his idiosyncratic edition of the *Analects*, assesses our philosophical tradition: "The study of the Confucian philosophy is of greater profit than that of the Greek because no time is wasted in idle discussion of errors. Aristotle gives, we may say, 90% of his time to errors."[97] We need only remember what a Platonic dialogue is like in order to understand what it was that misled Mr. Pound.

It does seem sometimes that little is accomplished in most of the dialogues but the repudiation, once again, of some error. After an error has been "authoritatively" repudiated by someone, why *should* we be encouraged to return again and again to its reconsideration? One familiar answer is that various fundamental questions are more knowable than their answers—and that the alternative to such questioning is to live an unexamined life which is hardly worth living.[98] But, the public-spirited Confucius might reply, this is but the most subtle and the most dangerous instance of swaggering by the rich. It is enough, and hard enough, to help most people live decent lives; that is the most one can hope for in most circumstances.

And, one also suspects, Confucius might have doubted that any answers, or for that matter any useful reformulations of questions, would be forthcoming if they had not yet come out of the long Chinese history prior to him. Thus, he might have believed, history suffices to suggest what "works" and what does not; it can help one to establish or to preserve a decent regime. This seems to have been the use to which Confucius put the history of his country.

Does it not take a new people, a presumptuous people, to look at fundamental questions afresh and to take them seriously again—or for the first time? Solon's ancient and hence worldly wise (Chinese-like?) Egyptian observed that the Greeks were always like children; Thucydides' Corinthians could complain of the Athenians that they were constantly in motion, taking no rest themselves and making sure no one else rested either.[99]

Dare we go one step further in our assessment of Confucius's curious reticence? Did he fear, and not without some justification, that if human beings insist upon raising fundamental questions, they will find themselves looking into the abyss—that they might indeed find answers, but not answers they can live with? Did Confucius glimpse the abyss which Friedrich Nietzsche, for example, found mankind suspended over? But being himself of a different temperament—a more cheerful and practical temperament—Confucius could prudently "step back"?[100]

Or perhaps Confucius simply said to himself, "This is the way human life is. There are many questions which are interesting but insoluble. So let's get on with the business of living, generation after generation. It is better for a community to have things settled roughly than it is to keep everything constantly in turmoil by trying to settle things perfectly or by trying to understand everything." And so there is the emphasis by him upon ritual and family and the established way. "Besides," he might have added, "most people can see, most of the time, when personal interest does not blind them, what proper conduct is."

Confucius does seem to say things like this here and there in the texts. Does he not, in this way, make some use of, even though he does not examine explicitly, what nature provides us? Nature thus manages to assert herself, *albeit in a somewhat limited manner*, through him.

Was Confucius correct to proceed as he did—to sacrifice, if he did, the intellectual virtues and the possibility, and challenge, of philosophy to the moral virtues and to domestic tranquility? The conditions for the emergence of genuine philosophy are rare and, we suspect, fleeting.

XIII.

Still, we have been taught to prize the truly human. It is significant that we can understand so much of what Confucius says. Rationality and humanity are reflected from the *Analects* across the ages, despite radically different customs and language. Should not that encourage us to believe, with classical philosophy, that there is indeed something natural—something independent of time, place, and circumstances—which governs mankind and which is worthy of serious and prolonged study?[101]

Would Confucius himself advise us against any extended study of his teachings? That is, he is not part of our own. He did teach that there is something presumptuous about sacrificing to a spirit which is not one's own. Would he not direct Americans to the Bible, to Shakespeare perhaps, and to the Declaration of Independence, the Constitution, and Lincoln?[102]

But we do study Confucius, in part in order to help us to understand what is natural in, and for, the human being, what the conditions for philosophy are, and are not, and perhaps even what the nature of nature is. A more mundane reason for studying Confucius should also be noticed: a study of him may be the best introduction to the character of the great Chinese people today just as the study of Dostoevsky may be the best introduction to the great Russian people today.

Our dedication in the West to inquiries into what has been thought and done elsewhere on the earth, as well as into what may be seen in the heavens above and below the earth—this daring, animating, and unsettling persistence—suggests that we may now be, for better and for worse, constitutionally unable to submit to an approach to the works of the mind which depends as much as Confucius's approach piously seems to do upon respect for what does happen to be one's own.

We have seen, in the course of examining various passages from the *Analects*, how Confucius interprets what people say—and this should alert us both to what Confucius himself says, to others and to us, and to what he may not dare to say or perhaps even to think. I again wonder whether there is involved in all this, showing through the text, an editor superior to Confucius, someone who depends upon the dispassionate reader to subject the text and Confucius himself to the most searching examination. It is that editor, after all, who has so arranged these recollections of Confucius as to have the opening and closing lines of the *Analects* quietly testify to the primacy of understanding in the affairs of human beings.[103]

I have already ventured to suggest that Confucius himself probably was not a philosopher but that one of his editors might have been more disposed than he could be toward a consideration of the fundamental questions which Confucius seems (almost as if by an instinct) to shy away from. But public manifestation, if not even private maturation, of a philosophical disposition may nevertheless have been inhibited even in such an editor by the pervasiveness and evident utility of Confucian piety.[104]

Notes

1. Plato, *Theaetetus* 173D–E. I remind readers that this discussion of Confucian thought was the first of the series on non-Western thought published by me in *The Great Ideas Today,* serving thereby as an introduction also to the half-dozen discussions that followed during that decade.

2. William T. De Bary and Ainslie T. Embree, *A Guide to the Oriental Classics* (New York: Columbia University Press, 1975), p. 120.

James Legge, the distinguished missionary-translator, seems to have been the deviser of the "Analects" title for a book which could also have been called "Collected Fragments" or "Digested Conversations." See *Confucian Analects, The Great Learning and the Doctrine of the Mean,* trans. James Legge (volume 1 of James Legge, ed., *The Chinese Classics* [Oxford: Clarendon Press, 1893]), p. 137n. I will be drawing, for the Legge notes, on the 1971 Dover Publications reprint of his 1893 edition. "There is not much doubt that *Lun Yu (Analects,* to use the English equivalent that Legge's translation has made so familiar) means 'Selected Sayings.'" *The Analects of Confucius,* trans. Arthur Waley (New York: Vintage Books, n.d.; originally published 1938), p. 21. Citations to the *Analects* will be by book and chapter (roman numerals and arabic numerals, respectively). See note 18 below. When page numbers are given by me for the Legge edition or for the Waley edition, the references are to editorial material.

I have found the following discussions to be useful: Herman L. Sinaiko, "The *Analects* of Confucius," in William T. De Bary, ed., *Approaches to the Oriental Classics* (New York: Columbia University Press, 1959); a subsequent unpublished lecture on Confucius by Mr. Sinaiko; Max Hamburger, "Aristotle and Confucius: A Comparison," *Journal of the History of Ideas,* vol. 20, p. 236 (April 1959); Kung-chuan Hsiao, *A History of Chinese Political Thought,* vol. 1 (Princeton, N.J.: Princeton University Press, 1978).

An earlier, shorter version of this chapter, and without these notes, was published in the *University of Chicago Magazine* (vol. 66, pp. 21–28 [1974]). (Unless otherwise indicated, all references to notes in any chapter in this collection are to the notes of that chapter.)

3. Legge does use "philosopher" at various places to designate Yu, Tsang shan, and Confucius himself. See, e.g., *Analects,* 1, 2, 4, 9, 12, 13; VIII, 3, 4, 5, 6, 7; IX, 2; XIV, 28; XIX, 16, 17, 19. See also Legge, *Analects,* pp. 2, 137 n.1, 138 n.2, 214 n. 20, 345 n. 13. "Sage" may be a better word in such places. See, e.g., *Analects,* IX, 6. I believe Waley usually uses "Master" where Legge uses "Philosopher."

4. "I will not here enter into the difficult question of how the dates (551–479 B.C.) later accepted as official were first arrived at." Waley, *Analects,* p. 16 n. 2. See also ibid., pp. 78–79. See, for a useful introduction to Confucius's life and works, Kung-chuan Hsiao, *A History of Chinese Political Thought,* vol. 1, pp. 79f., 86.

"The personal name of Master K'ung, or Confucius, was Ch'iu, and his formal name was Chung-ni." Ibid., p. 79. See note 35 below. Confucius's ancestry has been traced back by some to 2637 B.C. " The more moderate writers, however, content themselves with exhibiting his ancestry back to the commencement of the Chau dynasty, B.C. 1121." Legge, *Analects,* p. 56.

I have been told that there are alive today [1984] known direct lineal descendents of Confucius in the seventy-seventh generation.

5. Some even say that *none* of the sayings may be Confucius's. See Waley, *Analects*, p. 25. Some of the things attributed to him may even refer to events long after his death. See ibid., p. 30 n. 1. See also Plato, *Menexenus*.

6. See *Analects*, XVII, 19. See also Legge, *Analects*, pp. 3–4, 6–10, 15–16.

7. There are twenty books in the version of the *Analects* which has come down to us. Another (now lost) version had twenty-two books (that is, two in addition to the twenty we have). Still another version had twenty-one books (that is, with the present twentieth book divided into two books). See, on the organization of the *Analects*, notes 29 and 52 below. See also the text at notes 67 and 103 of this chapter.

8. See Plato, *Phaedrus* 274C et seq. (on the distortion in the living thought produced by writing) (*GBWW* [*Great Books of the Western World*], vol. 7, p. 138); Plato, *Seventh Letter* 344C (*GBWW*, vol. 7, p. 810). See also note 103 below.

9. "In an effort to understand nature, society, and man, Aristotle began where everyone should begin—with what he already knew in the light of his ordinary, commonplace experience. Beginning there, his thinking used notions that all of us possess, not because we were taught them in school, but because they are the common stock of human thought about anything and everything. We sometimes refer to these notions as our common sense about things. They are notions that we have formed as a result of the common experience we have in the course of our daily lives—experiences we have without any effort of inquiry on our part, experiences we all have simply because we are awake and conscious. In addition, these common notions are notions we are able to express in the common words we employ in everyday speech." Mortimer J. Adler, *Aristotle for Everybody* (New York: Macmillan, 1978), pp. xi–xii. "Aristotle's thinking *began* with common sense, but it did not *end* there. It went much further. It added to and surrounded common sense with insights and understandings that are not common at all. His understanding of things goes deeper than ours and sometimes soars higher. It is, in a word, *uncommon* common sense." Ibid., pp. xiii–xiv. See also ibid., pp. 165–67. See further on Aristotle, Leo Strauss, *The City and Man* (Chicago: Rand McNally, 1964), pp. 13f.

10. "Speaking generally, government is [not established by] device or cunning craftiness; human nature demands it. But in no other family of mankind is the characteristic so largely developed as in the Chinese. The love of order and quiet, and a willingness to submit to 'the powers that be,' eminently distinguish them. Foreign writers have often noticed this, and have attributed it to the influence of Confucius's doctrines as inculcating subordination; but it existed previous to his time. The character of the people moulded his system, more than it was moulded by it." Legge, *Analects*, p. 102. See notes 40, 77, 95, and 96 below.

11. See, on the commentaries made available, Legge, *Analects,* pp. 16f., 112f., 128f.; Waley, *Analects,* pp. 71f. See also note 29 below. Some of what I have just said about the circumstances in which Confucius found himself could be adapted to our discussion, in chapter 6 of this collection, to the advent and success of Muhammad.

12. "The Master [Confucius] said, 'The study of strange doctrines is injurious indeed!'" *Analects*, II, 16. Waley renders this chapter thus: "The Master said, 'He who sets to work upon a different strand destroys the whole fabric.'" See the text at note 102 of this chapter. See also note 104 below.

13. Of considerable interest, of course, are the discussions of Chinese thought by Montesquieu in *The Spirit of Laws* (*GBWW*, vol. 38) and by Hegel in *The Philosophy of History* (*GBWW*, vol. 46). Whether these thinkers attempted to understand the Chinese au-

thors as those authors understood themselves is another matter. Consider, as well, Eric Voegelin, *Order and History*, vol. 4 (Baton Rouge: Louisiana State University Press, 1974).

14. The specialness of the West—a specialness which may permit it and it alone truly to understand what has happened elsewhere—is suggested in a passage from a talk given at St. John's College:

> The most impressive alternative to philosophy in the life of Leo Strauss is summed up by the name of a city, Jerusalem, the holy city. What if the one thing most needful is not philosophic wisdom, but righteousness? This notion of the one thing most needful, Mr. Strauss argued, is not defensible if the world is not the creation of the just and loving God. Neither philosophy nor revealed religion, he argued, can refute one another; for, among other reasons, they disagree about the very principles or criteria of proof. . . . This mutual irrefutability and tension between philosophy and biblical revelation appeared to him to be the secret of the vitality of Western Civilization.

Laurence Berns, "Leo Strauss" *The College* (Annapolis, Md.: St. John's College, April 1970), p. 5. Compare Plato, *Euthyphro* (*GBWW*, vol. 7). See Mortimer J. Adler, *How to Think about God* (New York: Macmillan, 1980), pp. 31f., 56-59, 148–68. See as well chapter 3 of this collection, notes 7 and 79; notes 17, 38, 79, and 96 below. Consider also note 100 below. Consider as well note 24 of the Preface to this collection

15. Leo Strauss, *What Is Political Philosophy?* (Glencoe, Ill.: The Free Press, 1959), p. 39. See Kenneth L. Deutsch and John A. Murley, eds., *Leo Strauss, The Straussians, and the American Regime* (Lanham, Md.: Rowman & Littlefield, 1999).

16. Strauss, *What Is Political Philosophy?*, p. 14. He called this a provisional definition.

17. Ibid., p. 12. This last Strauss quotation brings Martin Heidegger to mind. See notes 100 and 102 below. See also note 91 of chapter 2 of this collection. See Legge, *Analects*, pp. 162–63 n. 22, for criticisms of a distinguished leader by the sages. Such criticisms remind one of the Socratic-Platonic criticisms of Pericles. See also Laurence Berns, "Heideggar and Strauss," *Interpretation*, vol. 27, pp. 99, 103 (1999–2000). See, on the relation between Reason and Revelation, ibid., pp. 103, 104 n. 9.

18. I myself have used four different English translations of the Analects, the principal Confucian text, in my effort to get a reliable notion of what might have been intended. They are, in order of usefulness, the translations by James Legge (in the Clarendon Press, later the Dover, edition), by Arthur Waley (in the Vintage edition), by Ezra Pound (in the New Directions edition), and by James R. Ware (in the Mentor edition). (Pound, it seems, drew considerably on translations by others.) Most of my quotations in this article are from the well-annotated Legge translation (without his accent marks). It is that translation which is reprinted, in its entirety (but without most of its notes), in the 1984 volume of *The Great Ideas Today*, the volume in which this chapter appeared.

See, on my citations to the Legge and Waley editions of the *Analects* in this chapter, note 1 above. I use roman numerals and arabic numerals for books and chapters, respectively, whereas Legge used roman numerals for both.

19. Thus, it can be said by Legge of *Analects*, IX, 18, "This [chapter] is a fragment, like many other chapters, of some conversation, and the subject thus illustrated must be supplied." Legge, *Analects*, p. 222 n. 18.

20. Even so, I provide (in my notes) the Waley translation for the shorter passages I comment upon. Waley renders *Analects*, XV, 18–19, thus:

The Master said, A gentleman is distressed by his own lack of capacity; he is never distressed at the failure of others to recognize his merits.

The Master said, A gentleman has reason to be distressed if he ends his days without making a reputation for himself.

The divergences possible in translations from the Chinese are suggested by the following inventory with respect to a term, *jen*, which is said to have in Confucian thought "profound and far-reaching significance and purpose": "Legge translates *jen* variously as 'perfect virtue' and as 'benevolence,' Waley as 'Goodness,' Creel as 'virtue,' Fung Yu-lan . . . as 'human-heartedness,' following Bedde, etc. W.T. Chan prefers 'humanity'; that is perhaps the closest equivalent semantically, but it is awkward to use." Kung-chuan Hsiao, *A History of Chinese Political Thought*, vol. 1, 101. See note 91 below (for a use of *jen*).

My preference for Legge depends in part on my impression that he was more apt than Waley to retain the rough, or troublesome, spots. Consider, for example, *Analects*, XIV, 36, commented on below in note 40. Waley seems to me to have smoothed over a teaching which Legge, as a devout Christian, was challenged by. See also the text at note 21 of this chapter. See as well note 51 below. But consider, in note 34 below, how Waley translates *Analects*, I, 15.

21. Waley, *Analects*, p. 197 n.3. A worthy challenge to one's powers of reconciliation may be found in such passages as *Analects*, XIII, 10–12 (the Legge notes are helpful here). See for samples of Christian reconciliations of texts, *The Table Talk of Martin Luther*, ed. Thomas S. Kepler (Grand Rapids, Mich.: Baker Book House, 1979), pp. 180, 207–8, 315–16.

22. Ezra Pound has it, "He said: The gentleman is irritated if his generation dies without weighing the worth of his name."

23. See, e.g., Plato, *Republic* 386C, 516D-E (*GBWW*, vol. 7, pp. 324, 389). Consider George Anastaplo, *The Constitutionalist: Notes on the First Amendment* (Dallas: Southern Methodist University Press, 1971), pp. 278–81.

24. Thus, Legge lays down this salutary caution, "But we are not at liberty to admit alterations of the text, unless, as received, it be absolutely unintelligible." *Analects*, p. 212 n. 12. (Legge makes this statement with respect to VIII, 12, in which he has the Master saying, "It is not easy to find a man who has learned for three years without coming to be good," and in which Waley has the Master saying something less difficult to understand, "One who will study for three years without thought of reward would be hard indeed to find.") See also Waley, *Analects*, p. 203 n. 3. See as well the text at note 51 of this chapter. See also note 103 below.

25. See, for additional observations bearing on the problem of reputation, *Analects*, I, 1, 16; IV, 14; IX, 22; XI, 25 (3); XII, 20; XIV, 18, 25, 32, 33; XV, 27; XVI, 12. See also Plato, *Apology*, 34D et seq. (*GBWW*, vol. 7, p. 208f.). See as well notes 42 and 86 below.

See, on nursery rhymes, Iona and Peter Opie, *The Oxford Dictionary of Nursery Rhymes* (Oxford: Clarendon Press, 1951), pp. 27-30, 44–45, 213–15, 404–5.

26. Consider, for example, the various ways in which we can be taken *to know*. See, e.g., Adler, *Aristotle for Everybody*, pp. 129–67. Friedrich Nietzsche's aphoristic presentations may be more on the Confucian model—with much, if not most, of the explicit argument left to be developed by the reader. See George Anastaplo, "The Forms of Our Knowing," in Douglas A. Ollivant, ed., *Jacques Maritain and the Many Ways of Knowing* (Catholic University Press, 2001).

27. For this reason, would not Confucius more easily be a subject of a novelist than would Socrates? See, e.g., note 52 below. The writers with whom we are familiar who might provide us with the best introduction to Confucius—at least by putting us in the proper mood—are the following three: the Aristophanes of *The Clouds* (*GBWW*, vol. 5), the Xenophon of the *Oeconomicus*, and the Machiavelli of *The Florentine History*, with Jane Austen providing the translation into English. The resulting compilation should be made up primarily of conversational exchanges, the circumstances and consequences of which are barely, if at all, indicated in the excerpts, which should *seem* more or less haphazardly arranged. Molly Bloom's remarkable soliloquy, in James Joyce's *Ulysses*, comes to mind. But see note 29 below. See also the text at notes 67 and 103 of this chapter. See as well note 89 of chapter 3 of this collection.

28. I should mention, before we proceed further, that scholarly opinion is divided about which of the books of the *Analects* are earlier, which later; which draw on Confucius, which do not. I am not competent to pass on these questions—and for our purposes I need not try. But the reader should know there *are* such scholarly differences: thus, some regard the first ten books of the *Analects* as "Confucian"; others consider books III through IX to be a whole, and an early whole; still others arrange things differently and eliminate entire books from the canon.

See Legge, *Analects*, pp. 10–13, 21; Waley, *Analects*, pp. 11, 21, 24. See note 7 above. Compare notes 29 and 52 below.

29. The tradition with respect to the *Analects*, which I attempt to draw upon in this chapter, was long ago put thus: "[The *Analects*] were recorded, and afterwards came a first-rate hand, who gave them the beautiful literary finish which we now witness, so that there is not a character which does not have its own indispensable place." Quoted in Legge, *Analects*, p. 16. On the other hand, Legge evidently expressed the general scholarly opinion of his day and ours when he said, "If one hand or one mind had digested the materials provided by many, the arrangement and style of the work would have been different. We should not have had the same remark appearing in several books, with little variation, and sometimes with none at all. [See e.g., *Analects*, VI, 25; XII, 15. But see note 38 (end) below.] Nor can we account on this supposition for such fragments as the last chapters of the ninth, tenth, and sixteenth books, and many others. No definite plan has been kept in view throughout. A degree of unity appears to belong to some books more than to others, and in general to the first ten more than to those which follow, but there is no progress of thought or illustration of subject from book to book. And even in those where the chapters have a common subject, they are thrown together at random more than on any plan." Ibid., pp. 16-17.

Is there a "definite plan . . . kept in view" throughout the *Analects*? One is not likely to be moved to look for an overall order in something that *does* appear so haphazard—unless one happens to notice how carefully wrought some of the parts are. I suspect that a proper account of the overall order of the *Analects* will have to come from someone who, being duly motivated, knows well both the Chinese language and Chinese political and literary history. Perhaps this chapter of mine can contribute to an informed motivation. See the text at notes 52, 67, 94, and 104 of this chapter. See also notes 31, 52, 81, and 103 below.

30. Waley renders *Analects*, I, 1, thus: "The Master said, To learn and at due times to repeat what one has learnt, is that not after all a pleasure? That friends should come to one from afar, is this not after all delightful? To remain unsoured even though one's merits are

unrecognized by others, is that not after all what is expected of a gentleman?" And Waley notes, "The 'after all' [in the first sentence here] implies 'even though one does not hold office.'" Waley, *Analects*, p. 83 n. 2.

31. Plato, *Apology of Socrates* 17A (Thomas G. West and Grace Starry West, trans.) (*GBWW*, vol. 7, p. 200). *Is* there a "definite plan" for the *Analects*? See note 29, above. If there is, it is for a work which, however utilitarian its overall appearance and general effect may be, does first come to view with an observation about the pleasure of learning. Does this not emphasize that which is distinctively human? See Adler, *Aristotle for Everybody*, pp. 6-9. See the text at note 92 of this chapter. See also note 100 below. See, on Plato's *Apology*, George Anastaplo, *Human Being and Citizen: Essays on Virtue, Freedom, and the Common Good* (Chicago: Swallow, 1975), p. 8.

32. Waley renders *Analects*, II, 17, thus: "The Master said, Yu, shall I teach you what knowledge is? When you know a thing, to recognize that you know it, and when you do not know a thing, to recognize that you do not know it. That is knowledge." Yu, we are told, is the "familiar name of the disciple Tsze-lu," whom we shall encounter in our exegesis of *Analects*, XI, 25 (in section VII of this chapter). See Waley, *Analects*, pp. 20, 91 n. 5. "That knowledge consists in knowing that one does not know is a frequent theme in early Chinese texts." Ibid., p. 91 n. 6. (It should be noticed that translators may not all use the same spelling of some of the Chinese names they provide us.)

33. We have already looked at the third sentence of this first chapter of book I of the *Analects*. See the text of this chapter between notes 20 and 21.

See, on friendship, Aristotle, *Nicomachean Ethics*, Bks. VIII and IX (*GBWW*, vol. 9, pp. 406–26); Anastaplo, *The Artist as Thinker: From Shakespeare to Joyce* (Athens, Ohio: Swallow Press/Ohio University Press, 1983), p. 310 ("Art and Mortality"); note 91 below. See also *Analects*, I, 8(3); Larry Arnhart, *Aristotle on Political Reasoning: A Commentary on the "Rhetoric"* (DeKalb, Ill.: Northern Illinois University Press, 1981), pp. 62–63. See as well Plato, *Laws* 756E-758A (*GBWW*, vol. 7, pp. 699–700).

34. Waley renders *Analects*, I, 15, thus:

> Tzu-kung said, "Poor without cadging, rich without swagger." What of that? The Master said, Not bad. But better still, "Poor, yet delighting in the Way; rich, yet a student of ritual. Tzu-kung said, The saying of the *Songs*,
>   As thing cut, as thing filed,
>   As thing chiselled, as thing polished
> refers, I suppose, to what you have just said? The Master said, Szu, now I can really begin to talk to you about the *Songs*, for when I allude to sayings of the past, you see what bearing they have on what was to come after.

See, on *Songs* (or *Book of Poetry*), note 42 below. See also note 95 below. See, on the use of both familiar and formal names in the same passage (as here), note 35 below.

35. This chapter reminds us that the names of the people in these texts should be taken into account, including the way formal and familiar names are used and when. See note 4, above. What are the traditions respecting each of these men appearing in colloquies with Confucius? What is said about them, and by them, in other chapters in the *Analects*? Legge notes for *Analects*, I, 15, for instance, "Tsze-kung had been poor, and then did not cringe. He became rich and was not proud. He asked Confucius about the style of character to which he had attained. Confucius allowed its worth, but sent him to higher attainments." Legge, *Analects*, p. 144 n. 15. See for related observations, *Analects*, XIII, 26; XIV, 11.

36. Waley uses "ritual" where Legge uses "rules of propriety." See, on rituals, note 38 below. The same terms may also be rendered as "rites." See Kung-chuan Hsiao, *A History of Chinese Political Thought*, I, 80 n. 5.

37. Consider Plato, *Republic* 329E-331D, 362D et seq. (*GBWW*, vol. 7, pp. 296–97, 313).

38. Ritual can mean that for many, if not for all, actions or situations, there is a proper response or way of conducting oneself. Thus, it can be said, "In bed, he did not lie like a corpse. At home, he did not put on any formal deportment." *Analects*, X, 16. Waley renders this, "In bed he avoids lying in the posture of a corpse. When at home he does not use ritual attitudes." See the text at notes 85–87 of this chapter. See also the text at notes 68–69 and at note 72 of this chapter.

See, for a sampling of the rituals that the Confucians dealt with, *Analects*, VI, 1; VII, 34; VIII, 4, 21; IX, 9, 10, 11; X (throughout this book); XIII, 3, XIV, 18, 44; XV, 4, 14, 32, 36, 41; XVII, 11. See, for an attempt by Confucius to ground a ritual in the natural, *Analects*, XVII, 21. Both Waley and Legge protest at the proposed derivation here. See note 85 below. But do they consider the possibility that Confucius knew, at least as well as did they, the limits of his salutary derivation? "The American tradition of popular government in the person of Lincoln [can be] seen to depend upon the statesman as prophet. And prophecy, as I learned from [Leo] Strauss, who had it from Maimonides—and ultimately from Plato's Athenian Stranger [in the *Laws*]—was the political name for political science." Henry V. Jaffa, *American Conservatism and the American Founding* (Durham, N.C.: Carolina Academic Press, 1984), p. 136. Compare Adler, *How to Think about God*, pp. 127–28. See also note 14 above, note 71 below. See as well note 80 below; chapter 3 of this collection, note 88; chapter 5 of this collection, notes 32 and 56; chapter 6 of this collection, note 21; appendix B of this collection, notes 50 and 88; epigraph, preface to this collection. The most extensive discussion of prophetology in this collection may be found in chapter 6 (e.g., the text at note 1). See note 26 of appendix C.

Confucius's advocacy of ritual observances evidently could become tiresome. Thus, one duke is said to have been dissuaded from assigning Confucius an office in his dukedom by the following argument (Legge, *Analects*, p. 69):

> Those scholars are impracticable and cannot be imitated. They are haughty and conceited of their own views, so that they will not be content in inferior positions. They set a high value on all funeral ceremonies, give way to their grief, and will waste their property on great burials, so that they would only be injurious to the common manners. This Mr. K'ung [Confucius] has a thousand peculiarities. It would take generations to exhaust all that he knows about the ceremonies of going up and going down. This is not the time to examine into his rules of propriety. If you, prince, wish to employ him to change the customs of Ch'i, you will not be making the people your primary consideration.

Compare *Analects*, IX, 3, 10. It should be instructive, with respect to the possible differences between ancient China and ancient Greece, to consider why the traveling Chinese scholars should have been so much identified with a respect for the customary, while at about the same time the traveling Greek scholars (or Sophists) should have been considered such a threat to the customary. Thus, Protagoras stirred up a scandal when he opened his work *On the Gods*, "About the gods I am not able to know either that they are, or that they are not, or what they are like in shape, the things preventing knowledge being many, such as the obscurity of the subject and that the life of man is short." See also the epigraph for this chapter from Plato's *Theaetetus* (*GBWW*, vol. 7, p. 529). One chapter which is repeated in the *Analects* emphasizes the importance in learned scholars of a respect for well-established ritual. See *Analects*, VI, 25; XII, 15; note 29 above. Is this not a salutary repetition for intellectuals? See notes 71 and 73 below. (Is not Confucius closer in those matters to Sophocles' Tiresias than to Plato's Socrates?)

39. See, e.g., *Analects*, VII, 19; XII, 1–2; XVIII, 2. See also Legge, *Analects*, p. 305 n. 38; Waley, *Analects*, p. 46.

40. A variation of the Golden Rule has been associated with Confucian teaching; see, e.g., *Analects*, IV, 15; V, 11, VI, 28, XV, 23. But consider *Analects*, XIV, 36:

> 1. Someone said, "What do you say concerning the principle that injury should be recompensed with kindness?"
> 2. The Master said, "With what then will you recompense kindness?
> 3. "Recompense injury with justice, and recompense kindness with kindness."

(Waley renders this chapter thus: "Someone said, What about the saying 'Meet resentment with inner power'? The Master said, In that case, how is one to meet inner power? Rather, meet resentment with upright dealing and meet inner power with inner power.") Legge comments on this chapter thus (*Analects*, p. 288 n. 36):

> How far the ethics of Confucius fall below our Christian standard is evident from this chapter, and even below Lao-tsze. The same expressions are attributed to Confucius in the Li Chi. . . . [It is there explained,] "He who returns good for evil is a man who is careful of his person," i.e., will try to avert danger from himself by such a course.

Analects, XV, 23 is translated in this fashion by Legge: "Tsze-kung asked, saying, 'Is there one word which may serve as a rule of practice for all one's life?' The Master said, 'Is not *reciprocity* such a word? What you do not want done to yourself, do not do to others.'" In his comment on this chapter, Legge suggests substituting "altruism" for "reciprocity." Ibid., p. 301 n. 23.

Legge's reservations about Confucius's lack of Christian charity are developed at ibid., pp. 109–11, culminating in the observation (ibid., p. 111):

> It is remarkable that Confucius . . . affirmed the duty of blood-revenge in the strongest and most unrestricted terms. . . . Sir John Davis has rightly called attention to this as one of the most objectionable principles of Confucius. The bad effects of it are evident even in the present day. Revenge is sweet to the Chinese. I have spoken of their readiness to submit to government, and [their] wish to live in peace, yet they do not like to resign even to government the "inquisition for blood." Where the ruling authority is feeble, as it is at present, individuals and clans take the law into their own hands, and whole districts are kept in a state of constant feud and warfare.

See, for a spirit similar in these respects to the Chinese, *Beowulf* 2020–69. See note 10 above. The "hardheadedness" I have observed in Confucius may be found in Aristotle as well. See, e.g., note 61 below. See also the text at note 91 of this chapter. Compare *Analects*, VI, 13. See as well Adler, *Aristotle for Everybody*, pp. 109f.

41. See *Analects*, VIII, 10. See also ibid., VI, 4; VIII, 13; XII, 7; XIII, 9; XV, I, 27; XVI, 1(10) (reproduced in section 9 of this chapter). See, as well, Kung-chuan Hsiao, *A History of Chinese Political Thought*, I, 108–10.

42. See, on Confucius's use of the ancients, ibid., I, 4 n. 4, 6–7, 10; *Analects*, II, 2; VII, 1; XVII, 5; Waley, *Analects*, pp. 51–52. Did not Confucius and his predecessors share

some ends? The first duties mentioned in the *Analects* are family based. See I, 2. The "eternal" may be reflected in the flow of generations. See, e.g., I, 13; II, 5, 21. See also note 89 below.

The poem evidently drawn upon by Tsze-kung may be found in Arthur Waley, *The Book of Songs* (New York: Grove Press, 1960), p. 46:

> Look at that little bay of the Ch'i,
> Its kitesfoot so delicately waving.
> Delicately fashioned is my lord,
> As thing cut, as thing filed,
> As thing chiseled, as thing polished.
> Oh, the grace, the elegance!
> Oh, the lustre, oh, the light!
> Delicately fashioned is my lord;
> Never for a moment can I forget him.
>
> Look at that little bay of the Ch'i,
> Its kitesfoot so fresh.
> Delicately fashioned is my lord,
> His ear-plugs are of precious stones,
> His cap-gems stand out like stars.
> Oh, the grace, the elegance!
> Oh, the lustre, the light!
> Delicately fashioned is my lord;
> Never for a moment can I forget him.
>
> Look at the little bay of the Ch'i,
> Its kitesfoot in their crowds.
> Delicately fashioned is my lord,
> As a thing of bronze, a thing of white metal,
> As a sceptre of jade, a disc of jade.
> How free, how easy
> He leant over his chariot-rail!
> How cleverly he chaffed and joked,
> And yet was never rude!

(Kitesfoot is a reedlike grass.) Is not the entire poem, with its appreciation of a finely wrought beauty, necessary to dwell upon in order to interpret fully this chapter (I, 15) of the *Analects*? Is a man of virtue to be considered as delicately fashioned and unforgettable? See the discussion of reputation in the text at note 25 of this chapter.

43. See *Analects*, VII, 1, 19; XVII, 16. An American might be reminded of what Abraham Lincoln did in the Gettysburg Address: "Four score and seven years ago" does make the country seem much more venerable than would have "A couple of generations ago" or "Eighty-seven years ago."

44. See *Analects*, VIII, 8.

45. I mention in passing the reservation about whether any of this was intended by the original poet! The poem may even have had four or more different things being worked upon. Or only one? See note 42 above.

46. Consider the Lincoln speech of January 27, 1838, "The Perpetuation of Our Political Institutions." Consider also Socrates' suggestion, in Plato's *Gorgias* (*GBWW*, vol. 7) that he was the greatest statesman in Greece.

47. See *Analects*, VII, 8 (note 95 below). See also Anastaplo, *The Constitutionalist*, pp. 735–36. Thus, the Confucian advice during our extended impeachment crisis in the 1970s could well have been, "Make Mr. Nixon go quietly, or leave him alone. It is obvious that the president is vulnerable and quite desperate. Is it good for the country to keep pushing him? After awhile, do we not hurt ourselves more than him?" See Anastaplo, *Human Being and Citizen*, pp. 160f. See also Anastaplo, "Legal Realism, the New Journalism, and *The Brethren*," *Duke Law Journal*, pp. 1045, 1069f (1983). The same advice could well have applied to the extended impeachment crisis in the 1990s.

48. Waley renders *Analects*, II, 24, thus: "The Master said, Just as to sacrifice to ancestors other than one's own is presumption, so to see what is right and not do it is cowardice." See note 100 below.

49. See Plato, *Republic* 427B et seq., 414B et seq. (*GBWW*, vol. 7, pp. 345f, 340f). See also the concluding passage in Lucretius's *On the Nature of Things* (*GBWW*, vol. 12) and the parallel description in Thucydides [*GBWW*, vol. 6] (with respect to "stealing" another's funeral fire). See as well notes 84 and 88 below.

50. See, e.g., Waley, *Analects*, p. 93 n. 1. See also Legge, *Analects*, pp. 99–101, which includes the observation (p. 100):

> It will not be supposed that I wish to advocate or to defend the practice of sacrificing to the dead. My object has been to point out how Confucius recognized it, without acknowledging the faith from which it must have originated, and how he enforced it as a matter of form or ceremony. It thus connects itself with the most serious charge that can be brought against him—the charge of insincerity.

But see note 47 above, notes 84 and 85 below. See also notes 86 and 88 below. See as well note 42 above.

51. See Legge, *Analects*, pp. 135, 184. Compare ibid., pp. 16–17; Waley, *Analects*, p. 172. See also notes 21, 24, and 29 above.

52. At times there are exhibited in the *Analects* suppressed as well as expressed passions, the susceptibility to which can be curious in a sage. See, e.g., ibid., VI, 8, 26; IX, 9, 17; XI, 8, 9; XIV, 10, 26, 46; XV, 12. See also Legge, *Analects*, pp. 78, 330 n. 25. But consider *Analects*, XVII, 3: "The Master said, 'There are only the wise of the highest class, and the stupid of the lowest class, who cannot be changed.'" (Waley renders this, "The Master said, It is only the very wisest and the very stupidest who cannot change.") Consider also the speech about the passions of Socrates by Alcibiades in Plato's *Symposium* (*GBWW*, vol. 7, pp. 169–72); Anastaplo, *The Artist as Thinker*, p. 249 (Xenophon epigraph).

The "personality" of Confucius may be related to how the *Analects* is organized. Book X, one of the two central books of the *Analects*, can be considered the most prosaic of the twenty books: it is devoted to various modes of conduct of Confucius, dealing with his dress, manners, food, etc., but with few of his sayings. See Legge, *Analects*, p. 89. (One can be reminded of some of Xenophon's accounts of Socrates. Consider also the last lines of Charles Darwin's *The Descent of Man*: " Man still bears in his bodily frame the indelible stamp of his lowly origin." [*GBWW*, vol. 49, p. 597.] Compare the Platonic teaching to the effect that the body is merely the temporary receptacle for man's soul.) Did the editor who put the *Analects* together want to remind his readers of a "human being" who was very much obliged to concern himself with material things and very much aware of his circumstances? Are not such obligations critical to the practical life, even on the highest level? See note 60 below, and the text at note 62 of this chapter.

The other central book, book XI, is also somewhat prosaic, even gossipy. It concerns itself with some of the more important "material things" and "circumstances" that Confucius had to work with and around—that is, various of his followers, who are reported on and assessed. Book XI concludes with chapter 25, perhaps the longest chapter in the *Analects*, which I comment on at length in section VII of this chapter. In that passage of the *Analects* the royal inclinations of four of Confucius's followers are exposed and analyzed. See, e.g., note 63 below. Legge observes (*Analects*, p. 237n), "With [book XI] there commences the second part of the *Analects*, commonly called the *Hsia Lun*. There is, however, no important authority for this division." But it seems to me, partly on the basis of what I have noticed in this note, that the traditional division does make sense. Someone who knows the language, literature, and history of China should be able to do much more than I can with these observations. That is, the *Analects* as a whole may be a well-ordered text, inviting and rewarding careful and imaginative study. (Is it not appropriate, by the way, that book XX [the final book] should represent the falling off that it does, with Confucius not appearing at all? But what of his spirit?) In any event, it is well to keep in mind the advice Montesquieu gives to his readers: "If they would search into the design of the author, they can do it in no other way so completely as by searching into the design of the work." Preface to *The Spirit of the Laws* (see *GBWW*, vol. 38, p. xxi). See notes 28 and 29 above.

53. See *Analects*, III, 6. See also Kung-chuan Hsiao, *A History of Chinese Political Thought*, I, 99.

54. Consider comparable matters in Judaism. Would not an Orthodox Jew also fail to find amusing some misbehavior of this kind? See note 89 below.

55. Consider *Analects*, III, 17:

1. Tsze-kung wished to do away with the offering of a sheep connected with the inauguration of the first day of each month.
2. The Master said, "Ts'ze, you love the sheep, I love the ceremony."

Waley renders this chapter thus:

Tzu-kung wanted to do away with the presentation of a sacrificial sheep at the Announcement of each New Moon. The Master said, Ssu! You grudge sheep, but I grudge ritual.

See, for further indications of Confucius's sense of humor, *Analects*, V, 20; IX, 2, XVII, 20. See also Legge, *Analects*, p. 79. See as well note 103 below.

56. See, e.g., Plato, *Apology*, 36C-37A (*GBWW*, vol. 7, p. 209).

57. See, e.g., *Analects*, IX, 28, XIV, 7, XV, 32, XVII, 8. Compare Adler, *Aristotle for Everybody*, p. 104.

58. See, on courage, *Analects*, VI, 13, VII, 10, VIII, 2, IX, 28, XI, 14, 25(4) (commented on by me in section VII of this chapter), XIV, 13, XVII, 8, 24. Consider the ambiguous treatment of courage in Aristotle's *Nicomachean Ethics*, bk. III (*GBWW*, vol. 9, pp. 361–64). See also Plato, *Republic* 430B (*GBWW*, vol. 7, p. 347); Adler, *Aristotle for Everybody*, pp. 103f.

59. See, on formal and familiar names, note 35 above. Waley uses "league" for "li" in section 5 of this chapter of the *Analects*. Consider, with respect to section 4 of this chapter, Legge, *Analects*, p. 140 n. 5: "A country of 1000 chariots was one of the largest fiefs of the empire, which could bring such an armament into the field."

60. One is reminded of the references to dress in sections 6 and 7 of this chapter of the *Analects* how much one simply does not know about what must have been taken for granted

by the original editor of the *Analects*. Legge notes (*Analects*, p. 249): "Capping was in China a custom similar to the assuming the *toga virilis* among the Romans." See note 52 above.

61. See Aristotle, *Nicomachean Ethics* 1123b8–12 (*GBWW*, vol. 9, p. 370):

> The man who thinks himself worthy of less than he is really worthy of is unduly humble, whether his deserts be great or moderate, or his deserts be small but his claims yet smaller. And the man whose deserts are great would seem *most* unduly humble; for what would he have done if they had been less?

See note 40 above, note 64 below.

62. See Machiavelli, *The Prince*, chap. 6 (*GBWW*, vol. 23, p. 8). See also the Lincoln "Perpetuation" speech, note 46 above.

63. Legge reports on our Number One in the following way (*Analects*, p. 86):

> In the year B.C. 479, Confucius had to mourn the death of another of his disciples, one of those who had been longest with him—the well-known Tsze-lu. He stands out a sort of Peter in the Confucian school, a man of impulse, prompt to speak and prompt to act. He gets many a check from the master, but there is evidently a strong sympathy between them. Tsze-lu uses a freedom with him on which none of the other disciples dares to venture, and there is not one among them all, for whom, if I may speak from my own feeling, the foreign student comes to form such a liking. A pleasant picture is presented to us in one passage of the *Analects* [XI, 12]. It is said, "The disciple Min was standing by his side, looking bland and precise; Tsze-lu (named Yu), looking bold and soldierly; Yen Yu and Tsze-kung, with a free and straightforward manner. The master was pleased, but he observed, 'Yu [Tsze-lu] there! he will not die a natural death.'"

But is it not clear, at least from *Analects*, XI, 25, that this is one Peter to whom the keys of the kingdom would *not* be entrusted?

64. See, e.g., *Analects*, V, 27; VII, 32; XVII, 19. Legge says, with respect to this last chapter, that "it is not easy to defend Confucius from the charge of presumption in comparing himself to heaven." *Analects*, p. 326 n. 19. But see note 61 above. There may be something Socratic in Confucius's remark, "I am fortunate! If I have any errors, people are sure to know them." *Analects*, VII, 30.

65. See, e.g., *Analects*, VIII, 12; XVII, 1. (Is this one of the rare times in the *Analects* that Confucius is bested in a discussion? Perhaps he wanted to be "bested," which meant he *would* be "argued into" taking office, but on his own terms.) See also ibid., XVII, 4; XIX, 25. (Is rule *the* test and the best use of one's talents?) See, on the sovereign as the "lonely one," Waley, *Analects*, p. 251. In any event, the two longest chapters in the *Analects* (IX, 25, and XVI, 1) seem to be devoted to discussions of ruling. See section IX of this chapter. See, on government service, *Analects* II, 21; V, 18; VII, 10, VIII, 12, 18; XIII, 10; XIV, 34; XVII, 1, 5; XVIII, 3, 7, 10; XIX, 1, 13. Compare note 91 below.

Is there in the four responses in *Analects*, XI, 25, progressively more concern for ritual? And does this, here at the end of book XI, point back to book X? See ibid., XII, 1 et seq. See also note 52 above.

66. Again we ask, Does Confucius smile at us or for us? Are we worthy of such smiling? Only if we notice it and sense that it must mean something? See note 95 below. See also notes 100 and 103 below.

67. See note 29 above (on "a first-rate hand, who gave [the *Analects*] the beautiful literary finish which we now witness"). See also the text at note 104 of this chapter; note 103, below.

68. See note 38 above. See also the text at note 85 of this chapter. See, on age, the text at note 70 of this chapter.

69. This is something like what tragedy does to critical passions in the audience—in order to achieve the appropriate cathartic effect. See Aristotle, *Poetics* (*GBWW*, vol. 9); Laurence Berns, "Aristotle's *Poetics*," in Joseph Cropsey, ed., *Ancients and Moderns* (New York: Basic Books, 1964). See also note 38 above.

70. It has been observed that, "in effect, all three [if not all four?] were asking for kingdoms." Waley, *Analects*, p. 161 n. 2. See, on Abraham Lincoln's constant ambition, Anastaplo, *Abraham Lincoln,* pp. 297–98. See, on the uses of *virtù* in Machiavelli, *The Prince*, ed. Leo Paul S. de Alvarez (Irving, Tex.: University of Dallas Press, 1980), pp. xi-xiv.

71. Waley, *Analects*, p. 200 n. 1. Waley renders *Analects*, XV, 32, thus:

The Master said, He whose wisdom brings him into power, needs Goodness, to secure that power. Else, though he get it, he will certainly lose it. He whose wisdom brings him into power and who has Goodness whereby to secure that power, if he has not dignity wherewith to approach the common people, they will not respect him. He whose wisdom has brought him into power, who has Goodness whereby to secure power and dignity wherewith to approach the common people, if he handles them contrary to the prescriptions of ritual, [he] is still a bad ruler.

See, on ritual, note 38 above.

72. See also, e.g., *Analects*, IV, 1; VI, 20; XIII, 5.

73. Waley renders *Analects*, VI, 18, thus: "The Master said, To prefer it [the Way] is better than only to know it. To delight in it is better than merely to prefer it." Compare note 100 below.

74. See also *Analects*, XVI, 7 (on what one is apt to be moved by in various stages of one's life). See as well note 91 below.

75. Compare *Analects*, IV, 4: "The Master said, 'If the will be set on virtue, there will be no practice of wickedness.'" Waley combines *Analects*, IV, 3–4, so as to read, "Of the adage 'Only a Good Man knows how to like people, knows how to dislike them,' the Master said, He whose heart is in the smallest degree set upon Goodness will dislike no one." Legge is reminded here of *I Epistle of John* 3:9: "Whosoever is born of God doth not commit sin." See, for the subjection of the exercise of will to the test of wisdom, Thomas Aquinas, *On Truth*, Q. 23. Compare *The Table Talk of Martin Luther*, pp. 7, 216. But see ibid., pp. 184f.

Consider also Alexis de Tocqueville, *Democracy in America*, trans. George Lawrence, ed. J. P. Mayer (Garden City, N.Y.: Doubleday, 1969), p. 538:

In France we are worried about the increasing rate of suicides; in America suicide is rare, but I am told that madness is commoner than anywhere else.

Those are different symptoms of the same malady.

The Americans do not kill themselves, however distressed they may be, because their religion forbids them to do so and because materialist philosophy is practically unknown to them, although the passion for prosperity is general.

Their will resists, but reason frequently gives way.

Consider, as well, ibid., pp. 534–35.

76. Confucius may be suggesting, "At least be honest with yourselves as to what is going on and as to what you want." This kind of suggestion may be seen as well in *Analects*, XI, 25 (commented upon by me in section VII of this chapter). Compare the text at note 77 of this chapter. See note 100 below.

77. Are there limits to obeying one's leader? See *Analects*, XI, 23; XVIII, 1. The right of revolution, as recognized by the Declaration of Independence, does not seem to be countenanced by Confucius. Does not such a right look, ultimately, to nature as a guide? See note 94 below; Legge, *Analects*, pp. 67–68, 106 ("The government which Confucius taught was a despotism, but of a modified character.") See also Kung-chuan Hsiao, *A History of Chinese Political Thought*, I, 105–6. See as well note 10 above.

78. See Waley, *Analects*, p. 202. Chau Zan has been identified as an ancient sage who lived long before Confucius.

79. See, e.g., Aristotle, *Politics*, 1284a28–34, 1311a20–22, 1313a38–41 (*GBWW*, vol. 12, pp. 482, 513, 516).

80. Does not Confucius anticipate here, and share in various ways, some of the illusions of the European Enlightenment? Here, too, the classical political philosopher would travel differently? See Aristotle, *Politics*, 1276a25–34, 1326a5 et seq., 1265a13–18 (*GBWW*, vol. 12, pp. 473, 530, 460). See also note 94 below.

One can say that Confucius did succeed in his way or "project," as did much later Thomas Aquinas in his? Both can be said to have addressed peoples of considerable scope. Consider Tocqueville's comments on the Chinese way in *Democracy in America*, p. 464. Consider, as well, Orville Schell, "A Reporter at Large," *New Yorker*, January 23, 1984, pp. 43, 84–85. Compare Seymour M. Hersh, *The Price of Power: Kissinger in the Nixon White House* (New York: Simon & Schuster, 1983), p. 501n. Mr. Kissinger may well have been correct here.

See also the text at note 89 of this chapter. See, as well, the text following note 102 of this chapter.

81. Would the Chinese reader in antiquity have known how the episode, if historical, was resolved? See, for example, the information available with respect to the matters touched upon in *Analects*, V, 21, 22; and VI, 4. Legge, *Analects*, p. 181 nn. 21, 22; p. 186 n. 4. See also note 29 above.

82. Book XVII of the *Analects* may continue to deal with some of the people dealt with in *Analects*, XVI, 1. See Legge, *Analects*, p. 317n: "As the last book [XVI] commenced with the presumption of the Head of the Chi family, who kept his prince in subjection, this [book XVII] begins with an account of an officer, who did for the Head of the Chi what he did for the duke of Lu. For this reason—some similarity in the subject-matter of the first chapters—this book, it is said, is placed after the former." See notes 29 and 52 above.

83. Waley renders *Analects*, XX, 3, thus: "The Master said, He who does not understand the will of Heaven cannot be regarded as a gentleman. He who does not know the rites cannot take his stand. He who does not understand words, cannot understand people." See the text at notes 57 and 58 of this chapter.

84. See, e.g., notes 38 and 49 above. Evidently, Confucius himself made no claim about supernatural powers. See *Analects*, II, 4(4), 23; IV, 8; VI, 8, 20; VII, 20; IX, 1, 5; XI, 11, 22; XII, 5; XIV, 37; XVI, 8. See also Legge, *Analects*, pp. 97-99, 101, 142 n. 10, 153 n. 23, 168 n. 8, 225, n. 28 (a comment by Legge on *Analects*, IX, 28, which is said by him to be "one of the sayings about virtue, which is only true when it is combined with trust in God"—the saying being, "The Master said, 'The wise are free from perplexities; the virtuous from anxiety; and the bold from fear.'" [This is rendered by Waley thus: "The Master said, He that is really Good can never be unhappy. He that is really wise can never be perplexed. He that is really brave is never afraid."]); Waley, *Analects*, pp. 31–32. Somewhat uncharacteristic are the uses of "God' and "sinner" in *Analects*, XX, 1 (or, in Waley's

version, the uses of "God" and "the guilty"). "And, the philosopher Mo Tzu, in denouncing the Confucians, made much of the point that they did not believe in spirits and gods." Kung-chuan Hsiao, *A History of Chinese Political Thought*, p. 96. See Montesquieu, *The Spirit of Laws*, XXIV, 19 (*GBWW*, vol. 38, pp. 205–6). See also notes 40 and 50 above, notes 88, 92, and 95 below. See as well note 100 below.

85. Compare Maimonides, *The Guide for the Perplexed*, III, 25–50. See *Analects*, III, 11. See also Legge, *Analects*, pp. 62, 65, 66, 328 n. 21. See as well notes 38, 69, and 72 above, note 95 below, and the text at notes 68–70 of this chapter.

86. Consider how a Christian missionary can comment on the death of Confucius:

> Such is the account which we have of the last hours of the great philosopher of China. His end was not unimpressive, but it was melancholy. He sank behind a cloud. Disappointed hopes made his soul bitter. The great ones of the kingdom had not received his teachings. No wife nor child was by to do the kindly offices of affection for him. Nor were his expectations of another life present with him as he passed through the dark valley. He uttered no prayer, and he betrayed no apprehensions.

Legge, *Analects*, p. 87. The melancholy and bitterness here, however, may be only in the eye of the beholder. See *The Table Talk of Martin Luther*, pp. 89, 93–94, 331–32. See also notes 40 and 50 above, notes 88 and 92 below, and the text following note 20 of this chapter. See as well note 100 below.

87. Waley sums up the *chun-tzu* (the "son of a ruler," or the "gentleman") in this fashion:

> Moderation in conduct and opinion is a well-known hallmark of the true gentleman: "The *chun-tzu* avoids the absolute, avoids the extreme." Mencius tells us that "Confucius was one who abstained from extremes." "To exceed is as bad as not to reach." [Note: *Analects*, XI, 15. Cf. XIII, 21.] . . . This conception of virtue as a middle way between two extremes is one which we have no difficulty in understanding: for it is familiar to us as part of our popular heritage from Greek philosophy. It is, however, one which rapidly disappears so soon as purely magical, non-social virtues are held in esteem. The reputation of an Indian ascetic, for example, is in proportion to the "excessiveness" of his behavior; and a society which admired St. Simeon on his pillar would not easily have understood either the ["Nothing in excess"] of the Classical Greeks or the "middle conduct" (*chung hsing*) inculcated by Confucius.

Waley, *Analects*, pp. 56–57. See *Analects*, VI, 27. See also note 9 above.

88. In Socrates' best city, as described in Plato's *Republic* (*GBWW*, vol. 7), a man may not even know who his parents are. And noble lies are relied upon by philosophers as rulers, not by philosophers as philosophers. Here are Christian assessments of this situation:

> What early Chinese literature, as also that of the Hebrews, condemns is "bearing false witness," i.e., telling lies that lead to harm. Other sorts of lies are ritually enjoined: for example, that of saying one is ill instead of bluntly refusing an invitation or declining to see a visitor. The necessity of this sort of lie is recognized by "society" in Europe; but not by the Church. Confucius once (XVII, 20) told a lie of this kind, and Soothill wrote (in 1910) concerning it, "That such laxity on the part of China's noblest Exemplar has fostered that disregard for truth for which this nation is so notorious, can hardly be denied." In this instance a man of the world would have understood Confucius better than a clergyman [E. Soothill] had done. In the passage concerned Confucius shows not "laxity" but on the contrary a strict attention to manners.

Waley, *Analects*, pp. 43–44. (Whether *Analects*, XVII, 20, is precisely as Waley understands it here is another question.) See notes 92 and 95 below. See also note 49 above.

89. See, on filial piety and mourning, *Analects*, e.g., XVIII, 14, 17-18. Does the considerable emphasis on mourning elevate the family at the expense of the social and political? See note 85 above. See also note 42 above. Does not Pericles' funeral talk, in book II of Thucydides' *Peloponnesian War*, assume that the political order should regulate the family even with respect to mourning? See note 94 below. See, on how Confucius dealt with his own son, *Analects*, XVI, 13. Consider also Legge's comment on this (*Analects*, p. 71):

> I can easily believe that this distant reserve was the rule which Confucius followed generally in his treatment of his son. A stern dignity is the quality which a father has to maintain [according to] his system. It is not to be without the element of kindness, but that must never go beyond the line of propriety. There is too little room left for the play and development of natural affection.

See the text at note 80 of this chapter. See also note 94 below. Compare Waley, *Analects*, p. 208 n. 2 (also commenting on *Analects*, XVI, 13):

> The reasons why a gentleman must not teach his own son are discussed in *Mencius*, IV, 1, XVIII. There is a definite ritual severance between father and son. A father may not carry his son in his arms. A son may not, when sacrifice is being made to his deceased father, act as the "medium" into whom the spirit of the deceased passes.

May not similar inhibitions be found in the Eastern Orthodox Church and in Judaism?

90. See the discussion of Plato's *Apology* in Anastaplo, *Human Being and Citizen*, pp. 8f. See also on Plato's *Crito*, ibid., pp. 203f. Does not the dominant religion of the West reinforce the inclination of philosophy to place the pursuit of truth above demands of family and of community? See, e.g., *Matthew* 4:21–22, 8:21–23, 10:37, 23:9; *Mark* 1:19–20, 3:31–35, 10:28–30, 13:12; *Luke* 9:59–62, 12:51–53, 14:26. See, on Taoism, note 19 of the preface to this collection; note 40 above; note 38 of chapter 5 of this collection. See also note 102 below.

91. It is in the first five books of Aristotle's *Nicomachean Ethics* (*GBWW*, vol. 9) that the moral virtues are discussed. See, on the Christian response to the "hardheadedness" of both Confucius and Aristotle, note 40 above. See, on the Confucian choosing between the vices (somewhat as Aristotle does), *Analects*, VII, 35; XI, 15, 26; XIII, 21. See also Waley, *Analects*, p. 241; note 87 above. See, on the relation of happiness to virtue (*somewhat* as for Aristotle), *Analects*, VI, 17, 21; VII, 15, 22. See also Adler, *Aristotle for Everybody*, pp. 76f., 199. See as well note 74 above.

Consider Kung-chuan Hsiao, *A History of Chinese Political Thought*, 1, 113:

> Plato also regarded ethics as the highest aspect of the state's existence, and his "philosopher king" ideal is close to Confucius' advocacy of the idea that governing and teaching are inseparable, and that the roles of ruler and preceptor must be combined. However, Plato's philosopher-king was to be a philosopher who valued knowledge above all, while Confucius's ruler-preceptor was a man of *jen* [note 20, above] who valued ethics above all. The ruler-preceptor was to employ ethics wherewith to transform the people, whereas the philosopher-king was to employ knowledge wherewith to rule the country. Both as men and in their modes of action they are different.

See ibid., pp. 88–89. Compare note 65 above.

92. The latter half of Aristotle's *Nicomachean Ethics* (*GBWW*, vol. 9) does include an extended discussion of friendship, which Confucius also discusses at length. Whether

friendship can be properly understood without a grasp of the intellectual virtues is another question. See, on Confucius and "the great problems of the human condition and destiny," Legge, *Analects*, pp. 97–98:

> He did not speculate on the creation of things or the end of them. He was not troubled to account for the origin of man, nor did he seek to know about his hereafter. He meddled neither with physics nor metaphysics [quoting from *Analects*, VII, 17, 24, and 20]. . . .
> Confucius is not to be blamed for his silence on the subjects here indicated. His ignorance of them was to a great extent his misfortune. He had not learned them. No report of them had come to him by the ear; no vision of them by the eye. And to his practical mind the toiling of thought amid uncertainties seemed worse than useless.
> The question has, indeed, been raised, whether he did not make changes in the ancient creed of China, but I cannot believe that he did so consciously and designedly. . . . [T]hat he suppressed or added, in order to bring in articles of belief originating with himself, is a thing not to be charged against him.

But see notes 95 and 100 below.

See also Kung-chuan Hsiao, *A History of Chinese Political Thought*, I, 7-9 n. 13, 113.

93. Confucius may be, in this as in several other respects, very much like Abraham Lincoln. See, e.g., notes 38, 43, 46, and 70 above, note 95 below, and the text at note 70 of this chapter. See, on the importance of the proper assignment of names and tasks, ibid., 1, 99–100; *Analects*, XII, 11; XIII, 3; XIV, 4; Lincoln, "Message to Congress in Special Session," July 4, 1861 ("It might seem at first thought to be of little importance whether the present movement at the South be called 'secession' or 'rebellion.' The movers, however, well understand the difference. At the beginning they knew they could never raise their treason to any respectable magnitude by any name which implies *violation* of law. . . . Accordingly, they commenced by an insidious debauching of the public mind. They invented an ingenious sophism, which, if conceded, was followed by perfectly logical steps through all the incidents to the complete destruction of the Union. . . . With rebellion thus sugarcoated, they have been drugging the public mind of their section for more than thirty years.") See also Tocqueville, *Democracy in America*, pp. 470–82. See, as well, Thucydides, *History of the Peloponnesian War*, book I, chap. 3, sec. 82 (*GBWW*, vol. 6, pp. 369–70). Compare *United Housing Foundation* v. *Forman*, 421 U.S. 837, at 847-51 (1975).

94. My hunch is that there is in the Chinese of Confucius no word which should be translated as "nature." But see, in the Waley translation of the *Analects*, XII, 20; XVII, 2; and in the Legge translation of the *Analects*, I, 12(1); IV, 15; V, 12; XI, 12; XIV, 6, 41; XVII, 2; XX, 2. See also Hajime Nakamura, "The Idea of Nature, East and West," *The Great Ideas Today*, pp. 234–303 (1980).

We have noticed that Confucius does not consider the best political community naturally limited in size. See the text at note 80 of this chapter. Indeed, one must wonder whether the very notion of *nature* eluded him, except perhaps as it is reflected in the family, of which he does make much (perhaps too much, the philosopher might suggest). See the text at note 89 of this chapter. If an emphasis is placed on the family, or on the salvation of the individual soul (as Christianity tends to do?), the size of the political community may not matter—and empire may even become attractive (if only as a permissive milieu in which families and souls are more apt to be left alone than they are in the *polis*?). See note 80 above. See also note 89 above.

95. See, on "difficult philosophical questions," Adler, *Aristotle for Everybody*, pp. 169 f. It is possible, of course, that Confucius went far beyond the position I have found it useful to discuss on this occasion. Confucius *is* said, in *Analects*, XV, 2, to "seek a unity all-pervading" (Waley: "one thread upon which [to] string everything"). See, for an indication of an esoteric teaching, *Analects*, VII, 8: "The Master said, 'I do not open up the truth to one who is not eager to get knowledge, nor help out anyone who is not anxious to explain himself. When I have presented one corner of a subject to anyone, and he cannot from it learn the other three, I do not repeat my lesson.'" (Waley renders this chapter thus: "The Master said, Only one who bursts with eagerness do I instruct; only one who bubbles with excitement, do I enlighten. If I hold up one corner and a man cannot come back to me with the other three, I do not continue the lesson.") See also *Analects*, II, 21; V, 12; VI, 19, 23; VIII, 1, 23; VIII, 9; XII, 3; XIII, 28; XV, 6, 7; note 34, above, and note 103 below. See, on prudence, ibid., VII, 10; XIV, 16; XV, 11. Compare ibid., VII, 24; XV, 16. "Chinese writers are eloquent in their praises of the sage for the combination of propriety, complaisance and firmness, which they see in his behavior [on a certain occasion]. To myself there seems nothing remarkable in it but a somewhat questionable dexterity." Legge, *Analects*, p. 70. Similarly, Stephen A. Douglas could say of Abraham Lincoln that he had "a fertile genius in devising language to conceal his thought." Sixth Joint Debate, Quincy, Illinois, October 13, 1858. See note 50 above.

In any event, the pointers in the *Analects* to an esoteric teaching, if they are that, are most ambiguous. It is prudent, therefore, to consider my discussion here as merely introductory and indeed tentative. See Leo Strauss, *Persecution and the Art of Writing* (Glencoe, Ill.: The Free Press, 1952).

Bearing on the problem of esotericism is Legge's concern with an occasional dissimulation by Confucius: "On the way [to a certain place], he was laid hold of . . . by a rebellious officer . . . and before he could get away, he was obliged to engage that he would not proceed thither. Thither, notwithstanding, he continued his route, and when Tsze-kung asked him whether it was right to violate the oath he had taken, he replied, 'It was a forced oath. The spirits do not hear such.'" Legge, *Analects*, p. 79. Legge then adds, "This is related by Sze-ma Ch'ien . . . and also in the 'Narratives of the School.' I would fain believe it is not true. The wonder is, that no Chinese critic should have set about disproving it." Ibid., p. 79 n. 6. Legge comments further on this episode in these terms:

What shall we say to the incident [in which Confucius deliberately broke] the oath which he had sworn, simply on the ground that it had been forced from him? I should be glad if I could find evidence on which to deny the truth of that occurrence. But it rests on the same authority as most other statements about him, and it is accepted as a fact by the people and scholars of China. It must have had, and it must still have, a very injurious influence upon them. Foreigners charge a habit of deceitfulness upon the nation and its government—on the justice or injustice of this charge I say nothing. For every word of falsehood and every act of insincerity, the guilty party must bear his own burden, but we cannot but regret the example of Confucius in this particular. It is with the Chinese and their sage, as it was with the Jews of old and their teachers. He that leads them has caused them to err, and destroyed the way of their paths.

But was not insincerity a natural result of the un-religion of Confucius? There are certain virtues which demand a true piety in order to their flourishing in the heart of man. Natural affection, the feeling of loyalty, and enlightened policy, may do much to build up and preserve a family and a state, but it requires more to maintain the love of truth, and make a lie, spoken or acted, to be shrunk from with shame. It requires in fact the living recognition of a God of truth, and all the sanctions of revealed religion. Unfortunately the Chinese have not had these, and the example of him to whom they bow down as the best and wisest of men, does not set them against dissimulation.

Ibid., pp. 100–101. Compare Plato, *Republic*, 331A-C, 414B et seq. (*GBWW*, vol. 7, pp. 297, 340); notes 49 and 84 above. I am reminded by all this of the criticisms in *The Interpreter's Bible* of the salutary deceptions by Rebekah in *Genesis*. Are the Jews and the Chinese more worldly, and hence more sensible, in these matters than the other-worldly Christian? The Chinese *are* sometimes spoken of as "the Jews of Asia." See note 88 above. See, on the remarkable Rebekah, George Anastaplo, "Law & Literature and the Bible: Explorations," 23 *Oklahoma City University Law Review* 515, 564 (1998).

96. See, on the need for the guide to salvation being presented in other than philosophical terms if most men are to be helped, Richard P. McKeon, *The Philosophy of Spinoza: The Unity of His Thought* (New York: Longmans, Green and Co., 1928), pp. 266–67. Consider also *Analects*, VIII, 9: "The Master said, 'The people may be made to follow a path of action, but they may not be made to understand it.'" (Waley renders this chapter thus: "The Master said, The common people can be made to follow [the Way]; they cannot be made to understand it.") Consider, as well, Pierre Bayle, *Historical and Critical Dictionary* ("Spinoza" entry); George Washington, "Farewell Address"; Tocqueville, *Democracy in America*, e.g., pp. 442–49.

97. Ezra Pound, *Confucius* (New York: New Directions, 1951), p. 191. See also Adler, *Aristotle for Everybody*, pp. ix–x:

It is in another way that philosophy is useful—to help us to understand things we already know, understand them better than we now understand them. That is why I think everybody should learn how to think philosophically.

For that purpose, there is no better teacher than Aristotle. I do not hesitate to recommend him as the teacher to begin with. The only other teacher that I might have chosen is Plato, but in my judgement he is second best. Plato raised almost all the questions that everyone should face; Aristotle raised them too and, in addition, gave us clearer answers to them. Plato taught Aristotle how to think philosophically, but Aristotle learned the lesson so well that he is the better teacher for all of us.

Compare Anastaplo, *Human Being and Citizen*, pp. 17f., 244 n. 45. But see *Analects*, XV, 30.

98. See Plato, *Apology*, 38A (*GBWW*, vol. 7, p. 210); Adler, *Aristotle for Everybody*, pp. 77-78. Should we not say that an unexamined life is not a fully human life?

99. See Plato, *Timaeus*, 22B (*GBWW*, vol. 7, p. 444); Thucydides, *History of the Peloponnesian War*, book I, chap. 3, sec. 70 (*GBWW*, vol. 6, p. 366). See also Tocqueville, *Democracy in America*, e.g., pp. 477-81. See as well the text at note 10 of chapter 2 of this collection.

100. See, on Confucius as the man who "knows it's no use, but keeps on doing it," *Analects*, XIV, 41. See also Kung-chuan Hsiao, *A History of Chinese Political Thought*, I, 91. See as well *Analects*, XVIII, 6. But see, on the influence of the superior man, ibid., XII, 19: "The relation between superiors and inferiors is like that between the wind and the grass. The grass must bend, when the wind blows across it." (Waley renders this passage thus: "The essence of the gentleman is that of wind; the essence of small people is that of grass. And when a wind passes over the grass, it cannot choose but bend.")

Thus, there is a sense in which Confucius's entire approach is deeply hypothetical. See notes 90 and 91 above. May not such an approach also be seen in some modern existentialists? See note 17 above, note 102 below.

See, on being able (for the sake of mental health) to "step back," the text at note 1 of chapter 1 of this collection.

See, on the need for the superior man to "keep on doing it" (no matter how burdensome), the concluding lines of *The Song of Roland*.

101. See Anastaplo, *The Constitutionalist*, pp. 546–48 n. 146, 612–16 n. 35, 640–43 n. 77, 790–71 n. 20 See also my discussion of obscenity in *Human Being and Citizen*, pp. 117f; my argument for the abolition of television in *The American Moralist: On Law, Ethics, and Government* (Athens, Ohio: Ohio University Press, 1992) p. 245; and my discussion of psychiatry and the law (and the status of nature) in ibid., p. 407.

102. I say "perhaps" about Shakespeare because of the unsettling opening to philosophy seen in *his* treatments of nature. See, on Shakespeare, Anastaplo, *The Constitutionalist*, p. 820; Anastaplo, *The Artist as Thinker*, pp. 496–97. See also Laurence Berns, "Gratitude, Nature, and Piety in *King Lear*," *Interpretation*, autumn 1972, p. 27; Harry V. Jaffa, "On Leo Strauss," *National Review*, December 7, 1973, p. 1355 ("And Shakespeare was the great vehicle within the Anglo-American world for the transmission of the essentially Socratic understanding of the civilization of the West.") See as well note 12 above, note 104 below.

One can see in Confucian thought a combination of the biblical "way" (but without revelation) and the classical "perspective" (but without philosophy). See notes 17 and 100 above. See also note 90 above.

103. See the text at note 67 of this chapter. See also note 29 above. In *Analects*, XV, 25, Confucius recalled that he could still remember "when a historiographer would leave a blank in his text" rather than fill in, on the basis of mere conjecture, any gap left in the manuscript. See Kung-chuan Hsiao, *A History of Chinese Political Thought*, I, 81. It so "happens" that later in this very sentence in the *Analects* there is a gap—which all the translations I have consulted have supplied words for! Was this blank left by Confucius, or by his authoritative compiler, as a kind of test of future editors and commentators— as well as a joke? See note 55 above. Certainly, it could be instructive as to how carefully the text is to be read. See, on playfulness, Anastaplo, "Notes toward an 'Apologia pro vita sua,'" *Interpretation*, May and September 1982, pp. 319, 338–39. See also note 95 above.

104. Consider *Analects*, III, 15, which suggests that the asking of certain questions about a ritual can itself be prescribed by ritual. And, it seems, Confucius was particularly good at asking questions. Ibid., I, 10. Would anyone who analyzes these texts as I have here be influenced by a philosophical view of things? And may not an early, perhaps the original, editor have seen the whole somewhat as I do on this occasion? Is such an awareness of the whole, on the part of the authoritative shaper of the *Analects*, presupposed by my mode of inquiry?

See, on the limitations as well as the attractions in Sophocles' *Antigone* (*GBWW*, vol. 5) of family-based piety, Anastaplo, *The Constitutionalist*, pp. 651 n. 91, 798–99 n. 32; Anastaplo, *The Artist as Thinker*, pp. 8, 144, 368–69 n. 12; Anastaplo, *The Thinker as Artist: From Homer to Plato and Aristotle* (Athens, Ohio: Ohio University Press, 1997), p. 391.

Consider, finally, Tocqueville, *Democracy in America*, p. 476:

A glance at writings left to us by the ancients is enough to show that those writers sometimes lacked variety and fertility in the choice of subjects and boldness, movement, and a power of generalization in their thought, but they were always admirably careful and skillful in detail. Nothing is written hurriedly or casually, but is always intended for connoisseurs and is always seeking an ideal beauty. No other literature puts in bolder relief just those qualities that democratic writers tend to lack, and therefore no other literature is better to be studied at such times. This study is the best antidote against the inherent defects of the times, whereas the good qualities natural to the age will blossom unintended.

This point should be clearly understood.

It may be good for the literature of one people to study that of another even though it has no bearing on their social and political needs.

See, on Tocqueville, Anastaplo, *Abraham Lincoln,* p. 81.

Chapter Five

Buddhist Thought

I had rather believe all the fables in the [Golden] Legend, and the Talmud, and the Alcoran than that this universal frame is without a mind. And therefore God never wrought miracle to convince [refute] atheism, because his ordinary works convince it. It is true, that a little philosophy inclineth man's mind to atheism, but depth in philosophy bringeth men's minds about to religion. For while the mind of man looketh upon second causes scattered, it may sometimes rest in them, and go no further; but when it beholdeth the chain of them, confederate and linked together, it must needs fly to Providence and Deity.

—Francis Bacon[1]

I.

What is there in the human soul that can be appealed to by radical self-abnegation, that comprehensive suppression of appetites which goes far beyond ordinary temperance? Perhaps efforts at self-abnegation have the appeal they sometimes do because they represent heroic attempts to control, far more than otherwise seems possible to most of us, the ever changing and unpredictable tribulations that flesh is heir to. The heroism of such efforts, characterized by both remarkable self-sacrifice and determined mastery, can attract (when it does not happen naturally to repel) those who yearn for models of greatness.

The turning point in the life of the founder of the Buddhist movement followed his being exposed to ordinary experiences that left him in a severe depression. He learned for the first time at age twenty-nine what most people learn as children. His doting father, the local ruler in a region in Nepal, had rigorously sheltered the young prince from disagreeable things. Siddhartha Gautama had been attractive and sensitive from youth; he lived in exquisite

147

ease; and he acquired at age sixteen a lovely wife and then thirteen years later an infant son.

In any movement numbering five hundred million (as the Buddhists do to-day) a wide variety of stories and belief can be anticipated. But there are some elements in these stories, especially about the life of Gautama, who came to be recognized as the Buddha (the Enlightened One), which seem to be generally accepted. Among the elements in the vast Buddhist literature of hundreds of thousands of pages is the standard account of how the career of the Buddha, at least during his sixth-century B.C. incarnation, got started.[2] Here is a summary of that account for the modern reader:

> One day, while out driving with his charioteer, [Gautama] saw "an aged man as bent as a roof gable, decrepit, leaning on a staff, tottering as he walked, afflicted and long past his prime." The charioteer, questioned by the Prince as to what had happened to the man, explained that he was old and that all men were subject to old age if they lived long enough. The Prince, greatly perturbed by this sight, went back to the palace and became absorbed in thought. Another day, again driving with his charioteer, he saw "a sick man, suffering and very ill, fallen and weltering in his own excreta, being lifted up by some. . . ." Because [Gautama] was perturbed, the charioteer explained, as before, that this was a sick man and that all men are subject to sickness. On a third occasion the Prince saw a dead body and again the charioteer provided the explanation. Finally, [Gautama] saw "a shaven-headed man, a wanderer who has gone forth, wearing the yellow robe." Impressed with the man's peaceful and serene demeanour, the Prince decided to leave home and go out into the world to discover the reason for such a display of serenity in the midst of misery.
>
> On his way back to the palace after seeing the yellow-robed ascetic, [Gautama] received the news of the birth of his son. . . . Upon receiving this news, the Prince decided to make what is known as the great renunciation: giving up the princely life to become a wandering ascetic.[3]

It should be noticed at the outset of our inquiry that physical pleasure is not dismissed by Buddhism as simply inconsequential. Rather, pleasure seems to be recognized as in a sense desirable, but not as truly possessable, no matter how many incarnations one has. So fleeting and otherwise illusory is pleasure bound to be that it is something to be routinely avoided.[4] Centuries after Gautama's traumatic experiences, a Buddhist monk could instruct a ruler, "Whoever, great king, orders his walk aright, grasps the course of the Aggregates [all the composite things in the world, including of course human beings]. Grasping their course, he sees therein Birth, he sees therein Old Age, he sees therein Disease, he sees therein Death. He sees therein nothing that is pleasant, nothing that is agreeable; from the beginning to the middle to the end he sees nothing therein which it is possible for him to lay hold of."[5]

The prospect of his inevitable decay moved Gautama to seek release by putting a stop to the endless series of lives that human beings can expect. Inevitable decay leads to the suffering critical to life on earth (and evidently elsewhere also). Gautama is celebrated as having addressed his followers in this fashion: "I teach only two things, disciples, the fact of suffering, and the possibility of escape from suffering."[6] A scholar can observe, therefore, that "the premise of Buddhism is that life is suffering, that suffering arises from desires or passions, and that desires or passions arise from the erroneous conviction that the ego exists."[7] Gautama is distinguished, it seems, by the intensity of his compassion for the dreadfulness of that suffering which all living things are destined to endure, suffering which is keyed to the mutability of all things. It also seems, however, that enough of our being usually endures to permit us to suffer, including that most exalted form of suffering identified as compassion.

Gautama's response to death may be usefully compared to that of Gilgamesh, the hero in the ancient Mesopotamian epic (at the other extreme, geographically, on the continent from that East Asia in which Buddhism has flourished). Gilgamesh, too, is confronted by death in a special way. Although, as an adventurous warrior, he has seen death before, it does not become "personal" for him until his beloved comrade is mortally stricken.[8]

The two heroes, Gilgamesh and Gautama, have quite different responses to their depressing discoveries. In neither case is a preoccupation with death dismissed as childish or unmanly. Rather, the audiences of these two stories are expected to accept the fact that the discovery of mortality and hence of the insubstantiality of all things is "naturally" traumatic. We have seen that Gilgamesh's response is to try to grasp life more firmly: he desperately seeks immortality, or deathlessness, searching for and finding the only survivors of the Great Flood. He secures from them access to a plant which wards off death. After losing this plant on the way home, however, he is reduced to political projects and to leaving a name for his city and hence for himself.[9]

We have also seen that Gautama, on the other hand, tries to secure release by a determined pursuit of selflessness. If life is the way that Gautama now knows it to be, he wants no part of it: it is clear to him that it is always better never to be born (or reborn) at all.[10] Or, as Albert Schweitzer has put it, "When [Gautama was] nine-and-twenty years of age he left his wife and child, and [as an ascetic] went forth 'from home into homelessness.' The thought that all birth leads only to suffering and death, and that the succession of births is endless, had robbed him of all joy in life. He now sought deliverance from reincarnation."[11]

Gautama, like Gilgamesh before him, can also be said to have had recourse to a political project, in that he founds a great monastic order that embodies the enlightened way he has discovered for an effective renunciation of life. It can even be said that monks are the only Buddhists in the proper sense of the word.[12] Certainly Gautama's discourses are ordinarily addressed to monks. He can be considered more successful as a founder than Gilgamesh, since Gilgamesh's very name suffered oblivion for thousands of years. Gautama, in founding or perhaps refounding, the yellow-robed monastic order, had to experiment, as Gilgamesh did, with an alternative (in Gautama's case, the alternative of radical asceticism) to the mode into which he finally settled.

II.

I attempt in this chapter to search for the core of Buddhism, particularly as it may be seen in the stories most intimately connected with Gautama himself.[13] We can do no more than sample here the vast literature that is available, literature that has no single text generally recognized to be as authoritative as are, say, the Bible, the Koran, the *Analects*, and perhaps the *Bhagavad Gītā* by their respective devotees.

Gautama's renunciation of household life initially took the form evidently traditional in Hindu society: not only did he leave his family in assuming the role of the homeless monk, but he so subjected himself to the rigors of extreme asceticism that he almost starved to death. What finally put a halt to these practices was his recognition that the enlightenment (Nirvana) he sought depends upon rational processes which are difficult to maintain if the body should be wrecked. "The human body, Gautama saw, was the one instrument man had through which to attain enlightenment."[14] Earlier, Gautama's father, partly because of some prophecies, had provided another approach for his son: he had sheltered him from all unpleasant things, offering him the best that wealth and position could provide, including a lovely wife.[15]

Gautama himself chose a middle way between the life of pleasure and the life of asceticism. He worked this out in a period of sustained contemplation (at the outset of his career, after his experimentation in radical asceticism) and was then prepared to deliver his first sermon (that at Benares). His first audience and initial converts consisted of five ascetics who had been appalled by Gautama's recent abandonment of the life of asceticism. The sermon included these observations:

> [There are] two extremes, monks, [which] are not to be practiced by one who has gone from the world. What are the two? That conjoined with the passions and luxury, low, vulgar, common, ignoble, and useless; and that conjoined with self-torture, painful, ignoble, and useless. Avoiding these two extremes the Tathagata [the Perfect

One, that is, the Buddha] has gained the enlightenment of the Middle Path, which produces insight and knowledge, and tends to calm, to higher knowledge, enlightenment, Nirvana.

And what, monks, is the Middle Path, of which the Tathagata has gained enlightenment, which produces insight and knowledge, and tends to calm, to higher knowledge, enlightenment, Nirvana? This is the noble Eightfold Way: namely, right view, right intention, right speech, right action, right livelihood, right effort, right mindfulness, right concentration. This, monks, is the Middle Path, of which the Tathagata has gained enlightenment, which produces insight and knowledge, and tends to calm, to higher knowledge, enlightenment, Nirvana.[16]

All this, Gautama explained in his inaugural sermon, is grounded in four truths:

Now this, monks, is the noble truth of pain: birth is painful; old age is painful, sickness is painful, death is painful, sorrow, lamentation, dejection, and despair are painful. Contact with unpleasant things is painful, not getting what one wishes is painful. In short the five groups of grasping are painful.

Now this, monks, is the noble truth of the cause of pain: the craving, which tends to rebirth, combined with pleasure and lust, finding pleasure here and there; namely, the craving for passion, the craving for existence, the craving for non-existence.

Now this, monks, is the noble truth of the cessation of pain, the cessation without a reminder of craving, the abandonment, forsaking, release, non-attachment.

Now this, monks, is the noble truth of the way that leads to the cessation of pain: this is the noble Eightfold Way; namely, right view, right intention, right speech, right action, right livelihood, right effort, right mindfulness, right concentration.[17]

The fourth noble truth leads again to an enumeration of the elements in the Eightfold Way. (Both enumeration and repetition are made much of in Buddhist accounts.) Several times in the course of this sermon Gautama can announce, "Thus, monks, among doctrines unheard before, in me sight and knowledge arose, wisdom arose, knowledge arose, light arose."[18]

The specialness of the career of Gautama is reflected in how his body can both be talked about in literature and represented in art. Consider this account:

We must now consider the Buddha in his *glorified body*. When he walked about as a human being, [Gautama] naturally looked like any other human being. But this ordinary human body of the Buddha was nothing but a kind of outer layer which both enveloped and hid his true personality, and which was quite accidental and almost negligible. It was not at all an adequate expression of the Buddha's own being. Hidden behind this outer shell was another kind of body, different in many ways from that of ordinary mortals, which could be seen only with the eye of faith. The Buddhists variously called it "the enjoyment body," "the unadulterated body," "the body which expresses the Buddha's own true nature." A list of 32 "marks of a superman," often supplemented by a list of 80 "subsidiary marks," described the most salient features of the Buddha's "glorious body." The list of the 32 marks is common to all schools, and it must be fairly old. The paintings and statues of the Buddha which we find in Buddhist art never depicted the human body visible to all, but they always try to represent the "glorious body" of the Buddha.[19]

Another scholar reports:

> The image of [Gautama], whether seated in meditation or standing (the two most common types of images), walking, or reclining in the hour of death, represents for the whole Asian world the equivalent of the Christ image for the West. Yet, interestingly enough, centuries passed after the Buddha's death before any representations of him as an actual physical being were conceived or executed. This was in keeping with an old [Buddhist] scripture that states, "The Buddha, who has gone beyond the fetters of the body, cannot be endowed by art with the likeness of a body." When an artist, in telling stories of the Master's life and teaching, found it necessary to indicate the Buddha's presence, he used only specific symbols: an empty throne, an umbrella (symbol of sovereignty), a *stupa* (mound for relics), the wheel of his first sermon, footprints. Even in such lively scenes as the future Buddha's departure from his father's palace, the horse—whose hoofs are being lifted up by divine beings to prevent all telltale sounds—departs riderless through the palace gates.[20]

The statues of the Buddha, which may be the most important things in Buddhist art, are indeed revealing, as may be seen in the pieces on display in museums such as the Art Institute of Chicago. He is usually presented in a seated position, serene, contemplative, complete, healthy, full-fleshed, in the prime of life but with no sexual energy suggested. The representation is low-keyed, with little in the way of "action," except in the form of meditation. The faces, not only of the Buddha, but also of those around him, tend to be expressionless. All this can be considered relaxed, impassive, resigned, at rest—almost insistingly so, if that is not a contradiction in terms. A timeless quality, not any particular time or place, is indicated: this is the way things are and should be. One occasionally encounters a graphic representation of the ascetic Gautama, reduced almost to skin and bones. Ordinarily, however, even the statues of the dying Buddha show a reclining, relaxed, full-fleshed, and anything but decrepit man, despite his eighty years.

Such statuary should be contrasted with that produced both by Hindus and Christians. Hindu statuary is replete with distorted bodies, multi-headed "people," sometimes violent actions (including intense lustful embraces), contorted features and even monstrosities. It is easy to see the calmer Buddhist approach as itself a determined reaction to prevailing Hindu excesses.[21]

Then, of course, there is the characteristic Christian portrayal of the agonized body on a cross, something quite foreign to typical Buddhist representations. The Christian can find the stoic detachment of the Buddhist trouble-some, as Albert Schweitzer, for one, did:

> For the Buddha's monks there can be no question of active love, if for no other reason, because it assumes that one loves something in the world and so in some way gives one's heart to it. But this would mean a limitation of freedom from earthly cares. How pathetic is the Buddha's saying: "Those who love nothing in the world are rich in joy and free from pain." To a father who has lost his little boy, he knows nothing better to say than: "What one loves brings woe and lamentation."
>
> He draws the ideal of monastic perfection with hard lines in the saying: "He who cares not for others, who has no relations, who controls himself, who is firmly fixed in the heart of truth, in whom the fundamental evils are extinguished, who has thrown hatred from him: him I call a Brahmin."[22]

Schweitzer goes on to say:

> Jesus and the Buddha have this in common, that their form of ethics, because it is under the influence of world and life negation, is not an ethic of action but an ethic of inner perfection. But in both the ethic of inner perfection is governed by the principle of love. It therefore carries within it the tendency to express itself in action and in this way has a certain affinity with world and life affirmation. With Jesus the ethic of the perfecting of the self commands active love: with the Buddha it does not get so far.
>
> It must be noted that the world and life negation of Jesus is in origin and in essence quite different from that of the Buddha. It does not rest on the distinction between material and immaterial Being, but abandons the natural world as evil, in the expectation that it will be transformed into a world that is supernatural and good. The world and life negation of Jesus is conditioned by ethics.[23]

The agonies of Jesus can be seen as expressive of that love for all mankind which Schweitzer finds lacking in the Buddhist approach. Consider what more can be said about that approach by a man such as Schweitzer with his celebrated dedication to "reverence for life":

> The Buddha says nothing about the question of the redemption of the world. Really we should expect him to voice the hope that in time all living creatures will enter Nirvana and that in this way the sorrowful process of coming and going will some day quite come to an end. But he takes into account the difficulty of imagining the world-Nirvana if, in accordance with the hypothesis of the doctrine of reincarnation, all being can only attain redemption by the circuitous route of a human existence capable of the highest knowledge.
>
> According to the Buddha, it already borders on the impossible that a human being who, as a result of evil-doing, enters into a non-human form of existence should later

be born again in human form, "because in the low forms of existence there is mutual murder and no good action." If a yoke with one opening be thrown into the sea and in that sea there is a one-eyed turtle which only rises to the surface once in every hundred years, there is much more probability, according to a parable of the Buddha, that this turtle will one day put its neck into this yoke than that the fool who has once sunk to low forms of existence will again attain to human existence.

The fact that the Buddha, the preacher of compassion, makes man only occupied with his own redemption, not with that of all living creatures, is a weakness of his teaching.[24]

Whether Schweitzer is correct about the lack of concern among the Buddhists for all living creatures, would not Gautama (who could even eat meat on occasion, if the animal had *not* been killed for him) have been inclined to criticize the Schweitzer approach as hardly an adherence to the Middle Way?

III.

Both Hindus and Christians consider themselves guided, in their concerns for a desirable continuity of their existence, by conformity to the will of the divine. Hindus must cope with a system in which one's life (or soul?) is inevitably repeated in one form or another again and again; Christians must cope with the condition of the immortal soul with a view to its perpetual existence after its single manifestation on earth.

Buddhists, on the other hand, make far less of a godhead or the divine. A man can be freed from his fetters by a rational system of thought and the way of life he determines to be appropriate for liberation, something which Gautama considered himself particularly adept at doing.[25] Buddhists also make far less, certainly less than do most Christians, of their individuality: it can and should be overcome. Thus it has been reported,

The Buddhists also preserved few names, because it was, in the best periods, bad form for a monk to make a name for himself by literary work. It did not matter to them *who* said something, but whether it was true, helpful and in keeping with tradition. Originality and innovation were not encouraged, and anonymity was a concomitant of sanctity.[26]

One is able, if properly disciplined, to release oneself from the cycle of deaths and rebirths: the prospect of an immortal life, as ordinarily understood, is not treasured; the chain of rebirth should and can be broken. Gautama himself is considered to have been able to grasp his lives past and (in compassionate interest in mankind) his lives yet to come on earth. Is it not assumed that if a man is fully and hence truly to control his life now, and to insure what is to happen to him ever after (as well as to be able to offfer guidance to others), then he needs to know everything about himself, which includes knowing all that has happened and that is yet to happen?[27] This ability to take control over one's "life" in the most decisive manner includes control over how one dies during any particular incarnation.[28]

All this should be contrasted to the Hindu teaching that Arjuna confronts in the *Bhagavad Gītā*: his natural compassion must be subordinated to his duty.[29] The Buddhist may deny that there is any substantial thing (a permanent ego) transmitted from one life to the next. But is there not a consciousness or "identity" to "collect" one's *karma*, that compendium of things fated to happen to someone?[30] The self-denying Gautama has "succeeded" in maintaining something of himself permanently, if only in the imaginations of his followers, for millennia now.

There are various Buddhist doctrines and practices which serve the end of liberation, of total self-control, which culminates in Nirvana, a condition of complete self-abnegation which is nevertheless (or because of this) blissful beyond description. The effort must be made, therefore, to overcome the demands of one's body and the allure of other bodies. If "one" does succeed in controlling one's body, one's individuality is suppressed, so much so that there would be nothing around to "enjoy" any heavenly benefits. This means, among other things, that the status even here on earth of marriage and of the family has to be radically depreciated, however much those institutions have permitted the production of the men and women who become monks and (in ancient times) nuns.

One may wonder what confidence there can be that the condition a man gets himself into here on earth will forever determine his eternal career, even to the extent of total extinction. It seems that the control one exercises over one's passions extends to the development of confidence that one is indeed on the right path, the path out of the universe, so to speak.[31] What routine control of one's passions can mean is suggested by an anecdote from Zen Buddhism:

> Two monks, one old, one young, came to a muddy ford where a beautiful girl was deliberating whether to cross. The elder monk grabbed her and, without a word, carried her across. As they continued on their way the younger, astonished at the sight of his companion touching a woman, kept chattering about it, until at last the elder monk exclaimed, "What? Are you still carrying that girl? I put her down as soon as we crossed the ford."[32]

IV.

At the core of the Buddhist position is the denial of any considerable or reliable goodness of human life on earth (or of any life anywhere?), at least so long as *life* does mean change, disintegration, and death (and, perhaps also, the awareness of these gloomy prospects for others as well). Gautama did not depend on revelation, it seems, in arriving at this assessment of human life, however much he relied upon the revelations of the Hindus for various assumptions and doctrines (if not experiences), as about reincarnation. In principle, it can be said, others could figure out (perhaps many had already figured out, but not publicly?) what Gautama did.[33] This is not to deny that the teachings that reason suffices to establish for a few might need (for the sake of the many) considerable embellishment by tales of miracles and of a saintly life.[34] The many may require, perhaps even desire, stories about the physical torments of hell.[35] What *is* to be made of the fierce punishments depicted for those souls in hell? Is that sort of thing consistent with assumptions about the insubstantiality of the ego? What does such fierceness itself reveal, whether among Buddhists or among Christians? Is it "politically" necessary for so rational a religion as Buddhism?[36] The common sense of Buddhism is suggested by another Zen Buddhist anecdote:

> Ex-Emperor: Gudo, what happens to the man of enlightenment and the man of illusion after death?
> Gudo: How should I know, sir?
> Ex-Emperor: Why, because you're a master!
> Gudo: Yes, sir, but no dead one![37]

Buddhist reservations about earthly life may be contrasted with the affirmation of life found among such peoples as the Jews, an affirmation which reflects the goodness that God Himself sees in the Creation depicted in *Genesis*. Does not philosophy back up this finding of revelation? Consider, for example, the Aristotelian recognition of the sweetness of existence.[38] True, Socrates, for one, had no overpowering desire to live. But he could see life among the dead, if one did survive death, as not unpleasant, especially if one could continue inquiring and learning.[39]

Is there not something unnatural in the insistence upon suffering as decisive to human life on earth? To insist upon this is to suggest that the only happiness one could reasonably hope for is release from all life. That there is something to this may be indicated by the old saying, made more of by some than by others, that philosophy prepares one for dying. The Buddhist approach to what life is truly like is suggested by this account:

> Most of us are inclined by nature to live in a fool's paradise, to look on the brighter side of life, and to minimize its unpleasant sides. To dwell on suffering runs normally counter to our inclinations. Usually, we cover up suffering with all kinds of "emotional curtains." For most of us life would be intolerable if we could see it as it is,

and if our mental perspective would emphasize its distasteful features as much as its gratifying ones. We like to keep distressing facts out of sight.[40]

The natural grasp of the goodness of existence, in the fashion of Aristotle, is questioned. It is seen as self-deception, sometimes even as deliberate self-deception. And yet can it be truly said that Aristotle was deceived—that he did not know those realities of life which Buddhists, like the rest of us, know well? Did he not see life—as we know it, with its mortality, pains, failures, and serious disappointments—as permitting growth, maturation, challenge, and genuine accomplishments?

Does this Aristotelian approach depend upon taking nature seriously, something which may be impossible to do if routine reincarnation is made much of? If nature is not taken seriously, bizarre results can come to be accepted by quite intelligent people. For example, a Buddha is commended for having given up his life in order that a starving tigress and her litter might live.[41] Or a nun plucks out an eye to discourage a persistent suitor drawn to her by the beauty of her eyes.[42] Then there is this story:

> In order that [a monk] should have no attachment to food, he is bidden to eat everything and anything which is thrown into his bowl; and the Venerable Pindola has been held up to the reverence of posterity for calmly eating a leper's thumb which had fallen into his bowl [upon "begging" his food the way monks do]. Monastic discipline would be undermined if monks would start to pick and choose their food.[43]

The acceptance of reincarnation as routine undermines in various ways any reliance upon nature—that nature which points to the goodness of a life keyed to our natural faculties. When one's "life" is seen as aeons long, it must be difficult to grasp it as a whole: control is difficult—as is any reliable knowledge and hence the possibility of genuine satisfaction with what one has done. The only effective control one can hope to exercise may be seen as the result of efforts to eliminate once and for all the sequence of lives in which we are enmeshed.

Without a proper grasp of nature, philosophy itself is not possible, however much is made by modern scholars and others of Buddhists as philosophers.[44] The ancient dialogue, *The Questions of Milinda* (which exhibits Greek influences), is often regarded as philosophical; but it is much more a kind of rhetoric, if not even sophistry, which reflects the cleverness and subtlety repeatedly evident in Buddhism. The difference that nature, or rather its absence, makes is suggested by this exchange:

> [Said the king:] Reverend Nagasena, you Buddhists say: "Far hotter than any ordinary fire is the Fire of Hell. A tiny stone, cast into any ordinary fire, will smoke for a whole day and not crumble. But a rock as big as a pagoda, cast into the Fire of Hell,

will crumble in an instant." But on the other hand you also say this: "As for the living beings that are reborn in Hell, no matter how many thousands of years they are
tormented therein, they go not to destruction." That is something I do not believe.

[Said the Elder:] . . . What do you think about this, great king? Do not the delicate princesses of the Greeks and of the Warriors and of the Brahmans and of the
householders eat pieces of meat that are hard and tough?

Yes, Reverend Sir, they do.

Now these hard substances, once inside of their abdomen, once in their belly, go
to destruction; do they not?

Yes, Reverend Sir, they do.

But does the embryo in their belly also go to destruction?

No indeed, Reverend Sir.

For what reason?

I suppose, Reverend Sir, it is because of the Power of Kamma [Karma] that it does
not go to destruction.

Precisely so, great king, because of the Power of Kamma, the denizens of Hell,
no matter how many thousands of years they are tormented in Hell, go not to destruction. Right there are they born, right there do they grow up, right there do they
die. Moreover, great king, this was said by the Exalted One: "He shall not die so long
as that Evil Kamma is not yet exhausted."

You are a clever man, Reverend Nagasena![45]

It is obvious, at least to us, that the physiology relied upon here is mistaken:
an embryo that is swallowed would be digested as any other meat would be.
Another way of putting it is to say that the womb is far different from the
stomach. The physiological error is not the interesting point here, but rather
the fact that the author and his readers are prepared to believe that there *could*
be diverse consequences following upon the activity of the same agent (in this
case, the stomach). Thus, flesh is digested ordinarily, but not in the case of the
embryo. This means that there can be, routinely, diverse effects resulting from
the same cause: critical to the way things are ordered is the role of kamma (or
karma), which affects much if not all of what happens to us. Nature is thereby
circumvented or ignored, a circumvention anticipated perhaps by what Gautama's father had attempted to do in shielding his son from exposure to evidence of human mortality.

One consequence of the lack of dependence upon nature is that simple understanding, or understanding for its own sake, does not seem to be made
much of in Buddhism. Again and again one can see in Buddhist thought an
emphasis upon inquiry for the sake of the practical. Theoretical inquiry is routinely disparaged.[46]

We can again see why compassion rather than reason is the human attribute ultimately to be prized. If reason is given the second place, and nature little or no place at all, then prudence, as well as political philosophy,
is not likely to be taken seriously. Are not grave political problems apt to

emerge when the best people in the community systematically neglect a concern for this world? It must be a concern for community-minded citizens when celibacy is encouraged and expected, on a large scale, for the true believers and hence for the most virtuous. This may be made even more acute when those who do separate themselves from worldly concerns live by "begging," appearing daily among the others in quite conspicuous garments.[47]

One result of all this seems to be the promotion of gentleness, making Buddhism perhaps the least violent in practice of the great religions known to us.[48] But to promote gentleness is to discourage spiritedness—and this raises, in still another way, the question of whether a proper political ordering is possible on Buddhist terms. Are not both justice and courage likely to be neglected in this case? Is not spiritedness as much a part of the natural whole as gentleness?[49]

One may ask as well what the status of beauty is when the things of this world, and the appearances of things, are systematically disparaged. Nothing, it would seem, can be taken at face value. This implies that common sense, which respects the surface of things, may not mean much. Still, is it not natural and wholesome to give beauty its due, whatever the chattering monk after the river ford (to say nothing of his elder companion) may have believed? Appearances *can* be deceiving—but we would not be moved to notice this if "appearance" and "reality" did not match to a considerable extent in the everyday world.[50]

V.

I have attempted to work out some implications of the Buddhist approach to life and death. Why did Gautama take the way he did? Is not this one major way "out," considering the prevailing opinions and conditions of his time? Those opinions included, we have seen, what seem to have been fixed, deeply held convictions about the workings of incarnations.[51]

Among the Hindus and those of like mind from whom Gautama emerged, it can be said, the prospect of a soul's repeatedly waging vital battles, generation after generation, appears to have led to resignation if not despair. This is dramatized in the *Bhagavad Gītā*, where Arjuna gets critical instruction from his charioteer. (Is there not an echo of this in Gautama's learning about life and death from *his* charioteer at age twenty-nine?) According to the ancient sources drawn upon in the *Gītā*, one's divinely required duty can call for extreme violence; one has a destiny to fulfill; one cannot simply take charge of one's life.[52] Gautama, on the other hand, figures out (almost as a corrective commentary upon the approach seen in the *Gītā*) that gentleness is called for, that one *can* take charge of one's life, that an effort to do so in the name of compassion is a move in the right direction, a move that Gautama was able in his time and circumstances to work out to its proper conclusion.

Perhaps, also, the prevalence and unavoidability of suffering in Gautama's day, reinforced by the violence and mutual exploitation implicit in a Hindu caste system which had become more and more rigid, stimulated a man temperamentally inclined toward compassion and gentleness to assert himself.[53] Is a new, more humane, political order, or at least a more humane set of social relations, reflected in the brotherhood promoted by Gautama?

However much of an innovator Gautama was, he may well have recognized the limits of innovation. We have noticed that much of by-then-ancient Hindu thought, including its cosmology, is taken for granted by Gautama, or at least by his followers. The critical difference is that Gautama pointed the way to a deliberate self-annihilation which permits one to avoid, if not to overcome, the hopelessness that the Hindu belief in reincarnation can degenerate into. Even if Gautama did not take the Hindu view seriously himself, was he not obliged to take seriously its temporal consequences?

To suggest how desperate things might have become in Gautama's time is to approach these matters with both the advantages and the limitations of an outsider, somewhat as an anthropologist might. This approach may even consider Gautama to have been something of an anthropologist himself. Or, alternatively if not additionally, Gautama can be approached for psychological study: was he a man whose character traits or psychic makeup required a total withdrawal from physical struggle, if not even from life itself? So intense may such a withdrawal be that one can, in the name of self-denial, exercise a powerful hold upon others.

VI.

The questions of the anthropologist and the psychologist must be ultimately subordinated to the question whether Gautama's way has hold of the truth about human things, to say nothing about divine things. That is, a proper study of Buddhism must consider whether the ideas Gautama developed are sound.

One place to begin in any such assessment is with the Buddhist—and before it the Hindu—belief in routine reincarnations. What *is* the evidence for all this? Is it not evidence which should, if valid, be available to us as well in the West? What experiences do we have, what things do we know, that point to, or away from, earthly reincarnations? What does nature, and one's natural grasp of things, say about a belief in routine reincarnations? That so many intensely believe in reincarnation cannot suffice to establish it, even though such extensive testimony does oblige us to consider this doctrine with care. Is it not significant that routine reincarnations rarely occur to us in the West as something to be taken seriously? We can suspect why how many could come to believe in it, if it is *not* so. But can we understand how so many who have heard again and again of reincarnation could fail to take it at all seriously, if it *is* so?[54]

Much is also made in Buddhism of meditation. This is related to the oft-stated opinion that Buddhism is a rational religion, however pious (in the ordinary sense) its people at large may be. Although meditation is not simply philosophy, it can include sustained thinking which permits one to work things out somewhat as philosophers do. Does not modern cosmology, with its vast time and space and perhaps with its notions about how life can emerge anywhere in the universe, lend support to the Hindu-Buddhist approach to things? We are still left with the question of how good the understanding of modern science, or of any cosmological view, can be without a sound, if not even a continually examined, grasp of nature. Is there something artificial or hypothetical, however salutary, about what modern scientists and perhaps ancient Buddhists do?

The thinking we see in Buddhism may be more that of the artist than that of the philosopher. Consider the significance of so many apt images and engaging stories in Buddhism. This is related to the status of the particulars of which artists make so much. How self-conscious is Gautama about these matters, deliberately relying on particulars, in the form of stories and against the background of his own life, in order to spread his message? Was he then an artist who was counter-Homeric in his inclinations, a poet who made peace and self-abnegation, not war and self-assertion, the stuff of *his* "Iliad"?[55] Did Gautama believe all that he said when he talked about the whole? Considerable common sense and a grasp of the natural order are exhibited in his approach to things, not least in the way he turned away from his original asceticism and then organized his monastic order.[56]

What is likely to happen to Buddhism in an age when modern science does even more hereafter than it already has done with its own immense (perhaps incomprehensible) cosmological scope and when image making is already practiced so extensively all around us? The answer to this question might depend, in part at least, upon whether conventional Buddhism is to be accounted for primarily in anthropological-political-psychological terms. Or is it to be accounted for as itself a significant grasp of the truth?[57]

VII.

We must also consider what the significance is of the tradition of esotericism in Buddhism, something which is referred to even in what Gautama is reported to have said as he was about to die: "What, then Ananda, does the order {of monks] expect of me? I have preached the truth without making any distinction between exoteric and esoteric doctrine; for in respect of the truth, Ananda, the Tathagata has no such thing as the closed fist of a teacher who keeps some things back."[58] Although Gautama and his immediate adherents disavowed esotericism, the many indications of and references to it oblige us to wonder what was truly going on among them.

Esotericism presupposes that, for one reason or another, a few can understand and use properly and hence may be taught what the many are not able to understand or to use properly. What did Gautama himself truly believe about the matters which he discussed? If we assume he was as intelligent as he is generally reputed to have been, we must reconsider what he said in the light of what we ourselves can see from the evidence, or lack of evidence, available to him.[59]

Did Gautama, in his extended meditation into the nature of things, see an abyss confronting the thinking human being? Was he terrified, or exhilarated, or at least challenged about the prospect of groundlessness? We must wonder whether Gautama anticipated at all the view of things that Friedrich Nietzsche developed in our own time.[60] But Gautama, we have seen, sought to rise above or dispense with *the eternal return*, whereas Nietzsche asserted it and evidently clung to it as his salvation, closer in a sense to the spirit of Gilgamesh in this respect than to that of Gautama. Both Gautama and Nietzsche try to take control of their lives with an exercise of the will (bordering, it can seem to the outsider, on madness) that extends to the past as well as to the future, perhaps even to the extent of inventing (or is it discerning?) both one's "personal" predecessors and one's "personal" successors in the chain of births and deaths. In neither case, perhaps, is philosophy taken fully seriously or on its own terms, especially insofar as philosophy presupposes both the eternity of the universe and the temporary appearances on the earth of individual souls. These souls can reasonably aim at happiness here and can look back at their lives on earth as, on net, good. In short, the philosopher can contemplate a natural wholeness to things. It would be considered odd (and probably unnatural?) by him to regard complete personal annihilation as *perfection*, however temporary particular lives dependent on bodies may naturally have to be.[61]

Gautama, whatever he himself may have believed, was obliged to take some "givens" seriously in prescribing for his community. Did he succeed in reshaping what had been a violent community? Or was it that Buddhism had to move on, in the centuries after its founding among the Hindus, to more receptive regions in Asia, thereby reaffirming elsewhere, rather than creating, a peaceful way of life?

We are left, then, with the puzzle of what Gautama truly believed and did, as well as of what the status of nature and of the desire to understand may be in his thought. Whatever esotericism he may have resorted to did permit him a very long life, a career evidently pursued without serious conflict or persecution. His "religion" could even be suspected in some quarters (and repeatedly across the millennia) of "atheism," without turning him and his followers into outcasts, perhaps in part because of the trappings of religion and self-sacrifice with which the activities of the conspicuous Buddhist monks are invested. In any event, Gautama's life *can* be presented without miracles; very little is said about the divine, except negatively perhaps in the form of a devil. That which is said about the supernatural tends to treat it as "natural." The human being, moreover, should not expect help from the divine but must work out his own salvation.[62]

Both conventional religion and traditional philosophy can be expected to exhibit one trait which Gautama very much exhibited as well: a determined pursuit of perfection. Whether the ordinary religious spirit or the familiar philosophical temperament can properly accept the form of perfection Gautama seemed to settle upon—the perfection of complete personal annihilation or nothingness—is a question worthy of further consideration. With this question we remind ourselves that there is much left to be learned by all of us about the very nature of things.[63]

Notes

1. Francis Bacon, *The Essayes or Counsels, Civill and Morall* (1625), essay XVI, "Of Atheism." Consider also Bacon, *The Essayes*, essay XVII, "Of Superstition," which includes these sentiments:

> It were better to have no opinion of God at all than such an opinion as is unworthy of him. For the one is unbelief, the other is contumely, and certainly superstition is the reproach of the Deity. . . . And as the contumely is greater towards God, so the danger is greater towards men. Atheism leaves a man to sense, to philosophy, to natural piety, to laws, to reputation, all which may be guides to an outward moral virtue, though religion were not, but superstition dismounts all these, and erecteth an absolute monarchy in the minds of men. Therefore atheism did never perturb states, for it makes men wary of themselves, as looking no further, and we see the times inclined to atheism (as the time of Augustus Caesar) were civil times. . . . There is a superstition in avoiding superstition, when men think to do best if they go furthest from the superstition formerly received; therefore care would be had that (as it fareth in ill purgings) the good be not taken away with the bad, which commonly is done when the people is the reformer.

Consider as well note 62 below.

I have found very helpful the criticism of this chapter by Mahinda Deegalle, a Buddhist monk from Sri Lanka doing research at the University of Chicago. See M. Deegalle, *Nirvana saha sadacaraya* (Sri Lanka: Dipani Piakasapa, 1986), pp. 90–92 (bibliography).

2. The Hindu doctrine of reincarnations, which figures prominently in Buddhist thought, is repeatedly drawn upon in this chapter. See chapter 3 of this collection. See also notes 51, 54, and 59 below.

The Hindu-Buddhist doctrine of Nirvana, as a state of extinction of desire and individual consciousness and as freedom from rebirth, is also drawn upon in this chapter. See W. Theodore de Bary, ed., *The Buddhist Tradition in India, China, and Japan* (New York: Vintage Books, 1969), pp. 9, 11–12, 21, 30; Albert Schweitzer, *Indian Thought and Its Development* (Boston: Beacon Press, 1956), pp. 99–106; Nancy Wilson Ross, *Three Ways of Indian Wisdom* (New York: Simon and Schuster, 1966), pp. 90, 113–14.

"Buddha" is not the name of a person but designates a type. "'Buddha' is Sanskrit for someone who is 'fully enlightened' about the nature and meaning of life. Numerous 'Buddhas' appear successively at suitable intervals. Buddhism sees itself not as the record of the sayings of one man who lived in Northern India about 500 B.C. His teachings are represented as the uniform results of an often repeated irruption of spiritual reality into this world." Edward Conze, ed., *Buddhist Scriptures* (Penguin Books, 1959), p. 19. See also note 51 below. On Buddhism, see Ross, *Three Ways,* p. 79:

> Buddhism, the religion of reason and meditation and the faith of approximately one fifth of humanity, was founded by the so-called "historic" Buddha, Siddhartha Gautama, a unique spiritual genius born in northeastern India at a date generally accepted as 563 B.C. Although in the land of its origin Buddhism was in time reabsorbed into the all-embracing Hinduism from which it sprang, it was destined to become and remain the dominant influence in vast sections of Asia, including Ceylon, Burma, Cambodia, Thailand, Vietnam, Laos, as well as Nepal, Sikkim, Tibet, Mongolia, China, Korea, and Japan.

Buddhism is said to be the major religious denomination of our fiftieth state, Hawaii. Ibid., p. 134.

3. *Encyclopaedia Britannica*, 15th ed., s.v. "Buddhism." "Gautama" is the Sanskrit spelling of a name spelled "Gotoma" in Pali, the other principal language of the earliest Buddhist literature. See also the accounts of Gautama's career in Conze, *Buddhist Scriptures*, pp. 39–40, 43; de Bary, ed., *The Buddhist Tradition*, pp. 6–7; Ross, *Three Ways*, pp. 84–87; and E. A. Burtt, *The Teachings of the Compassionate Buddha* (New York: Mentor Book, North American Library, 1982), pp. 20–21. The institution of monks in yellow robes preceded Gautama, just as monasteries preceded Saint Augustine, a key figure in the development of monastic life in Christendom. For the first five hundred years after the career of Gautama the Buddhist "Scriptures" may have been orally transmitted. Conze, *Buddhist Scriptures*, p. 11. "Buddhists possess nothing that corresponds to the 'New Testament.' The 'continuing tradition' is all that is clearly attested." Ibid., p. 11.

Parallels to the development of Christianity are suggested in this account of the early career of Buddhism:

> A first Buddhist council was summoned in the reign of [Emperor] Ashoka—about 240 B.C.—with a view to the settlement of sectarian disputes. It is clear that heresies had already arisen, for certain of Ashoka's edicts are concerned with the unfrocking of schismatics; and, indeed, we know that heresies were promulgated even during the life of the Buddha himself. In course of time we find that a large number of sects developed, all equally claiming to be followers of the true doctrine, just as has been the case with Christianity and every other great faith. The Buddhist sects are divided into two main groups: those of the Hinayana ("The Little Raft") and the Mahayana ("The Great Raft"). The former, whose scriptures are preserved in Pali, claim to represent the pure original teaching of Gautama, and do in the main preserve its rationalistic, monastic and puritanical features to a marked extent: the latter, whose scriptures are in Sanskrit, interpret the doctrine in another way, with a development that is mystical, theological and

devotional. The Hinayana had maintained its supremacy mainly in the South, particularly in Ceylon and Burma: the Mahayana mainly in the North, in Nepal and China. But it is misleading to speak of the two schools as definitely Southern and Northern.

Let us recall that according to the orthodox Hinayana, Gautama was regarded as a man like other men, and differed from others only in his intuitive penetration of the secret of life and sorrow, in his perception of things as they really are, as an eternal Becoming; with that knowledge he attained Nibbana [Nirvana], and for him the causes of birth [that is, reincarnation] were extinguished.

Ananda K. Coomaraswamy, *Buddha and the Gospel of Buddhism* (New York: Harper Torchbooks, Harper & Row, 1964), pp. 222–23. See note 56 below. Compare note 59 below. See, on Gautama's charioteer, the text at note 52 of this chapter.

4. See Conze, *Buddhist Scriptures*, pp. 222–24.

5. From *Questions of Milinda*, in Lucien Stryk, ed., *World of the Buddha: A Reader* (Garden City, N.Y.: Anchor Books, Doubleday & Company, 1969), p. 120. See, on *Questions of Milinda*, note 45 below. Had the anticipated birth of his child triggered Guatama's anxiety about disease, old age, and death?

How deeply rooted was Gautama's anxiety in the languages and way of life in which he and Buddhism were nurtured? See Guy Richard Welbon, *The Buddhist Nirvana and Its Western Interpreters* (Chicago: University of Chicago Press, 1968), pp. vii–viii:

According to the Buddhists, a man's lot in this life is characterized by suffering (Sanskrit: *duhkha*; Pali: *dukkha*). The texts make it clear that suffering is linked to ignorance. Indeed, in the Buddhist view, suffering and ignorance are invariably associated. The one is never found without the other. Most poignant and consequential among the aspects of ignorance, say the Buddhists, is man's failure to comprehend the basic truth about the phenomenal universe: no phenomenon is permanent—nothing abides. Ignorant of that truth, his proclivities (habitual thirst—*trsna, tanha*—for objects and experiences) nurtured accordingly, man lives out of harmony with himself, his fellows, his world. He suffers.

The Buddha is the compassionate physician, his pronouncements prescriptions. The Way of the Buddha is, in a manner of speaking, the way from disease to health. But of what does "health" in the Buddhist sense consist? To be sure, it is deliverance (*moksa, mokkha*) from suffering. It is described variously, most commonly as *nirvana* (*nibbana*).

Nirvana is the absence—the destruction—of suffering (*duhkhanirodha*). It involves the eradication of ignorance through the acquisition of wisdom (*sambodhi*)—knowledge, conceived classically in India not merely as intellection but as operational and effective knowledge. Yet, more specifically, more positively than the absence of debilities, what is nirvana? The ultimate aspiration of all Buddhists, their *summum bonum*, what is its "essential" nature? What does attainment to it involve for the existence of the previously suffering individual? One of the oldest in the history of ideas, that question, in its various modes, has been debated furiously by Buddhists and non-Buddhists alike.

See also note 32 below. In 1863 a French scholar announced,

Today, as in 1856, I am convinced that it is morally impossible that in Magadha in the sixth century before our era the son of Mayadevi [Gautama] preached the absolute annihilation of virtuous souls until six hundred years later in Galilee the son of Mary could come to preach the Gospel of their eternal beatitude.

Ibid., p. 81. See notes 47 and 57 below. Does Buddhism, seen in this way, mean that ours is a universe from which the very best are systematically removed? See the text at note 24 of this chapter.

6. See Ross, *Three Ways,* p. 81. See also the quotation under the photograph of the Buddha statue facing the title page of A. L. Herman, *An Introduction to Buddhist Thought: A Philosophical History of Indian Buddhism* (Lanham, Md.: University Press of America, 1982).

7. Laurence G. Thompson, *Chinese Religion, An Introduction* (Encino, Calif.: Dickerson, 1975), p. 95.

8. See, for the text of the *Gilgamesh* epic, *The Great Ideas Today,* vol. 1986.

9. See chapter 1 of this collection.

10. See Edward Conze, *Buddhism, Its Essence and Development* (New York: Harper Torchbooks, 1959), p. 63. See also note 61 below.

11. Schweitzer, *Indian Thought,* p. 89.

12. See Conze, *Buddhism,* p. 53; Conze, *Buddhist Scriptures,* p. 70; Richard A. Gard, ed., *Buddhism* (New York: George Braziller, 1962), p. 52.

13. See, for a useful account of Gautama's career, Conze, *Buddhist Scriptures,* pp. 19–66.

14. Ross, *Three Ways,* p. 88. See also *Encyclopeadia Britannica,* s.v. "Buddhism"; Conze, *Buddhist Scriptures,* pp. 45f.; Schweitzer, *Indian Thought,* pp. 92–93.

15. Is this a mild form of the sensuality of the boisterous Gilgamesh?

16. Burtt, *The Teachings,* pp. 29–30. The Tathagata is "he who has fully arrived," that is, the Perfect One (and hence *completely gone?*). This is a title of the Buddha. See also *Encyclopeadia Britannica,* s.v. "Buddhism"; de Bary, ed., *The Buddhist Tradition,* pp. 15–17.

17. Burtt, *The Teachings,* p. 30. See, on the significance of numbers, chapter 3 of this collection, notes 30, 33, and 34. See also note 57 below.

18. Burtt, *The Teachings,* ibid., p. 30. See also ibid., pp. 28, 65.

19. Conze, *Buddhism, Its Essence and Development,* p. 36.

20. Ross, *Three Ways,* p. 125; see also ibid., p. 95. There was a similar delay "before any representations of [Jesus] as an actual physical being were conceived or executed." Compare the concern from the outset of Moses Maimonides' *The Guide of the Perplexed.*

21. Compare the four-headed statue in Bangkok, which is the center of attraction to worshipers and which is evidently widely known in Southeast Asia as the "four-headed" Buddha. See *India News,* August 19, 1985, pp. 4, 5. See also *Ezekiel,* chap. 1. The Buddha has been assimilated into Hindu worship in various places.

Compare also Islam with its vigorous abjuration of human portraits, especially of sacred personages. See chapter 6 of this collection. That Buddhism is not readily assimilated into Islamic worship is suggested by what the Taliban did recently in Afghanistan to massive Buddhist statuary. One can be reminded, by the more "glorious" Buddhist statuary, of the statues of Greek gods. Consider as well how Socrates was portrayed—not as an athlete but as full-bodied, sturdy, self-possessed. See further on Buddhist statuary, Ross, *Three Ways,* pp. 125–27.

22. Schweitzer, *Indian Thought,* pp. 109–10. Even though Schweitzer is considered outdated and otherwise limited in his scholarship, he is drawn upon in this chapter to illustrate how prominent Westerners have responded to Eastern "schools" of thought to which they have been exposed.

23. Ibid., p. 113.

24. Ibid. See note 5 above.

25. See *Encyclopaedia Britannica,* s.v. "Buddhism"; de Bary, ed., *The Buddhist Tradition,* pp. 10–11; Conze, *Buddhist Scriptures,* pp. 52–54, 229f.

26. Conze, *Buddhism,* p. 30.

27. See Conze, *Buddhist Scriptures*, pp. 25–26, 31, 53f. See also ibid., pp. 237–42, 258f., on the eventual coming to earth of the final Buddha, Maitraya. See also note 33 below.

28. See Conze, *Buddhist Scriptures*, pp. 58f. See also Burtt, *The Teachings*, p. 48.

29. This is similar to what desperate defenders of the Jewish law said to the first Christians with respect to such matters as healing on the Sabbath. See the discussions of the trial of Jesus in Anastaplo, "On Trial: Explorations," 22 *Loyola University of Chicago Law Journal* 539 (1991). See also the discussions in that article of the trial of Adam and Eve and of the Binding of Isaac. See, on Arjuna and his "trial," chapter 3 of this collection.

30. See Thompson, *Chinese Religion*, pp. 83f. See also Anastaplo, *The American Moralist: On Law, Ethics, and Government* (Athens, Ohio: Ohio University Press, 1992), pp. 10–11.

31. See, on the certainty of having attained liberation, Conze, *Buddhist Scriptures*, p. 31.

32. Stryk, ed., *The World of the Buddha*, pp. 388–89. Zen Buddhism has been described as "a unique blend of Indian mysticism and Chinese naturalism sieved through the rather special mesh of the Japanese character." Ross, *Three Ways*, p. 139.

Compare, as a reminder of not only the immediate appeal of various urges, but also of the transcendent significance of the naturally erotic, William Butler Yeats's poem "Politics." See Anastaplo, *The American Moralist*, p. 497. See also notes 47 and 50 below. See, on nature, Anastaplo, *Human Being and Citizen: Essays on Virtue, Freedom, and the Common Good* (Athens, Ohio: Swallow Press/Ohio University Press, 1975), pp. 8, 46, 74, 203; Anastaplo, *The American Moralist*, p. 616; sections IV and VI of this chapter; note 62 below; the preface to this collection; appendix B of this collection.

It seems to have been easier for the older monk than it was for the younger monk not to grasp the girl as girl. Another Buddhist elder was asked (perhaps by a young man?), "Reverend Sir, have you seen a woman pass this way?" The elder responded, "Was it a woman, or a man that passed this way? I cannot tell. But this I know, a set of bones is travelling upon this road" (Coomaraswamy, *Buddha*, p. 159). Compare note 47 below (the world as "cemetery").

We are apt to regard as healthier the reminiscence of the repentant Augustine: he recalls that, as a young man, he had prayed, "Give me chastity and continence, but not yet." *Confessions*, VII, 7. See note 58 below. Gautama's efforts at renunciation seem in some ways more desperate than those of someone such as Augustine. The Buddhist's fundamental problem is with life itself, while the Christian's is with life in one's earthly body, something which should be easier to deal with than any thorough repudiation of existence itself. Socrates and Plato could also address, without being crippled by, the problem of the fetters of the body. See, on the sweetness of existence for the philosophers, the text at note 38 of this chapter. See also the text at note 1 of this chapter. See as well note 57 below.

Augustine may have been moderated somewhat in his heroic attempts at self-abnegation by the philosophical tradition which Christianity inherited, in however diluted and altered a form, along with the language of the New Testament. See, on how the Church was obliged to take more than it wanted of classical antiquity with the Latin language, Machiavelli, *Discourses*, II, 5. See, on the significance of Shakespeare for modern republicanism, Anastaplo, *The Constitution of 1787: A Commentary* (Baltimore: Johns Hopkins University Press, 1989), pp. 1, 74–88. See also note 5 above.

The Christian reliance upon an elevated individuality can be instructively contrasted with the Buddhist yearning for complete personal annihilation. See note 5 above. The student of great religious movements must wonder what can be accounted for, in each case, by the chance circumstances and the natural talents of inspired mortals. We cannot help but wonder, upon reflecting on the celebrated lives of Gautama and Augustine, what the good was that was truly being sought by each of them and whether it was indeed secured. We take as our point of departure here the observation by Aristotle, "All human beings have by their nature an appetite for knowing" *Metaphysics*, I, 1, trans. Eva T. H. Brann. See, on inspired mortals, chapter 4 of this collection, note 38.

33. Compare Conze, *Buddhist Scriptures*, pp. 126f. Gautama, it should again be noticed, is not said to be either the first or the last Buddha to appear on earth. See ibid., pp. 19–20, 30–33, 35–36, 49; Ross, *Three Ways*, p. 124. See also note 27 above. Is he, at least for human beings, central to all the Buddhas that will ever appear? Compare how Muhammad can be spoken of with respect to the line of prophets.

34. See Conze, *Buddhist Scriptures*, p. 57.

35. See ibid., pp. 221, 224f.

36. See the concluding section of Plato's *Gorgias* (*GBWW* [*Great Books of the Western World*], I: vol. 7, p. 252; II: vol. 6, p. 252 [chapter 1 of this collection, note 4]). See also the text at note 48 of this chapter. See, on the political services rendered by organized religion, Anastaplo, "Church and State: Explorations," 19 *Loyola University of Chicago Law Journal* 61 (1987). See also note 56 below.

Is Biblical-style revelation such as not to leave sufficient room for the reason, or the will, of the Buddha? Compare God's appearances to Moses and Jesus' appearance to Saul on the road to Damascus. Gautama, on the other hand, considers himself to have figured out the way to his distinctive doctrines. See de Bary, ed., *The Buddhist Tradition*, p. 360. Consider also the text at note 1 of this chapter. Do we move away from the spirit of Gautama if we assume that this Buddha was destined to appear, that the divine had provided for the enlightenment of mankind in due time? Is it to misconceive the fundamental claim of Gautama to a rational approach to consider as a problem, as is done in *Questions of Milinda* (note 45 below), whether the Buddha (meaning Gautama) ever lived?

37. Stryk, ed., *The World of the Buddha*, p. 399. Gudo's dates are A.D. 1579–1661.

38. See Aristotle, *Politics* 1278b25–29 (*GBWW* I: vol. 9, p. 476; II: vol. 8, p. 476); Anastaplo, *The American Moralist*, p. 600. The Confucian teaching seems far closer to Aristotle than to Buddhism with respect to these matters. See chapter 4 of this collection. See, on Chinese Taoism here, Thompson, *Chinese Religon,* p. 85. See also note 32 above, note 47 below. See as well note 19 of the preface to this collection, note 90 of chapter 4 of this collection.

39. See Anastaplo, *Human Being and Citizen*, p. 8. Consider (in Homer's *Odyssey*) the condition in which Odysseus found Achilles among the dead: Achilles' interests and limitations (unlike, say, those of Socrates) were such as to require bodies (his and those of others) for his personal fulfillment. Consider, also, the Confucian respect for old age. See, on Confucius, note 38 above.

40. Conze, *Buddhism,* p. 44.

41. See Conze, *Buddhist Scriptures*, pp. 24–26; Schweitzer, *Indian Thought*, p. 104; Ross, *Three Ways,* pp. 91–92.

42. See Burtt, *The Teachings*, pp. 80–83. See also *Matthew* 5:29. See, on some offending eyelids, Ross, *Three Ways,* p. 152.

43. Conze, *Buddhism,* 62. There is a tradition that Gautama died, in his eighties, of a tainted meal. Then there is the apt explanation by Sam Houston upon spitting out, at a formal dinner, the very hot food he had inadvertently taken into his mouth: "A damned fool would have swallowed that!" See, on nature, note 32 above.

44. See, e.g., Burtt, *The Teachings*, pp. 22, 25; Gard, ed., *Buddhism*, p. 14; de Bary, ed., *The Buddhist Tradition*, p. xvi.

45. Stryk, ed., *The World of the Buddha*, pp. 107–8. A variation upon this exchange uses, instead of delicate princesses, "female sharks and crocodiles and tortoises and peacocks and pigeons [that] swallow hard stones and gravel." Ibid., p. 107. See also Ross, *Three Ways*, p. 115. See, on *Questions of Milinda*, Stryk, ed., *The World of the Buddha*, p. 89:

> The non-canonical Pali work *Milindapannha (Questions of Milinda)* . . . is a collection of imaginary dialogues between Menander, Greek king of Bactria, 125–95 B.C. (there is some divergence of opinion regarding these dates), and the sage Nagasena, whose expositions of Buddhist teaching on the non-existence of the soul and Nibbana (Nirvana) are of significance to all interested in Buddhist philosophy.

However questionable Nagasena's handling of nature and natural processes may be, there *is* something commonsensical (and hence Aristotelian) about a common refrain, "That man might say whatever he would, but all the same." In the following passage taken from *Questions of Milinda*, where Nagasena explains to the king the continuity of the soul that is manifested in successive reincarnations:

> Great king, it is precisely as if some man or other were to take a lamp and were to climb to the attic of a thatched house and were to eat, and the lamp as it burned were to set fire to the thatch, and the thatch as it burned were to set fire to the house, and the house as it burned were to set fire to the village, and the village-folk were to catch that man and were to say, "Why, Master man, did you set fire to the village?" and the man were to say, "Friends, I didn't set fire to the village; the fire of the lamp by whose light I ate is one thing, but the fire that burned the village is another." Suppose they carried the dispute to you. Whose side, great king, would you take?
>
> The side of the village-folk, Reverend Sir.
>
> Why?
>
> That man might say whatever he would, but all the same, that last fire came straight from the first.
>
> Great king, it is precisely as if some man or other were to choose a young girl to be his wife and were to pay the purchase-money and were to go his way, and after a time that young girl were to become a grown woman, were to attain her majority, and then a second man were to pay the purchase-money and were to marry her, and the first man were to come and say, "But why, Master man, are you carrying off my wife?" and the second man were to say, "I am not carrying off your wife; that young girl of tender years whom you chose to be your wife and for whom you paid the purchase-money is one person; this grown woman who has attained her majority, whom I chose to be my wife and for whom I paid the purchase-money, is another person." Suppose they carried the dispute to you. Whose side, great king, would you take?
>
> The side of the first man, Reverend Sir.
>
> Why?
>
> That man might say whatever he would, but all the same, that grown woman came straight from that young girl.

Stryk, ed., *The World of the Buddha*, pp. 98–99. See note 62 below.

46. See, e.g., Burtt, *The Teachings*, pp. 32f.; de Bary, ed., *The Buddhist Tradition*, p. 18n.; Ross, *Three Ways*, p. 113; Conze, *Buddhism, Its Essence and Development*, p. 19; Schweitzer, *Indian Thought*, pp. 96–97. Compare Burtt, *The Teachings*, pp. 70–71.

47. See de Bary, ed., *The Buddhist Tradition*, pp. 27n., 32, 46–47, 72, 258; Schweitzer, *Indian Thought*, p. 112. See also Pliny, *Natural History*, V, xv, 73 (on "the remarkable

tribe" of celibate Essenes). Compare the Chinese concern about childlessness. See de Bary, ed., *The Buddhist Tradition*, pp. 133–34, 243, 247–51. The Buddhist repudiation of earthly existence is reflected in someone's regarding "the world of men [to be] no better than a cemetery, as being under the sway of old age and death, and as being always in distress," Conze, *Buddhist Scripture*, p. 224. See note 32 above ("a set of bones"). Although the better thinkers of antiquity in the West recognized the fragility of human life on earth along with the fragility of the earth itself, they could still take political life and prudence more seriously than Buddhism seems to. See Anastaplo, *The American Moralist*, pp. 100–102.

Is the use today of Buddhist monks as social workers and teachers a concession to modernity or to Western ways? Consider this summary of the European Enlightenment attitude toward Buddhism during the seventeenth and eighteenth centuries:

> Buddhism always appears simply as a "monstrous religion," as an "abominable sect" founded by a "very wicked man." It is a "plague," a "gangrene." Chinese philosophers and statesmen have had reason to combat it not only as a "ridiculous doctrine" but as a "moral monster and the destruction of civil society."

Welbon, *The Buddhist Nirvana*, See notes 5 and 38 above.

The future Buddha can be presented, as in an ancient statue in the Art Institute of Chicago, seated in a regal throne: he is ruling. This does suggest an opening to the political in traditional Buddhism. See note 56 below.

48. See, e.g., Burtt, *The Teachings*, p. 39. See also ibid., pp. 40f., on the virtues which are promoted. See as well Schweitzer, *Indian Thought*, pp. 100f., 115–16, 119. Compare the text at note 36 of this chapter. See, on suppressed spiritedness, the text at note 51 of chapter 2 of this collection.

49. See the discussion of conscientious objectors in Anastaplo, "Church and State: Explorations." See the discussion of the Vietnam War in Anastaplo, "Freedom of Speech and the First Amendment: Explorations," 21 *Texas Tech Law Review* 1941 (1990); Anastaplo, *The American Moralist*, pp. 108–21, 225–44. See, on the Gulf War, ibid., pp. xvi–xix, xxii, 225n. See also note 18 of appendix C of this collection.

50. See, on the beauty of Gautama, Conze, *Buddhist Scriptures*, pp. 35–36, 125, 129, 132. Consider this observation in Augustine's *The City of God* (X, 14) (*GBWW* I: vol. 18, p. 307; II: vol. 16, p. 358):

> The Platonist Plotinus discourses concerning providence and, from the beauty of flowers and foliage, proves that from the supreme God, whose beauty is unseen and ineffable, providence reaches down even to these earthly things here below; and he argues that all these frail and perishing things could not have so exquisite and elaborate a beauty were they not fashioned by Him whose unseen and unchangeable beauty continually pervades all things.

See also *Matthew* 6:23–30. Compare Augustine, *Confessions*, IV, 13. See, for "A Primer on the Good, the True, and the Beautiful," note 39 of appendix B of this collection. See also note 32 above.

51. See note 2 above, note 59 below. Did not Gautama welcome that kind of reincarnation that for him took the form of institutionalizing his spirit in the Buddhist monastery movement?

Compare the Socratic recourses to reincarnation in Plato's *Meno, Republic,* and *Phaedo* (but *not* at the end of Plato's *Apology*, where Socrates reviews the alternatives available to him upon his immediately impending death). Do not the conventional Platonic recourses to reincarnation seem, much more than do the conventional Hindu-Buddhist recourses, to be tentative stories which are enlisted in the service of philosophy? One does see in the Platonic dialogues an insistence upon the necessity, for philosophy (if not for the virtues generally), of rising decisively above the appetites of the body.

52. See, for the text of the *Bhagavad Gītā, The Great Ideas Today*, pp. 290–337 (1995). See also note 2 above. I am assuming here that although the *Bhagavad Gītā* was composed in about 300 B.C. (and hence after the career of Gautama, which was two or more centuries earlier), something of the story about the relation between Arjuna and his charioteer was known long before the composition of the *Gītā*. If I am mistaken here, the *Gītā* may be seen instead as an echo of the career of Gautama. See, on the Charioteer in the *Gītā*, chapter 3 of this collection, note 85.

53. It has been suggested, "On the metaphysical side, Buddhism is not fundamentally different from Hinduism. It stands in the same relation to Hinduism as Christianity to Judaism." Paul Thomas, *Epics, Myths, and Legends of India* (Bombay: D. B. Taraporevala Sons, 1960), p. 110. It has also been suggested that Gautama is like Martin Luther. See Schweitzer, *Indian Thought*, p. 91. See also ibid., pp. 134–37.

54. See, on reason, revelation, and nature in the *Bhagavad Gītā*, Anastaplo, "Church and State: Explorations," pp. 183–90.

The doctrine of reincarnations does not keep many (most?) of the faithful from regarding death much as we do in the West, as may be seen in the famous mustard seed parable. See Burtt, *The Teachings*, pp. 43–46; Ross, *Three Ways*, pp. 122, 133. See, on reincarnation experiences, Ian Stevenson, *Cases of the Reincarnation Type* (Charlottesville, Va.: University of Virginia Press, 1975, 1977).

55. But Homer could also have an *Odyssey*. Did Gautama, too, develop a companion piece, one which made much more of political considerations than radical self-abnegation would suggest? Is this seen perhaps in the rules devised for his Brotherhood?

56. Does not any long-established institution, especially if large numbers of people are recruited and trained, have to respond to and respect (in practice, if not in "theory") the dictates of nature? See note 52 above. Consider also the significance of the sometimes passionate Augustine's three decades of highly practical service as the Bishop of Hippo. See note 36 above, note 57 below.

See, on the importance of the Emperor Ashoka for the success of Buddhism, de Bary, ed., *The Buddhist Tradition*, pp. 7–8; Ross, *Three Ways*, pp. 125, 127; note 3 above. See also Machiavelli, *The Prince*, chap. 6: "Whence it comes to pass that all armed prophets conquer and the unarmed ones are ruined" (trans. Leo Paul S. de Alvarez) *(GBWW* I: vol. 23, p. 9; II: vol. 21, p. 9); chapter 4 of this collection, note 38.

57. A key question of fact for Buddhists could well be, Has Gautama ever returned "personally"? The significance of "personality" (or "consciousness" or "identity"), or lack of it, has been noticed with respect to Buddhist thought, and in such a way as to throw light on such Christian works of apparent self-abnegation as Augustine's *Confessions*:

> The denial of the ego or self is undoubtedly one of the Buddha's original tenets. From the viewpoint of Western mysticism, it seems to strike hard at what Underhill called a fundamental principle: the existence of a self capable of communion with God.

Richard Woods, "Buddhism, and Mysticism," *Mysterion, A Thomas More Newsletter*, no. 16, p. 3. Augustine, in the central chapter of the central book of his *Confessions* (a chapter which is, appropriately enough because of its subject matter, remarkably short), suggests,

> Also I considered all the other things that are of a lower order than yourself [God], and I saw that they have not absolute being in themselves, nor are they entirely without being. They are real insofar as they have their being from you, but unreal in the sense that they are not what you are. For it is only that which remains in being without change that truly is.

Confessions, VII, 11 (*GBWW* I: vol. 18, p. 49; II: vol. 16, p. 61). See note 5 above. See, on the significance of the number seven, Augustine, *The City of God*, XVII, 4 (*GBWW* I: vol. 18, pp. 451–55; II: vol. 16, pp. 514–18). See also note 17 above.

58. Burtt, *The Teachings*, pp. 48–49. See de Bary, ed., *The Buddhist Tradition*, pp. 28–29, 282, 287, 295; *Encyclopedia of Religion* (New York: Macmillan, 1987), vol. 2, pp. 172–81, 481, 526–27. See also chapter 2 of Wu Ch'êng-ên's *Monkey* tale for a critical reading by the Monkey King of significant esoteric signals ("Additions to the Great Books Library," *The Great Ideas Today*, pp. 314f (1992). See as well Welbon, *The Buddhist Nirvana*, pp. 139–41, 168. See further, ibid., pp. 299–300:

> The Buddha was not a philosopher. . . . Obviously, the Buddha was a genius as a soteriological tactician. Depending on the context and in particular the needs of the individual(s) to whom he spoke, his emphasis varied. To those full of self, his message was expressed negatively. To those full of fear, the message expressed confidence. To those full of suffering, the message expressed hope.

Was not Augustine, too, a master rhetorician? See note 32 above.

59. Many among the Buddhists tend to see Gautama as a divinity. Compare note 3 above. Certainly, he can seem to us as very thoughtful. What lessons, we may well consider, would be included among the esoteric teachings of Gautama? Our prime candidate is likely to be with respect to the widely accepted doctrine of reincarnations, the belief in which was a massive fact that had to be reckoned with by any would-be leader of Gautama's time and place. See notes 2, 51, and 52 above. If there really is no reincarnation of human souls, and if Gautama believed there are reincarnations, what do we make of any reports he might have made about having recollected his past (to say nothing of his future) existences? And if he did not believe there are reincarnations, what then?

60. See, on Nietzsche, Welbon, *The Buddhist Nirvana*, pp. 184–93; Anastaplo, *The American Moralist*, pp. 125–34. Does it matter, at least for most if not all practical purposes, whether the world is eternal and whether we know whether it is eternal? Consider this passage in Ross, *Three Ways*, p. 113:

> The Buddha's characteristic attitude toward those who overindulged themselves in speculating, theorizing and debating comes through most effectively in the story of a follower named Malunkyaputta. This monk, who had a restless, overactive mind, announced to the Buddha on one occasion that if he did not get some specific straightforward answers to his inquiries about First Causes, and in particular as to whether life was eternal or not eternal, he intended to give up the Sangha [the order of Buddhist monks] for good. The Buddha replied that such an attitude reminded him strongly of a man who, having been struck by a poisoned arrow, refuses to accept the services of a physician, or even to have the arrow removed, until he has made a lengthily detailed inquiry about who shot the arrow and how and why; or again, of a man in a burning house who refuses to put out the blaze, or even to leave the doomed edifice, until he has discovered who started the conflagration.

"Whether the dogma obtains, Malunkyaputta, that the world is eternal, or that the world is not eternal, there still remain birth, old age, death, sorrow, lamentations, misery, grief and despair—all the grim facts of human existence—for the extinction of which in the present life I am prescribing."

61. See Anastaplo, *The American Moralist*, pp. 5–6. See also the text at note 10 of this chapter.

62. See, on Buddhism and "atheism," Welbon, *The Buddhist Nirvana*, p. 312. Consider, on working out one's own salvation, the following counsel:

An ant is a wise creature for itself, but it is a shrewd [mischievous] thing in an orchard or garden. And certainly men that are great lovers of themselves waste the public. Divide with reason between self-love and society; and be so true to thyself as thou be not false to others, specially to thy king and country. It is a poor centre of a man's action, *himself*. It is [exactly like the earth]. For that only stands fast upon his own centre, whereas all things that have affinity with the heavens move upon the centre of another, which they benefit. The referring of all to a man's self is more tolerable in a sovereign prince, because themselves are not only themselves, but their good and evil is at the peril of the public fortune. But it is a desperate evil in a servant to a prince, or a citizen in a republic.

Francis Bacon, *The Essays or Counsels, Civill and Morall* (1625), essay XXIII, "Of Wisdom for a Man's Self." Consider also Bacon, *The Essays,* essay XXXVIII, "Of Nature in Men." See, on nature, notes 32 and 56 above. See also note 1 above. Consider, as well, in connection with the argument in the text at note 45 of this chapter, the womb-like stomach of Zeus noticed in the text at note 35 of appendix A of this collection.

63. To what extent does Gautama build *not* on nothingness but on a perhaps desperate effort to secure nothingness? Is there not something Cartesian about such determined self-centeredness, albeit in the ostensible service of complete personal annihilation? See note 57 above. See, on Descartes and modern science, Anastaplo, *The American Moralist*, pp. 83–102. See, on modern science, Anastaplo, *The Artist as Thinker: From Shakespeare to Joyce* (Athens, Ohio: Ohio University Press, 1983), pp. 250–53, 339–42, 496; appendix A of this collection. See, on the forms of our knowing, chapter 4 of this collection, note 26. See also the text at note 1 of this chapter.

Chapter Six

Islamic Thought: The Koran

Prophetology is a central teaching of [Maimonides'] *Guide of the Perplexed*. One gets an idea of its difficulties from the list of conditions which, according to Maimonides' teaching, the prophet must fulfill. The prophet must have at his command (1) a perfect intellect, (2) perfect morals, (3) a perfect power of imagination, (4) the faculty of daring, (5) the faculty of divination, and (6) the faculty of leadership (of men). What do these different conditions of prophecy have in common? Whence does this rhapsody gain a unitary, transparent order?

—Leo Strauss[1]

I.

It is likely that, for the reader who does not know Arabic, his first look into the Koran will be his last. The outsider does not feel that more will be gained by repeated readings of the Koran or that the considerable demands the text makes on the reader will ever decrease.[2] Thomas Carlyle, the great English historian, said of the book (in an essay on Muhammad, transmitter of the Koran to the Arab people), "[I]t is as toilsome reading as I ever undertook. A wearisome confused jumble, endless iterations, long-windedness, entanglement, most crude, incondite;—insupportable stupidity, in short!"[3] Edward Gibbon, another great historian, reports that Muhammad,

with the sword in one hand and the Koran in the other, erected his throne on the ruins of Christianity and of Rome. The genius of [this] Arabian prophet, the manners of his nation, and the spirit of his religion, involve the causes of the decline and fall of the Eastern [Roman] empire; and our eyes are curiously intent on one of the most memorable revolutions which have impressed a new and lasting character on the nations of the globe.[4]

Gibbon and Carlyle did consider Muhammad a great hero, one of mankind's greatest.[5] Are we not obliged, even if we accept Carlyle's harsh assessment of the Koran itself, to look with some care at what this prophet-hero (570–632 A.D.) left behind as the Word of God?[6]

The Koran (or Qur'ān) has been described in this fashion by the *Encyclopaedia Britannica*:

> The Qur'ān (Arabic: Reading or Recitation; often spelled Koran), the holy book of Islam, is regarded by believers as the true word of God as revealed to the Prophet Muhammad. In its written form it is accepted as the earthly reproduction of an uncreated and eternal heavenly original, according to the general view referred to in the Qur'ān itself as "the well-preserved tablet" . . . (Qur'ān 75:22). The word *qur'an* is derived from the verb *qara'a* "to read," "to recite," but there is probably also some connection with Syriac *qeryānā*, "reading," used for the scriptural lessons in the Syrian Church. In the Qur'ān itself the word is not used with reference to the book as a whole but only as a term for separate revelations or for the divine revelation in general. The Qur'ān is held in high esteem as the ultimate authority in all matters legal and religious and is generally regarded as infallible in all respects. Its Arabic language is thought to be unsurpassed in purity and beauty and to represent the highest ideal of style. To imitate the style of the Qur'ān is a sacrilege.[7]

This holy book is divided into one hundred and fourteen suras (chapters) of unequal length.[8] The suras revealed at Mecca during the earliest part of Muhammad's career are concerned with ethical and spiritual teachings and the Day of Judgment. The suras revealed at Medina during a later period in his career, especially after he was established as a powerful leader, are concerned with social legislation and political-moral principles for constituting and ordering the Community.[9] The *Britannica* description we have drawn upon continues:

> In length the Qur'ān is approximately comparable with the New Testament. For purposes of recitation during the holy month of Ramadan it is divided into 30 "portions" . . . one for each day of the month.[10] . . . With the exception of the first sura the so-called *fatihah* ("opening" of the book), which is a short prayer,[11] the [114] suras are arranged roughly according to length, sura 2 being the longest and the last two or three the shortest. Because the longest suras generally derive from the latter part of Muhammad's activity, the consequence of this arrangement is that the oldest suras are generally to be found toward the end of the book and the youngest generally appear at its beginning.
>
> In the accepted version of the Qur'ān now in use, each sura has a heading containing the following elements: (1) a title, which is usually derived from some conspicuous word in the sura, such as "The Cow," "The Bee," "The Poets," but usually not an indication of the contents of the whole chapter; (2) the *basmalah*, i.e., the formula-prayer "In the name of God, the Merciful, the Compassionate";[12] (3) an indication of whether the sura was revealed at Mecca or at Medina and the number of its verses;[13] and finally (4) in some cases one or more . . . detached letters [at the be-

ginning of the sura], the meaning of which has not been satisfactorily explained, though it is thought that they might stand for abbreviated words, indicate certain collections of suras, or have an esoteric significance.

We can well begin our own exploration of the Koran by recalling the work of another great hero, a giant among physicists, Isaac Newton. It has been said of his *Mathematical Principles of Natural Philosophy* that it is the culmination of attempts by such men as Galileo, Kepler, and Descartes to create a unified physics of terrestrial and celestial motion. The success of Newton's achievement made his work the basis of modern physical science down to our time. Is this not like Muhammad? Human beings have been thinking about nature for a very long time; similarly, they have been thinking about God for a very long time. The two inquiries may even be the same quest—into being and the basis of being—but with different standards or evidence relied upon in each case. Muhammad himself records that God had spoken of the flawlessness of heaven in this way: "[Have the unbelievers] not beheld heaven above them, how We have built it, and decked it out fair, and it has no cracks?" (50:6).[14]

There can be said to have appeared through Muhammad still another version of an inquiry, whether about nature or about God, which has always occupied the best minds. Was this version, "in the Arabic tongue"(46: 10–11), a refinement of what had gone before? Is it a culmination—or is it an inferior reflection? Muhammad is in some ways the most modern of the great religious prophets. Yet there has been incorporated in his teaching much of the old way which is otherwise generally repudiated. Were those incorporations reluctant accommodations by the Koran to pagan and other practices, or were they in the service of vigorous innovations if not even restorations? More needs to be said about this.

For the moment, it should be added that physics, like revelation, assumes a power greater than ourselves, which makes sense of things. But, one must wonder, is physics capable of dealing with the decisive question toward which all such inquiry can be said to be directed: What is the First Cause?[15]

II.

Muhammad, as transmitter, is in a great prophetic tradition—or, at least, he so considers himself. Other books, especially "the Torah and the Gospel," preceded the Koran (3:1–3; 34:30; 46:10–11). Eighteen enlightened men are set forth by the Koran as Muhammad's predecessors "in a straight path" (6:83–87).[16] His own coming is considered to have been prophesied by the last of the prophets before him, "Jesus, son of Mary" (61:5–9).[17] Moses, we are told by the Koran, called on his people to be *Muslims*—that is, to *surrender* to God. (10:84)[18]

Abraham, we are also told, prayed that his posterity would be made a *muslim* people—that is, "a nation submissive," surrendering itself to God (2:122–32). Abraham is described as neither a Jew nor a Christian, but rather as "a Muslim and one pure of faith; certainly he was never of the idolaters" (3:60).

The Jewish character of Koranic doctrines, especially in their most elevated aspects, may be seen in the short sura, "Sincere Religion" (112:1–4):

In the name of God, the Merciful, the Compassionate

> Say: "He is God, One,
>   God, the Everlasting Refuge,
> who has not begotten, and has not been begotten,
>   and equal to Him is not any one."[19]

Consider now the eleventh-century Jewish hymn, *Adon Olam*, one of the most popular hymns found in the Judaic ritual to this day. It includes these lines:

For He is one, no second shares
His nature or his loneliness;
Unending and beginningless;
All strength is His, all sway He bears.[20]

It has been noticed that Islam, like Christianity, is in some sense a Jewish sect, a derivation of sorts from traditional Judaism. But perhaps it should be added that modern Judaism may itself be influenced somewhat by Islam, by the determined monotheism promulgated by the Koran. The *Adon Olam* was written by a Jew in a Spain challenged by the Moors. Was he, as a Spanish poet, obliged to come to terms with both the Christian and the Islamic challenges to Judaism?[21]

The Koran reflects Christian sources as well, especially in its doctrines about eternal life and personal salvation. These elements may also be found in Judaism, but the emphasis there seems different. Life *here* does not seem to matter quite as much for the Muslims as it does for the Jews—and in this respect pious Muslims are more like pious Christians. Islam is perhaps more like Christianity also both in that there is considerable missionary fervor exhibited by it and in that one enters the fold by accepting the faith, not primarily by birth.[22] Islamic missionary zeal seems to have been expressed in a different way from that exhibited by the Christians, however. The message of the Koran, it still seems to many Christians, never converted many by itself; the aid of the sword was also required.[23] But, as Carlyle noticed, one has to *get* a sword.[24] The poetry,[25] if not the bare message of the Koran, has helped arm enterprising men, men who often seem tougher, at least today, than their Christian counterparts. Such toughness would perhaps be explained by Muslims as necessary for the merciful mission of rooting out, and keeping back, the idolatrous tendencies to which most human beings are subject.[26]

An even more critical difference between Islam and Christianity—after all, Christianity has also known the use of the sword—is that Islam denies the divinity of any being but Allah. Specifically, the divinity of Jesus is denied, a denial which is emphasized in the short sura I have already quoted in its entirety (112:1–4).[27] The Koran reports that the Jews have also believed in a son of God prior to Jesus, Ezra.[28] Not much is made of this by Muslims, however. It seems to be more an effort to undermine the Jews' monotheistic credentials for immediate polemical purposes than to address Judaism seriously.[29] Certainly, Muhammad himself is mortal; he is not even an intercessor with God; he is no more than a messenger (3:137).[30]

This is not to deny that Jesus is special (19:30; 48:55–60). We are told by the Koran that he was conceived by divine will in Mary, who remained a virgin (3:37–50; 19:16–37; 21:91; 43:57–64).[31] We are also told that he was not really killed by the Jews, but only a likeness of him (4:155–59). Still, Jesus is not eternal, but the Koran is.[32]

The Koran infuses Judaism with Christian and Arabic influences, just as Christianity had infused Judaism with Greek thought. These three great religions, it is obvious, are intimately related. This is evident in the Koran itself, with its many references to the Hebrew Bible and with some to the New Testament. It is also evident that Judaism was the great departure from the polytheism that was and is evident elsewhere in the world. How that came about remains for us a mystery.[33] What is not a mystery, though, is that there are remnants throughout the Koran of Jewish and Christian influences, however distorted or fragmentary (if not even idiosyncratic) those remnants may often seem to the Jew or to the Christian who knows the Bible.[34]

One must wonder whether Muhammad was to the Jews somewhat as Elijah Muhammad, of the Black Muslim movement in the United States, has seemed to many Muslims today: a self-defined successor of dubious credentials and muddled doctrines.[35] Or, is Muhammad another prophet in the Jewish tradition, despite his recourse to Arabic rather than to Hebrew for his prophetic utterances? Even more critical may be whether Muhammad, or his sources, really understood Jewish scriptures and traditions. But before we turn to the implications of this question, we should look further into the conditions out of which Islam seems to have originally developed.

III.

A considerable source for Islam (if only, sometimes, in reaction) was the medley of pagan religious opinions that antedated Muhammad in the Arabian

peninsula. Although these opinions were largely polytheistic and hence dif-
fuse in character, they were nevertheless influential, if only for the pilgrimages and rituals long associated with places such as Mecca. There must have
been, for Muhammad to draw upon, considerable ferment as well as numerous well-established religious forms among the Arabs of this region.[36]

Mecca matters a great deal to Muhammad. After all, it was the site, the Koran tells us, of the first temple ever founded for mankind, Kabba (Ka'bah), a
temple associated with the life of Abraham himself, the great ancestor of the
Arabs as well as of the Jews (3:90–93; 5:98).[37] The pilgrimages of Muslims
to Mecca continue to exhibit respect for the place most venerated by the idolaters before them (2:190–195).[38]

The message of Muhammad meant the end of pagan polytheism, at least in
the West. The last significant near-Western polytheism, in the seventh century, may well have been that found among the pre-Islamic Arabs. Was not a
program based on divine revelation the only safe way for any leader to reform
this fierce, idolatrous, and divided people?[39]

Without these various pre-Islamic influences—Christian, Jewish, and even
pagan—the teaching of the Koran would have had to have been more primitive than it was. There were three thousand years of experience and reflection
behind the Koran's innovations. Precisely what the now-suppressed pagan
contribution was to the Koran is considerably harder for us to spell out, from
the Koran itself, than what the Jewish and Christian contributions were. But
we cannot help but notice the pagan contribution, not least in the dramatic circling of the Kabba in Mecca.[40] What we make of the pagan contribution,
however, is another matter. It is tempting for moderns to allow "anthropology" to take over here—to allow ideas to be seen as the products of social,
economic, and other forces, not as things which have standing or authority on
their own.[41]

An anthropological approach is seen even in recent rearrangements by
scholars of the traditional text of the Koran. Its 114 suras are put by some in
chronological order, on the assumption that there is an ascertainable development in Muhammad's personal and political thought which must be taken into
account. But the suras of the Koran *were* arranged, evidently according to
some principle, by its original compilers—by people who had been fairly
close, it seems, to Muhammad.[42] Furthermore, it has been the Koran arranged
in a specific way, even if originally arbitrary, which has had the effect it has
had for centuries upon billions of people. Is it not presumptuous on the part
of scholars to rearrange matters, thereby depriving their readers of the Koran
of history?[43]

In principle, there is no *before* or *after* for a prophetic utterance, insofar as
it *is* the word of God.[44] Muhammad was known to "cancel" a text now and

then—but that is his doing, or God's, not a scholar's—and such cancellation *is* to be thought about.[45] The text as we have long had it is, if anything Koranic is, what God intended mankind to have. Is the text complete? Are all the suras now recorded those that Muhammad delivered the two decades that he prophesied? Perhaps not, but that may not matter: most of the original converts to Islam probably heard no more than occasional suras, just as most early Christians probably did not have either the complete New Testament or even any one of the four Gospels in its entirety.[46]

Dedication to one's own faith often means that the considered and long-accepted expressions of another's faith must also be taken seriously. Otherwise, the skepticism upon which anthropology tends to rely in these matters can become pervasive and critical. Does not every purported revelation have something of the truth about it, especially if it evokes a substantial and continuing response? Does it not at least reflect the nature of things, whatever may chance to be the physical circumstances, the personal motives, or the psychic condition of its transmitter?[47] Are prophets, spurious or otherwise, something like dreamers who incorporate parts of "reality" in their visions or like poets who imitate, rearrange, and thereby explain natural things?

The older anthropological approach, which sometimes seems to dominate the study of religion and religious experience today in the West, means that the possibility of the divine is denied or at least muted.[48] Muhammad's own character and history become more important than the thought he offers himself as the transmitter of. But, I again ask, did not the very character of that thought contribute significantly to its reception?

IV.

What more should be said, then, of Muhammad's teachings? Are they truly revelations? What is the whole *like* which the teachings of the Koran purport to illuminate? Does the divine permeate that whole?[49]

In properly considering these questions, which can help us think about revelation and about understanding itself, we are bound to notice what is now known as the "fact-value" distinction, the fashionable insistence by social scientists that only facts, not values, can be investigated and known. Values are said to be merely matters of opinion and taste, and hence not subject to serious examination and testing. But one's understanding of things—one's observation, not just assumption, of how things truly are—can very much affect the data one collects, how one regards that data, and what other data one regards as either irrelevant or unavailable.[50]

The most critical fact to be investigated and determined with respect to any-one's prophetic claims is whether they are true.[51] How *does* one go about decid-ing whether Muhammad's pronouncements are indeed the Word of God? Is there anything intrinsic to them which would identify them thus? Consider, for in-stance, the validity sometimes testified to by accurate predictions. There is, how-ever, relatively little predicting in the Koran.[52] There is also the problem, here as elsewhere, of the reliability of the account both of the reported predictions and of the reported outcomes of such predictions. In short, the reliability of ancient reports upon which everything may depend remains a serious problem.[53]

Then there are the assurances that miracles provide. The reliability of the reports of miracles is a serious problem as well. But no matter: there are no, or few, miracles, as ordinarily understood, associated with the life of Muham-mad, at least so far as Muhammad himself claimed them. Some victories and chastisements are linked to the will of God—but the battle accounts offered as evidence of divine intervention can themselves be accepted by the unbe-liever as plausible. Besides, it is recognized by Muhammad that the good do not always prosper, while the evil all too often do, at least for awhile—and so the workings of God need not always be evident here on earth.[54] To this, too, the unbeliever can assent.

Muhammad *is* said to have been transported to Jerusalem one night. But it seems that this can be understood as a dream (17:1).[55] Some of Muhammad's followers associate miraculous doings with him, including his bodily ascent into heaven at death, but such accounts do not seem to be either his doing or essential to his approach.[56] He does not deny the possibility of miracles—but he insists that Divine Messengers perform them only by leave of God (40:77). He does not claim to have been granted such leave. God, it seems, wanted to try it this time without signs: "Naught prevented Us from sending the signs [for Muhammad] but that the ancients cried lies to [earlier signs]" (17:62).

Muhammad's failure to perform miracles is to be contrasted with the mir-acles associated with the lives of Moses and Jesus (or with the life of Abra-ham, Muhammad's greatest predecessor in the millennia-long campaign against idols). Were things too stable—too late in the day—for miracles to "work," or to be claimed, by Muhammad's time? Perhaps the long period of idol worship in Arabia had got Arabs accustomed to divinities without the miraculous. After all, they had long been respectful of divinities which did lit-tle in response to rituals conducted in their names. In any case, it may be more difficult to make much of miracles in an account set down so soon after the revelations and the events it purports to record.[57]

Muhammad repeatedly encountered from Jews and Christians, as well as from others, the question, "What are your signs?" (e.g., 20:133; 25:5–11). Some suggested that he bring back the fathers as a sign (45:24). His repeated reply was that the earth itself is a great sign for man, the earth created by God, as is also His creation of life, of men and women, and of the generative process (26:6; 30:19–29; 45:25). Muhammad's lack of reliance upon miracles of his own (he did have to make considerable use, in effect, of Jewish and Christian miracles of earlier times) confirms him as somewhat of a modern. Or at least it inspires us to confront his teaching in itself, and hence its intrinsic merits, more seriously than we otherwise might.[58] We now turn to that teaching, beginning with a further consideration of the very nature of revelation itself.

V.

One vital "value" determination, on which many "facts" depend here, has to do with the character of divine intervention in human affairs. What does it mean to say that God speaks to man? The Lord, the Koran says, teaches man "that he knew not" (96:5). How does the Lord teach a man anything? How does—how would—God speak to man if He chose to do so? This is a problem one has to deal with, not only when one confronts any prophetic claim made by another, but even when one has what appears to be a divine contact oneself. Thus, Muhammad wondered whether he was crazy upon first finding himself encountering the angel Gabriel, who was to provide him with the messages from God that he was to transmit to his people.[59]

It is evident that Muhammad is very much moved by the wonders of everyday life–by birth and growth, by death, and by the wholeness of things. The world of everyday experience, the Koran argues, is a wonderful sign, just as the remarkable words that Muhammad is given to say are themselves the principal sign of his genuineness. Thus, things make sense: cause and effect, moral as well as physical, govern the universe. Chance is ruled out in the world, as is arbitrariness.[60]

Not only is chance ruled out, but the Koran teaches that the world and mankind have been created for a serious purpose, not in play (15:85; 21:16; 23:117; 44:38).[61] The overall justice of things is insisted upon. Thus, each age has its Book (2:81–83; 13:39). All peoples have warnings before they are destroyed; no people is ever punished without first being sent a Messenger (17:15–19; also, 6:130; 16:38; 45:30). The Koran is warning enough for the Arabs. Muhammad's contemporaries are many times reminded that the Koran is an Arabic Book especially provided for them (9:129; 12:1; 13:38; 16:105; 19:97; 26:195; 39:29; 42:5; 43:1; 44:1, 45; 62:2).[62]

What *is* one to make of Muhammad's series of revelations? How can *we* judge such things? Is a believer in natural right obliged to concede that there must be something genuinely appealing in Islam for it to have spread, and

survived, as it has?[63] That is, can one argue from such effects back to extraordinary (if not supernatural) causes? Carlyle observed that a false man cannot build
a religion which lasts so long for so many.[64] And Gibbon suggested that it is "not
the [original] propagation, but the permanency of [Muhammad's] religion, that
deserves our wonder."[65]

Muhammad's revelation is, we have noticed, not a teaching that denies
common experience. It does not insist that earthly prosperity and goodness
necessarily coincide (3:134–35; 18:44, 195–200). Moreover, since his is not
a revelation which depends upon special signs, it need not be discredited
when the age of signs passes. People always want signs, the Koran observes.
The Jews had even asked Moses to show them God Himself. This kind of appetite led them to the idolatry of the Golden Calf (4:150–53).[66]

Evidently Muhammad was taunted with the challenge that he have an angel appear to confirm his claims. He responded that angels cannot be used as
signs for all human beings to see. An angelic appearance to the world at large
would mean that things as we know them had come to an end (6:4–9). This
end, he elsewhere reminds his addressees, would create no problem for God,
who can destroy mankind and replace it (4:132–33). God does not need believers: He holds out a way of salvation not because of His need (nor perhaps
even because of His care?), but evidently because of His justice. Is there not
something sensible in Muhammad's suggestion about what the general appearance of angels would mean?[67]

Should there not be something sensible as well in *how* God speaks to man?
The response here of the Koran is cautious. "It belongs not to any mortal that
God should speak to him, except by revelation, or from behind a veil, or that
He should send a messenger and he reveal whatsoever He will, by His leave;
surely He is All-high, All-wise" (42:50). We should not be surprised, therefore, that the wisdom of God should lead Him to vary the form of His messages according to circumstances. Messengers, we are told, know things that
others cannot.[68]

Nor should we be surprised if divine expression should be of surpassing
beauty and elevation. Thus, one translator refers to the Koran as a sym-
phony.[69] The elevation of what a prophet says can help establish the genuineness of what he claims. Is not beauty significant in that it is a promise of excellence, an image of the perfect? But, we also know, beauty may be only skin
deep. The truth of what Muhammad says can be difficult to see, despite the
remarkable beauty of his language.

We put aside the problem of Muhammad's personal sincerity. That is not an
interesting problem. After all, whatever his own sincerity, there can be no
doubt about the sincerity of most of his followers for more than a millennium.[70] More interesting is the extent to which Muhammad understands Judaic

and Christian thought and the problem that this creates when we consider the genuineness of his supposed revelation. One problem here is whether what he has to say is little more than a muddled version of Judaism and Christianity.[71]

Can Muhammad's revelation be genuine—can it be from God—if he is so often wrong in his understanding of the Bible, of Judaism, and of Christianity? Of course, there is the prior question, Is he indeed wrong? He claims to correct what Jews and Christians have done, in their interpretations, with the Word entrusted to them. Does he know what the uncorrupted Word was? We can understand why he might differ from Christian interpreters of Jewish teachings: early non-Jewish Christians may have misunderstood such teachings, especially in that those Christians might not have been learned enough or subtle enough. But we should also consider the possibility that Jewish and Christian interpretations over the centuries may have been muddled in their own way, partly because of the changing circumstances of the Jews and Christians to whom the Word had been directed from time to time. Muhammad can be understood as clarifying what had been said, getting closer thereby to what God would want permanently understood.[72]

What is the significance, in this respect, of the Koranic claim that Muhammad is the last of the prophets (33:40)? Perhaps that means only that he is the last to add anything distinctive to what has already been revealed, that after him no other great religion will be established.[73] Once the Word has been properly refined and purified, all who follow will be saying substantially the same thing. Is not this consistent with the expectation that there may still be revelations of a provisional character for peoples in circumstances which do not permit them to profit from the Word in its more exalted forms? Would not the most exalted form depend upon the "nature" of the divine in its relations with human beings?

Critical to the nature of God is knowledge: He is the only One Who can say that something should *be* and *it is.* That is what Divine Creation means (3:53; 6:73; 16:42; 20:36; 36:82; 40:70). The unity of God is stressed by the Koran. It is seen dramatically in how Abraham deals with idols and in how the question of the divinity of Jesus is treated (21:50–70; 26:70–89; 112:1–4). The world is nothing but a manifestation of God's power and presence.[74] It is fitting, Muslims believe, that complete prostration before God should be routinely exhibited by the believer: men are mere slaves of God. The Koran is believed somehow to embody the divine: to know the Koran is to possess God, insofar as the human being can do so. The key duty seems to be belief in God, so defined, not the pilgrimages and the charity of which much is also made (9:18–20).[75]

The Koran is from God, otherwise it would contain "much inconsistency" (4:84). This, too, affirms that God is wise (6:73–74). Cannot it be properly said that the Koran is uncreated if it truly embodies the truth about God?[76] We can think about what God must be like: He must be one, unchanging, perfect. Still, is it not generally true that human beings can know most reliably what God *cannot* be? This means that He cannot be embodied in idols or otherwise grasped by the senses. Our grasp of what God is like, therefore, depends ultimately upon the understanding.[77]

VI.

There can be no doubt that Muhammad could and does move people. Does he touch in human beings a natural sense of awe? Is the beauty of the Koran sufficient to account for what Muhammad has accomplished? What desires does he appeal to? With such questions one is perhaps asking about the nature of rhetoric.[78]

Muhammad encountered throughout his life the "charges" that he was no more than a poet, or that he was possessed, or that he was even a forger. To the charge of forgery, he could simply answer, Let others produce something as good as this.[79] The charge of being a poet is particularly important, since there seems to have been a significant tradition of poetry among pre-Islamic Arabs.[80]

What does it mean to say that a poet, or any human being, is possessed or inspired? The poet tells the truth about things, with special emphasis upon particulars.[81] Particularity, or a responsiveness to diverse circumstances, is found also in the piecemeal delivery of the Koran to human beings.

Consider, further, the effect upon people of the first among them who discovered something revealing in wood or stone. Beauty, as a sign of excellence,[82] may provide as well an intimation of the divine. The Koran is so much the embodiment of the divine, we are told, that any mountain in which the Koran appeared would have humbled itself before it, "split asunder out of the fear of God" (59:21).

This does not mean, however, that a prophet, any more than a poet, need be fully aware of what he is up to. Even if Muhammad "meant" a physical heaven and a physical hell in his sermons, that may not have been what God truly made manifest through him.[83] Was Muhammad, whether prophet or poet, himself aware of what was meant? He did have considerable self-confidence, and he managed to convey that assurance to others.

To be inspired does not mean that one's own limitations may not get in one's way. In a sense, we all have access to the divine[84] even as we are more or less inhibited by personal deficiencies in the realization of human potential—in being able to give full expression to universal truths about the whole, about the oneness of things.

VII.

Some may recognize the universal as the most interesting subject for contemplation by the human mind. To many, however, the universal is either incomprehensible or uninteresting. That is, our limitations and predispositions do affect what we can see, what we can respond to. By looking at the consequences of another's limitations, we might better notice what our own opinions are like and what it is we take for granted. It will not do, I have suggested, to dismiss all supposed manifestations of the divine as superstitions, for that begs questions about the status of various insights and about that which serves as the core toward which all such insights might be directed. Even if Muhammad's "prophetic revelations" were spurious, we have noticed, they might appeal to people because they happen to draw on the truth, especially when they do not depend upon historical events.[85]

The word of God about unity and the universal must be tailored, if it is to do any good—which is to say, if it is to be accepted as the basis for conversion and belief—to the conditions of the people to whom it is directed. Those conditions, in the case of the Koran, included the language of the Arabs, their poetic appetites, and the traditions of a proud desert people for whom Mecca, a city sensitive to shifts in world trade and in political power, was vital long before Muhammad. The critical role of Mecca, we have seen, is explained because of the connection with Abraham that Muhammad insists upon. It is no accident, then, that even pagans made so much of that city.[86]

Do Arabic inclinations and limitations help account for the form of the Koran. It *is* fragmentary and repetitious, for the most part a collection of sermons, exhortations, meditations, prescriptions, and prohibitions. What does it mean that there is no sustained narrative, no evident "logical" development, no obviously coherent account of things?[87] This seemingly haphazard arrangement, seen often within individual suras as well, indicates what moved the Arabs, and how, at various times. These people *are* different from, say, the Greeks to whom the Christian message was first brought by Jewish believers. The differences are not superficial—and hence are likely to endure. Such differences are aside from, although they must be considerably reinforced by, the particular languages in which various messages are set forth.[88]

Is it not rare when the full or pure divine message, whatever it may be, makes itself known to mankind? Human circumstances do assert themselves, even though God Himself would not be affected by the different conditions which shape, or distort, revelatory messages about Him. Indeed, it would seem an ultimately mistaken if not an idolatrous notion of God which would have *Him* different according to conditions.

VIII.

It can further explain the reception of the Koran to indicate various ways, in response to Arabic conditions (and other chance elements), that the Koranic message is embodied in everyday life:

1. The status of poetry—or the passion-laden word—seems to be enhanced by the Koran. The visual arts had found expression among the pagans in idols. But, it is emphasized, such would-be gods have no share of creation, as well as no Book from or about them (35:35–38). The visual arts tend, therefore, to be restricted in Islam to calligraphy and to the architecture and the geometrically designed decoration of mosques; relatively little can be done with the human form. The Koran is more to be heard than to be read.[89]

To emphasize the heard, rather than the seen, may tend to make for a noisy if not even a boisterous community.[90] When passion-laden language matters as much as it seems to do for Arabs, would not that tend to discourage reliance upon prudence in political affairs?

2. A disciplined passion is routinely expressed among Muslims in family life and in the considerable respect paid to parents and elders. Would not this emphasis upon the family tend to provide a useful stability, despite the volatile character of passion, especially with respect to honor?[91]

Instruction in the Koran about family matters extends to the proper care of orphans as well as of strangers (4:40–41; 107:1–7).[92] The undutiful child is said to be rare.[93] There are proper and improper marriages. An illicit sexual liaison with a believing slave girl is to be preferred to marriage with an idolatress (2:220). Monastic life is condemned as not ordained by the prophets (57:26–27). These observations suggest that the Koranic teachings are for a people, its perpetuation, and governance.

Sexual propriety is vital. At the same time, sensuality is accepted and even incorporated in accounts of Paradise.[94] The legitimacy of satisfying one's desires with one's wives and with appropriate slaves is recognized (70:30).[95] (This is *said* to be emphasized in the recruitment of martyrs.)

3. Lest too much be made of Islamic sensuality, however, we should be reminded of Carlyle's observation that Muhammad did not establish the sensuality of his religion; rather, he curtailed what had long been there among the Arabs.[96]

Be that as it may, one is not to make too much of one's earthly self. Self-sacrifice is taken for granted, with heavenly rewards promised for exemplary exercises of the martial arts. Another form of self-sacrifice is alms-giving, which is routine. Still another form may be seen in the five-times-daily prayers, the abject prostrations before God on those occasions, and the willingness to witness (and even die) for one's faith at all costs.[97]

4. Reinforcement of the family, the inspired use of language, the ratification of the martial arts, and other forms of self-sacrifice combined to help make a nation of the Arabs. Or, as Carlyle put it, "To the Arab Nation [Islam] was as a birth from darkness into light; Arabia first became alive by means of it."[98]

Muhammad was, in effect, an early nationalist, perhaps the first major one of postpagan times. He gave sublime meaning to the Arabs' existence by enlisting them in the service of the one true God. Every nation, he insisted, should have its own Book (45:27).[99] Every people should have its own Messenger sent to it (16:37–39).[100]

To say that Muhammad helped establish a nation is not to say that the political community is for the Muslim supreme. It is evident in the Koran that constituted authority can be misguided, that the prosperous can be wrong. An Egyptian pharaoh is shown to have been mistaken in criticizing his subjects for having believed Moses without his permission (20:70–74). Still, it is evident, from the Koran and the institutions derived from it, that social relations and social character dominate even private matters. The equality among men which Muslims make so much of does not mean that each is permitted to do as he pleases. Rather, all men are equally entitled to be disciplined to become loyal members of the community of Islam.[101]

5. The Koranic condemnation of usury (that is, of charging any interest for loans), wherever it is enforced, tends to inhibit modern commercial development. The Koran criticizes those who insist that commercial trafficking and usury are alike (2:275–78).[102] The financial arrangements permitted by conventional (non-Islamic) banking practices are likely to be international, thereby subverting attachment to one's own as supreme. That commercial development which the Islamic prohibition of usury impedes may have a softening effect as well, playing down among non-Islamic peoples the role of honor in human affairs.

It is true of Muslims what is true of all peoples, that their way of life is very much shaped and affected by what is held up for esteem among them. The critical commandments laid down in the Koran are moral as well as religious.[103] Is not the status of justice itself seen in how God is regarded? He will not, we have seen, destroy human beings without cause and without fair warning.

6. We have already referred to the status of honor among Muslims. This affects their notions of friendship and of hospitality. It is often seen as well in their possessive attitude of Muslim men toward women: "Your women are a tillage for you" (2:223–24). Although a male orientation is evident throughout the Koran, things may be more complicated here than they seem to the outsider, especially since it may now be difficult to learn how much the rules set

down with respect to women (as in sura 4) are intended as ameliorations of what had prevailed among the Arabs before Muhammad.

We should notice, among other things, that the Koran urges improved treatment of daughters (16:60). Provision is made for believers, male or female; a respect for female believers is sometimes evident (3:193; 11:43). Consider also the effects of the requirement that there be four witnesses to a woman's sexual misconduct before various harsh punishments can be exacted of her (4:19; 24:4), of the requirement that all one's wives be treated alike (a serious restriction, in practice, on polygamy?) (4:128), and of the requirement that virtuous women be protected from slander and corruption (24:4, 11–19, 24, 30–33).[104]

It may well be that the impetus given toward "women's rights" by the Koran has made the resulting arrangements seem oppressive—especially when it is forgotten what conditions had had to be taken account of by the original liberator, conditions that the liberated if not presumptuous successors to the liberator today no longer have to contend with.[105]

Even so, it can seem, at least to the outsider, that "human being" for the Muslim means primarily the male. Still, *is* there not a basis in the Koran itself for improved treatment of women? It is far from clear that the status given women does not "work." To assess that status properly, one would have to be clear about the respective natures of men and women and of their proper relation.[106]

7. Finally, in this inventory of various ways that the Koranic message is embodied in everyday life, there are its many rituals and observances, including fasts and pilgrimages. These seem to appeal to, or at least to recognize, the bodily component of the human being; the passions are thereby ministered to; that which is recognized here is the material basis of, or counterpart to, the spiritual.[107]

Thus, circumcision is called for. Intimate physical contact is taken for granted. Dietary matters are dealt with. Is there not something to be said for distinguishing, even if only arbitrarily, between lawful and unlawful food?[108] It suggests that the appetites should not govern, that some principles should guide us to so elementary and pervasive an activity as eating or drinking. Relatively little *is* made of such matters in the Koran as a whole. But people need some rituals, some observances keyed to the body, and they make much of what there is in the Koran. Thus, the "intellectual" awareness of God's unity and bodilessness is supplemented by detailed rules about physical conduct between diverse human beings.[109] Still, there is in Islam a noble repudiation of attempts to exalt the physical unduly, even when it is manifested in the body of Muhammad himself. Consider the death scene, as reported by Gibbon, in which two of Muhammad's intimate companions contend as to how his corpse is to be regarded:

An expedition for the conquest of Syria was stopped by this mournful event; the army halted at the gates of Medina; the chiefs were assembled round their dying master. The city, more especially the house, of the prophet, was a scene of clamorous sorrow or silent despair: fanaticism alone could suggest a ray of hope and consolation. "How can he be dead, our witness, our intercessor, our mediator, with God? By God he is not dead: like Moses and Jesus, he is wrapt in a holy trance, and speedily will he return to his faithful people." The evidence of sense was disregarded; and Omar, unsheathing his scimitar, threatened to strike off the heads of the infidels who should dare to affirm that the prophet was no more. The tumult was appeased by the weight and moderation of Abubeker. "Is it Mohammed," said he to Omar and the multitude "or the God of Mohammed, whom you worship? The God of Mohammed liveth forever; but the apostle was a mortal like ourselves, and, according to his own prediction, he has experienced the common fate of mortality." He was piously interred by the hands of his nearest kinsman, on the same spot on which he expired; Medina has been sanctified by the death and burial of Mohammed; and the innumerable pilgrims of Mecca often turn aside from the way, to bow, in voluntary devotion, before the simple tomb of the prophet.[110]

IX.

One wonders, in considering ways of life, what the future is likely to be of this or that regime. What, in particular, lies ahead for Islam?

What, for example, are to be its relations with Israel (assuming, for the moment, that all Islam is united in a policy with respect to Israel, which it is not)? Relations may not be as bad as they sometimes appear: there is much in common between Islam and Judaism, both in themselves (for example, with respect to a rigorous doctrine about the unity of God) and in response to common threats. Also, one can reasonably hope that Arab honor may be relied on, if a genuine settlement in what we know as the Middle East is ever reached.[111]

The basis of Islamic reconciliation with Christians, in the places where they are in conflict, may be more questionable. (One thinks of Lebanon and Cyprus.) There are, for example, serious doctrinal divisions with respect to the status of Jesus. But then, Christians and Muslims also face common threats. Besides, serious divisions exist among Christians as well as to the status of Jesus.

The common threats faced by Judaism, Christianity, and Islam include the movement toward modern individuality, toward the skepticism emanating from modern science, and toward atheistic Marxism and its successors. Indeed, the most serious problem for Israel itself may not be any Muslim threat but rather the relegation, among the more sophisticated Israelis, of serious biblical (as distinguished from historical) concerns primarily to philologists, archaeologists, and anthroplogists.[112]

Modern science seems less of a threat in the long run directly to Islam than to Judaism and Christianity, although the typical Muslim fundamentalist, who is still moved by the "culture" of the desert, does not seem to appreciate this. We have seen that Islam originally relied less upon *new* miracles for its distinctive revelations. But to what extent does modern science threaten Islam indirectly? To what extent, that is, does Islam depend, at its foundations, upon miracle-laden Judaism and Christianity?

Before one can speak reliably about the future of Islam, three further questions should be considered. We need do no more than notice further these obviously momentous questions here:

What is God? This question, which has guided much of our discussion in this chapter, bears upon the problem of what signs and teachings are apt to be made manifest to human beings, and how. What teachings are needed for a new age, to reinforce old lessons and to adjust them to new circumstances? Are there extraordinary signs to be read? Will the more perceptive human beings be prepared to interpret them, and will they be listened to? These are the kinds of inquiries subsumed under the first of our three partially unanswered questions, What is God?

Our second partially unanswered question is, How does nature bear upon the form of religious revelations, upon the varying regional responses to such revelations, and upon the life-spans of the movements founded on them? The status of nature in Islamic thought seems to remain depressed, despite the instructive efforts by Islamic philosophers in the twelfth century or thereabouts.[113]

Our third, partially unanswered, question is, What, in fact, *is* Islam? Before one can speak with assurance about the future of Islam one must be aware of what is essential to it, what tendencies it has, and what provision it itself makes for change and accommodation without sacrifice of what is considered essential. One should study further the Koran, a text which we have begun to examine here with a view ultimately to an informed inquiry into the very nature of revelation and the divine.[114]

Notes

1. Leo Strauss, *Philosophy and Law: Essays Toward the Understanding of Maimonides and His Predecessors* (Philadelphia: Jewish Publication Society, 1987), p. 81. Moses Maimonides' standards suggest that the greatest (that is, the true?) prophets are not mere transmitters of the Word of God, however they may describe themselves. Is the prophet to be distinguished from the philosopher primarily by "the faculty of divination"? Is not that faculty, in any event, likely to be what people generally take to be distinctive to the prophet? See also Fazlur Rahman, *Prophecy in Islam: Philosophy and Orthodoxy* (Chicago: University of Chicago Press, 1958), p. 30; George Anastaplo, "Law & Literature and the Bible: Explorations," 23 *Oklahoma City University Law Review* 515, 521 (1998). See as well note 38 in chapter 4 of this collection; notes 21 and 53 below.

Maimonides, who is widely recognized as the greatest Jewish thinker since biblical times, has had his relations with Islam described in this way by Raymond L. Weiss:

Maimonides (1135–1204) developed his great powers of concentration and wrote his monumental works in spite of the severe hardships of the Exile and his own "poor original temperament and weak natural build." His birthplace of Cordoba, Spain, was conquered in 1148 by religious zealots, the Almohads, who forced non-Muslims to convert to Islam. Maimonides and his family managed to remain in Spain for some time, after which they moved to Morocco, and finally settled in Egypt, which was beyond the hegemony of the Almohads. . . . [He] turned to medicine to earn a livelihood for the whole family, and he eventually became a physician to the sultan's palace in Cairo. This position had political significance, for it gave him access to the vizier and other Muslim leaders when Jews were in a highly vulnerable position. Maimonides himself was exposed to peril because of the unorthodox character of his thought. . . .

Whatever danger he faced as a heterodox thinker and an alien living under Muslim rule, Maimonides was also able to reap the advantages of living in a Muslim world that had recovered the Aristotelian sciences. His intellectual kinship with the Muslim philosophers transcended the rigid boundaries set by religion. His agreement with them can be seen in a common opposition to the Mutakallimum, who used reason in a non-philosophical manner to defend the tenets of the revealed religion. . . .

The prophet's ultimate goal, like that of the wise man, is the intellectual perception of God. Although this goal is discussed briefly [in the work], *Eight Chapters* is concerned with the prophetic way of life, not with prophecy as such. As a work on ethics, it has a practical intent, laying down a way of life which, in principle, can be followed at any time. Maimonides does not assume that prophecy ceased forever with the close of the biblical period, but that it is an ever present possibility for men with the appropriate gifts and training. . . .

It is in this context that Maimonides forcefully condemns hedonism. If intellectual perception is the goal of human life, bodily pleasure becomes incidental. Man's ultimate goal requires a concern with the body's health rather than its pleasure.

[Further on,] Maimonides hints that the all-encompassing contemplative goal might occasionally conflict with the demands of the Law. He resolves the difficulty by appealing to a rabbinic teaching that sanctions a transgression when committed in obedience to the dictum: "In all your ways know Him" (*Prov.* 3:6). At this point, Maimonides says the goal is the truth. . . .

When Maimonides had spoken earlier of the moral vices as diseases of the soul, he had presupposed the philosophic understanding of the subject. [Later] he shows how the moral vices are viewed by the prophets. He quotes from Isaiah, who refers not to "moral vices" but to "sins" that separate man from God. Seen through the eyes of prophecy, the moral vices are like veils that hinder the contemplation of God. . . .

Maimonides never discusses the best regime as such, in the manner, say, of Plato in the *Republic*. He does describe the best *Jewish* regime in his account of the messianic era. . . . Maimonides' view of the end of days is not altogether alien to the thought of Plato, however, for the ultimate purpose of the messianic era is to enable men to pursue the contemplative life. Moreover, world peace will be brought about by a prophet-king who is reminiscent of Plato's philosopher-king. The messiah will combine extraordinary wisdom with political rule, which calls to mind Plato's view that the best regime can come into existence only if philosophers become kings or kings become philosophers.

The nations of the world will be attracted to the messiah because of his great wisdom and consummate justice. Jesus and Muhammad have already helped to lay the groundwork for the messianic era by directing a large portion of mankind toward the service of God. The messianic king will correct their mistakes and teach the nations the true way of the Lord. He will have to be not only a teacher, but also a political leader, indeed a statesman with great military skill. For peaceful means will not suffice to unify the nations and to usher in the messianic era. The messiah will have to engage in warfare, and his success in battle will be one of the signs that he is in fact the messianic king. On the whole, Maimonides gives a "naturalistic" account of how the messianic era will come into existence. . . .

Since human nature will not be transformed [in the messianic age], the Law will still be needed for moral training and the prevention of injustice. Although Maimonides is intentionally vague about the future global political order, he articulates the prophetic vision that mankind will remain divided into nations. A single religion will serve as the bond that unites them. Peace among individuals and nations will be furthered by an abundance of material goods. The promise of peace held out by Scripture is mainly based, however, upon the vision of a universal preoccupation with attaining knowledge of the deity, a goal that eliminates every reason for people to harm one another. The love of wisdom places humankind beyond the lure of moral vice. While moral virtue is instrumental for the contemplative life, the reverse is also true. Contemplation itself aids in preserving moral excellence.

Ethical Writings of Maimonides, Raymond L. Weiss, with Charles E. Butterworth, eds. (New York: New York University Press, 1975), pp. 1–2, 14, 15, 23–24, 24–25. See further, on Maimonides, the Introductory Essay by Leo Strauss in Moses Maimonides, *The Guide of the Perplexed*, Shlomo Pines, trans. (Chicago: University of Chicago Press, 1963). See also the essay on Maimonides in George Anastaplo, *The American Moralist: On Law, Ethics, and Government* (Athens, Ohio: Ohio University Press, (1992), p. 58.

I have found very helpful the criticism of this chapter by C. M. Naim of the University of Chicago.

2. The Koran is in this respect like T. S. Eliot's *Four Quartets,* a complicated religious poem that is very hard to understand and yet appeals to many because of passages which they cherish as beautiful expressions of their religious sentiments. See Anastaplo, "Law & Literature and the Moderns: Explorations," 20 *Northern Illinois University Law Review*, 251, 539 (2000). Also, the Koran is like Blaise Pascal's *Pensées* (*GBWW,* vol. 33, pp. 171a–352a) in its episodic character. See as well note 78 below. (*GBWW* refers to the *Great Books of the Western World* collection published by the *Encyclopædia Britannica*.)

3. "The Hero as Prophet; Mahomet; Islam," in Thomas Carlyle, *On Heroes, Hero-worship, and the Heroic in History* (London: Oxford University Press, 1904), p. 85 (first published in 1841). See, for the continuation of this passage, note 5 below. See also note 6 below.

4. Edward Gibbon, *History of the Decline and Fall of the Roman Empire* (New York: Modern Library, n.d.), vol. 3 (chap. 50.), p. 56 (*GBWW,* vol. 41, p. 220b). Gibbon's assessment of the Koran itself anticipates the Carlyle observation we have quoted (ibid., vol. 3, 85–86, *GBWW,* vol. 41, p. 231c–d):

In the spirit of enthusiasm or vanity, the prophet rests the truth of his mission on the merit of his book; audaciously challenges both men and angels to imitate the beauties of a single page; and presumes to assert that God alone could dictate this incomparable performance. [Koran: 17:90] This argument is most powerfully addressed to a devout Arabian, whose mind is attuned to faith and rapture; whose ear is delighted by the music of sounds; and whose ignorance is incapable of comparing the productions of human genius. The harmony and copiousness of style will not reach, in a [translation], the European infidel: he will peruse with impatience the endless incoherent rhapsody of fable, and precept, and declamation, which seldom excites a sentiment or an idea, which sometimes crawls in the dust, and is sometimes lost in the clouds. The divine attributes exalt the fancy of the Arabian missionary; but his loftiest strains must yield to the sublime simplicity of the book of Job, composed in a remote age, in the same country, and in the same language. If the composition of the Koran exceeds the faculties of a man, to what superior intelligence should we ascribe the Iliad of Homer, or the Philippics of Demosthenes?

See note 6 below. The passage we have quoted in the text from Carlyle continues in a way that separates him somewhat from Gibbon (*On Heroes*, pp. 85–87):

Nothing but a sense of duty could carry any European through the Koran. . . . It is true we have it under disadvantages: the Arabs see more method in it than we. Mahomet's followers found the Koran lying all in fractions, as it had been written-down at first promulgation; much of it, they say, on shoulder-blades of mutton, flung pell-mell into a chest: and they published it, without any discoverable order as to time or otherwise;—merely trying, as would seem, and this not very strictly, to put the longest chapters first. The real beginning of it, in that way, lies almost at the end: for the earliest portions were the shortest. Read in its historical sequence it perhaps would not be so bad. Much of it, too, they say, is rhythmic; a kind of wild chanting song, in the original. This may be a great point: much perhaps has been lost in the Translation here. Yet with every allowance, one feels it difficult to see how any mortal ever could consider this Koran as a Book written in Heaven, too good for the Earth; as a well-written book, or indeed as a *book* at all; and not a bewildered rhapsody: *written,* so far as writing goes, as badly as almost any book ever was! So much for national discrepancies, and the standard of taste.

Yet I should say, it was not unintelligible how the Arabs might so love it. When once you get this confused coil of a Koran fairly off your hands, and have it behind you at a distance, the essential type of it begins to disclose itself; and in this there is a merit quite other than the literary one. If a book comes from the heart, it will contrive to reach other hearts; all art and authorcraft are of small amount to that. One would say the primary character of the Koran is this of its *genuineness,* of its being a *bona-fide* book. [Some critics] have represented it as a mere bundle of juggleries; chapter after chapter got-up to excuse and varnish the author's successive sins, forward his ambitions and quackeries: but really it is time to dismiss all that. I do not assert Mahomet's continual sincerity: who is continually sincere? But I confess I can make nothing of the critic, in these times, who would accuse him to deceit *prepense;* of conscious deceit generally, or perhaps at all;—still more, of living in a mere element of conscious deceit, and writing this Koran as a forger and juggler would have done! Every candid eye, I think, will read the Koran far otherwise than so. It is the confused ferment of a great rude human soul; rude, untutored, that cannot even read: but fervent, earnest, struggling vehemently to utter itself in words. . . . We said 'stupid': yet natural stupidity is by no means the character of Mahomet's Book; it is natural uncultivation rather. . . . The panting breathless haste and vehemence of a man struggling in the thick of battle for life and salvation; this is the mood he is in! A headlong haste; for very magnitude of meaning, he cannot get himself articulated into words. The successive utterances of a soul in that mood, coloured by the various vicissitudes of three-and-twenty years; now well uttered, now worse: this is the Koran.

Muhammad, who died in his sixty-third year, is said to have begun his prophetic mission when he was forty. See, on the ordering of the suras in the Koran, notes 8 and 58 below.

5. A brief account of the life and works of Muhammad, taken from the *Encyclopaedia Britannica*, 15th ed. (1989 printing; vol. 8, pp. 396–97), describes the career of the man who delivered the Koran to his people:

Muhammad, in full ABŪ AL-QĀSIM MUHAMMAD IBN ˋABD ALIĀH IBN ˋABD AL-MUṬṬALIB IBN HĀSHIM (b. (?), 570, Mecca—d. June 8, 632, Medina), founder of the religion of Islām and of the Arab Empire, who initiated religious, social, and cultural developments of monumental significance in the history of mankind. . . .

During his early life in Mecca his merchant activities resulted in his marriage in about 595 to the wealthy widow Khadijah. He received his prophetic call in about 610 and began his religious activities among his friends and members of his own family. He began preaching publicly in about 613. The rise of Meccan opposition about 615 and the withdrawal of his clan's protection about 619 caused Muhammad to seek aid elsewhere. In 620 he began negotiations with clans in Medina, leading to his emigration *(hijrah)* there in 622. He eventually went to battle with his Meccan opponents and achieved, at the battle near Badr (624), his first military victory, which he interpreted as divine vindication of his prophethood. He again engaged his Meccan opponents at Uhud (625) and lost, but, in outwitting them at the siege of Medina (627), he further strengthened his position. The Treaty of al-Hudaybiyah (628) forced the Meccans to acknowledge his political authority and grant him concessions. Muhammad's following was meanwhile growing: and in January 630 he entered Mecca with 10,000 men. As he had also formed alliances with nomadic tribes scattered throughout the peninsula, he left, on his death, most of Arabia united and ready for spreading the faith in Syria and Iraq. Muhammad's divine revelation was recorded after his death in the Qur'ān [Koran], for which he claimed merely to be the earthly vehicle.

A fuller account of Muhammad's life is provided in ibid., 22: 1–5. See also Gibbon, *The Decline and Fall*, vol. 3, 75ff. (*GBWW*, vol. 41, p. 228a); Carlyle, pp. 67ff.; John L. Esposito, *Islam: The Straight Path* (New York: Oxford University Press, 1988), pp. 7ff.; John Bagot Glubb (Glubb Pasha), *Life and Times of Muhammad* (New York: Stein and Day, 1970). See, on Muhammad's death scene, the text taken from Gibbon at note 110 of this chapter. See also note 30 below.

6. I must, with Gibbon, "profess my total ignorance of the Oriental tongues" (*The Decline and Fall*, vol. 3, 56, n. 1). I take all my quotations from the Koran in this chapter from the translation by Arthur J. Arberry, *The Koran Interpreted* (New York: Macmillan, 1955). Arberry suggested in his preface (p. 12) that although "Gibbon and Carlyle were in their times remarkable for the liberality of their attitude toward Islam," they were prejudiced against the Koran by the inadequacy of the English translation they had to rely upon. See note 65 below.

See, on why *God* rather than *Allah* should be used in English texts to refer to the Muslim deity, Kenneth Cragg, *The Call of the Minaret* (New York: Oxford University Press, 1964), pp. 36–37:

> [*Allah*] is so far from its Arabic original, when pronounced with a thin English consonant and feeble vowels, that many an Arab Muslim would find it unrecognizable. But more important, there have grown up associations with the English usage of *Allah* that are sentimental, having to do more with melodrama than theology. These should be shunned. There may also be the idea in the user's mind that in referring to God in Islam as *Allah* he is distinguishing that Deity from the God whom Christian English denotes. . . .
>
> Since both Christian and Muslim faiths believe in One supreme sovereign Creator-God, they are obviously referring when they speak of Him, under whatever terms, to the same Being. . . . The differences, which undoubtedly exist, between the Muslim and the Christian understanding of God are far-reaching and must be patiently studied. . . .
>
> Before, however, leaving the Arabic term *Allah* in order to keep to the English equivalent God, we must investigate its precise literal meaning. The Arabic form *ilahun* meaning "a god" is similar to Hebrew and Aramaic words for deity. When used with the definite article *Al-llahu* meaning "The God" the *l* consonant of the article coalesces with the same letter in the first syllable of the word eliding the *i* sound to make *Al-lah*. . . .
>
> It is clear from the negative form [of the first part] of the Muslim creed, "There is no god except God" [LA-ILAHA-ILLA-ALLAH], that the existence and lordship of *Allah* were known and recognized in pre-Islamic Arabia. The Prophet's mission was not to proclaim God's existence but

to deny the existence of all lesser deities. The fact that Muhammad's own father bore the name `Abd-Allah, slave of God, demonstrates that God was known by that name prior to Islam. . . . But the people of Mecca did not understand or allow that God alone should be worshiped.

See, on the names of God, ibid., pp. 37–44. See, on the Muslim creed, notes 10 and 57 below.

Consider, also, the distinctions drawn between Jehovah and Allah in G. W. F. Hegel, *The Philosophy of History* (New York: Dover, 1956), pp. 356–57:

Only among the Jews have we observed the principle of pure Unity elevated to a thought; for only among them was adoration paid to the One, as an object of thought. This unity then remained, when the purification of the mind to the conception of abstract Spirit had been accomplished; but it was freed from the particularity by which the worship of Jehovah had been hampered. Jehovah was only the God of that one people—the God of Abraham, of Isaac and Jacob: only with the Jews had this God made a covenant: only to this people had he revealed himself. That speciality of relation was done away with in Mahometanism. In this spiritual universality, in this unlimited and indefinite purity and simplicity of conception, human personality has no other aim than the realization of this universality and simplicity. *Allah* has not the affirmative, limited aim of the Judaic God. The worship of the One is the only final aim of Mahometanism, and subjectivity has this worship for the sole occupation of its activity, combined with the design to subjugate secular existence to the One. . . . But Mahometanism is not the Hindoo, not the Monastic immersion in the Absolute. Subjectivity is here living and unlimited—an energy which enters into secular life with a purely negative purpose, and busies itself and interferes with the world, only in such a way as shall promote the pure adoration of the One. The object of Mahometan worship is purely intellectual; no image, no representation of Allah is tolerated. Mahomet is a prophet but still man—not elevated above human weaknesses. The leading features of Mahometanism involve this—that in actual existence nothing can become fixed, but that everything is destined to expand itself in activity and life in the boundless amplitude of the world, so that the worship of the One remains the only bond by which the whole is capable of uniting. In this expansion, this active energy, all limits, all national and caste distinctions vanish; no particular race, political claim of birth or possession is regarded—only *man* as a *believer.*

Is there any other major religion today which makes as little as Islam seems to do of the differences between the races or as much as Islam does of the differences between male and female? See notes 105 and 106 below.

The spelling of Muhammad's name varies according to the sources quoted in these notes. Some of the sources use the improper term "Mahometanism" or a version thereof to refer to Islam.

7. "Islam," *Encyclopaedia Britannica*, vol. 22, pp. 5–6. Although *Qur'ān* may be the more accurate transliteration of the title of the book. I use the spelling in this chapter that is likely to be familiar to most of my readers, *Koran*.

8. For the sake of uniformity, I use the word *sura* throughout this chapter. (*Sūrah* is used in the *Encyclopaedia Britannica* passage quoted in the text near note 10 of this chapter. Some authors capitalize the word.) "The word Sura occurs nine times in the Koran. . . . but it is not easy to determine whether it means a whole chapter, or part only of a chapter, or is used in the sense of 'revelation.'. . . It is understood . . . to have a primary reference to the succession of subjects or parts, like the *rows* of bricks in a wall." Koran, Everyman's Library edition, p. 19 n. 1.

See, on the ordering of the suras in the Koran, note 4 above, note 58 below, and the text at note 10 of this chapter.

9. See note 58 below. Mecca and Medina are nearly 250 miles, or about ten days journey on foot, apart. See, for the dates of Muhammad's association with each city, note 5 above. His emigration from Mecca to Medina in 622 (the *hijrah*) is taken to mark the beginning of the Muslim calendar, with the years thereafter dating from that momentous event. See, on Mecca, notes 37 and 86 below.

10. The following account of the Ramadan obligation is taken from the *Encyclopaedia Britannica* article on Islam (vol. 22, p. 13): "Fasting during the month of Ramadan (ninth month of the Muslim lunar calendar), laid down in the Qur'ān (2:183–85), is the fourth of the five pillars of the faith. [The first, second, third, and fifth pillars are the profession of faith, 'There is no god but God; Muhammad is the prophet of God'; the daily prayers (see notes 90 and 97 below); the systematic giving of alms; and a pilgrimage to Mecca.] Fasting [during Ramadan] begins at daybreak and ends at sunset, and during the day eating, drinking, and smoking are forbidden. The Qur'ān (2:185) states that it was in the month of Ramadan that the Qur'ān was revealed. Another verse of the Qur'ān (97:1) states that it was revealed 'on the night of determination,' which Muslims generally observe on the night of 26–27 Ramadan." See Lloyd A. Fallers, "Notes on an Advent Ramadan," *Journal of the American Academy of Religion,* 42, no. 1 (March 1974), p. 35. See also "Islam," *Encyclopedia of the Social Sciences* (1963), vol. 7, pp. 337f.; Cragg, *The Call of the Minaret,* pp. 113f.

11. The *fatihah,* as set forth in the Arberry translation, reads:

The Opening

In the Name of God, the Merciful, the Compassionate

Praise belongs to God, the Lord of all Being,
the All-merciful, the All-compassionate,
    The Master of the Day of Doom.

Thee only we serve; to Thee alone we pray for succour.
    Guide us in the straight path,
the path of those whom Thou hast blessed,
not of those against whom Thou art wrathful,
    nor of those who are astray.

12. Only one sura, the ninth, is not prefaced by the *basmalah.* It is usually explained that this is because what is now the ninth sura was originally added to what is now the eighth sura. Is there anything special about the ninth?

13. All of my citations in this chapter, unless otherwise indicated, are to the Koran and are by sura and verses. My verse citations have to be approximations, since the English translations available to me do not number each verse but rather count them off by fives or tens.

See, for a comprehensive survey of the verses in the Koran, note 58 below.

14. Compare *Deuteronomy* 4:5–6 (on what Moses is instructed by God to tell his people as his mission draws to an end):

Behold, I have taught you statutes and ordinances, even as the Lord my God commanded me, that ye should do so in the midst of the land, whither ye go in to possess it. Observe therefore and do them; for this is your wisdom and your understanding in the sight of the peoples, that, when they hear all these statutes, shall say: "Surely this great nation is a wise and understanding people."

See also *Job*, chap. 38; Anastaplo, "Law & Literature and the Bible," p. 640. See as well note 63 below. Isaac Newton's years of research into biblical prophecies, especially in the *Book of Daniel*, are instructive here—*not* so much for what he discovered, but rather for his persistence. See, on Newton, note 113 below.

15. Leo Strauss speaks, in the concluding sentence of *The City and Man* (Chicago: Rand McNally, 1964), p. 241, of "the all-important questions which is coeval with philosophy although the philosophers do not frequently pronounce it—the question *quid sit deus.*" See Anastaplo, *The Artist as Thinker: From Shakespeare to Joyce* (Athens, Ohio: Swallow Press/Ohio University Press, 1983), pp. 252–53; epigraph, preface to this collection; appendix A of this collection. See also Anastaplo, "Church and State: Explorations," 19 *Loyola University of Chicago Law Journal* 61–64 (1987). See as well note 109 below.

16. The eighteen enlightened men listed here as Muhammad's predecessors are Abraham, Isaac, Jacob, Noah, David, Solomon, Job, Joseph, Moses, Aaron, Zachariah, John, Jesus, Elias, Ishmael, Elisha, Jonah, and Lot (6:83–87). The order here is not chronological, just as in the Koran itself the suras are not collected in chronological order. See note 58 below.

One consequence of this arrangement is to place Moses and Aaron at the center of an array framed at its extremes by the kinsmen Abraham and Lot. Does not the Koran generally identify Muhammad with Moses or, more precisely, with both Moses and Aaron (in that Muhammad serves his people as those brothers together had served their people)? See note 35 below. Gibbon reports that the people in the age of Moses and those in the age of Muhammad "dwelt under similar tents, and conducted their horses, and camels, and sheep to the same springs and the same pastures" (vol. 3, 60; *GBWW*, vol. 41, p. 221c). See, on what the desert is like, ibid., pp. 57–58 (*GBWW*, vol. 41, pp. 220b–24a); also, note 90 below.

See, for other lists of Muhammad's predecessors, Koran 2:129; 19:6; 21:9. See, on the number 18, section V of chapter 3 of this collection.

17. Again and again in the Koran, Jesus is emphatically identified as "son of Mary." That is, he is to be regarded by Muslims as a mortal, albeit a special mortal, *not* as the Son of God. See note 81 below. There are respectable Christian theologians today who might agree to this proposition. See sura 112 (in the text at note 19 of this chapter). The response of the more old-fashioned Christian to the Koran is suggested by the notes provided by the Rev. J. M. Rodwell in the Everyman's Library edition of the Koran. See, for example, ibid., p. 406, n. 1, for the argument that Muhammad had misapplied to himself the promise that Jesus had made about a *Paracletos* (John 16:7; Koran 61:7).

18. See also Koran 10:90–91 (Pharaoh becomes one of "those that surrender"—that is, "muslim"). See Koran, Everyman's Library edition, p. 283 n. 1.

19. "Say" is the command by God to Muhammad in some of the suras as to what he is to transmit to his people. In most of the suras God is to be understood as speaking directly, albeit through Muhammad. (This "Sincere Religion" sura is entitled "The Unity" in the Everyman's Library edition of the Koran.) Thus, there is reported in the Koran much more "direct quotation" of God than there is in the Bible. In the Bible there is much more of a narrative, which reflects the greater role of the human element in the prophets involved, however inspired they may have been. The Muslim might argue that the much larger contribution by human beings to the Bible may help account for its being much easier to read. Another way of putting this is to say that God would "naturally" be harder to understand than fallible human beings who are much like ourselves.

20. The author of these lines is Solomon Iben Gabiral (1021–58). The English translation is by Israel Zangwill (1861–1926).

21. See, on the life of Jews under Islamic rule, Anastaplo, *Human Being and Citizen: Essays on Virtue, Freedom, and the Common Good* (Chicago: Swallow Press, 1975), pp. 159, 306 n. 30. Leo Strauss reported that his research on Gersonides' *Teaching as Prophecy* "led [him] from Maimonides to Islamic philosophers, of whom [he] studied several in Arabic manuscripts—and made [him] realize that the connection between medieval Jewish and Islamic teaching or prophecy and Plato's *Statesman* and *Laws* had not yet been thoroughly evaluated" (1933 letter, Leo Strauss Papers, Regenstein Library Archives, University of Chicago). See notes 1 and 13 above. The interesting philosophical developments in Islam seem not to have been in the Arab countries but at the extremes of the Muslim world in Spain and Iran. See chapter 4 of this collection, note 38.

The vigorous Islamic challenge to idolatry in any form may be reflected also in the iconoclastic controversy in the Eastern Orthodox Church. See, on the Nicene Creed and idolatry, note 34 below.

22. However, birth seems critical for providing one the opportunity, if not also the obligation, to become a Muslim. Are not the most "natural" Jews likewise those who are born Jews?

23. "Whence it comes to pass that all armed prophets conquer and the unarmed ones are ruined." Niccolò Machiavelli, *The Prince*, Leo Paul S. de Alvarez, trans. (Irving, Tex.: University of Dallas Press, 1980), chap. 6, p. 34 (*GBWW*, vol. 23, p. 9c). See Leo Strauss, *On Tyranny* (New York: Free Press, 1963), pp. 195f.

24. See Carlyle, *On Heroes*, p. 80.

25. Muhammad, we are told, had "to defend himself up to a very late period against the charge of being merely a Poet." Koran, Everyman's Library edition, p. 4. It seems to be generally recognized among scholars that the Arabs had, long before Muhammad, a remarkable poetic tradition, with great prestige assigned to poets. See, e.g., Gibbon, vol. 3, 68–69 (*GBWW*, vol. 11, p. 225a–d); Carlyle, *On Heroes*, p. 63 (on the importance among the Arabs of "poetic contests"). The significance of poetry for Islam continues to this day:

> Whether or not it may be agreed that "poets are the unofficial legislators of mankind," there is no gainsaying the fact that poets have played a prominent, in some instances indeed a leading part in that most exciting drama of modern times, the revolt of Islam—against internal corruption, and especially and most compellingly against external domination.

A. J. Arberry, *Aspects of Islamic Civilization* (Ann Arbor: University of Michigan Press, 1967), p. 378 (the "legislators" quotation draws upon Percy B. Shelley's *The Defense of Poetry*). A similar influence of poets seems to prevail among the Russians, as can be testified to by anyone who has ever attended a public performance by Yevgeny Yevtushenko.

26. Sura 26 has Abraham confronting his father and his people, warning them that it was not a sufficient reason to worship idols that their fathers had done so. The perverse will be consigned to Hell, at which time it shall be asked of them, "Where is that which you were serving apart from God? Do they [the idols?] help you or help themselves?" (26:91–91). One can find similar arguments in the Talmud. See note 30 below.

27. See the text at note 19 of this chapter. See also Koran 2:110; 3:52; 5:77, 109; 9:30; 17:112; 19:36, 93; 23:93; 25: 2; 72:3.

28. The Koran puts it thus (9:30–31):

The Jews say, "Ezra is the Son of God";
the Christians say, "The Messiah is the Son of God."
That is the utterance of their mouths, conforming
with the unbelievers before them. God assail them!
      How they are perverted!
They have taken their rabbis and their monks as lords
apart from God, and the Messiah, Mary's son—
and they were commanded to serve but One God;
there is no god but He.

29. See Koran, Everyman's Library edition, pp. 473–74 n. 8: "The Muhammadan tradition is that Ezra was raised to life after he had been 100 years dead, and dictated from memory the whole Jewish law, which had been lost during the captivity, to the scribes. That the Jews regarded Ezra as a son of God is due to Muhammad's own invention. . . . The Talmudists, however, use very exaggerated language concerning him. Thus, *Sanhedrin*, 21, 22, 'Ezra would have been fully worthy to have been the lawgiver, if Moses had not preceded him.' Josephus, *Ant*. XI. 5, 5, speaks of his high repute (*doxa*) with the people, and of his honorable burial."

30. Absolutely no physical representation of Muhammad is permitted, however much he is esteemed among Muslims. What does it mean that this is the one human being who absolutely must not be pictured? Compare the passage from Gibbon in the text at note 110 of this chapter.

Gibbon provides the following description of Muhammad (*Decline and Fall*, vol. 3, 78–79; *GBWW*, vol. 41, pp. 228d–29a):

According to the tradition of his companions, Mohammed was distinguished by the beauty of his person, an outward gift which is seldom despised, except by those to whom it has been refused. Before he spoke, the orator engaged on his side the affections of a public or private audience. They applauded his commanding presence, his majestic aspect, his piercing eye, his gracious smile, his flowing beard, his countenance that painted every sensation of the soul, and his gestures that enforced each expression of the tongue. In the familiar offices of life he scrupulously adhered to the grave and ceremonious politeness of his country: his respectful attention to the rich and powerful was dignified by his condescension and affability to the poorest citizens of Mecca: the frankness of his manner concealed the artifice of his views; and the habits of courtesy were imputed to personal friendship or universal benevolence. His memory was capacious and retentive; his wit easy and social; his imagination sublime; his judgment clear, rapid, and decisive. He possessed the courage both of thought and action; and, although his designs might gradually expand with his success, the first idea which he entertained of his divine mission bears the stamp of an original and superior genius.

See, for additional physical descriptions, ibid., vol. 3, 78–79 n. 75.

31. A note to Koran 3:48, in the Everyman's Library edition, speaks to this point (p. 391 n. 2):

Muhammad probably believed that God took the dead body of Jesus to Heaven—for three hours according to some—while the Jews crucified a man who resembled him. Sura 4:156. . . . It would also seem from Sura 19:34, that Muhammad supposed Jesus to have died a natural death, though it is nowhere said how long he continued in that state. The Muhammadans believe that Jesus on his return to earth at the end of the world will slay the Antichrist, die, and be raised again. A vacant place is reserved for his body in the Prophet's tomb at Medina.

See also the passage from Gibbon in the text at note 110 of this chapter. See as well note 72 below.

32. Is the Koran somehow like the Holy Ghost? Consider how Gibbon compares the Bible and the Koran and their transmitters as understood by their respective adherents (*The Decline and Fall*, vol. 3, 85; *GBWW*, vol. 41, p. 231b):

> The inspiration of the Hebrew prophets, of the apostles and evangelists of Christ, might not be incompatible with the exercise of their reason and memory; and the diversity of their genius is strongly marked in the style and composition of the books of the Old and New Testament. But Mohammed was content with a character more humble, yet more sublime, of a simple editor; the substance of the Koran, according to himself or his disciples, is uncreated and eternal; subsisting in the essence of the Deity, and inscribed with a pen of light on the table of his everlasting decrees. A paper copy, in a volume of silk and gems, was brought down to the lowest heaven by the angel Gabriel, who, under the Jewish economy, had indeed been despatched on the most important errands; and this trusty messenger successively revealed the chapters and verses to the Arabian prophet. Instead of a perpetual and perfect measure of the divine will, the fragments of the Koran were produced at the discretion of Mohammed; each revelation is suited to the emergencies of his policy or passion; and all contradiction is removed by the saving maxim that any text of Scripture is abrogated or modified by any subsequent passage.

Is there a danger of turning the book itself into an idol, especially if one understands Arabic well enough to be mesmerized by its eloquence? See note 45 below.

33. Similarly, ancient Greece had a great breakthrough with the discovery of *nature*. See, e.g., Anastaplo, *Human Being and Citizen*, p. 47 (quoting from Leo Strauss's article on natural law in the *International Encyclopedia of the Social Sciences*); appendix B of this collection. Consider, also, Nirad C. Chaudhuri, *The Continent of Circe: Being an Essay on the Peoples of India* (London: Chatto & Windus, 1965), p. 151:

> No greater nonsense has ever been talked than that about the profundity of Hindu thought. There is no such thing as thinking properly so called among the Hindus, for it is a faculty of the mind developed only in Greece, and exercised only by the heirs of the Greeks. . . . The real strength of the Hindu mind lies in its intuitive exaltations, and also in its empiric patterns of action.

See the text at note 113 of this chapter. See also chapter 3 of this collection, note 91.

34. The Christian clergyman who provided the notes for the Everyman's Library edition of the Koran offers many samples of supposed distortions. Compare how Carlyle deals with Islam (*On Heroes*, p. 74):

> [The soul of Islam] is properly the soul of Christianity;—for Islam is definable as a confused form of Christianity; had Christianity not been, neither had it [Islam] been.

Further on Carlyle says (ibid., p. 82),

> Mahomet's Creed we called a kind of Christianity; and really, if we look at the wild rapt earnestness with which it was believed and laid to heart, I should say a better kind than that of those miserable Syrian Sects, with their vain janglings about *Homoiousion* and *Homoousion*, the head full of worthless noise, the heart empty and dead! The truth of it is embedded in portentous error and falsehood; but the truth of it makes it be believed, not the falsehood: it succeeded by its truth.

And again (ibid., p. 100).

> On the whole, we will repeat that this Religion of Mahomet's is a kind of Christianity; has a genuine element of what is spiritually highest looking through it, not to be hidden by all its imperfections.

Of course, the devout Christian or Jew might ask, if Muhammad did get wrong elementary things about the Judaism and Christianity he depends upon, what does that suggest about the caliber, if not about the genuineness, of his inspiration? On the *Homoiousion* debate and the Nicene Creed, see Anastaplo, "Law & Literature and the Bible," p. 719.

35. I had occasion to conduct (with Mervin Block, a Chicago journalist) an hours-long interview of Elijah Muhammad, founder of the American Black Muslim Movement, not long before his death in 1975. His doggedness, which exploited his ability to improvise "arguments" to serve his ends, reminded me of determined Southerners persisting in the Lost Cause a generation ago. See Anastaplo, *Human Being and Citizen*, p. 310 n. 11. See also Koran, Everyman's Library edition, p. 128 n. 2. See, as well, Anastaplo, "Slavery and the Constitution: Explorations," 20 *Texas Tech Law Review* 677, 778 (1989).

The Muslims also bring to mind the Mormons, with two founding leaders who shared the functions that had been combined in Muhammad. See also note 16 above (on Moses-Aaron and Muhammad), note 57 below.

36. See for what preceded Muhammad in Arabia, Gibbon, *The Decline and Fall*, vol. 3, 70 (*GBWW*, vol. 41, p. 226b). See also chapter 1 of this collection (for some ancient Middle Eastern religious practices). The medley of religious "faiths" that Muhammad had available to draw upon included worship of heavenly bodies, fire worship, Judaism, Christianity, and various kinds of idol worship. See note 40 below.

The Muslim who preached to pagans made use of Jewish and Christian sources much as Christians who preached to pagans must have made use of Jewish sources. In neither case would the listeners know much about the traditions drawn upon—but they would tend to be impressed by them as beliefs more elevated than what they themselves had had.

37. The Arabs, at least since Muhammad, see many of themselves as descended from Abraham (or Ibrahim) through Ishmael (or Isma'il), the son depicted as an outcast in the Bible. See Esposito, *Islam*, p. 24:

> While Jews and Christians are descendants of Abraham and his wife Sarah through their son Isaac, Muslims trace their lineage back to Ismail, Abraham's first-born son by his Egyptian bondswoman, Hagar. Islamic tradition teaches that Abraham, pressured by Sarah who feared that Ismail, as first born, would overshadow Isaac, took Hager and Ismail to the vicinity of Mecca, where he left them on their own. Ismail became the progenitor of the Arabs in northern Arabia. When Abraham later returned, Ismail helped his father build the Kabba [in Mecca] as the first shrine to the one true God. Muslim tradition also holds that it was here at the Kabba that Abraham was to sacrifice his son. In contrast to the biblical tradition (*Genesis* 22), Islam designates Ismail rather than Isaac as the intended victim, spared by divine intervention.

See also W. Gunther Plaut, ed., *The Torah: A Modern Commentary* (New York: Union of American Hebrew Congregations, 1981), p. xxxii, n. 1:

> The Arabs regard themselves as descendants of Ishmael, Abraham's oldest son. Some of the Moslem teachers accused the Jews of misinterpreting (or even falsifying) the biblical text in

order to give preference to their ancestor Isaac. Similar charges, that Jews have tampered with
the Hebrew text of the Bible, were made by some early Christian thinkers.

See as well David K. Shipler, *Arab and Jew: Wounded Spirits in a Promised Land* (New
York: Times Books, Random House, 1986), pp. 151–52, 166–67. *Kabba* is spelled many
ways in the sources I quote. I try to use the same spelling in all of the quotations.

38. The Esposito account of Islam includes these descriptions of this holiest of places
(*Islam*, pp. 5–6, 93–94):

> The religion of Arabia [before Muhammad] reflected its tribal nature and social structure. Gods
> and goddesses served as protectors of individual tribes, and their spirits were associated with sa-
> cred objects—trees, stones, springs, and wells. Local tribal deities were feared and respected
> rather than loved, the objects of cultic rituals (sacrifice, pilgrimage, prayer) of supplication and
> propitiation celebrated in local shrines. Mecca possessed a central shrine of the gods, the Kabba,
> a cube-shaped building that housed the 360 idols of tribal patron deities, and was the site of a
> great annual pilgrimage and fair. While these deities were primary religious actors and objects
> of worship, beyond this tribal polytheism was a shared belief in Allah ("the god"). Allah, the
> supreme high god, was the creator and sustainer of life but remote from everyday concerns and
> thus not the object of cult or ritual. Associated with Allah were three goddesses who were the
> daughters of Allah: al-Lat, Manat, and al-Uzza. . . .
>
> Ramadan [note 10 above] is followed by the beginning of the pilgrimage season [for Mus-
> lims]. Every adult Muslim physically and financially able is expected to perform the pilgrimage
> (*hajj*) to Mecca at least once in his or her lifetime. The focus of the pilgrimage is the Kabba, the
> cube-shaped House of God, in which the sacred black stone is embedded. Muslim tradition
> teaches that the Kabba was originally built by the prophet Ibrahim (Abraham) and his son Is-
> mail. The black stone was given to Abraham by the angel Gabriel and thus is a symbol of God's
> covenant with Ismail and, by extension, the Muslim community. The Kabba was the object of
> pilgrimage during pre-Islamic times. Tradition tells us that one of the first things Muhammad
> did when he marched triumphantly into Mecca was to cleanse the Kabba of the tribal idols that
> it housed, thus restoring it to the worship of the one true God.
>
> The pilgrimage proper takes place during the twelfth month, Dha al-Hijja, of the Muslim lu-
> nar calendar. As with prayer, the pilgrimage requires ritual purification. . . . As the pilgrims near
> Mecca they shout, "I am here, O Lord, I am here!" As they enter Mecca, they proceed to the
> Grand Mosque, where the Kabba is located. Moving in a counterclockwise direction, they cir-
> cle (*tawaf*) the Kabba seven times. During the following days, a variety of ritual actions or cer-
> emonies take place—praying at the spot where Abraham, the patriarch and father of monothe-
> ism, stood; running between Safa and Marwa in commemoration of Hagar's frantic search for
> water for her son, Ismail; stoning the devil, three stone pillars that symbolize evil. An essential
> part of the pilgrimage is a visit to the Plain of Arafat, where, from noon to sunset, the pilgrims
> stand before God in repentance, seeking His forgiveness for themselves and all Muslims
> throughout the world. . . .
>
> The pilgrimage ends with the Feast of Sacrifice (*Id al-Adha*), known in Muslim piety as the Great
> Feast (*Id al-Kabir*). It commemorates God's command to Abraham to sacrifice his son Ismail. . . .
> The pilgrims ritually reenact Abraham's rejection of Satan's temptations to ignore God's command
> by again casting stones at the devil, represented by a pillar. Afterward, they sacrifice animals (sheep,
> goats, cattle, or camels) as Abraham was finally permitted to substitute a ram for his son.

See also Gibbon, *The Decline and Fall*, vol. 3, 71, 107 (*GBWW*, vol. 41, pp. 226c–d,
241b–c); Carlyle, *On Heroes*, pp. 64–66; Koran, Everyman's Library edition, p. 395 nn. 1,
2, p. 497 n. 1. See, on the ritual circling of the Kabba, note 40 below. See, on the three
"daughters of Allah" and on the black stone, note 45 below.

39. Consider how Lycurgus used Thales, the poet, to tame the Spartans and thus prepare them for a new regime. See Plutarch, *Lycurgus* (*GBWW*, vol. 14, pp. 32a–48b).

40. See note 38 above. This rapid circling of the Kabba, with an intensity that borders on frenzy, is said by some scholars to be left over from the actions of star worshipers who imitate thus the movement of the heavily bodies. Related to this was the housing of 360 idols in the Kabba, evidently for the days of the year in a lunar calendar. I have seen a documentary film of this exercise as performed by large throngs of pilgrims: it is a remarkable spectacle. See Cragg, *The Call of the Minaret*, pp. 116f. See also note 97 below.

41. The anthropological approach may be seen in uses made by scholars of Muhammad's supposed epilepsy and by their attribution of his visions of Houris in Paradise to his own supposedly frustrating marriage to an older woman. See, e.g., Koran, Everyman's Library edition, p. 21 n. 1, p. 76 n. 2. Even so, Muhammad is recorded as having always remembered his first wife with great respect, not least because she believed in his mission when no one else would. See notes 59, 95, and 105 below. Similar speculations have been ventured about Socrates.

42. Could not the compilers of the Koran, after Muhammad's death, be considered to have been inspired by God as much, or in the same way, as some have believed that the translators of the King James version of the Bible or the translators of the Septuagint to have been? The "higher criticism," with its concerns for dating, sources, and editorial motives in interpreting texts, has also been brought to bear upon the Bible, upon the works of Plato, and upon the works (indeed, upon the person) of Shakespeare. See Anastaplo, "Oh How Eric Voegelin Has Read Plato and Aristotle," *Independent Journal of Philosophy*, vol. 5/6, p. 85 (1988).

43. Are not the more devout among intelligent Muslims, however, likely to know the probable chronology of the suras, even though the suras are not physically arranged thus? But there *is* ambiguity with respect to various of the suras, especially since some of the suras we now have may have been made up of parts that became available through revelations on different occasions. See note 58 below.

44. See Arberry, *The Koran Interpreted*, vol. 2, preface, pp. 12–13, 15–16.

45. The most notorious supposed cancellation or abrogation by Muhammad was of the verses which have figured so dramatically in the recent controversial novel, *Satanic Verses* (New York: Viking, 1989), by Salman Rushdie. The article on Muhammad in the *Encyclopedia of Religion* (New York: Macmillan, 1987), vol. 10, p. 139, offers this account of the episode:

[The] incident of the "satanic verses" [is] recounted by early commentators on the Qur'an as an illustration of sura 22:51. The story is that, while Muhammad was wondering how the leading merchants could be induced to accept the Qur'anic messages, he received a fresh revelation (sura 53, *The Star*), of which a section permitted treating three pagan goddesses as having the power to intercede with God on behalf of their worshipers. The goddesses were al-Lat, al-'Uzza, and Manat, and all had shrines within a day or two's journey from Mecca. When Muhammad proclaimed this revelation in the presence of the leading men, they joined him at the end in prostrating themselves in worship. Later, however, the angel Gabriel came to Muhammad and made him realize that the verses permitting the goddesses' intercession were not a genuine revelation but had been "put upon his tongue" by Satan, and the true continuation of the sura was then revealed to him. This "abrogation" or cancellation of the satanic verses increased the opposition to Muhammad and his followers. Some Muslims today reject this whole story, but it is difficult to see how any Muslim could have invented it, or how a non-Muslim could have persuaded distinguished Muslim scholars to accept it.

A similar account may be found in the Koran, Everyman's Library edition, p. 69 n. 1, p. 70 n. 4, where the abrogated verses (said to have been originally at 53:19–20) are said to have been,

> These are the exalted females [or, sublime swans, i.e.,
>   mounting nearer and nearer to God]
> And truly their intercession may be expected.

It is said in Koran 22:52–53 (a later sura than sura 53) that Muhammad was told by God that he was not the first prophet to be deceived by Satan:

> We sent not ever any Messenger
> or Prophet before thee, but that Satan
> cast into his fancy, when he was fancying;
> but God annuls what Satan casts, then
> God confirms His signs—surely God is
>   All-knowing, All-wise—
> that He may make what Satan casts
> a trial for those in whose hearts
> is sickness, and those whose hearts
> are hard; and surely the evildoers are
>   in wide schism;
> and that they who have been given knowledge
> may know that it is the truth from thy Lord
> and believe in it, and so their hearts
> be humble unto Him; and assuredly
> God ever guides those who believe
>   to a straight path.

Another scholar sees both the black stone in the Kabba and the three goddesses (note 38 above) as local cult matters to which Muhammad had to consider accommodating himself:

> Foreign religious ideas must have been known practically everywhere [in Arabia], but the standing of their adherents, for the most part aliens or slaves, added little to their persuasiveness. The Arabian border districts had for centuries been a hotbed of sectarianism, and members of every branch of Eastern Christianity must have been represented among the uninstructed motley crowds that passed through or worked in Mecca. That spiritual unrest, that same dissatisfaction with traditional paganism and its threadbare comforts which had marked the last stage of the Roman Empire, seems to have gripped ever widening strata of the peninsula's population when we first meet with the records of pre-Islamic civilization.
>
> There had never been much of an emotional religious life of native origin and even less theological or philosophical speculation. The physiognomy of most of the many deities whose names have been preserved is indistinct. Nearly all are of local importance only; not one profited by an imaginative effort of his followers. Their nomadism tended to disrupt the relationship of the tribes to a god whose place of worship had for a time been in their territory. . . . The real attraction of the Kabba [in Mecca] to the worshiper was a black stone of unfathomable age encased in its walls, whose cult the Prophet felt constrained to adopt into the ritual of Islam, where it still lingers as a weird testimonial to Islam's failure to rid itself of the crude associations of its origins.
>
> More than localized validity and a somewhat individualized profile had been attained by three female divinities, referred to by the Koran as "Allah's daughters" [37:149, 53:21], Manat (Fate),

al-Lat ("*The Goddess*," probably originally a sun-goddess), and al-Uzza (the Venus or Morning Star). Although their personalities, too, were rather pale and would hardly have roused any pious fervor, they were so firmly ensconced in the minds of the Meccans that, in a curious swerve from his uncompromising monotheism, Mohammed at one time thought he could, by acknowledging their divine rank and power, induce his compatriots to desist from persecuting his ill-protected congregation [53: 19–23]. Soon, however, Mohammed repented of his weakness and characterized the goddesses as "nothing but names which you and your fathers have used" [53:23]. And it is precisely because their deities had shrunk to little more than names hedged in by the habits of superstitions awe that the Bedouins nowhere put up a fight for them when the Muslims dethroned and destroyed them.

Gustave E. von Grunebaum, *Medieval Islam: A Study in Cultural Orientation* (Chicago: University of Chicago Press, 1953), pp. 67–68. See, on the cancellation of texts, ibid., pp. 85–86. See, for another account of pre-Islamic religious opinions in Arabia, Esposito, *Islam*, pp. 4–7.

It is generally said today that Muslim scholars tend to reject the Satanic verses episode as unhistoric (compare Koran 6:112). Western scholars accept the episode, but they do not doubt Muhammad's sincerity. Indeed, cannot both the episode and the record of it be taken as evidence of Muhammad's integrity? A few Muslim scholars evidently argue that Satan *was* involved, in that he caused *the listeners* to hear the verses, not that the Prophet actually heard and spoke them. And, of course, there were the old-fashioned Christian critics of Islam who argued that all of Muhammad's verses were due to Satan. These radically different assessments do suggest that the gulf between Revelation and Reason may be difficult, if not impossible, to bridge. See note 53 below.

The literature on the Rushdie *Satanic Verses* controversy is extensive. See, e.g., *Sunday Times* (London), January 22, 1989, p. B5 ("There is a saying: You can say what you like about God, but be careful with Muhammad."); *New York Times Magazine*, January 29, 1989, p. 24; *New York Times Book Review*, January 29, 1989, p. 3; Steve Lohr, "Rushdie Expresses Regret to Muslims about His Novel," *New York Times*, February 19, 1989, p. 1; *Christian Science Monitor*, March 2, 1989, p. 13; *Chicago Tribune*, March 3, 1989, sec. 1, p. 21; Jimmy Carter, "Rushdie's Book Is an Insult," *New York Times*, March 5, 1989, sec. E, p. 23; "Vatican Newspaper Faults Rushdie Book," *New York Times*, March 7, 1989, p. 3 ("The very attachment to our own faith induces us to deplore that which is irreverent and blasphemous in the book's contents"); Cheryl Benard, "Rushdie's Critique Is as Old as Islam," *Wall Street Journal*, March 16, 1989, p. A16. See also note 62 below. See as well Dean E. Murphy, "Muslim Cleric Calls for Death of Author [Khalid Duran] Who Wrote on Islam," *New York Times*, June 30, 2001, p. A9.

46. Whatever the inspiration that directed either Muhammad or the original compilers of the Koran, the modern scholars who rearrange the text do not claim to be directed by God to act as they do. Or should it be said that God may nevertheless be behind what they are doing, leading them to adapt the Koran to radically new circumstances, including to modes of thought among Westerners quite different from those among the Arabs of Muhammad's time? See note 58 below. See as well Dean E. Murphy, "Muslim Cleric Calls for Death of Author [Khalid Duran] Who Wrote on Islam," *New York Times*, June 30, 2001, p. A9.

47. See Anastaplo, *The Constitutionalist: Notes on the First Amendment* (Dallas: Southern Methodist University Press, 1971), pp. 803–4 n. 38.

48. Sigmund Freud's *Moses and Monotheism* and Sir James Frazer's *The Golden Bough* come to mind. Compare the commentary on the *Book of Genesis* by Robert Sacks, published in installments in *Interpretation* in recent years, beginning with volume 8 of that journal.

49. What do the Koran and the career of Muhammad happen to reveal about the origins of other religions and about how one might think about them and about the divine? See, e.g., the text at note 53 of this chapter. See also note 57 below.

50. It affects also, I have suggested, what one does with Muhammad's own temperament, desires, and personal circumstances. See, on the risks one runs in using such terms as "values," Anastaplo, *"In re* Allan Bloom: A Respectful Dissent," *The Great Ideas Today*, pp. 269b–70a, n. 40 (1988). This and another review by me of the Bloom book, a review which discusses Mr. Bloom's opinions about race relations in the United States, are included in Robert L. Stone, ed., *Essays on "The Closing of the American Mind"* (Chicago: Chicago Review Press, 1989). See also note 113 below. See, generally, on the "fact-value" problem, Leo Strau*ss, Natural Right and History* (Chicago: University of Chicago Press, 1953).

51. Arberry records the opinion of an English convert to Islam: "It may be reasonably claimed that no Holy Scripture can be fairly presented by one who disbelieves its inspiration and its message." *The Koran Interpreted*, vol. 1, preface, p. 20.

52. Compare Koran 30: 1–3. But see Koran, Everyman's Library edition, p. 210 n. 4. See also ibid., p. 239 n. 1.

53. Maimonides' prophetology can become critical here. See the text at note 1 of this chapter. See also note 14 above. What does this, too, say about the gulf between Revelation and Reason? See note 45 above.

54. The *Book of Job* supports this observation. The references here are to particular workings of God, to be distinguished from the general workings or signs, such as the universe itself, generation, etc. See the text at note 58 of this chapter. See also Anastaplo, "Law & Literature and the Bible," p. 680.

55. Compare Gibbon, *The Decline and Fall*, vol. 3, 87 (*GBWW*, vol. 41, p. 232a–b).

56. See, for fanciful accounts of miracles associated with Muhammad which have been developed by some of his followers since his death, Gibbon, *The Decline and Fall*, vol. 3, 87–88 (*GBWW*, vol. 41, p. 232b–d); von Grunebaum, *Medieval Islam*, pp. 92ff. Compare Esposito, *Islam*, pp. 22–23:

> Since the Quran is God's book, the text of the Quran, like its author [that is, God?], is regarded as perfect, eternal, and unchangeable. This belief is the basis for the doctrine of the miracle of inimitability (*ijaz*) of the Quran, which asserts that the ideas, language, and style of the Quran cannot be reproduced. The Quran proclaims that even the combined efforts of human beings and jinns could not produce a comparable text (17:88). The Quran is regarded as the only miracle brought by the Prophet. Muslim tradition is replete with stories of those who converted to Islam on hearing its inimitable message and of those pagan poets who failed the Quranic challenge (10:37–38) to create verses comparable with those contained in the Quran. Indeed, throughout history, many Arab Christians have regarded it as the perfection of Arabic language and literature.

Compare, with respect to any bodily ascent by Muhammad into heaven at death, the Gibbon passage in the text at note 110 of this chapter.

57. Is one being somewhat "anthropological" in making such suggestions as these? Similar considerations apply to the emergence in the United States of the Mormon religious movement, a movement similar to the Muslim movement in many interesting respects. See note 35 above. Both movements can provide us instructive glimpses of what beginnings may be like in such matters, helping us to see better (and perhaps to appreciate even more?) the accomplishments of Abraham, Moses, and Jesus. See ap-

pendix A of this collection. Certainly, Muhammad can seem more impressive, the more one sees the uses made by or through him of the materials he had at hand. Also impressive is the respect he wins from so tough-minded if not even so cynical a scholar as Gibbon: "The faith which, under the name of *Islam*, he preached to his family and nation, is compounded of an eternal truth and a necessary fiction. THAT THERE IS ONLY ONE GOD, AND MOHAMMED IS THE APOSTLE OF GOD." (*The Decline and Fall*, vol. 3, 80–81; *GBWW*, vol. 41, p. 229c.) "It is not the propagation, but the permanency of his religion, that deserves our wonder: the same pure and perfect impression which he engraved at Mecca and Medina is preserved, after the revolutions of twelve centuries, by the Indian, the African, and the Turkish proselytes of the Koran." (Ibid., vol. 3, 129; *GBWW*, vol. 41, p. 252a) "The most bitter or most bigoted of his Christian or Jewish foes will surely allow that he assumed a false commission to inculcate a salutary doctrine, less perfect only than their own. He piously supposed, as the basis of his religion, the truth and sanctity of *their* prior revelations, the virtues and miracles of their founders. The idols of Arabia were broken before the throne of God." (Ibid., vol. 3, 130; *GBWW*, vol. 41, p. 252d.) See also Esposito, *Islam*, p. 15. See as well note 114 below.

58. The central verses of the Koran have an unresponsive people demanding of a prophet that he show them a sign (26: 185–91):

> They said, "Thou are merely one of those
> 			that are bewitched;
> thou are naught but a mortal, like us;
> indeed, we think that thou are
> 			one of the liars.
> Then drop down on us lumps from heaven, if thou art
> 			one of the truthful."
> He said, "My Lord knows very well
> 			what you are doing."
> But they cried him lies; then there seized them
> the chastisement of the Day of Shadow;
> assuredly it was the chastisement of
> 			a dreadful day.
> Surely in that is a sign,
> yet most of them are not believers.
> 			Surely thy Lord. He is
> the All-mighty, the All-compassionate.

I rely here, in locating the central verses in the Koran (turning around verses 186–87 of sura 26, fittingly entitled "The Poet"), upon standard verse counts as provided, for example, in the Everyman's Library and Penguin editions. (The totals, of approximately 6,230 lines, do differ slightly from one version to another of the Koran.) Is not this exchange, in sura 26, between Unbelievers and Prophet, at the heart of all the verses of the Koran as they happened to be arranged by the original compilers of the disjointed suras that Muhammad left behind? Should this providential placement of an exchange about prophecy and signs be itself regarded as a most instructive sign? (One can be reminded of what Homer does with the arrangement of the perhaps traditional "Catalogue of Ships" information in book 2 of the *Iliad*. See Anastaplo, *The Constitutionalist*, p. 807 n. 39. See also Anastaplo, *The Artist as Thinker*, pp. 11, 203, 384 n. 56.)

To ask for signs is to say, in effect, "You are *not* making sound arguments. Why should we take your word for what you are advocating?" There is a curious combination in the Koran of a generous acceptance by Muhammad of virtually all miracles in the Bible that happen to be known to him and a firm disavowal of any miracles that may be attributed to him personally—and yet, throughout the two decades of his mission, he reports himself in repeated direct contact with the Angel Gabriel.

To what, then, should the thoughtful modern attribute Muhammad's remarkable success as a founder? Perhaps to one or more of the following factors having been available to Muhammad: the faculty of divination; an inspired poetical gift; a captivating personality; extraordinary political-military skills; divine influence; the circumstances of the day, especially the heritage, interests, and passions of the Arabs; and chance. We can again see that the career of Muhammad, properly understood, may help us understand and assess the careers of other prophets and would-be prophets. To what extent did Muhammad, whether or not pursuant to immediate divine direction, do for the Arabs what Homer did for the Greeks? In both cases, a medley of preexisting opinions about the divine (among the Greeks and among the Semitic peoples, respectively) was reworked, refined, and made attractive. Consider the yet to be appreciated implications of the discovery a generation ago at Kenchreai, Greece, "of a large life-size mosaic portrait of a figure labeled 'Homer' in Greek, with some of the characteristics we associate with the figure of the Christ in later Byzantine art." This figure is from the third or fourth century A.D. See Anastaplo, *The Constitutionalist*, p. 552 n. 132.

Modern rearrangements of the suras conceal from view the revealing order left by the original Koranic compilers, whether due to divine guidance or to editorial skill or to chance. (Are the verse totals for each sura, with the verses themselves varying considerably in length, recorded in part for the kind of use made of them in this note?) In any event, it does not seem to have occurred to the scholars responsible for modern rearrangements of the Koranic suras that important clues might thus be sacrificed to their methodology. See note 16 above.

Many puzzles are left by the traditional arrangement of the suras, inviting speculation for more than a millennium now. See, e.g., Cragg, *The House of Islam* (New York: Dickenson, 1975), pp. 34–37. For the most part, the suras which come first in the Koran are the ones which had been most recently revealed at the time the Koran was compiled shortly after Muhammad's unexpected death. Were not the more recent suras apt to be the most useful, since they were more likely both to deal with immediate circumstances and to reflect Muhammad's latest thought?

It has been noticed that, by and large, the longer suras were put first by the compilers. Perhaps they were put first not simply because of their lengths but rather because of their subjects which did require more extensive treatment. Were not these also apt to be the suras most readily available in that their lengths made it more likely that they would be reduced to writing?

The latest suras are like the most recent statutes of a people, providing immediate guidance to the community, which is what in fact these longer suras do. The earlier (and generally more poetic) suras, on the other hand, had been more concerned to establish the faith, to win over allegiances; but once that and other missionary work had been done the primary concern became how those who had been converted would be governed. (Why did not the Israelites organize their Book similarly? Was their Book put together at a time when their faith was being challenged, when it was not primarily a question of governance but rather of belief, and for *that* the foundation text needed was the *Book of Genesis*?) Also, we must further wonder, is the orthodox arrangement of the suras most convenient for the systematic reading of the entire Koran through the thirty days of Ramadan? The more complicated, even tedious, suras are at the beginning, when everyone is fresh; the more beautiful, shorter suras, and very much to be anticipated, are at the end of the endeavor.

I have ventured several suggestions as to why the longest suras go first (after the brief invocation which is sura 1). The key to the overall arrangement may be sura 2, which is the longest. There are a number of things in sura 2 which may have made it particularly attractive as a front-runner (including cautions against imitating the Koran and guidance in various important matters). If sura 2 *was* chosen for its content (or for whatever reason), and if it happened to be the longest, this may have helped establish the pattern of giving priority to length (all other things being equal). (Candidates for special study are the central suras of the Koran, suras 57 and 58.)

A modern rearranger of the Koran observes with regret, "The text . . . as hitherto arranged, necessarily assumes the form of a most unreadable and incongruous patchwork . . . and conveys no idea whatever of the development and growth of any plan in the mind of the founder of Islam, or of the circumstances by which he was surrounded and influenced." (Koran, Everyman's Library edition, p. 2.) It is precisely this sort of scholarly approach to the Koran that the traditional order discourages. Even so, the cumbersome way that the compilers originally organized the Koran is generally taken as testimony to their honesty.

It may be difficult for us to be certain what moved the compilers. But whatever did, the resulting text "worked" remarkably well. Does the modern rearrangement of the suras in chronological order reflect a Western (if not Judaic-Christian) rationalistic approach? Is the Muslim (Arab?) approach more haphazard if not fatalistic, accepting more what happens to be at hand or moving in the direction that was first happened upon? Different senses of the universe and nature, or of God's relation to human beings, may be indicated thereby. See note 113 below.

In any event, the modern chronological ordering of the suras depends upon critical anthropological-historical-sociological (that is, scientific) methods designed to show a development in Muhammad's thought keyed to his circumstances. Is this in turn to assume that neither the original revelations to Muhammad nor the original Koranic arrangement by the compilers came from God? See note 41 above. A more pious approach to these matters may be seen in this observation by still another modern translator of the Koran:

> The arrangement is not easy to understand. Revelations of various dates and on different subjects are to be found together in one sura; verses of Medinah revelation are found in Meccan suras; some of the Medinah suras, though of late revelation, are placed first and the very early Meccan suras at the end. But the arrangement is not haphazard, as some have hastily supposed. Closer study will reveal a sequence and significance—as, for instance, with regard to the placing of the very early Meccan suras at the end. The inspiration of the Prophet progressed from inmost things to outward things, whereas most people find their way through outward things to things within.

Mohammed Marmaduke Pickthall, *The Meaning of the Glorious Koran* (New York: Mentor Books, 1953), pp. xxviii–xxix.

59. See, for the Muslim tradition as to how Muhammad responded to his "call," Esposito, *Islam*, p. 9:

He was both frightened and reluctant. Frightened by the unknown—for surely he did not expect such an experience. Reluctant, at first, because he feared he was possessed and that others would use such grounds and dismiss his claims as inspired by spirits, or *jinns*. Despondent and confused, Muhammad set out to kill himself but was stopped when he again heard the voice say, "O Muhammad! You are the messenger of God and I am Gabriel." This message was reinforced by his wife, Khadija, who reassured him that he was neither mad nor possessed; the messenger was from God and not a demon.

See also Carlyle, *On Heroes*, p. 76:

Long afterwards, Ayesha his young favorite wife, a woman who indeed distinguished herself among the Moslem, by all manner of qualities, through her whole long life; this young brilliant Ayesha was, one day, questioning him: "Now am not I better than Kadijah? She was a widow; old, and had lost her looks: you love me better than you did her?"—"No, by Allah!" answered Mahomet: "No, by Allah! She believed in me when none else would believe. In the whole world I had but one friend, and she was that!"

See as well "Islam," *Encyclopaedia Britannica* (1989), vol. 22, p. 2.

60. The issue of "free will or determinism" has developed among Muslims as it has among Christians. See, e.g., Gibbon, *The Decline and Fall*, vol. 3, 101 (*GBWW*, vol. 41, p. 238c):

The Koran inculcates, in the most absolute sense, the tenets of fate and predestination, which would extinguish both industry and virtue, if the actions of man were governed by his speculative belief. Yet their influence in every age has exalted the courage of the Saracens and Turks. The first companions of Mohammed advanced to battle with a fearless confidence: there is no danger where there is no chance: they were ordained to perish in their beds; or they were safe and invulnerable amidst the darts of the enemy.

Compare Esposito, *Islam*, pp. 70–71:

The determinists argued that the free will of human beings limited an omnipotent God. The advocates of free will countered that to deny free will ran counter to the sense of human accountability implicit in the notion of the Last Day and Judgment. Both sides were able to utilize Quaranic texts to justify their positions. On the one hand, human freedom is affirmed in such passages as, "Truth comes from your Lord. Let anyone who will, believe, and let anyone who wishes, disbelieve." (18:29) On the other hand, there are many verses that portray an all-powerful God who is responsible for all events: "God lets anyone He wishes go astray while He guides whoever he wishes." (35:8)

The status of free will *is* a problem. See, e.g., Koran 2:273; 3:25; 6:15, 25, 39, 111, 126; 10:45, 98–100; 64:11; 76–30; Ibrahim Abdel Meguid, *No One Sleeps in Alexandria*, trans Farouk Abdel Wahab (Cairo: The American University in Cairo Press, 1996), pp. 214–15. Indeed, one is often tempted to conclude that Muhammad rules out free will. Yet there is in the Satanic Iblis (or Eblis) a decisive willfulness (18:48):

And when We said to the angels, "Bow
yourselves to [the newly-created] Adam": so they bowed
themselves, save Iblis: he was one of
the jinn, and committed ungodliness
against his Lord's command.

See also Koran 2:33; 7:10; 15:30–40; 17:64–66; 38:70–80. "In the name Eblis (diabolos) and in the honour claimed for Adam as a kind of Godman, there are traces of a Christian original, as well as in the identification of the serpent with Satan." (Koran, Everyman's Library edition, p. 341 n. 3) "Muhammad appears, according to this text [18:48], to have considered Eblis not only as the father of the Djinn, but as one of their number. The truth appears to be that Muhammad derived his doctrines of the Genii from the Persian and Indian mythology, and attempted to identify them with the Satan and demons of the Semitic race." (Ibid., p. 185 n. 2) I have also heard the suggestion that Iblis refused to bow to Adam because he wanted to remain faithful to the One. See, on John Milton's Satan, Anastaplo, "Law & Literature and the Moderns," p. 261.

See, for a thoroughgoing determinism as well as for an indication of the array available of Indian divinities, chapter 3 of this collection.

61. There was no weariness by God after the six days of creation (50:38), just as there is no weariness in nature presumably in response to how things work. See, on nature, note 113 below and the text at note 113 of this chapter. See also the preface to this collection.

62. The Koran is seen as doing for the Arabs what Moses (and, at the outset, Jesus also?) had done for the Jews (46:11). But, it is insisted, no foreigner taught Muhammad what to say in the Koran (16:105). One can see, in the passion with which the memory of Muhammad is defended by Muslims (see note 45 above), the importance of cherishing one's own, something that Jews have long been aware of. Particularly instructive here is a 1962 talk by Leo Strauss at the University of Chicago Hillel House, "Why We Remain Jews: Can Jewish Faith and History Still Speak to Us?" See Kenneth Hart Green, ed., *Jewish Philosophy and the Crisis of Modernity* (Albany: State University of New York Press, 1997), p. 311. See also note 45 above, notes 93 and 112 below.

63. See, on natural right, Anastaplo, *Human Being and Citizen*, pp. 46, 74. See also note 14 above, appendix B of this collection. Are not the choice and implementation of a religion in large part political? See Anastaplo, "Church and State: Explorations," pp. 61–64, 88–90, 109–26, 145–63, 190–93. See also chapter 4 of this collection, note 38.

64. Carlyle, *On Heroes*, pp. 57–58. Compare the relatively little effect over the centuries of spectacular marauders such as Attila the Hun. Are the notorious sensual excesses of a Kernal Ataturk bound to subvert his influence in the long run? See note 95 below.

65. Gibbon, *The Decline and Fall*, vol. 3, 129 (*GBWW*, vol. 41, p. 252a). Also deserving of wonder is what someone with Gibbon's genius could do, even when poorly informed if not wrongheaded, with such materials as those available in the eighteenth century about the career and doctrines of a Muhammad. Consider, in turn, how Gibbon can comment on some of his predecessors (ibid., p. 131 n. 202):

> The writers of the Modern Universal History (vols. i and ii) have compiled in 850 folio pages the life of Mohammed and the annals of the caliphs. They enjoyed the advantage of reading, and sometimes correcting, the Arabic text; yet, notwithstanding their high-sounding boasts, I cannot find, after the conclusion of my work, that they have afforded me much (if any) additional information. The dull mass is not quickened by a spark of philosophy or taste; and the compilers indulge the criticism of acrimonious bigotry against Boulainvilliers, Sale, Gagnier, and all who have treated Mohammed with favour, or even justice.

See note 6 above.

66. Did not Moses also ask to see God? See Anastaplo, "Law & Literature and the Bible," p. 591. On The Golden Calf, see ibid., p. 604. Would Mohammad consider this a

corruption in the Hebrew text? See note 72 below. Consider, also, Semele's fatal request of Zeus and, in the *Bhagavad Gita*, Arjuna's revealing request of Krishna. On Semele, see Euripides, *Bacchae*; on Arjuna, see chapter 3 of this collection.

It is evident in the career of Muhammad, as drawn upon in the Koran, that earthly prosperity and goodness *can* coincide. Consider sura 108 ("Abundance": God speaking to Muhammad):

> In the Name of God, the Merciful, the Compassionate
> Surely We have given thee abundance;
> so pray unto the Lord and sacrifice.
> Surely he that hates thee, he is the one cut off.

This sura is said to be "a reply to those who had taunted Muhammad with the death of his two sons, as a mark of the divine displeasure." Koran, Everyman's Library edition, p. 30 n. 2.

67. Consider, the opening lines of sura 81 ("The Darkening"):

> When the sun shall be darkened,
> when the stars shall be thrown down,
> when the mountains shall be set moving,
> when the pregnant camels shall be neglected,
> when the savage beasts shall be mustered,
> when the seas shall be set boiling,
> when the souls shall be coupled,
> when the buried infant shall be asked for what sin she was slain,
> when the scrolls shall be unrolled,
> when heaven shall be stripped off,
> when Hell shall be set blazing,
> when Paradise shall be brought nigh,
> then shall a soul know what it has produced.

See also Koran 21:103 ("On the day when We shall roll up heaven as a scroll is rolled for the writings: as We originated the first creation, so We shall bring it back again"); sura 56 ("The Terror"). See, on the significance of UFO "visitations" and the like, Anastaplo, "Lessons for the Student of Law: The Oklahoma Lectures," 20 *Oklahoma City University Law Review* 19, 187 (1995). See also the text at note 68 of chapter 7 of this collection. See as well appendix C of this collection, note 140.

68. Even so, not all is told by God to or through His messengers all the time. Koran 3:173–74.

69. Arberry, *The Koran Interpreted*, preface, pp. 20–21. See also ibid., pp. 24–25, 28. What is one to make of the fact, if fact it is, that the Greek of Plato's dialogues is superior to that of the New Testament? How do the Hebrew of the Old Testament and the Arabic of the Koran compare? One scholar has observed,

> The Koran has been severely criticized for its stylistic inadequacies. The West has been almost unanimous on this count, and not a few Muslims have intimated their disappointment with its language and imagery.
>
> Some of this criticism is undoubtedly justified. Muhammad was not a writer of Plato's or an enthusiast of Amos' rank. His inspiration could hold its sublime level only for a short while before it was brought down to commonplace by exhaustion of the imaginative power or before it broke

up into disconnected paragraphs for lack of logical cogency. But the general charge of staleness, poverty of ideas, and repetitiousness is ill considered.

Von Grunebaum, *Medieval Islam*, p. 80. Consider, also, his observation:

> The effect of the literary advance which the Koran marks is heightened by a number of passages of sublime beauty. Many of the lines that seem rather commonplace to us must have been astounding and stirring to the contemporaries. But at all times this simile of the Lord and the mysterious aloofness of his splendor will penetrate to the innermost heart: "Allah is the light of the heavens and the earth; His light is like a niche in which is a lamp, the lamp in glass and the glass like a brilliant star, lit from a blessed tree, an olive neither of the East nor of the West whose oil would almost give light even though no fire did touch it; light upon light."

Ibid., p. 88 (citing Koran 24:35). Consider, as well, this distillation: "In the superhuman wisdom and justice of the Torah, the seeing Jew *sees*, and in the superhuman beauty of the Koran the seeing Muslim *sees*, that Revelation is real." Strauss, *Philosophy and Law*, p. 39.

70. Even if Muhammad believed himself to be an impostor, God may nevertheless have been using him. But consider what is said about "a perfect intellect" and "perfect morals" in the passages in the text at notes 1 and 95 of this chapter.

71. Muhammad claims to know what the prophets before him did not know, such as what passed among celestial beings on various occasions (Koran 38:69–88). Such claims may be seen as well in, among many other places, the *Gilgamesh* and Homer. On the *Gilgamesh*, see chapter 1 of this collection; on Homer, see Anastaplo, *The Thinker as Artist; From Homer to Plato and Aristotle* (Athens, Ohio: Ohio University Press, 1997), p. 13. See also note 78 below.

72. "Although God had revealed His will to Moses and the Hebrew prophets and later to Jesus, Muslims believe that the Scriptures of the Jewish community (Torah) and that of the Christian church (the Evangel or Gospel) were corrupted. The current texts of the Torah and the New Testament are regarded [by Muslims] as a composite of human fabrications mixed with divine revelation." Esposito, *Islam*, p. 21. "The Qur'an stresses the alleged falsification of the Scriptures by both Jews and Christians but in a way that usually indicates a derivative or insufficient understanding of the original ideas or facts. Among these are the Incarnation, which is categorically rejected, and the Crucifixion, said to be a Jewish distortion of the true event. According to Islamic dogma, another figure was crucified in the place of Jesus, who was himself taken to heaven." "Islam," *International Encyclopedia of the Social Sciences* (1968), vol. 8, p. 205. See note 31 above. See also von Grunebaum, *Medieval Islam*, pp. 78–79. In any event, Muslims believe that the Koran incorporates as much of Jewish and Christian scriptures as is necessary for Islam, correcting in the process what had become faulty in the transmission of those scriptures.

73. Islam has been (except perhaps for Marxism?) the last of the great religions founded thus far, the last before the onslaught upon religious faith of modern science and the way of life it tends to promote. The Muslim can insist that all kinds of modern developments (ranging from medical advances to moon walks) are anticipated in the Koran. Similar retroactive discoveries are made by Hindus who know their own texts. Such fanciful rationalizations suggest how powerful (and threatening?) the modern development is.

The Muslims, perhaps more than any other large-scale religious community today, tend to be fundamentalists. See note 97 below. This means, among other things, that religious restrictions, imagery, and standards figure much more prominently, if not even naively, in everyday life than we are now accustomed to in the West (except perhaps among the most observant of Orthodox Jews). Consider this report about the first Arab in space (Prince Sultan, a nephew of the king of Saudi Arabia, on the American space shuttle "Discovery"):

> Later in the flight, King Fahd and Prince Salman, governor of Riyadh and Prince Sultan's father, spoke by telephone to the 28-year-old Arab astronaut. King Fahd told the prince: "We are proud of your mission. It is a great achievement."
> "The best news I heard today is that you completed reading the Quran in space," Prince Sulman told his son.
> "I hope this will be a good deed for Islam, Muslims and the Arab Nation," replied the astronaut prince, who had studied most of the Quran, the holy book of Islam, and finished reading it in space.

Arab Perspective (August 1985), p. 6. See notes 90 and 97 below. Consider also the insistence by Martin Heidegger, "Only a god can save us." Interview (given in 1966, to be published posthumously) in *Der Spiegel* (1976), trans. in *Philosophy Today* (winter 1976, pp. 267–84). See the essay on Heidegger in Anastaplo, *The American Moralist*, p. 144.

74. See also Carlyle, *Heroes*, p. 91. The following passage from Thomas Aquinas, *On Truth* (Q. 23, A. 6, Reply), cautions us about what the power of God does and does not mean:

> Since justice is a certain "correctness," as Anselm says, or "equation," as the Philosopher [Aristotle] teaches, the essential character of justice must depend first of all upon that in which there is first found the character of a rule according to which the equality and correctness of justice is established in things. Now the will does not have the character of the first rule; it is rather a rule which itself has a rule, for it is directed by reason and the intellect. This is true not only in us but also in God, although in us the will is really distinct from the intellect. For this reason the will and its correctness are not the same thing. In God, however, the will is really identical with the intellect, and for this reason the correctness of His will is really the same as His will itself. Consequently the first thing upon which the essential character of all justice depends is the wisdom of the divine intellect, which constitutes things in their due proportion both to one another and to their cause. In this proportion the essential character of created justice consists. But to say that justice depends simply upon the will is to say that the divine will does not proceed according to the order of wisdom, and that is blasphemous.

See also Anastaplo, *The American Moralist*, p. 139.

75. Fundamental to the belief is the rigorous purging of idolatrous elements. See the text at note 26 of this chapter. See also Koran 21:53ff. Consider as well note 45 above and note 77 below.

76. If the Koran should be found to contain "much inconsistency," would that mean that it cannot be from God? That is, should a flawed Koran itself be believed about the significance of flaws? We can be reminded here of the ancient Cretan Paradox. See the passage quoted in the text at note 1 of this chapter. See also note 45 above.

77. See, Plato, *Republic*, books II and III, where the Homeric account of the gods is repeatedly corrected (*GBWW*, vol. 7, pp. 310c–41d). Consider, also, the opening chapters of Maimonides, *The Guide of the Perplexed.* See note 85 below.

78. See, on rhetoric, Plato, *Gorgias* (*GBWW*, vol. 7, pp. 252a–94c); Aristotle, *Rhetoric* (*GBWW*, vol. 9, pp. 593a–675c); Larry Arnhart, *Aristotle on Political Reasoning: A Com-*

mentary on the "Rhetoric" (DeKalb, Ill.: Northern Illinois University Press, 1981). See also chapters 3, 4, and 5 of this collection. See as well note 57 above, note 105 below. Is Muhammed, in critical respects, even like Homer as poetic theologian? See notes 2 and 71 above, note 80 below. See also the text at note 42 of chapter 7 of this collection.

79. See, for charges of forgery, plagiarism, poetry, and sorcery, Koran 2:100; 7:201–03; 10:2, 78; 11:10–18, 30–39; 16:24; 18:1–3; 25:9; 26:26; 31:4; 34:43; 37:33; 44:13; 52:32; 68:12, 51. Comparisons are made by Muhammad to charges made against Moses. We have noticed that a study of Muhammad and the Koran can help us begin to see what men such as Abraham and Moses were and were not like. See chapter 4 of this collection, note 38.

80. Were there, in pre-Islamic Arabic poetry, the hypnotic rhythms and engaging sounds found in the Koran? Consider also the source of knowledge among the Greeks (including in pre-Homeric stories) about particular named gods. See notes 58 and 78 above, note 89 below.

81. Thus, one sees graphic details in the Koran: "We indeed created man; and We know what his soul whispers within him, and We are nearer to him than the jugular vein" (50:15); "And eat and drink, until the white thread shows clearly to you from the black thread at the dawn" (2:183); "The Messiah, son of Mary, was only a messenger; messengers before him passed away; his mother was a just woman; they both ate food." (4:78; see note 17 above); "Surely those who disbelieve in Our signs—We shall certainly roast them at a Fire; as often as their skins are wholly burned, We shall give them in exchange other skins, that they may taste the chastisement" (4:38); "[T]hey bite at you their fingers, enraged" (3:117). See also the quotation from Koran 24:35 in note 69 above.

82. See "A Primer on the Good, the True, and the Beautiful," in note 39 of appendix B of this collection.

83. The poet who sings that his love is "like a red, red rose" would be horrified if this turned out to be literally true, with his beloved turning into a flower. See, on the limitations of gifted poets, the discussion of Plato's *Apology* in Anastaplo, *Human Being and Citizen*, p. 8. See, on the poems of Robert Burns, Anastaplo, "Law & Literature and the Moderns," part 5.

84. This may be true even if we should not be poets or prophets. Jacob Klein again and again, and not only in his probing of Plato's *Meno,* worked from and toward what "everyone knows." See Klein, *Lectures and Essays* (Annapolis, Md.: St. John's College Press, 1985); Anastaplo, *Human Being and Citizen*, p. 74. See also Anastaplo, "Teaching, Nature, and the Moral Virtues," *The Great Ideas Today*, p. 2 (1997).

85. See notes 70 and 83 above. The Maimonidean standards set forth in the passage in the text at note 1 of this chapter reflect the natural tension between Revelation and Reason (or between Poetry and Philosophy). Plato's *Republic* teaches that poets necessarily deceive in their (sometimes successful?) efforts to tell the truth. See also note 77 above.

86. See notes 9, 37, and 45 above. Similarly, the modern visitor to Delphi can recognize that if Apollo ever spoke to human beings, it could well have been there. Consider, also, what Saint Augustine says in *The City of God* about the partially valid intimations among the pagans about the true God.

87. Compare the obvious, more or less systematic, movements in the Torah and within each of the Gospels. See note 58 above.

88. See, on the arrangement of the suras in the Koran, note 58 above. See, on nature, note 33 above and the text at note 113 of this chapter. See also preface to this collection, appendix B of this collection.

89. See Koran 9:63:

And some of them hurt the Prophet, saying,
"He is an ear!" Say: "An ear of good for you;
he believes in God, and believes the believers,
and he is a mercy to the believers among you."

I have been told that Muslims enjoy reciting, and stretching out, the Koran, especially the *l* of "Allah."

90. One of my fondest memories of Cairo, where I was stationed with the United States Army Air Corps at the end of the Second World War, is of the way one could walk the crowded market streets without missing a note of the plaintive, drawn-out songs being broadcast on the radios played at high volume in one shop after another. Another memory is of the allure of the desert, both in Egypt and in Saudi Arabia (where I was also stationed), especially as the world cooled off at the end of a very hot day. This was in marked contrast to my experience earlier on Guam and other watery places in the Pacific. On Egypt, see chapter 2 of this collection.

The American visitor can find the public noise oppressive in Muslim countries as in places such as Rome. An American missionary has written to us from Indonesia,

Well, I tell you—this five times a day chanting from the Moslem mosque gets pretty irritating sometimes. Modern electronics has provided the amps and loudspeakers, and they seem to have no awareness of what we call public quiet and order. Far beyond the sound atmosphere we seem to feel from time to time the weight of the general religious, philosophical, and social atmosphere generated by what may be just the Muslim presence.

Were the Christian Middle Ages somewhat like this? Compare Cragg, *The Call of the Minaret*, p. 35; Shipler, *Arab and Jew*, p. 5. See note 73 above, note 97 below.

91. We, as officers stationed in Egypt and Saudi Arabia at the end of the Second World War (see note 90 above), had to be counseled not to risk abusing the hospitality of Egyptians or Arabs who invited us into their homes, where, for instance, the visitor's casual admiration of some object might oblige his host to give it to him. (Of course, the Muslim women had to be left strictly alone, advice we were *not* given in places such as England, Italy, France, Germany, and Liberia or on islands such as Guam, Okinawa, and Hawaii.) See, on abuse of hospitality, note 113 below.

See, on the low status of the idea of privacy in Middle Eastern communities, Anastaplo, "The Public Interest in Privacy: On Becoming and Being Human," 26 *DePaul Law Review*, 767, 777 n. 16.

92. This is said to reflect Muhammad's bitter experiences as an orphan. See note 5 above. See also Cragg, *The Call of the Minaret*, p. 97.

93. It is reported in the Koran, Everyman's Library edition, p. 415 n. 2:

An undutiful child is very seldom heard of among the Egyptians, or the Arabs in general. Sons scarcely ever sit, or eat, or smoke, in the presence of the father unless bidden to do so; and they often wait upon him and upon his guests at meals and on other occasions: they do not cease to act thus when they have become men.

(I observed similar deference and conduct with respect to parents in the Greek community in Cairo more than forty years ago. See note 90 above. See also Koran 18:24.) Muhammad is considered like a father to the Muslims, and his wives like their mothers. See note 45 above.

94. Thus we hear of ever-virgin Houris (44:53; 56:35). What can it mean that this use of sensuality is, as some suggest, only figurative? See Koran, Everyman's Library edition, p. 66 n. 6. See Montesquieu, *Persian Letters*. See also note 104 below. See, on Solomon, Anastaplo, "Law & Literature and the Bible," p. 653. Compare *The Song of Solomon*.

95. Are these attractions based on Persian luxuries? See Koran, Everyman's Library edition, p. 183 n. 5. Honey is set forth as having a special appeal (ibid., p. 205 n. 1; Koran 16:70). It, too, ministers to the passions, it seems. See note 104 below. Westerners are apt to have special problems reconciling Muhammad's reported sensuality, for which special permissive exemptions seem to have been developed, with conventional standards of piety (Koran 33:38–39), especially when his marriage with the youthful Ayesha is considered (Gibbon, *The Decline and Fall*, vol. 3, 117; *GBWW*, vol. 41, p. 245d). See the passage quoted in the text at note 1 of this chapter. See also notes 59, 64, and 70 above. "Perfume, confided [the Saudi Arabian King] Abdul Aziz, was one of his principal worldly delights. The other two were prayer and women, and in this the king felt he bore a certain resemblance to the Prophet Muhammad, who also drew great contentment from these three special joys." Robert Lacey, *The Kingdom* (New York: Harcourt, Brace, Jovanovich, 1981), p. 253.

96. Carlyle, *On Heroes*, pp. 92, 97. See, for how far back such sensuality can go in the Middle East, chapter 1 of this collection.

97. Daniel prayed three times a day toward Jerusalem (morning, noon, and evening). See *Psalms* 55:17. Muslims originally prayed toward Jerusalem, but Jerusalem was superseded by Mecca (2:137–39), perhaps after it became evident that the Jews were not going to be as receptive to Islam as Muhammad may have once hoped they would be. (How does this adjustment bear upon the current Palestinian claim to parts of the Old City of Jerusalem?) "Although the Qu'ran is silent on the subject, five daily prayers have been standard since the earliest period of Islam. Their times vary somewhat but usually come before dawn, just after midday, in midafternoon, after sunset, and at night, usually in the first minutes of darkness—hours seemingly calculated to avoid any hint of sun worship." "Islam," *International Encyclopedia of the Social Sciences* (1968), vol. 8, p. 206. See notes 10 and 90 above. See also Cragg, *The Call of the Minaret*, pp. 105ff.

The Muslim obligation to witness for one's faith at all costs resembles more that of the Christian than that of the Jew. (Consider the prudent advice given on apostasy by Maimonides.) "For these twelve centuries, [Islam] has been the religion and life-guidance of the fifth part of the whole kindred of Mankind. Above all things, it has been a religion heartily *believed*. These Arabs believe their religion, and try to live by it! No Christians, since the early ages, or only perhaps the English Puritans in modern times, have ever stood by their Faith as the Moslem do by theirs,—believing it wholly, fronting Time with it, and Eternity with it." Carlyle, *On Heroes*, pp. 100–101. See notes 73 and 90 above. I once heard Hans Kung remind an audience, upon being asked if he expected the Muslims to "open up" as the Roman Catholic Church has in recent decades, that it took centuries for the Roman church to do so. Recent troubling manifestations of the Muslim obligation to witness at all costs may be seen in the recourses to suicide bombings in the Middle East, North Africa, and the United States. See note 113 below.

98. Carlyle, *On Heroes*, p. 101. See note 114 below.

99. Consider the extent to which, or the way in which, *the* "Book" for Americans includes the Declaration of Independence, the Constitution, and the Gettysburg Address. See

Anastaplo, "We the People: The Rulers and the Ruled," *The Great Ideas Today*, pp. 53a–72b (1987); Anastaplo, *The Constitution of 1787: A Commen*tary (Baltimore: Johns Hopkins University Press, 1989); Anastaplo, *Abraham Lincoln: A Constitutional Biogrphy* (Lanham, Md.: Rowman & Littlefield, 1999), p. 229.

100. We have seen that Muhammad stressed that the Koran is Arabic in its language. One must wonder how far the Koran can be spread. Are there social as well as climatic and linguistic conditions which define the outer limits of its distribution without serious compromises in both doctrines and practices? See note 57 above, note 114 below.

101. The "church and state" distinctions we very much depend upon for domestic tranquility are not likely to mean much in most countries where the population is predominantly Muslim. Similarly, it can be said, no "temple and *polis*" distinction would have meant much in ancient Greece. See note 73 above. See chapter 3 of this collection, note 7.

Thomas Hobbes would have applauded the pharaoh who criticized his subjects for having believed Moses without his permission.

102. See, e.g., David Lamb, "Banking without Interest," *Sunday Star* (London), November 11, 1984, p. B3; "Arab Banking," *Financial Times* (London), October 24, 1988, sec. 3, p. 1; Muhammad Abdul-Rauf, *A Muslim's Reflections on Democratic Capitalism* (Washington, D.C.: American Enterprise Institute, 1984), pp. 22, 26; Peter T. Kilborn, "No Longer a Banker's Dream, the Saudi System Stagnates," *New York Times*, March 2, 1987, p. 28; Chibli Mallat, ed., *Islamic Law and Finance* (London: Graham & Trotman, 1988), p. 69; Howard L. Stovall, "Arab Commercial Law— Into the Future," 34 *International Lawyer* 839 (2000). "In due course of economic life, as in other areas, Islam has had recourse to legal fictions in order to avoid the paralyzing effects of the more rigorous Qur'anic prohibitions." "Islam," *International Encyclopedia of the Social Sciences* (1968), vol. 8, p. 215. "As a Malay once said about Muslim rules for division of property, Muhammad was thinking about camels, not fishing boats or rice lands." *American Anthropologist*, 83 (1981), p. 589.

103. For example, witnesses are to be truthful (4:134); thieves risk the loss of limbs (5:41).

104. It is typically said today by Muslim apologists that the Islamic system of polygamy provided fathers for orphans and husbands for widows, especially in the early days when there were many deaths in battle. I have heard several Muslims say that they have never personally known a Muslim man with more than one wife. See Cragg, *The Call of the Minaret*, p. 167.

105. Gibbon deals in this fashion with the rhetoric that Muhammad was obliged to employ in describing the paradise awaiting the believer (*On Heroes*, vol. 3, 92–93; *GBWW*, vol. 41, p. 234c–d:

> Seventy-two *Houris*, or black-eyed girls, of resplendent beauty, blooming youth, virgin purity, and exquisite sensibility, will be created for the use of the meanest believer; a moment of pleasure will be prolonged to a thousand years, and his faculties will be increased a hundred fold, to render him worthy of his felicity. Notwithstanding a vulgar prejudice, the gates of heaven will be open to both sexes; but Muhammad has not specified the male companions of the female elect, lest he should either alarm the jealousy of their former husbands, or disturb their felicity by the suspicion of an everlasting marriage.

See notes 57, 78, and 95 above, note 113 below. See also Abdul-Rauf, *A Muslim's Reflections,* p. 17; Koran 2:183 ("[women] are a vestment for you, and you are a vestment for them"). See as well Koran 3:193: "I waste not the labor of any that labours among you, be you male or female—the one of you is as the other." These words are said to be occasioned by one of Muhammad's wives having told him that God often praised the men, but not the women, who had fled their country for the faith (Koran, Everyman's Library edition, p. 404 n. 2).

Consider how opponents of American slavery had to speak about people of African descent, in the first half of the nineteenth century, if they were to remain politically effective. This is reflected in President Lincoln's recognition, at the outset of the Civil War, that much more support could be marshalled for saving the Union than for freeing the slaves.

106. See, e.g., Arberry, *Aspects of Islamic Civilization*, pp. 397f.; Anastaplo, "Women and the Law," in *The American Moralist*, p. 349. Be all this as it may, Islam does seem, to the typical Westerner, to subjugate women to an unnatural rule. Indeed, a heavily veiled woman can seem to the Westerner an entombed woman. Then there is *purdah*, a policy that keeps women from appearing in public. (This policy is not limited to Muslims but is made considerable use of by them.) There is a saying in Pakistan that a woman goes into her husband's home in a wedding dress and comes out in a coffin. See Mary Williams Salsh, "Pakistan Women Look to Bhutto to Improve a Harsh Existence," *Wall Street Journal*, May 3, 1989, p. 1. See also note 6 (end) above.

107. The American Unitarians, similar to the Muslims in a few respects, do not so provide for the material basis of the spiritual. Are not the Muslims more like Old Testament Israelites in this respect, but with far fewer restrictions and ritual observances? Compare note 113 below.

108. See, on culinary delights among the Muslims, Arberry, *Aspects of Islamic Civilization*, pp. 155ff.

109. "O believers, wine and arrow-shuffling, idols and divining-arrows are an abomination, some of Satan's work; so avoid it: haply so you will prosper" (5:93).

Our recognition of observances keyed to the body prompts recognition as well of the problem of what the best way of life is. The very best way requires things to be just right, including the physical dimensions of things, which provision is easy to disparage but hard to do without. See Plato, *Laws* (704–707; *GBWW*, vol. 7, pp. 677a–78a).

To speak thus of the best regime is to be reminded of differences between regimes. We are thus moved to wonder (as we have been throughout this collection) about our own way of life. One must wonder, also, how the best regime, which is keyed to human nature, is related to the perennially overriding question, What is God? See note 15 above. Does that, too, bear upon the question of regimes? Are some regimes better than others for and in addressing that question? Does the answer to that question affect our decision about the best regime and hence about how seriously we can take our own regime, or perhaps any regime here on earth?

110. Gibbon, *The Decline and Fall*, vol. 3, 113 (*GBWW*, vol. 41, p. 244a–b). See also Pickthall, *The Meaning of the Glorious Koran*, pp. xxvii–xxviii. See as well notes 30 and 31 above. The burial place of Moses, it could well be noticed here, is not known. See Anastaplo, "Law & Literature and the Bible," pp. 639–40.

111. See Anastaplo, *Human Being and Citizen*, p. 155. Compare Sol Schindler, "The Immutable Sands and Arab Clannishness," *Washington Times*, February 27, 1989, p. E9; Thomas Molner, "Islam on the Move," *Intercollegiate Review*, fall 1985, p. 17. Consider as well Hegel, *The Philosophy of History*, p. 358 (*GBWW*, vol. 46, p. 323a–b):

Abstraction swayed the minds of the Mahometans. Their object was, to establish an abstract worship, and they struggled for its accomplishment with the greatest enthusiasm. This enthusiasm was *Fanaticism*, that is, an enthusiasm for something abstract—for an abstract thought which sustains a negative position towards the established order of things. It is the essence of fanaticism to bear only a desolating destructive relation to the concrete; but that of Mahometanism was, at the same time, capable of the greatest elevation—an elevation free from all petty interests, and united with all the virtues that appertain to magnanimity and valor. *La religion et la terreur* was the principle in this case, as with Robespierre, *la liberté et la terreur*. But real life is nevertheless concrete, and introduces particular aims; conquest leads to sovereignty and wealth, to the conferring of prerogatives on a dynastic family, and to a union of individuals. But all this is only contingent and built on sand; it is to-day, and to-morrow is not. With all the passionate interest he shows, the Mahometan is really indifferent to this social fabric, and rushes on in the ceaseless whirl of fortune. . . . While Europeans are involved in a multitude of relations, and form, so to speak, "a bundle" of them—in Mahometanism the individual is *one* passion and *that alone*; he is superlatively cruel, cunning, bold, or generous.

See note 113 (end) below. See on Israel and the Gulf War, note 114 below.

112. "Faced with the choice of an Orthodoxy affirming the God of Abraham, Creator of heaven and earth, or an unconditionally political (and therefore atheist) Zionism, the modern Jew is left at an intolerable impasse." Ralph Lerner, foreword, in Strauss, *Philosophy and Law*, p. 19. See note 62 above.

113. See Anastaplo, *The Artist as Thinker*, p. 262. "It was not only in the course of human history that evidences of God's power and purposes were to be found—an encouragement to Muslims in later centuries to trace and record the course of history. The created world surrounding man on all sides abounded in signs of God—a powerful stimulus to scientists and philosophers when their studies revived in Islam." Arberry, *Aspects of Islamic Civilization*, p. 44. See, on the contribution of Islam to the revival of philosophy in Europe before the Renaissance, Koran, Everyman's Library edition, p. ix. Is Islam able to appreciate, however, "the reverence-producing splendor of modern science and mathematics"? Anastaplo, "*In re* Allan Bloom: A Respectful Dissent," *The Great Ideas Today*, vol. 1988, p. 268 n. 25 (quoting Eva Brann) (see note 50, above). I suspect not—at least, not yet. Whether this is strength or weakness, bad or good, is a question requiring extensive consideration. Is there not something Heideggerian, and hence perhaps self-deluding, about the Islamic theocratic project? See note 73 above. See also note 33 above.

See, on the nature of nature, Klein, *Lectures and Essays*, p. 219. See also appendix B of this collection. A useful beginning to the study of the Islamic understanding of nature as it bears upon the conduct of human affairs may be made by considering the following episode from the career of a central Asia king:

> Ebrahim ibn Adham's saintly career began in the following manner. He was king of Balkh, and a whole world was under his command; forty gold swords and forty gold maces were carried before and behind him. One night he was asleep on his royal couch. At midnight the roof of the apartment vibrated as if someone was walking on the roof.
>
> "Who is there?" he shouted.
>
> "A friend," came the reply. "I have lost a camel, and am searching for it on the roof."
>
> "Fool, do you look for a camel on the roof?" cried Ebrahim.
>
> "Heedless one," answered the voice, "do you seek for God in silken clothes, asleep on a golden couch?"

John B. Christopher, *The Islamic Tradition* (New York: Harper & Row, 1972), p. 89 (taken from A. J. Arberry, trans., *Muslim Saints and Mystics* [Chicago: University of Chicago Press, 1966], pp. 63–65). Is there not something Socratic about the way this lesson is developed? But what is curious about the story is how it moves from this more or less naturalistic beginning through a variety of bizarre experiences to a mystical rejuvenation for the terror-stricken king. Thus, it sometimes seems to the outsider that for the "Arab mind," reason goes only so far before something unpredictable, if not undisciplined, emerges. Or, as seen in the September 11, 2001, hijackings, discipline can be put to the most monstrous uses, calling into question the very spirit of martyrdom. Perhaps the most distressed by those dreadful events were the multitudes of truly pious muslims all over the world who must endure the shame, for years to come, of the shocking abuse of American hospitality by their demented coreligionists, the kind of hospitality that Islam and its Prophet have always cherished. It is the duty of prudent Muslims everywhere to remind their peoples what the "Laws of Nature and of Nature's God" both call for and forbid. See note 26 of appendix C of this collection.

Another useful beginning to the study of the Islamic understanding of nature may be made by examining the much-told, and most curious, story told once again in Arberry, *Aspects of Civilization*, p. 188. (It is revealing that the slave girl involved there is never consulted about her personal preferences with respect to the two men desperate to possess her. See note 105 above.) The limitations even in the West of a reliance upon nature and hence reason may be seen in the nineteenth-century American hymn "The Last Words of Copernicus":

Ye golden lamps of Heav'n, farewell,
With all your feeble light;
Farewell thou ever changing moon,
Pale empress of the night.
And thou refulgent orb of day,
In brighter flames array'd,
My soul which springs beyond thy sphere,
No more demands thy aid.

Original Sacred Harp (Bremen, Ga.: Sacred Harp, 1987), p. 119. See appendix A of this collection. Also instructive, with respect to Jews, Christians, and Muslims, is Gotthold E. Lessing's *Nathan the Wise* and Judah Halevi's *The Kuzari*. See Anastaplo, "Law & Literature and the Bible," p. 530. It has been suggested that Muhammad wanted "a doctrine that should present to mankind Judaism divested of its Mosaic ceremonial and Christianity divested of the Atonement and the Trinity." Koran, Everyman's Library edition, p. 14. Is this a kind of natural religion, but susceptible in its abstractness to wide-ranging fanaticism? See notes 97, 111 above.

See, on nature in Islamic thought, Sir Mohammad Iqbal, *The Reconstruction of Religious Thought in Islam* (London: Oxford University Press, 1934), e.g., pp. 53–54, 76, 120–22. "What we call Nature or the not-self is only a fleeting moment in the life of God. His 'I-amness' is independent, elemental, absolute. Of such a self it is impossible for us to form an adequate conception. . . . Nature is to the Divine Self as character is to the human self. In the picturesque phrase of the Quran it is the habit of Allah. From the human point of view it is an interpretation which, in our present situation, we put on the creative activity of the Absolute Ego. . . . Nature, then, must be understood as a living, ever-growing organism whose growth has no final external limits. Its only limit is internal, e.g . . . the immanent self which animates and sustains the whole. . . . The knowledge of Nature is the knowledge of God's behaviour. In our observation of Nature we are virtually seeking a kind of intimacy with the Absolute Ego; and this is only another form of worship." Ibid., pp. 53–54. Nature, as something growing (that is, changing) does *not* appear to be the nature we are accustomed to. One must wonder what Arabic term is rendered here as *nature* and how it is used, if at all, in the Koran. See, for a useful guide to Islamic philosophical materials, Ralph Lerner and Muhsin Mahdi, eds., *Medieval Political Philosophy* (New York: Free Press of Glencoe, 1963). See, on Isaac Newton, nature, and modern science, Anastaplo, book review, *The Great Ideas Today*, p. 448 (1997). The work being done on Alfarabi by Christopher A. Colmo, of Dominican University, is most promising.

114. The Koran was brought forward, we have seen, as a distinctively Arabic revelation for the people of Arabia. Must one, in order to understand Islam, have to consider whether its success aroused expectations among the Arabs that were bound to be disappointed, especially if Islam's very success subverted the political enterprise upon which an enduring happiness here on earth may depend for a people? See the text at note 98 of this chapter. Consider how Gibbon describes the political fate of the Arabs, continuing the passage from him with which we end note 57 above:

> The idols of Arabia were broken before the throne of God; the blood of human victims was expiated by prayer, and fasting, and alms, the laudable or innocent arts of devotion; and his rewards and punishments of a future life were painted by the images most congenial to an ignorant and carnal generation. Mohammed was, perhaps, incapable of dictating a moral and political system for the use of his countrymen: but he breathed among the faithful a spirit of charity and friendship; recommended the practice of the social virtues; and checked, by his laws and precepts, the thirst of revenge, and the oppression of widows and orphans. The hostile tribes were united in faith and obedience, and the valour which had been idly spent in domestic quarrels was vigorously directed against a foreign enemy. *Had the impulse been less powerful,* Arabia, free at home, and formidable abroad, might have flourished under a succession of her native monarchs. *Her sovereignty was lost by the extent and rapidity of conquest.* The colonies of the nation were scattered over the East and West, and their blood was mingled with the blood of their converts and captives. After the reign of three caliphs, the throne was transported from Medina to the valley of Damascus and the banks of the Tigris; the holy cities were violated by impious war; Arabia was ruled by the rod of a subject, perhaps of a stranger; and the Bedoweens of the desert, awakening from their dream of dominion, resumed their old and solitary independence.

The Decline and Fall, vol. 3, 130–31; *GBWW*, vol. 41, pp. 252d-53c (emphases added). It remains to be seen what the long-term effects of oil-generated wealth does to the character and aspirations of "the Bedoweens of the desert." See, on the 1990–1991 Gulf War, Anastaplo, "On Freedom: Explorations," 17 *Oklahoma City University Law Review* 465, 589, 604 (1992). I have prepared for the *Claremont Review of Books* an article, "Islam in the United States." Consider, as to what can be expected from Islam at its most productive, Dennis Overbye, "How Islam Won, and Lost, the Lead in Science," *New York Times*, October 30, 2001, p. D1. See also Akbar Ahmed and Lawrence Rosen, "Islam, Academe, and Freedom of the Mind," *The Chronicle of Higher Education*, November 2, 2001, p. B11.

See, on the status of nature generally, appendix B of this collection.

Chapter Seven

North American Indian Thought

Speak of me as I am. Nothing extenuate,
Nor set down aught in malice. Then must you speak
Of one that loved not wisely, but too well;
   ... of one whose hand,
Like the base Judean, threw a pearl away
Richer than all his tribe ...

          —Othello[1]

I.

It can be saddening to review collections of North American Indian myths, legends and stories, even though there is much in that legacy which can be a source of wonder and delight.[2] What is saddening is that human beings as imaginative and as interesting as these native American peoples are should have, for so long and so vigorously, been treated as mere savages. They were, therefore, routinely beaten into submission wherever they were not simply exterminated.[3]

It is sobering to recognize how rich and varied an Indian heritage there has been "out there," much of which is now mangled. Even so, a remarkable array of tales is still available to us, with many inventive and good-natured episodes on display. But however considerable the material that has survived, in some form or other, much more seems to have been lost.

Europeans on this continent have always had a curious way of dealing with the Indians they encountered. On the one hand, Indians could routinely be regarded as dangerous savages who were virtually impossible to civilize. On the other hand, Indian names and Indian heroes could eventually be shown respect, so much so that ordinary people can now be proud of the Indian blood they might have in their veins. Indian names *are* all around us: Massachusetts,

Ohio, Michigan, Illinois, Chicago, Wisconsin, Iowa, the Mississippi, and Seattle. Yet the best of what the Indians had to offer is but dimly perceived by most of us.

Alexis de Tocqueville and scholars influenced by him have noticed the somewhat aristocratic character of Indian life, a way of life that usually preferred hunting and war to agriculture and commerce.[4] But this approach to the Indians, however sympathetic it is in some respects, neglects the richness of their life, something which I attempt to suggest in this chapter. The Indians generally appeared at their most formidable, if not at their worst, as strangers and enemies; they appeared more and more civilized and hence worthy of respect as one got to know them, at least until disease and demoralization wrecked their various ways of life.

The peoples I refer to as North American Indians, whatever the proper names for them should be,[5] were scattered across what we now know as the contiguous forty-eight states of the American Union. There is far too much intriguing material left by them for me to exhaust my subject in this chapter. Much of what I say will have to disregard critical differences among the many Indian tribes.[6]

II.

A sampling from a dozen stories should serve to illustrate the surprising things that the Indians have had to offer the human race. In most cases it is probably impossible to determine how far back these things go—but it does seem that some Indian stories, occasionally in several versions, have origins long before the coming of the Europeans. A marvelous, sometimes a dark, imagination is evident here, as in the uses the Indians made of European stories.

The Snohomish (in the Northwest) say that people were not pleased with the way the Creator had made the world:

> The sky was so low that the tall people bumped their heads against it. Sometimes people would do what was forbidden by climbing up high in the trees and, learning their own words, enter the Sky World.
>
> Finally the wise men of all the different tribes had a meeting to see what they could do about lifting the sky. They agreed that the people should get together and try to push it up higher.
>
> "We can do it," a wise man of the council said, "if we all push at the same time. We will need all the people and all the animals and all the birds when we push." . . .
> Everyone made poles from the giant fir trees to use in pushing against the sky.[7]

They pushed all together again and again until they managed to get the sky up to where it has been ever since.[8]

The Nez Percé say that "before there were any people in the world, the different animals and trees lived and moved about and talked together just like human beings. The pine trees had the secret of fire and guarded it jealously, so that no matter how cold it was, they alone could warm themselves."[9] But Beaver managed to steal a live coal:

> The pines immediately raised a hue and cry and started after him. Whenever he was hard pressed, Beaver darted from side to side to dodge his pursuers, and when he had a good start, he kept a straight course. The Grande Ronde River [in Idaho] preserves the direction Beaver took in his flight, and this is why it is tortuous in some parts of its course and straight in others.
>
> After running for a long time, the pines grew tired. So most of them halted in a body on the river banks, where they remain in great numbers to this day, forming a growth so dense that hunters can hardly get through. A few pines kept chasing Beaver, but they finally gave out one after another, and they remain scattered at intervals along the banks of the river in the places where they stopped.[10]

A story from northern California reports that at one time early in the life of the earth, "It did not thunder or lighting, since there were no trees to be struck."[11]

An Acoma story says that in the beginning two female human beings were born underground. They eventually made their way to the earth's surface and its light, taking with them two baskets they had found "full of presents: seeds of all kinds, and little images of many animals."[12] This was the means used by the Creator of the world to supply the earth with living things. Eventually one of the sisters took dirt from her basket in order to give life to many gods. "And so everything was as it should be."[13]

A Modoc account of the origins of life on earth includes this report:

> The [Chief of the Sky Spirits] broke off the small end of his giant [walking] stick and threw the pieces into the rivers. The longer pieces turned into beaver and otter; the smaller pieces became fish. When the leaves dropped from the trees, he picked them up, blew upon them, and so made the birds.[14]

Notice what this and like accounts assume about the common elements shared by all living things.[15]

The Papago tell what happened when the Creator was saddened by his recognition of the inevitable deterioration of things:

> One day the Creator was resting, sitting, watching some children at play in a village. The children laughed and sang, yet as he watched them, the Creator's heart was sad. He was thinking: "These children will grow old. Their skin will become wrinkled. Their hair will turn gray. Their teeth will fall out. The young hunter's arm will fail. These lovely young girls will grow ugly and fat. The playful puppies will become blind,

mangy dogs. And those wonderful flowers—yellow and blue, red and purple—will fade. The leaves from the trees will fall and dry up. Already they are turning yellow." Thus the Creator grew sadder and sadder. It was in the fall, and the thought of the coming winter, with its cold and lack of game and green things, made his heart heavy.[16]

The stage is now set for some benevolent experimentation:

Yet it was still warm, and the sun was shining. The Creator watched the play of sunlight and shadow on the ground, the yellow leaves being carried here and there by the wind. He saw the blueness of the sky, the whiteness of some cornmeal ground by the women. Suddenly he smiled. "All those colors, they ought to be preserved. I'll make something to gladden my heart, something for these children to look at and enjoy."

The Creator took out his bag and started gathering things: a spot of sunlight, a handful of blue from the sky, the whiteness of the cornmeal, the shadow of playing children, the blackness of a beautiful girl's hair, the yellow of the falling leaves, the green of the pine needles, the red, purple, and orange of the flowers around him. All these he put into his bag. As an afterthought, he put the songs of the birds in, too.

Then he walked over to the grassy spot where the children were playing. "Children, little children, this is for you," and he gave them his bag. "Open it; there's something nice inside," he told them.

The children opened the bag, and at once hundreds and hundreds of colored butterflies flew out, dancing around the children's heads, settling on their hair, fluttering up again to sip from this or that flower. And the children, enchanted, said that they had never seen anything so beautiful.[17]

This charming account continues with an awareness of the limitations of this Creator:

The butterflies began to sing, and the children listened smiling.

But then a songbird came flying, settling on the Creator's shoulder, scolding him, saying: "It's not right to give our songs to these new, pretty things. You told us when you made us that every bird would have his own song. And now you've passed them all around. Isn't it enough that you gave your new playthings the colors of the rainbow?"

"You're right," said the Creator. "I made one song for each bird, and I shouldn't have taken what belongs to you."

So the Creator took the songs away from the butterflies, and that's why they are silent. "They're beautiful even so!" he said.[18]

This "correction" in the creative endeavor testifies to something seen again and again in Indian stories: the trial-and-error approach that even the most exalted personages have to rely upon. The Europeans who dealt so vigorously, if not even harshly, with the Indians they confronted in the New World had an infallible divinity to model themselves upon.[19] These Europeans probably could not imagine how imaginative their primitive enemies were—and how the Indians' divinities could be reasoned with and even corrected.

A Flathead story, which may have its counterparts in other parts of the world, goes like this:

> Coyote was walking one day when he met Old Woman. She greeted him and asked where he was headed.
>
> "Just roaming around," said Coyote.
>
> "You better stop going that way, or you'll meet a giant who kills everybody."
>
> "Oh, giants don't frighten me," said Coyote (who had never met one). "I always kill them. I'll fight this one too, and make an end of him."
>
> "He's bigger and closer than you think," said Old Woman.
>
> "I don't care," said Coyote, deciding that a giant would be about as big as a bull moose and calculating that he could kill one easily.
>
> So Coyote said good-bye to Old Woman and went ahead, whistling a tune. On his way he saw a large fallen branch that looked like a club. Picking it up, he said to himself, "I'll hit the giant over the head with this. It's big enough and heavy enough to kill him." He walked on and came to a huge cave right in the middle of the path. Whistling merrily, he went in.
>
> Suddenly Coyote met a woman who was crawling along on the ground. "What's the matter?" he asked.
>
> "I'm starving," she said, "and too weak to walk. What are you doing with that stick?"
>
> "I'm going to kill the giant with it," said Coyote, and he asked if she knew where he was hiding.
>
> Feeble as she was, the woman laughed. "You're already in the giant's belly."
>
> "How can I be in his belly?" asked Coyote. "I haven't even met him."
>
> "You probably thought it was a cave when you walked into his mouth," the woman said, and sighed. "It's easy to walk in, but nobody ever walks out. This giant is so big you can't take him in with your eyes. His belly fills a whole valley."[20]

Coyote must improvise, which improvisation extends not only to feeding his fellow prisoners by carving fat off the walls of the "cave" they are in, but also to contriving a mode of killing the giant that would permit them all to escape. The darker side of the often childlike Indian imagination becomes more evident here.[21]

A Penobscot tale from Maine, on the origins of corn and tobacco, goes like this:

> A famine came upon the people and the streams and lakes dried up. No one knew what to do to make it different. At length a maid of great beauty appeared and one of the young men married her. But she soon became sad and retiring and spent much time in a secret place. Her husband followed her one day and discovered that she went to the forest and met a snake, her lover. He was sad, but he did not accuse her; he loved her so much he did not wish to hurt her feelings. He followed her, however, and she wept when she was discovered. Clinging to her ankle was a long green blade of a plant resembling grass. She then declared that she had a mission to perform and that he must promise to follow her instructions; if so, he would obtain a blessing that would comfort his mind in sorrow and nourish his body in want, and bless the people in time to come.

She told him to kill her with a stone axe, and to drag her body seven times among the stumps of a clearing in the forest until the flesh was stripped from the bones, and finally to bury the bones in the center of the clearing. He was told to return to his wigwam and wait seven days before going again to the spot. During this period she promised to visit him in a dream and instruct him what to do afterward. He obeyed her. In his dream she told him that she was the mother of corn and tobacco and gave him instructions how to prepare these plants to be eaten and smoked. After seven days he went to the clearing and found the corn plant rising above the ground and the leaves of the tobacco plant coming forth. When the corn had borne fruit and the silk of the corn ear had turned yellow he recognized in it the resemblance to his dead wife. Thus originated the cultivation of corn and tobacco. These plants have nourished the bodies of the Indians ever since and comforted their minds in trouble.[22]

We are likely to be troubled by the willingness of the loving husband to kill his wife and then shred her body as he had been directed by her to do. Was this made easier for the tribe to accept because she had been discovered in a compromising relation? This reminds us that most of the stories have moral presuppositions upon which they draw, although another version of this story from the same tribe has no hint of apparent misconduct on the woman's part.[23] A much more benign version of the same story is told by the Osage, which has the stately elk so moved by joy on one occasion that he rolled over and over on the earth: "[A]ll his loose hairs clung to the soil. The hairs grew, and from them sprang beans, corn, potatoes, and wild turnips, and then all the grasses and trees."[24]

A Tlingit story records the fate of a giant who loved to kill human beings, eat their flesh, and drink their blood. A man kills the giant when he discovers that the giant's heart is in his left heel.

Yet the giant still spoke. "Though I'm dead, though you killed me, I'm going to keep on eating you and all the other humans in the world forever!"

"That's what you think!" said the man, "I'm about to make sure that you never eat anyone again." He cut the giant's body into pieces and burned each one in the fire. Then he took the ashes and threw them into the air for the winds to scatter.

Instantly each of the particles turned into a mosquito. The cloud of ashes became a cloud of mosquitos, and from their midst the man heard the giant's voice laughing, saying, "Yes, I'll eat you people until the end of time."

And as the monster spoke, the man felt a sting, and a mosquito started sucking his blood, and then many mosquitoes stung him, and he began to scratch himself.[25]

Are we to understand, by the way, that the "dead" giant required the deceived man's cooperation in order to be transformed into the ubiquitous mosquitoes?[26]

Transformations of a different kind are reported in an Iroquois story about Raweno, the Everything-Maker, when he was busy creating various animals. He was working on Rabbit, and Rabbit was saying: "I want nice long legs and long ears like a deer, and sharp fangs and claws like a panther." "I do them up the way they want to be; I give them what they ask for," said Raweno. He was working on Rabbit's hind legs, making them long the way Rabbit had asked all his legs to be. It was at this moment that Raweno became angry at the yet unformed Owl for pestering him and for refusing to shut his eyes while Raweno worked on Rabbit:

> [Raweno] grabbed Owl, pulling him down from his branch, stuffing his head deep into his body, shaking him until his eyes grew big with fright, pulling at his ears until they were sticking up at both sides of his head.
>
> "There," said Raweno, "that'll teach you. Now you won't be able to crane your neck to watch things you shouldn't watch. Now you have big ears to listen when someone tells you what not to do. Now you have big eyes—but not so big that you can watch me, because you'll be awake only at night, and I work by day. And your feathers won't be red like cardinal's, but gray like this"—and Raweno rubbed Owl all over with mud—"as punishment for your disobedience." So Owl flew off, pouting: "Whoo, whoo, whoo."
>
> Then Raweno turned back to finish Rabbit, but Rabbit had been so terrified by Raweno's anger, even though it was not directed at him, that he ran off half done. As a consequence, only Rabbit's hind legs are long, and he has to hop about instead of walking and running. Also, because he took fright then, Rabbit has remained afraid of most everything, and he never got the claws and fangs he asked for in order to defend himself. Had he not run away then, Rabbit would have been an altogether different animal.
>
> As for Owl, he remained as Raweno had shaped him in anger—with big eyes, a short neck, and ears sticking up on the sides of his head. On top of everything, he has to sleep during the day and come out only at night.[27]

We may well wonder what it means to say that both Rabbit and Owl existed or could make requests before they were formed as we know them.[28]

A Wintu tale indicates how grotesque American Indian tales could become. A young woman, out where she was not supposed to be, had a finger stuck by a splinter while cutting maple bark. She sucked the blood and spat it out. The story continues:

> Then more blood came, and though she sucked and sucked, she could not stop the flow. Meanwhile the sun began to set. She kept on sucking until early evening, unable to help herself. Suddenly she happened to swallow blood and smelled the fat. It tasted sweet. So she ate her little finger, and then ate her whole hand. Then she devoured both her hands. Then she ate her leg, ate both her legs. Then she ate up her whole body. Then her head alone was left.[29]

But the head rolled along, voraciously consuming everything it encountered—until it fell into a river, where a riffle pike jumped up and swallowed it.[30]

A Blackfoot story tells about the fateful decision of another woman. Old Man created the woman and the child. After he gave them the power of speech the woman and Old Man had this encounter:

> At once the woman asked: "What is that state we are in, walking, moving, breathing, eating?"
> "That is life," said Old Man. "Before, you were just lumps of mud. Now, you live."
> "When we were lumps of mud, were we alive then," asked the woman.
> "No," said Old Man, "you were not alive."
> "What do you call the state we were in then?" asked the woman.
> "It is called death," answered Old Man. "When you are not alive, then you are dead."
> "Will we be alive always?" asked the woman. "Will we go on living forever, or shall we be dead again at some time?
> Old Man pondered. He said: "I didn't think about that at all. Let's decide it right now. Here's a buffalo chip. If it floats, then people will die and come back to life four days later."
> "No," said the woman. "This buffalo chip will dissolve in the water. I'll throw in this stone. If it floats, we'll live forever and there will be no death. If it sinks, then we'll die." The woman didn't know anything yet, because she had been walking on earth for just a few hours. She didn't know about stones and water, so she threw the stone into the river and it sank.
> "You made a choice there," said Old Man. "Now nothing can be done about it. Now people will die."[31]

It should be immediately noticed that women are *not* usually considered the principal or original source of human afflictions in the Indian stories.[32] Rather, women are often looked to by the community for wisdom and guidance. What women do, we can be told, is as great as what warriors do.[33] And, we are shown, women can sacrifice themselves for their loved ones and the community, as one Multnomah maiden did when her people were threatened by an epidemic. Her body was found at the foot of the cliff from which she had thrown herself in compliance with a prophecy. She took "the moon coming up over the trees across the river" as a token that her self-sacrifice was called for. We complete this sampling of North American Indian materials with the conclusion of the self-sacrificing maiden's story:

> Then her father prayed to the Great Spirit, "Show us some token that my daughter's spirit has been welcomed into the land of the spirits."
> Almost at once they heard the sound of water above. All the people looked up to the cliff. A stream of water, silvery white, was coming over the edge of the rock. It broke into floating mist and then fell to their feet. The stream continued to float down in a high and beautiful waterfall.
> For many summers the white water has dropped from the cliff into the pool below. Sometimes in winter the spirit of the brave and beautiful maiden comes back to see the waterfall. Dressed in white, she stands among the trees at one side of Multnomah

Falls. There she looks upon the place where she made her great sacrifice and thus saved her lover and her people from death.[34]

She, unlike the woman who acted in ignorance about the properties of stones in water, can be said to have known what she was doing. She, like her father after her, had asked for a token ratifying her sacrifice. It is instructive to notice that the ratification in each case was nothing that we now consider extraordinary: the moon coming up over the trees in her case, the waterfall in his case.[35]

III.

I will be commenting on various elements in the sampling of a dozen stories I have just provided. Dozens upon dozens of equally intriguing stories could have been chosen. One frequently used element in Indian tales is clever improvisation, as may be seen in the way that Coyote adapted himself to having wandered into the stomach of the giant. Improvisation as a way of life may be seen in the figure of the Trickster, whether he be a divinity, a human being, or an animal.[36]

Here is how a leading American anthropologist has described the world-wide Trickster figure:

Few myths have so wide a distribution as the one known by the name of *The Trickster*. . . . For few can we so confidently assert that they belong to the oldest expressions of mankind. Few other myths have persisted with their fundamental content unchanged. The Trickster myth is found in clearly recognizable form among the simplest aboriginal tribes and among the complex. We encounter it among the ancient Greeks, the Chinese, the Japanese and in the Semitic world. Many of the Trickster's traits were perpetuated in the figure of the mediaeval jester, and have survived right up to the present day in the Punch-and-Judy plays and in the clown. Although repeatedly combined with other myths and frequently drastically reorganized and reinterpreted, its basic plot seems always to have succeeded in reasserting itself.

Manifestly we are here in the presence of a figure and a theme or themes which have had a special and permanent appeal and an unusual attraction for mankind from the very beginnings of civilization. In what must be regarded as its earliest and most archaic form, as found among the North American Indians, Trickster is at one and the same time creator and destroyer, giver and negator, he who dupes others and who is always duped himself. He wills nothing consciously. At all times he is constrained to behave as he does from impulses over which he has no control. He knows neither good nor evil, yet he is responsible for both. He possesses no values, moral or social, is at the mercy of his passions and appetites, yet through his actions all values come into being. But not only he, so our myth tells us, possesses these traits. So, likewise, do the other figures of the plot connected with him: the animals, the various supernatural beings and monsters, and man.[37]

The curious adventures of which Trickster is capable may be seen in this episode from the Winnebago Trickster Cycle:

> Soon [the buffalo] sank in the mire and Trickster was immediately upon him with his knife and killed him. Then he dragged him over to a cluster of wood and skinned him. Throughout all these operations he used his right arm only.
>
> In the midst of these operations suddenly his left arm grabbed the buffalo. "Give that back to me, it is mine! Stop that or I will use my knife on you!" So spoke the right arm. "I will cut you to pieces, that is what I will do to you," continued the right arm. Thereupon the left arm released its hold. But, shortly after, the left arm again grabbed hold of the right arm. This time it grabbed hold of his wrist just at the moment that the right arm had commenced to skin the buffalo. Again and again this was repeated. In this manner did Trickster make both his arms quarrel. That quarrel soon turned into a vicious fight and the left arm was badly cut up. "Oh, oh! Why did I do this? Why have I done this? I have made myself suffer!" The left arm was indeed bleeding profusely.[38]

It is significant, perhaps, that the Trickster can be regarded as "possibly the most important single figure in North American Indian lore," "the pre-eminent figure in all his bewildering yet wonderful complexity."[39] Supernatural spirits seem to enjoy a good laugh.[40] The complicated intellectual activity seen in the Trickster testifies further to the liveliness of the Indian imagination. The tales can be quite sophisticated, with a high level of verbal skills, anything but crude emanations from the morose savages the Indians are sometimes taken to be.[41]

It is also significant, perhaps, that there is among the American Indians no "national" story, no major intertribal accounts of a great adventure, of authoritative theology, or of moral doctrine. Thus, there is nothing comparable to what Homer and Hesiod could do among the Greeks, Confucius among the Chinese, or Muhammad among the Arabs. With hundreds of languages spoken by the various "indigenous" peoples of what is now the United States, there may have been no nation from which "national" poets could emerge.[42]

Why, then, should the Trickster have mattered as much as he evidently did among the Indians? (Although women can play tricks, the Trickster, is, I believe, almost always, if not always, a male.) Odysseus can be described by Homer as a man of many wiles, but is there not much more to him than those wiles? Cronus and Prometheus can be several times referred to as tricksters by Hesiod (in his *Theogony*), but they can be handled by Zeus, who is also much more than a trickster. The modern Greeks have a trickster hero in Karaghiozis, the shadow-play character, but they also make much, even more, of Alexander the Great, the commander who could be reluctant to "steal a victory."[43] Moreover, whatever the Indian fascination with the Trickster, much is made in North American Indian stories both of keeping one's promises and of the perfidy of the white man.

To make as much of the Trickster as the Indians do—much more than is made of him among other peoples perhaps—may reflect a special view of the universe, a view which relies more upon will and less upon understanding than we are accustomed to. It relies more upon magic than upon science in accounting for what happens among human beings. This may have had something to do with the inability of Indians, by and large, to adjust usefully to technological challenges.[44]

Thus one must notice, in considering the place of the Trickster in Indian stories, not only what the Trickster provides, but also, and perhaps more important, what he takes the place of or excludes. The primacy of the Trickster in Indian lore, including as it does what can only be called divine shenanigans, is to suggest the intimate combination of the high and the low, perhaps even the denial of a difference in principle between the high and the low, at the very least an indifference to the distinction.[45]

IV.

What we would consider low may be seen in the bawdiness frequently found in Indian stories. But we should notice that the English-language oral tradition has not been without its robust bawdiness at times.[46] The Indian oral corpus, or what is left of it, happens to have been recorded at a time when people generally were more open than they have been until recently in speaking about sexual matters.[47]

The North American Indians do seem to have been life-enjoying peoples, even though their ways of life often left them on the brink of annihilation from famine or disease. But their enjoyment could sometimes turn around grim-sounding themes. For example, stories of grinding teeth where men least want women to have them are found everywhere in the New World. There are Asian and European equivalents, but they are not as vivid as here.[48]

At times, Indian stories seem cruder than those we are used to seeing in print; sometimes, indeed, they can be terrible in their implications. The terrible, if not even the ugly, may be seen, for example, in an incestuous exploitation of a horrified sister by her persistent brother which accounts for the relation of the pursuing male moon and the fleeing female sun in the heavens.[49]

But *comic* sexuality may be much more prevalent, as in a story about keeping the Devil in the Inferno which could well have gone back to Boccaccio.[50] A discussion of the merits of reclaiming stolen wives—a question debated in European literature, too, as in the case of Helen of Troy—is instructive, particularly when it is pointed out what kind of wife is thought by others to be worth stealing.[51]

However questionable some of the bawdiness in the Indian stories may seem, the dominant impression there can be of the childlike, the naive, and the innocent,[52] quite unlike the sleazy sophistication to which we have had to become accustomed in recent decades. The healthiness of Indian sexuality may be seen in the announcement recorded by one narrator upon the discovery of sexual pleasure: "It's too good to be properly described."[53] This would be a good motto for our time, discouraging the desperate efforts at depiction of sexuality that are encountered all around us.[54]

V.

Sexuality is not as critical among the Indians as it has often been among Europeans in accounting for the origins of things.[55] For the Indians, it seems, a single creation or a single series of events does not suffice to explain the complexity of the world or the existence of evil.[56] It is several times indicated that thinking and naming made things appear.[57]

Much is made of water in various Indian accounts of the beginning, perhaps reflecting thereby either the memory of a gigantic flood or some collective awareness of, say, experience in the womb, or both. The earth is sometimes said to have been made of mud brought up by some animal from deep beneath the water.[58] The heavenly bodies, and especially constellations, can be repeatedly explained (as in some ancient Greek stories) in terms of the consequences of earthly episodes.[59]

The ways in which human beings are said to have originated are many. Often, depending upon the tribe and the circumstances, human beings are traced back to particular animals. (Totems or taboos can result from these associations.) Even stranger for us today are the stories, such as we have seen, which have crops dependent upon human bones or upon the shredding of "human" flesh.[60] In various ways, that is, the affinity among earth, vegetation, and man is indicated.

Also strange for us are those Indian stories which have the Creator, rather than a surrogate, sacrificing himself for the good of mankind. Thus, one creator has himself killed so that people will not want to live forever, with the bad consequences of immortality.[61]

It can be difficult to read the Indian stories with the discipline and imagination they probably require. They tend to be terse and subtle; much was evidently left to the audience; much is taken for granted, especially since it was usually an audience accustomed to elaborating upon the tales it heard.[62] Various of the stories I have retold here had moral lessons to teach, or at least moral presuppositions upon which they depended and which they reinforced.

There is evident again and again in the Indian stories a lively concern for the sacred, the beautiful (including the erotic), the healthy, and the common good.[63]

VI.

The common good depends, in practice, on an awareness of limits set by nature, if not also on goals suggested by nature. Whatever the Indian understanding of nature, which I will soon say something about, a kind of natural law or a respect for something like natural right may be seen at work among the Indians. This is evident in the lessons taught by the stories they told, as well as in the way their communities were organized.[64]

They knew, for example, how various animals, birds, and insects conduct themselves and what various plants do and are good for. *They sensed, that is, what can and cannot be.* We notice that they put the more outlandish stories in the long-distant past. Is it not prudent in these matters to assume that most peoples, or at least the intelligent storytellers they instinctively depend upon, have a minimum of common sense?

It is often said that the Indians lived "close to nature."[65] Even though one may wonder how close to nature a people can be who do not really know what nature is, it is probably true that nature asserts herself even when she is not recognized as such or understood. This can be reassuring: we can expect that long-established peoples have managed to work out sensible ways of life, however difficult a tradition-bound people may find it to adjust quickly when they confront an abrupt and massive change in circumstances.[66]

The sensibleness of the Indians may be seen in the ways they generally organized their lives, treasured various things, and talked about how they should conduct themselves. They were for centuries a better-ordered people than Europeans originally imagined them to be. The self-interest of Europeans often made it difficult for them to see clearly those evidently aboriginal peoples who seemed to stand in the way of what the Europeans took to be (and may well have been, on the whole) salutary economic and political developments.[67]

Is there not something sensible as well in the Caddo creation story in which a woman is told by a voice how to plant and harvest corn? The voice, which is never heard again thereafter, concludes, "Now you have everything you need. Now you can live. Now you will have children and form a new generation. If you, woman, should plant corn, and something other than corn comes up, then know that the world will come to its end."[68] We can see here an awareness of what we call the natural process, just as the author of the Hebrew Bible (with no word for *nature* available to him either) exhibits such an awareness in reporting that animals and plants appear according to their own kind.[69]

VII.

A former United States Commissioner of Indian Affairs was moved to say this about the Indians in 1947:

> They had what the world has lost. They have it now.
>
> What the world has lost, the world must have again, lest it die. Not many years are left to have or have not, to recapture the lost ingredient. . . .
>
> What, in our human world, is this power to live? It is the ancient, lost reverence and passion for human personality, joined with the ancient, lost reverence and passion for the earth and its web of life.
>
> This indivisible reverence and passion is what the American Indians almost universally had; and representative groups of them have it still.
>
> They had and have this power for living which our modern world has lost—as world-view and self-view, as tradition and institution, as practical philosophy dominating their societies and as an art supreme among all the arts.[70]

Such recognition of the Indian "reverence and passion for the earth and its web of life" as may be seen here can lead people to speak of Indians as very close to nature, as open to and respectful of nature. But the Indian perspective, important though it may be, is more that of the outdoorsman than that of the naturalist. For better or for worse, it is not the scientific approach, which (so far as we know) is ultimately Southern European in origin. The Indians can remind us here of the Egyptians and the Babylonians with their vast quantities of observations about the heavens, observations that the scientifically minded Greeks were evidently able to put to a more theoretical use than had been done by those who had originally compiled them.[71]

Our study of Indian thought permits us better to appreciate what nature and the systematic study of nature mean. Science, we can again see, is a Greek way of talking about nature. By and large, the Indians were far more interested in a practical grasp of things than in a theoretical understanding of the world. In fact, we must wonder, is it possible to have genuine theoretical interests if one does not know what *nature* is?[72] The Indians, it seems, were more attuned to art than to science and were more interested in evocative stories than in any systematic understanding of things. Did they "believe in" their stories about why the animals, including human beings, and the earth and heavens are the way they are? If they had alternative explanations which they took seriously, they do not show up in the anthologies I have seen of materials collected from them over the past five centuries.

What is implied by that nature which the Indians do not seem to have spoken of? *Nature* means, among other things, that there need be no beginning or end to the movements and combinations of matter and their consequences.[73] For example, death is shown in various Indian stories to have been invented or chosen rather than being intrinsic to things.[74] Much the same may be seen with respect to the origins of, or any living being's access to, the sun, light and fire, all of which can be said to depend upon animal or other decisions and efforts. On the other hand, a reliance upon nature, or *not* looking to particular events as decisive, implies the conquest of time, the depreciation of history.[75]

The Indian approach, I have suggested, means that the way things look, their attributes, the way they are and act, are all keyed to events, or acts of will, not to something innate in things. This applies, I have also suggested, not only to human beings and other living things, but also to features of the land, sea, and sky. Even the earth can be spoken of as having once been a human being.[76] It is taken for granted in many Indian stories that human beings were once much closer to the animals than they are now.

The colors and shapes of animals, their behavior (for example, how the Coyote runs), the ways trees and other vegetation are, and what the terrain is like—all of these can be traced back to particular humanlike events.[77] Once, indeed, not only the animals and trees could feel and talk but even rocks.[78] For example, it could matter to a large rock whether it had a blanket to cover it, so much so that it could go rolling after Coyote when he took back the blanket which he had previously bestowed upon the rock.[79]

A Tewa tale suggests the collaboration between human beings and other living things in dealing with what we would call natural forces. It is an account of how Tiny Flower and his wife White Corn were rescued by birds when they fled from the "personage with great powers, whose duty it was to make rain, thunder, and clouds every day," a great personage who had stolen White Corn for his mate.[80] He had been killed by the couple but he was able to come back to life and to pursue them:

It was not long before the sky darkened and thunder and lightning began to play all around White Corn and Tiny Flower as they ran.

When they passed the river with red water, rain had caught up with them. By the time they reached Yunque, it was falling faster and faster. Tiny Flower urged White Corn to keep running, for they were just a mile away from home.

The Rio Grande was the next river they crossed, and hail began to fall. All kinds of birds were circling above them, but they kept running. They had only a few hundred yards to go when the hail became so heavy that they could not move.

Tiny Flower and White Corn lay on the ground, and all the birds that had been following—crows, eagles, hawks, owls, sparrows, and more—swooped down and protected the man and woman with their spread wings. The birds that were on top of this

great canopy were struck by hail and became spotted, while the ones underneath, like
the crows, kept their solid colors. When the rain and hail stopped, Tiny Flower promised the birds that in the next four days he would bring them four deer to eat.[81]

All this is not to deny that the Indians knew—perhaps far better than most
Europeans knew—how some things were and acted in nature. But their understanding of things was still fundamentally different. This is reflected in the
importance of transformations in their scheme of things: there are repeated
shiftings from one thing to another, shiftings back and forth, reflecting the underlying connections among things that they insist upon, the ultimate oneness
of things.[82] In the Bible, transformations of this kind (such as water into wine)
are rare—and they can be designated as miracles.[83]

The significance of sometimes bizarre shiftings among species in Indian
stories suggests that there is no fixed nature, *nor* any Darwininan notion of
evolution or adaptation.[84] We have already noticed Indian stories in which
there is no natural basis of, or cause for, death. The cause of the eventual end
of the world can be put in terms of Beaver steadily gnawing at the center pole
that holds up everything, gnawing faster when he is angry.[85] The shiftings go
even further, as may be seen in the movements back and forth between life
and death. One consequence of this is the critical place for ghosts and spirits
in Indian stories. A human being can be married to someone who turns out to
be a snake or a grizzly bear or an eagle or a ghost. Yet it can be said, in recognition of the fundamental difference between life and death, that the dead live
in darkness and that it is far better to be alive.[86]

To describe and account for things as the Indians tended to do is, I have suggested, not to recognize the primacy of the rational, at least as we "Europeans"
understand the rational.[87] I have further suggested that the Indians may not truly
have seen things as they are, however familiar they were with them. Thus, we
have stories in which the Morning Star and the Evening Star are regarded as different, with their mating producing the first human being.[88]

How much, then, *did* the Indians know about nature as nature? Their limitations here may be seen in the attribution of speech and hence reason to all
living things at one time or another. Their view of nature reminds us that the
observation of facts and a lively imagination cannot suffice for understanding.[89] One consequence of the emphasis upon choice and history that I have
described is that chance becomes critical, with a "personalization" of much of
what one observes. History, or rather memory, was more important for the Indians (as for the Jews?) than for European (that is, Hellenized) Christians. But
the European emphasis upon reason, especially in the service of religious
faith, could also mean that a concern with the baleful effects of witchcraft
could be far more important for the Europeans than for the Indians.[90]

That is, the age of reason could produce epidemics of monsters to which the Indian psyche may have developed an immunity.

VIII.

We must consider further, if only briefly, the significance of the North American Indians' lack of access either to nature or to a substantial substitute for it. (Substantial substitutes do seem to have been developed among the ancient Chinese and Hindus and among the ancient Israelites.) The Indians rely upon magic and formulas in place of a wisdom keyed to nature, however much of a sound moral sense there is in much of what they believe. Their ritualistic approach to things may be seen in their almost obsessive emphasis upon the number *four*.[91] This number seems to be intimately related to the four cardinal directions, directions which work with the movement from the rising to the setting of the sun. (This may reflect the importance of physical mobility for most Indians.) It is in keeping with the emphasis upon *willing* rather than upon *discovering* that the four directions can be said to have been *made*, not found.[92] The four directions can also be accounted for by the way that four monsters once happened to fall.[93]

To question the ultimate wisdom of the Indian approach to things is not to question their nobility. Indeed, there is often some tension, as is evident in the Greek tragedies, between the noble and the wise.[94] Was it not the noble strain in the Indians that Tocqueville could identify as aristocratic and that could contribute, when suppressed, to their demoralization? Self-esteem very much matters in these situations, and repeated defeats can be devastating to the spirited soul. Wisdom, on the other hand, permits sensibleness and compromises—that is to say, prudence.[95]

The American statesman could have said of the Indians in North America in the eighteenth and nineteenth centuries what the Roman statesman could say of the tribes in Britain more than a millennium earlier: "Our greatest advantage in coping with tribes so powerful is that they do not act in concert. Seldom is it that two or three states meet together to ward off a common danger. Thus, while they fight singly, all are conquered."[96]

I have suggested that an enduring prudence probably depends upon an overall grasp of things grounded in an awareness (whether or not articulated) of nature. The Indian tales we have, which are often like either war stories or accounts of athletic contests among us today, tend to close off inquiries rather than to suggest questions. An underlying problem here, which is difficult to address properly, is what the appropriate use by the human race has been since 1492 of the vast resources of the Western Hemisphere. It was, and still is, difficult to be both fair and persuasive in dealing with this problem.[97]

IX.

The most dramatic characteristic of the Indian way of life may have been its interest in war and hunting, interests related to the somewhat aristocratic tenor of that way of life.[98] Various warlike activities, such as horse-stealing forays, were evidently regarded by the Indians as fit diversions for their young men. No doubt there were considerable differences among tribes, with some of them adept in subsistence farming, but there were fundamental similarities as well, especially when Indians were compared to Europeans. It proved difficult for Europeans to accommodate themselves to Indian ways of thinking and of acting. One striking similarity among the Indians is that there is relatively little discussion in their surviving materials about forms of government or about political decisions, except perhaps in connection with devising tactics for war or the hunt.[99]

The typical European response to the Indians in the seventeenth and eighteenth centuries is reflected in the way they are described in the Declaration of Independence of 1776, where one of the grievances against the king of Great Britain is the following:

> He has excited domestic Insurrections amongst us, and has endeavoured to bring on the Inhabitants of our Frontiers, the merciless Indian Savages, whose known Rule of Warfare, is an undistinguished Destruction, of all Ages, Sexes and Conditions.[100]

The critical places where the Indians were encountered in those days, we can see here, were "our Frontiers," for it was there that the Europeans were constantly pressing to enlarge their holdings.

What particularly colored the European perception of the Indians, it seems, was their appetite for the scalps of the enemy, an appetite that could also indulge itself in the torture of prisoners.[101] It is true that Chief Joseph's Nez Percé warriors, in their late nineteenth-century battles with the United States Army, never took scalps.[102] But did not this Nez Percé practice condemn by implication most of the other Indian tribes?[103]

One Indian story after another seems to take it for granted that scalping is perfectly proper. Why did it matter so much to them?[104] This is not to deny that far worse things were done to the Indians, and for much longer, by the Europeans than the Indians were ever *able* to do to the Europeans who found scalping so abhorrent. Scalping did seem the thing for young men to do: they would set out on an expedition to slaughter unknown men and to collect scalps of alien peoples as tokens of their courage and prowess in war.[105] In one story, the heroes can be depicted as laboring under a tremendous burden of scalps while they continue to look for "the scalp of all scalps" with which to cap their exploits.[106] It is almost as an afterthought that they can be instructed that they should stop killing innocent people.[107]

The importance of displaying one's prowess may be seen in the curious Indian institution of the *coup*, the mere touching of an enemy in battle, even while killing is going on all around.[108] This is related to the respect shown by Indians for the courage of enemies, even of those whom they felt obliged to torture to death. Their sense of honor did not preclude recourse to deception, as may be seen in the respect shown for the cunning of various tricksters.[109] Still, the Indians were easily deceived by Europeans, while they themselves got an undeserved reputation for treachery.[110]

It should also be noticed that conflicts between Indian tribes were rarely wars of extermination. Fighting could be seen almost as sport to which warriors could be urged by their women.[111] The argument could even be made that a diversity of language was good in that it permitted men to fight, something that permits proper fulfillment of the male. Besides, without war there would develop such ills as an excess of population.[112]

But whatever the failings of the Indians in this respect, we have noticed that the depredations of the Europeans could be far worse. This is testified to by the mostly futile injunction laid down in the Northwest Ordinance of 1787, where it is said,

> The utmost good faith shall always be observed towards the Indians; their lands and property shall never be taken from them without their consent; and in their property, rights, and liberty, they never shall be invaded or disturbed, unless in just and lawful wars authorized by Congress; but laws founded in justice and humanity shall from time to time be made, for preventing wrongs being done to them; and for preserving peace and friendship with them.[113]

It may well be, as we shall see, that the principles of the Europeans were in critical respects superior to those of the Indians. But, by and large, the Indians were probably more conscientious in living up to their principles than the Europeans were in living up to theirs.[114]

X.

Indian principles, we have noticed, make much of fighting. They would fit more easily into the world of Homer's *Iliad* than into the world either of Homer's *Odyssey* or of Hesiod's *Works and Days*.[115] Many of the tribes could despise, as Chief Joseph did, "the white half-men who scratch in the ground."[116] Yet does not agriculture serve as the basis of civilization as we know it?

Indian principles also taught that those who misbehave are apt to suffer. Youngsters could hear the moral, "You see, because you wanted nothing for yourself, everything has come to you."[117] It is also taught that the good are entitled to use deception in crippling and otherwise restraining the wicked.[118]

We have also noticed the importance for the Indians of the sacrifice of oneself for the community. One's tribe could be considered the favored people of the Creator. The original names of many of the tribes mean, in their respective languages, "*the* people" or "the real people." Each tribe evidently considered itself to have a sacred trust, with appropriate spirits to look after it.[119]

Individuality, as we know it, seems to have been discouraged. The young man, upon maturing, might be left alone for days at a time on a vision-quest.[120] This was done in order to permit his soul to commune with the spirits of his people, to learn what he had in him, and to dedicate himself properly to the common purpose. It was not designed to develop traits of independence and personal initiative, which do not seem to have been valued. Neither the principles nor the experiences of the Indians supported the opinion of Europeans, especially the Europeans on this continent, that an enlightened self-interest could be depended upon to promote the common good.[121] Nor did the Indians see the common good as much as the Europeans did in terms of an ever-rising standard of living.[122]

However much the Indians made of subordination of oneself to the communal interest, tribes did find it difficult to unite properly in dealing with common threats.[123] This was a problem that was independent of the presence of the European: the Indians north of the Rio Grande had had thousands of years to develop before 1492. These North American Indians can be seen as having by then, if left to themselves, probably taken their intellectual and social development as far as their principles and aspirations called for and permitted. We are obliged to wonder, in a way perhaps which they did not, what the truly human life consists of.

XI.

There is not, among the Indians north of the Rio Grande, the same evident sense of a high civilization that may be seen in, say, ancient China or ancient India. The American Indian perception of civilization is much closer to that of Huck Finn, who, "light[s] out for the Territory ahead of the rest" in order to escape civilization, having "been there before" and not finding it to his liking.[124]

Indian adaptations to what the Europeans have had to offer have been mixed. The horse was quickly taken on and put to good use, the gun to perhaps less good use, and alcohol to disastrous use.[125] Technology and agriculture have, by and large, *not* been in the spirit of the Indian way of life.[126]

The most important thing that the Europeans could have offered the Indians was philosophy—and hence a truly informed awareness of what is fully human. This is related to ethics, or a thoughtful morality, but it is not limited to that. One consequence of the philosophical approach, which of course most Europeans neglected then as they do now,[127] is that it obliges one to question the importance of "one's own." Philosophy, in however diluted a form, makes itself felt among many people in the West through Christianity. Christianity itself builds somewhat on Platonic and Aristotelian thought, or the life of the mind.[128] Since the life of the mind as we know it has never been critical to the Indian way of life, it may help to explain why the Indians as a people have not been particularly interested in Christianity. It did not help, of course, that many of the "Christians" that the Indians first encountered, and suffered from, were self-serving hypocrites. Even so, I suspect that the emphasis upon the Great Spirit one now finds in Indian stories has been shaped in part by the influence of Christianity. Islam, with its more militant tones and its greater reliance upon a pre-Koranic poetic tradition, might have done better in some ways than Christianity among North American Indians in the sixteenth and seventeenth centuries.[129]

And so we must face up to the challenge implicit in much that I have noticed: is not the European way of life ultimately preferable to the typical Indian way of life? One cannot assess the Indian way properly, or its response to the European alternative, until one addresses this question squarely, even if it cannot be readily answered. Did the Indians fail to recognize as superior the things that make one more fully human? Have the Indians failed to appreciate the best of the Europeans at least as much as the Europeans have failed to appreciate the best of the Indians? There may be mutual failures here: the fault may be greater among the Europeans, but the damage may be greater among the Indians.[130]

Much of what we have just now been considering can be seen to address the question of why Aristotle believed that the *polis* (rather than either a nomadic tribe or a small village, on the one hand, or a massive city or an empire, on the other) is the natural habitat for the human being.[131]

XII.

We must wonder, of course, how much we can truly grasp of what Indian life was like before it was corrupted by extensive contact with the Europeans. Of the Indian materials we now have, how much has been filtered through European eyes and consciousness?[132] Would it not be natural for the somewhat Europeanized Indians themselves to repudiate whatever elements of their heritage now look dubious? And have some of the more potent stories been diluted, especially those that rely upon an audience of a proper character and experience? With such questions the workings and significance of an oral tradition can be investigated.

Then there is the simple problem of adequate translations of what the Indians used to say, especially since many of the Indian languages are themselves either extinct or at risk even among Indians.[133] The very names now given to tribes, and perhaps even the very term *tribe*, can be challenged as themselves distortions. The word *Indian* itself depended of course on a European misconception of how far west Christopher Columbus had gotten when he finally reached land. There may be a happy accident here, however, in that the name *Indian* did happen to anticipate what is now generally taken to be the case, that the North American Indians came here more than twenty thousand years ago from Asia.[134]

We may well wonder what traces there are in Indian languages, customs, and stories of their distant Asian connections. These should be further studied, not least for what they can suggest about the way of life that preceded the now dominant Chinese and Hindu ways of life on the Asian mainland.[135] Also, we can perhaps learn thereby what might have happened in various parts of Europe and the Middle East before the development of the forms of civilization found in Egypt and Greece. We can at least see the stuff out of which later, more sophisticated, stories and cosmologies developed, even as we recognize that something truly mysterious happened when human beings first became aware not only of nature, but (perhaps even more significant) of their awareness of that awareness, an awareness which includes the recognition that nature has her salutary effects even on those who are but dimly aware of her.[136]

XIII.

I bring this account to a close by speaking briefly about the future of the Indians in the United States. We owe a debt to the anthropologists who have done so much to help salvage the materials that we now have of what would otherwise almost certainly and even more rapidly have been a vanishing Indian heritage. These anthropologists, some of whom now are themselves Indians, have been vigilant in their efforts to counteract to some extent the depredations visited upon the North American Indians by all too many politicians in the service of thoughtless and self-serving non-Indian constituents.[137]

Anthropologists and politicians alike are both in need of correction here. The politicians have generally failed to appreciate the merits of the Indians; the anthropologists have generally failed to appreciate their defects. The former erred on the side of realism, the latter erred on the side of brotherhood. Still, however defective the Indian grasp of the world, it can be superior to what many among us today stand for who go in for consumerism and for a mindless addiction to our conventional "leisure-time activities."[138]

It is appropriate to notice, considering our own concerns these days, that the Indians of old may have something vital to contribute to the currently fashionable environmental movement. We all, Indians and non-Indians alike, can learn from what the Indians once somehow knew. They had access to the real treasures of North America, not just the gold, fur, and agricultural products that the Europeans yearned for. It is remarkable what a rich trove of stories there are still all around us among the Indians, stories that Europeans by and large have been unaware of for centuries.[139] Rich as that treasure trove may be, however, it is obvious that few of our forebears would have come over here to learn what the Indians had to teach. Still, it may be that the Indians can be fully seen for the first time, by Indians as well as by non-Indians, only because of the inquiring spirit nourished by the philosophical mode that the European way of life both permits and encourages.[140]

The Indian can help us become more intimate with the land, as well as with the earliest manifestations of humanity on this planet. One Brule Sioux story observes that the white man needs to have "earth wisdom, making him listen to what the trees and grass tell him."[141] A proper study of Indians can help non-Indians see themselves better, including the African Americans who have had their complex heritage shattered even more than that of the American Indians has been.[142]

The last sentiments here come from Indians. First, there is a talk (evidently a non-Indian rendering in poetic terms of a talk) to the governor of Washington Territory in 1854 by the great Dwamish chief, Seattle. It is an eloquent talk in which we should be able to hear (despite its Europeanization) various of the elements of Indian thought that I have attempted to sketch in this chapter. We should be able to hear as well the pious accents of ancient Sparta, Troy, and Rome, especially in the following excerpt:

> To us the ashes of our ancestors are sacred and their resting place is hallowed ground. You wander far from the graves of your ancestors and seemingly without regret. . . .
>
> Your dead cease to love you and the land of their nativity as soon as they pass the portals of the tomb and wander way beyond the stars. They are soon forgotten and never return. Our dead never forget the beautiful world that gave them being.[143]

Finally, there is a fragment from a Dakota poet, an Indian who echoes here a timeless teaching by Socrates:

> You cannot harm me,
> you cannot harm
> one who has dreamed a dream like mine[144]

Notes

1. William Shakespeare, *Othello,* V ii, 342-28 (GBWW [Great Books of the Western World], I: vol. 27, p. 243; II: vol. 25, p. 243 [chapter 1 of this collection, note 4]). "Judean" has been said to refer to an infidel or disbeliever—perhaps to Herod, who slew Marianne in a fit of jealousy, or to Judas Iscariot, the betrayer of Jesus. Some editors prefer "Indian" to "Judaen." See David Bevington, *The Complete Works of Shakespeare* (Glenview, Ill.: Scott, Foresman and Co., 1980), p. 1167.

2. In this chapter I deal primarily with the Indian tribes north of the Rio Grande and south of the Arctic, emphasizing aspects of North American Indian thought that I do not find in most accounts. South of the Rio Grande the remarkable social institutions among the Aztecs, Incas, and Mayas were critically, indeed fatally, compromised by their systematic reliance upon human sacrifice. See, with respect to troubling archaeological finds in Colorado and elsewhere in the Southwest, Bruce Bower, "The Cannibal's Signature," *Science News*, January 2, 1993, p. 12, ibid., February 27, 1993, p. 131. See, on the traumatic effects of the occasional resort to human sacrifice among the Greeks and Romans, Plutarch, *Life of Themistocles*, XIII, 2–3, *Life of Pelopidas*, XXI, 1, XXII, 2, *Life of Marcellus*, II, 3–4, *Life of Philopoemen*, XXI, 5. See also notes 66 and 87 below.

See, on nomenclature, notes 5 and 6 below, and section XII of this chapter. Unless otherwise indicated, all references to notes in any chapter in this collection are to the notes of that chapter.

I have been encouraged by the reponse to this chapter by Leslie G. Freeman of the University of Chicago.

3. The "Indian count" in 1990 was 1,516,540 (for thirty-nine states and the District of Columbia). See Dirk Johnson, "Census Finds Many Claiming New Identity: Indian," *New York Times*, March 5, 1991, p. A10. See also note 6 below.

4. See, for an instructive discussion from a Tocquevillian (and hence somewhat prudential) perspective of the policies of the government of the United States toward the Indians, Ralph Lerner, *The Thinking Revolutionary: Principle and Practice in the New Republic* (Ithaca, N.Y.: Cornell University Press, 1987), pp. 139f, 174f. See also the text at notes 95 and 114 of this chapter, and notes 96, 98, 121, and 140 below. Comments on the Lerner book may be found in note 97 below. See, for a review of the book, George Anastaplo, "Law, Education, and Legal Education: Explorations," 37 *Brandeis Law Journal* 585, 704–22 (1998–1999).

5. I will often refer to these peoples or nations by the names of their tribes. See section XII of this chapter. See, on the number of people involved, note 3 above, note 6 below, and the text at note 42 of this chapter. (*Tribes* is the term used for the Indians collectively in the Constitution of the United States. See the Commerce Clause in Article I, Section 8.) "'Indian,' by the way, seems to be a generic term that Indians themselves use freely, perhaps because it's been around for centuries and carries little cultural baggage for them. The terms 'Native Americans' and, in Canada, 'Natives' are OK, too, but those also were invented by whites—of a politically correct academic tribe." Henry Kisor, book review (of Thomas King, *Green Grass, Running Water*), *Chicago Sun-Times*, Book Week, February 14, 1993, p. 14.

6. "Over a million Indians occupied the area covered today by the forty-eight states, but [their] physical and cultural variations were many. Red men came in as many differ-

ent sizes and shapes and skin tones as the whites who were about to overwhelm them. The only features the Indians had in common were black hair, brown eyes, and some shade of brown skin. The Winnebagos were noted for their large heads, the Utes for their squat, powerful frames; the Crows for their height. These physical variations, coupled with the hundreds of different dialects spoken (although scholars have classified them in six major language groups) offer the best evidence that the migration from Asia began perhaps 30,000 years ago and included many fragments of Asiatic peoples." William T. Hagan, *American Indians* (Chicago: University of Chicago Press, 1979), pp. 2–3. See, also, the text at notes 42 and 133 of this chapter. The populations south of the Rio Grande were much larger, with perhaps twenty million Indians in the whole of the Western Hemisphere. See "American Indians," *Encyclopædia Britannica*, 15th ed. (1988 printing), vol. 13, p. 311. Did introduction of the English language permit Indian tribes to communicate among themselves to a degree never possible before in North America? See Hagan, *American Indians*, p. 134. Did something like this also happen in India?

7. Richard Erdoes and Alfonso Ortiz, eds., *American Indian Myths and Legends* (New York: Pantheon Books, 1984), p. 96. The "liberating" effect of "learning their own words" can remind us both of the story of the eating of the forbidden fruit in the Garden of Eden and of the story of the building of the Tower of Babel. See Anastaplo, "On Trial: Explorations," 22 *Loyola University of Chicago Law Journal* 765, 767–784 (1991); the text at note 57 of this chapter. Also instructive here is the cooperation assumed between "all the people and all the animals and all the birds." See the text at note 15 of this chapter.

8. Erdoes and Ortiz, eds., *American Indian Myths*, p. 96. It is *said* in the story that the word for *lift together* (*Ya-hoh*) is the same in all the Indian languages. See also the Papago account of the career of Montezuma and the consequent raising of the sun so as to produce winters. Ibid., pp. 487–89. The Cherokee tribe, on the other hand, tell about first having had to bring the sun down closer to the earth for light and heat and then having had to raise it "to the height of four men" to make the sun bearable. In the process the crawfish had its flesh turned red, making it inedible. Ibid., pp. 105–7.

9. Ibid., p. 343.

10. Ibid., p. 343. See the text at note 77 of this chapter. Why did the pine trees hoard fire as they did? Partly to protect themselves from forest fires?

11. Ibid., p. 108.

12. Ibid., p. 98.

13. Ibid., p. 105. An editorial note here adds, "The Hopis tell this as the tale of Bahana, the lost White Brother, replacing the sisters with brothers throughout. This version from Acoma shows Spanish influence in the mention of 'sin,' a concept unknown on this continent until after Columbus; the role of the snake in tempting Nao-tsiti [in the Acoma version] may also be colored by knowledge of the Bible." See Anastaplo, "Rome, Piety, and Law: Explorations," 38 *Loyola University of New Orleans Law Review* 1, 113 (1993). See also the passage quoted in the text at note 22 of this chapter.

To say that "everything was as it should be" suggests an intuition (ancient or more recent?) about the nature of nature. See note 15 of this chapter. See also sections VI and VII of this chapter.

14. Erdoes and Ortiz, eds., *American Indian Myths*, pp. 85–86. See also the passage quoted in the text at note 17 of this chapter,

15. Perhaps nonliving things are also included, as in the accounts by modern scientists. See note 7 above, note 78 below, the text at notes 79 and 82 of this chapter.

16. Ibid., pp. 407–8.

17. Ibid., 408. See also the passage quoted in the text at note 14 of this chapter.

18. Ibid., p. 408. Is not natural right implied in the birds' argument, invoking as they do the justice of respecting contractual undertakings? See also the text at note 64 of this chapter. See as well appendix B of this collection.

19. On the trial-and-error approach by God seen in the Bible, see Robert Sacks, "The Lion and the Ass: A Commentary on the Book of Genesis," *Interpretation*, vol. 8, pp. 29f (1980). On the implications here of *Jonah*, see Anastaplo, "On Trial," pp. 821–30. See, also, ibid, p. 783.

20. Erdoes and Ortiz, eds., *American Indian Myths*, p. 223. It is not indicated how the giant digests anyone who may be alive inside his stomach.

21. We can be reminded here of the encounter between Odysseus and the Cyclops in Homer's *Odyssey*. See, on imagination generally, Eva T. H. Brann, *The World of the Imagination: Sum and Substance* (Savage, Md.: Rowman & Littlefield Publishers, 1991).

22. Frederick W. Turner III, ed., *The Portable North American Indian Reader* (New York: Penguin Books, 1974), pp. 25–26. Did the killng of the wife with an axe and the shredding of her body suggest that her husband was not really a loving, but rather a furious, spouse? Is there here a sublimated form of cannibalism as well? Compare *Genesis* 3:20 (on Eve as "the mother of all living"). See also note 13 above, the passage quoted in the text at notes 34 and 60 of this chapter.

23. See Erdoes and Ortiz, eds., *American Indian Myths*, pp. 12–13.

24. Ibid., p. 119. See, for a grimmer version of this kind of story, accounting for the development of medicine, Turner, ed., *Portable North American Indian Reader*, pp. 28–29.

25. Erdoes and Ortiz, eds., *American Indian Myths*, pp. 192–93. We can be reminded here of the vulnerability of Achilles because of *his* heel.

26. We can be reminded here of how Oedipus's determined (if not even frantic) effort to avoid a prophecy contributed materially to its fulfillment. See Anastaplo, "On Trial," pp. 830–46. See, for another account of the origins of mosquitos, Turner, ed., *North American Indian Reader*, p. 31.

27. Erdoes and Ortiz, eds., *American Indian Myths*, pp. 398–99. Consider how, in this and other Indian stories, the accounting for various parts of a body compares with modern evolutionary accounts. See the text at note 84 of this chapter. See also note 89 below. See, on tricks played with eyeballs and why Veeho ends up with mismatched eyeballs, ibid., pp. 379–81.

Will seems to be critical in understanding the whole in the Indian accounts. See the text at notes 76 and 92 of this chapter.

28. How is all this related to the soul that passes from one body to another (sometimes human, sometimes nonhuman) in Hindu thought? See chapter 3 of this collection.

29. Erdoes and Ortiz, eds., *American Indian Myths*, p. 210.

30. Ibid. See, on the chase of a severed head, ibid., pp. 230–34. See, also, the text at note 79 of this chapter.

31. Ibid., p. 470. The nature of stones and of water is drawn upon here. Should we be reminded again of Eve and her fateful choice? See, for another version of this story, Turner, ed., *Portable North American Indian Reader*, p. 160. Variations are probably inevitable when an oral tradition is relied upon. (This may be seen as well in the Greek stories, as with respect to the career of Helen of Troy. See, on how Helen's abduction might

be regarded, the text at note 51 of this chapter.) How death began is a question frequently addressed in Indian stories. See the text at note 74 of this chapter.

32. Compare, for example, the stories we have about Eve and about Pandora. See Anastaplo, "On Trial," pp. 778–79.

33. See Erdoes and Ortiz, eds., *American Indian Myths*, p. 50.

34. Ibid., p. 308. See also the passages quoted in the text at notes 22 and 60 of this chapter.

35. Is the waterfall token ambiguous? Did it just then begin to flow? A similar inquiry can be made about the moon coming up over the trees when it did. Compare, for the tests with the fleece devised by Gideon, *Judges* 6:36–41. See text at note 50 of appendix A.

36. Consider the opening lines of Homer's *Odyssey*. See note 21, above, the text at notes 43 and 109 of this chapter.

37. Paul Radin, *The Trickster: A Study in American Indian Mythology* (New York: Bell, 1956), p. ix. Do the Western Hemisphere Indians, by having retained archaic forms of stories that had long been superseded on the Asian mainland, permit us to investigate both the power and the limitations of primitive thought? See, on tricksters, Plutarch, *Life of Numa, Pompilius* XV, 3–4.

See the text at note 135 of this chapter. (*GBWW*, I: vol. 14, p. 57; II: vol. 13, p. 57).

38. Radin, *The Trickster*, p. 8. See, also, the text at note 58 of this chapter.

39. Turner, ed., *Portable North American Indian Reader*, pp. 30, 106.

40. See William K. Powers, *Beyond the Vision: Essays on American Indian Culture* (Norman: University of Oklahoma Press, 1987), p. l2.

41. See, e.g., Karl Kroeber, ed., *Traditional Literatures of the American Indian* (Lincoln: University of Nebraska Press, 1981), pp. 12–13.

42. See ibid., p. 45. See also notes 3 and 6, above. See as well note 78 of chapter 6 of this collection and part one of appendix A of this collection.

43. See, also, Plutarch, *Life of Marcellus*, XXII, 5. Alexander the Great appears in the Karaghiozis stories. On one occasion, the ever-wily Karaghiozis even tries to palm off one of Alexander's conquests as his own. See, on the Karaghiozis theater, Sotiris Spatharis, *Behind the White Screen* (New York: Red Dust, 1976).

44. See, on the relation of technology to the modern natural sciences, the opening speeches of Galileo's *Dialogues on Two New Sciences*.

45. See, on the relation of the high to the low, Leo Strauss, *Spinoza's Critique of Religion* (New York: Schocken Books, 1965), p. 2: "It is safer to try to understand the low in the light of the high than the high in the light of the low. In doing the latter one necessarily distorts the high, whereas in doing the former one does not deprive the low of the freedom to reveal itself fully as what it is." See note 132 below, and the text at note 140 of this chapter.

46. Consider, for example, the stories that Abraham Lincoln told "among the boys." See Charnwood, *Abraham Lincoln* (Garden City, N.Y.: Garden City Publishing Co., 1929), pp. 12–13.

47. See, on obscenity, Anastaplo, *Human Being and Citizen: Essays on Virtue, Freedom, and the Common Good* (Chicago: Swallow Press, 1975), p. 117. See also note 54 below.

48. See Alice Marriott and Carol K. Rachlin, *Plains Indians Mythology* (New York: New American Library, 1975), pp. 15, 18–19. See, also, Erdoes and Ortiz, eds., *American Indian Myths*, pp. 284–85, 363; Turner, ed., *Portable North American Indian Reader*, p. 128.

49. See Erdoes and Ortiz, eds., *American Indian Myths*, pp. 160–62. Consider, also, Herodotus, *The History*, I, 199 (*GBWW*, I: vol. 6, p. 45; II: vol. 5, p. 45); Anastaplo, "Rome, Piety, and Law," pp. 127, 137, (Apollo and Daphne).

50. See Erdoes and Ortiz, eds., *American Indian Myths*, p. 358; Boccaccio, *The Decameron*, III, 10. See, for a grimmer story, adapted perhaps from European sources, Erdoes and Ortiz, eds., *American Indian Myths*, pp. 315f.

51. See ibid., p. 93. See, also, Herodotus, *The History*, I, 1–4 (*GBWW*, I: vol. 6, pp. 1–2; II: vol. 5, pp. 1–2); Homer, *Iliad*, Book I (*GBWW*, I: vol. 4, pp. 3–9; II, vol. 3, pp. 3–9); the text at note 80 of this chapter; note 98, below.

52. See, e.g., *Wisconsin* v. *Yoder*, 406 U.S. 205, 247 n. 5 (1972).

53. Erdoes and Ortiz, p. 45. See also, Anastaplo, *The Constitutionalist: Notes on the First Amendment* (Dallas: Southern Methodist University Press, 1971), p. 548 n. 126.

54. See appendix B of this collection. It is reported, about the discovery of sexual pleasure, that its original discoverers did not have to encourage others: "When [they] got back to camp, they found nobody there. All the male creatures and the women beings had already paired off and gone someplace, each pair to their own spot. They didn't need to be told about this new thing; they had already found out." Erdoes and Ortiz, eds., *American Indian Myths*, p. 45. The private character of "this new thing" is taken for granted. See, on that freedom of expression which can be subversive of a healthy privacy, Anastaplo, *Amendments to the Constitution of the United States: A Commentary* (Baltimore: Johns Hopkins University Press, 1995), p. 47. See also note 47, above.

55 See, e.g., Anastaplo, *The Constitutionalist*, pp. 803–4 n. 38; Anastaplo, *The American Moralist: On Law, Ethics, and Government* (Athens, Ohio: Ohio University Press, 1992), pp. 135–38.

56. See Turner, ed., *Portable North American Indian Reader*, pp. 36f.

57. See, e.g., Erdoes and Ortiz, eds., *American Indian Myths*, p. 111. See also *Genesis* 2:18–24, 3:20; Anastaplo, *The Artist as Thinker: From Shakespeare to Joyce* (Chicago: Swallow Press, 1983), pp. 357–62; note 7 above.

58 See, e.g., Marriott and Rachlin, *Plains Indians Mythology*, pp. 30f. See also the text at note 13 of this chapter.

59. See, e.g., Erdoes and Ortiz, eds., *American Indian Myths*, pp. 96–97, 174–75, 205–9, 296–97. See also note 82 below.

60. See, e.g., ibid., pp. 12–13; the passage quoted in the text at note 22 of this chapter. Compare the Binding of Isaac and the Sacrifice of Jesus. See Anastaplo, "On Trial," pp. 854–73, 882–919. Consider also the sowing of the dragon's teeth to produce the ancestors of the Thebans in Greece. See note 37 above.

61. See Erdoes and Ortiz, eds., *American Indian Myths*, pp. 78f.

62. See, on the reading of the Confucian *Analects*, chapter 4 of this collection. Consider how we fill out, with the help of our personal experiences and our imagination, radio accounts of basketball, baseball, or football plays. See, on the improvisations and interpretations by storytellers, Kroeber, ed., *Traditional Literatures,* pp. 49–56. See also the text at note 76 of chapter 2 of this collection.

63. See, on the relation between the sacred and the common good, Anastaplo, *The American Moralist*, pp. 144–60, 341–48, 516–36; Anastaplo, "Rome, Piety, and Law," pp. 113f. See also note 46 of chapter 2 of this collection.

64. See, on natural right, Leo Strauss, *Natural Right and History* (Chicago: University of Chicago Press, 1953); Anastaplo, *Human Being and Citizen*, pp. 46–60, 74–86. See also note 18 above, notes 72 and 73 below. See as well appendix B of this collection.

65. See, e.g., Erdoes and Ortiz, eds., *American Indian Myths*, p. 128.

66. The frightful aberration of systematic human sacrifice challenges us. Is not this, even when institutionalized, a form of insanity? See Anastaplo, "Rome, Piety, and Law," pp. 114–15; Anastaplo, "On Trial," p. 977 (on the Nuremberg Trial); note 2 above, note 87 below.

67. See, for Abraham Lincoln on the blinding effects of self-interest, *The Collected Works of Abraham Lincoln*, Roy A. Basler, ed. (New Brunswick, N. J.: Rutgers University Press, 1953), vol. 4, 3, 9, 15–16; Anastaplo, "Slavery and the Constitution: Explorations," 20 *Texas Tech Law Review* 677, 732–53 (1989). See also notes 97 and 123, below. See as well the text at note 121 of this chapter.

68. Erdoes and Ortiz, eds., *American Indian Myths*, p. 122. See the text at note 83 of this chapter. See also the text at note 67 of chapter 6 of this collection.

69. See *Genesis* 1–2.

70. John Collier, *The Indians of the Americas* (New York: W. W. Norton, 1947), pp. 15–16. See, on Commissioner Collier's policies, Hagan, *American Indians*, pp. 155–61.

71. Consider, also, Johannes Kepler's use of Tycho Brahe's data. See the text at note 88 of this chapter. See also chapters 1 and 2 of this collection.

72. See, on the nature of nature, Jacob Klein, *Lectures and Essays* (Annapolis, Md.: St. John's College Press, 1985), pp. 219–39; Anastaplo, *The American Moralist*, pp. 412–15. See also note 64 above, appendix A of this collection, note 143.

73. "For though in nature nothing really exists besides individual bodies, performing pure individual acts according to a fixed law, yet in philosophy this very law, and the investigation, discovery, and explanation of it, is the foundation as well of knowledge as of operation." Francis Bacon, *The New Organon*, book II, aphorism 2. See, on whether the world had a beginning, appendices A and B of this collection. See also note 64 above.

74. See, e.g., Erdoes and Ortiz, eds., *American Indian Myths*, pp. 79–80. Consider also the stories about the roles of Coyote and others in bringing death into the world. See, e.g., Kroeber, ed., *Traditional Literatures*, pp. 26–34. See as well the text at notes 31 and 84 of this chapter.

75. It has been argued that this sense of nature, with its depreciation of singularity, is more Cartesian than Newtonian. See Thomas K. Simpson, "Science as Mystery: A Speculative Reading of Newton's *Principia*," *The Great Ideas Today*, pp. 119–21 (1992). See also chapter 6 of this collection, note 113; appendix A of this collection.

76. See Erdoes and Ortiz, eds., *American Indian Myths*, p. 14. Consider the Greek *Gaea* and our *Mother Earth*.

77 See, e.g., the passage quoted in the text at note 10 of this chapter.

78. See ibid., pp. 85–87. Thus, a Pueblo woman can say, "We were here before the rocks were hard." See the text at note 15 of this chapter.

79. See ibid., p. 337. See also the passage quoted in the text at note 29 of this chapter. Consider the care with which the Japanese select rocks for their gardens.

80. See ibid., p. 285. See also the text at note 51 of this chapter.

81. Ibid., pp. 289–90. See, on why human babies take a year or so to walk, ibid., p. 151.

82. "My imagination brings me to speak of forms changing into new bodies." Ovid, *Metamorphoses*, I, 1–2. See also Montesquieu, *The Spirit of the Laws*, Book 28 (epigraph) (*GBWW*, I: vol. 38, pp. 230–62; II: vol. 35, pp. 230–62); the text at notes 15 and 59 of this chapter. See as well chapter 2 of this collection. Compare the text at note 68 of this chapter.

83. Consider, also, the occasional resurrection in the Bible. Does not something material have to be there first for the biblical miracle to work on, perhaps even (some have argued) for the introductory miracle in *Genesis* 1? See the text at note 68 of this chapter.

84. See the text at notes 27 and 73 of this chapter.

85. See Erdoes and Ortiz, eds., *American Indian Myths*, p. 484.

86. See ibid., p. 442. One can be reminded of Achilles' complaints to Odysseus in Hades. See Homer, *Odyssey*, Book XI (*GBWW*, I: vol. 4, pp. 243–49; II: vol. 3, pp. 406–18).

87. One side effect may be the rareness of madness (as we usually know it) in the Indian stories we have. Compare, e.g., Erdoes and Ortiz, eds., *American Indian Myths*, p. 434; note 66 above. What is to be made of the deadly recourse to alcohol for which Indians became notorious? See, on madness, Anastaplo, *The Artist as Thinker*, pp. v, 338–39.

88. See Marriott and Rachlin, *Plains Indians Mythology*, pp. 16–19. How did the Greeks, or perhaps the Egyptians or Babylonians before them, learn that the Morning Star and the Evening Star were the same? See the text at note 71 of this chapter.

The Indians (with the possible exceptions, among those north of the Rio Grande, of some tribes in the American Southwest) were also confused about the relation between the length of the year and the periods of the moon, evidently not appreciating that the year (with its seasons) is not keyed primarily to the movements of the moon. See Marriott and Rachlin, eds., *Plains Indians Mythology*, p. 13. But then, even our students today (including students in sophisticated adult education programs) are often not aware of this either. Another way of putting this is to say that, once the earth settled into the orbit it now has around the sun, the earthly year would have been virtually the same length as now even if the moon had never existed. Consider, however, R. Monastersky, "Tilted: Stable Earth, Chaotic Mars," *Science News*, February 27, 1993, p. 132.

89. Observation alone can tempt one to say, for example, that since bears can walk like people they must be the ancestors of human beings. See Marriott and Rachlin, *Plains Indians Mythology*, pp. 43f. See also note 27 above.

90. See, on the European witchhunting craze, Anastaplo, "Church and State: Explorations," 19 *Loyola University of Chicago Law Journal* 61, 65–86 (1987). Some early Christian observers of the native peoples in North America did tend to see them as "perfect children of the Devil." See Increase Mather, *A Brief History of the War with the Indians in New-England* (1676), in Richard Slotkin and James K. Folsom, eds., *So Dreadful a Judgment: Puritan Responses to King Philip's War 1676–1677* (Middletown, Conn.: Wesleyan University Press, 1978), p. 116. See, on the Indians as believers in ghosts and witches, Samuel Cole Williams, ed., *Adair's History of the American Indians* (New York: Promontory Press, 1930), pp. 38–39. See, on the Indians as devil worshippers, Roy Harvey Pearce, "The 'Ruines of Mankind': The Indian Mind and the Puritan Mind," *Journal of the History of Ideas*, vol. 13, p. 200 (1952).

91. See, e.g., the text at note 81 of this chapter. See, on the importance of *five* among the Chinese and of *five* and *eight* among the Hindus, chapters 4 and 3 of this collection.

92. See Erdoes and Ortiz, eds., *American Indian Myths*, p. 77f. See also note 27 above.

93. See, ibid., p. 121. See also, on the directions, ibid., pp. 38–39, 50, 59. Four winds can be spoken of as related to the four directions, with the winds dependent upon the moods, or will, of Ga-oh. See ibid., pp. 40, 42.

94. See Anastaplo, *The Constitutionalist*, p. 171 n. 3, p. 798 n. 32. See also Anastaplo, "On Trial," pp. 846–49.

95. See note 4 above, note 97 below.

96. Tacitus, *Life of Agricola*, sec. 12. See the text at note 123 of this chapter. A critical difference, in the long run, may have been that Agricola and his successors provided a liberal education for the sons of the British chiefs that the Romans conquered. See ibid., sec. 21. Compare Hagan, *American Indians*, p. 11; *The Annals of America*, vol. 1, pp. 497–98 (Benjamin Franklin on the futility of educating the Indians).

97. Consider, for example, what a king of the Gauls once said to the Romans:

> The Clusians wrong us in that, being able to till only a small parcel of earth, they yet are bent on holding a large one, and will not share it with us, who are strangers, many in number and poor. This is the wrong which ye too suffered, O Romans, formerly at the hands of the Albans, Fidenates, and Ardeates, and now lately at the hands of the Veientines, Capenates, and many of the Faliscans and Volscians. Ye march against these peoples, and if they will not share their goods with you, ye enslave them, despoil them, and raze their cities to the ground; not that in so doing ye are in any wise cruel or unjust, nay, ye are but obeying that most ancient of all laws which gives to the stronger the goods of his weaker neighbours, the world over, beginning with God himself and ending with the beasts that perish. For these too are so endowed by nature that the stronger seeks to have more than the weaker. Cease ye, therefore, to pity the Clusians when we besiege them, that ye may not teach the Gauls to be kind and full of pity towards those who are wronged by the Romans.

Plutarch, *Life of Camillus*, XVII, 2–4. Those sympathetic to the Israeli cause in the Middle East at this time can make like arguments with respect to the Holy Land. See Anastaplo, *Human Being and City*, pp. 155–59.

Consider, also, John Winthrop's observations about New England in 1629 (Pearce, "The 'Ruines of Mankind,'" p. 203):

> [T]he whole earth is the Lord's garden, and he hath given it to the sons of Adam to be tilled and improved by them. Why then should we stand starving here for the places of habitation, (many men spending as much labor and cost to recover or keep sometimes an acre or two of lands as would procure him many many hundreds of acres, as good or better, in another place), and in the mean time suffer whole countries, as profitable for the use of man, to lie waste without any improvement.

The principal point of view worked from in the instructive discussion, of the American governments' Indian policies, provided in Ralph Lerner's The Thinking Revolutionary (note 3, above) is that of the white statesman. This means, according to Mr. Lerner, that things pretty much "had" to turn out the way they did, however more gently (if not decently) they could have been done. Supreme Court and other judicial determinations (ibid., pp. 142–47) did not matter much here, except perhaps as the basis for later reparations and other such reconsiderations, long after the Indians had been neutralized. A critical problem may be seen in what is ruled out at the outset of Mr. Lerner's discussion of Indian policies: the "patently inadequate points of view—that of avaricious Indian-haters, or of sentimental white humanitarians, or of sullen and beleaguered natives. " Ibid., p. 139. Compare the impression upon the reader, however, if other terms had been used here: for example, "sympathetic" instead of "sentimental," and "aggrieved" and "pillaged" instead of "sullen" and "beleaguered." Certainly, the Lerner analysis is *not* presented from the point of view either of the conscientious Indian statesman or of a desperate people with grievances at least as serious as those which are collected in, say, the Declaration of Independence.

(Even with respect to the "avaricious Indian-haters," is it not likely that the *avarice* fueled the *hatred,* rather than the other way around? And avarice was not limited to those of violent tendencies.) "A more appropriate perspective," we are told by Mr. Lerner, "is that of the white statesman who tried to shape national policy toward the Indians in the early years of the republic." Ibid., p. 139. The perspective of even the better American statesman, however, was rarely that either of the victims or of those few who spoke on their behalf. No major statesman is identified as having been willing to risk his career in order to protect the Indians, especially since the Indians were early and mostly regarded as dangerous and unproductive savages. The spirited aspect, obviously an important aspect, of the lives of the Indian peoples could be run through the all-too-often distorted souls of influential victimizers who had a great personal interest in driving the Indians further and further west. In such matters it can indeed be noticed that "the thoughtful, as distinguished from the influential, are always few." Ibid., p. x. Even fewer, it seems, are those moved by "the spirit of martyrdom." Ibid., p. 67 n. 10. See the text at note 137 of this chapter. See also note 67 above, note 123 below. The career of Sam Houston, who was both friendly to Indians and hostile to Texas secession from the Union, deserves consideration here. So does the career of the saintly John Woolman. See note 142 below. See, on Sam Houston, Hagan, *American Indians,* p. 98; Anastaplo, "Lessons for the Student of Law: The Oklahoma Lectures," 20 *Oklahoma City University Law Review* 17, 163 (1995).

98. The Indians were considerably more relaxed about the chastity of their wives, however, than were the medieval aristocrats with whom they have been sometimes compared. See the text at note 51 of this chapter. Plutarch observes that the Persians, like other barbarian nations, are jealous about their women. See *Life of Themistocles,* XXVI, 3–4.

99. One can be reminded, by the activities of young Indians, of the training of Spartan youth. See, e.g., Plutarch, *Life of Lycurgus,* XVIII, 1, XXII, 2–3; *Adair's History,* p. 428. Unsuccessful attempts have been made to emphasize the influence upon the Constitutional Convention of 1787 of the Albany Plan (and hence of Indian political thought).

100. The "domestic Insurrections" referred to here were slave uprisings.

101. See, on the refinements of scalping and torture (and not only by Indians), *Adair's History,* pp. 158, 318, 415–19, 454, 460. See, also, Hagan, *American Indians,* pp. 8, 15, 17, 22, 36, 106, 119; Slotkin and Folson, eds., *So Dreadful a Judgment,* pp. 90, 107, 115–17, 213, 218, 318, 326, 332; notes 110 and 129 below. Compare Plutarch, *Life of Lycurgus,* XXII, 5 (*GBWW,* I: vol. 14, p. 44; II: vol. 13, p. 14).

102. See Robert Penn Warren, *Chief Joseph of the Nez Percé Who Called Themselves the Nimipu "The Real People"* (New York: Random House, 1983), pp. 17, 54–55.

103. Although the Nez Percé were unfortunate in being associated in the public mind with the other Indian tribes, their Chief Joseph "was probably the only defeated Indian chief ever to be feted at a banquet shortly after his capture." Hagan, *American Indians,* p. 116.

104. We might ask as well why the notches on one's gun mattered in the Old West and why so much was made in the United States Army Air Crops during the Second World War of insignia on airplane fuselages recording bombing missions and fighter-pilot "kills."

105. See Turner, ed., *Portable North American Indian Reader,* pp. 51f.

106. Ibid., pp. 52–53.

107. See ibid., pp. 53–54.

108. Compare, for the Greek use of trophies, Plutarch, *Life of Timoleon,* XXIX, 4, XXXI, 6–7, XXXVI, 6, *Life of Pelopidas,* XVII, 4–5.

109. Consider, on the multitribal story of why the tails of prairie dogs are short, Marriott and Rachlin, *Plains Indians Mythology*, pp. 75f. The prairie dogs did learn to post guards thereafter. See also ibid., pp. 57f. See, on the Trickster, section 2 of this chapter.

110. On the other hand, James Fenimore Cooper could conclude chapter 30 of *The Last of the Mohicans* with an invocation of "the inviolable laws of Indian hospitality." He could also describe, as at the beginning of chapter 33 of this novel, "evidence of the ruthless results which attend Indian vengeance." See note 101 above, notes 129 and 139 below. See, on the variety of experiences of Europeans held captive by Indians, Annette Kolodny, "Among the Indians: The Uses of Captivity," *New York Times Book Review*, January 31, 1993, p. 1. Particularly instructive is Mary Rowlandson's famous account of her captivity, during which she suffered the extreme privations of her captors while being treated with more courtesy than had been expected by her. See Slotkin and Folsom, eds., *So Dreadful a Judgment*, pp. 301f. See, on abuse of hospitality, note 113 of chapter 6.

111. The resort to systematic human sacrifice by the Aztecs and others was foreign to the spirit of most Indian tribes in North America, even where cruel tortures were indulged in. See note 2 above.

112. See Erdoes and Ortiz, eds., *American Indian Myths*, pp. 92–94.

113. Northwest Ordinance, Article III. See Anastaplo, *The Constitution of 1787: A Commentary* (Baltimore: Johns Hopkins University Press, 1989), p. 263. See also Anastaplo, *Abraham Lincoln*, pp. 39, 69.

114. This is conduct on the part of the Indians consistent with their being regarded as aristocratic. See the text at note 4 of this chapter. Was not the typical European immigrant, or his descendant, much more apt to be plebeian and hence pragmatic (as well as moralistic)? See the text at note 127 of this chapter.

115. See the text at notes 42 and 129 of this chapter.

116. Warren, *Chief Joseph*, p. 51.

117. Marriott and Rachlin, *Plains Indians Mythology*, p. 55.

118. See Erdoes and Ortiz, eds., *American Indian Myths*, pp. 77f. We can be reminded here both of the relation between Jacob and Esau and of the counsel of Niccolò Machiavelli.

119. See, e.g., note 102 above. The same may be seen with such peoples as the ancient Chinese and the modern Greeks.

120. See, e.g., the third paragraph of the passage quoted in note 143 below. Compare, on individualism, note 140 below.

121. See, on the central chapter (on "interest well understood") in Tocqueville's *Democracy in America*, Anastaplo, *Abraham Lincoln*, p. 81. See also the text at note 67 of this chapter.

122. Did the old Indians ever consider this possible—or did change mean for them, at best, a few material gains and many spiritual losses? Compare the theme of perpetual progress often emphasized by political campaigns in the United States.

123. See the passage quoted in the text at note 96 of this chapter. The limitations of the Indians were such that they could neither understand the best nor anticipate the worst of what the Europeans had to offer. See note 97 above, note 132 below. See also the text at note 130 of this chapter.

124. See Mark Twain, *Adventures of Huckleberry Finn*, final paragraph. It should be remembered, however, that the deadliest villain in Mark Twain's *Adventures of Tom Sawyer* is Injun Joe.

125. See, on the horse, Marriott and Rachlin, *Plains Indians Mythology*, p. 89. Europeans in North America continue to fall victim to the horse (in the form of the automobile), to the gun, and to alcohol (which now includes other drugs as well).

126. Hopeful reports on the Indians' receptivity to an agricultural way of life were a regular feature of President Jefferson's annual messages to Congress. When Indian tribes did attempt to settle down to that way of life, they were not well received by Europeans eager for their lands. See, e.g., Hagan, *American Indians*, pp. 68–69, 73–81, 88–91, 130.

See, for the opinion in some circles that the Indians were really descended from the ancient Jews, *Adair's History*, pp. xxviii-xxx, 16f, 143–44, 153f. Did this kind of opinion influence the development of Mormon doctrines in the nineteenth century?

127. See, e.g., note 114 above.

128. See, on the relation of Christianity and philosophy, Anastaplo, *The American Moralist*, pp. 78, 125–34, 346–47. Should not the life of the mind be distinguished somewhat from the life of the imagination?

129. See, on the Koran, chapter 6 of this collection. A pious Quaker, disturbed by how missionaries to the Indians conducted themselves, counselled, "To reach a full-blooded Indian, send after him a full-blooded Christian." Hagan, *American Indians*, p. 129. See Slotkin and Folsom, eds., *So Dreadful a Judgment*, pp. 303–4; *The Annals of America*, vol. 1, pp. 92f (on the hopelessness of efforts to convert the Indians, who are described as "altogether inhuman, more then barbarous, far exceeding the African"), 315, 443f.

130. See notes 97 and 123 above, note 132 below.

131. See Aristotle, *Politics*, book I; Anastaplo, *The American Moralist*, pp. 20–26.

132. Have not the Europeans, with all their faults, been better able to understand the Indians, with all their virtues, than the Indians have been able to understand the Europeans? See Hagan, *American Indians*, p. 15. See also note 123 above, the text at notes 130 and 140 of this chapter.

133. See, e.g., Mark Abley, "The Prospects for the Huron Language," *Times Literary Supplement*, August 7, 1992, p. 4. See also note 6 above.

134. See, on the word *Indian*, note 5 above. Are Indians yet to be vindicated spiritually by the rapidly growing Asian presence in this country? The dispossession of the Japanese (including Japanese American) on the West Coast of the United States during the Second World War imitated in some respects what had been done to the Indians during the nineteenth century.

135. See, on Hindu and Chinese thought, chapters 3 and 4 of this collection. See also note 37 above.

136. See, e.g., the text at note 66 of this chapter.

137. See, e.g., note 97 above.

138. One of the more heartening things I have heard about the American Indians today is that they have almost no interest in television. That may turn out to be their secret weapon if they are to have the kind of resurgence that should benefit both them and their non-Indian fellow citizens in this country. See, on the abolition of broadcast television, Anastaplo, *The American Moralist*, pp. 245–74.

139. I am reminded of the shortwave emissions from all over the world that can pass through and around us all the time without our ever being aware of them. Europeans in this country who had read the popular novels of James Fenimore Cooper should have been

aware of more than they were. Consider, for example, the Indian nobility displayed in the closing chapters of *The Last of the Mohicans*. See note 110 above. An instructive intro-duction to Cooper's work is provided in Catherine H. Zuckert, *Natural Right and the American Imagination: Political Philosophy in Novel Form* (Savage, Md.: Rowman & Lit-tlefield Publishers, 1990).

140. See, for the virtues and limitations of the Indians' aristocratic way of life, ibid., pp. 20f. See also notes 45, 97, and 132 above. "Like many a chief before and after him, Pon-tiac had found the individualism of the Indian an unsurmountable obstacle [in organizing them]." Hagan, *American Indians*, p. 26. See also ibid., pp. 56 (Tecumseh as "a man with a breadth of vision rare among Indians"), 61, 90. Compare, on Indian individualism, the text at note 120 of this chapter.

141. See Erdoes and Ortiz, eds., *American Indian Myths*, p. 495.

142. See, on law, civilization, and African American circumstances, Anastaplo, *Human Being and Citizen*, pp. 175–99. See also chapter 2 of this collection. See, on the career of John Woolman as a determined civilizer, George Anastaplo, "Legal Education, Econom-ics, and Law School Governance: Explorations," 46 *South Dakota Law Review*, appendix B (2001).

143. Turner, ed., *Portable North American Indian Reader*, p. 252. The Seattle excerpt in the text is taken from the following (substantially Europeanized) passage (ibid., pp. 251–53):

> Yonder sky that has wept tears of compassion upon my people for centuries untold, and which to us appears changeless and eternal, may change. Today is fair. Tomorrow it may be overcast with clouds. My words are like the stars that never change. Whatever Seattle says the great chief at Washington [the President of the United States] can rely upon with as much certainty as he can upon the return of the sun or the seasons. The White Chief [the Governor] says that Big Chief at Washington sends us greetings of friendship and goodwill. That is kind of him for we know he has little need of our friendship in return. His people are many. They are like the grass that covers vast prairies. My people are few. They resemble the scattering trees of a storm-swept plain. . . . I will not dwell on, nor mourn over, our untimely decay, nor reproach our paleface brothers with hastening it, as we too may have been somewhat to blame. . . .
>
> Your God is not our God. Your God loves your people and hates mine. He folds his strong and protecting arms lovingly about the paleface and leads him by the hand as a father leads his infant son—but he has forsaken his red children—if they really are His. Our God, the Great Spirit, seems also to have forsaken us. . . . We are two distinct races with separate origins and separate destinies. There is little in common between us.
>
> To us the ashes of our ancestors are sacred and their resting place is hallowed ground. You wander far from the graves of your ancestors and seemingly without regret. Your religion was written upon tables of stone by the iron finger of your God so that you could not forget. The Red Man could never comprehend nor remember it. Our religion is the traditions of our ancestors—the dreams of our old men, given them in solemn hours of night by the Great Spirit; and the vi-sions of our sachems; and it is written in the hearts of our people.
>
> Your dead cease to love you and the land of their nativity as soon as they pass the portals of the tomb and wander way beyond the stars. They are soon forgotten and never return. Our dead never forget the beautiful world that gave them being.
>
> Every part of this soil is sacred in the estimation of my people. Every hillside, every valley, every plain and grove, has been hallowed by some sad or happy event in days long vanished. The very dust upon which you now stand responds more lovingly to their footsteps than to yours, because it is rich with the blood of our ancestors and our bare feet are conscious of the sympathetic touch. Even the little children who lived here and rejoiced here for a brief season

will love these somber solitudes and at eventide they greet shadowy returning spirits. And when the last Red Man shall have perished, and the memory of my tribe shall have become a myth among the White Men, these shores will swarm with the invisible dead of my tribe, and when your children's children think themselves alone in the field, the store, the shop, upon the highway, or in the silence of the pathless woods, they will not be alone. At night when the streets of your cities and villages are silent and you think them deserted, they will throng with the returning hosts that once filled and still love this beautiful land. The White Man will never be alone.

Let him be just and deal kindly with my people, for the dead are not powerless. Dead, did I say? There is no death, only a change of worlds.

See, on death and dying, Anastaplo, *Human Being and Citizen*, pp. 212–21. See also note 13 above. See, on the relations between the dead and the living, Aristotle, *Nicomachean Ethics*, 1101a21 sq.

144. Turner, p. 239. See, on Socrates and the city, Anastaplo, *Human Being and Citizen*, pp. 8–29, 203–13.

Appendix A

On Beginnings

> You certainly are Romans who claim that your wars are so fortunate because
> they are just, and pride yourselves not so much on their outcome, in that you
> gain the victory, as upon their beginnings, because you do not undertake wars
> without cause.
>
> —The Rhodians[1]

Introduction

Our sampling of accounts of beginnings includes, on this occasion, a poem by
Hesiod, a book of the Hebrew Bible, and the work of a contemporary scientist.[2] Before we discuss these beginnings we should consider, however
briefly, what usually permits the beginning of a recognition of the very idea
of beginning. The variety in the more or less inspired accounts of beginnings
collected in this appendix may suggest what if anything is constant, if not
"always," about beginnings.

There may have to be, if only as a practical matter, some change that is visible if there is to be an observation of, or productive speculation about, beginnings. But, on the other hand, for change itself to be noticeable, is not substantial stability required as well?

It also seems that an *end* is implicit in the notion of *beginning*.[3] *End* can refer to something temporal, something at the other extremity of the process
which starts with the beginning. *End* can refer as well to the purpose for
which something exists or is done. The end of a thing, in both senses of *end*,
may thereby be implied in its beginning.[4]

261

The beginning of a thing may assume not only a termination or conclusion. It may assume as well something prior to the beginning, something which brought about a beginning or for the sake of which something begins. We venture here upon the theology of our perhaps most influential ancients, both Greek and Judaic.

Language seems to be needed if there is to be the recognition, to say nothing of the examination, of any beginning. Rationality, or at least the potential for rationality, seems to be required for language. That potential, in turn, seems to depend for its proper realization upon a community, or at least upon that minimum of social cohesiveness provided by the family.[5]

Poets draw upon, as well as shape, the language of a people. Poetry, however much it (like music) charms audiences by its mode of expression, depends upon and serves an opinion of what the world is like.[6] Each of the three works surveyed in this appendix stands somewhat alone, instructive though it may be to notice the light cast by each on the other two as we consider what each suggests about beginnings.

Before we delve into the beginnings and doings of particular poets, we should notice (and not only in anticipation of part 3 of this appendix) the understanding of things advanced by scientists dedicated to the study of nature. The *nature* which is studied—the apprehension of which permits scientific inquiry—may imply perpetuity.

That is, a reliance upon nature could mean that there is no temporal beginning to the things of the world. Why may not matter, if not also the universe itself, be regarded as are, say, numbers and geometrical relations? That is, there *are* things always available to be discovered, separated out, and studied, if not even to be manipulated and otherwise used.[7]

Does *nature* also suggest *purpose* or *meaning*? Some argue that nature can guide us in how we should act. We can, it is said, be helped by nature to make sense of things not only by what we study, but also by how we are shaped by the way we conduct ourselves.[8]

The poet is usually to be distinguished from the scientist in these matters. We can see here an opposition similar to, if not quite the same as, that identified by Moses Maimonides as existing between the philosophers and those faithful to the Law of Moses, an irreconcilable opposition which rests, it seems, on an opinion as to whether the world had a beginning in time by having been brought into existence out of nothing by God.[9] In these matters, the poets tend to be the allies of the faithful, especially those poets who undertake to describe the bearing of the divine upon human affairs. With these observations we are prepared to turn to Hesiod, a Greek poet who, like the authors of the Hebrew Bible, never uses the word *nature*.[10]

Part One. Hesiod's *Theogony*

The noble voice of Calliope, whom Hesiod called chiefest of the Muses, has sounded steadily since Homer. It has not sounded all of the time, but whenever it has sounded it has given strength to those through whom it spoke. It is the source of great poetry—of great story . . .

—Mark Van Doren[11]

I.

Although little is known about Hesiod, we may know more about his personal life—as a resident of that part of Greece known as the Boeotia to which his father had emigrated from Asia Minor—than we do about any other author of his time. An encyclopedist records the following additional information:

Hesiod (Gr., Hesiodos; fl. c. 730-700 B.C.E.), one of the earliest recorded Greek poets. The earlier of his two surviving poems, *Theogony*, is of interest to students of Greek religion as an attempt to catalog the gods in the form of a genealogy, starting with the beginning of the world [this may not be quite so] and describing the power struggles that led to Zeus' kingship among the gods. . . .

Hesiod's other poem, *Works and Days*, is a compendium of moral and practical advice. Here Zeus is prominent as the all-seeing god of righteousness who rewards honesty and industry and punishes injustice.

Also attributed to Hesiod was a poem that actually dated only from the sixth century B.C.E., the *Catalog of Women*, which dealt with heroic genealogies issuing from unions between gods and mortal women. It enjoyed a status similar to that of the *Theogony*, but it survives only in fragments.[12]

A much earlier introduction to Hesiod is provided us by Herodotus, in fifth-century Greece. He says in his *History*:

Whence each of [the gods to whom the Greeks sacrifice] came into existence, or whether they were for ever, and what kind of shape they had were not known until the day before yesterday, if I may use the expression; for I believe that Homer and Hesiod were four hundred years before my time—and no more than that. It is they who gave to the gods the special names for their descent from their ancestors and divided among them their honors, their arts, and their shapes. Those who are spoken of as poets before Homer and Hesiod were, in my opinion, later born.[13]

It should be noticed that Herodotus does not say that Homer and Hesiod invented or even discovered the gods, but only that they offered the Greeks a clear picture of the forms, functions, and relationships of the gods.[14] It should also be noticed that there remains to this day some uncertainty as to who was earlier, Homer or Hesiod. There may be an instructive uncertainty here: in one sense, Homer is prior, but in another, Hesiod is.[15]

It should be noticed as well that there is in Homer no systematic account of the beginning of the gods, to say nothing of the beginning of the universe or of cosmic forces. There is not even much attention paid explicitly by Homer to the beginning of the Great War in which the Achaeans and the Trojans find themselves. Rather, there is in Homer's *Iliad* a detailed account of the beginning of a quarrel, between Achilles and Agamemnon, late in a very long war. This leads to a detailed account of one episode in that war, an extended episode which says much about the overall war, if not also about the world itself.[16]

Why is not Homer openly concerned about the beginning of things? Is it partly because this does not seem to be a concern of his characters? *They* take the world, including the gods, as *given*. Whether or not the gods are really *given* for Homer personally, he is willing to make them seem so, even as he presents events and results in such a way that few if any of them may require the much-spoken-of gods for them to be understood in human terms. This does not deny that Homer presents events and their consequences in the terms of human beings who are very much open to the gods.[17]

Much of what Homer, or a particularly gifted predecessor, does can be understood to prepare the way for Hesiod: the language is developed, a poetic meter, the hexameter, is established, and the audience is shaped. This can be said even though Hesiod seems more primitive, and hence earlier, than Homer in some respects, especially with his cataloguing of gods and others.[18]

II.

We can now look more directly at Hesiod and his beginnings by returning to the account of the *Theogony* in our encyclopedist:

> The cosmogony begins with Chaos ("yawning space"), Earth, [Tartarus,] and Eros (the principle of sexual love—a precondition of genealogical development). The first ruler of the world is Ouranos ("Heaven"). His persistent intercourse with Earth [who had generated him on her own] hinders the birth of his children, the Titans, until Kronos, the youngest, castrates him. Kronos later tries to suppress his own children by swallowing them, but Zeus, the youngest, is saved and makes Kronos regurgitate the others. The younger gods [led by Zeus] defeat the Titans after a ten-year war and consign them to Tartarus, below the earth, so that they no longer play a part in the world's affairs.[19]

Our encyclopedist then adds:

> This saga of successive rulers is evidently related to mythical accounts known from older Hittite and Babylonian sources. Hesiod's genealogy names some three hundred gods. Besides cosmic entities (Night, Sea, Rivers, etc.) and gods of myth and cult, it includes personified abstractions such as Strife, Deceit, Victory, and Death. Several alternative theogonies came into existence in the three centuries after Hesiod, but his remained the most widely read.[20]

Hesiod's account of the origins of the things which he can see and has heard about culminates in the emergence of the supreme and now supposedly unchallengeable rule of Zeus. Here, as elsewhere, the end may help shape the beginning, providing that by which the poet takes his bearings. Gods other than those Hesiod mentions are worshiped elsewhere, such as the Egyptian divinities, but these, whatever Hesiod may have heard or thought about them, are ignored by him.

Hesiod works, then, with what he observes: the earth beneath, the heaven above (which always keeps its distance), perhaps the under-earth, and those erotic relations among living beings which are so critical for "peopling" the world. Along with these can be observed human beings and "evidences" among the Boeotians, if not among the Greeks at large, of the divine, such as shrines, altars, and stories about the gods, as well as their names. Also to be observed is how things do not stay the same: sometimes considerable effort is needed in order to keep things going; sometimes all the effort immediately available cannot be used effectively to preserve things as they have been. This may suggest that the element of chaos is always near, if not with, us. Among the vulnerable things, Hesiod could notice, are the gods themselves, as memories and other signs survive of divinities which have been permanently, or at least long, eclipsed.

It can be gathered from Hesiod's account that it was difficult, if not impossible, to celebrate properly any divinities who appeared before Zeus and his colleagues manifested themselves. That is, Zeus is recognized as responsible for the song and perhaps the poetry critical to any celebrations that are likely to depend upon and endure as extended if not comprehensive accounts of the gods.[21] Thus, in order for Hesiod to present his account of the beginnings (or birth) of the gods, he must describe, however briefly, how he himself got *to be*—that is, how *he* began as a singer or, as we would say, as a poet. Without the inspiration available from the Muses, daughters of Zeus, Hesiod would be like most if not all human beings everywhere, merely a "belly" living as little more than an animal dominated by pleasure, fear, and pain.[22]

Piety, in Hesiod's time, consists then of celebrating the regime of Zeus, which is comprehensive in its ministering to the potential that human beings have for maturation, understanding, and justice.[23]

III.

Why does not Hesiod say that the divine is always? Can this be said, with sustainable plausibility, only about a single unchanging god? Hesiod inherits a theology which includes not only Zeus as dominant, but also a history both of other divinities and of how Zeus's current ascendancy was established. Perhaps any divine history that is going to be interesting as a story requires a variety of named gods who rise and fall. Almighty Zeus himself first comes to view in the *Theogony* as Kronion ("son of Knonos"); even he cannot be understood completely on his own.[24]

It has been noticed that the "Succession Myth" forms the backbone of Hesiod's *Theogony*: "It relates how Ouranos was overcome by Kronos, and how Kronos with his Titans was in his turn overcome by Zeus. It is not told as a self-contained piece, but in separate episodes, as each generation of gods arises."[25] An account is given by Hesiod of Ouranos's eighteen children by Earth and Kronos's six children by Rhea, before the poet turns to the struggles of Zeus to establish himself and thereafter to secure himself in his rule.[26]

The overall account begins, as has been said, with Chaos, Earth, Tartarus, and Eros somehow emerging, evidently each of the four separately from the other three, into effective being.[27] Nothing seems to be said by Hesiod about what was prior to these four. Nor does anything seem to be said by him about what caused Chaos, Earth, Tartarus, and Eros to come into being, if that is what they did, or to manifest themselves when and where they did.[28]

There is about Chaos, Earth, Tartarus, and Eros something more durable, if not eternal, than there is about the divinities that come to view, beginning with Ouranos, who is produced by Earth on her own, and followed by the children of Earth and Ouranos, especially Kronos, and followed in turn by the children of Kronos and his sister Rhea, especially Zeus. The sequence begins with Earth's production of Ouranos (or Heaven or Sky)—this makes sense, not only in that the Earth provides the stage upon which all of this action takes place, but also in that what the sky is, as distinguished from all the vastness of the universe, is somehow keyed to the dimensions of the earth, with Ouranos completely covering Earth.[29]

Nothing is said about "the place" where all of these beings appear. Does their very appearance, "wherever," establish *the* place?[30] Does Earth emerge to provide a place for gods as well as for human beings? She does produce Ouranos on her own, but not Tartarus and Eros which emerge after her, perhaps in relation to her. That is, Tartarus's location is defined by Earth's. Eros exerts an influence among beings on or near Earth, including among the Olympian gods. Chaos is always there, it seems, perhaps as an alternative. It is after Chaos, or alongside Chaos, but *not* necessarily *out of*

Chaos, that the generations of divinities and human beings manifest themselves.[31]

We are left to wonder what it may be, what it is that is "always," which accounts for the emergence of Chaos and Earth, each of which has the capacity to produce others on her own, others who will then be able to help engender still others.[32]

IV.

The gods, including those who are supreme for a while, do not emerge independently as Earth seems to do (along with Chaos, Tartarus, and Eros). Instead, the gods who are shown as, in turn, supreme (Ouranos, Kronos, and Zeus) are generated by others.[33] We can wonder whether only generated beings can have fates. (Again we might ask, What if anything is it that is "always" which is responsible for the fates?) In their susceptibility to fate the generated gods resemble human beings. Ouranos, Kronos, and perhaps Zeus were fated to be overthrown—and each took measures which (in the case of Ouranos and Kronos) might have made their overthrow even more likely.[34]

The vulnerability of these deathless gods—Ouranos, Kronos, if not also Zeus—may be related to their having been generated: that is, each has come out of another; they were, before they manifested themselves, confined in another. Perhaps this makes them susceptible to being confined thereafter by adversaries, most obviously so in the case of Kronos. Kronos and his siblings are confined by their father Ouranos in the womb of their mother Earth; Kronos in turn swallows and thereby confines his children, all but Zeus, in his womblike stomach.[35]

What about the fate of Zeus? He, like Kronos before him, is warned by Earth and Ouranos that a son of his would surpass him. And he, like Ouranos and Kronos before him, takes preventive measures, using in effect the technique relied upon by his grandfather and father, but doing it more effectively. Here is how this is summed up:

> Zeus is now elected king of the gods. He apportions their functions, and undertakes a series of marriages to establish order and security in the new regime. His first wife, Metis, is destined to bear a son stronger than Zeus; but Zeus, instead of waiting to swallow the child, as Kronos had done, swallows Metis, thus halting the cycle of succession. (881-929)[36]

We are left to wonder precisely how the prophecy to Zeus had been put. For instance, did it say that *if* he had a son by Metis, he would be overthrown by him?[37] Hesiod does not address this question: one is left to wonder whether it interested him. We do learn that Metis, when she was swallowed by Zeus, was already with child by him—and this is what leads to Athena being born from the head of Zeus.

Perhaps Zeus, in swallowing Metis (or *Cleverness?*), incorporates prudence within himself, thereby personally becoming something other than what he had been. Perhaps, indeed, Zeus can even be said to have been supplanted in this sense. Does Hesiod understand that the reign of Zeus, perhaps because of his defensive prudence, is dedicated to justice much more than the preceding reigns of Ouranos and Kronos had been?[38]

V.

It has been said, as we have seen, that succession struggles among the gods dominate the *Theogony*. Other stories are told, some at considerable length, but the succession struggles provide the core around which the other stories are organized. We see in Homer's *Iliad* how Zeus can "physically" threaten the other Olympian gods effectively.[39]

But Earth cannot be overcome in the way that, say, Ouranos can be. Earth does provide the stage upon or around which all of the named gods act. And it is on Earth that *we* have seen the eclipse of Zeus since the time of Hesiod and Homer. Does this suggest that Zeus never "really" existed? Or is it a fulfillment of the prophecy about any son that Zeus may have by Metis? Did that son somehow get conceived, in one sense or another of *conceived?*

There is here a way of accounting for the prophecy to Zeus which a Christian Hesiod might, in the spirit, say, of St. Augustine, try to do something with. That is, something mysterious can be said to have gone on here, of which the pagans could have had no more than intimations, something consistent perhaps with the deification of the *Logos* recorded in the opening chapter of the *Gospel of John*, a gospel in which classical Greek influences are quite evident.[40]

VI.

Human beings are secondary in the account laid out in the *Theogony*: there is not evident in that poem the concern with human beings that can be seen elsewhere in inspired texts, such as in the Christian Gospels. The life of human beings is described more in Hesiod's *Works and Days*, with much said there about everyday life.[41] A different succession story may be seen there, with five stages of mortals described.

Five seems to be an inauspicious number for Hesiod, with the fifth stage of mortals on Earth representing quite a decline from the opening golden and silver ages.[42] Perhaps *five* can be seen as well in the development of *Theogony*, which is a kind of "works and days" survey for the gods: these are the stages, in turn, of (1) Chaos, Earth, Tartarus, and Eros; (2) Ouranos and his progeny; (3) Kronos and his progeny, which may have been, in some ways, the best time for human beings; (4) Zeus and his divine wives and progeny, as well as the progeny of Zeus and other divinities with mortals; and (5) the career, perhaps yet to come, of Zeus's son by Metis, which would be a departure, if not a decline, from that age of Zeus which Hesiod is commissioned by the Muses to celebrate.[43]

Thus, the correspondences between Hesiod's two great poems may be worth exploring. Further correspondences include the fact that there is in both poems the suggestion that femaleness is an affliction among human beings, if not also among the gods. Still, does not femaleness testify to male incompleteness and hence to the vulnerability of human beings? (Is not the female, more than the male, able to produce offspring alone?) Furthermore, Earth and Rhea are critical to the overthrow of Ouranos and Kronos. The biblical parallels here, going back to the Garden of Eden, can be intriguing.[44]

The correspondences between *Theogony* and *Works and Days* may include indications that the gods are somewhat dependent upon human beings, and not only for sacrifice and worship. When human beings change, especially in the opinions they hold, so may the gods change somehow, if not even disappear. Besides, the gods of Hesiod and Homer are said to have the physical forms, and all too often the passions, of human beings.

We can again be reminded of Maimonides, not least for his insistence that the God of the Bible should never be understood to have a human form or human attributes.[45] In addition, we have been taught, "The Bible is the document of the greatest effort ever made to deprive all heavenly bodies of all possibility of divine worship."[46] Even so, we should also be reminded, as has been said, "In the poetry of Homer, Hesiod, and Aeschylus, the myths of the gods are a source of order."[47]

VII.

We return, as we prepare to close the first part of our inquiry on this occasion, to the questions touched upon at the outset of this appendix on beginnings: Is an end implied by *any* beginning? Is there expected, in the temporal sense, an end to the gods depicted by Hesiod and Homer? And is there, in the sense of the purpose of their existence, an end or aim?

Little, if anything, is suggested in Hesiod about the immortality of human souls, whatever may be understood about those rare mortals, such as Zeus's son, Heracles, who are eventually transformed into immortals. What should be expected of the cosmos that is described in the *Theogony*? Should it be expected to continue forever?

Chaos and Earth, we are told in the *Theogony*, did come into view, if not into being, evidently on their own. Might they somehow go away eventually, perhaps to return and leave over and over? Is there, for example, something about Chaos, Earth, and Eros, if not also about the particular gods generated in Hesiod's account—is there something which endures, however hidden from view these beings may be from time to time, just as can be said about the Ideas which are perpetually available to be discovered and to shape and nourish reason?[48]

Although Hesiod and Homer do not seem to recognize and address such questions explicitly, they can be said to have helped prepare the ground for the philosophers who would first discover these and like questions to be so much in the very nature of things that they are properly the end of the account which an inspired poet may offer as a beginning.[49]

Part Two. The Bible

> And Gideon said unto God, "If Thou wilt save Israel by my hand, as Thou hast spoken, behold I will put a fleece of wool on the threshing-floor; if there be dew on the fleece only, and it be dry upon all the ground, then shall I know that Thou wilt save Israel by my hand, as Thou hast spoken." And it was so; for he rose up early on the morrow, and pressed the fleece together, and wrung dew out of the fleece, a bowlful of water. And Gideon said unto God, "Let not Thine anger be kindled against me; and I will speak but this once: let me make trial, I pray Thee, but this once more with the fleece; let it now be dry only upon the fleece, and upon all the ground let there be dew." And God did so that night; for it was dry upon the fleece only, but there was dew on all the ground.
>
> —Anonymous[50]

We need do no more on this occasion than remind the reader of beginnings in the Bible, thereby pointing up aspects of the Hesiodic account in part 1 of this appendix and preparing the ground for the scientific account in part 3. Our principal source here is the *Book of Genesis*, the very name of which refers to origins or beginnings.[51]

Seven forms of beginnings are either described or anticipated in *Genesis*. First, there is the beginning of the world itself, as set forth in the first chapter of *Genesis*.[52] Then there is the beginning of the human race, with its twofold creation and its indelible experiences in the Garden of Eden.[53] Then there is the beginning of the troubled career of the human race outside of the Garden, starting with the fatal conflict between Cain and Abel and ending with the devastating Flood attributed to human wickedness.[54]

A new beginning for the human race follows in *Genesis* after the Flood, leaving the descendants of Noah subject to the Noahide Law which can be said to continue to govern most of mankind.[55] Then there is the beginning of the people of Israel, the descendants of Abraham, Isaac, and Jacob, who are to have a special relation with God, with profound implications for the rest of the human race.[56] Then there is, in *Genesis*, an anticipation of the beginning, or liberation from Egypt and Egyptian ways and hence the revitalization, of the people of Israel under the leadership of Moses and his successors who promulgate and administer a comprehensive system of laws for the life and well-being of a designated people.[57]

Finally there is, also as an anticipation in *Genesis*, the beginning of the career of the people of Israel in the Promised Land and thereafter, with exiles and returns, with priests and kings, with triumphs and disasters.[58]

In all seven of these accounts, it seems to be assumed that things cannot be properly understood without some recognition of whatever beginnings they may have had. Each of these accounts has inspired libraries of commentaries, which testifies both to their richness and to their elusiveness.

The first two words of the Septuagint, a pre-Christian Greek translation of the Hebrew Bible, are *En arché* ("In the beginning").[59] Christian theology evidently drew upon this *Genesis* account by using the same Greek words to open the *Gospel of John*—but there, instead of the making of the world by God being "in the beginning," the Word—*Logos*, or the divine itself—was "in the beginning."[60]

This reminds us, if reminder we need, that there is no account in *Genesis* of the beginning of the divine: the divine seems to have been regarded as existing "always"—and hence as mysterious. We have seen in the *Theogony*, as we can see in many other such accounts elsewhere, how the gods came into being, whatever there may have always been "somewhere" or "somehow" before the birth of the named gods described by Hesiod.

I turn now—not without an awareness of my limitations as a layman here—to the way that modern science can approach these matters, that way of accounting for things which combines somehow the emergence of the idea of nature in classical Greece and the almost instinctive respect for rationality in the Bible.[61]

That is, the world of the Bible—whether the Hebrew Bible or the Greek Bible—is more or less orderly, especially when compared to the worlds of the great nonbiblical religions of the human race. Due recognition should be given to the considerable physical stability as well as to the challenging shrewdness evident in the Bible, both of which elements may be seen in the career of Gideon. Both of these—in the forms of an acceptance of the idea of nature, developed among the Greeks, and of a respect for rational discourse, evident in the Bible—are very much taken for granted by modern science, as well as by its predecessors.[62]

Part Three. Modern Science

It can scarcely be denied that at the present time physics and philosophy, two sciences of recognized durability, each handed down in a continuous tradition, are estranged from one another; they oppose one another more or less uncomprehendingly. By the Nineteenth Century a real and hence effective mutual understanding between philosophers and physicists concerning the methods, presuppositions, and meaning of physical research had already become basically impossible; this remained true even when both parties, with great goodwill and great earnestness, tried to reach a clear understanding of these issues.

—Jacob Klein[63]

I.

There is in modern cosmology far less of an opportunity than in other sciences to have theories guided and validated either by experiments or by how attempted applications "work." There is, instead, an unleashing among cosmologists of an imagination, poetic or rhetorical in some respects, that can be a key to professional success. The layman rarely senses how little the cosmologists have available to go on and how much something akin to fantasy has to be relied upon by them. Although most physics today is much more sober, a glance at contemporary cosmology can help the layman, who can be quite uncritical in response to spectacular announcements by scientists, to notice some of the temptations to which all of modern science may be subject.[64]

Consider, as a particularly dramatic illustration, a remarkably popular book by an English cosmologist, Stephen Hawking's *A Brief History of Time*.[65] His book comes to us with the authority—or is it the burden?—of more than two years on the *New York Times* best-seller list.

An examination of the Hawking book can be a useful way to investigate a few aspects of the character of modern science and what it is we seek by our recourse to science. Are we truly wiser (and not only about beginnings), we must wonder, because of books such as this and the work they report?[66]

A Brief History of Time and its remarkable author have been conveniently described for us by the publisher in words that sometimes echo the author's. I draw here upon the opening and closing paragraphs of the dust jacket of the book (first published in 1988):

> Stephen W. Hawking has achieved international prominence as one of the great minds of the twentieth century. Now, for the first time, he has written a popular work exploring the outer limits of our knowledge of astrophysics and the nature of time and the universe. The result is a truly enlightening book: a classic introduction to today's most important scientific ideas about the cosmos, and a unique opportunity to experience the intellect of one of the most imaginative, influential thinkers of our age.
>
> From the vantage point of the wheelchair where he has spent the last twenty years trapped by Lou Gehrig's disease, Professor Hawking himself has transformed our view of the universe. His groundbreaking research into black holes offers clues to that elusive moment when the universe was born. Now, in the incisive style which is his trademark, Professor Hawking shows us how mankind's "world picture" evolved from the time of Aristotle through the 1915 breakthrough of Albert Einstein, to the exciting ideas of today's prominent young physicists.
>
> . . . *A Brief History of Time* is a landmark book written for those of us who prefer words to equations. Told by an extraordinary contributor to the ideas of humankind, this is the story of the ultimate quest for knowledge, the ongoing search for the secrets at the heart of time and space.
>
> Stephen W. Hawking is forty-six years old. He was born on the [three-hundredth] anniversary of Galileo's death, holds Newton's chair as Lucasian Professor of Mathematics at Cambridge University, and is widely regarded as the most brilliant theoretical physicist since Einstein.[67]

This somewhat extravagant description of book and author by the publisher is accentuated by the eerie picture of the author on the cover.

The contents of the Hawking book are further suggested by the following passage on its dust jacket:

> Was there a beginning of time? Will there be an end? Is the universe infinite? Or does it have boundaries? With these fundamental questions in mind, Hawking reviews the great theories of the cosmos—and all the puzzles, paradoxes and contradictions still unresolved. With great care he explains Galileo's and Newton's discoveries.
>
> Next he takes us step-by-step through Einstein's general theory of relativity (which concerns the extraordinarily vast) and then moves on to the other great theory of our century, quantum mechanics (which concerns the extraordinarily tiny). And last, he explores the worldwide effort to combine the two into a single quantum theory of gravity, the unified theory, which should resolve all the mysteries left unsolved—and he tells why he believes that momentous discovery is not far off.
>
> Professor Hawking also travels into the exotic realms of deep space, distant galaxies, black holes, quarks, GUTs, particles with "flavors" and "spin," antimatter, and

the "arrows of time"—and intrigues us with their unexpected implications. He reveals the unsettling possibilities of time running backward when an expanding universe collapses, a universe with as many as eleven dimensions, a theory of a "no-
boundary" universe that may replace the big bang theory and a God who may be
increasingly fenced in by new discoveries—who may be the prime mover in the creation of it all.[68]

Many of the things said here by the publisher about the Hawking book are
of general interest to us, commenting as they in effect do upon the modern
scientific approach. Hawking's special interests and theories may pass in
time, but the scientific project continues. We may usefully consider that project by observing various features of it as exhibited in this book.

A prominent feature of the scientific project today is its abandonment—
perhaps, from its point of view, its necessary abandonment—of what is generally regarded as common sense. The ancient scientist was much more respectful of that common sense, and this is sometimes seen today to have
contributed to his limitations. Modern physical scientists consider themselves
fortunate to have been liberated from such restraints.[69]

Still, common sense continues to be relied upon, for much is inherited from
our predecessors without our recognizing it. But since we often do not notice
what is indeed inherited, we sometimes make inadequate use of it, if only in
our efforts to understand what we are doing.[70] Modern scientists can seem
rather amateurish, therefore, in explaining the basis or presuppositions for the
wonderful things they do come up with.

Consider how much common sense, as commonly understood, is still with
us even in the most exotic scientific activities today. Elementary observing and
counting depend upon ordinary experience. Common sense is needed to direct
us to the relevant observations, to determine how many observations suffice,[71]
even to assure us that a particular collection of data is from our laboratory assistant, not from, say, our stockbroker. Common sense is needed as well in
hooking up equipment, in reading dials, in deciding how accurate one has to
be, in sorting out aberrations. In addition, common sense has to be drawn upon
in what is to be understood as cause and effect and in what is to be understood
as a contradiction, if not also in what the significance of contradictions is.[72]

I now put my commonsense point in another form: what is the role of judgment in science? Albert Einstein's old-fashioned reservations about critical
modern theories should be taken more seriously than younger scientists today
evidently do. God, he insisted, "does not throw dice."[73] If one does *not* have
deep common sense and good judgment, can one be reliably "in tune" with
nature and the universe? I will have more to say about this further on.

The ancients (because they had far less evidence to work with?) seem to
have been more sober than modern scientists in assessments of the alterna-

tives they confronted. The practical judgment of the ancients was more evident even in theoretical matters. We may be more accustomed than they to a kind of madness in speculative work, from which our proliferating science-fiction literature and fantasy films are derivations.[74] One consequence of the differences between ancients and moderns is that the rate of change, for reigning theories as well as far everyday practice, was much lower for the ancients than it is for us.

The modern propensity for innovation may be seen in the series of novelties conjured up by Hawking in his relatively short career, some of which novelties have already had to be repudiated by him. Another way of putting this reservation is to say that Hawking is astonishingly brilliant, especially as a puzzle solver, but not truly thoughtful.[75] Still another way of putting all this is to observe that I do not recall another book from a man of his stature with so many questionable comments in it.[76] One does not always have the impression of a mature mind at work here. This may be related to the prominence in these matters, as noticed on the dust jacket and reported in the book, of young physicists. The role here of mathematics may also contribute to the overall effect.[77]

II.

It is important to notice the contributions of modern technology, itself dependent upon and permitted by modern science, in developing scientific discoveries.[78] In fact, the character of "discoveries" is likely to be affected by the "character" of the technology relied upon. There may be a self-perpetuating spiral here. Whether such a spiral is up or down remains to be seen.

We should be reminded again and again of how slim the physical evidence is that is usually exploited for the most fanciful cosmological speculations, a practice that can be said to go back to Ptolemy and his colleagues. (The contemporary scientist is apt to observe here that the modern evidence is much better than that which supports either Hesiod or *Genesis*). We should also be reminded that the fundamental alternatives about the cosmos, including with respect to its extent and its origins, may have been noticed long, long ago. It does not seem to me that Hawking and his associates appreciate what their predecessors routinely faced up to—and in sophisticated ways.

One consequence of the volatility of modern scientific thought is that bizarre things tend to be promoted, which should not be surprising whenever ingenuity and innovation are encouraged and rewarded. Radical changes can be made, as with respect to Hubble's Constant—changes which require stupendous curtailment or enlargement of the estimated age, extent or "population" of the universe. These remarkable changes, which *are* consistent with a large body of established mathematical theory, can sometimes seem to be made without blinking an eye.[79]

Hawking does caution against jumping to conclusions; he encourages people to admit their mistakes. But is not much of modern science (or at least those who describe it to the public) peculiarly susceptible to rashness and consequent bad judgment?[80] Again, one wonders whether all this is conducive to the sobriety and thoughtfulness that may be necessary for a sound grasp of fundamental issues in science just as in, say, theology.

Hawking may be most obviously a modern scientist in his inability to grasp what predecessors such as Aristotle said, an inability that reveals his own limitations. Whenever he reaches back—if not even to Isaac Newton, certainly to before Newton—he is apt to be sloppy if not simply wrong.[81]

Consider, for example, his remarks about why Aristotle believed the earth to be at rest. Aristotle is seen, here as elsewhere, to have been "mystical."[82] There is no recognition of what we have long been told about the parallax with respect to the fixed stars expected to be observed if the earth is really in a great orbit around the sun, and about the significance of the inability of observers of Aristotle's day and for centuries thereafter, with their equipment, to detect such parallax. Much of what is said by Hawking about predecessors such as Aristotle and Ptolemy is trivial stuff, evidently picked up from unreliable "pop" history.[83] Yet various experts seem to have let him get away with this sort of thing, both before and after publication of this book. Why is that? Because they do not know better themselves? Or because they do not believe it matters? I suspect there is something of both explanations here.

It is a sign of bad judgment not to be more careful in these matters, not to check things out, and perhaps most important (as Socrates taught us) not to be aware of how much one does not know. It is this bad judgment which contributes to a mode of scientific endeavor that permits, if it does not actually encourage, all kinds of wild things to be tossed around and regarded as profound efforts. Another way of putting these observations is to suggest that all too many competent scientists today do not appreciate that the best of their ancient predecessors may have been at least as intelligent as they are.

The three biographies appended to Hawking's book confirm that his limitations are not confined to reports on the ancients. In those biographies, three of the modern heroes of science, Einstein, Galileo, and Newton, are dealt with.[84] For many readers, the Hawking biographies may be the only extended accounts they will ever have of these men. This is not fair either to these men or to the typical reader. Newton, for example, is dramatized as a sadistic self-seeker.[85]

An intelligent high school student with access to standard reference works could be expected to do better than Hawking (or his research assistant) does here. Such a student might also ask himself what the purpose of such biographies might be, something which is far from clear in this book. The "history" thereby provided is rather flimsy.[86]

What, according to Hawking, are scientists really after? One thing that scientists seem to be after, he indicates, is the Nobel Prize. The reader can be surprised by how often Hawking feels compelled to mention that this or that discovery had earned a Nobel.

Related to this may be the use he makes of chance relations, such as the fact that he was born three hundred years after Galileo died.[87] Similar connections are made with Newton. We can suspect here the spirit of astrology, perhaps not surprising in an age when so much is made, and not only by pollsters, of numbers.[88]

Even as Hawking connects himself with Galileo and Newton, he shows himself "with it" in comments and illustrations which draw upon passing fancies. In all this, in short, a lack of seriousness may be detected.

I have touched upon various things that contribute to the popular success of the book, a success which may be a tribute as well to the recognized eminence of Hawking as a physicist. The successful mixture here of the high and the low is similar to what we can observe in other surprising best-sellers from recognized scholars. In such cases, the authors can have previously shown themselves to be capable of much more competent work.[89]

What *do* readers get from the Hawking book? They are both flattered and reassured. They are led to believe that they now understand things that they did not understand before or, at least, that they have been exposed to some wonderful things.

But I must wonder if much is gotten in the way of a serious understanding of things. There is much in the book which is serious sounding, but a good deal of that is really incomprehensible.[90] Indeed, much of the book must be unintelligible for most of its purchasers.[91] Furthermore, the typical reader is likely to be misled as to what the fundamental alternatives are in facing the cosmological questions that are glanced at in the Hawking book, fundamental alternatives that have been developed long ago and far more competently elsewhere.

III.

Hawking and his colleagues, I have suggested, do not appreciate how naive they can be. They are certainly intelligent, even gifted, hardworking, and imaginative. Yet, I have also suggested, they all too often lack the kind of productive sobriety that obliges one to take the world seriously and that disciplines flights of fancy. They sometimes seem far from accomplished in their grasp of how the thoughtful investigate serious matters, and of how they promulgate their discoveries and conjectures.

Another way of putting my reservations is to suggest that Hawking and his associates do not know what a real book is like.[92] One who is not practiced in reading carefully is unlikely to write with the greatest care.[93] Is the cosmos of the modern cosmologist as shallow as his book? If it is not, then the modern cosmologist may not be equipped to have a soulful encounter with the cosmos. No doubt, competent scientific work can be done without the utmost seriousness—but are not great souls required for the highest activities?[94]

It may not be possible to read or write with the greatest care if one is imbued with our modern prejudices. One such prejudice is that of the Enlightenment, as illustrated in the concluding paragraph of the Hawking volume. It is there suggested that "if we do discover a complete theory [which concerns both the extraordinarily vast and the extraordinarily tiny], it should in time be understandable in broad principle by everyone, not just a few scientists." Hawking goes on, "Then we shall all, philosophers, scientists, and just ordinary people, be able to take part in the discussion of the question of why it is that we and the universe exist."[95]

Such egalitarian sentiments are found elsewhere in the volume as well. This hope or expectation is very much in the Enlightenment tradition, and it may be reflected in the intriguing popularity of this volume. It is not recognized, however, what the limits are as to how many can grasp the most serious things. That is, the limits placed here both by nature and by circumstances are not taken into account.

Related to this can be the irresponsibility exhibited by all too many intellectuals in how they present what they come to believe. The social, moral, and psychic consequences of ideas are not properly assessed.

We have been told that 85 percent of all the scientists who have ever lived are alive today. Their influence is evident and so are their marvelous works. But since they are usually no more thoughtful than most of their fellow citizens, the dubious consequences of many of their innovations, in their intellectual as well as in their technological manifestations, are also evident.

The immaturity, even the not-infrequent juvenile cast of expression, among contemporary scientists may be sanctioned, if not encouraged, by the insulating effects of the mathematics so critical to modern scientific activity. The spirit here is very much that of games, especially of those sports in which much is made of record keeping and of statistics.[96] The childishness evident in contemporary scientific enterprises may well be accompanied by, and depend for success upon, considerable ingenuity and a laudable integrity.

Childishness is not unrelated to the self-centeredness that sometimes seems to be, in principle, at the heart of the scientific method today. Self-centeredness may be seen in the anthropic-principle explanations of the universe as understood by contemporary scientists.[97] It sometimes seems to be believed that things exist only if there is, in principle, a human observer.[98]

Common sense does *not* say what contemporary cosmologists, if not physicists, generally seem to say, "If I *cannot* know it, it does not exist—or, at least, it has no consequences."[99] Nor does such a spirit (which can remind one of Plato's Meno) encourage genuine inquiry, but rather limits us to looking into matters that promise "results."[100] We all know that what may seem to be the limits of "knowability" in one generation may be superseded in another—and yet what is "real" is hardly likely to have changed over the years.[101]

Besides, is it true what is often said by cosmologists, that we cannot possibly know anything about what happened before the Big Bang? May there not have been, for instance, an extraordinary compacting then of the matter that resulted in the Big Bang? What can be known about *that*, if it did happen? It will not do to say that "events before the big bang can have no consequences," for informed conjectures about such events, however difficult they may be to grasp "scientifically" and thus "verify," can affect the grasp we have of the whole.[102]

The anthropic-principle explanations taken up by some modern scientists are not of the kind seen in the *Book of Genesis*. Nor do they seem of the kind which sees reason as vital to the universe, as that to which energy can be said to be naturally moving. One implication of the anthropic-principle approach seems to be that if anything had been even a little different in the laws of physics, conditions would be hard if not impossible for human beings as we know them. This might bear upon the status of the Ideas in the world.[103]

To argue, as some do, that only the measurable exists so as to be knowable is to make too much of the way—the remarkably productive way—we do happen to approach scientific inquiries today. Hawking recognizes, "In effect, we have redefined the task of science to be the discovery of laws that will enable us to predict events."[104] Various animals effectively "predict" events—and yet they surely do not understand what is going on.[105]

The earth, we are often reminded, is no longer regarded as at the center of the universe. It sometimes seems, however, that the centrality of the earth has been replaced by the centrality of the scientist: for whatever *he* cannot measure does not exist, at least for practical purposes if not also for human understanding. The predictability made so much of by the scientist does rely considerably upon measuring.[106]

That which can be measured is no doubt important. But if genuine understanding is not truly limited to that, even in scientific endeavors, then for scientists to proceed as they do is to subvert the possibility of human excellence. Reviewers of the Hawking volume do not seem to be aware of the serious epistemological problems left both by what he says and by the way he says it.

I conclude my primary critique of this volume by saying that it is hard for me to see that we know more because of all this. It does not seem to be generally appreciated, I have argued, how slim the evidence is that Hawking builds upon or how even slimmer is all too many scientists' understanding of what it means *to know*. The approach and spirit of current cosmology may effectively cut us off from the most thoughtful awareness of the fundamental issues posed by the inquiries touched upon here. There may even be something unnatural in making so much of so little in the way that modern cosmologists "have" to do, exciting though it may sometimes be.[107]

IV.

What, one may well ask, does nature suggest here? Although I will continue to comment upon the Hawking volume, it is only fair, after the criticisms I have presumed to make, to put myself at risk by venturing now some "cosmological" speculations of my own.

Nature, taken by herself, means (to repeat) that there need be neither a beginning nor an end to the universe.[108] This in turn means, as Hawking sometimes seems to recognize, that there need be no beginning of time, however limited the means may be in one set of circumstances or another for noticing or measuring the passage of time. Nature seen in this way is opposed, at least in spirit, to the professional, not necessarily any personal, self-centeredness of modern scientists. Thus, nature and self-centeredness contend for the central position in the human soul, if not in the universe.[109]

A somewhat different, perhaps laudable, kind of self-centeredness may also be seen in the goal set by Hawking, which is "to know why we are here and where we come from."[110] Much is made here and elsewhere of the universe as a place in which human beings live.[111] But, as both Hesiod and the Bible (as well as philosophy) have taught us, human beings may not be the highest things in the universe, and so to understand the universe primarily in human terms may not give it its due.[112]

Nor may it do to frame a study of the universe, or even of physics, as a history of *time*. To put it thus may make far too much of process and of human perceptions, not enough either of substance or of principles. This is not to suggest that it is unnatural for time to be made so much of by human beings who regard themselves as personally vulnerable.

But does not nature also direct us to look for those enduring things by which we can take our bearings as we notice and deal with the transitory? Hawking has in his volume a brief account of the origins of life on earth, with the eventual emergence of mammals.[113] This *seems* to me far easier to grasp than the astronomical, or cosmological, conjectures that he and his colleagues offer us, and it was fairly easy to grasp as well (however much it was opposed) when first developed by Charles Darwin and his associates a century and a half ago.[114] It also seems to me that this greater ease depends in part upon the fact that nature and a commonsense awareness of things may be closer to the surface of this evolutionary account than they are to the surface of many of the cosmological and other speculations of our physicists.

Is it not easier to believe that life on earth had a beginning, and even that the earth itself had a beginning, than it is to believe that the universe did? Aristotle evidently believed that the human understanding of things depends upon the opinion that the visible universe is eternal—that is, that it is more or less unchanging.[115] Since this evidently is not so, Aristotle seems to be vulnerable. But perhaps a sound intuition was at work in Aristotle, which may be appreciated when we recognize that "visibility" may extend far beyond what he could be immediately aware of in his circumstances.[116]

In some sense, then, things may always have been as they are now, with a variety of forms available for the enduring substance of the universe. The ancients who looked to cycles—ancients such as some of the Platonists and perhaps Lucretius—may also have been sound in their intuition.[117]

V.

Hawking talks at times (we have noticed) about a beginning of time with the Big Bang and at other times only about an ascertainable time beginning with the Big Bang. More seems to be made of the former than of the latter, as is reflected in the dust-jacket summary I have quoted. Would not the tenor and force of Hawking's argument change significantly if *the* beginning he makes so much of were simply recognized as merely the *most recent* cataclysmic "beginning," and as such no more than a useful starting point for our inquiries?

If we take the Big Bang seriously, must we not also consider the implications of something that has been called the Big Crunch—that concentration of matter which eventually led to the Big Bang? And why should we believe that we happen to be the beneficiaries of, or "tuned in" to, the only occasion that this sequence came about? Is not this too self-centered or otherwise unimaginative on our part?[118]

If, on the other hand, a cyclical pattern of Big Crunches and Big Bangs is assumed, what follows? Whether there was a beginning of time may be intimately related to whether there is a beginning of space. Here we can be reminded of Lucretius and his tireless spear thrower, repeatedly pushing back the "frontiers" of the universe.[119]

To argue as I have done just now is to speak from the perspective of human reason—albeit, perhaps, an unsophisticated reason—contemplating nature. We must leave open, at least at this point of our inquiry, the question of whether there is a genuine divine revelation—and, if so, which one of the many revelations that have been offered *it* may be—instructing us about a single beginning of time.[120]

However beginning-less (and hence infinite?) both time and space may be, it is hard, perhaps impossible, to imagine infinite matter. Do our cosmologists try to imagine that? I am not sure. They do talk about infinite density— the Big Crunch concentration of all matter into one point— at the time of, that is, culminating in, the Big Bang. If their calculations show all matter in the universe compacted to virtually a point—and if they mean this literally—my natural inclination (a kind of untutored defensiveness?) is to suggest that they had better calculate again. Lucretius was particularly insistent upon the good sense of recognizing what cannot be.[121]

We are investigating, in effect, the nature of science, that great work of the mind which is distinctively Western both in its origins and in its presuppositions. We should not forget that science must, like all reasoning, begin with premises which cannot themselves be demonstrated. Related to this is the fact that Newton, for example, does not define the matter of which he makes so much. No doubt, he could have done so, but the thing(s) in terms of which he did define matter would in turn have had to be left undefined. Perhaps he preferred to leave as his principal undefined premises those things which are sufficiently available to us by our natural grasp of the everyday world.[122]

The comprehensive account of the universe that the modern cosmologist aims at, as seen in the loose talk at the end of the Hawking volume about knowing "the mind of God," may be, in principle, impossible to attain. I suspect that it is also impossible to comprehend—that is, to grasp, describe, or understand—either the smallest element in the universe or the largest, that is, the universe itself. To try to comprehend them is like trying to demonstrate the premises that one uses. I do not pretend to *know* whether matter is infinitely divisible (whatever that may mean), but I have long wondered whether any ultimate "particle" can be both found and identified as such.[123]

I suspect that we see in the celebrated Uncertainty Principle of Werner Heisenberg a reflection of the impossibility of avoiding a dependence upon premises.[124] The ambition of modern cosmologists makes them less thoughtful than they might otherwise be, for it keeps them from recognizing and perhaps refining the premises they must inevitably depend upon.

VI.

Critical to our Hawking volume is a discussion of black holes. One can become particularly aware, upon considering the basis for the imaginative discourses we have had in recent years about black holes, how slim the basis for much scientific speculation has indeed had to be.[125]

Perhaps related to this state of affairs is what is said by modern cosmologists about chaos.[126] It is difficult to see, especially if the stuff of the universe does oscillate between Big Crunch and Big Bang, that any state can be considered truly chaotic. I again ask: Is it not possible, if not even probable, that matter, or at least the idea of matter, has always *been*, and hence has always been susceptible to the same "rules"? Why would the rules ever change, except in accordance with a rule of rules, or a cosmic constitutionalism?

Chaos may be, therefore, only a way of talking about our unsettling ignorance about any particular state of things. Among the things implicit in each state of things is the eventual emergence not only of life but even of reason. The potential for, if not even an "inclination" toward the emergence of, reasoning is thus always present in the universe.[127]

But to say that reason always *is*, in some form or other, does not mean that reason should be able on its own to understand the whole, including why the whole exists at all. The eternity of the universe probably cannot be demonstrated. But it does seem to be conceivable, whatever that may mean. And it may be vain, if not maddening, to wonder, or to insist upon wondering, why things "have" to exist at all. That is, there may be no place to stand upon in answering such a question.[128] Again, it is prudent to leave open the possibility of what genuine revelation may be able to teach us about such matters.

Is it not possible that matter has to be as it is, just as numbers have to be as they are, and perhaps reason (and not only human reason) as well? To what extent, or in what way, reason depends upon matter is another question better left perhaps for another occasion.[129]

It is possible (I again conjecture) that even the divine, however conceived, might be obliged to accept matter as well as number for what they are. One reading of the opening chapter of the *Book of Genesis* finds matter already in existence when the creation described there begins.[130] Also, when the days are being counted during Creation Week, it does not seem that the numbers drawn upon there, culminating in *seven*, are being created as well.

It may not make sense, therefore, to pursue very far the inquiry of why matter exists. Numbers can be used in describing the operations of matter—but, I again venture to suggest, we should be careful not to assume that the most important things to be known about anything, including matter, come to view only by way of measurements, with or without experiments.

Numbers can give us the appearance of orderliness and even of comprehensiveness, especially as they are projected indefinitely. But an awareness of important aspects of things may be sacrificed in the process. Consider, for example, the limitations of a census taker in grasping the spirit of a people. Consider, also, this suggestion by Bertrand Russell: "Physics is mathematical not because we know so much about the physical world, but because we know so little: it is only its mathematical properties that we can discover."[131]

VII.

One defect to be guarded against, especially by the more clever and talented among us, *is* presumptuousness. Presumptuousness is dependent, in part, upon a failure to appreciate what is assumed or presupposed—or, more generally speaking, upon a failure to recognize what has gone before or is always.

Thoughtfulness *is* needed for the most serious grasp of things. An awareness of one's limitations can contribute to, even if it does not guarantee, thoughtfulness. Such an awareness is far less likely to be secured if one is presumptuous—if, for example, one has been imbued with scientific doctrines which hold out the prospect of a comprehensive understanding of everything, including the very process and form of that understanding.

Why are people today as interested in cosmology as they evidently are? No doubt they simply want to know about the grandest things. That is natural enough. Perhaps also they seek material confirmation or reassurance about eternal matters, including as they bear upon the standards by which they live and understand. That, too, is natural enough. But does modern cosmology provide the means to grasp these things? Is there not a limit to what can be learned, even by a select few, about such things in this way?

The appeal for us of Hawking's fortitude and perseverance in the face of great personal adversity is a reflection of our own awareness of, and respect for, the significance and enduring worth of various virtues. Do we not have from him, here, access to something much more solid, even magnificently so, than the cosmological doctrines spun out of the flimsy data that even the most gifted scientists seem destined to have to settle for—and to replace from time to time?[132]

It is instructive here to be reminded that Socrates moved, in the course of his career, from such inquiries as contemplation of the heavens to a concern primarily with human things.[133] It is hardly likely that access to such instruments as electron microscopes and radio telescopes would have induced him to conduct himself otherwise.

To turn to human things, as Socrates says that he did, includes an effort to know oneself. Unless one knows oneself it may be difficult, if not impossible, to know reliably any other thing—for how can one be certain otherwise that one's own psyche does not distort what one believes one sees or how one reasons about such things?

But as one comes to know oneself and hence what it means to know, one may also learn that the whole cannot be truly and fully known by human beings. This may be one reason Socrates can speak of *philo*sophy or *love* of wisdom, not of wisdom itself, as that which characterizes the thoughtful human being.[134]

The evident limitations of even the most thoughtful may encourage many human beings to look to some faith in the divine as a way of providing them a meaningful universe. But if one is unsettled by the prospect of a universe without beginning, how does recourse to a God without beginning take care of one's sense of groundlessness?

It may be answered that God is unchanging, while matter, and hence the universe, is always changing. There is a sense, however, in which an eternal material universe, however varied its forms, is as unchanging as a divinity which is forever.[135] One may have to look elsewhere, then, for justification of that faith in the divine which has meant so much to so many for so long.

The "mind of God" talk of which so much is made in the Hawking volume and elsewhere can seem the essence of presumptuousness. It may be intended as a kind of piety, of course, however misconceived it may be. The fundamental innocence of such statements today is testified to, in effect, by the lack of reproof for these particular statements from most reviewers of the Hawking volume. Evidently this kind of talk is not taken to mean what it might have once been taken to mean.

The perhaps unbridgeable gulf, and hence the prudence of a truce, between Reason and Revelation may not be generally appreciated these days, however fundamental that gulf has been for millennia in Western thought.[136] The popular appeal of the Hawking volume may rest in part upon its being perceived as siding, in the name of science, with theology against philosophy, however much Christian theology in the West once considered itself in principle compatible with philosophy, thereby distinguishing itself in still another way from the various "schools" of non-Western thought.

Something of the divine is elicited by the enormous numbers invoked by the cosmologist. Thus we can be told, as if we are being offered a revelation, which should mean something to us, that a thousand billion stars have already been accounted for.[137] Are not numbers on this scale, whether applied to stars or galaxies or distances or time, simply incomprehensible, if not literally nonsense?

Numbers of this scope do suggest the magnitude of the divine. But they may not suggest the awesomeness of the truly holy, partly because they are numbers which are repeatedly being revised, almost (it can sometimes *seem*) at the whim of the cosmologist.[138]

How does the mythology of the modern cosmologists compare with the theology of our ancients, whether Greek or Judaic? We have to understand the old better than we now do in order to be able to answer this question—and for that understanding, a grasp of what each of these ways of thinking takes to be the *beginning* should be useful, if not even essential. Also useful here can be at least an informed awareness of what the non-Western "schools" of thought have revealed across millennia.

Be that as it may, we can see, in the considerable popular response to the kind of story of the universe told in the Hawking volume, why the Bible can be said to be "the document of the greatest effort ever made to deprive all heavenly bodies of all possibility of divine worship."[139]

Be that too as it may, we must wonder if the old mythology, if mythology it be, is keyed more to human capacities and expectations than is the new. One reliable model in responding to the speculations of modern cosmologists may well be that of Socrates' sober response to the ambitious speculations of Anaxagoras.[140]

Conclusion

Morale among physical scientists can be high, however much their efforts can remind one at times of the high-minded but ill-fated Children's Crusade. The enthusiasm of gifted students is stimulated, in large part, by the considerable talents and obvious dedication of their teachers, by the noble hope that the general understanding as well as the material conditions of mankind will be enhanced, and by the plausible perception that much has already been accomplished because of the technology generated by science. The more thoughtful scientists are not unaware of some of the reservations I have sketched on this occasion about the modern scientific project.[141] Particularly challenging is the question of what it is that the scientist is entitled to believe and to say on the basis of the evidence which happens to be available to him.[142]

To what extent should continual examination of the evidence that can be mustered in support of scientific speculation include assessments of the technology to which these speculations have contributed? We can still see, in various parts of Europe, North Africa, and the Middle East, Roman aqueducts, perhaps often repaired if not rebuilt since antiquity, that carry water as they did thousands of years ago. The technology of the Romans has continued to work long after the natural sciences of their day were superseded if not even discredited. It is instructive thus to notice that a "theory" may "work"—it may have substantial practical applications—even if not strictly or fully true. Many are the marvels associated with modern science—not least with the technology inspired by and otherwise keyed to modern science—but these marvels should not be taken to validate that science, certainly not to validate it unqualifiedly when it speculates about the beginnings of things. Similar comments can be made about the religious foundations upon which great enterprises have been reared and sustained for centuries, if not even for millennia, all over the world.

A story I once heard at the weekly physics department colloquium at the University of Chicago, which I have attended regularly for decades, assures us (as do other stories) that some scientists are alert to the follies to which unbridled speculation can lead: Two American engineers who had made fortunes developed a passion for archaeology. This led them to purchase villas in Rome where they could excavate to their hearts' content. Their zeal was rewarded. One of the engineers came to the other with exciting news. Excavations on his grounds had turned up some ancient metal strings. This proved, he was pleased to report, that the ancient Romans had invented the telephone as well as the aqueducts for which they were already admired by everybody. The other engineer was inspired by this report to dig further on his own grounds. Eventually, he too had exciting news to report. He had dug all over and had found nothing. "Then why are you so excited?" his friend asked. "Don't you realize what this means?" came the reply. "The Romans must have invented the radio also!" Scientists intend to remind us by such stories about the difficulty, as well as the allure, of discovering the true beginnings, and hence the very nature, of things, even as we keep in mind these propositions:

> Philosophy in the strict and classical sense is quest for the eternal order or for the eternal cause or causes of all things. It presupposes then that there is an eternal and unchangeable order within which History [including the "history" of Big Crunches and Big Bangs?] takes place and which is not in any way affected by History.[143]

Notes

1. Hugo Grotius, *The Law of War and Peace*, II, i, 1 (quoting remarks recorded by Titus Livy from a speech made to the Romans by the Rhodians). This appendix is an

expanded version of an article, "On Beginnings," published in volume 1998 of *The Great Ideas Today*. See also George Anastaplo, "Law & Literature and the Bible: Explorations," 23 *Oklahoma City University Law Review* 515, 787 (1998).

2. Our scientist, a cosmologist (discussed in part 3 of this appendix, "On Beginnings"), is *not* representative of physical scientists today, whose speculations tend to be much less spectacular. But cosmology does fit in nicely with the poetic and biblical accounts considered in parts 1 and 2 of this appendix, as well as with the "systems" discussed elsewhere in this collection. Although cosmology may not be representative of disciplines such as "ordinary" physics, it does suggest the direction in which science is moving, with speculations about the most minute and immediate things matching, in their inventiveness, speculations about the grandest and most remote things. See the text at notes 80, 95, and 123 of this appendix. (All references to notes in this appendix are, unless otherwise indicated, to the notes in appendix A of this collection.)

3. Quintillian, Seneca, and many others have observed that everything ends that has a beginning. See, e.g., *Genesis* 3:19. Consider, also, the opening line of T. S. Eliot's *East Coker*: "In my beginning is my end." Consider, as well, the opening lines of his *Burnt Norton*. See, on these poems, George Anastaplo, "Law & Literature and the Moderns: Explorations," 20 *Northern Illinois University Law Review* 251, 539 (2000).

4. Must there be an ultimate "particle"? If not, what (in a particle-theory approach) provides the foundation for such substantial steadiness as we observe and do depend upon in the world? So far as we know, and perhaps so far as most of us can imagine, all material particles can be divided. If there is an ultimate particle, therefore, is it likely to be material? Rather, may it not be somehow immaterial? And, if so, how is the marvelous transition effected between the immaterial and the material? Do we touch here upon the "mystery" of the relation between body and soul? See notes 117 and 143 below. See, on the soul, appendix B of this collection, part 1. See, on the *ultron*, note 123 below.

5. The languages essential for rationality, as well as for responsible families, seem to depend upon community. This suggests the limits to radical individualism. See the text at note 128 of this appendix.

6. See, on Homer as the educator of Greece, George Anastaplo, *The Thinker as Artist: From Homer to Plato and Aristotle* (Athens, Ohio: Ohio University Press, 1997). See, also, the text at note 11 of this appendix.

7. See the text at note 142 of this appendix. See, on nature, ibid., p. 399. See also the text at notes 62, 108, and 115 of this appendix. I have been told that Leopold Kronecker said, "God created the natural numbers [1, 2, 3, etc.]. Everything else is man's handiwork." Compare the text at note 129 of appendix A.

8. See, e.g., Leon John Roos, "Natural Law and Natural Right in Thomas Aquinas and Aristotle" (University of Chicago doctoral dissertation, 1971). See also appendix B of this collection (e.g., note 17 of appendix B).

9. See Moses Maimonides, *The Guide of the Perplexed*, II, 15 sq.

10. Homer uses *nature* only once, and that use is curious. See *Odyssey*, X, 303. See also the text at note 62 of this appendix.

11. Mark Van Doren, *The Noble Voice: A Study of Ten Great Poems* (New York: Henry Holt, 1946), p. xi. See Anastaplo, *The Artist as Thinker: From Shakespeare to Joyce* (Athens, Ohio: Ohio University Press, 1983). See also note 5 above.

12. *Encyclopedia of Religion* (New York: Macmillan, 1987), vol. 6, 307–8. See the text at note 47 of this appendix.

13. Herodotus, *History*, II, 53, David Grene, trans. (Chicago: University of Chicago Press, 1987).

14. See R. M. Frazer, *The Poems of Hesiod* (Norman: University of Oklahoma Press, 1983), p. 13.

15. See, for a challenging discussion of Hesiod, Seth Benardete, "The First Crisis in First Philosophy," 18 *Graduate Faculty Philosophy Journal* 237 (1995) (New School for Social Research). The Benardete challenges here begin with the unfortunate opening line, "Virtually everyone knows that Aristotle sometimes lies." But see note 21 below.

16. Similarly, in Homer's *Odyssey*, the story begins late in the course of Odysseus's effort to return home. By the sixth book, in this twenty-four-book epic, Odysseus reaches the next-to-last stop on his voyage home. This bears upon whether the Homeric epics were "folk" productions. See Anastaplo, *The Thinker as Artist*, pp. 367f.

17. See, e.g., ibid., pp. 13f. Virgil's *Aeneid* seems critically different in this as in other respects.

18. The Catalogue of Ships, in Book II of Homer's *Iliad* (see Anastaplo, *The Thinker as Artist*, pp. 23, 37–39, 375–77), can be seen as a Boeotian element adopted (and transformed) by Homer. In any event, Homer can be taken to suggest that human beings almost always, if not always, find themselves in the midst of *some* struggle.

19. *Encyclopedia of Religion*, vol. 6, 307–8. Dante, in his *Divine Comedy*, even immobilizes Titans-like beings at the bottom of the Inferno. Elsewhere, as in Homer, Zeus can be referred to as the oldest of the Olympians. Does he, because of his superior power, act and regard himself as the oldest, even though he is sometimes said (in other stories, such as Hesiod's) to be the youngest of the Olympians?

20. *Encyclopedia of Religion*, vol. 6, 308. See, on the Babylonian and Hittite sources, chapter 1 of this collection.

21. Poets (or prophets, who may sometimes be the same as poets?) had sung of other gods, but not as effectively (that is, as truly?) as Hesiod can. Thus, as the Muses told Hesiod, the Muses "know how to speak many false things as though they were true." Hesiod, *Theogony* 26 sq. Perhaps this helps account for the dubious stories about the gods which have been challenged. See, e.g., Plato, *Republic*, Books II–III. See, also, Virgil, *Aeneid*, VI, 893-96. John Milton argues, in his *Areopagitica*, that the truth is much more likely to prevail than is error in a fair contest. See note 15 above. See, on prophecy, chapter 4 of this collection, note 38.

22. See Hesiod, *Theogony* 26 sq.

23. See the text at note 47 of this appendix.

24. See Hesiod, *Theogony* 4.

25. M. L. West, ed., Hesiod, *Theogony* (Oxford: Clarendon Press, 1966), p. 18.

26. See ibid., pp. 17–18.

27. Eros is critical to the generating to be done later by divine as well as by human couples; Tartarus becomes important later as a place to be used by Zeus to confine permanently his defeated challengers. See Hesiod, *Theogony* 713 sq. See, also, Virgil, *Aeneid*, Book VI.

28. Nor is anything said about any other place but Earth and its environs (which could include where the gods are most of the time). See Aristotle, *Physics* 225a sq. See, also, the text at note 143 of this appendix.

29. See Hesiod, *Theogony* 126 sq.

30. We recall that the Lord could be referred to, in ancient Hebrew, as "the place."

31. See, on Chaos, the text at note 126 of this appendix.

32. We have similar questions about what preceded the Big Bang examined in part 3 of this appendix on beginnings.

33. See Hesiod, *Theogony* 126 sq., 453 sq., 491 sq.

34. They are in this respect like Oedipus, whose (presumptuous?) efforts to avoid his fate may have made that fate come about in the worst possible way. That too, by the way, is a Boeotian story, and one in which, like the story of Ouranos, a son mates with his mother to produce a much-troubled dynasty. See, on Sophocles' Oedipus, Anastaplo, "On Trial: Explorations," 22 *Loyola University of Chicago Law Journal* 765, 821f (1991); Anastaplo, *The Thinker as Artist*, pp. 3, 6–8, 119–28, 400.

35. See note 33 above. See also the text at note 45 of chapter 3 of this collection.

36. West, ed., Hesiod, *Theogony*, p. 19.

37. Was this the kind of prophecy that Laius, the father of Oedipus, had had?

38. See the text at note 47 of this appendix.

39. See, e.g., Homer, *Iliad*, XV, 48 sq.

40. See, on *Logos* and the *Gospel of John*, the text at note 60 of this appendix. See also Anastaplo, "Law & Literature and the Bible," p. 692. See, on St. Augustine, Anastaplo, "Teaching, Nature, and the Moral Virtues," *The Great Ideas Today* 2, 9f (1997); Anastaplo, "Rome, Piety, and Law: Explorations," 39 *Loyola University of New Orleans Law Review* 2, 83 (1993).

41. See Stephanie A. Nelson, "An Honest Living: Farming and Ethics in Hesiod's" *Works and Days Georgics*" (University of Chicago doctoral dissertation, 1992).

42. See, on *five* in Hindu accounts, chapter 3 of this collection, note 33.

43. This is perhaps somewhat like Pindar, Hesiod's fellow Boeotian, being commissioned to celebrate the winners of the great athletic games. See Anastaplo, *The Thinker as Artist*, pp. 76f. See also Anastaplo, *The American Moralist: On Law, Ethics, and Government* (Athens, Ohio: Ohio University Press, 1992), pp. 51f.

44. Consider, for example, the decisive career of Rebekah. See Anastaplo, "Law & Literature and the Bible," p. 564. Consider, also, the story about Eros told by "Aristophanes" in Plato's *Symposium*. See, Anastaplo, *The Thinker as Artist*, pp. 171f.

45. See Maimoidies, *The Guide of the Perplexed*, I, 1 sq. See, on Maimonides, Anastaplo, *The American Moralist*, p. 58. See also chapter 6 of this collection, note 1.

46. Leo Strauss, *Jewish Philosophy and the Crisis of Modernity*, Kenneth Hart Green, ed. (Albany: State University of New York Press, 1997), p. 293. See, for a review of this book, Anastaplo, "Law & Literature and the Bible," p. 778. See also the text at note 139 of this appendix. See as well note 40 of chapter 6 of this collection.

47. Charles Segal, *Dionysian Poetics and Euripides' "Bacchae"* (Princeton, N.J.: Princeton University Press, 1982), p. 339. See also the text at notes 12 and 38 of this appendix.

48. See, on the Doctrine of the Ideas, Anastaplo, *The Thinker as Artist*, pp. 307f, 397. See also the text at notes 3 and 127 of this appendix.

49. See the text at note 143 of this appendix. Parmenides helped open up the West to nature and hence philosophy. He shows himself, in a Homeric-style poem, introduced to his topics by a goddess. This can remind the reader of Hesiod's initiation by the Muses. See, on Parmenides "as the first extant author deserving to be called a philosopher in a present-day sense of the word," David Gallop, ed., *Parmenides of Elea* (Toronto: University of Toronto Press, 1984), p. 3. The evident coextensiveness, for Parmenides, of *thinking* and *being* suggests that "beginning," as distinguished from that which is "always" or eternal, may be for him little more than an illusion, except that the process of change itself

may be eternal. See the text at note 116 of this appendix. See also note 135 below. See, for a useful introduction to Parmenides and to the Platonic dialogue by that name, Albert Keith Whitaker, *Plato's Parmenides* (Newburyport, Mass.: Focus Philosophical Library, 1996). See, also, the discussions of Parmenides by Martin Heidegger, Jacob Klein, Karl Reinhardt, and Kurt Riezler.

50. *Judges* 6: 36–40. Compare *Judges* 6: 14–24.

51. The traditional Hebrew name for this book is *In the Beginning*. The title *Genesis* is a much later usage from the Greek. The other four books of the Torah are also called traditionally by the word or words that appear first in the text. See the text at note 59 of this appendix. See also Robert Sacks, "The Lion and the Ass: A Commentary on the Book of Genesis," 8 *Interpretation* 29f (1980). See as well note 40 above.

52. See, e.g., Strauss, *Jewish Philosophy and the Crisis of Modernity*, pp. 359f.

53. See, e.g., Anastaplo, "On Trial," pp. 767f.

54. See, e.g., Anastaplo, "Law & Literature and the Bible," p. 548.

55. See, e.g., Anastaplo, "Lessons for the Student of Law: The Oklahoma Lectures," 20 *Oklahoma City University Law Review* 17, 97f (1995); Anastaplo, "Law & Literature and the Bible," p. 680.

56. See, e.g., Anastaplo, "On Trial," p. 854f; Anastaplo, "Law & Literature and the Bible," pp. 564, 580. See also note 44 above.

57. See, e.g., ibid., pp. 591, 604, 613.

58. See, e.g., ibid., pp. 641, 653, 665. Indeed, it can sometimes seem, much of the Hebrew Bible is written for a people that is somehow "abroad."

59. *Arche* is the term evident in such English words as *archetype, architect,* and *architectonic.* See note 51 above. Some readers of the Hebrew text have it open, "When God began to create . . ."

60. Should this be understood as God *speaking* or *thinking*? See the text at note 40 of this appendix. Goethe has his Faust open a book and begin to speak thus:

It says: "In the beginning was the *Word*."
[Geschrieben steht: "Im Anfang was das Wort!"]
Already I am stopped. It seems absurd.
The *Word* does not deserve the highest prize,
I must translate it otherwise
If I am well inspired and not blind.
It says: "In the beginning was the *Mind* [der Sinn]!"
Ponder that first line, wait and see,
Lest you should write too hastily.
Is mind the all-creating source?
It ought to say: "In the beginning there was *Force* [die Kraft]!"
Yet something warns me as I grasp the pen,
That my translation must be changed again.
The spirit helps me. Now it is exact.
I write: "In the beginning was the *Act* [die Tat]!"

Johann Wolfgang von Goethe, *Faust*, Walter Kaufmann, trans. (Garden City, N.Y.: Anchor Books, Doubleday, 1963), p. 153.

61. See, on miracles in the New Testament, Anastaplo, "Law & Literature and the Bible," p. 692. See also Anastaplo, "On Trial," pp. 882f, 900f.

62. See, on Gideon, the text at note 50 of this appendix. See also note 133 below. Compare Robert Graves, introduction, *Larousse Encyclopedia of Mythology* (London: Paul Hamlyn Limited, 1951), p. v:

> Mythology is the study of whatever religious or heroic legends are so foreign to a student's experience that he cannot believe them to be true. Hence the English adjective "mythical," meaning "incredible"; and hence the omission from standard European mythologies, such as this, of all Biblical narratives even when closely paralleled by myths from Persia, Babylonia, Egypt and Greece; and of all hagiological legends.

See Anastaplo, "On Trial," pp. 821f, 882f, 900f. Most of the major religions of the world, when compared to those grounded in the Bible, can seem rather "wild" to us in the West. See, e.g., notes 20, 42 above. See, for what the West is accustomed to, Anastaplo, "Law & Literature and the Christian Heritage: Explorations," 40 *Brandeis Law Journal* (forthcoming). An exception, although it may not really be a "religion," is the Confucian way. See, e.g., chapter 4 of this collection. See, also, the text at note 136 of this appendix.

63. Jacob Klein, *Lectures and Essays* (Annapolis, Md.: St. John's College Press, 1985), p. 1. I have found very helpful the comments made by often *quite* critical readers of part 3 of this appendix on beginnings. Those readers include Laurence Berns of St. John's College, Peter Braunfeld of the University of Illinois, Keith S. Cleveland of Columbia College of Chicago, and Stephen Vanderslice of Louisiana State University, as well as Nikilesh Banerjee, Hellmut Fritzsche, Edward Kibblewhite, Joseph J. O'Gallagher, Robert G. Sachs, and Noel M. Swerdlow of the University of Chicago. See note 109 below.

64. A mature physicist (who is not himself a cosmologist) has told me that one did not hear much if any talk, forty years ago, about the age of the universe; there was little talk then of a "beginning." But, he insists, observational evidence is now available, primarily because of the work earlier of Edwin Hubble, arguing for the steady expansion of the universe, and because of the discovery in the 1960s of the cosmic background radiation, which suggests a beginning of time—that is, the Big Bang. (This "beginning of time," we shall see further on, seems to mean to cosmologists today the beginning of *knowability*. See the text at notes 98–100 of this appendix.) It is hard, this physicist can add, to fathom either a finite universe, in time or space, or an infinite universe, in time. See note 80 below. On the risks of *imagination*, as noticed by Enrico Fermi, see the *Interpretation* book review cited in note 70 below.

65. The full title of the Hawking book is *A Brief History of Time: From the Big Bang to Black Holes*. It was first published, by Bantam Books, in 1988, and subsequently revised. See note 89 (end) below. See, for recent speculations about these matters, "Papers from a National Academy of Sciences Colloquium on the Age of the Universe, Dark Matter, and Structure Formation," 95 *Proceedings of the National Academy of Science USA* 1 (1995).

66. See note 107 below. See also the text at note 94 of this appendix.

67. See, for "A Brief History of *A Brief History*," Stephen Hawking, *Black Holes and Baby Universes* (New York: Bantam Books, 1993), p. 33f. See also the text at note 87 of this appendix.

68. See, on the challenging mission of combining the extraordinarily vast and the extraordinarily tiny, the text at note 95 of this appendix. See also note 1 above, and the text at note 123 of this appendix.

69. Has our "common sense," if not even our "intuition," been shaped by such grand innovations as Newton's system of the world? For example, what we accept as his law of

inertia can be said to have defied "common sense": that is, everyday observation is that things moving on earth come to a stop unless pushed or pulled further. See also notes 116 and 126 below. Still, consider how current scientific speculations can be regarded:

> Contemporary cosmologists feel free to say anything that pops into their heads. Unhappy examples are everywhere: absurd schemes to model time on the basis of the complex numbers, as in Stephen Hawking's *A Brief History of Time*; bizarre and ugly contraptions for cosmic inflation; universes multiplying beyond the reach of observation; white holes, black holes, worm holes, and naked singularities; theories of every stripe and variety, all of them uncorrected by any criticism beyond the trivial.

David Berlinski, "Was There a Big Bang?" *Commentary*, February 1998, p. 38. But see note 80 below. See also note 131 below.

70. See, e.g., the commentaries in the Joe Sachs translation of Aristotle's *Physics* (New Brunswick, N.J.: Rutgers University Press, 1995). See also my discussion of this useful edition of the *Physics* in 26 *Interpretation* 275 (1999). (This review was originally commissioned by the *St. John's College Review*, which discovered it could not use it.)

71. Statistical theory is important here, as is a distinction between discovery and verification. No, or few, rules govern discovery—one inspired conjecture might suffice—while, on the other hand, fairly strict rules may govern what is accepted as verification. Be that as it may, the contemporary physicist can insist that precise measurement is impossible. See note 143 below.

72. See the text at note 121 of this appendix. The Hawking career puts to a severe test the ancient prescription of *mens sana in corpore sano*. Hawking himself has had to compensate for a dreadful disease for which he was in no way responsible. See Hawking, *Black Holes and Baby Universes*, pp. 21–26. It is a disease which has made him, in key respects, very much a creature of modernity—not only in his reliance upon more and more technology for survival and communication, but also in his being able to divorce his mental activity to a remarkable degree from bodily activity and hence from the material element. (One can be reminded of René Descartes, one of the founders of modern science, who argued that scientific progress required the investigator to abstract from his body and his circumstances. See Anastaplo, *The American Moralist*, pp. 83f. See also Anastaplo, "The Forms of Our Knowing: A Somewhat Socratic Introduction," part 2 in Douglas A. Ollivant, ed., *Jacques Maritain and the Many Ways of Knowing*, an American Maritain Association publication [Catholic University of America Press, 2001]). One can wonder whether a radical independence from the body contributes to a spectacular imaginative power, if not to even more such power than is called for by the available facts. See note 122 below. Socrates does seem to argue that if the soul withdraws from the body (that is, dies?), it should, if properly prepared while still alive, be able to think better—but such speculations came from a Socrates who always did have a sound body—and his having such a body may have contributed to the sobriety that can be seen underlying even his most imaginative ventures. However impressive Hawking's intellectual achievements may be, they are likely to be superseded within decades, given the volatility of modern science, while the remarkable achievements of the spirit that he has exhibited should be celebrated for generations if not for centuries. See the text at note 132 of this appendix. See also note 117 below. Compare note 36 of appendix B of this collection.

73. Consider, for example, this comment by Einstein in a letter to Max Born, December 12, 1926:

Quantum mechanics is certainly imposing. But an inner voice tells me that it is not yet the real thing. The theory says a lot, but does not really bring us any closer to the secret of the Old One. I, at any rate, am convinced that He does not throw dice.

Ronald W. Clark, *Einstein: The Life and Times* (New York: World, 1971), p. 340. See also ibid., p. 396 ("God is subtle but he is not malicious."). See, on the Enlightenment and deism, Edward O. Wilson, "Back from Chaos," *Atlantic Monthly*, March 1998, p. 52. Compare note 89 below. See as well note 143 below.

74. See Eva T. H. Brann, *The World of the Imagination* (Savage, Md: Rowman & Littlefield, 1991), pp. 603–31. See also ibid., pp. 579-600. See as well notes 95 and 140 below. See, for the rigor employed by the very best of the ancients in using fully the relatively little evidence that was then available about the heavens, Aristotle, *De Caelo*. See also notes 97 and 114 below.

75. The puzzles of modern physicists are largely technological in character and are dictated in various ways by technology, even as solutions tend to expand technology.

76. He starts well enough (on page 1) with the charming story about the tower of turtles, but he is all too often flip thereafter. Consider, for example, what is said about astronauts falling into black holes, about the risks run at a Vatican conference, about such things as *Penthouse* and *Private Eye*, about various of the ancients, and about the biographies of great predecessors. I will return to some of these matters. See also note 66 above.

77. See section 3 of part 3 of this appendix on beginnings. Hawking is said to rely less on mathematics, even in his professional papers, than do most of his colleagues. See Jeremy Bernstein, "Cosmology," *New Yorker*, June 6, 1988, p. 118.

78. See Hawking, *A Brief History of Time*, p. 85. The engineering art seems to be a vital part of contemporary physics. See also note 75 above.

79. Consider the implications of such changes while the accompanying technology continues to work. Indeed, much of the technology can be opaque. We sometimes "know" that if we do A and B, our result will "always" be C, without our having the least idea why. See, for puzzlement about the attraction of masses, Anastaplo, "Lessons for the Student of Law," pp. 157-58. See, also, the conclusion of this appendix on beginnings. See, as well, the text at note 138 of this appendix. See, on Hubble's Constant and its elusiveness, Donald Goldsmith, *Einstein's Greatest Blunder? The Cosmological Constant and Other Fudge Factors in the Physics of the Universe* (Cambridge, Mass.: Harvard University Press, 1995), pp. 90f.

80. A particularly dramatic instance was the Cold Fusion scandal of the late 1980s. But the scientific community itself dealt with *this* aberration decisively. See, e.g., John R. Huizenga, *Cold Fusion: The Scientific Fiasco of the Century* (Rochester, N.Y.: University of Rochester Press, 1992). Consider, also, this report by the eminent scientist (notes 84 and 107 below) who first popularized contemporary cosmology:

It is conceivable that some of the skeptics will turn out to be right about the big bang theory, but this seems unlikely. [Martin] Rees cautiously gives odds of only 10 to 1 in favor of the big bang, but he quotes Yakov Zeldovitch as saying that the big bang is as certain "as that the Earth goes round the Sun." At least within the past century, no other major theory that became the consensus view of physicists or astronomers—in the way that the big bang theory has—has ever turned out to be simply wrong. Our theories have often turned out to be valid only in a more limited context than we had thought, or valid for reasons that we had not understood. But they are not simply wrong—not in the way, for instance, that the cosmology of Ptolemy or Dante is wrong. Consensus is forced on us by nature itself, not by some orthodox scientific establishment.

Steven Weinberg, "Before the Big Bang," *New York Review of Books*, June 12, 1997, p. 20. See also the text at note 125 of this appendix. See, on the "originality" of the moderns, G. M. D. Anastaplo, book review, 82 *Isis* 713 (1991). See also note 122 below. See as well note 131 below.

81. This seems to be due to a combination of carelessness, ignorance, and presumptuousness. See, e.g., Martin Gardner, "The Ultimate Turtle," *New York Review of Books*, June 16, 1998, pp. 17–18. See also note 84 below.

82. See, e.g., Hawking, *A Brief History of Time*, p. 2. See, on Aristotle's *Physics*, note 70 above.

83. This is evidently done, in part, to bolster the "history" anticipated in the title to the book. See the text at note 86 of this appendix.

84. Consider these observations by Jeremy Bernstein ("Cosmology," pp. 121–22):

As much as I like Hawking's book [*A Brief History of Time*], I would be remiss if I didn't point out an important way in which it might be improved. Hawking has a somewhat impressionistic view of the history of recent science. Very few active scientists—Steven Weinberg is an exception, and that is one of the reasons why his book [*The First Three Minutes*] (note 107 below)] is so good—actually take the trouble to read the papers of their early predecessors. A kind of folklore builds up which bears only a tangential relationship to reality, and when someone with the scientific prestige of Hawking repeats these legends it gives them credibility.

85. See Hawking, *A Brief History of Time*, pp. 181-82. See, for the grandeur of Newton's work, Subrahmanyan Chandrasekhar, *Newton's "Principia" for the Common Reader* (Oxford: Clarendon Press, 1995); Anastaplo, book review, *The Great Ideas Today* 448 (1997). See, on Newton as a "lion" for Chandrasekhar, Anastaplo, "Thursday Afternoons," in Kameshwar C. Wali, ed., *S. Chandrasekhar: The Man behind the Legend* (London: Imperial College Press, 1997), p. 125. See also note 31 of chapter 3 of this collection; note 92 below.

86. See note 83 above. See also the text at note 143 of this appendix.

87. See Hawking, *A Brief History of Time*, p. 116. See also the text at note 67 of this appendix.

88. See, e.g., Anastaplo, *The Constitutionalist: Notes on the First Amendment* (Dallas: Southern Methodist University Press, 1971), pp. 806–8; Anastaplo, "Thursday Afternoons," p. 126 n. 2.

89. See, e.g., Stephen Hawking, "The Unification of Physics," *The Great Ideas Today* 2 (1984). Compare ibid., p. 4:

Einstein spent most of the last forty years of his life trying to construct a unified theory of physics. He failed partly because not enough was known about nuclear forces and partly because he could not accept the limits on our ability to predict events, limits which are implied by the quantum mechanical uncertainty principle. He said: "God does not play dice." Yet, all the experimental evidence suggests that God does. In any case, we now know a lot more than Einstein did, and there are grounds for cautious optimism that a complete, unified theory is in sight. Were I a gambling man, I would bet even odds that we can find such a theory by the end of this century, if we do not blow ourselves up first.

See note 73 above, the text at note 124 of this appendix. See also Anastaplo, *"In re* Allan Bloom: A Respectful Dissent," *The Great Ideas Today,* p. 252 (1988); Robert L. Stone, ed.,

Essays on "The Closing of the American Mind" (Chicago: Chicago Review Press, 1989), pp. 225f, 267f; Anastaplo, "'McCarthyism,' The Cold War, and Their Aftermath," 43 *South Dakota Law Review* 103, 111–13 (and related appendices) (1998). See as well Bill Goldstein, "Let Us Now Praise Books Well Sold but Seldom Read," *New York Times*, July 15, 2000, p. A19.

90. Jeremy Bernstein, himself a scientist with literary accomplishments, considers *A Brief History of Time* "charming and lucid." "Cosmology," p. 117. See note 84 above.

91. Compare Hawking, *Black Holes and Baby Universes*, p. 38.

92. This limitation is reflected in how the typical physics colloquium is presented these days, with an inordinate reliance upon slides and other such visual aids. One exception during the past decade or so was a lecture by Subrahmanyan Chandrasekhar, at the weekly physics colloquium at the University of Chicago, which featured his filling of yards of blackboard with mathematical expressions (and all from memory). See note 85 above.

93. See Leo Strauss, *Persecution and the Art of Writing* (Glencoe, Ill.: Free Press, 1952).

94. May not great souls be discerned in scientists such as Galileo Galilei, Isaac Newton, Albert Einstein, Erwin Schrödinger, Leo Szilard, Enrico Fermi, Subrahmanyan Chandrasekhar, and perhaps C. F. von Weizsacher, Werner Heisenberg, and Niels Bohr? See note 109 below. See, on Schrödinger, note 131 below.

95. Hawking, *A Brief History of Time*, p. 175. Consider the cautions in Anastaplo, "Scientific Integrity, UFOs, and the Spirit of the Law," in "Lessons for the Student of Law," p. 187. See also the text at note 74 of this appendix.

96. An illuminating anticipation of the Hawking volume in this respect is James D. Watson's *The Double Helix* (New York: Atheneum, 1986), in which the contest for winning the Nobel Prize awaiting the successful description of the DNA molecule is vividly presented by one of the exuberant winners. See, on sports today, Anastaplo, "Law & Literature and the Bible," p. 860.

97. See Hawking, *A Brief History of Time*, pp. 124–25:

> There are two versions of the anthropic principle, the weak and the strong. The weak anthropic principle states that in a universe that is large or infinite in space and/or time, the conditions necessary for the development of intelligent life will be met only in certain regions that are limited in space and time. The intelligent beings in these regions should therefore not be surprised if they observe that their locality in the universe satisfies the conditions that are necessary for their existence.
>
> . . . According [to the strong version of the anthropic principle], there are either many different universes or many different regions of a single universe, each with its own initial configuration and, perhaps, with its own set of laws of science. In most of these universes the conditions would not be right for the development of complicated organisms; only in the few universes that are like ours would intelligent beings develop and ask the question: "Why is the universe the way we see it?" The answer is then simple: If it had been different, we would not be here!

See, also, John D. Barrow and Frank J. Tipler, *The Anthropic Cosmological Principle* (Oxford: Clarendon Press, 1986); Jacques Demaret and Dominique Lambert, *Le Principe Anthropique: L'Homme est-il le centre de l'Univers?* (Paris: Armand Colin, 1994); Michael A. Corey, *God and the New Cosmology: The Anthropic Argument* (Lanham, Md.: Rowman & Littlefield, 1993); Bernstein, "Cosmology," p. 118. See as well the text at notes 103, 111, and 127 of this appendix.

It should be noticed that Hesiod, if not also the creation story in *Genesis*, can seem rather childish to some moderns. See note 74 above.

98. Thus, Hawking can observe (*A Brief History of Times*, p. 46), "As far as we are concerned, events before the big bang can have no consequences." This can seem to be an inverse of that aspect of the Uncertainty Principle which has the object observed altered by the very act of observing it. See note 124 below. See also note 118 below.

Peter Braunfeld has observed, "Although a few of the best mathematicians I know are modest, many of them are just the opposite. Doing mathematics (or science) can be a lonely, risky business, and arrogance can help you to keep at it."

99. See Brann, *The World of the Imagination*, p. 175. See also note 64 above.

100. Modern scientists sometimes act as if they are bound by the laws of evidence in courts of law. See, on Plato's Meno, Anastaplo, "Teaching, Nature, and the Moral Virtues," pp. 2f.

101. Nor do the things that have been discovered stop "existing" when they happen to be forgotten by all living human beings for awhile?

102. See the text at note 118 of this appendix.

103. See notes 48, 97 above. See also note 126 below.

104. Hawking, *A Brief History of Time*, p. 173. The sentence quoted concludes, "up to the limits set by the uncertainty principle." See note 124 below.

105. Human beings, too, can predict events, or can proceed confidently with the predictions by others, that they do not understand.

106. Compare Plato, *Republic* 602D sq.

107. The most cautious, and hence most reliable, of the popular accounts here still seems to be Steven Weinberg, *The First Three Minutes: A Modern View of the Origin of the Universe* (New York: Basic Books, 1977). See notes 80 and 84 above. The physicists I have consulted for the Hawking part of this appendix speak well of the Weinberg book.

108. See, e.g., Plato, *Timaeus* 27C sq.; Anastaplo, *The Thinker as Artist*, pp. 279f; note 70 above. See also the text at note 7 of this appendix. See as well appendix B of this collection.

109. See, on the self, Anastaplo, *Human Being and Citizen*, pp. 87f. See also note 94 above. Thus, one of the scientists who read this appendix concluded his comments with this observation, "The only true beginning and end is our own individual birth and death."

110. Hawking, *A Brief History of Time*, p. 13. What would Hawking consider sufficient answers to these questions, and why?

111. See, e.g., ibid., p. 171. See also note 97 above.

112. See Plato, *Apology of Socrates*; Aristotle, *Nicomachean Ethics*, Book VI; Anastaplo, *Human Being and Citizen*, p. 8; Anastaplo, *The Thinker as Artist*, p. 318.

113. See Hawking, *A Brief History of Time*, pp. 120–21.

114. The National Academy of Sciences has recently recommended that evolution should be taught in public schools as "the most important concept in modern biology." "Scientific Panel Urges Teaching of Evolution," *Chicago Tribune*, April 10, 1998, sec. 1, p. 13. See also Larry Arnhart, *Darwinian Natural Right* (Albany: State University of New York Press, 1998); Anastaplo, *The Artist as Thinker*, pp. 482f. Can the advocates of "creation science" justify settling on any particular revelation about Creation among the many that have long been available around the world? See the text at note 120 of this appendix. See also Anastaplo, *The American Moralist*, pp. 341–44; note 143 below. Consider as well how "evolution" theory is drawn upon in the following 1957 poem, "Sally," by Sara Prince Anastaplo:

Hooray, hooray, hooray!
Let the old bands play!

The only talking baby is
In this world to stay!

She screeches, she crows,
She works her mouth and toes,
She arches neck and back,
Full of what she knows.

"Last year, gilled, I floated in the dark.
What was really me, except a hungry spark
Coaxing, 'Become, be-oh-something
For a lark'?

"So this spring
I kick and sing.
Finny sisters mild,
Furry brothers wild,
Bow to my choice,
I am a human child!"

Be all this as it may, cosmologists can say, Darwin is easier to understand because his theory is largely qualitative, so it doesn't presuppose a technical facility with sophisticted mathematics. Besides, he is talking about the everyday world, the very world our common sense was honed to cope with. It is when we want to think about the world of the subatomic or the world of galaxies, or the world of unimaginable densities and forces that common sense deserts us, and mathematics is our only tool, cosmologists would add.

115. See Leo Strauss, *Natural Right and History* (Chicago: University of Chicago Press, 1953), p. 8; Klein, *Lectures and Essays*, pp. 114, 187f. See also the text at note 7 of this appendix. Hawking himself seems open to the possibility, if not even to the likelihood, of a universe without a beginning or an end.

116. See note 49 above, the text at note 135 of this appendix. Does the discovery that light has a velocity play a role here? Thomas Aquinas and others, including *perhaps* Galileo, basing themselves on everyday experience, seem to have considered light's transmission as instantaneous. See Anastaplo, "The Forms of Our Knowing," part 1. See also note 69 above, note 126 below.

117. I have sometimes wondered what sense we can have of, or what "feel" we can have for, the matter that our bodies are composed of—what intuition we can have, if any, of the eternity that that matter has "experienced." See note 72 above, the text at note 129 of this appendix. Does this contribute to a sense of personal invulnerability?

118. Recent conjectures by some cosmologists have the universe expanding indefinitely, thereby making another Big Crunch unlikely, if not impossible. See, e.g., George Johnson, "Once Upon a Time, There Was a Big Bang Theory," *New York Times*, March 8, 1998, p. 3 (WK). But even more recent conjectures about the mass of neutrinos can perhaps be taken to suggest otherwise. See, e.g., Simon Singh, "The Proof Is in the Neutrino," *New York Times*, June 16, 1998, p. A31. Is it not far too early to be confident about any of these conjectures? See the text at note 138 of this appendix. Perhaps, indeed, the nature of things may be such as to make it impossible, in practice, for human beings, to arrive at a permanent stopping place. This may be related to the Uncertainty Principle rediscovered in our time by Werner Heisenberg. See note 123 below; the text at note 124 of this appendix. See also note 98 above.

119. See Lucretius, *On the Nature of Things*, I, 958 sq.

120. See the book review cited in note 46 above. If one grasps one cycle of Big Crunch and Big Bang, has one (in principle) grasped them all? See also note 114 above.

121. See Lucretius, *On the Nature of Things*, I, 72 sq. See, also, ibid., I, 536 sq., V, 55 sq. See as well the text at note 72 of this appendix.

Still, it should be noticed that cosmologists may extrapolate the universe back to a point only in the sense of a *limit*. As long as the universe is finite, it makes sense to them to speak of the laws of physics. But they might not attempt to apply those laws to a genuine point.

122. Laurence Berns has observed, in commenting on this passage, "It may be possible to overrate demonstration (even in mathematics). As Leo Strauss once put it, 'Order and orderliness are very nice, but I prefer illumination.'" See note 72 above.

123. See, on the *ultron* that I have posited, Anastaplo, *The Artist as Thinker*, pp. 252–53:

Is there any reason to doubt that physicists will, if they continue as they have in the Twentieth Century, achieve, again and again, "decisive breakthroughs" in dividing subatomic "particles"? But what future, or genuine understanding, is there in *that*? I believe it would be fruitful for physicists—that is, for a few of the more imaginative among them—to consider seriously the nature of what we can call the "ultron." What must this ultimate particle be like (if indeed, it is a particle and not an idea or a principle)? For is not an "ultron" implied by the endeavors of our physicists, by their recourse to more and more ingenious (and expensive) equipment and experiments? Or are we to assume an infinite regress (sometimes called progress) and no standing place or starting point? Or, to put this question still another way, what is it that permits the universe to be and to be (if it is) intelligible? To ask such questions is to raise fundamental questions about what Leo Strauss called the "modern project." [Originally published in 1974.]

See notes 4, 118 above. It remains to be seen what can be made of recent talk about the minimum *length* that things may have. Are the dimensions of the *ultron* thus conjectured? See, e.g., T. D. Lee, "Physics in Terms of Difference Equations," in J. de Boer, E. Dal, and O. Ulfbeck, eds. *The Lessons of Quantum Theory*, (Elsevier Science Publishers B.V., 1986), p. 181. In any event, there *is* the question put in Plato's *Theaetetus* (203B): "But how will one say the elements of the element?"

124. See, e.g., William C. Price and Seymour S. Chissick, eds., *The Uncertainty Principle and Foundations of Quantum Mechanics: A Fifty Years' Survey* (London: John Wiley & Sons, 1977). See, also, Malcolm P. Sharp, "Crosskey, Anastaplo, and Meiklejohn on the United States Constitution," 20 *University of Chicago Law School Record* 14, 18 n. 52 (1973). See, as well, notes 98, 118 above.

125. See, e.g., Anastaplo, book review, *The Great Ideas Today* 450 (1997). See also note 80 above.

126. See, on chaos, part 1 of this appendix on beginnings. How is contemporary *chaos* theory related to the talk one hears from some physicists today about many "universes"? The physicists with whom I have discussed such talk have not been receptive to my suggestion that there "must" then be a universe of universes, which "regulates" and accounts for the relations among "universes." This notion is similar both to the notion of "a rule of rules" and to the notion of the *ultron* (note 123, above). See also notes 64, 69, and 120 above; the text accompanying note 135 of this appendix.

127. See note 97 above. See also note 48 above.

128. See the text at note 4 of this appendix.

129. See Anastaplo, *The Thinker as Artist*, p. 178. See also notes 72 and 117 above. See as well note 7 above. Of course, most people (including mathematicians) would insist that matter and numbers exist in somewhat different ways.

130. See Sacks, "The Lion and the Ass," pp. 32–33. See also Plato, *Timaeus* 30C sq., 35B sq.

131. See Anastaplo, *The Artist as Thinker*, p. 252, note 77 above. I was astonished to hear a Nobel Laureate in Physics ask, in the course of one of the physics colloquia at the University of Chicago during the 2000–2001 academic year, whether the experiment just described provided at last some evidence that black holes actually exist. Evidently not! Scientists do wonder, from time to time, about what is really going on. See, on "alarming prospects" (and anticipations of the Cosmic Radiation Background discovery and current Inflation Theory?), Erwin Schrödinger, "The Proper Vibrations of the Expanding Universe," 6 *Physica* 899 (October 1939).

132. See note 72 above. See also note 36 of appendix B of this collection.

133. This redirection of his thought is recalled by Socrates on his last day, as recorded in Plato's *Phaedo*. But had he not been obliged to think through a notion of the whole, however provisional, which allowed or accounted for the rationality, however limited it may be, found in the human things? See the text at note 62 of this appendix.

134. See, on what Socrates *did* know, Anastaplo, "Freedom of Speech and the First Amendment: Explorations," 21 *Texas Tech Law Review* 1941, 1945f (1990).

135. Are we not accustomed to expect the laws of nature to work everywhere and always? See the text at note 116 of of this appendix. See also notes 49 and 126, above.

136. See, e.g., Anastaplo, *The Artist as Thinker*, pp. 265–66. See also the text at note 62 of this appendix. See as well chapter 4 of this collection, note 38; appendix C of this collection, note 88.

137. See Hawking, *A Brief History of Time*, p. 37. Others can speak with apparent confidence of fifty billion *galaxies*, still others of a million million galaxies.

138. See the text at note 79 of this appendix. See also note 118 above.

139. See the text at note 46 of this appendix. See also Klein, *Lectures and Essays*, pp. 109f.

140. See Plato, *Phaedo* 97B sq. See also note 62 above. Has some science fiction literature provided a better mythology than the cosmologists in that it may make the cosmos *seem* more accessible for human beings? See the text at note 74 of this appendix. See, as a restrained sample of what the tabloid press can do with modern cosmology, "The Great Debate," *Weekly World News*, May 5, 1998, pp. 36f. See also chapter 6 of this collection, note 67. Compare William Burton, "The Beginnings of the End: The Omega Factor," *University of Chicago Magazine*, April 1998, pp. 20f.

141. See, e.g., note 94 above.

142. See, e.g., Hellmut Fritzsche, "Of Things That Are Not," in John A. Murley, Robert L. Stone, and William T. Braithwaite, eds., *Law and Philosophy: The Practice of Theory* (Athens, Ohio: Ohio University Press, 1992), pp. 3f.

143. Strauss, *Jewish Philosophy and the Crisis of Modernity*, p. 471. See note 49 above. The concerns that scientists have about what is and is not established may be seen in the opening paragraphs of a famous paper by Albert Einstein and two colleagues:

> Any serious consideration of a physical theory must take into account the distinction between the objective reality, which is independent of any theory, and the physical concepts with which

the theory operates. These concepts are intended to correspond with the objective reality, and by means of these concepts we picture this reality to ourselves.

In attempting to judge the success of a physical theory, we may ask ourselves two questions: (1) "Is the theory correct?" and (2) "Is the description given by the theory complete?" It is only in the case in which positive answers may be given to both of these questions, that the concepts of the theory may be said to be satisfactory. The correctness of the theory is judged by the degree of agreement between the conclusions of the theory and human experience. This experience, which alone enables us to make inferences about reality, in physics takes the form of experiment and measurement. It is the second question that we wish to consider here, as applied to quantum mechanics.

Whatever the meaning assigned to the term *complete*, the following requirement for a complete theory seems to be a necessary one: *every element of the physical reality must have a counterpart in the physical theory.* We shall call this the condition of completeness. The second question is thus easily answered, as soon as we are able to decide what are the elements of the physical reality.

The elements of the physical reality cannot be determined by *a priori* philosophical considerations, but must be found by an appeal to results of experiments and measurements. A comprehensive definition of reality is, however, unnecessary for our purpose. We shall be satisfied with the following criterion, which we regard as reasonable. *If, without in any way disturbing a system, we can predict with certainty, (i.e., with probability equal to unity) the value of a physical quantity, then there exists an element of physical reality corresponding to this physical quantity.* It seems to us that this criterion, while far from exhausting all possible ways of recognizing a physical reality, at least provides us with one such way, whenever the conditions set down in it occur. Regarded not as a necessary, but merely as a sufficient, condition of reality, this criterion is in agreement with classical as well as quantum-mechanical ideas of reality.

A. Einstein, B. Podolsky, and N. Rosen, "Can Quantum-Mechanical Description of Physical Reality Be Considered Complete?" *Physical Review*, vol. 47, pp. 777–78 (1935).

We end this inquiry by reminding ourselves of the profound political and social consequences of conflicting presuppositions, even within the West, about human beginnings, as may be seen in the Bible (e.g., *Genesis* 2:18, 11:1 sq.), Plato (e.g., *Symposium* 189C sq.), Aristotle, *Politics* (e.g., 1253al sq.), Lucretius, Hobbes/Locke, Jean-Jacques Rousseau, and Charles Darwin. These disparate consequences are reflected in, for example, the status of "individuality," ancient and modern. See Anastaplo, *The American Moralist*, p. 23. See also notes 62 and 114 above. Such differences may be related, at bottom, to questions about the proper, if not the natural, relation of soul to body. See notes 4 and 72 above.

On the Human Soul, Nature, and the Moral Virtues

Part One. Is The Self Grounded In The Soul?

If one wants to have a taste of death,
let him sleep with his shoes on.

–Rabbi Samuel[1]

I.

The noun *self*, as it is likely to be used by us these days, is defined as "the union of elements such as body, emotions, thoughts, and sensations that constitute the individuality and identity of a person."[2] A standard dictionary follows up this definition with a list of some two hundred combinations in which *self* is used, ranging from *self-abasement* through *self-generated* to *self-worshiper*. Thereafter some three hundred additional terms are provided, ranging from *self-abandoned* and *self-absorbed* through *self-image*, *self-interest*, and *selfish* to *self-winding* and *self-worth*.

The same dictionary devotes only a dozen entries to forms of the term *soul*, such as *soul brother*, *souled*, *soul food*, *soulful*, *soul kiss*, *soulless*, *soul mate*, *soul music*, and *soul-searching*. *Soul* itself is defined as "the immaterial essence, animating principle, or actuating cause of an individual life." This is followed up with "the spiritual principle embodied in human beings, all rational and spiritual beings, or the universe." It is symptomatic of modern times that so much is made of *self*, compared to *soul*, however intimately these terms may be related.

The relations between these two terms, *self* and *soul*, are suggested by the following observations:

> The *self* is what emerges when much is made of what is called *individuality* among us. (Notice that we do use in this connection the term *self* more than the old-fashioned term, *soul*.) An emphasis upon individuality means, among other things, that we should attempt to intensify the experiences of the self. But, I suggest, if the emphasis is placed upon individuality and its expression, we are bound to have schisms of the soul; indeed, we *should* have such schisms, if only to give each part of the soul something of what it yearns for. . . . [This diversity of responses seems the way, for some, to complete self-fulfillment.]
>
> Is not *soul* critically different from *self?* *Self*, as I have indicated, is somehow intimately related to individuality. *Soul*, on the other hand, points to what is common or general, to a principle, to a natural function, to a standard to be realized. The full development of the soul means a lessening of selfness, of individuality—a conformity of oneself to the very best.[3]

It may follow from these observations of mine that, when one's soul is fully developed, one's childhood and personal history do not matter much. But such disciplined development, however much it looks to a model or standard of excellence, might be regarded by many moderns as a kind of death, a notion to which we should return on this occasion.[4]

The *self*, at least as we have come to know it, seems to be that which results from the soul's collaboration with the body. Another way of putting this is to say that the self exhibits the effects of the body upon the soul. Still another way of putting this is to say that the self is the soul with critical elements diluted if not even bleached out. The supreme activity of the soul, as once understood, was divine contemplation or philosophical understanding. Insofar as one grasps the most important things, therefore, one is like all others who grasp those things.

Self, on the other hand, looks more to the particular, the parochial, the personal (including the familial). It can be odd, however, to think of this identifiable entity, or this form of self-consciousness, enduring forever. Terms such as *self-preservation* and *self-sacrifice* contend for preeminence here. This bears upon the pathos that can be heard in the inscription found on John Keats's gravestone in a Roman cemetery: "Here lies one whose name is writ in water." Our particularity is both attractive and vulnerable. Even royalty may have their names forgotten. The recent discovery of the large tomb for dozens of the sons of Ramses II may temporarily revive their memory; but this tomb reminds us of the multitudes of others, royalty as well as peasantry, who have left no recognizable individual traces. The soulless self, to which we have become accustomed, tends in its emphasis upon particularity to be unduly materialistic or mechanistic—and as such it tends to make difficult, if not impossible, that form of self-fulfillment found through self-knowing.

I will interweave more or less technical observations about the self and the soul with reminders of what are for us common experiences—our experiences with identical twins, with fatigue, and with old-fashioned movies. This interweaving is an effort to flesh out my technical observations. I offer thereby a body, or a set of illustrations, which might help us see better the soul, or the principles, of this discourse.[5]

II.

A couple of weeks ago I saw, across the room from me at a physics lecture, a man with whom I have long had a nodding acquaintance, a man whom I had seen at such lectures before. I nodded; he did not. That left me with a minor mystery. Perhaps he had not noticed me or my greeting. A few minutes later, another man came into the room: *he* was my man. When I saw the "original," the other man was at once exposed as an inadvertent imposter. No nodding back and forth was needed to confirm what I could at once grasp. This is an experience we have all had, testifying to our remarkable ability to distinguish, eventually if not immediately, among the multitudes of particulars by which we happen to be confronted all the time. These two men sat together. Perhaps they were relatives.

My next pair were decidedly relatives, so much so that they could seem to be one person instead of two. They were identical twins, in their sixties perhaps, seated across from me, a couple of months ago, on a Chicago elevated train. Nature and art combined to make each of these women appear the duplicate of the other. Facial features, including coloring of skin and hair, body build and weight—all seemed the same; style of hair, clothing, shoes and stockings, handbags—all were exactly the same. So were the ways they talked, gestured, moved their heads, rose to leave, and walked. They were coordinated in their movements the way birds in flight can be, making it difficult if not impossible for the observer to determine who had taken the lead in any change of course. (It may be worth noticing that neither woman wore a wedding ring.)

So much duplication reflects considerable deliberate effort. There can be something uncanny about such deliberateness, especially when it is likely that it has gone on for five or six decades. At the same time, it is so compulsive a duplication that it hardly looks deliberate. One can wonder whether either of these woman can truly be seen so long as the other is present. One can even wonder whether either of them can see her self as separate from the other's.

The following day I happened upon another pair of identical twins just off Michigan Avenue (behind the Tribune Tower). (They seemed to be heading toward the National Broadcasting Company Tower.) Once again, everything was in duplicate—including, perhaps most astonishingly, the crosses marked on their foreheads. It was Ash Wednesday. What makes this astonishing is that Christianity does stand for personal choice, or individuality—and yet here were two women who had evidently moved in tandem, if not in lockstep, from their mother's womb.

These two women were certainly different from the two I had seen the day before elsewhere in the city. But it became impossible for me to *feel* certain about this, whatever the divergences there may have been between the two pairs. That is, I had encountered on successive days two sets of twins who were so much alike in their twinness that I could even wonder if the two pairs had been the same pair—just as one can wonder whether a pair of identical twins is really one person. Twinness becomes so much the dominant characteristic that one pair of twins can be confused with another seen elsewhere, at least so long as they are of the same gender and of roughly the same age and size.

It can be sobering, as well as instructive, to be reminded of how much one's material as well as one's social circumstances (including bodily features) matter. Such external identity can affect elements of the soul. We can see here how much determinism, or a kind of mechanism, may figure into what we are and how we conduct ourselves. In what ways, if at all, does each such twin have a will or a self of her own, something that is truly particular and distinctive? Do not such twins remind us of the determinism that modern science tends to consider decisive, not only in the physical world but also (to a considerable extent) for human beings?[6]

However differentiated most, if not all, people we know may be, the further away in time or space people are, the more alike and undifferentiated they can seem to us. This applies both to the multitudes that die in massacres and famines and to the dozens of sons that Ramses buried during his half century on the Egyptian throne. A more benign image of this kind of coordination is that of the Rockettes who dance in Radio City. I always found peculiar the stories of wealthy men in the audience who would take a fancy to this or that Rockette, even though these women were trained to look so much alike to the masculine eye.

Also peculiar may be what the mass media are doing to whatever commendable individuality our fellow citizens had once had. Is this what is likely to happen to the self when its rootedness in the soul is abandoned? Perhaps many of the disturbances that we encounter these days reflect desperate efforts on the part of people, beginning with youngsters, to come alive by being a "somebody" distinguishable from others. (Another pair of identical twins I encountered on the streets of Chicago a fortnight ago were very much like those of an earlier generation that I have described. These two women were in their late twenties. Although everything was again the same—hair style, brown raincoats, shoes and socks, and the way they walked—they did carry their purses and bags on different sides.)

III.

Before continuing with other common experiences that may throw light on the *self*, I return (however briefly) to a more technical discussion of the matter, beginning with observations from the "Personal Identity" entry in the *Encyclopedia of Philosophy*, where it is said that the word *self* is

> sometimes used to mean the whole series of a person's inner mental states and sometimes, more restrictedly, the spiritual substance to which the philosopher says they belong. The use of the word "self," however, has the effect of confining the question to the unity of the mind and of preventing the answer from relying on the temporal persistence of the body. This has made the unity problem seem intractable, especially when the fleetingness of mental images, feelings, and the like is contrasted with the temporal persistence their owner needs in order even to engage in the relatively lengthy processes of dreaming, reasoning, or scrutinizing the external world.

The amount of dictionary space usually devoted to forms of the term *self*, when compared to that devoted to forms of the term *soul*, testifies (I have suggested) to the modern preoccupation with self. It is hard to find in ancient Greek a word for *self*.[7] Similar observations might be made about the somewhat related modern terms *conscience* and *privacy*.

There is, in the term *self*, an emphasis upon the uniqueness, or specialness, of *me*. If the self is emphasized, dignity becomes critical, and we hear much of privacy and of self-fulfillment. If, on the other hand, the soul is emphasized, virtue becomes critical, and we hear more of citizenship and patriotism—and of the need to avoid corruption of the soul.

There may be seen, in the emergence of the self out of a Christian view of the soul and its personal relation to God, an attempt to add to temporal discourse that divine interest in humanity exhibited in the Bible. Ancient philosophy did not seem to offer to human beings at large what the Bible did. Christianity has emphasized, more than Judaism evidently does, the immortality of the soul, which means that the self has its individuality both enhanced and perpetuated forever.

Modern philosophers, such as Thomas Hobbes and René Descartes (and perhaps Niccolò Machiavelli), work far more than ancient philosophers did from the interests, if not the autonomy, of the individual. Self-consciousness may even be relied upon as the foundation of all that seems to be known. Radical inwardness, which may hold the seeds of madness, does promise certainty about the things that can be known, things related to one's awareness of one's own existence, perhaps also of one's self-interest. [8]

When individuality is at the core both of philosophy and of political action, much more is likely to be made of self-expression as the source of the greatest satisfaction, with the common good and a sense of excellence being displaced as the end of liberty. (Another form of this may be the deeply compromised self-assertiveness advocated by Martin Heidegger, however learned he may have been about ancient things.) The old-fashioned approach, on the other hand, had the thoughtful man recognizing that the more thoughtful he is, the less likely he is to be unique or "individual" or indeed mortal. That is, he recognizes that "he" has been, as thinker, "here" "before," and that "he" will "return." Only the accidental and essentially superfluous is "individual" and hence vulnerable. Philosophers, then, tend to resemble one another—but not in the way that my identical twins do. It may even be said that that which is most significantly immortal in the universe is the reasoning being who contemplates the principles of things, not the individual characterized by chance, errors, and personal attachments.[9] Still, people who are taught to make as much as we do of both liberty and equality are apt to resist arguments which not only urge restraints upon us, but also consider some states of the soul inferior to others. This resistance can mean that it is more important to be oneself than it is to be good. Modern economic as well as political conditions permit, if they do not even promote, self-expression. On the other hand, the old-fashioned approach assumed, that which is the best among human beings is not the unique or the individual, but rather that which most resembles the Good.[10]

By now you have probably again become tired of more or less technical observations. It is time, then, to return to something more familiar—and it is appropriate that that should be concerned with the all-too-common experience of fatigue.

IV.

Fatigue, when examined properly, can help us see what both the body and the soul contribute to what is known as the self. The body may be most in evidence when it is defective or exhausted. Some may argue that the body is even more in evidence when one is engaged in erotic relations—but are not what make erotic relations most engaging the elements that are not physical?

When one is not tired, one simply makes use of one's body without noticing it. (It is like the experience of seeing things: the soul sees, or so it seems, not the eyes.) Fatigue can not only keep one from being able to do some things; it can also sap one of the will to try to do those things, so much so as to induce a kind of heaviness if not even depression. Things can sometimes appear hopeless, with one's ability to think clearly impaired. Mistakes in recollection, calculation, and judgment can result. It is encouraging in such circumstances to recall that one has felt this way before and that a short nap, or if need be a night's rest, can make all the difference in the world.[11]

Fatigue, then, may have its uses, including the obvious one of requiring the body to be replenished and restored to the working order most useful for the soul. (We anticipate here the problem of whether the soul can function as soul if there is not a body for it to work through, and not only when dealing with the material universe.) Another, however unnoticed, use of fatigue is that of permitting us to see how the soul does differ from the body, especially when one finds oneself wanting to do things that the body is not up to, at least for the moment. (An illness is, in a sense, a kind of extended fatigue.) That is, fatigue can help or permit one to see past one's body—to see what is essential, or what is best, in one's total makeup.

Something odd can happen in these circumstances. I have found, when I have turned to studying my own fatigue, that I am not hampered in the same way (or to the same degree) by fatigue as I am when studying other things that my fatigue keeps me from pursuing for the moment. Indeed, fatigue tends to be lifted somewhat when I examine fatigue itself—as if fatigue wants to elude examination. A kind of refreshment, if only temporarily and for limited purposes, can result.

Be that as it may, does not the soul assert itself in such a process, as something that exists somewhat independently of the body and hence of the fatigue to which the body is susceptible? Indeed, is not the soul as such never fatigued, especially if it is purified, or is in the process of being purified, of ignorance and of desires and attachments that are associated with its own and other bodies?

V.

Much more can no doubt be said about the workings of fatigue, a condition which may be an anticipation of the process of dying. Fortunately, however, the lessons one can learn from fatigue about the relations between soul and body do not depend upon serious illness or upon old age when death appears imminent. I trust that enough has been said by me about fatigue, at least for the moment, in this effort to suggest what the soul is like independent of the body, that soul which is apt to be neglected in modern accounts of the self.

It is only prudent, however, to acknowledge again the apparent need of the soul for *some* body with which to associate itself. This has to be done lest one be carried away by the notion that the sooner a soul can divest itself of its body, the sooner that soul can come to its full realization. A precious perfume may be worth much more than the glass bottle which contains it. But, so far as we know, some bottle is needed if the perfume is not to be dissipated and lose its effectiveness. Is it the same for the soul in its relation to some body? (Is this, in effect, an argument against serial reincarnations?)

Even so, death (or the collapse of the body) poses much more of a threat to the self than it does to the soul. For the self, I have argued, depends much more upon the individual and hence upon the accidental than does the soul—and this means that a body is critical not only for the existence of the self (as it may be for the practical existence of the soul), but also for the special form of the self. That is, the soul can sometimes rise above its body in a way, or to a degree, that the self cannot.

VI.

The self is illuminated not only when the body undergoes the debilitation of fatigue or serious illness, but also when it is furthest from that condition—that is, when the body is fresh and vital, even more so when the body is beautiful. Again, we can refresh ourselves by turning from a technical discussion to a reliance upon something familiar, in this case, a film classic which I happened to see recently: *National Velvet*.

A youthful Elizabeth Taylor (Velvet) is devoted to a horse; a youthful Mickey Rooney is devoted to her—and is persuaded by her to help prepare her horse to compete in the Grand National. Velvet herself (albeit incognito) has to ride the horse in England's premier race—and we are prepared to see her win it, whatever the rules ordain thereafter.

The collaboration of body and soul depicted in this movie points to a peak, or to what seems to be a peak. Beautiful bodies (both human and animal) are used to suggest virtuous souls, reminding us that the beautiful is in some way a promise of the good. We are reminded also of how art relies upon the use of bodies in order to talk about souls.

We are reminded as well—and this can be sad here—we are reminded of the limits of this collaboration of body and soul when we reflect upon what happens as adults to many gifted child actors. Attractive young people may be taught how to *look* good, but they may never learn how to *be* good. Evidently, such actors may not be able to see their own movies, and be lifted up by them, in the way that the typical moviegoer might be.

Critical to the way actors and their directors proceed are the images that are presented on the screen, images of the virtues upon which the effectiveness of a movie may depend. Decisive here is not the condition of the soul of any actor but rather the *persona* that is offered to the public. It is the elevation, as well as the concealment, of the person that is vital to the modern notion of the self. That may be one reason why we have so many celebrities and so few great-souled men and women to contemplate.[12]

VII.

We depend upon our poets, as well as upon the occasional philosopher, to remind us of what we somehow know about the soul and its relation to the body. The philosopher's efforts here *are* apt to be technical and hence not easily profited from or even endured by most people. The artist, on the other hand, can be memorable in what is presented to us, however much that presentation may require analysis for its full appreciation.

The workings of the soul, with a minimum of reliance upon the body, may be discerned in a story told by Mark Twain in *Life on the Mississippi* (chapter 11) about a veteran pilot's taking a steamboat through a difficult passage on the river. This pilot had entered the pilothouse, during a night that was "particularly drizzly, sullen, and dark," to offer to replace the pilot who was on duty, saying,

> Let me take her, George; I've seen this place since you have, and it is so crooked that I reckon I can run it myself easier than I could tell you how to do it.

To this the other pilot replied,

> It is kind of you, and I swear *I* am willing. I haven't got another drop of perspiration left in me. I have been spinning around and around the wheel like a squirrel. It is so dark I can't tell which way she is swinging till she is coming around like a whirligig.

The relieved pilot stayed in the pilothouse to watch his colleague work, finally exclaiming upon being shown a "marvel of steering," "Well, I thought I knew how to steer a steamboat, but that was another mistake of mine." Even more remarkable displays of the pilot's art thereafter moved the professional observer to proclaim, "That's the sweetest piece of piloting that was ever done on the Mississippi River! I wouldn't believe it could be done, if I hadn't seen it."

It turns out, however, that this marvelous piloting was done by a man caught up in a fit of sleepwalking. Others are appalled upon learning what had happened, but the pilot who had witnessed the feats of his colleague pronounces this magisterial judgment:

> Well, I think I'll stay by next time he has one of those fits. And I hope he'll have them often. You just ought to have seen him take this boat through Helena crossing. *I* never saw anything so gaudy before. And if he can do such gold-leaf, kid-glove, diamond-breastpin piloting when he is sound asleep, what *couldn't* he do if he was dead!

We *can* imagine this episode happening as it is described, with the soul of the sleepwalking pilot exerting itself unencumbered by the inhibitions that might ordinarily have been prompted by the body's sense of its vulnerability. Even so, our laughter, upon hearing "logical deduction" carried to this extreme— "And if he can do such . . . piloting when he is sound asleep, what *couldn't* he do if he was dead!"—our laughter testifies to our natural awareness that (so far as we can tell from our experience) the human does depend upon a living body, however much the soul rises above it on occasion.

Still, it may be prudent, in a materialistic age when catering to the *self* prevails, to err on the side of making too little of the *body*, thereby making it more likely that the *soul* will perpetually be given its due.[13]

Part Two. Are the Moral Virtues Grounded in Nature?

> All good men whom I know have taught me that we do not commit a grievous error if we make it our purpose to be as good as possible.
>
> —Leo Strauss[14]

I.

Are the moral virtues grounded in nature? The common understanding of the three terms I have just used—*moral virtues, nature,* and *grounded*—suffices for our immediate purpose. It is on the basis of that understanding that our question is first likely to engage us.[15]

This question is an ancient one. But it may be dramatized by modern science—and by our contemporary doubts, related perhaps to the effects of science, about the knowability and the authority of nature, at least with respect to human affairs.[16] The question with which we start here is likely to generate many other questions whenever a serious effort is made to clarify the issues by which one may be confronted upon delving into the question of the relation between nature and the moral virtues.

Nature, as it has long been understood, is consistent with the notion of the eternity, in one form or another, of the physical universe. This notion is reinforced, or made more plausible, by the vast extent of time and space that modern science lays out before us.

Related to this notion of the eternity of the universe, for most if not all practical purposes, is the evidence offered us for the accidental origins of the human race, as well as of other species here on earth. The substantial anatomical correspondence between several other species and the human species is now evidently taken for granted by most biologists. We notice in passing that we do not consider the other species of animals known to us to have much if anything to do with the moral virtues, however much what they do, or "have to do," may be grounded in nature.[17]

The more that is made of evolution, the more likely it seems to the modern scientist that the origins of the human species did depend upon somewhat fortuitous combinations of matter. (This tendency is reinforced by the radically materialistic bent, at least up to now, of modern science.) These material combinations, about which disciplines such as physics and chemistry have much to say, make it possible, if not likely, that our passions and appetites, with which the moral virtues are very much concerned, are in large part due to physical causes.

These currently pervasive opinions suggest to some that there may be other forms of life elsewhere in the far reaches of the universe, even as cautions are heard about the exceedingly rare combination of material factors that permits life to emerge and sustain itself here.[18] But may there not be forms of life that we can do little more than imagine, if even that? Those who believe in angels, for example, cannot tell us much, if anything, about the "chemistry" of those (living yet bodiless?) beings.

Thus, the possibility of life elsewhere in the universe—aside, of course, from what has long been believed to be found in such "places" as Hades, the Inferno, Purgatory, Paradise, and the Elysian Fields—is no longer dismissed as merely fanciful. That is, it is said, the vastness of the universe, in both time and space, makes other life possible if not even likely here and there. What is not said as often is that that very vastness makes physical contact between those loci of life virtually impossible, assuming that the speed of light is indeed the upper limit of the speed of all matter in motion (and hence of the transmission of information?) in the universe.[19]

What do such scientific findings and speculations tend to do to the traditional reliance upon any ancient divine revelation which ministers to the guidance and care of one particular set of immortal souls, the human species on our planet? The significance not only of individual human souls, but also of the human species itself becomes harder for some to take seriously now that our scientists try to tell us about billions upon billions of galaxies, among which even our tremendous galaxy, let alone our solar system, can seem inconsequential.

What difference does it make, and to whom, how other rational beings conduct themselves, especially in circumstances when we are not immediately or personally concerned? This is related to questions about the goodness or enduring worth of personal conduct that no one else ever knows about. Another way of putting this is to wonder whether a study of nature may help our theoretical understanding, as distinguished from our practical judgment, leading to the possibility that the only reliable grasp of things by the reason of human beings may be intellectual, not moral.

What difference does it make now, or ever, what was thought, said, or done by the immeasurable multitudes of "persons" we can be sure lived, on the earth if not elsewhere also, at various times in the past? What, if anything, does the immense expansion of the human perspective of time and space witnessed in the twentieth century do to our ability and willingness to regard the moral virtues as grounded in nature—that is, as matters to be taken seriously by the dispassionate observer? May not the movements of distant and often long-gone stars and planets be easier to understand, if not ultimately more interesting?

II.

Let us come back down to the earth itself by considering our question about the grounding of the moral virtues from a much more limited, even prosaic, perspective, however much that perspective may be influenced by the remarkable cosmological speculations of our day.

What should or does guide us in what we do? To some extent—at times, to a considerable extent—we are moved by familiar pleasures and pains. Related to this is the desire to avoid death, or at least a painful death. All this can be keyed to personal advantage or to communal advantage, or to both.

If a species had not had an intense, sometimes all-consuming, desire for self-preservation, it probably would not either have emerged into self-replicating life or have been able to perpetuate itself very long thereafter, however it might have originated. A pain/pleasure guidance related to this desire is seen in nonhuman forms of life as well—and it has many benefits, as well as creating problems. Biologists can find it useful to approach instinctive conduct as if it were purposive, serving thereby the overall interests of a species if not also of individual members of the species.

Arguments are rarely needed to persuade the typical human being to seek and increase pleasures or to avoid and reduce pains.[20] Arguments are much more likely to be needed to encourage, if not even to require, someone to forego some pleasures and to undergo some pains. Most of us learn early in life that some immediate pleasures can bring on severe pains, or can deprive us of other more substantial pleasures. It is in the arguments related to these matters that morality, as ordinarily understood, can come to view.

The enjoyment of pleasure, if not also the avoidance of pain, has been said to be seen in its most satisfying, if not also in its most enduring, form (at least on earth) in the activity of the genuine philosopher. Of course, other kinds of activities are regarded by many as more enjoyable. But, it can be argued, only those who have had some experience of the range of activities to which human beings have always been drawn can reliably rank them with a view to what they may contribute to the most effective use of one's talents and hence to a general satisfaction with one's life.

The most serious alternative, if not even opposition, to philosophy, at least among worldly pursuits, is offered by a political life and its ambitions and rewards. But the pleasure available to a few in politics is too dependent upon others to be reliable—and for this, and for other, reasons it may be illusory in what it offers.[21]

Many more would look to bodily gratifications, and especially sexuality, as the source of the most intense, all-engrossing pleasures. But this sort of pleasure is notoriously brief—and, all too often, it does not deliver what it promises. Even so, there is a *knowing* element in sexuality which beguiles us, and to which the long-recognized role of *eros* in philosophy is probably related. In addition, sexuality can help us learn what knowing is, including a self-confident knowing of ourselves.[22]

In any event, philosophy is critical to the ability to make sure that one's soul is in proper condition. It can help one know oneself well enough to make allowances for one's limitations and circumstances, thereby making it more likely that one will act as one should.

The ranking of the principal human pursuits, by those who have experienced enough of each to be able to judge among them, extends also to the subjects investigated by the inquiring mind. It comes to be observed that there is something intrinsic to various subjects, with some perceivable as higher and others as lower. Both the crossword puzzler and the cosmologist work with "wholes" (as well as with holes)—but is it not obvious to most of us which pursuit is intrinsically higher?

Nature provides, or at least seems to provide, guidance as to what it means to know, as to what is most worth knowing, and as to the premises and forms of reasoning needed for learning and knowing. Someone such as St. Augustine would argue that the supernatural is also vital here, that its "personal" intervention may be not only instructive but even essential if there is to be reliable understanding.

III.

We have reminded ourselves of the pleasures and pains, or limitations, of the body and also of the mind. We can now turn directly, however tentatively, to the critical question of the status of, or the grounding for, the moral virtues. Is there a sense of moral goodness that is not keyed to, or is not in the service primarily of, either personal or communal interests and advantages as ordinarily understood? We might well ask, as *the* test for exercising the virtues for their own sake, what basis may there be among us for personal self-sacrifice?

If nature is at work here, the human being may be inclined or directed toward morality, self-sacrificing or otherwise, without appreciating how or why this is so. This would be seen, for example, among those who have never discovered or thought much about *nature*. Our question may appear then as largely theoretical. But the way we answer it may affect how morality, or the rules dependent upon and serving morality, should be regarded. Care must be taken not to subvert the hold upon a people of the established morality of their time and place, a morality that does tend to be respected on the highest level as worth practicing for itself alone. The "realistic" opinions here of a few may eventually have profound consequences.

This development can become acute if there should be an undermining of conventions and tradition, or the old way, with respect to morality by modern science. This may be related to the long-recognized tension between the pursuit of the common good (or justice) and the quest for truth (or the noble).[23]

Be that as it may, is there something about morality that provides pleasure in somewhat the way that there are physical pleasures, whether personal or shared, and intellectual pleasures, whether in the form of theology or in the form of philosophy? Is there even something about morality that provides an attraction, generating something other than pleasure, which is superior to pleasure in whatever form? This may be what Immanuel Kant was reaching for in his reflections on *duty*?[24]

The pleasure related to the exercise of the moral virtues may be more complicated than either the pleasures of the soul or those of the body. Are not the pleasures associated with the moral virtues sometimes less "single-minded" than those other pleasures—and hence, in a sense, more vulnerable? It can be difficult to sustain a compatible combination of "thought" and "feeling."[25]

IV.

To recapitulate: There are pleasures of the body that may be enjoyed somewhat with little or no thinking required. This may be observed in all kinds of living things as well as in what happens to and with our bodies as we sleep. Even so, the mind may be very much required for, as well as involved in, the more interesting of the bodily pleasures.

There are also pleasures which are posited for the disembodied soul (for example, in heaven), and which one can anticipate somewhat here on earth, forgetting in moments of ecstasy one's body, time, place, or other circumstances. One or more of the intellectual virtues may guide the use of the mind on such occasions.

What, if any, basis is there, then, for morality in nature? A digression may be of some use as we refine this question further. Aside from the question of whether morality is grounded in nature, there is the intriguing question, which I can do little more than allude to here, of whether nature herself should be obeyed, assuming that nature makes her guidance known.

Does not nature make us feel that we should obey her? But is it right or necessary that we should obey? Should we do so only because nature moves us to do so? If we cannot help acting one way rather than another in a particular situation, where is the moral element in that action? Still, one should take care here (whatever Kant may seem to tell us) not to disparage a proper habituation and its consequences.

Enough, at least for the moment, for this digression. What if any basis is there for morality in nature? There is a natural basis for morality in the sense that nature provides physical equipment, parts of the soul, and perhaps inclinations and instincts which make us open to moral considerations and guidance.

This openness seems to be largely confined on earth to human beings among the living things we know by direct observation. Nature permits human beings to use moral teachings, including the curbing of various pleasures, to serve various ends. Human beings can also clarify, as no other animal that we know can, the principles on the basis of which they act. This suggests that there is something intrinsic to human beings which makes them open to moral teachings, whatever the sources of morality. But what does nature herself say about those sources?

An inquiry as to the sources of morality is related to what the standards and rules are and to why we should observe those standards and obey those rules. We have anticipated what is sometimes said, even by quite respectable students of this subject. Morality, it can be said by some, is exclusively instrumental or ministerial; it is not something worth having, exercising, or honoring for its own sake, but only, if at all, for its consequences.

Less of a problem, in a sense, is the radical nihilist for whom not even philosophy means much if anything. Such a nihilist is both harder and easier to deal with here. We put him to one side as perhaps virtually impossible to argue with, addressing instead those who recognize a grounding in nature for philosophy, or the intellectual virtues, but not for the moral virtues.

This position may be one consequence of the modern insistence, as may be seen in René Descartes, upon an unprecedented standard of certainty in all subjects of inquiry. Is moral discourse incapable of appearing precise and hence certain enough for modern tastes? We have not been concerned here with whether the moral virtues should be ranked as high as, if not higher than, the intellectual or philosophic virtues, but rather with whether the moral virtues have any grounding in nature as knowable things worth having for their own sake.[26]

Much can be said for the proposition that the moral virtues are indeed largely instrumental and properly so, especially since most, if not all, of the virtues depend upon conventions or have obvious practical consequences. No matter what the sources, impulses, or motivation involved, conventions and consequences are often critical in determining how one should act. For example, several virtues depend upon how property is dealt with: but what *is* property and what may be done with it very much depend upon ever-changing laws.[27]

Those who argue for the exclusively instrumental character of the moral virtues sometimes refer to obviously thoughtful people who are said to endorse this argument. But when one happens to observe such men and women close up, what does one see? They feel obliged to pronounce moral judgments, sometimes about ancient or long-past events or actors, sometimes about twentieth-century events (such as what the Nazis did in their death camps), and sometimes about individuals they know personally. These men and women can pronounce moral judgments in such a way as not to seem to regard morality as merely instrumental. A genuine moral feeling, as if grounded in nature, is expressed, sometimes spontaneously.[28]

Besides, when we consider someone such as Socrates, for whom the life of the inquiring mind seemed most worthy of the human being, we remember that he was prepared on more than one occasion to risk his life, and hence the opportunity to continue philosophizing here on earth, for the sake of moral rectitude.[29] This kind of self-sacrificing response, in defiance of the city's "teaching" of the moment, seems to be an endorsement of the moral virtues for their own sake, something that the moral skeptics of our time cannot easily explain away.

Furthermore, there is a problem in regarding the intellectual virtues to be grounded in nature, but not the moral virtues. Do not the philosopher's honesty and willingness to run risks in pursuit of the truth seem to have some of the characteristics of the moral virtues?[30] In addition, if the intellectual virtues do depend, as Socrates argued, upon an erotic element, what guides that element? Is it guided in the interest of nature-grounded philosophy—and, if so, does nature indirectly shape the erotic? The erotic, I have suggested, may connect the realm of the intellectual virtues to the realm of the moral virtues.

It has been argued that we cannot see critical actions if we do not grasp and take seriously the moral element in those actions.[31] But how seriously can the moral virtues be taken if they are regarded as merely instrumental? Consider as well the *noble*, that which seems to be worth having and savoring for its own sake. Is it that which makes it easier for us to see, for example, that it is better that a man be treated unjustly than that he be unjust himself?

V.

However all this may be, there are difficulties, if not risks, in considering morality as exclusively instrumental, especially if this opinion becomes widely accepted. For one thing, morality cannot be effectively instrumental if it is believed to be merely instrumental. We may want morality to be regarded as more than instrumental because we sense that it is important, that it is vulnerable, and that it is most effective when it is regarded as grounded in nature (or, to somewhat the same effect, in divine revelation).

Our deepest concerns here may reflect an instinctive, or natural, opening in us to morality. To recognize what we have said about the appeal of the moral virtues is to recognize some grounding in nature for them. This recognition may be required if there is to be an effective response to the challenges posed by Thrasymachus and perhaps Polemarchus in book I of Plato's *Republic*, by Glaucon and Adeimantus in book II of the same dialogue, and by Polus and Callicles in Plato's *Gorgias*. Those vigorous challenges suggest that "everyone knows" that if you can "get away with" injustice, with no one else ever knowing of it, you may seem to have the best of two worlds: others are thus encouraged to be respectful of justice, which contributes to your personal security, while you enjoy things that would not otherwise be available to you.

"Be realistic," we are told by those who believe they know what it is that truly moves people. But may there not be a naturally moral component to facing up to the truth? Those who regard the intellectual virtues as grounded in nature probably rely somewhat upon the moral virtues in the conduct and assessment of the inquiries which the intellectual virtues require and glory in. Furthermore, do not the challenges posed by Thrasymachus and others somehow draw upon something natural in us? Intellectual honesty is invoked or relied upon by Socrates' challengers, as if that is something which all should respect.

If the moral virtues are not grounded in nature, then they are at best only instrumental, borrowing their dignity from the activity they may happen to serve. Thus, morality would be grounded in nature, but only indirectly, in that it is in the service of natural desires (whether of the body or of the mind, if not of the community as well in forming a city). Thus, also, the moral virtues would have no intrinsic dignity.

If morality is indeed only something to be *used*, does not that tend to make the *will* paramount? An insistence upon the decisiveness of the will in human, if not also in divine, affairs is perhaps distinctively modern. Critical here seems to be the opinion that man makes everything, including his "values."[32] This opinion is reinforced by the growing popular awareness, partly because of modern science and its technology, of the remarkable variety of ways of human life around the world.

VI.

What does the variety of conventions show, that variety which seems so much the manifestation of chance in human life and which is made so much of by "realists"? However varied these conventions may be, do not their similarities suggest that there may be something natural at work here?

First, there is the very fact that almost all, if not all, communities have moral guides, as if they are intrinsic to human beings or at least to their associations. Both this fact and the variety of ways have long been evident, as may be seen in Homer, Herodotus, the Bible, Livy, and Lucretius.

Second, there is a remarkable compatibility among the many moral codes around the world, even for peoples who evidently were not in touch with each other during their formative stages centuries, if not millennia, ago. Critical details of a code here or there may depend upon geography, climate, and other chance circumstances. But we can usually see the sense of most rules in the circumstances in which we find them. Thus, there is sometimes available an indication of what the basis was, in a particular community, of the determination to adopt the moral code relied upon, a basis which includes elements that we can recognize as defensible if not even as praiseworthy. This can help us get to the roots of a moral code.[33]

Third, there is the prevalence of the notion that one *should* be virtuous, whatever the specifics of the morality of a time or place may be. When a convention is questioned, moreover, this is usually done on the basis of moral standards that are generally accepted. We can be troubled by someone who casually disregards the long-established morals of his time and place, even when we have serious reservations about the political regime under which he lives.

Often, we have noticed, the moral code of a people is rooted in some form of divine revelation. Which revelation governs where may be largely a matter of chance (except, it should be conceded, for the true revelation). No doubt, acceptance of revelation may be in part due to ignorance and fear, reinforced by intimidating glimpses of the abyss. But there may also be a natural appetite for revelation—or for that which revelation provides, a comprehensive view of the whole reinforced by divine authority. It may be related to that natural desire to know of which Aristotle spoke.[34]

A caution is in order here. Care must be taken in making use of divine revelation, or of any other expression of an authoritative will, to support rules of conduct, lest that use, if deemed indispensable, undermine the grounding of morality in nature. Besides, is not nature useful in shaping us, including our religious organizations and other communities, day in and day out? Care must be taken, that is, lest religion come to be regarded as little more than a super-convention, not itself consistent with nature.

And if, as happens in the course of centuries to all but perhaps the true religion, purported revelations here and there come to be questioned (or worn out) and replaced, what becomes of the status of morality? One problem here is suggested by the tendency in some quarters today to see a public promotion of morality as a way of surreptitiously foisting revealed, as distinguished from natural, religion upon the citizen body.

Nature may express herself through the believer, even when the believer no longer considers nature sufficient as a guide. (There has long been talk in the Western world of "a fallen nature.") Does the believer, like the modern realist, tend to undermine reliance upon nature? Does not the believer tend to believe that, without revelation, life is ultimately meaningless and hopeless, as well as immediately fragile? He does not recognize any natural basis of morality—or perhaps the intrinsic goodness even of the rational life. It is in this direction that nihilism may lie.

Does the believer, like the modern scientist, also make too much of the tenuousness of the human species in the absence of divine providence? What is the significance of the fact, if fact it is, that all we have and can know, and even the possibility of knowing, is temporary and provisional, with everything that we depend upon (including memory) doomed to deterioration and annihilation? Yet if matter/energy is eternal, is not the potential always "here" for "us" to appear again and again? That is, is there not something natural about our very being, including our aspirations, however fortuitous any particular appearance and form of a species and its yearnings may be?

VII.

We should not conclude this inquiry without noticing the question of what the basis is of the choice of a code when rules of conduct are offered as divine commands, or as super conventions.

If a "divine" code is contrived by human beings, there may be either delusion or deliberate deception at work there. In either case, the moral soundness or worth of the enterprise can be suspected—unless there is a noble illusion involved, which may be salutary in its effect as well as in its intention. Even the invention by human beings of gods may reveal a divine spark or urge in our species, something that is naturally there in both the prophet (or poet) and his audience.

If a moral code is truly from God, there is still the question of how God chooses what He does. It need not be—indeed, it probably should not be—considered as arbitrary.[35] Why should that to which God looks in framing a moral code be considered different from that which nature, in its perfection, also offers for our guidance?

If divine intervention is put to one side, what does a finite earthly existence, with no reliable prospect of immortal life, do to our sense of the meaningfulness of life here? It may depend partly upon whether the *prevalent* appetite for immortal life and salvation is not natural but rather cultivated, and if so how.[36]

We have moved from asking whether morality is good in itself to whether human life, with nothing following personally after death, is good in itself? These may be related questions. Have not human beings usually had the vivid sense that existence is a good thing if not burdened by great calamities and pains?[37] If we are naturally attracted to human life, should we not also be naturally drawn to the moral code that evidently makes human life work well and be well? If this is "instrumentalism," it is so on a very high level which dignifies the moral virtues, virtually making them worth practicing for their own sake.

An inquiry into the natural basis for morality could well inspire us to wonder, if only in passing, whether there is something immoral in questioning the natural basis for morality, unless perhaps one insists at the same time upon the divine basis of morality. If there *is* a natural basis for morality, is there something wrong, morally or intellectually or both with those who explicitly deny, and perhaps thereby subvert reliance upon, such a basis?

We can wonder, furthermore, whether there is something deeply wrong with those who are not simply open to the good. Do some intellectuals "allow" their speculative appetites to overcome their moral sensibilities when they consider, or at least talk about, these matters? A comment by John Van Doren on the arguments I have developed here offers a salutary corrective to contemporary skepticism:

I am not sure it can be *proved* that the moral virtues are grounded in nature, but the evidence of our persistent and spontaneous response to injustice, say, powerfully suggests that they are. This response may not be everywhere the same, or as strong, but that is only to acknowledge that cultural beliefs and convictions can affect it. I think it can be found usually, however skewed, even in such cases. There exists a pervasive human sense of "ought," to some end or ends, which is defied only with embarrassment or bravado, both of which are forms of recognition—or if they are not, we say men are acting inhumanly. To say nothing of the fact that, if the moral virtues were not grounded in nature, there would be no way to teach them, that is, awaken us to them, except as rote lessons. Some of our moralists would be willing to settle for this, to be sure.[38]

Ultimately critical here may be the question whether there is *an idea of the good* that guides all actions as well as all serious inquiry and thought. We recall the opening passages of the *Nicomachean Ethics* and the *Politics* of Aristotle, with their insistence that every pursuit is thought to aim at some good. If Aristotle is correct in what he thus says again and again, does not that reveal a natural opening in human beings to the good—and hence to the moral virtues? The virtues, if seen in this way, may not be exclusively instrumental, however useful they may indeed be.

Even our pleasures and pains continually teach us, or illustrate for us, the idea of the good. Is not that idea vital to the philosophic inquiry which we have noticed that some do concede to be grounded in nature, reinforcing thereby that enduring sense of rightness which moral choices naturally seem to us to rest upon and to serve?

At the very least, then, there may be nothing wrong, depending of course upon how one goes about it, in affirming, or reaffirming, the natural basis for a sensible morality.[39]

Part Three. Natural Law or Natural Right?

And in His will is our peace:
it is that sea to which all things move,
both what it creates and what nature makes.

—Dante Alighieri[40]

I.

Any advocacy of enduring standards of right and wrong stands in refreshing opposition to the intellectual fashions of our day, fashions that make much of positivism and relativism.[41] Commonsensical moral standards are routinely drawn upon by politicians, lawyers, and judges for their public utterances, no matter what they may have heard in political science and jurisprudence courses while they were still in school. It is not surprising that ordinary conversation also draws on these long-established standards.[42]

Substantial support for the traditional position may be found in both the constitutional thought and the legal heritage of the English-speaking peoples. Consider, for example how contracts could be spoken of in 1805 by American judges reared in the common law:

> This is a contract; and although a state is a party it ought to be construed according to those well-established principles which regulate contracts generally.
>
> The state [in this case] is in the situation of a person who holds forth to the world the conditions, on which he is willing to sell his property.
>
> If he should couch his propositions in such ambiguous terms, that they might be understood differently, in consequence of which sales were to be made, and the purchase money paid, he would come with an ill grace into court, to insist on a latent and obscure meaning, which should give him back his property, and permit him to retain the purchase money. All those principles of equity, and of fair dealing, which constitute the basis of judicial proceedings, require that courts should lean against such a construction.[43]

Fair dealing had been reaffirmed, a generation before, in the Preamble to the Constitution of 1787 where the establishment of justice is listed among the ends of government.[44] A reliance upon the common law, and hence upon enduring standards of right and wrong, is evident throughout the Constitution.[45]

Also evident throughout the Constitution is the assumption that these enduring standards may be used for judging the Constitution as well. That assumption is implied not only in the provisions for amending the Constitution, but also in the process by which the Constitution had been drafted and ratified. Something outside the Constitution provides a basis for judgments to be made about the document itself. Furthermore, the Ninth and Tenth Amendments recognize that there are claims, rights, and principles prior to and independent of the Constitution and its Bill of Rights.[46]

Constitutional law scholars who resist "originalist" interpretations of the Constitution tend to be positivistic in orientation: they are likely to insist that the Constitution is what the judges *say* it is.[47] But to what are their judges themselves supposed to look in determining what to *say*? In addition, some of our contemporary positivists can advocate the protection of more rights than are explicitly set forth in what judges may happen to say that the Constitution and Bill of Rights provide for. To what do such positivists look in determining what to advocate here?

II.

That there are enduring standards of right and wrong is further suggested by our ability to understand, if not even to endorse, everyday moral judgments made centuries ago. Where do such standards ultimately come from? What are they based upon? It was once widely believed in the Western World that the principal sources of, or authorities for, enduring standards were *revelation* and *nature*.[48]

The contributions of revelation may be seen in the sacred texts and teachings of religious institutions.[49] The directives developed from these sources by statesmen, as well as by recognized spiritual authorities, may be fairly clear and straightforward.[50] The contributions of nature may be more uncertain insofar as the dictates of nature, which can sometimes be difficult to determine, have no obviously authoritative interpreters.

However different, in critical respects, revelation and nature may be, it is not unusual—it may even be natural—for those who are grounded in one of these to find themselves cooperating to a considerable extent with those grounded in the other. St. Paul, for example, observed that some of the moral precepts developed by pagan rationalists in Athens were consistent with the rules provided by the revelation available to Jews and Christians.[51]

This is not to deny, however, that the moralist grounded in nature and the moralist grounded in revelation sometimes part company when an effort is made to understand what is truly going on or how things really are. Differences of opinion about first principles may sometimes become evident, if not even vigorous, when particular cases have to be dealt with.[52]

III.

Natural law tries to combine the approach of those grounded in nature and the approach of those grounded in revelation.[53] Does not the combination somehow depend upon the proposition that it is natural to be guided here by revelation? Also, does not revelation tend to teach that nature, or what has long been believed by a community, should be respected?

The authority of revelation might thus be used to reinforce the dictates of nature among a people.[54] On the other hand, an undue emphasis upon revelation might tend to undermine respect for or reliance upon nature, aside from whatever the effect may be of any explicit religious opinion that nature does not suffice as the ultimate guide for human action.

Natural law, insofar as it prescribes law of a very high order or on the highest authority, may have a tendency to promote a kind of positivism, albeit an exalted positivism. Consider, for example, the story in *Genesis* of Adam and Eve. God no doubt had His reasons for the Prohibition laid down in the Garden of Eden.[55]

God's reasons for this fateful prohibition, however, need not be understood by human beings. Nor, it seems, need it be understood why God should always be obeyed. The important things seem to have been that there *was* an announced rule and that it was known to have come from God, *not* what the basis or the purpose of the divine directive was. Much the same can be said of the request made to Abraham by God with respect to the sacrifice of Isaac.[56]

Although we may not be expected to figure out many of God's reasons and purposes, it is believed by some of the more sensitive souls among us that human beings have long if not "always" been in trouble, that they have profound disabilities. These sensitive observers surmise that there must have been some critical misstep to account for such a sad state of affairs.[57] A just God, if not also an initial golden age, may be taken for granted here.

IV.

Central to our inquiry in this context is the pious human being's observation that neither nature nor revelation needed to exist in the first place.[58] Is there not, however, something missing from the traditional understanding of nature when it is not regarded as intrinsic to things and hence perhaps even necessary? That is, can nature, fully realized, be understood to have had a beginning—and is not a temporal beginning for nature implied in any observation that nature did not need to exist?

On the other hand, is it not conceivable that the matter upon which nature and the world so much depend is like, for instance, the numbers which we *can* accept as "always" having had the relations among themselves that they now do, not merely as having begun to be what they are at some time or other? Even so, particular *manifestations* of combinations of material things, just like the particular *manifestations* or applications of the relations to one another of various numbers, can begin and end. Something critical happens to the attributes of nature, however, when nature itself is regarded as not having had "to exist in the first place." This does seem to suggest that nature has had, or at least could have had, a beginning.

The underlying question here, then, is about the very nature of Being. However much this question might be refined, it can be difficult, if not impossible, to answer because the premises or presuppositions of the inquiry cannot themselves be demonstrated. Being itself is lodged, so to speak, in those first principles. Something indemonstrable must be intuited and grasped for the inquiry to be able to proceed. There can be no place upon which an inquirer might "stand" in demonstrating, for example, the eternity (if not even the existence) of any first principle.[59]

Need nature, or its material world, have had a beginning? It can seem inconceivable to most, if not to all, human beings that the world, at least as we know it, did not have a beginning. Would a world without a beginning be like the Divine? The Divine too may be "accepted," but cannot truly be conceived, as having had no beginning. Thus, anything that is taken *as always having been* may be ultimately incomprehensible by us.[60] We cannot say more about this mystery before we consider the significance of the traditional understanding of *natural right*.

V.

Classical natural right seems to be grounded in nature and reason.[61] It is to be distinguished from traditional natural law, which (as we have seen) depends much more on revelation. Natural right looks ultimately to the best regime on earth, and hence tends to be more political than does natural law, while natural law looks ultimately to personal salvation, with political citizenship and the best earthly regime taking second place to concerns about one's personal fate after death.

Thomas Aquinas and his successors seem to prefer the term *natural law* to the term *natural right* when dealing with the matters discussed here. Both of these terms have always been available to Thomists, and yet *natural right* is rarely used by them. It should be instructive, therefore, to consider both some possible causes and a few implications of the use of the term *natural law* by someone as authoritative as St. Thomas.

First, then, let us consider the possible causes of any Thomistic preference for the use of the term *natural law*. This inquiry touches upon long-standing questions about law, about nature, and about the relation of reason to revelation.

1. Three-fourths of Thomas's celebrated *Treatise on Law*, in his *Summa Theologica*,[62] is devoted to a detailed discussion of the Divine Law—to a discussion, that is, of the Old Law and the New Law found, respectively, in what we call the Old and New Testaments. Thus, the directives and guidance provided by nature and ascertainable by human reason are regarded as *law* perhaps in part to fit in with that reliance upon the Old Law and the New Law which dominates the complete *Treatise on Law*.

2. The Old Law can be said to be built around the Decalogue. The Decalogue, we are told in the *Treatise on Law*, incorporates, among other commands, the principal precepts with which nature instructs human beings about

their conduct.[63] Because the Decalogue is a body of laws, the precepts of nature that may be incorporated in the Decalogue should also be called *law*.

3. Or, put another way, if God (in the Decalogue and elsewhere) delivered *His* principal precepts in the form of laws, why should not nature do so also? A revelation, such as the Decalogue, is not an argument or a demonstration; it is not presented as something figured out in the way that *natural right* tends to be.[64] Rather, a revelation lays down guidance which takes the form of commandments or *laws*.

4. Furthermore, there is implied by the use of *natural law* a community, or an established way of life, which also guides human beings. This is not unrelated, perhaps, to the importance of the Church in the spiritual guidance of human beings: a man cannot, on his own, devise and follow the course which leads to personal salvation. Not even the Scriptures suffice to guide him. Rather, eternal salvation depends upon his acting in conformity to, and in company with, the Church. Similarly, the temporal guidance of human beings is rooted in a community, that community implied by any reliance upon law. To speak of *natural right*, on the other hand, tends to make more of the self-sufficiency of the best human beings, of those who can figure out what the right thing to do is and who then do it because of its intrinsic rightness. Such self-sufficiency may be exhibited in its highest form in the life of the philosopher. Such a life, in which worship of a miracles-working divinity does not figure largely if at all, may be played down when natural *law* is spoken of.

5. A lawgiver is implied when *natural law* is used. This implication conforms to the teaching, evident throughout the *Summa Theologica*, that the world (whether or not eternal) and everything in it are established and governed by an eternal Lawgiver.[65] That Lawgiver lays down firm if not inflexible directives, including the natural law for the moral guidance of mankind. Natural right, on the other hand, tends to be more flexible in its terms and tone, placing a greater emphasis upon prudence and the use of one's judgment in varying circumstances. This may seem to go against the spirit of the teaching that the Divine Lawgiver, and He alone, has the prerogative of suspending the operation of His rules. Such suspensions, or miracles, are believed to provide foundations for both the Old Testament and the New Testament.[66]

6. To rely on natural *law* is to retain and to encourage, in the very name of this set of transcendent standards, a respect for law itself. Natural right, on the other hand, can be easily seen (if, in most cases, mistakenly seen) to be somewhat in opposition to human law. If the inclination of the classical natural-right approach *is* to be somewhat skeptical of law, then any endorsement of that approach might lead some to begin to question law generally, and not just human law but perhaps even the Old and the New Law grounded in the Scriptures. For this reason too, some might say, it is better to reinforce the dignity

of law generally by labeling as "natural law" that guide to human conduct which is provided by nature.

7. Still another reason for the preference for "natural law" may be seen in the status of nature itself in Thomas's scheme of things.[67] That is, "natural law" fits in better than does "natural right" with what Thomas usually considers nature to be. Nature, thus conceived, is not ultimately autonomous. Behind nature is a Being endowed with knowledge and intelligence and, of course, will.[68] That will can even find expression in miracles. To speak of the Divine Will is to speak of Something that is commanding, Something that is laying down (as well as suspending?) the law, yet Something that is incomprehensible except to the extent that It chooses to reveal Itself. It is not to speak, as the natural-right people speak, of naturally ascertainable standards of intrinsic rightness. To speak as the natural-right people tend to do is to suggest that nature *is* somehow independent of the Divine and hence, in principle, considerably if not even sufficiently knowable by the human reason unaided by revelation.

These, then, have been some seven possible causes of the use by Thomas and his successors of the term *natural law* in preference to the term *natural right*. This inquiry may be further developed by considering, if only briefly, a few more implications of the preference (for whatever reasons) for *natural law* over *natural right*. At the root of the sovereignty of natural law for Thomas, I have suggested, may be the will of God—and that is, in principle, inscrutable. God is evidently not moved to do what He does by any necessity either of His nature or of any other nature.[69] His will is the cause of all things.[70]

We have seen that nature does not seem to mean for the Thomist what it meant for the Classical thinkers. It is not simply "on its own." Natural *law* qualifies whatever thrust of necessity there may otherwise be in the term *nature*, inasmuch as *law* implies will and choice, not necessity, on the part of the lawgiver. That is, law draws on, or *is*, a convention; it need not rest clearly or always on what is natural.

Natural law reminds us, therefore, that at the very foundation of things is Something which is not limited, Something which is not operating according to nature—and therefore Something which cannot be grasped by the unaided or natural faculties of human beings. Natural right, on the other hand, is more likely than natural law to imply that the fundamental things of the world *can* be adequately investigated by human reason on its own.

All this means, among other things, that revelation is needed to complete the natural law, or at least to reinforce it, if not even to establish it. It has been suggested that the entire notion of natural law, in the Thomistic sense, is—in fact, if not in intention—a dictate of reason "informed by faith."[71]

We have noticed that natural law, because of its ultimate reliance upon rev-elation and upon the particularity and the will that are implied in revelation, may tend to be more doctrinaire, less flexible, than natural right. Natural right, we have also noticed, may make more of prudence than does the guid-ance provided by revelation.

VI.

A persistent question here is as to the ultimate basis for the authority of na-ture. Why, indeed, should we be guided by "the authority of nature"—and what, in fact, can that mean? If one accepts revelation, nature can perhaps be understood as the divine means for informing all peoples, not just those priv-ileged to have had a special revelation vouchsafed to them. Nature can thus be seen to have some authority whether or not an explicit revelation is avail-able or accepted.

Whether or not there is any valid revelation available at any particular time or place, does not nature naturally make us inclined to respect the natural—and to respect as well that which can easily seem to be natural, such as the an-cestral? Certainly, intuitions with respect to right and wrong can seem natural, however much one's circumstances may affect what one happens to intuit.[72]

The limitations of nature for Thomas are reflected in what he has to say about the need that even the most philosophical have for revelation. We touch here upon matters that are critical to any attempt to consider the relation of reason to revelation. Thomas repeatedly indicates that the ends at which hu-man beings ultimately aim are life eternal and the bliss possible only in such a life. That bliss seems to find its fulfillment in a vision of God. But human beings, Thomas also indicates again and again, are not capable of attaining such a vision and such bliss on their own.[73]

Thomas's manifest teaching is, therefore, that the natural ability of human beings to reason about or to God is severely limited. For example, the natu-ral reason cannot lead us to see what the Trinity is like, or perhaps even that it *is*. He warns that it may undermine the Faith for believers to try to estab-lish things by reason that simply cannot be established that way.[74]

A critical question here may be whether human beings are *naturally* aware that more is needed for a solid happiness than can be secured by the use of their natural powers alone. Thomas sometimes seems on the verge of sug-gesting that the human being may naturally yearn for a bliss which can come only through biblical revelation.[75]

Were the more astute Classical thinkers, then, able to become *aware* (albeit in a melancholy manner) of a natural desire for something more than was attainable by them through philosophy or through an eminently virtuous way of life based solely upon nature and reason? Such a natural yearning would mean, among other things, that (according to the Classical thinkers) insofar as nature provides nothing in vain,[76] nature itself points (however obscurely) to that divine order of things described in biblical revelation.[77]

If there *is* a natural yearning here, should not nature also provide the means of its satisfaction? Or is any such yearning not truly natural but rather the result of a misguided imagination? Is too much sometimes made here, in effect, of the natural desire for self-preservation?

Individual perpetuation without a body raises, as we have seen in part 1 of this appendix, serious difficulties for the possibility of a soul capable of enjoying *any* bliss. The consequent need for a doctrine of reincarnation—a doctrine positing a return of the soul to a resurrected body or (as in the East) to a series of new bodies—can make us wonder whether the self one is most likely to be concerned about (that is, one's own) truly survives death. On the other hand, one might also wonder, are the revelations offered mankind—revelations which provide assurances and guidance with respect to these matters—clearly beyond the natural powers of human beings to develop? What, in short, *are* the ultimate sources of both the yearnings and the teachings that Thomas makes so much of?

Furthermore, what is the ultimate source of Thomas's arguments about the nature of faith and of revelation? The faith that he invokes again and again depends (he says) not on reasoning but on that divine guidance which is made available to mankind because of the grace of God.[78] Thomas's insistence here upon authority as decisive again reminds us of something that is vital to law. To speak as he does of natural law, rather than of natural right, is to invoke authority in still another way—and, by doing so, he points once again to God and to the Faith necessary if one is to approach God fully.

Thus, in various ways, Thomas and his successors argue that something more is needed, if human beings are to prosper, than the conclusions arrived at by even the most astute human reasoning about the natural and the divine. Particularly to be guarded against, it would seem, are the self-sufficiency and perhaps even the pride that seem to characterize those among us who ground themselves both in the natural-right teaching and in the philosophy which that teaching depends upon and can be said to serve.[79]

VII.

Whether there happens to be a genuine revelation available to a people, the philosopher might argue, natural right could itself lead to the development of an appropriate religion, perhaps also of a plausible revelation to support it.[80]

The imagination that human beings naturally have can be used, especially if divine guidance should be available, to fashion persuasive revelations in the service of that which is naturally right.[81]

I have suggested that the tendency of the revelation-based natural-law approach, especially when compared to the Classical natural-right approach, is to be less political and to be more concerned with personal salvation and individual choice. There is a risk in such circumstances of encouraging, in all too many people, self-centeredness, or at least a lack of serious involvement in the political community (except, perhaps, to the extent that the religious community is itself a form of political association). An emphasis upon personal salvation can take the form, in our more skeptical age, of a celebration of natural or human rights—that is, of claims made against or upon the community for the sake of "autonomous individuality." This is, as Leo Strauss has said, a shift in emphasis "from man's duties to his rights."[82] Even so, the more or less modern natural-law approach is probably closer in its revelation-inspired individualism to the modern natural-rights approach than it is to the Classical natural-right approach that the natural-law approach in effect replaces.[83]

The pious man, in order to counter the selfishness that might otherwise be legitimated by the modern approaches, may follow the authority of the Second Vatican Council and of Pope John Paul II in making much of a "free gift of self" as somehow the peak of personal endeavor and sacrifice.[84] This encourages human beings to get closer to that inner goodness of creation in which God is All.

The ancient Greeks, from whom Classical natural right stems, would rarely talk thus, considering such talk apolitical, if not even antipolitical.[85] "Gift of self" talk seems to depend on revelation—or at least on a scheme of things in which the Divine (however revealed or intuited) is dominant and, probably, active. Is there not something unnatural, or at least not-natural, about this "gift of self"? When the worship of God is approached thus, nature may be ultimately repudiated in still another way.

An instructive guide to the Christian conception of the place of gifts in human life may be found in a letter by St. Paul to the Corinthians:

> Now there are varieties of gifts, but the same Spirit; and there are varieties of service, but the same Lord; and there are varieties of working, but it is the same God who inspires them all in every one. To each is given the manifestation of the Spirit for the common good. To one is given through the Spirit the utterance of wisdom, and to another the utterance of knowledge according to the same Spirit, to another faith by the same Spirit, to another gifts of healing by the one Spirit, to another the working of miracles, to another prophecy, to another the ability to distinguish between spirits, to another various kinds of tongues, to another the interpretation of

tongues. All these are inspired by one and the same Spirit, who apportions to each one individually as he wills.[86]

Nine gifts are inventoried here by St. Paul. Wisdom is placed at the outset: it seems to be essential for organizing all things, including one's understanding of the spiritual things to which human beings may reasonably aspire. Miracles are at the core of this array of gifts. Are not miracles at the core, too, of the Christian experience generally, if only by providing the critical foundations for eliminating dubious revelations?[87] The perhaps unavoidable particularity of miracles makes it difficult, if not in principle impossible, to subject them to systematic investigation.

May we not see, in St. Paul's instructive ordering of gifts, implicit testimony to the pervasiveness, if not to the ultimate sovereignty, of reason in human affairs? His account, properly understood, may even suggest what natural right, or philosophy, can do to supply the lack of, if not even to strengthen, genuine revelation. In any event, St. Paul's invocation of the common good looks to the great political ends to which natural right has always been dedicated.[88]

Notes

1. *The Jewish Encyclopedia* (New York: KTAV Publishing House), 4: 486 (*Yoma* 78b). Part One of appendix B is based on a talk given at the Lenoir-Rhyne College Humanities Conference, Wildacres Conference Center, Little Switzerland, North Carolina, May 18, 1995. (All references to notes in this appendix are, unless otherwise indicated, to the notes in appendix B of this collection.)

2. The text drawn upon here is *Webster's Ninth New Collegiate Dictionary*.

3. George Anastaplo, *The Artist as Thinker: From Shakespeare to Joyce* (Athens, Ohio: Ohio University Press, 1983), pp. 221, 222. See, on the uses of *soul* today even by religious writers, appendix C of this collection, in the text at note 21.

4. See, on death and dying, George Anastaplo, *Human Being and Citizen: Essays on Virtue, Freedom, and the Common Good* (Chicago: Swallow Press, 1975), p. 214.

5. See Anastaplo, *Human Being and Citizen*, pp. 87–96 (on the soulless "self"); Anastaplo, *The American Moralist: On Law, Ethics, and Government* (Athens, Ohio: Ohio University Press, 1992), pp. 3–19, 582–91.

6. Immanuel Kant tried to work out a doctrine of personal responsibility that is compatible with scientific determinism. See, e.g., Anastaplo, *The American Moralist*, pp. 27–32. Does not liberal democracy depend upon the assumption that there are choices to be made and that political as well as personal responsibility follows upon such choices?

7. Some try to use the Greek word *psychos* for *self*, but that is not right. Perhaps a variation of *autos* would be possible. See the opening words of Plato's *Phaedo*. In Latin, a variation of *persona*, or mask, might be used. See note 12 below. When we use *psyche*, we look more to passions which should be ministered to than to any model by which the soul (including its passions) should be guided.

8. See, e.g., Anastaplo, *Human Being and Citizen*, p. 220; *The Artist as Thinker*, p. 224; *The American Moralist*, pp. 86–87; Anastaplo, "The Forms of Our Knowing: A Somewhat Socratic Introduction," in D. A. Ollivant, ed., *Jacques Maritain and the Many Ways of Knowing* (American Maritain Society publication, Catholic University Press, 2001). See also appendix A of this collection, note 72; Anastaplo, "Samplings," 27 *Political Science Reviewer* 346, 389f. ("Thomas Hobbes and Madness"). I am using in the text here the terms *philosophy* and *philosopher* in a broad sense. See the text at note 21 of appendix B of this collection. This bears on the title of this collection, *But Not Philosophy*, where a "narrow" (or most rigorous) sense of philosophy is drawn upon.

9. See, e.g., Anastaplo, *Human Being and Citizen*, p. 317 n. 4; *The American Moralist*, p. 137. See, on Martin Heidegger, ibid., p. 144; Horst Mewes, "Leo Strauss and Martin Heidegger: Greek Antiquity and the Meaning of Modernity," in Peter Graf Kielmansegg, Horst Mewes, and Elisabeth Glaser-Schmidt, eds., *Hannah Arendt and Leo Strauss* (New York: Cambridge University Press, 1995), p. 105. Consider this observation.

> Yet while according to Plato and Aristotle *to be* in the highest sense means to be *always*, Heidegger contends that *to be* in the highest sense means *to exist*, that is to say, *to be* in the manner in which man *is*: *to be* in the highest sense is constituted by mortality.

Leo Strauss, *The Rebirth of Classical Political Rationalism* (Chicago: University of Chicago Press, 1989), p. 37. See appendix C of this collection, note 26. See also note 13 below.

10. See, on distinctively modern terms, Anastaplo, *The American Moralist*, p. 142. See, on conscience, ibid., p. 133; Anastaplo, *Human Being and Citizen*, p. 275; appendix C of this collection. See, on the self, ibid., p. 90; *The Artist as Thinker*, p. 403 n. 112; *The American Moralist*, p. 230. See, on self-expression, *Human Being and Citizen*, p. 135; *The Artist as Thinker*, p. 6. See, on individuality and virtue, *Human Being and Citizen*, p. 293 n. 13. See, on individuality and immortality, ibid., p. 317 n. 4. See, on privacy, *The American Moralist*, p. 230. See, on Machiavelli and individuality, *The Artist as Thinker*, p. 438 n. 194. See, on the relation between the Good and the unique, ibid. p. 413 n. 145, p. 431 n. 175. See, on modern economics, Anastaplo, "Legal Education, Economics, and Law School Governance: Explorations," 46 *South Dakota Law Review* (2000).

11. See Anastaplo, *The Artist as Thinker*, p. 291; *Human Being and Citizen*, pp. 219, 316 n. 2.

12. See, on the limitations of the cinema, Anastaplo, *The Artist as Thinker*, pp. 322–30; *The American Moralist*, p. 245; Anastaplo, "Can Beauty 'Hallow Even the Bloodiest Tomahawk'?" *The Critic*, winter 1993, p. 2 (with commentary on Flannery O'Connor, Ernest Hemingway, and *The Silence of the Lambs*). On the *person*, see Anastaplo, "John Quincy Adams Revisited," 25 *Oklahoma City University Law Review* 119, 178, (2000).

13. If the body is made too much of, a preoccupation with self-preservation (or with one's identity) is likely to develop, thereby making the best in us more vulnerable than it should be. See note 9, above. See, on death and dying, note 4 above. Compare note 25 below. My 1998 Lenoir-Rhyne College Humanities Conference talk, entitled "On Identity," included these observations:

> An emphasis upon "identity" may be related to, or may depend upon or lead into, what we know as "existentialism." This can be considered an "identity-producing" or "identity-defining" approach. It could well be called "identityism" instead of "existentialism." (It is here that *commitment* is made much of, as well as an emphasis upon the *self*.)

Underlying these modern developments is the acceptance of the notion of individualism as a very good thing. One form that individualism takes is that of modern art, which does so much with subjectivity and a repudiation of traditional notions. A related form of individualism may be discerned in the shift, in constitutional law, from the traditional term *freedom of speech* to a much more fashionable term today, *freedom of expression*. This is a shift from citizens who are concerned with an activity aimed primarily at serving the common good to human beings who are concerned most of all with an activity aimed at permitting personal gratification. This is related to an emphasis upon *creativity*, which is to be distinguished from regarding art as *an imitation of nature*.

Again and again we see, in these shifts in vocabulary, the opinion—a sometimes desperate opinion—that one is "essentially" on one's own in this world.

See, on existentialism, Anastaplo, *The American Moralist*, pp. 139–45. See also appendix C of this collection, note 26. The "On Identity" talk is included in Anastaplo, "Lawyers, First Principles, and Contemporary Challenges: Explorations," 19 *Northern Illinois University Law Review* 353, 458–59 (1999).

14. Hugh S. Moorhead, ed., *The Meaning of Life* (Chicago: Chicago Review Press, p. 1988), p. 188 (a quotation of April 8, 1953). See also ibid., p. 18; note 28 below. See, on "natural valuations," note 37 below.

Part 2 of appendix B is based on a talk given at the Center for Christianity and the Common Good, the University of Dallas, Irving, Texas, September 15, 1995. See Anastaplo, "Teaching, Nature, and the Moral Virtues," *The Great Ideas Today* 23–26 (1997). The considerable changes since 1995 have been influenced by suggestions from Clifford A. Bates, Jr., Laurence Berns, Keith Cleveland, Christopher A. Colmo, Thomas Engeman, Harry V. Jaffa, and John Van Doren.

15. See, on nature and natural right, Leo Strauss, *Natural Right and History* (Chicago: University of Chicago Press, 1953); Yves R. Simon, *The Definition of Moral Virtue*, ed. Yukan Kuic (New York: Fordham University Press, 1986); Anastaplo, *Human Being and Citizen*, pp. 74f; Anastaplo, *The American Moralist*, p. 616. See also note 28 below. See as well part 3 of appendix B of this collection.

16. See, e.g., Anastaplo. *The American Moralist*, p. 83; note 8 above. Recent dramatic announcements, with perhaps profound implications for our understanding of the nature of nature, are the reports that mammals have been cloned. See, e.g., Gina Kolata, "Scientist Reports First Cloning Ever of Adult Mammal," *New York Times*, February 23, 1997, p. 1; Michael Specter and Gina Kolata, "After Decades and Many Missteps, Cloning Success," *New York Times*, March 3, 1997, p. A1. Roman Catholic theologians argue, however, that a distinctive soul for the cloned human being would still have to be provided by God.

17. See, e.g., Larry Arnhart, *Darwinian Natural Right: The Biological Ethics of Human Nature* (Albany: State University of New York Press, 1998); Frans deWaal, *Goodnatured: The Origin of Right and Wrong in Humans and Other Animals* (Cambridge, Mass.: Harvard University Press, 1996).

18. Speculations, in the scientific literature of recent decades, about what is called the Anthropic Principle spell out such cautions. See Anastaplo, book review, *The Great Ideas Today* 448 (1997) (on Subrahmanyan Chandrasekhar's study of Isaac Newton's *Principia*). See also part 3 of appendix A of this collection.

19. Still, it may be instructive to consider here how long it takes for any change in the gravitational pull of a body to be felt elsewhere. Is this "transmission" also limited by the

speed of light? See George Anastaplo, "Lessons for the Student of Law: The Oklahoma Lectures," 20 *Oklahoma City University Law Review* 19, 187 (1995).

20. A few severely inhibited people may have to be encouraged to let themselves enjoy, now and then, the physical pleasures legitimately available to them. See note 39 below. Even if the various species on earth are regarded as created, this evidently would not insure their perpetuity—or so it would seem from the evidence we have of extinct species.

21. See, on the limitations of even someone such as Alexander the Great, George Anastaplo, *The Constitutionalist: Notes on the First Amendment* (Dallas: Southern Methodist University Press, 1971).

22. See, e.g., Shakespeare, *Julius Caesar*, I, ii, 51–62; *Antony and Cleopatra*, I, iii, 35.

23. See Anastaplo, *The Thinker as Artist: From Homer to Plato and Aristotle* (Athens, Ohio: Ohio University Press, 1997), p. 182.

24. See Anastaplo, *The American Moralist*, p. 27. See, also, ibid., p. 582. Are the attractions of heaven, as conventionally understood, based upon familiar pleasures of various kinds—and upon the avoidance of familiar pains? See note 36 below. See also Aristotle, *Nicomachean Ethics* 1099a12, 1104b4–9, 1153b10–19.

25. If neither the body nor the soul of the human being can exist separately, is the soul directed in its conduct by nature (if only because of the body, which "everyone" recognizes is constantly shaped by nature)? Similar to this body-soul relation may be that between "individual" and "society." See, on the relation of "self" to "soul," Anastaplo, *Human Being and Citizen*, p. 87. See also part 1 of appendix B of this collection.

26. Augustine seems to have regarded the moral virtues, guided by the conscience, as more solid than the intellectual virtues. Thinkers such as René Descartes, Thomas Hobbes, and Baruch Spinoza looked to mathematics for models of certainty for their inquiries even into human things. See note 8 above.

27. Aristotle, for one, was aware of the variability of justice. But if there is a best regime, itself grounded in nature, would justice be as variable there as he recognizes it to be in the everyday world? Be that as it may, the decent human being respects others' opinions to a considerable extent, avoiding as much as possible being thought "offensive." See, on "the best regime" in Aristotle's *Politics*, Harry V. Jaffa, "Aristotle (384–322 B.C.)," in Leo Strauss and Joseph Cropsey, eds., *History of Political Philosophy* (Chicago: Rand McNally, 1972), p. 64.

28. See, e.g., Anastaplo, "Lessons for the Student of Law," p. 179; Strauss, *Natural Right and History*, p. x. See also the epigraph in the text at note 14 of appendix B of this collection.

29. See, e.g., Plato, *Apology* 32A-E.

30. Thomas Aquinas, however, spoke of prudence as the only intellectual virtue which includes the moral virtues. See George Anastaplo, "On Freedom: Explorations," 17 *Oklahoma City University Law Review* 465, 681–82 (1992).

31. See Anastaplo, *The Artist as Thinker*, pp. 1f.

32. In American law, this opinion may be seen developed in the writings of Oliver Wendell Holmes, Jr., and in cases such as *Erie Railroad Company* v. *Tompkins*, 304 U.S. 64 (1938). See George Anastaplo, *The Constitution of 1787: A Commentary* (Baltimore: Johns Hopkins University Press, 1989), pp. 128–37; William T. Braithwaite, "The Common Law and the Judicial Power: An Introduction to *Swift-Erie*," in John A. Murley, Robert L. Stone, and William T. Braithwaite, eds., *Law and Philosophy: The Practice of Theory* (Athens, Ohio: Ohio University Press, 1992), p. 774.

33. This should be evident in the seven introductions to non-Western thought I have provided for this collection. See also appendix C of this collection.

34. It may also be related to the Aristotelian notion that a well-formed moral character seems itself to be a way of knowing what otherwise might not be known. I have, throughout these remarks, set aside Kant's possible argument that if morality is grounded in nature, then it cannot be *known* to be good in itself. (He does seem to want to establish that the moral law is simply good in itself.) I sense that he may not be an altogether reliable ally for the Aristotelian in these matters, especially if the Kantian doctrine should tend to leave good *intentions* as sovereign in moral matters.

35. See, e.g., Thomas Aquinas, *On Truth*, Q. 23, A 6, c. (quoted in note 74 of chapter 6 of this collection). See also note 70 below.

36. Few if any, it can be said, want immortality in the form of an eternally unchanging life. Would not such a life be too dependent upon a soul's memories for its activities and pleasures? See note 24, above. Consider the implications of the newspaper story about the French woman who was said to be the world's oldest person. The story concluded, "Though blind, virtually deaf and confined to a wheelchair, she retains a good appetite and has her hair done once a week." "World's Oldest Person Celebrates 122nd with Cake," *Chicago Tribune*, February 22, 1997, sec. 1, p. 15. (She died later in 1997.) Compare note 72 of appendix A of this collection; the text at note 132 of appendix A of this collection.

37. See Aristotle, *Politics* 1278b25–26; Anastaplo, *The American Moralist*, pp. 596–601. See, also, Leo Strauss, *The Political Philosophy of Hobbes* (Chicago: University of Chicago Press, 1952; Phoenix edition, 1963), pp. 124–25. See, on "the truth hidden [for Plato] in the natural valuations," ibid., p. 163.

38. See, for the perspective from which this comment is made, John Van Doren, "Poetic Justice," *The Great Ideas Today* 258 (1996); also, the foreword to this collection. See as well Anastaplo, "The O. J. Simpson Case Revisited," 28 *Loyola University of Chicago Law Journal* 461 (1997).

39. See, for cautions with respect to moral crusades, Anastaplo, *The American Moralist*, p. 327; Anastaplo, book review, *The Great Ideas Today* 464 (1996). See also note 20 above, note 48 below. See, on the Idea of the Good, Anastaplo, *The Thinker as Artist*, pp. 303–17, 396. See, on morality and chance circumstances (including the beginnings), the text at note 33 of this appendix. See, also, appendix A of this collection; note 51 below. See as well note 60 below. The following memorandum, "A Primer on the Good, the True, and the Beautiful" (which I prepared in 1976), bears upon the issues discussed in this appendix:

i.

We make much today of something called open-mindedness. But should we not take care lest a civilized willingness to hear out arguments become nothing more than a perverse mindlessness?

One is asked again and again by liberated intellectuals, especially when serious matters are under discussion, "Who is to say who is right?" This tiresome rhetorical question usually implies that one is entitled to do no more than express the preferences one happens to have. To pass judgment on another—to speak of right and wrong—is considered provincial, if not even bigoted.

"Right" and "wrong," as well as "good" and "bad," are explained away by the liberated as merely conventional ways of indicating one's preferences, the preferences determined (for the most part, if not altogether) by one's environment. Indeed, these advanced thinkers are incapable of any sustained argument, independent of "arbitrary" religious and legal prohibitions, against even such a practice (to take an extreme case) as a routine indulgence in cannibalism.

Such open-minded people (who, of course, happen personally to abhor cannibalism and other such social aberrations) do consider themselves *thinkers*. That is, the old-fashioned respect— perhaps an almost instinctive respect—for man's nature continues to assert itself in their implicit assumption that thinking is both possible and desirable. Thus, it is assumed proper, if not necessary, for men and women to attempt to think. Is it not also assumed that there are correct and incorrect conclusions following from the thinking one might attempt?

ii.

Many open-minded people do have decided opinions critical of social injustice, of bigotry, and (perhaps above all) of those who are not open-minded. But why should one bother to complain about what others are (or are not) doing or saying if right and wrong are but matters of opinion, if human beings have no defensible basis for the choices they make about the good and the bad? Why should one bother to try to "improve" things if one's preferences cannot be other than a matter of chance?

A matter of chance? If one's preferences are decisively determined by one's environment, and if one's environment and hence upbringing are essentially matters of chance, what basis *is* there for preferring or promoting one environment over another, for preferring one set of preferences over another? Will not whatever we change into be as much subject to chance (with *its* successor eventually becoming as appealing to some partisans) as whatever we may now happen to be? So, again, why bother to change things?

Why bother, if there is not something in the nature of man which demands (or at least permits) an ordering of alternatives, which suggests a hierarchy of better and worse ways of shaping, developing, and preserving both men and their communities? What sense does it make to speak of "progress" if men do not have some sense—if only a dim awareness—of what the very best would be for human beings?

Perhaps, then, we ought to replace open-mindedness by simple-mindedness. The paralyzing open-mindedness criticized here depends upon and reinforces a determined, if not suicidal, thoughtlessness. A proper simple-mindedness, on the other hand, may at least have the merit of acknowledging the primacy of mind, and hence of thinking, in human affairs.

iii.

Who *is* to say who is right? The simple-minded answer is, "Whoever knows what is right." But, it should at once be recognized, there are all kinds of foolish people who *believe* themselves to know what is right. Is not even this, however, a reflection of the human being's natural yearning for, and perhaps openness to, goodness and truth? (Beauty, it can be suggested in passing, may be the pleasure-inducing manifestation, often in corporeal form, of the good or of the true.)

We must distinguish, therefore, between those who know what is right and those who mistakenly believe themselves to know. It is one thing to recognize that it is often difficult to know what is right or good; it is quite another to conclude from this long-familiar difficulty that it is always impossible to know what is right or good.

To recognize this vital distinction, as well as the perils of unexamined dogmatism, is to give ourselves an opportunity to begin to understand what can indeed be known and done about human beings. Such understanding, to which serious education should be directed, rests upon:

1. an array of refined intellectual skills (as well as psychic maturity);
2. a body of carefully sifted information (including information about the obvious and the self-evident, as well as about the apparently self-evident);
3. an awareness of the fundamental questions thoughtful human beings have always recognized to be worthy of repeated investigation.

See Anastaplo, *The Artist as Thinker*, pp. 275–78. See also note 74 below.

40. Alighieri Dante, *Paradiso*, III, 85–87. Consider also the reference in the Declaration of Independence to "the Laws of Nature and of Nature's God."

Part 3 of appendix B is adapted from an article, "Natural Law or Natural Right? An Apreciation of James V. Schall, S.J.," 38 *Loyola of New Orleans Law Review* 915–30 (1993).

41. The essay by James V. Schall that originally provided the occasion for this discussion is his 1992 Brendan Brown Lecture at Loyola University of New Orleans Law School. See Schall, "On Being Dissatisfied with Compromises: Natural Law and Human Rights," 38 *Loyola of New Orleans Law Review* 289 (1992). For extended consideration of these matters, see Leo Strauss, *Natural Right and History* (Chicago: University of Chicago Press, 1953). See, also, Peter Stanford, "The Holy See-Saw," *Guardian Weekend* (London), December 12, 1992, 26; Alan Cowell, "Challenge to the Faithful," *New York Times Magazine*, December 27, 1992, 1C.

42. This is evident upon considering, for example, the political speeches of Abraham Lincoln. See George Anastaplo, *Abraham Lincoln: A Constitutional Biography* (Lanham, Md.: Rowman & Littlefield, 1999), pp. 149f.

43. *Huidekoper's Lessee* v. *Douglass*, 7 U.S. (3 Cranch) 1, at 70–71 (1805) (Chief Justice Marshall). See, on *Huidekoper*, William W. Crosskey, *Politics and the Constitution in the History of the United States* (Chicago: University of Chicago Press, 1953), pp. 719–53. See also Anastaplo, "Mr. Crosskey, the American Constitution, and the Natures of Things," 15 *Loyola University of Chicago Law Journal* 181, 209 (1984); *Marbury* v. *Madison*, 5 U.S. (1 Cranch) 169 (1803). Consider as well the oath for judges provided in Section 8 of the Judiciary Act of 1789. See, on the legal heritage of the English-speaking peoples, Anastaplo, ed., *Liberty, Equality and Modern Constitutionalism: A Source Book* (Newburyport, Mass.: R. Pullins/Focus, 1999).

44. See, on the Preamble to the Constitution, Anastaplo, *The Constitution of 1787*, pp. 13–25; Anastaplo, *The Amendments to the Constitution: A Commentary* (Baltimore: Johns Hopkins University Press, 1995), p. 462. See, also, Anastaplo, "Constitutionalism, The Rule of Rules: Explorations," 39 *Brandeis Law Journal* 179, 230 (2000).

45. See Anastaplo, *Human Being and Citizen*, pp. 46–60, 74–86; *The Constitution of 1787*, pp. 124–48. See, also, Braithwaite, "The Common Law and the Judicial Power," in Murley, Stone, and Braithwaite, eds., *Law and Philosophy*, p. 774.

46. See Anastaplo, *The Constitution of 1787*, pp. 179–95, *The Amendments to the Constitution*, pp. 92–106, 228–38. See also note 64 below.

47. Compare Malcolm P. Sharp, "Crosskey, Anastaplo, and Meiklejohn on the United States Constitution," 20 *University of Chicago Law School Record* 1 (1973). See, on the

pitfalls of "originalism," George Anastaplo, "*In re* Antonin Scalia," 28 *Perspectives in Political Science* 22 (1999). See, on positivism and legal realism, Anastaplo, "Legal Education, Economics, and Law School Governances: Appendix G.

48. See, on nature, Anastaplo, *The American Moralist*, pp. 412–17, 616. Compare Joseph Cropsey, *Political Philosophy and the Issues of Politics* (Chicago: University of Chicago Press, 1977), p. 221. See also part 2 of this appendix.

49. See Anastaplo, *The American Moralist*, pp. 58–79. See also note 46 above, note 64 below.

50. See, on the relation of prophecy to statesmanship, Leo Strauss, "Some Remarks on the Political Science of Maimonides and Farabi," 18 *Interpretation* 3 (1990). See, also George Anastaplo, "Church and State: Explorations," 19 *Loyola University of Chicago Law Journal* 61 (1987); Anastaplo, *The American Moralist*, pp. 20–26, 58–79, 214–22, 516–36, 582–601; Anastaplo, "On Trial: Explorations," 22 *Loyola University of Chicago Law Journal* 763, 765, 767–84, 821–30, 854–73, 882–969, 977–94 (1991); chapter 4 of this collection, note 38; notes 56, 88 below.

51. See, e.g., *Romans* 2:14, *Acts* 17:23. See also Augustine, *City of God*, book 8, chapters 9–12, book 18, chapter 41. Consider the parts of the Ten Commandments (or Decalogue) that the Noahites were expected to respect. See, on the Decalogue, note 63 below. See, on the moral tradition associated with the Jewish and Christian religions, Alan Donagan, *The Theory of Morality* (Chicago: University of Chicago Press, 1977), p. xv. See also Anastaplo, "Law & Literature and the Bible: Explorations," 23 *Oklahoma City University Law Review* 515 (1998); note 39 above, note 64 below. See as well appendix C of this collection.

52. See Anastaplo, *Human Being and Citizen*, pp. 46–60, *The American Moralist*, pp. 345–48. The tension can become particularly acute here when the revelation invoked does not happen to be the true revelation.

53. See Schall, "On Being Dissatisfied," pp. 296–97, 304–06.

54. See, e.g., Plato, *Republic* 414B sq., 427B-C; Plato, *Laws* 624A sq.; Aristotle, *Politics* 1331a19–30, 1335b12–17. See also note 88 below.

55. See Anastaplo, "On Trial," pp. 767–84.

56. See, ibid., pp. 854–73; Anastaplo, *The American Moralist*, pp. 68–69.

57. See Anastaplo, "On Trial," p. 769.

58. See Schall, "On Being Disssatisfied," p. 303.

59. See Anastaplo, *The American Moralist*, pp. 144–60.

60. See Anastaplo, *The Artist as Thinker*, pp. 252–53. See, on "the ineluctable necessities" of death without which "no life, no human life, no good life, is possible," ibid., p. 271 (quoting Leo Strauss). See also notes 39 and 51 above.

61. See, e.g., Schall, "On Being Dissastisfied," p. 292.

62. A convenient English translation of much of the *Summa Theologica* may be found in volumes 17 and 18 of *Great Books of the Western World*, published by the Encyclopaedia Britannica (second edition, 1990). Thomas's *Treatise on Law* makes up Questions 90 through 108 of Part I of the Second Part of his *Summa Theologica*. Popular editions of the *Treatise on Law* are usually limited today to Questions 90 through 97. See, on the *Treatise on Law*, Anastaplo, "Lawyers, First Principles, and Contemporary Challenges," p. 431.

63. See Thomas Aquinas, *Treatise on Law*, Question 91, Article 5, Question 98, Articles 5 and 6, Question 99, Articles 2 and 4, Question 100, Articles 1, 3, 6, 7, and 8. The Decalogue refers to the Ten Commandments given to Moses. See *Exodus* 20:1–17,

Deuteronomy 5:6–21. See also note 51 above. See, on the Ten Commandments, Anastaplo, "Law & Literature and the Bible," p. 613.

64. But consider the far-reaching implications of *Deuteronomy* 4:6: "Observe therefore and do them [the Lord's statutes and ordinances]; for this is your wisdom and your understanding in the sight of the peoples, that when they hear all these statutes, shall say, 'Surely this great nation is a wise and understanding people.'" Is it not implied here that nonbelievers can, on their own, recognize the sensibleness, indeed the wisdom, of the Mosaic code *once it is established*? See Aquinas, *Treatise on Law*, Question 100, Article 7; Anastaplo, *The American Moralist*, pp. 60, 63–64, 74–77; "On Trial," pp. 770, 1035–36 n. 19. See also note 51 above, notes 74, 80, and 88 below. See, on the determination of the biblical canon, note 88 below.

Our investigation of the differences between *natural law* and *natural right* is complicated by the use of *law of nature* by the physical scientists. Consider the far-reaching implications of Francis Bacon, *The New Organon*, Book One, Aphorism II: "[I]n nature nothing really exists besides individual bodies, performing pure individual acts according to a fixed law."

65. See, e.g., Thomas Aquinas, *Summa Theologica*, Part One, Question 46, Article 2.

66. See, e.g., ibid., Part II of the Second Part, Question 2; Article 9, reply to Objection 3. It has been noticed by students of these matters that the term *natural law* implies an active agency, whereas Aristotle, as perhaps the most noteworthy source of what later developed into the natural-right/natural-law doctrines, speaks only of that intrinsic rightness to which I have referred. See Harry V. Jaffa, *Thomism and Aristotelianism—A Study of the Commentary by Thomas Aquinas on the Nicomachean Ethics* (Chicago: University of Chicago Press, 1952), p. 174. See also Anastaplo, *The American Moralist*, p. 100; section VIII of part 3 of this appendix.

67. See, e.g., Ernest L. Fortin, "St. Thomas Aquinas," in Strauss and Cropsey, eds., *History of Political Philosophy* (second edition), pp. 227–23, 233–46.

68. See, e.g., ibid., pp. 243–45, 240; Thomas Aquinas, *Summa Theologica*, First Part, Question 2.

69. Ibid, First Part, Question 19, Articles 3 and 4.

70. Ibid, First Part, Question 25. There is no cause of the will of God. See ibid., First Part, Question 19. See, also, ibid., First Part, Question 46. Compare Thomas Aquinas, *On Truth*, Question 23, Answer 6. See note 35 above. Consider, on Lucifer's defiant "I will not serve," Anastaplo, *The Artist as Thinker*, pp. 228, 231–32. Consider also Anastaplo, "Law & Literature and the Moderns: Explorations," 20 *Northern Illinois University Law Review*, 261 (2000).

71. See Jaffa, *Thomism and Aristotelianism*, p. 192. Compare the definition of *law* in Question 90, Article 4, of Thomas's *Treatise on Law*: law "is nothing else than an ordinance of reason for the common good, made by him who has care of the community, and promulgated."

72. This may be related to the more or less modern phenomenon of *conscience*, which also can seem like natural intuition once it is deeply rooted in a way of life. See Anastaplo, *The American Moralist*, p. 607; "On Trial," p. 1076 n. 628. See also note 48 above.

73. See Thomas Aquinas, *Treatise on Law*, Question 91, Article 4. See also Thomas Aquinas, *Summa Theologica*, First Part, Question 12.

74. See, e.g., ibid., First Part, Question 32. See, on the severe limitations of the natural ability to *reason* about the highest good, ibid., First Part, Question 12. Yet it sometimes

seems that Thomas suggests that a few human beings may be naturally endowed with the capacity to have, without the aid of scriptural revelation, the vision of God required for attainment of the greatest bliss. See, e.g., First Part, Question 23, Article 7, Reply to Objection 3. See also note 64 above. What can those Few provide as guidance for the Many with respect to the Good? See note 39 above, note 88 below.

75. See Thomas Aquinas, *Treatise on Law*, Question 91, Article 4. See also note 45 above. See, for what Augustine does with this, Anastaplo, "Teaching, Nature, and the Moral Virtues," *The Great Ideas Today* 2, 9–23 (1997). See, on this natural yearning, Anastaplo, "Law & Literature and the Bible: Explorations," p. 738.

76. See, e.g., Isaac Newton, *Principia*, Book Three, "Rules of Reasoning in Philosophy," I; Aristotle, *Politics* 1252b2. See, also, Anastaplo, "Church and State," pp. 123–24.

77. See, e.g., Augustine, *The City of God*, Book 3, Chapters 11 and 23, Book 10, Chapter 16, and Book 22, Chapter 11.

78. See Thomas Aquinas, *Summa Theologica*, Part I of the Second Part, Question 109.

79. See the arguments of the Philosopher in the opening pages of Judah Halevi's *The Kuzari*. See also Anastaplo, "On How Eric Voegelin Read Plato and Aristotle," 5/6 *Independent Journal of Philosophy* 85 (1988); Anastaplo, "Seven Questions for Professor Jaffa," in Harry V. Jaffa, ed., *Original Intent and the Framers of the Constitution* (Washington, D.C.: Regnery Gateway, 1994), pp. 182–94, 196–97. See, on non-Western serial reincarnations, chapters 3 and 5 of this collection; Anastaplo, "Church and State," p.183.

80. See Anastaplo, "Church and State," pp. 109–26, 183–90. Compare "Bertrand Arthur William Russell," *Encyclopedia of Philosophy*, vol. 7, pp. 235, 254–56 (1967). See note 87 below.

81. See note 88 below. See, on imagination generally, Eva Brann, *The World of the Imagination: Sum and Substance* (Savage, Md.: Rowman & Littlefield, 1991).

82. See Schall, "On Being Dissatisfied," p. 289 (quoting from Leo Strauss, *Platonic Political Philosophy* [Chicago: University of Chicago Press, 1983], p. 144).

83. See, e.g., Schall, "On Being Dissatisfied," pp. 305–6. See, also, Anastaplo, *Human Being and Citizen*, pp. 46–60. So influential is the "natural rights" approach that it is difficult to keep editors from changing "natural right" to "natural rights." See, for such an unfortunate change, the title to my article in 38 *Loyola of New Orleans Law Review* 915 (1993).

84. See Schall, "On Being Dissatisfied," p. 308. See, on the relation of the self to the soul, part of this appendix.

85. See, e.g., Jaffa, *Thomism and Aristotelianism*, epigraph from Winston Churchill: "It is baffling to reflect that what men call honour does not correspond always to Christian ethics." See also ibid., pp. 192–93; notes 76 and 80 above.

86. *I Corinthians* 12:4–11 (Revised Standard Version). One can be reminded, by the references to "various kinds of tongues" and to "the interpretation of tongues," of the inspired babbling by the Pythia at Delphi and to how the priests of Apollo interpreted such babbling. See, on Delphi, Anastaplo, *The Thinker as Artist*, p. 93.

87. See the text at note 66 of this appendix. More can be said, but not here, about St. Paul's ordering of gifts in *I Corinthians* 12. Aristotle observed that it is the business of the wise man to order. *Metaphysics* 982a18. See also note 46 above. See as well the text at note 80 of this appendix.

88. See Jaffa, "Aristotle," in Leo Strauss and Joseph Cropsey, eds., *History of Political Philosophy* 2d ed, (Chicago: Rand McNally Co., 1972), pp. 68–72, 125–28. See, also, Anastaplo, *The American Moralist*, pp. 37–50, 217, 531–32; Anastaplo, "On Trial," 1052 n. 309, 1054 n. 348, 1060 n. 450, 1064 n. 501, 1117–18 n. 900. Consider the opening sentences of Leo Strauss, "Some Remarks on the Political Science of Maimonides and Farabi," at 4:

> There is, in the philosophy of Mainomides as well as in that of his Muslim masters and his Jewish disciples, a political science. The principal teaching of this science is summarized in the following theses: Men need, in order to live, guidance and, as a result, a law; they need, in order to live well, to attain happiness, a divine law which guides them not only, like the human law, toward peace and moral perfection, but further toward the understanding of the supreme truths and thereby toward supreme perfection; the divine law is given to men by (the intermediary of) a man who is a "prophet," i.e., one who combines in his person all the essential qualities of the philosopher as well as those of the legislator and king; the activity proper to the prophet is legislation.

See also ibid., pp. 10–20. Prophecy, it has been argued, was the political name for political science. This Farabian, if not also Maimonidean, account of prophecy suggests that revelation, its assessment, and its applications lie within the province of statesmanship, especially that statesmanship which is grounded in the natural-right tradition. It may also suggest that the true, or full, prophet is ultimately a statesman, a pious man who must routinely take his bearings by considerations of justice and the common good. The role of wisdom in establishing a plausible biblical canon becomes apparent upon assessing such dubious proposals as W. B. Yeats's *A Vision* (1937). See Leo Strauss, *The Rebirth of Classical Political Rationalism* (Chicago: University of Chicago Press, 1989), pp. 223–24; Anastaplo, "Law and Literature and the Moderns," p. 473; Anastaplo, "Law and Literature and the Bible," p. 719 (on the Nicene Creed). See also notes 50, 54, 64, 75 above. See as well chapter 4 of this collection, note 38; the text at note 136 of appendix A of this collection; the text at note 24 of appendix C of this collection; epigraph, preface to this collection.

In opposition to the position taken in this appendix are various modern thinkers. See, e.g., Robert S. Hill, "David Hume," in Strauss and Cropsey, eds., *History of Political Philosophy*, p. 509. Compare Leo Strauss, *Natural Right and History* (Chicago: University of Chicago Press, 1953); Anastaplo, "A Primer on the God, the True, and the Beautiful," (incorporated in note 39 of this appendix).

Appendix C

On the Use, Neglect, and Abuse of Veils: The Parliaments of the World's Religions

I never saw you in the sun or shade,
Lady, remove your veil
After you knew the wish that makes me pale
By which all other wills from my heart fade.

While I was hiding the fair thoughts I bore,
That have undone my mind in this desire,
I saw compassion shine upon your face;
But when Love made you conscious of my fire
The blond hair became veiled and was no more,
The loving look closed in itself its grace.
What I most longed for finds its hiding-place
In you; the veil rules me,
Which to my death, hot or cold though it be,
Covers your eyes' sweet light as with a shade.

—Petrarch[1]

Religious differences have often fueled long and bitter conflicts. Our Age of Enlightenment, beginning perhaps in the seventeenth century, has attempted to dampen down such conflicts by promoting commerce, encouraging religious skepticism, and having recourse to interfaith accommodations. Nevertheless, the beneficial effects of religious discipline continue to be desired: moral and social effects that depend upon religion being taken seriously.

The first half of this appendix, describing for the most part what I happened to observe of the 1993 convocation in Chicago, Illinois, of the Parliament of the World's Religions, presents an assembly dedicated, for the sake of universal peace, to the advancement of toleration and cooperation across a broad range of religious and other diversity. The second half of this appendix, examining the principal statement issued in the name of that assembly, assesses

345

both modern interfaith thought and the prospects of reconciliation grounded in such thought.[2]

Both a general enlightenment grounded in modern science and an abundance of religious faiths continue to enlist the allegiance of multitudes. Whether current accommodations can truly be both global and effective depends, in part, upon whether people can know the whole in such a way as to permit them to act sensibly in many different circumstances.

I.

Chicago's Palmer House was occupied in August 1993 by delegates to the second Parliament of the World's Religions, many of them in colorful costumes that we usually see only in pictures. At times the colors, noises, incense, and culinary odors turned the corridors of this hotel into "instant Asia," a rather exhilarating place. The concluding public event of the Parliament was a well-received talk by an amiable Dalai Lama in Grant Park the evening of September 4.[3]

The Parliament of the World's Religions brought together more than eight thousand participants for five hundred meetings between August 28 and September 5, 1993. The participants, representing more than one hundred and twenty-five faiths, came from fifty-six countries, with evidently the largest contingents from India and the United States.

The 1993 Parliament followed, by a century, the first such convention of the world's religions in September 1893, also held in Chicago. The 1893 effort (a Pentecost of sorts) extended over seventeen days and resulted in voluminous publications. That Parliament, with four hundred delegates from forty-one religious traditions and denominations and with thousands in its audiences, was one of the splendors of the great 1893 Columbian Exposition.[4]

Critical to the 1893 meeting of religious leaders had been an emphasis upon religious unity and brotherhood. Each religious group participating in that Parliament was permitted to display itself. The use of the term *parliament* presupposed the equality of the constituent members, a presupposition that evidently troubled many Christians in this country who did not want to surrender their own faith's ancient claim to preeminence among the world's religions. By 1993 there was far less need for foreign, especially Asian, groups to introduce themselves to the West. The 1893 Parliament had been far more intriguing in that many of the foreign sects represented in Chicago that year were barely known in the United States. Those sects now have large permanent outposts in Chicago as elsewhere in this country. (African groups were not adequately represented at either Parliament. Perhaps in 2093?)

We can sense, upon comparing the 1893 and the 1993 Parliaments, the intellectual and social movements there had been during the intervening century among the members of the principal world religions. The influence upon everyone today of great wars, drawing upon and promoting profound economic and technological changes, is evident in how religious, as well as other, subjects came to be discussed in the late twentieth century. The accepted verities of earlier times are no longer relied upon to the extent that they once were.

Another difference between the 1893 and the 1993 Parliaments in Chicago was that the earlier proceedings appeared to be more religious or spiritual in tone than the later, even as their scholarship was more serious. Related to this difference is the fact that respectable divinity schools in Chicago seemed to have little to do with the 1993 Parliament convening in their own city. For this and other reasons, there may have been more of a carnival atmosphere during the 1993 proceedings (with its determined celebration of diversity), even though the 1893 proceedings had been conducted as part of a spectacular world's fair.

II.

One difficulty in arranging any convocation of the world's religions is with the very phrase, *the world's religions*. That term tends to lump together a variety of ways of organized worship, implicitly playing down (if not even negating) the specialness that most, if not all, of these associations see in themselves. To lump them all together may be to distort them somewhat: they tend thereby to be seen from the outside. They can even be spoken of as "lifestyles."

What we call a religion may not have originally been considered as *a religion*—that is, as an instance of a species—but rather it was often considered as a vital part of *the* way of life of a people. An indication of the many fundamental differences there are here may be seen in this part of a protest submitted (on August 31, 1993) to the Council for the Parliament on behalf of some of the Buddhist participants in the Parliament:

> Having listened to invocations, prayers and benedictions offered by religious leaders of different host committees during the Opening Plenary and having attended the evening Plenary on Interfaith Understanding, we could not help but feel that the 1993 Parliament of the World's Religions is being held for the worshippers of Almighty and Creator God and efforts are being made towards "achieving oneness under God."
>
> Further, with great astonishment we watched leaders of different religious traditions define all religions as religions of God and unwittingly rank Buddha with God. We found this lack of knowledge and insensitivity all the more surprising because we, the religious leaders of the world, are invited to this Parliament in order to

promote mutual understanding and respect, and we are supposed to be celebrating one hundred years of interfaith dialogue and understanding![5]

This protest included the following recommendation, a recommendation which suggests how even the most ancient sects have been influenced in our time by modern social science:

> Language and communication skills are important elements in bringing about agreement and cooperation. We must train ourselves to be sensitive to each other and learn to use language that is inclusive and all embracing. We suggest we use "Great Being" or "power of the transcendent" or "Higher Spiritual Authority" instead of "God" in reference to the ultimate spiritual reality. We are open to other suggestions and discussions on this matter.

The reference here to "the transcendent" can remind us of the influence of Ralph Waldo Emerson, an early Western student of Eastern texts and perhaps the first prominent American prophet of "interfaith dialogue." Consider, for example, Emerson's remarks about the relation between God and nature in his 1841 essay, "The Over-Soul":

> These questions which we lust to ask about the future are a confession of sin. God has no answer for them. No answer in words can reply to a question of things. It is not in an arbitrary "decree of God," but in the nature of man, that a veil shuts down on the facts of to-morrow: for the soul will not have us read any other cipher but that of cause and effect. By this veil which curtains events it instructs the children of men to live in to-day. The only mode of obtaining an answer to these questions of the senses is to forego all low curiosity, and, accepting the tide of being which floats us into the secret of nature, work and live, work and live, and all unawares the advancing soul has built and forged for itself a new condition, and the question and the answer are one.

We will return to the use and abuse of veils. Further on in his essay the individualism-minded Emerson says,

> Let man then learn the revelation of all nature and all thought to his heart; this, namely, that the Highest dwells with him; that the sources of nature are in his own mind, if the sentiment of duty is there. But if he would know what the great God speaketh, he must "go into his closet and shut the door," as Jesus said. God will not make himself manifest to cowards. He must greatly listen to himself, withdrawing himself from all the accents of other men's devotion. . . .
>
> It makes no difference whether the appeal is to numbers or to one. The faith that stands on authority is not faith. The reliance on authority measures the decline of religion, the withdrawal of the soul.

It remains an important question whether the transcendent, or interfaith, approach seen in Emerson and his successors can ever help anyone to see and "feel" any particular religion as its truly faithful have long done.

The now-fashionable interfaith approach to the world's religions does reflect a tendency to see each of them from the outside. However attractive such an approach can be, it should be recognized that particularity and immediacy are essential to an association if it is to be taken seriously by its members generation after generation—if it is to have the richness which promotes the deep attachments and inspires the great sacrifices that can mean so much for people.[6]

Another way of putting the typical true believer's reservations about the interfaith approach to religion is to observe that that approach may be too rationalistic. Still another way of putting this is to observe that it is not vigorous enough, which may be related to a general slackening of spirit. It is a web of particulars that usually binds together most people through bad times as well as good, however sympathetic they may like to be, and indeed should usually be, toward what is happening "everywhere else" in the world.

The interfaith approach tends to collapse, or at least to disregard, the differences that individual partisans naturally take seriously—differences between "us" and "them," between "the truly divine" and "all the other projections of the divine," between a world in which divinity is seen to act in human affairs and a world in which no such action is ever discerned.

III.

Particularity and intense allegiances lead to variety, energy, and serious alternatives. No doubt, this variety can be traced, at least in part, to different climes and other circumstances. No doubt, also, a major impetus for the interfaith movement in recent centuries has been the history of violence and atrocities in large part attributable to religious differences between peoples. Bosnia and its neighbors immediately come to mind today, and then Northern Ireland, the Middle East, Cyprus, India, Tibet, and several parts of the former Soviet Union.

So deep-rooted are these differences that it was surprising that there were so few expressions of hostility among the delegates in Chicago during this 1993 Parliament. (There *were* Hindu protests in response to expressions of Kashmir-related and Sikh grievances.) Perhaps the calm in Chicago reflects that spirit in this country which still tends to contain the political conflicts arising between differing religious associations. One could even hear delegates from far away sing "We Shall Overcome" and invoke the First Amendment to the American Constitution both to justify provocative speech and to promote mutual toleration. Also, a general good will, even a determined good will, could be observed among the delegates: most people very much wanted to be, and obviously were, on their best behavior.

The sectarian outbursts we do observe from time to time, even in this country, remind us of political differences around the world which are grounded in long-standing religious differences. One suspects that the religions which are important in the lives of peoples may themselves really be peculiarly sensitive aspects of the political life of the communities involved.

IV.

The religious practices of one people can be difficult for others to accept. Take, for example, one of the most "philosophical" of the religions of mankind, Zoroastrianism (or the Parsi faith), which comes out of ancient Persia and India.[7] The adherents of that faith, who were ably represented at the 1993 Parliament, come to view as preeminently rationalistic. There may be a problem, however, with the ethnocentric emphasis by the adherents to this religion: it seems to be virtually impossible to become a Zoroastrian if one is not born into the faith. This is justified, today, as a temporary restriction—but it does point to the significance of bodies in the lives of human beings. This approach may be difficult for outsiders to reconcile with the general philosophical inclinations of this faith.

Also somewhat philosophical in appearance, but likely to be much more troubling to outsiders, is that seeming disregard (if not disrespect) for the body seen in the traditional Zoroastrian practice of leaving the corpses of their dead for the vultures to eat, a practice evidently still followed by them in Bombay. Herodotus long ago observed that differences in burial practices can be disturbing from one people to another.

The Zoroastrians explained to me, at one of their panels, that this ancient practice respected the cycle of nature, even as it pointed up the transitory character of the body for the human being. This practice was likened to what some North American Indian tribes did with their dead and even to what animals do.[8]

A Hindu who was present defended the ancient Zoroastrian practice by also likening it to the prompt cremation (within twenty-four hours of death) called for in India. The Zoroastrians I talked with (some of whom are now settled, as prosperous businessmen, in Chicago suburbs) seemed to be eager to emphasize that cremation is pretty much the practice resorted to by most Zoroastrians outside of India today.

V.

People, in explaining their own, can usually be trusted to appreciate whatever merits it may have, especially since they are not likely to see their own as others do. When one hears their explanations—which are usually so self-assured that they may not sound defensive—one recognizes, as Aristotle did, that all human beings aim by their actions at some good.[9] It is a good that they have aimed at which permits a people to explain calmly, and even to justify, what can be most shocking to others.

If an association is long established, it is almost certain that it will be able to justify its ways as good and moral. Such justification is routine. I have even heard career gangsters on trial quoted as speaking thus, perhaps not insincerely, about their violent way of life. I am reminded here of another remark by Emerson in his "Over-Soul" essay:

> We grant that human life is mean, but how did we find out that it was mean? What is the ground of this uneasiness of ours; of this old discontent? What is the universal sense of want and ignorance, but the fine innuendo by which the great soul makes its enormous claim?

There seems to be a common set of criteria about morality and the common good, recognizable down to our day, that can be drawn upon for such justifications. How those criteria are expressed may well depend upon the spirit and vocabulary of the time. Today, for example, *nature* is made much of in fashioning explanations: one could hear nature referred to again and again by partisans of one religion after another at the 1993 Parliament, even though the traditions out of which such partisans come never had the Western idea of nature as part of their understanding until modern times. But then, the need as well as the opportunity to provide the kinds of explanations they now provide may also be a modern development.

The often superficial use today of *nature* for this purpose may be traced back to, among others, Emerson, who is hardly superficial himself. The idea of nature may cut against the grain of the fundamental tenets of some, if not all, of the ancient faiths: nature suggests that there is a principle of rest and motion, accounting for how things are, which is independent of any superintending intelligence. There seems to be something Emersonian also in the Declaration of a Global Ethic that was prepared for the 1993 Parliament of the World's Religions. The conscientious social worker with global responsibilities may be heard again and again in the Declaration. I will return to that document in the second half of this appendix. (Excerpts from the document are provided in the addendum to this appendix.)

Certainly *not* in the spirit of that interfaith Declaration, which is determinedly modernist in its accents, were such striking sights, on view at the Palmer House, as the heavy (however voluntary) veiling by which some Muslim women were distinguished and the abject (however joyful) veneration shown by some Hindus to their holy men and holy women.

Other unusual things were on display, of course, including the shaving of heads of men and women by some sects and the never-cut hair of other sectarians. But the heavily veiled Muslim woman may have been the most troubling, especially when observed in a Western setting. (That setting included, at the Parliament, the presence of *most* Muslim women dressed in the Western style.) One could—upon seeing what appeared to be a humble young woman shrouded in black cloth, with only her eyes, eyebrows, and hands (taking notes) showing—one could even get the impression of someone who had been buried alive.[10]

However many times the Westerner sees such veiling (which can cover the entire head), it can be hard to get used to. And yet I have heard a heavily veiled woman at the University of Chicago explain to a gathering of graduate students, for hours at a time, the salutary purposes served by this practice. Some women can even wax enthusiastic about it, acclaiming it as a form of liberation from the pressures routinely exerted upon them by the typical male response to feminine beauty. Plausible opinions about human nature are drawn upon in such explanations.

The desire and ability of one people after another to have recourse to widely accepted moral criteria in justifying their distinctive practices can be reassuring. This suggests that something more or less natural with respect to goodness *is* available for everyone to apprehend and draw upon. It is this commonality in moral impulse that interfaith movements attempt to put to use worldwide. Here is how Emerson, in his "Over-Soul" essay, saw the commonality at work in "religious" experience (emphasis added):

A thrill passes through all men at the reception of new truth, or at the performance of a great action, *which comes out of the heart of nature*. In these communications the power to see is not separated from the will to do, but the insight proceeds from obedience, and the obedience proceeds from a joyful perception. Every moment when the individual feels himself invaded by it is memorable. Always, I believe, by the necessity of our constitution a certain enthusiasm attends the individual's consciousness of that divine presence. The character and duration of this enthusiasm varies with the state of the individual, from an ecstasy and trance and prophetic inspiration,—which is its rarer appearance, to the faintest glow of virtuous emotion, in which form it warms, like our household fires, all the families and associations of men, and makes society possible. A certain tendency to insanity has always attended the opening of the religious sense in men, as if "blasted with excess of light." The trances of Socrates; the "union" of Plotinus; the vision of Porphyry; the conversion of Paul; the aurora of Behmen; the convulsions of George Fox and his Quakers; the illuminations of Emanuel Swedenborg, are of this kind. What was in the case of these remarkable persons a ravishment, has, in innumerable instances in common life, been exhibited in less striking manner.

Whether a Socrates can be adequately dealt with, or understood, in these terms is an underlying question posed by this appendix.[11]

The general recourse by interfaith-minded peoples to moral criteria can be troubling as well as reassuring. This reminds us of the problems faced in attempting to reconcile contending "tribes" who are firmly grounded in their respective ways. Invariably, in the panels I attended at the Parliament, the members of a sect defended their own practices, confident in the soundness of the way they had "always" done things. This was evident also in the materials I collected from dozens of organizations represented at the Palmer House. The most that the typical association did by way of accommodation was to try to "understand" the others, which usually consisted in translating what others say or do into its own terms. One could find something natural in this as well, just as there is something natural in the troublesome impulses or passions that nature can nevertheless guide us in checking or transforming.

The difficulties with others' ways of life can be readily noticed. But it should be noticed as well that *they* do not usually regard them as difficulties. This should alert us to the difficulties that our own ways may really have.

VI.

Even more fundamental differences than those between religions, and the practices of different religions, can be those between religious and nonreligious (if not antireligious) associations. This too can raise questions about what *religion* truly means.[12]

Such differences were dramatized by the withdrawal from the 1993 Parliament by the Chicago representatives of the Eastern Orthodox Church, primarily because of the leeway allowed during the meetings to avowed witches and neopagans. The trouble evidently began, for these Greek Americans, with some of the invocations pronounced during the opening ceremonies, if not before. The prospect of a Grant Park moon-worshipping ceremony midway through the Parliament contributed to the decision of these Eastern Orthodox delegates to withdraw. Evangelical and other fundamentalist Christians, as well as Southern Baptists, Christian Scientists, and Orthodox Jews (with their long-standing reservations about interfaith dialogue), stayed clear of this enterprise altogether, as had their counterparts in 1893. Roman Catholic representatives, led by the archbishop of the Chicago diocese, remained obviously uncomfortable participants throughout. Mainline Protestantism was not as prominent in 1993 as it had been in 1893.

One of the problems for the conventionally pious in the 1993 Parliament was the apparent "craziness" (as some put it) of various participants, including a few perhaps who could be considered to be spoofing much of what was going on at the Palmer House. Nor did the presence of voodoo, UFO enthusiasts, and perhaps satanists help matters. But much of this was marginal, compared to what was implied by the neopagans and witches: they stood for an earthy passion, as exhibited in well-executed songs and dances I observed one morning in the Empire Room at the Palmer House. One could get a hint from their cavorting (including the dancing of a sensuous woman, dressed in dazzling white), what the lure had been both of the bacchanals that appealed to the ancient Greeks and of the Canaanites and other practices into which the Israelites repeatedly strayed. Although abominations may naturally follow from such practices, they can entice us at their outset because of the all-too-human passions they draw upon and exploit. We are reminded here of the insistence by the founder of the Salvation Army, in developing his organization's musical offerings, that the Devil should not be permitted to have all the good tunes.

The question remains as to what the community may properly do to promote restraint and to curb hedonism, whether or not that hedonism is legitimated by something called religion. Related questions may be posed as to whether any sect should ever have the final say in a civilized community about how children are treated medically and educated.[13]

VII.

My sensuous woman, dressed in close-fitting white, can seem to many an effective refutation of my veiled woman, dressed in loose-fitting black. But do not all healthy communities of any size, if they are to endure, depend upon veils? That is, each community has vital matters or relations that are likely to be kept from public view. That which is veiled is, in a sense, taken for granted, perhaps even cherished: it is not likely to be open to thorough examination by everyone. Precisely what is to be veiled, and how, may depend upon the particularities (including the fortuitous circumstances) to which I have referred.

Among the things to be veiled by communities may be the unverifiable stories that lie at their foundations. Chance may be critical here, especially as to what has been established and how. Chance may also have helped determine what I was personally able to observe during my own Palmer House visits. Even so, it was striking for me to notice, as I went from one group to another, how much was made by most groups of charismatic founders.

Interfaith movements find it difficult, if not impossible, to treat the revered founders of various faiths with anything like the veneration that the partisans of such faiths like to exhibit. We have noticed that an interfaith approach tends to blur or to transcend the differences between sects—but at the risk of draining from sectarians their vitality. Whatever may happen to a few people with exceptional talents, this devitalization of received doctrines and practices can undermine a community's dedication to the moral virtues and to civic duties.[14]

On the other hand, the vitality offered, and to some extent delivered, by earthbound movements (such as the neopagans and witches on display at the Palmer House) may naturally lead to the arousal of more and more expectations that lead in turn to suicidal desperation. Veils may even help protect us from being led astray by beauties that are only apparent or, at least, are far more limited in time or in effect than they seem to be.

In short, it would be imprudent to insist that neither the woman in black nor the woman in white has anything worthwhile to offer us. But it might also be imprudent to rely upon either of these exotic women to provide authoritative guidance about what we should take from the likes of them and their partisans, especially as we strive for mutual understanding and an enduring world peace.

We can well be reminded here of questions that are addressed by the most thoughtful. Some of those questions have always been dealt with, one way or another, by the religions of the world. However much one may have to approach those religions as an outsider, one may still be helped thereby to get to know oneself better.

That is, we should strive to see nature in her wondrous complexity, including how natural impulses take a variety of forms in different situations. There is something natural both in concealing and in uncovering what nature offers. In all this the human being of a philosophical inclination must take care not to seem cavalier about the moral and related religious concerns of his fellow citizens, however likely it may be that those concerns have been shaped by chance circumstances.

VIII.

The most serious part of the 1993 Parliament, aside perhaps from the concluding address in Grant Park by the Dalai Lama, was intended to be the Declaration of a Global Ethic signed by two hundred and fifty religious leaders from around the world. This document, the original draft of which had been prepared before the Parliament convened, was reviewed by the leaders of participating groups during the Parliament.[15]

The Declaration opens with a description of the present deplorable condition of humankind and invokes "ancient guidelines for human behavior which are found in the teachings of the religions of the world and which are the condition for a sustainable world order." The signers, who identify themselves as "women and men who have embraced the precepts and practices of the world's religions," "make a commitment to respect life and dignity, individuality and diversity, so that every person is treated humanely, without exception." At the same time they "condemn aggression and hatred in the name of religion." They further "commit" themselves to "a culture of nonviolence, respect, justice and peace." (p. 11, col. 1 [p. 15])

The Declaration is then devoted to "The Principles of a Global Ethic." These principles are gathered under four headings, with four "commitments" listed under the third heading. This is how the principles are arranged (after the Preamble):

I. No new global order without a new global ethic!
II. A fundamental demand: Every human being must be treated humanely.
III. Irrevocable directives
   1. Commitment to a Culture of Nonviolence and Respect for Life
   2. Commitment to a Culture of Solidarity and a Just Economic Order
   3. Commitment to a Culture of Tolerance and a Life of Truthfulness
   4. Commitment to a Culture of Equal Rights and Partnership Between Men and Women.
IV. A Transformation of Consciousness!

It is also instructive to notice what is *not* to be found in this Declaration. There is no reference to the 1893 Parliament of the World's Religions which had inspired the 1993 Parliament. There are no quotations from, or even references to, religious authorities such as the Bible, except for drawing upon old prohibitions which are now cast in positive terms.[16] There are nowhere any names of persons, whether religious founders, theologians, or philosophers. Care is taken, it seems, lest it appear that any particular religion or any part of the world is displayed as authoritative (even though the Declaration is decidedly Western in tone). This is in marked contrast to the 1893 Parliament where, for example, the Lord's Prayer of Christendom was repeatedly heard, including at the end of the final plenary session when that prayer was recited under the guidance of the most eminent Chicago rabbi of that day.[17]

In short, we can see in the 1993 Declaration what, in matters of interfaith interests, is the effect of working primarily from what is generally shared by all, or almost all, of the participants.

IX.

One of the things generally shared can be said to be the only document explicitly identified in the 1993 Declaration (p. 11, col. 3):

We are convinced of the fundamental unity of the human family on Earth. We recall the 1948 Universal Declaration of Human Rights of the United Nations. What is formally proclaimed [there] on the level of rights, we wish to confirm and deepen here from the perspective of an ethic: the full realization of the intrinsic dignity of the human person, the inalienable freedom and equality in principle of all humans, and the necessary solidarity and interdependence of all humans with each other.

The 1948 Universal Declaration drew upon the history and statements of principles of various people, also primarily in the Western world. It is "history," of course, which helps account as well for many of the troublesome, even deadly, conflicts around the world, just as it helps account for the richness of diverse traditions, thereby making matters even more difficult to deal with sensibly.

The Declaration of Human Rights is not a substitute for either a constitution or a foreign policy, although it questions in principle the legitimacy of separateness and, hence, of any foreign policy and perhaps of most constitutions. The 1948 Declaration did provide, for the people noble enough to acknowledge its aspirations but astute enough to recognize its limitations, a basis for moving mankind away from the edge of the nuclear-war abyss at which it found itself and toward a world order which permits human beings to survive with some dignity.[18]

X.

What kind of human life and world order is presupposed by the Declaration of a Global Ethic? Did those who prepared and signed the document address and answer this question?

The emphasis is on egalitarianism, peace and justice, with personal safety and material prosperity important also. A social conscience, much more than old-fashioned religious sensibilities, seems to inform this Declaration. What happens in this world (not in the world to come) seems to be all that is taken into account.

The good presupposed by the Declaration of a Global Ethic is not that of either personal salvation or eternal life. Although suggestions are made about individual conduct, there is no emphasis upon the preeminently virtuous human being. We must again wonder what kind of human being results from the criticisms and prescriptions found in the 1993 Declaration.

The dominant tone of the Declaration of a Global Ethic is *not* that of joy or of hopefulness, unlike the documents of the 1893 proceedings. There is here no reaffirmation of the goodness of life, of creation, or of human society, except by implication through the disavowal of conditions that are regarded as intolerable.

Pervading the 1993 Declaration of a Global Ethic is a determined, almost desperate, repudiation of the misery by which the world is engulfed. The depths of that misery are suggested, with some afflictions referred to several times. There is here little if any of that exaltation found in prophetic works such as the books of *Job* and *Isaiah*, an exaltation grounded in the majesty of the Divinity looked to for both chastisement and elevation.

The grounding of the Declaration is distinctively modern, emphasizing as it does *not* the *summum bonum* but rather the *summum malum*, the supreme not-good which is to be avoided or overcome. Is it not the tendency of modern realism to make much of the bad as the more "real"? A salutary corrective is provided by an Aristotle who could recognize the sweetness of existence.[19]

But it is not a celebration of existence that shapes the Declaration. Nor is anything said of any heavenly prospects promised by a reliable or at least persuasive revelation. Rather the emphasis is, following upon the tortured words opening the Declaration, on the *agony* of the world. It seems to be assumed that there is significantly more agony now than heretofore, perhaps much more than ever before for a larger proportion of human beings worldwide. Yet are there not billions more human beings living in some comfort and safety on earth today than ever before in the history of this planet?

It would be neither humane nor politic to deny the legitimacy of any concern today for human rights and for the alleviation of the considerable human misery always all around us. But it would be neither prudent nor instructive to ignore the fundamental challenge that can be posed even to that laudable concern. Such a challenge is suggested, not without some perverseness, by a Nietzschean nihilist's comment on the significance of the awesome Battle of Verdun (February–July 1916) during the First World War:

Nations, like individuals, reach their peak and then die spiritually, if not physically. Prussia and France reached their peak at Verdun (just as the United States probably reached its peak during the Civil War). . . .

Like most moderns, the French used [their modern] freedom to create egalitarian institutions grounded in universal human rights. The Prussians, however, used [this] freedom to create monarchical institutions rigidly subordinating their individual freedom to duty to throne and *Reich*. Thus Prussia radically opposed the popular (*Volkisch*) demands of most modern regimes, whether democratic, communist or nazi. At Verdun, these two most opposed versions of modern freedom, the Prussian and the popular, fought modernity's grand, tragic fight. Compared to that struggle of Titans, its prelude and aftermath—in Prussia, in France and in the modern world as a whole—remains a farce, a stayr play. Insofar as modernity's freedom can inspire political grandeur, it fought itself out at Verdun.

Was Verdun worth it? Not to those preferring peace to war. Verdun was war at its grimmest and most implacable: "They shall not pass!" . . . At Verdun, the French, and especially the Prussian, legions were not fighting for world peace. Both realized that neither would ever yield so long as a Falkenhayn or a Nivelle were in command. Between their Prussia and France, there was no possibility of lasting peace. Like Achilles, the Prussians preferred a heroic death to a life in which they peacefully shared the Rhine with France. . . . Verdun's life-or-death resolve always will move a Prussian Achilles far more deeply than the humanitarian goals of the American, French and Russian Revolutions. It brought out the best in the combatants, not their best as human beings, but as Prussians and Frenchmen. In this crucial sense, Verdun was a Prussian, not a French battle. No less than the Prussians, the French at Verdun subordinated humanitarian, global considerations to the demands of Duty! Honor! Country![20]

One might begin one's response to this instructive challenge by juxtaposing Homer's Odysseus to Homer's Achilles. After all, the wise poet (who can be presumed to have known both of his characters well) does seem to prefer the somewhat humanitarian (and yet shrewd and tough) Odysseus to the much more war-loving Achilles.

XI.

From the point of view of the Apostle of Verdun, the world's troubles today are little more than pale reflections of the deeper contest at Verdun, a contest that represents the clash of fundamental principles. What, according to the men and women of the Declaration of a Global Ethic, are the underlying causes of the world's troubles today?

Certainly, the causes of the universal agony are not put these days in terms of original sin, of fate, or even of "the human condition," explanations which might have been offered a century ago. Even though greed is singled out for criticism in the Declaration, the fundamental flaws do not seem to be in human beings as such. Rather, the problem is primarily with institutions such as governments, organized religions, and large-scale economic enterprises, and with the respectable leaders of all such associations.

It seems to be assumed in the Declaration that almost all that needs to be done to relieve the dreadful plight of multitudes of victims is a changing of the will of those to whom this Declaration is addressed. For one thing, it seems to be said, our leaders should start behaving themselves. There does not seem to be any awareness of the considerable effort and time needed both to establish proper institutions (religious as well as political) and to develop that character and competence in the people required to make sensible use of such institutions.

Divine revelation, of the kind that those of religious faith have traditionally relied upon, is not featured in this Declaration. It is curious that this document, signed by hundreds of religious leaders from around the world, manages to avoid using the word *God* altogether, settling instead for many invocations of *ancient religions* and for one use of the term *Ultimate Reality*. Indicative of how fashionable the lowest common denominator can be in such matters is the fact that the word *soul* is used but once in the Declaration, and even then only in quotation marks.[21]

Another way of characterizing the approach of the Declaration to the world's troubles is to say that it represents an effort to circumvent politics. The virtual repudiation of politics is implicit in the repeated insistence upon total disarmament and the repeated disavowal of the use of force. This is related to the implicit disparagement of contemporary capitalism throughout the document. In both cases, the fruits of efficient political and economic organization seem to be desired without recognizing either the institutions that are needed or the costs that have to be borne in producing such fruits.[22]

In any event, all large-scale institutions are suspect. Reforms, often in the form of what we now call "downsizing" and "personalizing," are looked to. But are the accomplishments of political men and women sufficiently appreciated, accomplishments which permit, for example, the calling and holding of such an ambitious conference as the Parliament of the World's Religions—and in reliable physical comfort and unquestioned personal safety? The routine accomplishments of politicians and social organizations, which we very much take for granted, often conceal from view the effects of chance in human affairs.

Still another way of putting one's assessment of the Declaration of a Global Ethic is to notice that no high level of political philosophy is drawn upon there. The problems, as well as the possibilities, of statecraft are not noticed, including those problems which may oblige the conscientious statesman to be more receptive to the necessity of deception and the use of veils, for the sake of the common good, than the Declaration seems to be.[23]

XII.

Insensitivity to both the possibilities and the pitfalls of politics carries over into how organized religion is treated in the Declaration. May this naturally follow if it should not be recognized that the typical religion is, at least in part, a form of political organization?

There are, in the Declaration, the repeated invocations of ancient religions to which I have referred. It is assumed that those ancient religions have much in common, especially when they prescribe how human beings should live. But may not the same be said about well-established political orders?

However much the ancient religions do have in common, they can also serve (we have noticed) as the underlying causes of the deadly enmities which are deplored in the Declaration. Those fundamental differences are recognized only intermittently in the Declaration, and then with the expectation that they can be transformed, virtually by acts of will, into no more than minor disturbances. It does not seem to be sufficiently recognized that the divergent ways of lives to which great multitudes owe allegiance are rooted, in effect, in divergent and passionate opinions about the very nature of things.

What are the sources of the great ancient religions of the human race? Most of them invoke divine revelation in some form. Prophecy, it has been suggested, is the political name for political science.[24] Others can speak of revelation as a form of poetry, a divinely inspired poetry perhaps, however much poetry itself depends upon a kind of deception. We can be reminded by these observations that little is said about the arts in the Declaration of a Global Ethic.

It is significant that religious leaders of stature could be persuaded to subscribe to a declaration that ignored, if it did not tacitly repudiate, much that is associated with traditional doctrine and worship. This kind of consensus, in these circumstances, seems to be possible (barring an apparently unprecedented divine intervention that moves everyone, or almost everyone, at once) only if the primary concern should be with salvation in this world.[25]

Another way of putting these observations is to suggest that there is little if anything distinctively religious about the concerns and solutions expressed in the Declaration, however sincere and even high-minded those concerns no doubt are. That which had been distinctively religious in the ancient faiths which are repeatedly referred to in the Declaration has given way, at least on this occasion and perhaps even generally among the more sophisticated religionists today, to the prevailing modern mode of thinking—and a recognition of this can make study of the Declaration particularly instructive.

XIII.

The leading minds of the Parliament of the World's Religions emphasized, as modernists, human beings and the Earth. (Earth, which is referred to, usually capitalized, a score of times in the Declaration of a Global Ethic, seems to have taken the place of God. It is appropriate that environmental groups and earth-worshipping societies should have been publicized as much as they were during the 1993 Parliament.) The fashionable tilt in the proceedings could be seen in the Declaration's determined uses of "women and men," with only a few uses of "men and women."

Intermediate institutions, religious as well as secular, are played down. There is instead an emphasis upon extremes: the individual and the worldwide. It is as if all mankind is to be regarded as working out its thought and way of life together. But, it can be argued, it is in the intermediate that human beings truly live—in the intermediate political and religious associations which make much of particulars (and hence of errors, as well as of intimate and otherwise fulfilling relations).

The "universal" orientation of the Declaration testifies to what worldwide struggles, commerce, music, communications, and entertainment (including highly publicized sporting events) did to us all in the twentieth century. Among the consequences of the remarkable technology to which we have become accustomed is the subversion both of humanity and of community. Another consequence of these developments is that a kind of sociology has replaced old-fashioned theology and philosophy, with the conscientious social worker replacing both the prophet and the politician as a reliable guide to right action.

If any "philosophical" position informs the Declaration, it is probably that of existentialism. Decades of loose talk, not least in the Academy, are reflected here, most tellingly revealed perhaps in the repeated recourse in the Declaration to the "authentically human." (Other revealing usages are *commitment* and *values*.) *Authenticity* has found its way into the theological vocabulary of our time in large part, it seems, through the influence of Martin Heidegger, another thinker whose remarkable attributes did not include a sound understanding of politics. He, too, thought he could either overcome or do without politics—but he succeeded only in being used, sadly misused in his self-centered naiveté, by politicians out of the gutter.[26]

A repudiation of Heidegger's political masters and their cruel intensification of partisan politics does not require repudiation of politics altogether, just as a repudiation of such a diabolical institution as the Inquisition does not require repudiation of religion altogether. The genuinely (as distinguished from the authentically?) human depends for most people upon some political/religious order. By far the most attractive feature of the 1993 Parliament of the World's Religions was not the argument made on behalf of a global consciousness but rather the character of the colorful representatives on exhibit from around the world. Those personable men and women, ever so dedicated and for the most part good-natured and high-minded, emanated from ways of life that have for centuries (if not for millennia) been much more substantial than any way of life likely to be tailored to the principles drawn upon in their Declaration of a Global Ethic.

The depreciation of politics and government implicit in this Declaration means, in effect, a depreciation also of prudence—and of that guidance grounded in nature by which prudence takes its bearings. The sentimentalized, if not even denatured, nature that is several times referred to in the Declaration of a Global Ethic does not promote either the tough mindedness or the precision which reason requires if it is to contribute to both sound speculation and sensible politics. It is not surprising that the 1993 Parliament, having failed to draw upon anything like an idea of nature with substance, also failed to invoke anything beyond nature—that is, a form of the supernatural to which faith and reverence could be plausibly accorded by serious human beings. The inadequacy of the idea of nature in the Declaration of a Global Ethic may be intimately related to the inadequacy of its idea of the divine (in whatever language). Unless the world should happen to be vouchsafed still another grand new revelation, the idea of the divine is not likely to be recovered and put to proper use worldwide until the idea of nature is carefully reexamined and somehow restored.

Addendum

Illustrative of the arguments and tone of the 1993 Declaration of a Global Ethic are the following passages (drawn by me from successive parts of the document) (see, for the texts cited, note 2 below):

1. The world is in agony. The agony is so pervasive and urgent that we are compelled to name its manifestations so that the depth of this pain may be made clear.
   Peace eludes us—the planet is being destroyed—neighbours live in fear—women and men are estranged from each other—children die!
   This is abhorrent!
   We condemn the abuses of earth's ecosystems.
   We condemn the poverty that stifles life's potential; the hunger that weakens the human body; the economic disparities that threaten so many families with ruin.
   We condemn the social disarray of the nations; the disregard for justice that pushes citizens to the margin; the anarchy overtaking our communities; and the insane death of children from violence. In particular, we condemn aggression and hatred in the name of religion.
   But this agony need not be.
   It need not be because the basis for an ethic already exists. This ethic offers the possibility of a better individual and global order, and leads individuals away from despair and societies away from chaos.
   We are women and men who have embraced the precepts and practices of the world's religions.
   We affirm that a common set of core values is found in the teachings of the religions, and that these form the basis of a global ethic.
   We affirm that this truth is already known, but yet to be lived in heart and action.
   We affirm that there is an irrevocable, unconditional norm for all areas of life, for families and communities, for races, nations and religions. There already exist ancient guidelines for human behavior which are found in the teachings of the religions of the world and which are the condition for a sustainable world order.
   [p. 11, col. 1 (pp. 14–15); opening passage of the Declaration]

2. Our world is experiencing a fundamental crisis: a crisis in global economy, global ecology, and global politics. The lack of a grand vision, the tangle of unresolved problems, political paralysis, mediocre political leadership with little insight or foresight, and in general too little sense for the commonweal are seen everywhere: Too many old answers to new challenges. [p. 11, col. 2 (p. 17)]

3. As religious and spiritual persons we base our lives on an Ultimate Reality and draw spiritual power and hope therefrom, in trust, in prayer or meditation, in word or silence. We have a special responsibility for the welfare of all humanity and care for the planet Earth. We do not consider ourselves better than other women and men, but we trust that the ancient wisdom of our religions can point the way for the future. [p. 11, col. 3 (p. 19)]

4. By a global ethic we do not mean a global ideology or a single unified religion beyond all existing religions, and certainly not the domination of one religion over all others. By a global ethic we mean a fundamental consensus on binding values, irrevocable standards, and personal attitudes. Without such a fundamental consensus on an ethic, sooner or later every community will be threatened by chaos or dictatorship, and individuals will despair. [pp. 11–12 (p. 21)]

5. We do not wish to gloss over or ignore the serious differences among the individual religions. However, they should not hinder us from proclaiming publicly those things which we already hold in common and which we jointly affirm, each on the basis of our own religious or ethical grounds. . . . The spiritual powers of the religions can offer a fundamental sense of trust, a ground of meaning, ultimate standards, and a spiritual home. Of course religions are credible only when they eliminate those conflicts which spring from the religions themselves, dismantling mutual arrogance, mistrust, prejudice and even hostile images, and thus demonstrate respect for the traditions, holy places, feasts, and rituals of people who believe differently. [p. 12, col. 1 (p. 22)]

6. No one stands "above good and evil"—no human being, no social class, no influential interest group, no cartel, no police apparatus, no army and no state. On the contrary; possessed of reason and conscience, every human is obliged to behave in a genuinely human fashion, to do good and avoid evil! . . . [W]e wish to recall irrevocable, unconditional ethical norms. These should not be bonds and chains, but helps and supports for people to find and realize once again their lives' direction, values, orientations and meaning. [p. 12, col. 2 (p. 23)]

7. Every form of egoism should be rejected; all selfishness, whether individual or collective, whether in the form of class thinking, racism, nationalism or sexism. We condemn these because they prevent humans from being authentically human. Self-determination and self-realization are thoroughly legitimate so long as they are not separated from human self-responsibility and global responsibility, that is, from responsibility for fellow humans and for the planet Earth. [p. 12, col. 3 (p. 24)]

8. As human beings, we have a special responsibility—especially with a view to future generations—for Earth and the cosmos, for the air, water, and soil. We are all intertwined together in this cosmos and we are all dependent on each other. Each one of us depends on the welfare of all. Therefore, the dominance of hu-

manity over nature and the cosmos must not be encouraged. Instead, we must cultivate living in harmony with nature and the cosmos. [p. 13, col. 1 (p. 26)]

9. If the plight of the poorest billions of humans on this planet, particularly women and children, is to be improved, the world economy must be structured more justly. Individual good deeds and assistance projects, indispensable though they be, are insufficient. The participation of all states and the authority of international organizations are needed to build just economic institutions. [p. 13, col. 2 (p. 28)]

10. We must value a sense of moderation and modesty instead of an unquenchable greed for money, prestige and consumption! In greed, humans lose their "souls," their freedom, their composure, their inner peace, and thus that which makes them human. [p. 13, col. 3 (p. 29)]

11. Numberless women and men of all regions and religions strive to lead lives of honesty and truthfulness. Nevertheless, all over the world we find endless lies and deceit, swindling and hypocrisy, ideology and demagoguery. [p. 13, col. 3 (p. 29)]

12. A universal consensus on many disputed ethical questions (from bio- and sexual ethics through mass media and scientific ethics to economic and political ethics) will be difficult to attain. Nevertheless, even for many controversial questions, suitable solutions should be attainable in the spirit of the fundamental principles we have jointly developed here. [p. 14, col. 3 (p. 35)]

13. In conclusion, we appeal to all the inhabitants of this planet. Earth cannot be changed for the better unless the consciousness of individuals is changed. We pledge to work for such transformation in individual and collective consciousness, for the awakening of our spiritual powers through reflection, meditation, prayer or positive thinking, for a conversion of the heart. Together we can move mountains! Without a willingness to take risks and a readiness to sacrifice there can be no fundamental change in our situation! Therefore, we commit ourselves to a common global ethic, to better mutual understanding, as well as to socially beneficial peace-fostering and Earth-friendly ways of life. We invite all men and women, whether religious or not, to do the same. [p. 14, col. 3 (p. 36); closing passage of the Declaration]

Notes

1. Petrarch, "Sonnet No. 14" in *Sonnets and Songs*, trans. Anna Maria Armi (New York: Grosset & Dunlap, 1968), p. 13.

A few other forms of *veil* can usefully be noticed here. John Quincy Adams said, "Plutarch reasons well, but he leaves too much of the mysterious veil over his subjects." The subjects referred to by Adams include the workings of the supernatural. See Meyer Reinhold, *Classica Americana: The Greek and Roman Heritage in the United States* (Detroit: Wayne State University Press, 1984), p. 250. W. E. B. Du Bois, in *The Souls of Black Folk*, confronts the Veil behind which the Negro is kept in the United States (in the last paragraph of the book he writes, "[T]hen anon in His good times America shall rend the Veil and the prisoned shall go free." See also Nathaniel Hawthorne, "The Minister's Black Veil." See, on Captain Ahab's blasphemous desire to "strike through the mask," Herman Melville, *Moby Dick*, chap. 34; George Anastaplo, *The Constitutionalist: Notes on the First Amendment* (Dallas: Southern Methodist University Press, 1971), pp. 363–64. See also note 10 below. (All references to notes in this appendix are, unless otherwise indicated, to the notes in appendix C of this collection.)

2. This statement, the Declaration of a Global Ethic, was signed by most, not all, of the religious leaders attending the 1993 Parliament. My discussion of the Declaration, which begins in section VIII of this appendix, uses primarily citations (by page and column) to the final version of the document as published in the *National Catholic Reporter*, September 23, 1993, pp. 11–14. (The document's original pagination is also used.)

Signers of the Declaration have been listed under these headings: Bahai; Brahma Kumaris; Buddhism; Christianity; Native religions; Hinduism; Jainism; Judaism; Islam; Neopagans; Sikhs; Taoists; Theosophists; Zorastrians; Interreligious organizations. See Hans Küng and Karl-Josef Kuschel, eds., *A Global Ethic: The Declaration of the Parliament of the World's Religions* (New York: Continuum, 1993), pp. 37–39

Some of the press coverage of the Parliament was unfortunate. Perhaps this helps account for the troubling reference to the convention by Andrew Greeley as "the World Parliament freak show here in Chicago." *Chicago Sun-Times*, September 12, 1993, p. 48. The Parliament was far more interesting, and much more important, than Father Greeley was led to believe.

3. Also well received were the services of the quite accommodating Palmer House hotel staff. I have found instructive the articles about the Parliament published in the *Chicago Sun-Times*, the *Chicago Tribune*, the *New York Times*, the *New World*, and the *Washington Post*, as well as the reports prepared by Andrew Patner for the *Forward* (including an account of a somewhat contrived controversy involving Louis Farrakhan of the Nation of Islam). See, on the Dalai Lama's Grant Park talk, note 15 below.

4. It suggests a decline in the self-confidence of Chicago's leaders that they could not manage to mount the efforts necessary to put on in 1993 anything comparable to the Columbian Exposition a century before. See Anastaplo, "Law, Education, and Legal Education: Explorations," 37 *Brandeis Law Journal* 583, 618 (1999–2000). See, for materials drawn from the publications of the 1893 Parliament, Richard Hughes Seager, ed., *The Dawn of Religious Pluralism: Voices from the World's Parliament of Religions, 1893* (LaSalle, Ill.: Open Court, 1993). See also note 17 below. The 1893 proceedings can now be recognized as largely "American" and "Presbyterian" in spirit. See note 12 below. One critical result of the 1993 Parliament has been to induce us to take the 1893 Parliament more seriously.

5. See, on Buddhism, chapter 5 of this collection. See also the text at note 21 of this appendix.

6. I am reminded of Aristotle's critique of the arrangement in Plato's *Republic* whereby everyone would consider as siblings all others in the *polis* of roughly the same age. It is better, Aristotle indicates, to be related to a cousin, as commonly understood, than to be related to a "brother," as Socrates prescribes. See Aristotle, *Politics* 1261a10–1262b35 (commenting on Plato, *Republic* 423E, 457C, 462B).

7. See, on Zoroastrianism, the entry in the *Encyclopedia of Religion*.

8. See, on the limits of modeling oneself upon the animals, Aristophanes, *Clouds* 1425–1432. See, on the North American Indians, chapter 7 of this collection.

The enduring problems here are suggested by the front-page story in the *New York Times* for August 26, 1993, p. A1, a story (by Isabel Wilkerson, "Cruel Flood: It Tore at Graves, and at Hearts") that can remind us of the burial-related sentiments that helped shape Sophocles' *Antigone* and William Faulkner's *As I Lay Dying.* This newspaper story describes what happened in Hardin, Missouri when the Missouri River washed away the local cemetery:

> When the Missouri River barreled through town like white-water rapids this summer, and grain bins and City Hall and the Assembly of God church and houses and barns gave way and there were no telephones or electricity or running water, people in this tiny farm town thought they knew all about the power of nature.
>
> Then the unthinkable happened. The river washed away about two-thirds of the cemetery where just about anybody who ever lived and died here was buried. The river carved out a crater 50 feet deep where the cemetery used to be. It took cottonwood trees and the brick entryway and carried close to 900 caskets and burial vaults downstream toward St. Louis and the Mississippi.
>
> The remains of whole families floated away, their two-ton burial vaults coming to rest in tree limbs, on highways, along railroad tracks and in beanfields two and three towns away.
>
> "You cannot accept the magnitude of it until you're standing in it," said Dean Snow, the Ray County coroner. He said it may take years to find all the remains.
>
> Now people who lost everything else to the flood are left to weep for the parents they mourned decades ago, the stillborn children they never saw grow up, the husbands taken from them in farm accidents, the mothers who died in childbirth. It is as if the people have died all over again and the survivors must grieve anew.

Further on it is reported,

> About 1,500 people buried at the Hardin Cemetery, once a pristine landscape nine acres across and now a muddy lake where minnows and snapping turtles live alongside broken headstones and toppled graves. The disaster was all the more astonishing because Hardin is not even a river town. It is some five miles north of the Missouri.
>
> Since it was founded in 1810, the cemetery had survived tornadoes, floods and the Civil War. No other cemetery in the country has been uprooted like this, officials of the American Cemetery Association say. Local people see the occurrence as near-biblical.
>
> "It makes you think, 'What is God saying to us?'" said Bess Meador, a retired nurse with two husbands in the cemetery. "What is it we're doing that we shouldn't be doing? You look at that cemetery and you feel so helpless."

One more passage rounds out this account for our immediate purpose:

> As people here await word on the recovery effort, some are trying to figure out what to do with the cemetery. Some want to extend it into the adjacent cornfields and maybe put water lilies in the lake the river made as a memorial to those lost to the floods. Others want to move the entire cemetery, including the intact graves, to higher ground. Some want to have a new mass funeral service after more bodies have been found. . . .
>
> [For some people] these are hallowed grounds. . . . [One man] anxiously paced the cemetery in search of his father and stillborn son. He got to the edge of the cliff and saw the earth carved out in the spot where they should be.
>
> "My baby and my dad are gone," [he] said, his eyes red and watery. "We've been hoping for five weeks they were safe. The way things are broken up down there, I don't know if they'll ever be recovered."

He wiped his eyes and headed back to the road, walking over dead corn shucks and wheat stubble, to break the news to his wife.

The meaning of "safe" here may well be pondered, illuminating as it does the general appeal that religions naturally have.

The traumatic effects of this Missouri episode remind us of what family ties can mean. One may wonder how the Zoroastrian approach looks in the light of this kind of situation. And how is the trauma here related to our considerable concern about appearances and about health, to which a disproportionate part of our material (if not also our spiritual) resources is allocated. Still, it is not unusual for a people, ancient as well as modern, to be very much concerned to preserve the integrity of its graveyards (and hence the "safety" of their dead), however unconcerned a Socrates could profess himself to be about what became of *his* corpse after his death.

9. See the opening sentences of Aristotle's *Nicomachean Ethics* and of Aristotle's *Politics*. See also Larry Arnhart, *Aristotle on Political Reasoning: A Commentary on the "Rhetoric"* (DeKalb, Ill.: Northern Illinois University Press, 1981).

10. A special kind of veil was worn by three Jain women I saw at the Palmer House: a mask, or perhaps a token for a mask, is placed over the nostrils and mouth to protect vulnerable insects from being taken into the body. See, on the intricacies of Muslim life, Naguib Mahfouz, *The Cairo Trilogy*. See also chapter 6 of this collection. A different form of burial of the living may be seen in the way that the caste system can still work in India for the Untouchables. See, e.g., Anastaplo, "Church and State: Explorations," 19 *Loyola University of Chicago Law Journal* 61, 188 (1987); chapter 3 of this collection. Consider also the effects of racial prejudice in the United States. See, e.g., Ralph Ellison, *Invisible Man*.

11. See, on Socrates, Anastaplo, *Human Being and Citizen: Essays on Virtue, Freedom, and the Common Good* (Chicago: Swallow Press, 1975), pp. 8, 203; Anastaplo, "Freedom of Speech and the First Amendment: Explorations," 21 *Texas Tech Law Review* 1941, 1945–58 (1990) (reprinted in James L. Swanson, ed., *First Amendment Law Handbook, 1993–94 Edition* [New York: Clark Boardman Callaghan, 1993], pp. 63–73).

12. These fundamental differences may have been less acute at the 1893 Parliament of the World's Religions from which various borderline associations as well as some genuine religions which were considered troublesome had been excluded. See note 4 above. Among those excluded in 1893 had been North American Indian groups, who were given places of honor in the 1993 opening ceremonies. The 1993 Parliament also saw a greater emphasis upon private meditation.

The "star" of the 1893 Parliament was the Indian Swami, Vivekananda. See the entries on the Parliament and on Vivekananda in the *Encyclopedia of Religion*. See also Martin E. Marty, *Pilgrims in Their Own Land: 500 years of Religion in America* (Boston: Little, Brown, 1984), pp. 281–84, 315, 345–47, 450–55. "I have often wondered why the Parliament of Religions, which has been all but forgotten here in Chicago, has remained so vivid in the memories of many religious people in other parts of the world." Joseph M. Kitagawa, *The 1893 World's Parliament of Religions and Its Legacy* (Chicago: The John Nuveen Lecture, 1983), p. 1.

13. See, e.g., Anastaplo, "Church and State: Explorations," p. 61; Anastaplo, "Rome, Piety, and Law: Explorations," 39 *Loyola of New Orleans Law Review* 2 (1993). These issues have recently been dramatized by the case in England of conjoined twins, both of

whom were expected to die soon if not separated and one of whom would die at once if separated. See Warren Hoge, "Siamese Twin Is Separated; 'Sadly Dies' to Save Sister," *New York Times*, November 8, 2000, p. A5.

"But our social science, if it is to be of any use, must be addressed to Moslems and Jews as well as to Christians, to Buddhists and Hindus as well as to believers in the Bible; it must, finally, be addressed 'not only to those who enjoy the blessings and consolation of revealed religion, but also to those who face the mysteries of human destiny alone.'" Harry V. Jaffa, *Thomism and Aristotelianism: A Study of the Commentary by Thomas Aquinas on the Nicomachean Ethics* (Chicago: University of Chicago Press, 1953), p. 193 (quoting from Winston Churchill's address at the Mid-century Convocation of the Massachusetts Institute of Technology, *New York Times*, April 1, 1949).

See, for a photograph of the dancing "sensuous women dressed in white," at the 1993 Parliament of the World's Religions, *The Great Ideas Today*, p. 42 (1994). See also notes 19 and 73 of chapter 1 of this collection.

14. "Whatever may be conceded to the influence of refined education on minds of peculiar structure, reason and experience both forbid us to expect that national morality can prevail in exclusion of religious principle." George Washington, Farewell Address (1796). Anastaplo, "Constitutionalism, The Rule of Rules: Explorations," 39 *Brandeis Law Journal*, 179, 298 (2000–2001). See also note 23 below.

Another observation, somewhat to the same effect, was made by Francis Bacon, but with a recognition of the special claims and consequences of biblical religions:

Religion being the chief band of human society, it is a happy thing when it itself is well contained within the true band of Unity. The quarrels and divisions about religion were evils unknown to the heathen. The reason was because the religion of the heathen consisted rather in rites and ceremonies than in any constant belief. For you may imagine what kind of faith theirs was when the chief doctors and fathers of their church were the poets. But the true God hath this attribute, that he is a *jealous God*, and therefore his worship and religion will endure no mixture nor partner. We shall therefore speak a few words concerning the Unity of the Church, what are the Fruits thereof, what the Bounds, and what the Means.

I include, in a 1976 discussion of the Mayflower Compact, my observation:

What, then, should be the proper relation of prudence to piety? Is not one of these ultimately more sensitive to the best in human nature, and to human possibilities, including the possibility of human error, than the other? It is the law of the sea (and of the air, I believe) that the more maneuverable craft should give way to the less. This certainty makes sense if one concludes that both "crafts" are needed for the well-being of the human race.

Anastaplo, "Constitutionalism, The Rule of Rules," p. 228.

15. The author of the original draft of the 5,000-word Declaration was the Swiss-born Roman Catholic theologian, Professor Hans Küng of the University of Tubingen. "I never worked so many months for so few words," said Father Küng. Peter Steinfels, "More Diversity Than Harmony at Religious Assembly," *New York Times*, September 7, 1993, p. A15.

Father Küng was warned by friends that he, by trying to say everything, would end up saying nothing. His assessment of the Declaration included these remarks: "It is certainly the first time in the history of humankind that a body of this importance tries to lay down principles for understanding, principles for behavior which . . . can also be supported by non-believers. . . . To be quite frank, I was always rather skeptical that this whole thing would be achieved. But there was no objection to any important point, and that was a happy surprise." Laurie Goodstein, *Washington Post*, September 2, 1993, p. A3. See note 13 above. See, for anticipations of the Declaration, Hans Küng and Jürgen Mortmann, eds., *The Ethics of World Religions and Human Rights* (London: SCM Press, 1990).

The controversial abortion, euthanasia, and world-population issues were skirted in the Declaration. The Dalai Lama, in his Grant Park talk, offered a "non-violent birth-control" solution: "More monks and more nuns." See note 22 below. See, for a charming photograph of the Dalai Lama with the mayor of Chicago, *The Great Ideas Today*, p. 33 (1994).

16. Thus, "What you do not wish done to yourself, do not do to other!" becomes "What you wish done to yourself, do to other!" (p. 12, col. 3); "You shall not kill!" becomes "Have respect for life!" (p. 12, col. 3); "You shall not steal!" becomes "Deal honestly and fairly!" (p. 13, col. 2); "You shall not lie!" becomes "Speak and act truthfully!" (p. 14, col. 1); and "You shall not commit sexual immorality!" becomes "Respect and love one another!" (p. 14, col. 2).

17. See John Henry Barrows, ed., *The World's Parliament of Religion* (Chicago: Parliament Publishing Company, 1893), pp. 186–87. This rabbi's family became so much "mainstream American" that one of his quite talented grandsons, who was never readily identifiable with the practice of any religious faith, could become president of the University of Chicago and attorney general of the United States. See Anastaplo, "Legal Education, Economics, and Law School Governance: Explorations," 46 *South Dakota Law Review*, appendix G (2001). See also Hayim Goren Perlmuter, *Siblings: Rabbinic Judaism and Early Christianity at their Beginnings* (New York: Paulist Press, 1989).

18. See, on the Universal Declaration of Human Rights, Anastaplo, "How to Read the Constitution of the United States," 17 *Loyola University of Chicago Law Journal* 1, 55–64 (1985). One follow-up to the 1993 Parliament of the World's Religions, and the personal contacts made there, may eventually be a "United Nations of Religions," with a special interest in conflict resolution. See, on the 1991 Gulf War and "a new world order," Anastaplo, "On Freedom: Explorations," 17 *Oklahoma City University Law Review* 465, 589–630 (1992). See also Anastaplo, "First Impressions," 26 *Political Science Reviewer* 248 (1999). See as well note 49 of chapter 5 of this collection.

19. See Aristotle, *Politics* 1278b25–29. See also Anastaplo, *The American Moralist: On Law, Ethics, and Government* (Athens, Ohio: Ohio University Press, 1992), pp. 599–601.

20. Harry Neumann, *Liberalism* (Durham, N.C.: Carolina Academic Press, 1991), pp. 292–94. Compare, ibid., pp. xii–xxiii. The distinctly French spirit may better be seen in the 1914 Battle of the Marne, Paris taxicabs and all. See, on the follies of the First World War, Anastaplo, *Campus Hate-Speech Codes, Natural Right, and Twentieth-Century Atrocities* (Lewiston, N.Y.: Edwin Mellen Press, 1999), p. 49 ("Did Anyone 'In Charge' Know What He Was Doing? The Thirty Years War of the Twentieth Century").

21. "In greed, humans lose their 'souls,' their freedom, their composure, their inner peace and thus that which makes them human." (p. 13, col. 3) See, on the uses of *soul* today, appendix A of this collection. See, on the avoidance of "God" in the 1993 Declaration, the text at note 5 of this appendix. Compare, for the references to the Divine in the Declaration of Independence, Anastaplo, *Abraham Lincoln: A Constitutional Biography* (Lanham, Md.: Rowman & Littlefield, 1999), pp. 25–26.

22. See, e.g., Anastaplo, *The American Moralist*, pp. 345–48; Anastaplo, "Rome, Piety, and Law," pp. 121–37 (this bears on the population issue referred to in note 15 above). See,

on the use and abuse of economics, Anastaplo, "Legal Education, Economics, and Law School Governance: Explorations," 46 *South Dakota Law Review* (forthcoming).

23. See, e.g., Plato, *Republic* 414D. See, on noble lies, Anastaplo, *The American Moralist*, pp. 27–32, 616. See also note 14 above.

24. See chapter 4 of this collection, note 38; appendix B of this collection, note 88. See also appendix B of this collection, note 64.

25. Far more robust, and with a more enduring appeal, is the single-minded (however intolerant) faith displayed in such spiritual masterpieces as John Bunyan's *The Pilgrim's Progress*, something which can be not only noticed but even admired by those of other faiths. See Anastaplo, *The Artist as Thinker: From Shakespeare to Joyce* (Athens, Ohio: Ohio University Press, 1983), p. 75. The more tolerant Christian conviction underlying the first Parliament of the World's Religions was expressed this way in 1893: "It is not true that all religions are equally good; but neither is it true that all religions except one are no good at all." Barrows, ed., *The World's Parliament of Religions*, p. 19. See, on the controversial implications of the plurality of religions, John Edward Sullivan, "The Idea of Religion," *The Great Ideas Today*, p. 275 (1978). How far toleration has been carried in the United States can be seen in the unanimity with which the United States Supreme Court declared a city ordinance unconstitutional which had forbidden the use of animal sacrifices in public religious services. See *Church of the Lukumi Babalu Aye v. City of Hialeah*, 508 U.S. 520 (1993). What is particularly significant here is not only what the Supreme Court did but, perhaps even more, that a cult made up of recent immigrants had been emboldened to announce that it intended to conduct highly offensive (and publicly evident) animal sacrifices in this country.

26. See, on existentialism and on Martin Heidegger, Anastaplo, *The American Moralist*, pp. 139–44; appendix B of this collection, notes 9, 13; appendix C of this collection, note 109. (The Existentialism of the Declaration seems, here and there, to have been influenced by Marxist terminology.) See, on the dreadful crimes of Heidegger's political masters and the Nuremberg Trial, Anastaplo, "On Trial: Explorations," 22 *Loyola University of Chicago Law Journal* 763, 977 (1991). Rabbi Emil Fackenheim, in his presentation at the 1993 Parliament of the World's Religions, traced the roots of the Holocaust to the idolatry of modern times. See, e.g., the text following upon note 12 of appendix C. See also epigraph, preface to this collection.

I had occasion to prepare for July 4, 2001, this commentary on another, even more prominent, Declaration ("On Reading, Once Again, the Declaration of Independence"):

It is again the time of year for celebrating the birth of the United States of America, a celebration which often includes public readings from the Declaration of Independence. Most professional speakers on such occasions recognize that the typical audience is likely to respond favorably only to the opening and closing passages of the Declaration. It is there that general principles are stated and that decisive actions are announced.

Thus, at the outset of the Declaration there is this solemn invocation: "When in the Course of human Events, it becomes necessary for one People to dissolve the Political Bands which have connected them with another, and to assume among the Powers of the Earth, the separate and equal Station to which the Laws of Nature and of Nature's God entitle them, a decent Respect to the Opinions of Mankind requires that they should declare the causes which impel them to the Separation. We hold these Truths to be self-evident, that all Men are created equal, that they are endowed by their Creator with certain unalienable Rights, that among these are Life, Liberty, and the Pursuit of Happiness—That to secure these Rights, Governments are instituted among Men, deriving their just Powers from the Consent of the Governed." And at the conclusion of the Declaration it is announced: "That these United Colonies are, and of right ought to be, Free and Independent States . . . and that [as such] they have full Power to levy War, conclude Peace, contract Alliances, establish Commerce, and to do all other Acts and Things which Independent States may of right do."

The Declaration of Independence gets to this fateful announcement only after having drawn upon that great political remedy which we know as "the right of revolution." It had been said in the Declaration, immediately after it was argued that Governments derive "their just Powers from the Consent of the Governed," "that whenever any Form of Government becomes destructive of these Ends, it is the Right of the People to alter or to abolish it, and to institute new Government."

The venerable right of revolution can be both threatening and reassuring. It is threatening because it can seem to undermine long-established ways of life. This can disturb those conscientious citizens who are concerned, as all everywhere should be, about Law and Order. But it is reassuring in that it reminds everyone of the natural, if not even divinely-ordained, right of a people to good government and of their right as well to get rid of bad government.

Above all, the right of revolution is an authoritative confirmation that there are indeed principles of proper government and a good life applicable to all mankind. It is thereby insisted, in effect that there naturally exist standards of good and bad, of right and wrong, which are ultimately independent of what any particular government might happen to acknowledge, to endorse, or to act upon.

Often overlooked during ceremonial readings of the Declaration of Independence is the array of two dozen grievances literally at the core of the document. It is "natural" enough that this array should be skipped today: many of these grievances are not rhetorically appealing; some of them seem outdated and otherwise hard to understand. But it is in that array of grievances that one sees now, as one could see then, how the fundamental principles invoked at the outset of the document had been in effect repudiated by the British government in its dealings with its North American Colonies.

It is important to be reminded that an invocation of principles is not enough: such invocations have to be backed up by facts. Individuals may have rights, of course, but so does the community at large, including the right not to have a decent government disturbed for "light and transient Causes." It is this distinction that President Lincoln insisted upon, in 1861, when he argued that the South simply did not have at that time just cause for invoking any right of revolution. It is never enough for any faction simply to say, "We don't like what is happening—and so we quit!"

Thus we can see both in the beginning and in the ending of the Declaration of Independence the elevated heights to which the proclamation of liberty and the cause of legitimate government can soar. But we can see at the heart of the Declaration that disciplined respect for relevant facts upon which a decade of struggle had been grounded prior to that memorable Fourth of July in 1776.

It is such discipline that political life is always in need of, especially at a time when there can be a lot of loose talk, some of it even highminded talk, taking the place of informed and reasoned discourse. The salutary rigor of the authors of the Declaration of Independence is testified to, therefore, by their allocation of more than half of their founding constitutional statement to a recital of the grievances which would provide "the Facts" necessary to "be submitted to a candid World."

See note 88 of appendix B of this collection.

A few months later we all, because of the montrous September 2001 assaults with hijacked airliners on New York City and Washington D.C., had occasion to assess the principles by which others may be dreadfully misled. We must now ponder how any religion-related fudamentalism should be addressed which may promote murderous, even suicidal, inclinations. Security measures, legal sanctions, and military responses— however useful they are at times—cannot reliably tame the deepest passions responsible for the conduct that is properly abhorred by civilized people everywhere. Insofar as disturbing movements do happen to be grounded in long-established religious opinions, it is necessary to enlist spiritual leaders who can explain to their evidenty demented coreligionists that their particular faith (or way of feeling and thinking) simply does not countenance, but rather has long condemned, the kind of reckless destructiveness witnessed in New York City and Washington.

Leo Strauss has suggested that "the only question which ultimately matters" is whether "the Bible or philosophy is right." *Is* this so? It may depend partly upon what one takes the Bible, or revelation, to include and whether any other (that is, nonbiblical) revelations are to be taken seriously. How are the various schools of non-Western thought, especially when they invoke revelation, to be regarded vis-à-vis philosophy? Do any of them have pathological features in need of treatment? Certainly, the Strauss suggestion here seems to depend upon his extaordinary capacity for theoretical pursuits and upon his happening to be personally grounded in Judaism. Leo Strauss may be usefully compared to Mortimer J. Adler (see the Dedication for this volume), who too was born a Jew and who evidently died a Roman Catholic. For him the conflict between reason and revelation seems to have been moderated, if not even eliminated, by Thomas Aquinas. Be that as it may, is a reliable thoughtfulness presupposed whenever reason and revelation are placed in juxtaposition, including an awareness (guided by nature) of what the truly divine surely does not call for or permit? That is, should both genuine prudence and an inspired revelation tend to direct one to the same judgment in any particular situation? In any event, the prudent statesman (or responsible prophet) may well emphasize different things to different peoples with respect to the same matter. Consider, for example, this statement by Alfarabi a millennium ago:

So let it be clear to you that the idea of the Philosopher, Supreme Ruler, Prince, Legislator, and *Iman* is but a single idea. No matter which of these words you take, if you proceed to look at what each of them signifies among the majority of those who speak our language [Arabic], you will find that they all finally agree by signifying one and the same thing.

Alfarabi, *Philosophy of Plato and Aristotle,* trans. Muhsin Mahdi (Ithaca, N.Y.: Cornell Universty Press, 1962), p. 47. See also note 38 of chapter 4 of this collection. It is salutary to be reminded here of Aristotle's recognition of the natural sweetness of existence. See note 19 above. See also Aristotle, *Nicomachean Ethics* 1161a17–18.

Do we tend to see religious fundamentalism as particularly dangerous among Muslims today partly because we are not personally threatened by what other peoples routinely do to each other in the non-Western world? (See, e.g., the text at note 51 of chapter 2 of this collection.) Be that as it may, Muslims in the United States and elsewhere are beginning to be suspected in some quarters in somewhat the way that the North American Indians were by many Europeans two centuries ago. Should not the traditional Muslim respect for both honor and hospitality be appealed to by those who shape the opinions of Islam? See note 113 of chapter 6 of this collection. See on Christian fundamentalists in the United States, George Anastaplo, *The American Moralist: On Law, Ethics, and Government* (Athens, Ohio: Ohio University Press, 1992), p. 327. See also Steven Erlanger, "Italy's Premier Calls Western Civilization Superior to Islamic World," *New York Times,*

September 27, 2001, p. 28; James Blitz, "Italian Premier Attacked for Islam Comments," *Financial Times,* London, September 27, 2001, p. 4; Benjamin Netanyahu, "The West Must Stand Tall," *Chicago Sun-Times,* September 28, 2001, p. 47 (excerpted from testimony to a committee of the United States House of Representatives, September 20, 2001). Compare the discussion of Lessing's *Nathan the Wise* in Anastaplo, "Law & Literature and the Moderns," p. 288.

A sustainable challenge to and fruitful cooperation with dedicated partisans of another school of thought than our own depends, in part, upon a recognition of what seems to be essential to that school. It is such a recognition to which the introductions in this collection attempt to contribute. It is assumed throughout this collection that the dictates of nature have had, for millennia, an effect upon the social organization and the sensibilities of even those peoples whose age-old doctrines do not depend upon (and may well even be antithetical to) an explicit awareness of nature. It is this salutary effect of nature which helps outsiders, as well as insiders, to question obviously inhumane and ultimately self-destructive measures in response to festering grievances. Particularly in need of thoughtful analysis is a pervasive resentment not only of involuntary and degrading poverty but (perhaps even more) of the challenges posed by modernity to long-established and somehow cherished ways of life. (Is this still another, somewhat romantic, Lost Cause?) The West, including its beleaguered outposts such as Israel and Taiwan, is identified as the liberty-enhancing agent of a science-and-technology-dominated modernity. The unsettling suicidal attacks we have been seeing in recent years are the desperate measures of the weak, not of the strong. Even the four hijacked airliners did not inflict upon the United States in September 2001 any damage commensurate with the psychic and financial harm done nationally by much of the response (some of it unbecoming) to those attacks in this country.

It is prudent to be cautious in offering to others even something that may be, in critical respects, better than what they have traditionally relied upon. Virtually any *working* social order, I have argued, is grounded somewhat in nature, even as it incorporates critical errors. It is well to remember, in any event, that Arabs, for example, did much to help revive classical philosophy in the West. It is also prudent to be aware of the highly provocative damage routinely inflicted upon the weak, albeit in good faith, by the strong in their righteousness. There *are* serious grievances worldwide that need to be properly addressed.

In short, we may now be better able than our *immediate* predecessors to recognize that statesmanship depends upon a sound use of rhetoric and prophetology, which should in turn be guided by the obligation to exhibit "a decent Respect to the Opinions of Mankind." See, e.g., note 38 of chapter 4 of this collection. We must proceed in the confident expectation that "a candid World" will respect words and deeds which determinedly adhere to "the Laws of Nature and of Nature's God." The prescriptions for the twenty-first century which I venture to offer in this concluding note of this collection have been anticipated by Winston Churchill's exhortation in the middle of the twentieth century: "Our social science, if it is to be of any use, must be addressed to Muslims and Jews as well as to Christians, to Buddhists and Hindus as well as to believers in the Bible." See note 13 of appendix C of this collection. See, on the religious heritage of the West, George Anastaplo, "Law & Literature and the Bible: Explorations," 23 *Oklahoma City University Law Review* 515–867 (1998) (to be published as a book of respectful readings of the Bible by Rowman & Littlefield). See, on the limitations of even the best earthly regime, Anastaplo, *The Constitutionalist: Notes on the First Amendment* (Dallas: Southern Methodist University Press, 1971), pp. 278–81. See, on the Good, the True, and the Beautiful, note 39 of appendix B of this collection.

Index

Aaron, 199, 203
Abdul Aziz, 219
Abdul-Rauf, Muhammad, 220
Abley, Mark, 258
abortion, 65, 370
Abraham, 178, 180, 182, 185, 187, 197,
    199–200, 204, 208, 217, 222, 252, 271,
    326. *See also* Bible; Christianity;
    Islam; Judaism
Abrahams, Roger D., 58, 62
Abubeker, 191
abyss, 123, 162, 321
Achebe, Chinua, 40, 42, 47, 53, 64
Achilles, 13, 15, 17, 21, 168, 250, 254,
    264, 359. *See also* Homer
Acoma tribe, 249
Acyuta, 72–75, 89, 91–92
Adair's History, 256, 258
Adam and Eve, 21, 94, 167, 213, 249, 326
Adams, John Quincy, 334, 365
Adeimantus, 319
Adler, M. J., xiv, xviii–xx, 88, 95–97,
    126–28, 130–32, 135, 140, 142–43,
    373. *See also* the dedication for this
    volume
Adon Olam, 178
Aeschylus, 19, 24, 50, 269
Aesop, 32–33, 46–47, 64
Africa, viii–ix, xvi–xvii, xx, 31–65, 209,
    258, 346

African Americans, 32, 47–48, 52–54, 57,
    64, 221, 247, 259
African thought, 31–65. *See also* Africa
Agamemnon, 19, 264
agony of the world, 358
Agricola, 255
agriculture, 243
Ahab, Captain, 366
Ahmed, Akbar, 224
AIDS epidemic, 55, 61
Akkadian, 14, 16, 19, 24–25
Albany Plan, 256
Alcibiades, 134
alcohol, drugs, 244–45, 258
Alexander the Great, 15, 23, 32, 234, 251,
    336
Alfarabi (Farabi), 223–24, 340, 343,
    373–74
Allah, 196–97. *See also* divine; Islam
al-Lal (a "daughter" of Allah), 204–7
Almohads, 193
al-'Uzza (a "daughter" of Allah), 204–7
Amos, 214
Analects, ix, xviii, 16, 30, 39, 55, 67, 85,
    99–145, 150
Anand, Mulk Raj, 95
Ananda, 162
anarchy, 120
Anastaplo, George, Bibliographies, xix,
    397

Anastaplo, George Malcolm Davidson, 295
Anastaplo, Sara Maria, 297–98
Anastaplo, Sara Prince, 1, 13, 297–98
Anaxagoras, 286
ancestral, 104, 109–10, 112, 114, 121
Ancoma tribe, 227
ancient city, xiii. *See also polis*
angels, 313. *See also* Gabriel; Islam
animal sacrifices, 371. *See also* rituals
animism, 42–44, 59
Ankeny, Rachel N., xix
Anselm, 216
anthropic cosmological principle, xviii, 246–47, 279–80, 296, 313, 335
anthropology, xviii, 101, 160–61, 180–81, 191, 205, 208, 211
Antigone, 21, 52, 367–68
Anu (father of Ishtar), 3, 6, 11, 17, 28–36
Aphrodite, 3, 19. *See also* eros, erotic; Ishtar
Apollo, 24, 51, 217, 342
Aptheker, Herbert, 62
Aquinas, Thomas. *See* Thomas Aquinas
Arabs, xii, 22, 28, 31–32, 39, 175, 180–81, 187, 190, 194–95, 200, 203–4, 206–10, 216, 218, 224, 372–74. *See also* Islam
Arberry, Arthur J., 196, 200, 205, 208, 214, 221–23
archaeology, 191, 248, 287
aristocracy, 226, 241–42, 257, 259
Aristophanes, 29, 129, 290, 366
Aristotle, xv, xix, xxii, 13, 25, 56, 59, 79, 88–89, 95–96, 104, 111, 121–22, 125–26, 130, 132, 135–38, 140–41, 143, 156–57, 168–69, 193, 216, 245, 258, 260, 273, 276, 281, 289, 293–95, 297, 301, 321, 323, 334, 336–37, 340–42, 350, 366, 368, 370, 373. *See also* philosophy; Plato; Socrates
Arjuna, 28, 67–98, 155, 159, 171, 214
Armi, Anna Maria, 365
Arnhart, Larry, xiv–xv, xix, 60–61, 130, 216, 297, 335, 368
Arnott, Kathleen, 54, 56, 58–59, 62–63, 65

Aronson, Jason, 24
art and probability, 59. *See also* poetry
artistry, 81–83, 161. *See also* poetry
asceticism, 148–50, 152, 161
Ashoka, Emperor, 164, 171
Ashurbanipal, 14, 16
Assyria, 14, 17, 19
Astarte (Ishtar), 18. *See also* Ishtar
astrology, 37
astronomy, astrophysicists, xx, 73. *See also* science, modern
Athavale, V. B., 87
atheism, 55, 84, 97, 163, 191, 222, 347–48. *See also* divine; philosophy; rhetoric
Athena, 3, 87, 268
Athens, ancient, 67, 105, 123
Atrahasis (Utnapishtim), 20, 27. *See also* Utnapaishtim
Attila the Hun, 213
Augustine, St., 164, 167–68, 170–72, 217, 268, 290, 315–16, 336, 340, 342
Augustus Caesar. *See* Octavius
Austen, Jane, 18, 129
authenticity, 362. *See also* existentialism
autonomy, 307. *See also* individualism
Awoonor, Kofi, 54
Ayesha (a wife of Muhammad), 212, 219. *See also* Kemal Ataturk
Aztecs, 248, 257. *See also* human sacrifice

Babel, Tower of, 249. *See also* Genesis
Babylonia, 14, 16, 19, 24, 238, 265, 289, 292
bacchanals. *See* sensuous woman dressed in white
Bacon, Francis, 147, 163, 173, 253, 341, 369
Bahrain, 22
Bancroft, Frederic, 54
Banerjee, Nikilesh, 292
Bangkok, 166
Barrow, John D., 296
Barrows, John Henry, 370–71
Basham, A. L., 85–90, 94–95, 98
Bates, Clifford A., Jr. 335

bawdiness, 235–36, 251
Bayle, Pierre, 143
beauty, 133, 145, 159, 170, 177, 184, 186, 310, 337–39, 352, 372. *See also* eros, erotic; philosophy
Beaver, 240
beginnings, xi, xix, xxi–xxii, 178, 236, 239, 253, 261–301, 326–27
Behmen, Jacob, 352
being, 177, 326–27. *See also* philosophy
Belgium, 61
Bellow, Saul, 56
Benard, Cheryl, 207
Benardete, Seth G., 92, 289
Bennet, Elizabeth, 18
Bennett, Lerone Jr., 52–53
Beowulf, 132
Berlin, 32
Berlinski, David, 293
Berlusconi, Silvio, 373–74
Bernal, Martin, 51
Berns, Laurence, 25, 28, 57, 65, 96, 127, 137, 144, 292, 299, 335
Bernstein, Jeremy, 294–96
Berry, Jack, 63
best regime, 139, 193, 221, 327, 336, 372
Bevington, David, 248
Bhagavad Gītā, xviii, 16, 28, 30, 39, 55, 67–98, 150, 155, 159, 171, 214
Bharata, 91
Bhishma, 70
Bible, xv, xviii, xxii, 13–18, 20–21, 26, 28, 39, 44, 46, 55, 63, 68, 89–90, 92, 94, 124, 127, 137, 139–40, 143–44, 150, 156, 164, 166–68, 170, 176–77, 179, 181, 191, 193, 197–99, 202–5, 210–11, 214, 217, 228, 237–38, 240, 249–51, 252–53, 257, 261–62, 268–72, 279–80, 283, 288, 290–92, 296, 301, 307, 320, 326–31, 340–43, 356, 358, 369, 373–74. *See also* Chrisianity; Judaism
Big Bang, 274, 279, 281–83, 287, 290, 292, 294, 296, 298–99
Big Crunch, 279, 281–83, 287, 298–99
Bilgamesh (Gilgamesh), 13
Bill of Rights (U.S.), 324
Binding of Isaac, 252, 326. *See also*

Abraham; Rebekah; Sarah
biology, modern, 297. *See also* evolution, theory of
Black Holes, 273, 283, 292–94, 300
Black Muslim movement (U.S.), 179
Blackfoot tribe, 232
Blitz, James, 374
Block, Mervin, 203
Bloom, Allan, 208, 277, 295–96
Bloom, Molly, 97, 129
Boccaccio, Giovanni, 235, 252
body and soul, 29, 33, 35, 38, 50, 70, 87–88, 99, 134, 190, 288, 293, 301, 304, 308–12, 350, 371–72
Boeotia, 263, 265, 289–90
Bohr, Niels, 296
Bolle, Kees W., 86, 88, 91, 93
bombing, annihilation, 41
Book of the Dead, The, 36
Boreas, xvii
Born, Max, 293
Bosnia, 349
Bower, Bruce, 248
Brahe, Tycho, 253
Brahman, 71–73
Braithwaite, William T., 13, 51, 300, 336, 339
Brandeis, Louis D., 27
Brann, Eva T. H., 168, 222, 250, 294, 297
Braunfeld, Peter, 292, 297
Britain, 241, 255
Brown, Calvin S., 16
Brule Sioux tribe, 247
Buddhist thought, xi, 15, 52, 55, 97, 147–73, 347–48, 366, 369, 374
Budge, E. A. Wallis, 51
Buitenen, J. A. B. van: *See* van Buitenen, J. A. B.
Bull of Heaven, 4, 19–20, 25–26, 28
Bunyan, John, 371
Burke, Edmund, 69, 88
Burma, 164–65
Burns, Robert, 217
Burton, William, 300
Burtt, E. A., 164, 166–67, 169–72
butterflies, creation of, 227–28
Butterworth, Charles E., 194

Caddo tribe, 237
Cain and Abel, 27. *See also Genesis*
Cairo, Egypt, 32, 49, 217
Callicles, 319
Calliopi, 263
Cambodia, 164
campus hate-speech codes, xviii
Canaanites, 14, 18, 354
cannibalism, 41, 53, 59, 250
capitalism, 359–60
Carlyle, Thomas, 175–76, 178, 184, 188–89, 194–96, 200, 202–4, 212–13, 216, 219
Carroll, Lewis, 88
Carter, Jimmy, 207
Carter, Steven R., 56
caste system, 94–95, 97, 160, 368
Catalogue of Ships, 209, 289. *See also* Homer
causualty, cause and effect, xvii, 42, 44–45, 183, 274. *See also* rationalism
celebrities, 311
cemetery, Hardin, Missouri, 367–68
censorship, 92
Ceres, 3
certainty, standard of, 318, 336. *See also* miracles; revelation; philosophy
Ceylon, 164
Chaerephon, xxii
Chan, W. T., 128
chance, 14, 17, 23, 99, 101, 119, 181, 183, 210–11, 240, 277, 294–95, 320–21, 337–38, 354–55, 360, 371–72
Chandrasekhar, Subrahmanyan, 90, 295–96, 335
Chaos, xi, 264–67, 269–70, 283, 289, 299
charioteers, instructive, 148, 159, 165, 171
charismatic elements, 354–55
charity, 185, 188
Charnwood, Lord, 251
Chatterji, M., 91, 94, 96
Chau Zan, 116–18, 138
Chauduri, Nirad C., 202
Cherokee tribe, 249
Chesterton, G. K., 28
Chicago, Illinois, 32, 226

Children's Crusade, 286. *See also* science, modern
Chi-lu (Yu), 116–19
Chimera, xviii
China, Chinese, 32, 95, 124, 131, 138–39, 142–43, 164–65, 167, 241, 244, 246, 254, 257–58, 374. *See also* Confucian thought
Chissick, Seymour S., 299
Ch'iu (Confucius), 125
Christ, 88, 152, 202, 210. *See also* Jesus
Christian Scientists, 353
Christianity, xv, xxi–xxii, 9, 18, 24, 33–34, 37, 39, 44, 49–51, 63, 85, 87–88, 94–95, 132, 137–43, 152–54, 156, 164–65, 167, 171, 175, 177–85, 187, 191, 196, 199, 201–3, 206–7, 209, 211–13, 215, 218–19, 223, 240, 245, 254, 258, 268, 271, 285, 290, 306–7, 315–16, 323–33, 339–43, 353, 356, 369, 373–74. *See also* Bible; Judaism
Christopher, John B., 222
Chung-ni (Confucius), 125
Church of the Lukumi Babalu Aye v. *City of Hialeah* (1993), 371
Churchill, Winston S., 98, 342, 369, 374
Circe, 20
circumcision, 190. *See also* rituals
Civil War (U.S.), 49, 141, 203, 221, 256, 350, 371
Clark, Ronald W., 294
classical writings, 145
Cleveland, Keith S., 292, 335
cloning, 335
Clytemnestra, 19
Cold Fusion fiasco, 294
Cold War, xviii
Cole, Frank, 50
Collier, John, 238, 253
Colmo, Christopher A., 223–24, 335
Columbian Exposition, 346, 366
Columbus, Christopher, 242, 246, 249
commerce, 14, 345, 362, 371
commitment, 334, 356, 362
common sense, xx, 96, 126, 159, 161, 169, 237, 274, 279, 282, 292–93, 298,

323–24. *See also* philosophy;
prudence; rationalism; science, modern
comparative literature, xviii
compassion, 149, 154, 158–60
Confucian thought, ix, xiii, xvi, xviii, 16,
29–30, 39, 85, 99–145, 168, 234, 292
Conrad, Joseph, 53
conscience, 307, 334, 336, 341, 364. *See
also* Christianity
Constitution, constitutionalism (U.S.), xxi,
14, 49, 124, 167, 219, 324
constitutionalism, cosmic, 283
consumerism, 247
Conze, Edward, 164–70
Coomaraswamy, Ananda K., 164–65, 167
Cooper, James Fenimore, 257–59
Corey, Michael A., 296
Corinthians, 123
corn, creation of, 229–30
cosmic radiation background, 292, 300.
See also science, modern
cosmology, cosmos, 120, 161, 272–87,
292–301
Cottrell, Leonard, 16–17
courage, virtue of, 110–11, 113, 120,
134–35, 159, 243
Cowell, Alan, 339
Coyote, 229, 233, 239, 253
Cragg, Kenneth, 196–98, 205, 210,
218–20
creation, creationism, xi, xxi–xxii, 62, 86,
141, 156, 183, 185, 188, 213–14, 222,
226–28, 230–32, 236–37, 239–40, 262,
283, 291, 297, 332, 336. *See also*
Bible; evolution, theory of
Creel, H. G., 128
Cretan Paradox, 216
Cronin, James W., 300
Cronus, 234
Cropsey, Joseph, 57, 96–97, 137, 336,
340, 343
Crusskey, William Winslow, 299, 339
Crow tribe, 249
Crucifixion, 215
custom, xv
Cyclops, 250
cynicism, 108

Cyprus, 191, 349
Cyrus, King, 21

Dakar, 32
Dakota tribe, 247
Dalai Lama, 346, 355, 366, 370
Daley, Richard M., 370
Daly, Lloyd W., 50
Damascus, 224
Daniel, 219
Däniken, Erich von. *See* von Däniken,
Erich
Dante Alighieri, 93, 289, 294, 323, 339
Danton, John, 61
Daphne, 252
Darcy and Elizabeth Bennet, 18
Darius, King, 23
Darwin, Charles, 134, 240, 281, 297–98,
301, 335. *See also* evolution, theory
of
David, King, 13, 199
Davis, Sir John, 132
de Alvarez, Leo Paul S., 14, 23, 92, 137,
171, 206
death, xix, 2, 4, 6–9, 11–15, 20–22, 24,
28–30, 33–34, 36–37, 52, 56, 77, 91,
94, 104, 120, 148–49, 151, 154–56,
158–59, 162, 165, 167–68, 170–71,
183, 232, 236, 239–40, 247, 251, 253,
259–60, 293, 297, 303–4, 309–10, 312,
314, 322, 327, 333–34, 340, 345, 350,
367–68, 371–74. *See also* natural,
nature; philosophy
de Bary, W. T., 125, 164, 166, 168–72
Decalogue. *See* Ten Commandments
de Coulanges, Fustel, xiii
Declaration of a Global Ethic (1993),
345–46, 351, 355–65, 369–71
Declaration of Independence (1776), 4, 8,
65, 124, 138, 141, 219, 224, 242, 255,
339, 370–72
Deegalle, Mahanda, 113
Delilah, 18
Delphic Oracle, xviii, 51, 217, 342
Demaret, Jacques, 296
Democritus, 65
Demosthenes, 195

Descartes, René, 173, 177, 253, 293, 307, 318, 336
despotism, 138
determinism, 212–13. *See also* fate; free will; will, act of
Deutsch, Eliot, 84–85, 91, 93–94
Deutsch, Kenneth L., xvii, 127, 397
Devil, 354. *See also* Satan
de Waal, Frans, 335
Dhananjaya, 94
Dhritarāshtra, King, 97
Dickens, Charles, 88
dietary rules, 157, 190
dignity, 137, 307, 356. *See also* individualism
Diodorus, 25
Diogenes Laertius, 65
Diotima, 24
discovery, ix, 241, 293, 297. *See also* science, modern
Divine, xi, xiii–xvii, xxi, 2–4, 8–11, 17–18, 20, 23, 25, 27–29, 33, 35–37, 42, 49, 51, 55, 58–59, 67–98, 120, 126–27, 131, 138, 147, 160, 163, 166, 168, 72, 175–224, 261–72, 282–83, 285–92, 294–95, 321–23, 326–31, 341–43, 345–73. See also Bible; Christianity; Juadaism; Islam; prophecy, prophetology
DNA molecule, 296
Donagan, Alan, 340
Doniger, Wendy, 85, 93, 96
Dostoyevsky, Fyodor, 124
Douglas, Stephen A., 142
Douglass, Frederick, 53, 61
Doyle, A. Conan, 27-28
Draupadi, 88
Dreams, 2, 6, 10, 18–19, 28, 30, 181–82
Drona, 70
Du Bois, W. E. B., 48, 54, 64, 365
Duran, Khalid, 207
Duryodhana, 92, 95
Dwamish tribe, 247

Ea, 20, 27–28
Earth, 264, 266–70, 289
East, xxii

Eastern Orthodox Church, 140, 200, 353
Eblis. *See* Iblis
Ebrahim bin Adham, 227–28
economics, 308, 334, 359–60, 371. *See also* onions, consumption of
Edgerton, Franklin, 86, 88–89, 91, 93–95
egalitarianism, equality, 48, 278, 308, 346, 350, 357, 371
Egidu, R. N., 56
Egypt, Egyptians, ix, xvii, xx–xxii, 23, 26, 31–38, 49–52, 123, 218, 238, 246, 254, 265, 271, 292, 306
Egyptian thought, 31–38, 49–52
Ehvenreich, Barbare, 60
Eightfold Way, 151
Einstein, Albert, 273–74, 276, 293–96, 300–301
Elamites, 14
Elements of the element, 299. *See also* ultron
Elias, 199
Elijah Muhammad, 179, 203
Eliot, T. S., 85, 194, 288
Elisha, 199
Ellison, Ralph, 368
Elpenor, 21
Emancipation Proclamation (1862–1863), 49
Embree, Ainslie T., 125
Emerson, Ralph W., 95, 348, 351–52
energy, 321
Engeman, Thomas, 335
Enkidu, 2–7, 9–10, 12, 18–22, 24–26, 28–30, 149
Enlightenment, 44, 138, 170, 278, 294, 345
Enlil, 9, 11, 27, 29
environmental movement, 247, 361
Epicureans, 97
epistemology, xiii–xxii, 279–80. *See also* philosophy
equality. *See* egalitarianism, equality
Erdoes, Richard, 249–54, 257, 259
Erie Railroad Co. v. *Tompkins* (1938), 336
Erlanger, Steven, 373
Eros, erotic, xxi, 2, 5–9, 11–12, 14, 17–18, 26–28, 33–34, 47, 50–51, 59, 167,

235–37, 251, 264–67, 269–70, 289–90, 308, 315, 319. *See also* beauty; philosophy
Esau, 257
Eskimos, 57
esotericism, 87, 142, 161–63, 172, 177. *See also* rhetoric; philosophy
Esposito, John L., 196, 203, 207, 209, 211–12, 215
Essenes, 170
eternity of the world, 162, 172–73, 313. See also creation; evolution, theory of; natural, nature
Ethiopia, 31, 33
Etrech. *See* Uruk
Euphrates River, 14, 17, 23, 25
Euripides, 19–20, 28, 214
euthanasia, 370. *See also* death; divine; natural law, natural right
Eve, 250–51. *See also Genesis*
evolution, theory of, xi, xix, 161, 250, 281, 297–98, 313–14. *See also* creation, creationism; Darwin, Charles
existence, natural sweetness of, 156–57, 167, 322, 358, 370, 373. *See also* death; natural, nature; philosophy; salvation, personal
existentialism, 144, 334–35, 362, 371
experimentation, 284, 301
Ezra, 179, 201

Fackenheim, Emil, 371
facts-values distinction. *See* "values"
Fahd, King, 216
Fallers, Lloyd A., 60, 198
family, 121, 123, 140–41, 150, 155, 188–89, 262, 288
fanaticism, 221–22. *See also* hijacking airliners
Farabi. *See* Alfarabi
Farrakhan, Louis, 366
fate, 22, 67–98, 267, 290, 359. *See also* chance; divine
fatigue, 305, 309
Faulkner, William, 367
Faust, Drew Gilpin, 53
Feagles, Anita, 26

Feinberg, Leonard, 94
female element, 12. *See also* women, status of
Fermi, Enrico, 292, 296
First Amendment (U.S.), xxi, 349
First Cause, xv, 177. *See also* divine
First World War, 358–59, 370
Flathead tribe, 229
flattery, 109–11. *See also* rhetoric
Flood, the Great, 2, 4, 6–7, 9–10, 17–20, 27–28, 30, 149, 271
Folsom, James K., 254, 256–58
Forster, 94, 96–98
Fortin, Ernest L., 341
Fox, George, 352
France, 22–23, 137, 358–59
Frankfort, H. and H. A., 23, 26
Franklin, Benjamin, 255
Frazer, R. M., 289
Frazier, Sir James, 207
free will, 212. *See also* fate; will, act of
freedom of expression, 252, 335
freedom of speech, 335. *See also* First Amendment
Freeman, Leslie G., 248
French, Howard W., 54, 64–65
French Revolution, 221–22, 358–59
Freud, Sigmund, 207
friendship, 46–47, 106, 130, 140, 189
Fritzsche, Hellmut, 51, 292, 300
Fuller, Amanda E., xix
fundamentalists, 353, 371–72
funeral industry (U.S.), 34
Fung Yu-lan, 128
Furies, 24
Fustel de Coulanges, xiii

Gabriel, 183, 202, 204–5, 210, 212. *See also* Koran; Muhammad
Gadamer, Hans-Georg, 87–88
Galileo Galilei, 56, 177, 251, 273, 276–77, 296, 298
Gallop, David, 290
Gamble, Clive, 52
gambling, 94
Gandhi, Mohandas, 95, 98
Ganges River, 77, 94

gangsters, self-image of, 351
Gard, Richard A., 166, 169
Garden of Eden, 249, 269, 271, 326
Gardner, John, 15–16, 19–20, 22, 24,
    27–28
Gardner, Martin, 295
Garelli, Paul, 22
Gaughin, Paul, 62
Gauls, 255
Gautama, Siddhartha (Gotama), 52,
    147–73
Gelb, I. J., 23
Genesis, 2, 17, 20, 26, 143, 156, 167, 211,
    249–50, 252–53, 270–72, 275, 279,
    283, 288, 291, 296, 301, 326. See also
    Bible; divine
gentleman, 139, 143. See also honor;
    hospitality; hospitality, abuse of
Germans, 41, 59
Gersonides, 200
Gettysburg Address, 133, 219
Ghana, 46–47, 54, 64–65
Gibbon, Edward, 49–50, 175–76, 184,
    190–91, 194, 196, 199–204, 208–9,
    212–13, 219– 21, 224, 272, 292
Gideon, 251, 270
Gilgamesh epic, Gligamesh, ix, xviii, xxi,
    1–30, 52–53, 149–50, 162, 166, 215
Glaser-Schmidt, Elisabeth, 334
Glaucon, 319
globalization, xvii
Glubb, John Bagot, 196
God. *See* divine
God and the throwing of dice, 274, 289,
    294–95. *See also* chance; natural,
    nature
Goethe, Johann Wolfgang, von, 291
Golden Age, 57, 326
Golden Calf, 184, 213
Golden Rule, 132
Goldsmith, Donald, 294
Goldstein, Bill, 296
good, goodness, xiv, 137, 310, 312, 323,
    337–39, 374. See also divine; natural
    law, natural right; rhetoric
Goodstein, Laurie, 370
Gordon, Cyrus H., 26

Gorgias, xxii
Gorgon, xviii
Gormly, John, 28
Gotama. *See* Guatama, Siddhartha
Gourevitch, Victor, 18, 66, 146, 344. *See
    also* esotericism; morality for its own
    sake
Grande Ronde River, 227
Graves, Robert, 292
Great Renunciation, 148
Great Spirit, 245, 259. *See also* divine
Greece, ancient, xi, xiii–xv, xix, xxii, 23,
    26, 31–33, 38, 44, 46–47, 49, 52, 56,
    100, 123, 131, 139, 166, 187, 202, 220,
    236, 238, 240, 246, 248, 250, 254,
    262–63, 286, 288, 292, 307, 332, 354
Greece, modern, 47, 63, 218, 234, 257.
    See also Nicene Creed
Greek Americans, 353
Greeley, Andrew, 366
Green, Kenneth Hart, xx, xxi, 17, 24, 97,
    213, 290
Greene, Graham, 87
Grene, David, 289
Grotius, Hugo, 287
Grunebaum, Gustav E. von. *See* von
    Grunebaum, Gustav E.
Guam, 218
Gudo, 156
Gulf War, 170, 222, 224, 370. *See also*
    hijacking airliners

Hades, 21
Hagan, William T., 248–49, 253, 255–56,
    258–59
Hagar, 203–4. *See also* Ishmael
Haile Selassie, Emperor, 60
Haiti, 63
Halevi, Judah, 223, 342
Hamburger, Max, 125
happiness, xix, 140, 372. *See also*
    existence, natural sweetness of
Harding, Vincent, 54, 62
Hawaii, 164, 218
Hawking, Stephen W., xx, 261, 272–88,
    292–301
Hawthorne, Nathaniel, 366

Hazlett, Thomas W., 61
Hector, 17
Hegel, G. W. F., xiii, xxi, 52, 85, 93, 98,
    100–101, 126, 197, 221–22
Heidegger, Martin, 65, 127, 216, 222, 291,
    308, 334, 362, 371
Heidel, Alexander, 14–17, 20–22, 26
Heisenberg, Werner, 282, 296, 298
Helen of Troy, 235, 250–51
Hell, 157–58
Hemingway, Ernest, 334
Heracles, 15, 27, 88–89, 270
Herman, A. L., 85, 90, 95, 166
Herod, 248
Herodotus, xxi, 24, 33, 52, 252, 263, 289,
    320, 350
Hersh, Seymour M., 138
Hesiod, 234, 243, 261–70, 275, 280,
    288–90, 296
Heyerdahl, Thor, 22
high and the low, 24, 57, 235, 277. *See
    also* Strauss, Leo
hijacking airliners (September 11, 2001),
    xxii, 223–24, 371–72. *See also*
    hospitality, abuse of; human sacrifice
Hill, Robert S., 343
Hinayana, The (The Little Raft), 164–65
Hindu thought, Hinduism, ix, xi, xvi, 30,
    34–35, 50, 67–98, 150, 152, 154–56,
    159–61, 163–64, 166–67, 171, 197,
    202, 213, 215, 241, 246, 250, 254, 258,
    290, 349–51, 369, 374
Hippolytus, 19–20, 28
history, 122–23, 239–40, 287, 295, 357.
    See also chance; divine; materialism
Hitler, Adolf, 61. *See also* Nazis
Hittites, 14, 19, 22, 265, 289
Hobbes, Thomas, 57, 220, 301, 307, 334, 336
Hoge, Warren, 369
holidays, 28
Holmes, Mycroft, 27
Holmes, Oliver Wendell, Jr., 336
Holmes, Sherlock, 27
Holy Ghost, Holy Spirit, 18, 202. *See also*
    Trinity
Homer, xxi–xxii, 13, 15–17, 20–21, 29,
    39, 51, 55, 68, 87, 92, 102, 110, 161,

168, 171, 195, 209–10, 215–17, 234,
    243, 250–52, 254, 263–64, 268–70,
    288–90, 320, 359
homosexuality, 26. *See also* natural,
    nature
honor, 189, 191, 224, 243, 371–72
Hopi tribe, 249
hospitality, status of, 189, 218, 223, 257;
    abuse of, 372–74. *See also* human
    sacrifice
Housmann, Per, 41
Houston, Sam, 168–69, 256
Hsiao, Kung-chuan. *See* Kung-chuan
    Hsiao
Hubble, Edward (Hubble's Constant), 275,
    292, 294
Huck Finn, 244
Huidekoper's Lessee v. *Douglass* (1805),
    339
Huizenga, John R., 294
human sacrifice, 64, 248, 253, 257. *See
    also* hijacking airliners; hospitality,
    abuse of; natural law, natural right
Humbaba, 2, 5, 7, 9, 19, 21, 26
Humboldt, Wilhelm von. *See* von
    Humboldt, Wilhelm
Hume, David, 343
Huxley, Aldous, 27

Iblis (Eblis), 212–13
Ibrahim. *See* Abraham
Iconoclastic Controversy, 200
idealism, 108. *See also* realism
Ideas, Doctrine of, xxii, 180, 186, 270,
    279, 290
identical twins, 305–7
idolatry, 178, 182, 184–88, 200, 202–5,
    209, 216, 224
Illinois, 226
immortality of the soul, 7–8, 11, 34–35,
    141, 149, 178, 236, 307–8, 313–14,
    322, 330–31, 334, 336–37, 342, 357
impeachment, presidential, 134
incarnation, 75, 87–88, 215. *See also*
    reincarnation
Incas, 248
incest, 235, 290

India, 38, 80, 88, 95, 98, 139, 164–65, 202, 209, 213, 214, 249, 346, 349–50, 368. *See also* Hindu thought
Indians, North American, viii–ix, xx, 31, 40, 43, 49, 56–58, 61–62, 225–60, 350, 366, 368, 373. *See also* references to Indian tribes
individualism, 33, 42–43, 61, 154–55, 164, 167–68, 191, 244, 259, 288, 301, 303–4, 306–8, 310, 333–34, 348, 356, 361
Indonesia, 218
industrialization, 44
Injun Joe, 257
Inquisition, 362
insanity, 137, 212, 223, 253–54, 283, 352. *See also* madness
intellectuals, 131–32. *See also* sophistry
Interfaith accommodations, 345–72
Iqbal, Sir Mohammad, 223
Iran, 19
Iraq, 15, 17, 22, 196
Ireland, Northern, 349
Iroquois tribe, 230–31
Isaac, 167, 197, 199, 203, 252, 271, 326. *See also* Abraham; Judaism; Rebekah
Isaiah, 193, 358
Ishmael (Ismail), 199, 203–4
Ishtar, 2–6, 9, 11–12, 17–20, 22, 24–25, 28–30
Isis, 50–52
Islam, ix, xi, xv, xxi, 28, 34, 37, 39, 49–50, 52, 60, 63, 94, 126, 166, 175–224, 245, 351–53, 369, 372–74. *See also* Koran; Muhammad
Israel, modern, 191, 222, 255, 372–74. *See also* Judaism
Israelites. *See* Bible; Judaism

Jackson, Michael, vii
Jacob, 197, 257, 271. *See also* Isaac; Rebekah
Jacobsen, Thorkild, 23
Jaffa, Harry V., 131, 144, 199, 335–36, 341–43, 369
Jahadhmy, Ali A., 60
Jains, 95, 368

James, Adeola, 54, 58
Japan, 164, 167, 253
Japanese in the United States, 258
Jefferson, Thomas, 258
Jerusalem, 17, 127, 182, 219. *See also* Bible; Islamic Thought; Judaism
Jesus, 100, 153, 165–66, 168, 177, 179, 182, 185, 191, 193, 199, 201, 208, 213, 215, 217, 248, 252, 348. *See also* Bible; Christ; Christianity; Judaism
Jews. *See* Bible; Jesus; Judaism
Joan of Arc, xix
Job, xi, 96, 194–95, 199, 208, 358
Jog, N. C., 98
John, (Gospel of), 199
John Paul II, Pope, 332
Johnson, Dirk, 248
Johnson, George, 298
Jonah, 199, 250
Joseph, Chief, 242–43, 256
Joseph, son of Jacob, 63, 199
Josephus, 201
Joyce, James, 13, 97, 129
Judaism, xv, xxi, 9, 17–18, 24, 49, 51, 57, 64, 85, 90, 95, 120, 135, 140, 143, 156, 167, 171, 177–80, 182–85, 187, 191, 193, 197, 200–201, 203, 209–11, 213, 215–16, 219, 221–23, 240, 255, 262, 270–72, 286, 307, 340, 353–54, 356, 369–71, 373–74. *See also* Bible; Christianity; Jesus
Judas Iscariot, 184–85, 248
Judiciary Act of 1789, 339
justice, virtue of, xiv–xv, 42, 110–11, 132, 159, 183–84, 189, 216, 223, 243, 250, 265, 268, 316, 319, 323–24, 336, 343, 357, 365, 371–72. *See also* natural law, natural right

Kabba, 180, 203–6. *See also* Mecca
Kant, Immanuel, 89, 95, 316–17, 333, 337
Karaghiosis puppet theatre, 234, 251
Karandikar, 87
Karma (Kamma), 155, 158
Kashmir, 349
Kaufmann, Walter, 291
Kauvavas, 66–68

Keats, John, 304
Keller, Bill, 61, 65
Kemal Ataturk, 213
Kenchreai discovery, 210
Kepler, Johannes, 177, 253
Kepler, Thomas S., 128
Khadijah (a wife of Muhammad), 195,
    205, 212
Khair, Gajanan S., 88, 90, 92
Kibblewhite, Edward, 292, 297
Kielmansegg, Peter Graf, 334
Kilborn, Peter T., 220
kindness not reciprocated, 40–41
King, Thomas, 248
King James translation, Bible, 205
King Lear, 144
Kipling, Rudyard, vii
Kirk, G. S., 21, 25, 29–30
Kisor, Henry, 248
Kissinger, Henry, 138
Kitagawa, Joseph M., 368
Klein, Jacob, 217, 222, 253, 272, 291–92,
    298, 300
Kolata, Gina, 335
Koldny, Annette, 257
Koran (Qur'ān), ix, xi, 24, 39, 55, 164,
    175–224. *See also* Islam; Muhammad
Kramer, Samuel Noah, 13–14, 16, 20–21,
    24–25
Krishna, 67–98, 214
Kroeber, Karl, 251–53
Kronecker, Leopold, 288
Kronus, 264, 267–69
Küng, Hans, 219, 366, 369–70
Kung-chuan Hsiao, 125, 128, 131–32,
    135, 138–41, 143–44
K'ung Fu'tzu, 100
Kung-his Hwa (Ch'ih), 111–14
Kunti, 91
Kupona, Mwana, 60
Kuschel, Karl-Josef, 366
Kytle, Calvin, 95

Lacey, Robert, 219
Laius, 290
Lamb, David, 220
Lambert, Dominique, 296

Lambert, W. G., 22
Lambo, Thomas Adeoye, 60, 64
Landsberger, Benno, 19
Langdon, S. H., 25
Laos, 164
Lao-tze, 132
Lawrence, George, 137
lawyers, xix
Lebanon, 19, 191
Lee, T. D., 299
legal realism, 340. *See also* positivism;
    natural law, natural right
Legge, James, 103, 105, 116, 125–26,
    128–32, 134–38, 140–43
Lenin, Nikolai, 34
Leonard, William Ellery, 16, 18–19, 21
Lerner, Ralph, 222–23, 248, 255–56
Lessing, Gotthold E., 223
Levi, Edward H., 356, 370
Liberia, 32, 49, 218
liberty, freedom, 101, 308, 358, 371–72,
    374. *See also* individualism
Libya, 31
Lichtheim, Miriam, 51
lifestyles, 347
light, speed of, 298, 313, 335–36. *See also*
    science, modern
Lincoln, Abraham, 49, 110, 124, 131, 133,
    136–37, 141–42, 221, 251, 253, 339, 372
Livy, Titus, 14, 287, 320
Locke, John, 301
Logos, 268, 271, 290
Lohr, Steve, 207
London, 32, 49
Lord's Prayer, 356
Lost Cause, 203, 374. *See also* suicide
Lot, 199
love, 18. *See also* eros, the erotic
Loyola University of Chicago School of
    Law, xviii
Lucifer, 93, 341. *See also* Satan
Lucretius, 97, 134, 281–82, 299, 301, 320.
    See also materialism; matter; science,
    modern
Lugalbando, 15
Luther, Martin, 128, 137, 139, 171
Lycurgus, 205

Machiavelli, Niccolò, 14, 22–23, 92, 129,
    136–37, 167, 171, 200, 257, 307. See
    also morality for its own sake;
    prudence
madness, 162, 307, 334, 371–72. See also
    insanity; rationalism; reason
magic, 35, 38, 42, 44–45, 63, 83, 139,
    235, 241. See also miracles; rituals
Mahabharata, The, 68–69, 72–73, 87, 93,
    95, 98
Mahayana (The Great Raft), 164–65
Mahdi, Muhsin, 223, 373
Mahfouz, Naguib, 31, 40, 49–50, 368
"Mahometanism," 197
Maier, John, 10, 15–16, 19–20, 22, 24,
    27–28
Maimonides, Moses, 94, 99, 131, 166,
    175, 192–94, 200, 215–17, 219, 262,
    269, 288, 290, 340, 343
Maitraya (the final Buddha), 167
Malamat, Abraham, 19
Mallat, Chibli, 220
Malunkyaputta, 172–73
Manat (a "daughter" of Allah), 204–7
Manniche, Lise, 50
Mao Tse-tung, 50
Marbury v. Madison (1803), 339
Marks, John H., 13
Marne, Battle of, 370
Marriott, Alice, 251–52, 254, 257–58
Marshall, John, 324, 339
Marshall Field's, 19
Marty, Martin E., 368
martyrdom, 188, 223–24, 229–30, 232–33,
    244, 256, 372–74. See also
    Christianity; Islamic thought; New
    York City, attack on; suicide
Marxism, 191, 215, 371
Mary, mother of Jesus, 177, 179, 199, 201,
    217
Mascaro, Juan, 87, 96
Mason, Herbert, 13–15
Master K'ung (Confucius), 100
Masters, Judith R. and Roger D., 17–18
materialism, xiii, 304, 312–13. See also
    body and soul

mathematics, 222, 262, 275–76, 278, 294,
    297–99, 336. See also numbers,
    numerology
Mather, Increase, 254
matter, 282–85, 288, 298, 300, 321, 326.
    See also science, modern; ultron
Mayans, 248
Mayer, J. P., 137
Mayflower Compact, 369
Mbiti, John S., 51–52, 55, 59–62, 64
"McCarthyism," xviii
McKeon, Richard P., 143
measurement, 279, 284, 293, 301
Mecca, 176, 180, 187, 195–98, 201,
    203–5, 209, 211, 219
Medina, 176, 191, 196–98, 201, 209, 211,
    224
meditation, 161, 162, 164
Meguid, Ibrahim Adbel, 212
Mehta, Ved, vii, 95
Meiklejohn, Alexander, 299
Melville, Herman, 366
Menander, King of Bactria, 169
Mencius, 139–40
Meno, 279, 297
Merchant of Venice, The, 24
Mesopotamian thought, 1–30
Messiah, 193–94
Metis, 267–69
Mewes, Horst, 334
Mill, John Stuart, vii
Miller, J. L., 18
Miller, M. S., 18
Milton, John, 213, 289
miracles, 93, 156, 163, 182–83, 192,
    208–10, 240, 291, 328–29, 332–33.
    See also divine; prophecy,
    prophetology; rhetoric
Mishra, Umesha, 87
Mo Tzu, 139
moderation, virtue of, 114–15, 120–21,
    139, 167
Moduc tribe, 227
Molière, 110
Molner, Thomas, 221
Monastersky, R., 254

Mongolia, 164
Monkey King, 172
Montesquieu, xxi, 28, 126, 135, 219, 253
Montezuma, 249
Moore, Henry, 21
Moorty, S. S., 87
morality for its own sake, 317–22
Moran, William L., 14–15, 21
Mormons (The Church of Jesus Christ of Latter-Day Saints), 203, 208, 258
mortality, xix, xxi, 149. *See also* death; immortality; Nirvana; salvation, personal
Mortmann, Jurgen, 370
Moses, 92, 96, 168, 177, 182, 184, 189, 191, 198–99, 203, 207–8, 213, 215, 217, 220–21, 262, 271, 340–41. *See also* Bible; Judaism
mosquitos, creation of, 230
Mountbatten, Lord, 60
Mozart, Wolfgang Amadeus, 51
Muehl, John F., 94–95
Muhammad, xix, 28, 126, 168, 175–224, 234, 371–72. *See also* Islam; Koran
Muhando, Penina, 58
Muir, Edwin, 26, 53
Muir, Willa, 63
Muller, F. Max, 90, 93, 96–97
multiculturalism, vii, xiii, 313. *See also* chance
Multnomah tribe, 232
Murley, John A., xvii, 13, 51, 127, 300, 336, 339, 397
Murphy, Dean E., 207
Muses, 265, 269, 289–90
Muslim, 177–78, 368. *See also* Islamic thought
mutakallimum, 193
myth, xvii–xviii

Negasena, 157–58, 169
Naim, C. M., 194
Nakamura, Hajime, 141
names, naming, 135, 141, 225–26, 236, 244, 246, 248, 255–56, 258, 263, 265, 304. *See also* philosophy; rhetoric

Narayan, R. K., 87–88, 90, 93–95
Nation of Islam. *See* Black Muslim Movement (U.S.)
national security, nationalism, 118, 189, 372–74
"Native Americans," ix, 248
natural, nature, x–xii, xiv–xvii, xix–xxii, 2, 5, 7–8, 12, 16–17, 20, 22–23, 25–27, 29–30, 33, 38, 43, 46, 48, 53, 59–60, 62, 81–83, 85, 87, 94–99, 104–5, 108, 115, 121–24, 126–27, 131, 136, 138, 140–41, 147, 149, 151, 152, 156–63, 167, 169, 171, 173, 177, 180–81, 185–86, 190, 192, 199–200, 202, 211, 213, 222–23, 237–41, 245–46, 249–50, 253, 255, 262, 271, 274, 278, 280, 282, 284, 287–88, 290, 294, 300–301, 303–43, 348–53, 355, 361–63, 365, 368–69, 371–74
natural law, natural right, xiv–xv, xviii–xx, 183–84, 202, 213, 224, 237, 250, 252, 297, 303–43, 371
natural rights, 332, 342
nature, fallen, 321. *See also* original sin
Nazis, 41, 59, 318, 362. *See also* Judaism; Nuremberg Trial
négritude, 56
Negroes, 48
Nehru, Jawaharlal, 80, 85–86, 94–96
Nelson, Stephanie A., 290
Nepal, 164–65
Netanyahu, Benjamin, 374
Neumann, Harry, 358–59, 370
Nevins, Allan, 54
New York City, attack on, 32, 223, 371–72
Newton, Isaac, 177, 199, 224, 253, 273, 276, 282, 292–93, 295–96, 335, 342
Nez Percé tribe, 227, 242, 256
Ngugi wa Thiong'o, 56
Nicene Creed, 200, 203, 343. *See also* Christianity
Nietzsche, Friedrich, 94–96, 123, 128, 162, 172, 358
nihilism, 108, 318, 321, 358
Nile River, 23, 32, 37–38
Nineveh, 2, 12, 15–16

Ninsun, mother of Gilgamesh, 9, 15, 19,
    21, 25
Ninth Amendment, U.S. Constitution, 324
Nirvana (Nibbana), 34–35, 50, 77, 82–83,
    150–51, 153–55, 157, 163–65, 167,
    169. *See also* reincarnation, doctrine of
Nixon, Richard M., 133
Noah, 2, 16, 20, 27, 199, 271. *See also*
    Utnapishtim
Nobel Prize, 277, 296, 397
noble, nobility, 241, 316
noble lie, 139, 142–43, 172, 289, 316,
    319–20, 322, 354–55, 360, 371. *See
    also* poetry; prudence; rhetoric
non-being, nothingness, xxi. *See also*
    beginnings; divine; Nirvana; numbers,
    numerology; prophecy, prophetology
North American Indian thought, 225–60
Northwest Ordinance of 1787, 243, 257
Nott, Josiah C., 53, 62
Nubians, 31
nuclear war, 357. *See also* chance;
    insanity; madness; prudence
numbers, numerology, 12, 29, 72–74,
    90–91, 93–94, 166, 172, 222, 241, 254,
    262, 269, 275–78, 283–84, 288, 290,
    293–94, 297–300, 326, 336. *See also*
    divine; playfulness
Nuremberg Trial, 253. *See also* justice;
    Nazis
nursery rhymes, 104, 128. *See also* noble
    lies; poetry; prophecy, prophetology;
    rhetoric

oaths, 142–43
obscenity, 26, 144, 235–36, 261. See also
    bawdiness; eros, erotic
O'Connor, Flannery, 334
Octavius, 163
Odysseus, xxi, 20–21, 42, 168, 250, 254,
    289, 290, 359. *See also* Homer
Oedipus, 63, 89
O'Flaherty, Wendy D. *See* Doniger,
    Wendy
O'Gallagher, Joseph J., 202
Ogundipe-Leslie, Molara, 53
Okie, Susan, 61

Okinawa, 218
Olafor, Fedelis U., 54
Ollivant, Douglas A., 128, 293, 334
Omar, 191
onions, consumption of, 23. *See also*
    economics
Opie, Iona and Peter, 128
Oppenheim, A. Leo, 28
Orestes, 19
Organ, Troy, 95
original sin, 326, 359. *See also* nature,
    fallen; sin, sins
originalism, 324
Orithyia, xvii
Ortiz, Alfonso, 249–54, 257, 259
Osage tribe, 230
Osiris, 35–37, 50–52. *See also* Egyptian
    thought
Othello, 225
Ouranos (Sky), 264, 266–68, 290
Overbye, Dennis, 224
Ovid, 253
owls, 231. *See also* creation

pacifism, 170
pagans, 177, 179–80, 187, 203, 208, 268,
    325, 354–55, 369
Palestine, 32
Palmer House, Chicago, 346, 354–55,
    366, 368
Pandavas, 67–68, 92, 94
Pandora, xi, 251
Pangle, Thomas L., xxii
Panini, 90
Papago tribe, 227, 249
parallax and the fixed stars, 276
Paris, 32
Parliaments of the World's Religions
    (1893–1993), xvi, xxii, 345–72
Parmenides, 290–91
Parsis, 350. *See also* Zoroastrianism
Partha, 91–93
Pascal, Blaise, 194
Patner, Andrew, 58, 366
Patroclus, 17
Paul, St., 168, 325, 332–33, 342, 352
Pearce, Roy Harvey, 254–55

Pegasus, xviii
Peloponnesian War, 100. *See also*
    Thucydides
Penobscot tribe, 229–30
Pericles, 127, 140
Perlmuter, Hayim Goren, 370
Persia, 100, 213, 219, 256, 292, 350
Persian Gulf, 17
person, 311, 334. *See also* individualism
Peter, St., 136
Petrarch, 345, 365
Pfaff, William, 61
Phaedrus, xvii–xviii
philanthropy, 122
Philistines, 18
Philoctetes, 88–89
philosopher–king, 140. *See also* Confucian
    thought
philosophy, xiii–xvii, xix, xxi–xxii, 5,
    12–15, 26–27, 30, 37, 44–45, 48, 67,
    81–83, 85, 87–88, 96–99, 101–2,
    104–5, 109, 111, 114–15, 118,
    120–27, 137–41, 143–44, 147,
    156–59, 161–63, 167, 171–72,
    180–81, 192–93, 199–200, 222,
    245–47, 258, 262, 270, 272, 280, 285,
    290, 304, 307–8, 311, 315–16,
    318–19, 323, 328, 330–31, 333–34,
    342–43, 350, 355, 360, 362–63,
    371–74
Philostratus, 88, 90, 94–96
physics, 96, 141, 177. *See also* science,
    modern
Picasso, Pablo, 14
Pickthall, Mohammed Marmaduke, 211,
    221
piety, xix, 79, 92, 106, 124, 140, 223, 265,
    285, 326, 343, 369. *See also* divine;
    religion; rituals
Pindar, 99, 162, 290
Pines, Shlomo, 194
Plato, xvii–xviii, xxi–xxii, 13, 24, 27–28,
    33, 37, 50–51, 67, 84, 87–90, 95, 99,
    103–6, 111, 122, 125–28, 130–31,
    133–35, 139–40, 143, 167–68, 171,
    193, 200, 205, 214, 216–17, 221, 245,
    279, 281, 289–91, 297, 299–301, 319,

333–34, 336–37, 340, 366, 374. *See
    also* Aristotle; philosophy; Socrates
Plaut, W. Gunther, 203–4
playfulness, 144
pleasure and pain, 105–6
Pliny the Elder, 31, 49, 170
Plotinus, 170, 362
Plutarch, 36, 50–51, 248, 251, 255–56, 365
Podolsky, B., 301
poetry, 22, 59, 181, 186–88, 200, 210,
    217, 262–63, 272, 289, 311, 322, 361.
    See also noble lies; prophecy,
    prophetology; rhetoric
Polemarchus, 319
polis, xiii, 119, 121, 141, 220, 245
"political correctness," xviii
political life, 170. *See also* prudence
Polus, 319
polygamy, 61, 190, 220. *See also* natural,
    nature; prudence
Pontiac, Chief, 259
Pope, Alexander, 65
Porphyry, 352
Poseidon, 28
positivism, 323–26, 340. *See also* realism,
    reality
Pound, Ezra, 127–28, 143
poverty, 116, 118, 371–72. *See also*
    property; rich and poor
Powers, William K., 251
Prabhupada, A. C. Bhaktivendanta Swami,
    89–90
Preamble, U.S. Constitution, 324
predestination, 212
predictions, 182, 279. *See also* prophecy,
    prophetology
Presbyterians, 366
Price, William C., 299
Pritchard, James B., 16, 30
privacy, 218, 252, 307, 334
process, 280
progress, idea of, 257, 299, 338. *See also*
    chance
Prometheus, 234
property, 113–14
prophecy, prophetology, xxi, 9, 97, 131,
    171, 175, 180–83, 186, 192–93, 200,

208–10, 289, 322, 332, 340, 343, 361, 373–74. *See also* divine; poetry; prudence; reason and revelation; rhetoric
propriety, rules of, 112–14, 120
Protegoras, 131
Protestantism, 353
prudence, xiv–xv, xx, 5, 23, 24, 56, 104, 123, 142, 158–59, 170, 188, 219, 237, 241, 268, 283, 285, 312, 318, 324, 328, 330, 336, 355, 358, 360, 362, 369, 371–74. *See also* common sense; natural, nature
Prussia, 358–59
psychoanalysis, psychology, 28, 160
Ptolemy, 275–76, 294
Pueblo tribe, 253
Punch and Judy plays, 233
Puritans, English, 219
Pushkin, Alexander, 64
Pygmies, 31–32, 37, 48–49. *See also* Turnbull, Colin
Pylades, 19
pyramids of Egypt, 33, 50
Pythagorean thought, 87
Pythia, 342

Quakers, 258, 352
quantum mechanics, 273, 294–95, 299. *See also* science modern
Quintillian, 288
Qur'ān, 176, 196–97. *See also* Koran

rabbits, 230–31. *See also* creation
Rachlin, Carol K., 251–52, 254, 257–58
"racism," xviii
Radin, Max, 56–57
Radin, Paul, 233, 251
Rahman, Fazlur, 192
Ramadan, 198, 204, 211
Ramayana, 89
Ramses, 304, 306
rationalism, rationalists, rationality, xi–xii, xxii, 211, 240, 262, 288, 300, 325, 349–50. *See also* causality, cause and effect; common sense; reason
Rauch, Jonathan, 51

Raweno, 230–31
reading, art of, xiii, xx–xxi, 278
realism, reality, 57, 104, 108, 246, 300–301, 316, 319, 321, 358. *See also* natural, nature
reason, xv, xx, xxii, 35, 114, 168, 283, 285, 341, 373
reason and revelation, 87, 96, 127, 207–8, 217, 285, 371–72. *See also* divine; prophecy; prudence; reason; revelation; rhetoric
Rebekah, 143, 290. *See also* Isaac; Judaism
reciprocity, 132. *See also* justice
Rees, Martin, 294
reincarnation, doctrine of, 34, 85–88, 148–49, 153, 156–57, 159–61, 163, 169–72, 250, 310, 331, 342. *See also* Buddhist thought; Hindu thought; Nirvana
Reinhardt, Karl, 291
Reinhold, Meyer, 365
relativity, theory of, 273
religion, xx, xxii, 345–72. *See also* divine; prophecy
renunciation, 71–72, 150. *See also* Buddhist thought
republican form of government, 167
reputation, 128, 133
resurrection, 35, 37, 42, 253
revelation, xv, xxii, 36–37, 127, 143–44, 156, 171, 177, 180–81, 183–85, 187, 192–93, 197, 211, 215, 282–83, 319, 321, 325–33, 340–42, 358–61, 363, 371–374. *See also* divine; prophecy; reason and revelation
revenge, 132
revolution, right of, 138, 141, 371, 371–74. *See also* Declaration of Independence
Rhea, 132
rhetoric, xvi, xxi, 186, 216–17, 272, 368, 371–72. *See also* noble lies; poetry; prophecy, prophetology; revelation
Rhodians, 261, 287
rich and poor, 107–10, 120, 122. *See also* poverty; property

riddles, 44–45
Riezler, Kurt, 291
Rig Veda, 86
Rilke, R. M., 21
righteousness, 127. *See also* Judaism
rituals, 12, 36, 38, 108–10, 113–15, 117,
 120–23, 131–32, 134, 136–37, 139–40,
 144, 180, 182, 190, 204–5. *See also*
 divine; piety; religion
Robespierre, M. F., 222
Rockettes, 306. *See also* sensuous woman
 dressed in white
Rodwell, J. M., 199
Rohter, Larry, 63
Roman Catholics, 353
Rome, ancient, 9, 23, 31–32, 44, 241,
 247–48, 255, 261, 287
Rome, modern, 218
Rooney, Mickey, 310
Roos, Leon John, 288
Rosen, Lawrence, 224
Rosen, N., 301
Rosetta Stone, 32
Ross, Nancy Wilson, 164, 166–69, 171–72
Rousseau, Jean-Jacques, xxi, 17, 301
Rowlandson, Mary, 257
Rubin, William, 60
Rushdie, Salman, 205, 207
Russell, Bertrand, 284, 342
Russia, 57, 124
Russian Revolution, 359
Rutz, Cynthia L., xix
Rwanda, 41, 59. *See also* African thought;
 World Trade Center assault

Sabbath observances, 167
Sachs, Joe, 293
Sachs, Robert G., 292
Sacks, Robert, 17, 207, 250, 291, 300
sacrifices, 110, 134–35. *See also* rituals
St. John's College, xix
Salsh, Mary Williams, 221
Salvation Army, 354
salvation, personal, 357–58. *See also*
 Christianity; individualism; Islam;
 Nirvana
Samkara, 82, 89

Samson, 18
Samuel, Rabbi, 303
Sanjaya, 83–84, 86
Santeria cult, 44
Sanyana, 97
Saracens, 211
Sarah, 203. *See also* Abraham; Isaac;
 Judaism
Sargeant, Winthrop, 86–87, 90, 97
Satan, 205–7, 212–13, 221. *See also* Devil
satanic verses, 205–7
satanists, 354
Saudi Arabia, 32, 216, 218
Saul. *See* Paul, St.
Scalia, Antonin E., 340
scalping, 242, 256. *See also* Indians, North
 American
Schall, James V., 339–40, 342
Schell, Orville, 138
Schindler, Sol, 221
Schleh, Eugene, 56, 64
Schmidt, William E., 59
Schrödinger, Erwin, 296, 300
Schweitzer, Albert, 149, 153–54, 164, 166,
 169–71
science, ancient, 254. *See also* Aristotle
science fiction, 275, 300
science, modern, xv, xviii, 161, 173, 177,
 191–92, 215, 222, 224, 238, 249, 251,
 262, 271–87, 292–301, 312–13,
 320–21, 341, 346
Scotland, 63
Seager, Richard Hughes, 366
Seattle, Chief, 247, 259–60
Seattle, Washington, 226
Segal, Charles, 269, 290
self, 171, 297, 303–12, 332–36, 342. *See
 also* soul, human
self-abnegation, 147, 161, 167, 171. *See
 also* Buddhist thought
self-assertion, 308–9. *See also* Heidegger,
 Martin
self-centeredness, 279–81, 284–85, 332
self-consciousness, 307
self-expression, 304, 308, 334
self-interest, 244, 253, 259, 307–8
selfishness, 41

self-preservation, 304, 307, 331, 334
self-sacrifice, 316, 318. *See also* suicide
Semele, 214
Semiramis, 25
Seneca, 288
Senegal, 32, 41, 49
Senghor, Leopold Sedar, 59–60, 64
sensuous woman dressed in white, 354,
    369. *See also* Rockettes
September 11, 2001, assault. *See*
    hospitality, abuse of
Septuagint, 205, 271. *See also* Bible
serpent, 4, 20–21, 27
sexuality, 25–26, 252, 315, 352
Shakespeare, William, xxi, 13, 24, 64,
    124, 144, 167, 205, 225, 248, 336
Shamash, 4, 19, 28
Sharp, Malcolm P., 299, 339, 397
Shelley, Percy B., 29, 200
Sherman, Elizabeth J., 51
Shillington, Kevin, 60
Shipler, David K., 204
Shiva, 86
Siddhartha, Prince. *See* Gautama,
    Siddhartha
sight, 93, 308–9
signs. *See* miracles; rhetoric
Sikh, 349
Sikkim, 164
Silverberg, Robert, 25
Simon, Yves R., xix, 335
Simpson, O. J., 337
Simpson, Thomas K., 253
sin, sins, 193, 249, 326, 359
Sin (moon god), 30
Sin Leqi-Unninni, 30
Sinaiko, Herman L., 125
Singh, Simon, 298
Sinuhe, 50
skepticism, 181, 191, 318, 322–23, 345
slavery, 37, 39, 41, 43, 53–55, 61–62, 65,
    203, 221, 253
Slavs, 39
Slotkin, Richard, 254, 256–58
Sly, Liz, 61
Smith, Adam, 62
Snohomish tribe, 226

social sciences, vii, 348
Socrates, ix, xiv, xvii–xviii, xxii, 21, 24,
    27, 29, 37, 49, 51–52, 67, 84, 96,
    99–100, 105–6, 110–11, 117, 121, 127,
    129–30, 133–34, 136, 139–40, 144,
    156, 166–68, 171, 205, 222, 247, 260,
    276, 285–86, 293, 300, 318–20,
    352–53, 366, 368
Solomon, King, 28, 199, 219
Solomon Iben Gabiral, 200
Solon, 123
Song of Roland, The, 144
Soothill, E., 139
sophistry, 157. See also intellectuals
Sophocles, 21, 52, 88–89, 131–32, 144,
    290, 367
sorcery, 38, 42, 63
soul, human, xxii, 303–43, 348, 351,
    360, 365, 390. *See also* body and
    soul; self
Southern Baptists, 353
Soviet Union, 349
Soyinka, Wole, 40, 59, 61
Spain, 23
Sparta, 205, 247, 256
Spatharis, Sotiris, 251
Specter, Michael, 335
speculation, modern, 274–75. *See also*
    poetry
Speiser, E. A., 2, 16, 18
Spinoza, Baruch, 143, 336. *See also*
    Judaism
spirit world, 60
spiritedness, 159, 170, 241, 256. *See also*
    Indians, North American; Sparta
sports, 296, 362
Stalin, Josef, 61
Stanford, Ann, 87, 90–91, 93
Stanford, Peter, 339
Steinfels, Peter, 369
Sterba, James B., 87
Stevenson, Jan, 171
Stockton, Frank R., 62
Stone, Robert L., 13, 51, 208, 295, 300,
    332, 339, 397
Storing, Herbert J., 53, 61
Stovall, Howard L., 220

Strauss, Leo, xvii, xx, xxii, 17, 24, 57, 65, 97, 101–2, 126–27, 131, 142, 144, 175, 192, 194, 199–200, 202, 208, 213, 215, 252, 269, 286–87, 290–91, 296, 298, 299–301, 312, 332, 334–37, 339–40, 343, 371–74. *See also* the dedication for this volume
Stryk, Lucien, 165, 167–70
Sudan, 36
suffering, 147–49
suicide, 137, 223, 355, 372–74. *See also* Islamic thought; martyrdom; Rome, ancient
Sumeria, 14–16, 20–23, 25
summum bonum, summum malum, 358
superstition, 163, 187
Swanson, James L., 368
Swedenborg, Emanuel, 352
sweetness of existence. *See* existence, natural sweetness of
Swerdlow, Noel M., 292
Syria, 19, 196
Sze-ma Ch'ien, 142
Szilard, Leo, 296
Szu (Tsu-kung), 130

taboos, 236
Tacitus, 241, 255
Taiwan, 374
Taliban, Afghanistan, 166. *See also* Islam
Talmud, 200–201. *See also* Judaism
Tammuz, 23, 25
Taoism, xxi, 140, 168
Tartarus, 264, 266–67, 269, 289
Tathaga (the Perfect One), 150–51, 162, 166. *See also* Buddhist thought
Taylor, Elizabeth, 310
technology, xvii, 275, 285–87, 285, 293–94, 320, 371–72. *See also* science, modern
Tecumseh, Chief, 259
television, abolition of, 58, 144, 258. *See also* virtues, intellectual; virtues, moral
temperance, virtue of, 147
temple-harlotry, 6, 9, 18, 24, 28
Ten Commandments, 327–28, 340–41, 356, 370

Tenth Amendment (U.S.), 324
Tewa tribe, 239
Thailand, 164
Thales, 205
Thebes (Greece), 252
Thomas Aquinas, St., 96, 137–38, 216, 288, 298, 327–31, 336–37, 340–42, 369, 373
Thomas, Paul, 171
Thompson, Laurence G., 148, 166–68
Thompson, R. Campbell, 13, 15–17, 19, 22, 24–25, 30
Thompson, Robert Farris, 53, 58, 63, 65
Thrasymachus, 319
Thuscydides, 123, 134, 140–41, 143
Tibet, vii, 164, 349
Tigay, Jeffrey H., 13–17, 20–21, 23–27, 29–30
Tigris River, 224
Tipler, Frank J., 296
Tiresias, 132
Titans, 264, 266, 289
Titus Livy, 14, 287
Tlingit tribe, 230
tobacco, 229–30. *See also* suicide
Tocqueville, Alexis de, 137–38, 141, 143, 145, 226, 241, 248, 257
Torre, Michael D., xix
Tosca, 58
totem, 236
Toynbee, Arnold J., 86–87
tragedy, 34, 50, 96, 137, 241
transmigration of souls, 85–86. *See also* Hindu thought; reincarnation
tribalism, 42
Trickster, 42, 233–35, 243, 251, 257
Trinity, 88, 179, 223, 330. *See also* divine; Holy Ghost, Holy Spirit
Trojan War, Troy, 17, 247, 264
truth-telling, 142–43
Tsang Hsi (Tien), 111–14
Tsze-kung (Tzu-kung, Ts'ze), 107–8, 132, 33, 135, 142
Tsze-lu (Yu), 111–14, 130, 136
Turkey, 22–23, 209, 211, 213
Turnbull, Colin, 48–49, 52, 61, 65. *See also* Pygmies

Turner, Frederick W., III, 250–52, 256, 259–60
turtles, tower of, 294
Twain, Mark, 257, 311–12
twins, conjoined, 368–69
tyranny, 108, 120. *See also* television, abolition of
Tzu-kung, 130

ultron, 282, 288, 299. *See also* science, modern
Uncertainty Principle, 282, 295, 297–98. *See also* Heisenberg, Werner
understanding, 181. *See also* philosophy
Unidentified Flying Objects (UFOs), 214, 296, 354
Unified Theory, 273. *See also* science, modern
Unitarians, 221
United Housing Foundation v. *Forman* (1975), 141
United Nations, 357, 370
Universal Declaration of Human Rights, the (1948), 357, 370
University of Chicago, xiii–xiv, xviii
untouchables, 95, 368. *See also* Hinduism
Upanishads, The, 68–69, 86–87, 96, 98. *See also* Hindu thought
Uruk (Etrech, Waka), 2, 4, 6, 11, 15, 17–18, 20, 22, 25, 28–29
Ushana, 92
usury, Islam, 189. *See also* noble lies
Utes tribe, 249
utilitarianism, 122, 124
Utnapishtim, 2, 4, 6–11, 14–15, 18, 20–22, 24, 26–30, 149; boatman of, 4, 21, 24; wife of, 4, 8–9, 20, 27–28

Vaidya, C. V., 87
"values," 181, 183, 208, 320, 362
van Buitenen, J. A. B., 86–87, 89–91, 93–97
Van Doren, John, vii–xii, xviii–xix, 322–23, 335, 337
Van Doren, Mark, 263, 288
Vanderslice, Stephen, 292

Vedas, The, 68, 86
veils, 111, 184, 193
Venus, 28
Verdun, Battle of, 358–59
Vestal Virgins, 9
Vietnam War, 164, 170
Virgil, 16, 289
virtù, 137
virtues, intellectual, 121, 123, 141, 336. *See also* prudence
virtues, moral, 79, 115, 121, 123, 138–40, 163, 170–71, 244–45, 284, 307, 312–23, 335–39, 355, 357. *See also* prudence
Vishnu, 68, 76–77, 82, 86
Vivekananda, 368
Voegelin, Eric, 29, 127, 205, 342
von Däniken, Erich, 51
von Grunebaum, Gustave E., 206–8, 214–15
von Humboldt, Wilhelm, 85
von Weizsacher, C. F., 296
Voodoo, 44, 63, 354
Vyasa, 83, 91–92, 94, 97

Wahab, Farouk Abdel, 212
Waka, 17. *See* Uruk
Waley, Arthur, 103, 107, 110, 115, 120, 125–43
Wali, Kameshwar C., 295
Ware, James R., 127
Warren, Robert Penn, 256–57
Washington, Augustus, 53
Washington, D.C., attack on, 223, 371–72
Washington, George, 53, 110, 143, 369
Watson, James D., 296
Weaver, Richard M., 43, 62
Weinberg, Steven, 294–95, 297
Weiss, Raymond L., 193–94
Weizsacher, C. F. von. *See* von Weizsacher, C. F.
Welbon, Guy Richard, 165, 170, 172–73
West, Grace Starry, 84, 130
West, M. L., 289
West, Thomas G., 84, 130
Whitaker, Albert Keith, 291

Wilkerson, Isabel, 367–68
will, act of, xi, 137, 162, 168, 235, 241, 250, 320–21, 329, 341, 359, 361
Williams, Samuel Cole, 254
Wilson, Edward O., 294
Winnebago tribe, 234, 249
Winthrop, John, 255
Wintu tribe, 231
Wisconsin v. *Yoder* (1972), 252
wisdom, 111, 241. *See also* prudence; rationalism; reason and revelation
witchcraft, witches, 42–44, 60, 62, 64–65, 240–41, 254, 354–55
women, status of, xix, 12, 24, 40–41, 60, 189–90, 197, 212, 220–21, 223, 232, 269, 352–56, 361
Woods, Richard, 171–72
Woolf, Virginia, 54
Woolman, John, 256, 259
World Trade Center assault, 223, 372–74. *See also* hijacking airliners; hospitality, abuse of; suicide
world's religions, the, xviii, 345–72
Wright, G. Ernest, 14

writing, consequences of, 126
Wu Ch'êng-ên, 172

Xenophon, 21, 95, 129, 134

Yeats, William Butler, 15, 167, 343
Yevtushenko, Yevgeny, 200
Yoruba, 53, 58–59, 63, 65
Yu (Tsze-lu). *See* Tsze-lu (Yu)

Zachariah, 199
Zangwill, Israel, 200
Zan Yu (Ch'iu), 116–19
Zan Yu (Yen Yu), 111–14
Zeldovitch, Yakov, 294
Zen Buddhism, 155–56, 167
Zeus, 15, 17, 29, 89, 173, 214, 234, 263–70, 289. *See also* divine
Zhisui Li, 50
Ziegler, Philip, 60
Zionism, 222. *See also* Judaism
Zoroastrianism, 350, 366, 368
Zuchert, Catherine H., 259
Zulus, 38, 48

About the Author

George Anastaplo was born in St. Louis, Missouri, in 1925 and grew up in Southern Illinois. After serving three years as an aviation cadet and flying officer during and just after the Second World War, he earned the A.B., J.D., and Ph.D. degrees from the University of Chicago. He is currently lecturer in the liberal arts at the University of Chicago, professor of law at Loyola University Chicago, and professor emeritus of political science and of philosophy at Dominican University.

His publications include a dozen books and more than a dozen book-length law review collections. His scholarship was reviewed in seven articles in the 1997 volume of the *Political Science Reviewer*. A two-volume Festschrift, *Law and Philosophy*, was issued in his honor in 1992 by the Ohio University Press. Between 1980 and 1992 he was nominated annually for the Nobel Peace Prize by a Chicago-based committee that had as its initial spokesman Malcolm P. Sharp (1897–1980), professor emeritus of the University of Chicago Law School.

Professor Anastaplo's career is assessed in a chapter in *Leo Strauss, the Straussians, and the American Regime* (Rowman & Littlefield, 1999). A bibliography of his work is included in the 1992 Fetschrift, *Law and Philosophy* (vol. II, pp. 1073–1145). See also "George Anastaplo: An Autobiographical Bibliography (1947–2001)," 20 *Northern Illinois University Law Review* 581–710 (2000); "George Anastaplo: Tables of Contents for his Books and Published Collections (1950–2001)," 39 *Brandeis Law Journal* 219–87 (2000–2001).